To Will Peppitt,

enjoy this story
of which many
charactrs are
known to you —

Jamie d'Antiox
31/3/16

NEIGHBOURS' NONSENSE

Bradley Jamieson

ARCADIAN LIFESTYLE

This book is dedicated to the faraway neighbours
who didn't make it into this book, and to the closest
neighbours of all, my children.

A heap of rocks is better than a neighbour.
 - Arabian proverb

When I was twenty-seven, I was looking to buy my first house. I
found the perfect place in East Grinstead: a palatial building, with a
stream nearby, surrounded by three acres of gardens and rolling hills.
The house had antique mahogany doors and marble mosaic floors. It
had a swimming pool, seven bedrooms and three receptions. It was
a dream come true. I drove out to the property with my heart in my
throat, ridiculously excited at the prospect of living there.

When I first stepped out of the car, I was charmed. Everything
seemed to be as described, even exceeding my expectations, and
I asked to be handed the letter of intent, so I could sign at once.
However, as the papers were handed to me, I heard the most terrible
squealing noise, accompanied by an awful, overwhelming stench.
At that very moment, a train screamed past in the field immediately
behind us. That was how I found out the nature of my neighbours in
this seemingly perfect property: a pig farm and a train track.

The lesson here is that one must be intensely careful both about
where one lives and whom one lives next to. I have travelled to one
hundred and forty countries, and lived in almost a third of these.
Every house and apartment I have lived in has come with its own
crop of neighbours, but I stress that this book is not limited to my
experience with these individuals; on the contrary, I have also
written about the neighbours I have acquired in trains, guest houses,
beaches, while staying with relatives, in hospitals, and on planes.
Some of them were permanent, some of them were transient; some
I knew for years and years, some for only a single night. And that's
just talking about immediate neighbours! If I were to extend the
parameters of this book to people who lived a mile down the road,
it would have been interminable. I have also limited this account to
my own neighbours, although, upon hearing I was compiling this
book, many acquaintances of mine volunteered their own hilarious

and painful narratives.

'Why would anybody want to write a book about neighbours?' some might ask. 'Aren't they all relatively nice?' 'Won't it be terribly boring?' These people have not had the neighbours I have had. Most people, however, will jump on the bandwagon at this point in the conversation. 'Oh, I once had a crazy neighbour!' they will tell me. 'Maybe you should put him in your book!' Of course, I have to tell them I have limited these stories to my personal experience. Furthermore, I have left out a few tales that would land me solidly in legal trouble. Beyond that, I have kept only the stories which seemed particularly funny, informative, or dramatic. I have had many, many other neighbours whom I have deemed unworthy of commentary.

The way in which neighbourly habits vary from country to country is in itself worthy of discussion. Upon arriving in a new house in America, one will usually be welcomed on the very first day by neighbours bearing hampers of food, while in Switzerland one might live next to someone for fifty-two years and know neither their name nor their occupation. The neighbourly stereotypes that appear are amusing in their consistency. Thus, the French I have encountered in this book seem to make obnoxious, smelly or noisy neighbours, but are almost all excellent cooks. I have met *frontaliers* driving from France into Switzerland who throw rubbish out of car windows, and others who empty it into neighbours' gardens. The English value their privacy above all, and are prepared to squabble for years over grass cuttings or property delimitations. Yet there are, of course, plenty of exceptions to these rules: after all, how else would I have come up with two hundred stories?

CONTENTS

TOM AND JOE, THE PRIESTS

Tom and Joe were two of the friendliest men I've met, and also two of the heaviest drinkers. They were Irish priests, the former my wife's cousin and the latter a friend of his, and they lived just down the road from me in Sussex in the mid-1970s, shortly after my marriage. Fitting the stereotype of the partying Irish perfectly, they were great fun to be around and were dedicated drinking partners. Even though I was teetotal, they seemed to love coming over to my house for a drink, or the occasional large meal. Whenever they turned up, I swear they would say, 'Go on, Bradley, how about a Scotch!' before they even said hello.

Often they would cook together: large, indulgent meals, as if they were farmers or builders. Steak, fish pie, and copious amounts of roast potatoes were some of their favourites. They liked big meals with an Irish touch. While they were cooking, they would knock back a few shots of whiskey, following each one up with a beer. 'Go on, let's have another chaser, then!' they would say. The way they drank them, it seemed you could never have just one chaser: you had to chase it with another. They would have four or five of these of an evening, get merry, and tell increasingly long and ridiculous jokes. Joe was the quieter man when sober, but he was definitely the heavier drinker, and the funnier drunk. Unsurprisingly, the pair span endless amusing yarns about their particular approach to priesthood. It fitted in quite nicely with a long tradition of Irish jokes about religious figures with a taste for alcohol.

'So a man goes to the doctor, and at the end of their session he says, "I'm very sorry Mr O'Flaherty, but I can't diagnose your trouble. I think it must be drink."'

Joe would usually pause before the punchline to take a swig of beer, then deliver:

'"Don't worry about it, Dr Cullen, I'll come back when you're sober," said O' Flaherty.'

And Tom would fall about laughing uproariously, while Joe smiled serenely. I heard some of these jokes so many times I could have repeated them word for word.

Now, I didn't mind this raucous party spirit. There seems to be a specific branch of Irish Catholicism that embraces this approach to life and priesthood, and these two men embodied it completely. They were quite a pair. They had the drinking habits of college boys mixed with the earnestness of Labradors. Both had dark hair and light eyes: they could have been brothers. Both had come from very religious families, one from Kilkenny and the other from County Mayo.

Tom, who was Father O'Brien to most people, was about thirty years old, tall and muscular. He was actually the head priest at the local convent just down the road. He and Joe were the only two men allowed in there. Often, nunneries will employ just one or two of the opposite sex to help with security, or teaching, or even just to help receive male guests. I could not have imagined when I first met them that they were the sort of men to be trusted so completely by the order, but there was obviously more to them than met the eye.

Tom managed to be beloved within the convent and still be respected by the nuns and feared by the head sisters, despite being half their age! Sometimes he and Joe would cook in the priory kitchen, and they were always very popular despite their unorthodox ways. Tom, although the younger of the pair, actually made his way further up the Church hierarchy than Joe. I suppose he was slightly more ambitious, and perhaps a bit more quick-witted, which served him well. Even before the promotion, he often ended up doing the job of a more senior priest.

Joe played the role of the sidekick in this friendship. He obviously admired Tom hugely, and agreed with everything he said. All the time I knew them, they were quite inseparable. They were true free spirits, giving the idea of pilgrimage a quite unusual meaning. Often, they would set out on these great journeys, 'exploring Christendom!' Tom would call it, with a twinkle in his eye. They loved to come home and tell me their lengthy stories, showing me all their pictures and respective sunburns. Even the dark-haired Irish are not built for the sun!

They 'visited cathedrals in the South of France', which meant that they mostly toured the beaches and the bars, popping into the great Catholic monuments on the way. They 'went to gospel mass in Florida,' went canoeing, and ate alligator steak in diners. I can just imagine them clapping along in some ridiculous robes with a gospel choir. They were true *bon vivants*, missionaries in a very modern sense. They spread the word of God mostly, as far as I could tell, by striking up conversation with people they met on their travels.

Years later, Tom came to stay with me and my wife in Paris. He was particularly fascinated by the darkest aspects of moral decline. He asked me to accompany him to the Pigalle district in Paris, as his usual sidekick Joe was not with him. We walked through the dark streets with their red lights warily. Tom, always keen to document his adventures, had his camera with him. He had been taking pictures along the street, through the windows, and of the streetwalkers themselves, when all at once, one of the ladies jumped on him, not in an attempted seduction, but to drag the camera from his shoulder. 'No pictures!' she was shouting, in a strong French accent, her feather boa dragging on the ground as she grappled with Tom: 'You must give me the film!' Suddenly, a broad-shouldered man with a gun appeared by her side and threatened us. Luckily, I convinced my friend to give up the film, and we made a swift exit.

That was probably the most un-Christian of their adventures. Their fascination with moral decline always seemed strange to me, especially considering their own casual approach to pleasures which many would consider sinful. It amuses me how many of their jokes I can still remember, particularly from one of the last evenings I spent with the two of them.

'So an Irish priest is driving a little unsteadily down a country road, right, and he gets pulled over,' Joe said. We were sitting in a restaurant, probably driving the other customers crazy. 'The policeman smells alcohol on the priest's breath, and then sees the empty wine bottle on the floor of the car.'

'Is this a familiar scene, Father O'Callahan?' Tom cut in, mischievously.

'Hush now, Father O'Brien,' Joe retorted. 'Let me tell Bradley my joke. So the cop says, "Sir, have you been drinking?" "Just water," says the priest. The copper says, "Then why do I smell wine?" The priest looks at the bottle and says, "Good God! He's done it again!"'

The two priests fell about laughing. I must admit I cracked a smile myself, although I did find myself wondering how on earth the two men fit their serious religious calling with their ridiculous sense of humour.

Sadly, time passed, and this cheerful set of rituals slowly became less and less regular. I found out that Tom, now in his forties, had left the church to marry a divorced lady with a son. He then became a family man, and found that it suited him. From then on, I no longer thought of him as a religious man, but simply as a friend who enjoyed good food and many drinks.

Joe, however, remained in the church. I met him again some fifteen years later, and he seemed much older than his age. The loss of his travelling and drinking partner had been tough for him. He didn't seem to have found anyone like Tom to keep him company in his fun-loving approach to priesthood. When I last saw him, he had gone grey, and seemed a little lonely. We talked for hours about all the great times he had had with his partner Tommy O'Brien, and about their travels together.

'But are you still finding fulfilment in your work for the church?' I asked him over dinner.

'Oh, I suppose I am,' he replied, looking forlornly out of the window. 'It's just not the same anymore. You know Tommy and I started at the same time, we came to this path the same way. And then he left it.'

'I suppose, in a way, you were both rather unlikely choices for priesthood,' I ventured.

He smiled wryly.

'I do believe we were,' he said quietly.

France is a country of culinary delights, but also of culinary philosophy. The French like to eat, and cook, but above all they like to talk about food. Almost every time I meet a Frenchman, I start the conversation with a commentary on food, just as I would bring up the weather first with an English neighbour. No Frenchman is interested in the weather, but the best way to boil an egg? The perfect combination of seasonings for steak tartare? Where to find the cheapest pears? How they're stuffing the quail for dinner? These topics seem capable of occupying them for hours.

I had a neighbour in my early days in France whose favourite culinary topic was more specifically how terrible my own non-French cooking was. He had particular issues with the concept of the barbecue.

'What are you doing burning up that nice meat like that?' he would ask me with a sneer. 'You're like a caveman! It's disgusting!'

'Of course eating your steak *bleu* and dripping with blood is the height of civilisation,' I retorted, but he only laughed.

'*Un bon steak*, a good steak is a sacred thing. You do not throw it in the flames!'

This neighbour's name was Pierre. He was short, rotund, and endowed with a small moustache. He never seemed to run out of topics to argue about.

'Oh, you cannot use these plastic cheeses! They are like cheese for children!' he would tell me another time, in that patronising tone Frenchmen cultivate specifically for talking to foreigners.

'It's cheddar,' I replied. 'It's a perfectly respectable cheese.'

'*Non, non, non,*' he would say, his little moustache bouncing up and down. 'The English do not know how to make cheese. They know how to make plastic.'

'Are you telling me that stinking, oozing Pont l'Évêque and Roquefort are the high mark of culinary quality? That the only good cheese is a half-rotten cheese?'

The moustache would bristle, the eyes would pop, and Pierre would grow red in the face.

'The only good cheese,' he retorted, 'is a cheese you can smell. Anything else is a joke!' He spat out the last word.

Sometimes, these pointless fights would go on for an hour at a time. Every time Pierre turned up on my doorstep, an argument was inevitable. It was as if he was some kind of belligerent medieval knight, turning up on my doorstep with a sausage instead of a sword. And every time, they would end the same way.

'So,' he would say, and he would walk over to my fridge and open it, without asking. 'What kind of junk have we got here? What kind of decent meal can we make?'

He would bury his head in the fridge like a foraging badger, occasionally looking up with a grunt to toss things over his shoulder. He would pull out whatever he could find: a hunk of brie, a shank of lamb, capers, butter, crumbs.

'What is this *sweetcorn*,' he might grumble from the depths of the fridge. '*Le maïs*. That's for pigs. American nonsense.'

Another time it might be: 'Ugh, feta. *Qu'est-ce que c'est ce truc?* What is this thing? This is not a real French cheese.'

Then the chopping and the mess-making would begin as he attempted to cook with flamboyant brio and absolutely no skill. Sometimes he would try to concoct some unusual stew based on something a friend had mentioned, but without remembering exactly what the ingredients were. On other occasions he would improvise a semblance of some dish he had once come across in a magazine, throwing in whatever bits and bobs he could find: half a head of broccoli, some leftover chicken, a leg of lamb. Some of the combinations were dreadful. He never asked for permission to help himself to the edible contents of my kitchen, and he never asked for my opinion on the cooking, but, strangely, although he occasionally made fun of the contents of my fridge, he still seemed quite happy to make use of them. The Fighting usually happened about once a week, often on the weekend, and almost inevitably ended with The Cooking.

At first, I didn't mind so much. Neither did my wife, although she had her own opinion about Pierre. I remember her saying once:

'Well, he's all right.' Then she paused. 'I mean, he's obviously a fool. And he can't cook.'

'That's a little harsh, isn't it?' I responded, being in a rather good mood with him at the time, although I tended to agree with her. 'I mean, he's rough, and a little rude... But we just have a sort of man-to-man friendship, you know. Like those school friends who don't have very much in common and bond over rough games like football or baseball. Or like brothers who punch each other.'

'Yes,' she said with a smile, 'Boys who break the kitchen cabinets. Boys making a mess.'

'Hey,' I said, 'it's not my mess. I'm not the one cooking.'

She laughed. 'Now you really sound like brothers.'

The dishes Pierre produced for me were, almost without exception, disgusting. They almost always consisted of a piece of meat fried in too much oil, with a dull assortment of spices piled on, or of some sort of overly rich stew. I ate them without too much complaint, even though it was obviously getting in the way of me having a nice family dinner with my wife. One day, however, Pierre went too far.

On that particular day, he had decided to make one of his questionable stews when we didn't have a particularly full fridge. The result was disastrous. The sauce was greasy, he put in three cloves of garlic, which I hate, and, most offensively, he served it up with some sort of stale bread.

'Pierre,' I said, 'this bread is three days old.'

'I know,' he replied, without looking up. Beads of grease dripped from his moustache. 'You have no fresh bread.'

'We have no fresh bread?' I blew my top. 'We? Can you hear what you are saying? You come into my house and eat all my family's food, every week, without asking. You then criticise our supplies, and you wouldn't even spend a franc to go down the road to buy a decent baguette so we could enjoy this god-awful, greasy, garlicky stew!' I drew a deep breath. 'You contribute nothing. You've made a terrible mess in the kitchen, which I'll have to clean up after you've left. Everything you take from the fridge might have been needed by my wife to make a wonderfully tasty dish. One that I actually like. One that we will enjoy together. Why don't you go back to your wife and cook *her* this poisonous muck?'

Pierre had stayed quiet throughout this outburst. He wiped his moustache on the back of his hand before responding.

'Only an Englishman would dislike garlic,' he said. 'Garlic is the spirit of French cuisine. And you're right, this stew is dreadful, but there was nothing decent in your fridge. And you should appreciate it, you selfish man. I've no-one else to cook for. I've been separated from my wife for two years.'

'Well with breath like that I can see why!'

'Well I wouldn't kiss *your* old wife no matter what she'd been eating!'

There was a pause. We glowered at each other. As the heat of the exchange began to subside, I realised the underlying message.

'Wait, you live alone?' I thought aloud. 'So you come here just to eat? It's not a culinary duel, it's not about intellectual or cultural advancement. We're not even friends! I'm just some guy you use for sustenance! I'm just the man whose bread you steal!'

This seemed to knock some of the fight out of Pierre.

'That's not fair,' he said. 'I do consider you a friend. Even if your taste in food is a bit strange.' He looked down a little, and hesitated before continuing. 'I'm just lonely. I would like to be friends with you. The culinary thing is just a means of trying to get a social life. If you feel that way, I can stop coming round.'

The moustache drooped uncharacteristically.

'Oh, Pierre,' I said, 'I'm sorry I said that. I didn't know about your wife. Look, of course we can be friends. You can even continue to cook at my house. Just give me advance notice before you come, and tell me what you're going to cook so I can have the right ingredients for you. All right? And please, no more garlic.'

He grinned. The moustache bounced a little.

'OK,' he said. 'How about we make a *boeuf bourguignon* next weekend?'

Pierre continued to visit me, but less frequently, perhaps only once a month. We planned some recipes together, and produced a few decent meals. And from then on, he always brought his own baguette.

GERHARD AND GILLETTE

When I lived and worked in New York, my colleagues and I went through a phase of exchanging our apartments. This was an occasion for a change of scene: new restaurants to go to, new landmarks to enjoy, and new neighbours to be met. American neighbours are always friendly and eager to get to know each other. If someone went to a new flat in London for three or four months, I can almost guarantee that they would most likely only come across one or two of their neighbours at most, and those probably by accident. This was not the case in New York City. Even in the big cities, Americans talk to each other. They are curious, they are loud, and they want to get to know every detail of your life.

Thus, when I moved into a flat on the West Side of Manhattan, I met my first neighbour almost immediately: a German man by the name of Gerhard. I'm quite sure this was on my first or second day since moving into the new flat, after coming back from a long day's work. Huffing and puffing from the exertion of coming up the stairs, Gerhard greeted me with an exuberant smile and an unforgettable first line.

'You are aware that I have a much bigger terrace than yours?' he asked me, in thickly accented English. I almost burst out laughing at this bizarre apparition.

'Hello,' I said cautiously. 'I'm Bradley.'

'I know!' he practically shouted. 'Our old neighbour told us he was running away and sending us a measly substitute. We thought we should find out what we had got ourselves into.'

Somewhat bewildered, I smiled and shrugged a little. 'Well, here I am.'

'The apartment's nice,' Gerhard continued, 'but you really are going to be disappointed as soon as you see our place. Oh, we have such a wonderful terrace! Come and have a look! We'll make you some coffee. And sausages. My wife has bought the most wonderful little German veal sausages today!'

Although it was quite late, I was rather charmed by the man's vivacity. I threw on a jacket, and prepared to follow my new neighbour down the stairs. As I locked the door to my flat, I could still hear him talking. 'Classic little bratwursts,' he was saying. 'They will be so nice with a potato salad. You can see all the lights of the city from our terrace! It's quite mild for the time of year. Perhaps we can interest you in some sort of cold beverage, too.'

I shook my head. Even when I was a full flight of stairs away, he didn't seem to want to stop talking to me. I found the door open, and walked in slowly. I could still hear Gerhard talking, although he seemed to have directed the flow of his conversation away from me and back towards his wife, who was presumably the usual recipient. The apartment was lovely, with high ceilings and big glass windows that let in the glow of the city lights stretching away into the distance. The furniture was rather beat-up, but it was obviously a carefully thought-out selection, and there were rugs and art posters on all the walls.

'It's a lovely apartment,' I told Gerhard as I stepped into the well-lit kitchen, where he was standing with a slender blonde woman in a floor-length print dress. He practically twirled around at the sound of my voice, a large drink held in each hand.

'Bradley!' he exclaimed. 'You are here! I am so glad you like our little apartment. Most of the decoration is the work of my wife, Stella. This is a glass of *bowle*, a traditional German fruit drink! We are so glad you have come down to see us.'

His wife smiled gently. 'Don't mind my husband's chattering. Please, make yourself at home. Sit down on the couch.'

'No, no,' Gerhard interjected. 'He must come out to the balcony! He must look out at the lights! Then we can have all the time we want for chatting.'

I smiled wryly at Stella. 'I'd love to,' I said.

'See, right there is the Festival Hall,' he explained. 'These are all the boring buildings, we don't look at them, but you can watch all the little people going in and out! It's great fun, living here. I love living in New York.'

'I'm rather fond of it myself,' I replied. Before I could add anything else to that effect, Gerhard had continued:

'We went to a wonderful concert there last week; all Bernstein. Very good fun. Good American music. Of course, it's a good German name, too! American Jews pronouncing everything wrong, forgetting their roots. Can't make a decent dumpling. The music was great, though, lots of brass, lots of noise.'

I sipped my red fruit drink quite happily, letting the tide of chatter wash over me.

His wife came and stood next to me at the railing. 'Sometimes, his speed of conversation slows down to seventy miles per hour,' she said with a little smile.

I glanced over at her. She really was an exceptionally beautiful woman. 'Is this about a hundred, then?'

'Oh, yes. I'd say a hundred and ten. He really loves having company over, and new neighbours are his favourite kind. I'd say there's no keeping him in check now.'

'... and we really should make some of those dumplings in stew, Stella!' Gerhard finished, obviously having wandered off on his own train of thought whilst his wife and I were quietly conversing. He didn't seem to mind our obvious lack of attention. Clearly, his own ear was enough to give him the illusion of interest; there was something quite inspiring about his confidence.

'Yes, darling,' she replied. 'Maybe not right this second, though. Will you check on the sausages in the oven? I'll settle our guest in.'

'Are you sure you won't stay on the balcony a bit longer? Isn't it large and splendid?'

I agreed with him, but as the evening was growing chilly, we moved inside. The rest of the night passed very pleasantly, and by the end, I suspected we would stay friends.

'I'll come visit you again soon,' Gerhard confirmed cheerily as he showed me to the door at the end of the night. 'Maybe we could have coffee this weekend.'

'Sure,' I said. 'Perhaps you'll allow me to show you the charms of my own, smaller, balcony?'

Gerhard laughed. 'You can try, but you'll never convince me I haven't got the best deal around!'

The next time I saw him, he greeted me with another of his unexpected lines.

'How do you like the way I've shaved?' he asked me, proffering his chin with a childish grin.

'What do you mean?' I had to ask.

'The way I've shaved!' he repeated. 'Look at my skin, it's like a baby's bottom!'

I resisted the urge to laugh as he grabbed my hand and ran it along his face. 'See? Can you feel it? Have you ever felt a smoother face?'

'Well, I haven't run my hand over many grown men's faces,' I replied, 'but yes, I would have to admit that this is pretty smooth.'

'My wife loves it!' he added with a wink. 'Do you want to know why I'm quite so smooth right now?'

'Tell me all about it.' It was a Saturday morning, after all, and I had nothing particularly urgent to accomplish. After all, Gerhard had proved to be quite an entertaining neighbour so far.

'I've bought a new razor,' he confided excitedly. 'Gillette have just produced this new double blade. It's fantastic. Look at that face of yours! All that weekend stubble. It's because you're using a single blade.'

'Well, I would personally argue that it's probably because I haven't shaved yet this morning...' I protested gently. Gerhard waved my objections away.

'Have you ever used a double blade?' he asked me.

'I have not,' I admitted.

'I've got six of them in my pocket!' he told me, brandishing them excitedly. 'Look, just hold one. See how the blade slides back into the handle?' I edged back a little, hoping that Gerhard's enthusiasm would not be so careless as to actually draw any blood. 'Don't be shy,' he cried out, 'take one!' Gingerly, I selected one of the razors and looked at it more closely.

'Are you sure I won't wound myself with this?'

'Oh no,' he said airily, 'it's perfectly safe. It's designed that way, you see. It gives you the closest shave possible. Furthermore,' he continued, putting on his best salesman's voice, 'the blade will last you for a good twenty-five shaves.'

I had to admit I was impressed. 'Most of my blades only last three or four days,' I told him.

'Ah, that's because of your rugged face!' he joked. 'You could light a match on that cheek of yours! It's like James Bond's!'

I laughed. 'I told you, I haven't shaved this morning!'

'That's what they all say,' he replied, waggling his head back and forth.

I looked at the item closely. 'It looks pretty dangerous to me. I'm not sure I would know how to use it, frankly. I'll probably end up with blood all over the place. Then I'll really look like James Bond!'

He laughed, then frowned thoughtfully. 'Why don't you come downstairs with me and I'll show you.'

'Couldn't you show me in my apartment?' I couldn't resist asking.

'Well, I could,' he said, 'but of course our bathroom is so much larger than yours.'

We crowded around the well-lit mirror in his admittedly large and luminous bathroom. He had an old-fashioned brush with badger bristles, and a large pot of foam, which he used to anoint both our faces liberally.

'I can't remember the last time I shaved next to somebody,' I said. 'Probably college, when several of us were late for some lecture.'

'Such a shame it's a lost tradition,' Gerhard said sadly. 'This means no-one shares their shaving wisdom anymore! Of course,' he added, brightening slightly, 'this also means that the secret of the Gillette double-bladed razor is safe in this building, for now.'

'What on earth are you boys doing?' Stella called over from the lounge. 'I'm trying to get some work done over here, but with all this racket going on in the bathroom... it sounds as though I might be missing the party!' She appeared at the door with her glasses pushed up on her head, and immediately dissolved into giggles. 'Oh, you two look just like big babies playing!'

I considered the scene from her point of view: two bankers, in their early-to-mid-twenties, standing in the bathroom trying to shave their faces together. I had to laugh. 'Your husband is giving me an important lesson,' I explained.

'What, you've never shaved before?' she asked in her sweet, heavy German accent. 'Do you mean that that baby face of yours comes naturally?'

'Who are you calling baby-faced?' Gerhard asked, turning to her with sad puppy eyes. 'I am the only one with a face this smooth!' He frowned. 'Maybe I shouldn't teach you after all,' he mused aloud. 'What if my wife starts meeting other men with faces as smooth as mine?'

Stella laughed tenderly, and laid a hand on his back. 'Don't worry, darling,' she said, 'I will never stroke their faces, so I will never know. You are safe.'

Gerhard sniffed. 'Well, I should certainly hope so! Meanwhile, you are distracting us. All this shaving foam is going to dry on our faces, and then we will make quite a sight!' He turned back to me. 'Now, all you have to do is this.' He began running the razor over his face. He then guided me through the first few swipes with my own new razor, and I got the hang of it almost immediately. 'See, it's easy!'

'It's almost as if I've been doing this every morning for all of my adult life,' I commented dryly.

Gerhard looked over suspiciously. 'Are you making fun of me? I'm giving you a great tip here, you know.'

'Oh, I know,' I said hastily. 'You must admit there is something amusing about this scene, though.'

'Yes,' he replied. 'And my bathroom is definitely bigger than yours.'

In the end, I mastered the technique quickly, even finishing before Gerhard did, which annoyed him slightly. Throughout the whole so-called lesson, the most amusing thing was my neighbour's apparent complete inability to stop talking. He talked about shaving, he talked about his childhood, he talked about his plans for lunch, the weekend, and the rest of his time in New York. He talked about scenes in films where characters shaved, he talked about advertising to men, he talked about investments in shaving products. It was very impressive, the way he rattled off this endless stream of consciousness in what was still a somewhat foreign language to him. He talked so fast and so constantly that I found myself worrying he would cut himself, as his chin and lips kept moving up and down at such high speeds. However, he obviously had a great deal of practice, and finished his routine unscathed.

Still, the whole incident made an impression on me. From that time on, I never used any other razor than Gillette's double-blade. That is, up until Gillette developed their next advancements like triple blades, built-in lubricating strips and rotating razor heads... At that time, however, the double-bladed Gillette razor was the best I had ever used. In fact, I thought it was so extraordinary I bought Gillette shares and made a lot of money on it! Actually, I am quite sure I still have one or two somewhere in my bathroom...

ARNOLD AND HOLLY

I met Arnold and Holly when I lived in a country house in Sussex as a student. They were a lovely old couple, both in their early seventies, sweet old folks with white hair. I would often see them coming back to their farmhouse from country walks on the Sussex downs, hand in hand. They were the sort of people you could tell had been together all their lives, simply from the way they looked at each other.

I was rather fond of the old couple, and would often invite them in for a drink. Every time this happened, I found it hugely entertaining. It was as if they had never had a drink in their lives, although considering their obvious taste for it, this was clearly not the case.

'Would you like a drink?' I would offer, as I ushered them into the lounge.

'Ooh, whisky please,' Holly would say at once, with her sweet lilting voice. She would always pretend to be surprised by the offer, but was obviously expecting it. Sometimes she would grin, a little cheekily, and ask: 'What sort do you have?'

Other times it might be Arnold, who answered jovially:

'Well, why not! How about a little whisky?'

Now, I don't drink myself, but I always make sure I have a well-stocked cupboard for occasional guests. This would include probably three or four decent whiskies, and one or two rather good ones. Holly and Arnold always picked the oldest, watching with delight as I poured the amber liquid over ice, perhaps a Johnnie Walker or an Auchentoshan. I didn't mind in the least. They weren't very well off, so I always felt it must be a bit of a treat for them. Besides, I did enjoy their company.

Holly was a cheerful old lady, really a delight to be around. Sipping her whisky rather swiftly, if daintily, she would tell me long stories about her grandfather's time in Scotland and pass on nuggets from his extensive knowledge of malts.

'Now don't call it Scotch,' she would warn me, even though I never did. 'Americans invented Scotch. These are fine single malts you have. It's an ancient drink. Even the cheapest bottle will be at least three years old. This delight we're drinking here,' she would say, pointing at her glass, forgetting that I was not partaking in a drink, 'is a great deal more ancient than that. A truly respectable whisky.' She would nod away happily, her nose turning a little red.

Once she told me all about the process of distilling a single malt: how you mash the barley with water to create the sugars, how you dry it over a peat fire to obtain that distinctive smoky flavour.

'My grandfather's favourite malt was from the Hebrides,' she told me once. 'They store the casks in open storerooms along the sea-coast there, so the salty air can flavour the alcohol.'

'The very spirit of Scotland!' I nodded. Holly grinned delightedly.

Other times she would recount long family stories, some of them hers, some of them her husband's. They were obviously very close, and had spent a lifetime sharing tales. She always called him 'honey,' except when she got a bit merry on the old Auchentoshan, and switched to 'Arnie'.

Arnold once offered to teach me the piano. I took a few lessons, and discovered quite quickly that I was useless, but I did keep trying for two or three years. They had a slightly worn second-hand piano, which they might have inherited. It had a few sticky keys, but made a delightful sound nonetheless. I loved the music, and I never give up without first having a good try. Besides, Arnold was such a sweet man and a dedicated teacher, and he did it all for free. All he wanted in exchange for the lessons was to be invited to my parties, and it was always a pleasure to have them there.

'You must accept some money!' I told him once after we finished our little lesson. 'Even just a few pounds.'

But he would hear nothing of it.

'No, Bradley, I don't want your money. Just keep inviting me to your fine get-togethers and I'll be a happy man.'

'I don't want to waste your time!' I worried.

He laughed that big laugh of his.

'Your piano-playing may not be world class, but your parties certainly are.'

Holly and Arnold always came together, hovering shyly outside as the guests milled about conversing and eating canapés. Even if the door was open they would knock and wait, as if they weren't quite sure this was the right party, despite their having come to my house a hundred times before.

I would come and let them in, in just the same way as when they came round in the afternoon.

'Now how about a drink?' I would say, as always.

Holly would tug timidly at the hem of her dress and murmur, as if she'd just thought of it: 'Oh, a little whisky would be lovely, if it's no trouble.'

Arnold would lean in to put an arm around her waist, and lean towards me to add, sometimes in a terribly fake Scottish accent, 'Quite fancy a wee dram meself!'

It was like a well-rehearsed play. I would coax them into the party, and once I had poured them each a generous glassful they would visibly relax. She would soften right up, leaning into her husband's shoulder and telling me over and over what a nice time they were having.

My friends found them very entertaining, and occasionally liked to remind me of one occasion when Arnold had had a few more whiskies than usual, and said goodbye to all the guests twice. He kissed them all on both cheeks, while Holly chased him around the room, stumbling a little and apologising in her sweet old lady voice.

'Oh, Arnie,' she kept saying, 'do come on home now!'

I suppose he was just trying to get his money's worth for the piano lessons, Though usually it was Holly who drank the most. Every Christmas, I would give them an envelope as a present. I wonder if most of it went on whisky.

Several years later, in the seventies, with my own musical ventures far behind me, I decided to look for a piano teacher for my three-year-old daughter. I had advertised in all the usual places, but was having no luck. Then, one evening, as I was looking for something in the drinks cabinet for some dinner guests of ours, I suddenly remembered the neighbour from my student days who had given me lessons in exchange for whisky.

I looked him up in the phone book and found him much the same, still living in the same house.

'Bradley, is that you?' he said, recognising my voice right away. His voice hadn't changed at all either, even though we were both five years older then.

He seemed happy to hear from me. We reminisced about those years in Sussex, the walks, the parties in the evening. Eventually it was Arnold who brought me back to the real topic of our discussion.

'But tell me, old friend, to what do I owe the pleasure of this phone call?'

'I won't beat around the bush. Are you still teaching piano?'

Arnold seemed amused. 'So are you looking to start up your piano career, again?'

I laughed. 'No, I think my concert pianist days are behind me, now. But I have a little daughter who might have more talent than me.'

He agreed with delight, and I could not have been happier. He was absolutely wonderful with her. He made a gentle but serious teacher all at once, sitting next to her, making sure she did everything right. It became evident that she had all the musical talent her father lacked, and progressed spectacularly with Arnold's help; by the time she was six years old she was reading music and could play a few little pieces. One day we held a mini concert for the family and invited all her friends. Her abilities really were quite remarkable.

Sadly, when we moved to Paris, my daughter gave up on the piano lessons, and though she still plays some of the things she learnt when she was six, she has hardly touched the piano in the thirty years since then.

I was glad, nonetheless, that I had looked up Arnold and Holly, as it was lovely to catch up with the old couple. This time I managed to convince my old friend to accept some money for the lessons, but you can imagine what they answered when I said, 'Now how about a drink?'

'Oh, a little whisky would be nice!'

When living in one of the most glamorous parts of the south of France, it's hardly a surprise to find oneself surrounded by somewhat eccentric neighbours, including neighbours with motorcycles. Most often, one might encounter groups of youths in Ray-Bans and leather jackets, driving down to the beach with their blonde girlfriends. One might also come across ageing rock-star types, who also have pretty young things on their arm to compensate for the fact that their skin is starting to wrinkle, and that years of drinking are taking their toll on their hearts. But one would probably not be expecting Henri, the most unlikely owner of a Harley-Davidson I have ever met.

Henri was eighty years old, tall and slender, with pure white hair. He did technically fulfil the much-younger-girlfriend requirement, as his lovely wife Jennifer, an avid gardener, was in her sixties. She was his second wife; a delicate thing, who spoke excellent English and spent most of her time in a sun-hat, pottering among the bougainvillea and roses that filled their ocean-side garden. We often conversed over the fence as we looked after our flowerbeds; she seemed to enjoy giving me tips on rose-pruning and fertilising.

Henri had made his money in the Bordeaux wine district, and also spoke fantastic English, as much of his wine distribution market was situated in the US. He always claimed to be more of a Norman than a Frenchman, even though he was Arcachon-born and bred. He had been rather successful flogging trendy *mono-cépages* to the old-school American upper-crust, who disdained the New World vintages of Chile, Australia and California. He had thus made a name for himself and accumulated considerable savings, with which he had purchased the house immediately next to mine. We often chatted in the warm Côte d'Azur evenings, with the sound of the waves in the background.

The unusual thing about Henri, however, was that he didn't own a car.

'But how do you manage this in St Tropez?' I asked in amazement, when I first found out about this oddity. 'It's a city of hills, with almost no public transport! There's no train station, and I would be surprised if there were many buses to be found!'

'Ah, my friend,' he said smoothly, laying a hand on my shoulder, 'but I have a Harley-Davidson!' Despite his many years rubbing shoulders with the rich and powerful of America, he still pronounced the classic motorcycle's name *à la Française*, with rough rolled Rs and an inaudible H. 'I love my *'arley*,' he told me with a grin. 'It's a classic. Like me, it does not age.'

Henri's Harley-Davidson was the most impressive-looking I had ever seen, with a 1300 CC engine and a fat, black body that evoked crews of tattooed Hell's Angels and 1960s films. But did Henri go blasting along the hills at 200 kilometres per hour? No. What Henri liked to do was chug around on this huge motorcycle at about ten kilometres per hour, often going so slowly that he could stop just by putting his foot on the ground rather than braking. Oh, he did have his lovely younger lady on the back of his motorcycle, Jennifer tucked in gracefully behind him in a summer dress. But there would be no leather jackets, torn-up jeans or slicked-back hair for him. Henri rode his motorcycle in an outfit better suited to a gentleman attending a polo match, or taking a stroll on a boardwalk: perhaps a beautiful white suit and a dark red silk tie, or a light blue linen jacket with wide pinstripes and cream chinos, and always a beautiful pair of hand-tooled Italian leather shoes. His hair was always impeccably trimmed; one of our acquaintances once told me he went to the hairdresser's twice a week. He really looked more like an eighty-year-old top model than like a biker!

Henri was the only person I ever met in St Tropez who went fishing. He enjoyed taking his little boat out and sitting in the sun, whistling peacefully and bobbing on the bay, oblivious to the chaos on the beaches. Henri lived a careful and healthy life, usually eating salads and the occasional freshly-caught grilled fish, and only allowing himself the indulgence of one fine scotch a day. He cut a truly dashing shape on the little backstreets of St Tropez, strolling from one café to the next, from one restaurant to the next, not even to eat or drink anything but just to catch up with all of his neighbours and their gossip.

If I ever ran into him on one of his little outings, he would always make sure to stop and say hello, and have a brief chat about the weather, the wind on the beach, and what quiet little retirement activities he had planned for the day. We would usually speak

French, although we occasionally slipped into English, especially when his wife was around, as Jennifer loved to practice her language skills from school. After we had caught up, he would usually offer me a ride; if one was Henri's friend or neighbour, one could simply hop on the back and be anywhere in the city within seven minutes, rarely getting caught in traffic, whereas it would usually take a good half hour at least by car. I enjoyed Henri's company hugely. They were truly pleasant occasions; he might even speed up to twenty kilometres per hour for the sake of the company. A little breeze would blow in his hair, and he would smile, doing what he loved best.

Our friendship continued for almost another decade of us being neighbours. Henri was always in excellent health due to his regular exercise and healthy eating. But one day, Jennifer appeared at my front door, wearing a black dress and with her eyes a little red. She managed a sweet smile and handed me a black card, embossed in gold. I knew at once that Henri had passed away.

'I'm so sorry,' I told her gently. 'Henri was very dear to me.'

'He died in his sleep,' she said. 'We've been planning this for ten years. We have prepared everything: now I will sell the house and the motorcycle and move out. *C'est la vie,*' she added with a little shrug. 'He had a good life. All eighty-seven years of it.'

'What are you going to do, then?'

'Well, I'll focus on trying to sell the house first. Then I think I will head back to Bordeaux and retire by the sea there. It's where I grew up, you see. I think it should be where I spend my last years.'

'Listen, let me know when you start advertising the house. I have a friend who has been looking for a long time, and she's a gardener as well. I suspect she might be interested.'

As it turned out, she was. My friend, who worked in the jewellery and cosmetic business, loved the house as soon as she saw it, and was especially charmed by the gorgeous old rose bushes in the garden. The house was sold within three weeks, and Jennifer was able to move to her beloved Bordeaux.

I didn't go to Henri's funeral, as I had to travel the next day, but I sent flowers, and I still often think fondly of my friend the charming and unusual motorcyclist.

In France, it is traditional for companies to give gifts to their clientele around the Christmas period. These gifts cannot be of a capital nature, as giving jewellery, money or expensive furniture would be considered bribery. One cannot, even in France, simply hand over a gold Rolex, an Art Nouveau vase or a mahogany desk. Companies and employees alike are not allowed to accept such offerings. However, various consumables somehow seem to fall under some kind of traditional loophole. These include all sorts of products that would be difficult for a *bon vivant* to refuse: foie gras from the Dordogne, Belgian chocolates and Russian caviar, for instance, as well as cases of fresh oysters, fancy German stollen, Swedish smoked salmon, and candied chestnuts. They also inevitably feature a large selection of fine wines and spirits.

I first learned of this charming tradition in the early 1970s, when I had an important role at the head of a leading French bank. I was in charge of the company's multinational clientele, which included big-name oil, cement, glass and construction companies, as well as industrial and aerospace corporations. These were all vast, successful international organisations, and as such they all tended to dedicate generous amounts of funds to giving luxury gifts around Christmas. If my aim in my choice of bank partners had been simply to get the best festive offerings, my array of clients would have appeared to be particularly successful. The typical décor of the corridor and gallery that led to my apartment approximately from the first day of Advent onwards was stacks and stacks of wine cases and chocolate boxes. The stairwell of our building in the seventh *arrondissement* was filled from floor to ceiling with magnums of Champagne from the 1950s and 1960s, whole cases of cognac and Armagnac from the Dordogne, expensive bottles of Scotch whiskey, and rare bottles of wine like Cheval Blanc, Château d'Yquem, Château Margaux or Mouton Rothschild. Every single one of these bottles was probably worth over a hundred dollars; probably more like five hundred dollars in the case of the Cheval Blanc. Scattered between these cases and bottles, there were pots of jam and honey wrapped with crimson and gold ribbons, expensive foreign cakes in cellophane, piles of chocolate boxes from Neuhaus and Oberweis, full of hundreds of pralines and truffles and cognac creams and candied orange peel. All this was crammed together under my stairwell! My wife would come in every day and pick up the chocolates and the smaller offerings, in order to stack them under our family Christmas tree. It wasn't the biggest apartment, though, and eventually space would run out. Still, the gifts would keep on coming until the corridor was full of veritable pyramids of luxury goods, sometimes to the point where we could hardly get through them to our front door.

I had no reason to complain about the generosity of these partners, but there was one small reason that some of these gifts less than thrilled me: there wasn't a single person in our family who drank alcohol. My wife and I had never been drinkers, and when we had children, we even stopped serving it at our dinner parties. There wasn't a drop of booze to be found in our entire apartment. Thus, these extravagant alcoholic presents were essentially wasted on our household, building up in the corridor as uselessly as if we had been allergic to them, or didn't know how to open the bottles. Our solutions were limited, as it would have been considered rude to return these gifts to the sender. In any case, I would almost immediately lose track of which gift came from which company. The sheer volume of the offerings was too high for there to be any way to carry them somewhere to give away; in any case, to whom could one offer hundreds of bottles of wine? The answer occurred to me one day when I was clambering over a case of Pouilly-Fuissé in the corridor: I had no need to look further than my very doorstep. I was surrounded by people who might enjoy these bottles very much. It might be a way to befriend a few more neighbours as well!

This is how, in the winter of 1972, I became the most popular man in all the six floors of our building. I called round every door in the block, carrying a case of wine or cognac to each and every one. Of course, all the neighbours were thrilled at the arrival of this strange sort of alcoholic Santa Claus! Most of these people would be hosting dinners throughout the festive season and sitting around with their extended families by the fireplace, so the timing was excellent. Everyone asked me in, although many people kept trying to offer me a glass of the very drinks I was trying to get rid of so desperately! No-one could believe I was simply giving away these beautiful bottles of wines and liquor for free. I toured round the fifteen or sixteen apartments in total, leaving cases with a note outside the two doors that had remained closed. In the end, I really did feel a bit like Santa Claus. I walked back up to our own apartment through the far tidier corridors feeling a real touch of the Christmas spirit – although presumably not as much as my neighbours would be once they opened the bottles!

Later, looking back on those hectic weeks, I realised there were some downsides to this solution. For one thing, I hadn't anticipated the effect I might produce on some families by presenting them with a whole case of expensive alcohol. For a time, I was a bit concerned that I might have converted several people in the building into drunks! This worry came from one occasion when I caught the concierge sipping Mouton Cadet behind the front desk at eleven in the morning. Amusingly, the concierge had actually confiscated some of the boxes for his personal use long before I even began my distribution. I assumed he would have felt a little guilty upon receiving this gift as well, but in truth he probably just rubbed his hands together and got out his corkscrew. I thought these gifts would last most households for months and months, but I suspect the concierge drank his personal stash before the end of January. Nearly every time I saw the man, he seemed to be drunk. Of course, it was impossible to tell if his inebriation was down to the finest brandies or vodka from Lidl. I continued to give him the boxes, anyway. It was Christmas, after all. So what if my neighbours then spent the whole year just drinking my expensive wines and liqueur, which would normally have been totally out of their budget?

Of course, another thing I hadn't counted on was the fact that these neighbours wouldn't forget such an event easily. From October the very next year, people would accost me in the street or the hall, asking how my Christmas preparations were going or even overtly saying: 'Don't forget me!' It was all in all quite amusing. Everyone was suspiciously friendly at all times, but this escalated to ridiculous levels as soon as the weather started to get cold. They were like children, really, trying to behave just in time to be worthy of their Christmas presents. If I'd had any favours I needed to ask for, I could have had anything I wanted. As I didn't require anything from any of them at that time, not even a cup of sugar or a ride to work, I was simply the most popular man in the building without having to do anything at all. This continued for four years, until we moved out, and in that whole time, the beneficial effects of my solution never wore off. I suspect that, for a while at least, I was everybody's favourite neighbour.

MY NEIGHBOUR, THE TOYOTA

In this book, in almost all of my stories, the neighbours are human. There are, however, a few noteworthy exceptions. Like many, this neighbour arrived by surprise in the middle of the night, and, like some, stayed for years and years, slowly ageing and going to pieces. However, in this particular story, my neighbour was a small, red Toyota.

Our bank had a guesthouse in Riyadh to entertain guests, where I would stay if I travelled over from Paris to do business. It was a welcome change, in a city which was known to have some of the worst hotels in the world in the 1970s. The guesthouse was modest, but clean and modern, with a beautiful swimming pool out back that offered some comfort from the unremitting dry heat of the city. Sometimes the wind would blow the sand around for months at a time. It was often around fifty-five degrees Fahrenheit in the shade, and so dry that at times one's mouth would feel glued shut: Riyadh has its own sort of climate, much less humid than other parts of the state. I did love that pool, which somehow was kept beautifully clean of the dust and sand so ubiquitous in a windy desert. I would often sneak in a quick dip between appointments in the afternoon, and sometimes liked to swim there first thing in the morning as well.

One morning, I woke up early and tiptoed outside, only to find a car in the swimming pool. To say I was surprised would be an understatement. It was – or had been – a red Toyota, which had obviously suffered some kind of impressive accident before flipping over into the water, where it was now bleeding oil and dirt. I sighed. This was not the first time I had been stopped from swimming by things being in there: a noisy family, or a bunch of leaves, but this was something else. My main concern was how on earth the car had got there. I worked out that the incident must have occurred during the evening, while I was out to dinner. I figured that I wouldn't have seen it when I came back, as it was dark by the time I walked home, though the fact that I would have walked past this beast without seeing it was somewhat disturbing. I walked back to my room, already beginning to sweat from the morning heat. I thought I should probably call the police, as I could see no sign that the situation was being dealt with. However, I decided to go and knock on my neighbours' door first, on the off chance they might have been at home when the incident occurred, or otherwise have more information about it.

My neighbour, a young woman I had crossed paths with a few times, opened the door at once with a friendly and inquisitive smile.

'I'm sorry to bother you,' I said. 'I was just wondering if you knew anything about the car. In the pool.'

She laughed. 'Oh, so you noticed!'

'Do you know what happened?'

'Didn't you know? There was a big accident last night, with two cars colliding head on. It was horrible, a real car crash like in the movies. One of them didn't stop at the sign, on the street corner.'

'The stop sign that's covered by the trees?'

'That's the one.'

'Nobody ever stops at that sign.'

'I know, they don't,' she sighed. 'It was the middle of the night, too, so it was completely dark. We heard the screech of brakes, and a bang, and then the most terrific crashing noise. It didn't even sound like a splash, just like it had fallen into the garden. But we ran outside and of course everything was soaked, and the car was upside down in the pool. It was so bizarre!'

'I can imagine. I can't believe I missed all of this. And a Toyota, too. What a rare sight for Saudi Arabia!'

'They've become more common of late. Although of course the shiny American classics are still the most prevalent! Still, you missed quite the fuss. Apparently the car jumped straight over the fence after the collision. It didn't even destroy the fence, just bent it a bit! That was how fast it was going at the time it hit the other car.'

I shivered a little at the thought. 'The other car must have been much bigger, then, considering the state this one is in.'

'Oh, yes. It totalled it. The ambulance carried away two bodies. It was all pretty scary.' The neighbour shook her head, obviously still quite upset at the memory.

'Sorry, I don't mean to make you mull over such a horrible incident. I really just wanted to make sure everything was being taken care of. I was out to dinner when it happened, you see.'

She nodded. 'I guessed. There's hardly any other way you would have been able to miss the event. There was a huge crowd here yesterday.'

'So is someone going to take care of removing the car itself?'

'Oh, of course they will, probably later today. I mean, it's going to ruin the pool if it's not taken out! The police said they would send someone over from a local garage to take care of it.'

Perhaps unsurprisingly for a fairly quiet neighbourhood in Riyadh, nobody came that day. However, nor did anyone show up for the next few days. Eventually, I grew tired of watching our once-lovely swimming pool fill with oil and rust. I called the police.

'Are you going to do anything about the car in our swimming pool?' I asked them.

'We have many other cars to deal with,' they replied vaguely. 'There are many accidents all over the city. Most of the cars are on busy streets or in populated neighbourhoods. This one doesn't need to be moved quite so urgently.'

'Well, it's going to ruin the swimming pool permanently, and that's going to be expensive.'

'Your swimming pool is not our priority, sir,' they replied rather rudely. 'We'll get there eventually.'

I waited another two days, in hopes that they would deliver on their word, but nobody turned up or even phoned to follow up. I was worried the pool was being permanently damaged. Eventually, I gave up and called a garage service. I got them to tow the car out of the pool, which was a rather messy and impressive operation overall. As they had nowhere to take the wreck, they simply threw it right across the street, where it landed and stayed.

We kept that guesthouse for three years, and the car was never removed from across the street. We never found out to whom the car had belonged, or what happened to them. Gradually, sand accumulated all around it. Between the effects of the sun, the wind, the sand and the passing of time, the car began to disintegrate. Spare parts were stolen by passing thieves and opportunists: the engine and the wheels first, then other miscellaneous pieces. The rest of the car disintegrated into rust, from lying in a pool for almost a week and then being thrown out into the burning Saudi sun. Slowly, the car was eaten up: after three years spent in that street, it had almost completely disappeared. The little Toyota was my neighbour for a long time, but nothing lasts forever. As it says in the Book of Common Prayer: ashes to ashes, dust to dust. Or, in this particular case, sand to sand!

My friend Raymond was a great French artist of Italian extraction, whose large atelier sat right next door to our bank in western Paris. We first met when the bank commissioned a series of large paintings from him to hang in our lobby, and quickly bonded over our shared love of art. He was something of an expert on the subject of the history of art, which has always been of great interest for me. Many of our casual conversations in the hallways of the bank ended with us in a café down the road, talking animatedly over espressos.

We became good friends, and he taught me an element of friendship that I'd never thought about or really recognised before: that commitment to spending time with a person was an essential and necessary element of friendship. These were Raymond's two distinguishing features: his love of small, hand-rolled Italian cigars, and his dedication to the organisational level of his acquaintance.

'Never leave a friend without arranging to meet again, or you might not be friends when you next meet. It's just like any kind of relationship, people underestimate this. You have to set a friendship up and devote time to it,' he told me.

'Can't you just assume that you'll be in touch?'

'Never assume anything. Once you finish a conversation, a meeting, lunch or dinner – even if you run into each other in the street – you set up the chronology of your friendship. The next appointment, the next phone call, the next coffee. The next move, like a board game.'

'A board game that you plan ahead in your agenda? I don't think that would be a very good game!'

'Don't be clever, Bradley. You writers are all the same! Here's a better metaphor for you: you can't just plant a seed and then expect it to grow. You have to water it. Well, at least occasionally.'

'What, you mean some friendships are more like a cactus?'

He laughed. 'Exactly. Friendships are strange plants. Some you water with coffee, some with wine. I have you down in my notebook as the coffee sort.'

We used to meet up at least twice a year or so in the seventies and early eighties, and always had great fun. In fact, even once the commission was long finished, we continued to meet up every few months for years and years. His love of Picasso and Dalí matched my own love of William Morris, Charles Rennie Mackintosh and Valtat: our eras of interest may have been very different, but we enjoyed sharing our knowledge of our respective periods. We swapped anecdotes about our favourite painters' lives, and details about our favourite paintings. Raymond was the expert, of course, and I ended up learning as much from our coffees and evenings together as I would if I had started taking an art class!

I learned another lesson from Raymond, however, which was the importance of hard work even to the most chaotic-seeming of artists. Most days, I quickly learned, Raymond worked on his art all day, and often long into the night as well. He was an incredibly productive and driven man, even when he wasn't working towards a commission or finishing a project. He devoted as much time and attention to sketching up the first draft of a new idea on the drawing board as he did to applying the final coat of paint to some detail of a sculpture. Nothing he did felt incidental or rushed, and he did not hesitate to destroy works that he was unhappy with in order to start afresh.

His atelier was full of his current and newly-finished projects. It was a vast place, over a thousand square metres, which was a tremendous amount of space to find in Paris even in those days. It had incredibly high ceilings, and from this gained an almost palatial air, a sort of mixture of neoclassical and modern art. The black–and–white diamond tiles on the floor, combined with the marble columns, were the unusual setting for Raymond's sprawling sculptures. These sculptures really were quite exceptional things. One of the most memorable looked like a prehistoric animal from one side, a sort of carnivorous-looking alligator with sharp plaster teeth, while anyone approaching from the window-side of the room would only see an innocuous scene of beauties walking on the St Tropez beach, the flutter of their scarves preserved in carved stone. Everything was sculpted by hand, by Raymond himself: in those days, there was no trend to employ a cabinet of assistants for each and every project. He knew his materials, and he used a vast spectrum of them: from marble and glass to cast bronze and plastic.

He even used wood, which wasn't really in fashion then, and which gave some of his pieces an almost religious air. I recall a series of Germanic-looking sculptures referring to New Testament stories. Each of these scenes was carved out of stained oak, but this classic backdrop was offset with crude and modern-looking animals made out of contrasting colourful materials. 'You have to surprise your onlooker,' Raymond told me as I marvelled over these strange sculptures. 'I want to convey the deep seriousness of life as a moral human being, but also the surreal aspects of it, the strangeness, the beauty.'

'I could imagine this might be inspired by Dali,' I said thoughtfully, 'this sort of sense of unfamiliarity in the context of what looks like a well-known scene.'

'Exactly,' he said, picking up a cigar and lighting it. 'Everyone will recognise these Biblical scenes, even if they're almost unrecognisable in composition. All you need are the key scenes: the cross, the bread and wine, the fish... You couldn't miss these Christian symbols. I just like to wrong-foot my audience at the point of recognition.'

'With a plastic snake?' I asked with a smile, suddenly noticing an uncharacteristic addition to one of the pieces.

Raymond was unfazed. 'Sometimes. Other times, I just want to draw attention to the power relations implied in these scenes. The balance of human life: innocence and aggression, misery and wealth, power and weakness.'

'All art is concerned in some way with these things,' I pondered aloud. 'Perhaps you just highlight this incongruity with some of these superimpositions.'

'That's exactly what I aim to do. It's nice to be able to discuss these things with someone who has some sense of the historicity of these ideas. Many of my biggest fans are just drawn to the modernity, the madness of it, without understanding what I'm reacting against.'

'I don't even think you're just reacting against these old ideas. You're embracing them, giving them a new form. Think of your beloved Picasso: people have been painting the human form for millennia. He just presented it in a new light, from new angles.'

'You old flatterer, you,' Raymond chuckled. 'This is the real reason I keep you around.'

'No, I mean it,' I replied. 'I think it's fascinating. Because in a sense, you're a very conventional man: much of your art is for sale, and exposed in banks or city halls. But I think you're quietly subversive.

I think there's more of the Picasso or the Dalí in you than most of your clients realise. For instance, I noticed something when you mentioned the idea of the balance of human life. One of the motifs you come back to often is that duality of success versus poverty, strength versus feebleness. It's quite political: I've become aware that there's a lot of imagery of slaves and masters, for instance.'

There was a twinkle in Raymond's eye. 'Are you accusing me of bringing socialist imagery into the banks of France? I wouldn't dream of such a thing.'

Raymond was a truly balanced man, both in his choice of projects and his choice of materials. This did not mean he was a man without surprises. I remember asking him one day: 'If you spend all your time working, what do you do for entertainment? I know you love your work, but surely you must need a break sometime? Some amusement?'

'You're right, my dear friend,' Raymond chortled. 'Why don't I show you? Come over to the atelier when I'm painting tonight. I'll procure some of my most beloved amusement on the side. You'll love the painting, actually; it's a history of Charles de Gaulle that has been commissioned by the French government.'

'You mean you're entertained while you paint? That wasn't quite what I had imagined.'

He tutted jokingly. 'No questions, my friend. You will see tonight.'

When I arrived at his atelier that night, the lights were blazing and the rich smell of coffee filled the air. Raymond was halfway up a small stepladder, adding the finishing touches to De Gaulle's moustache. The painting was quite impressive, and seemed to have covered part of Raymond's white smock as well as most of the large canvas.

'Don't you look where you put the paint, you old scoundrel?' I greeted him as I walked in. 'There's more paint on you than on De Gaulle! Are you sure you should be entertained quite so thoroughly?'

'Bradley!' he greeted me expansively. 'Welcome to my den of mysteries. In just one moment, I will reveal the secret of my private life. Then you will understand the mess. The artist's most secret form of entertainment! Now, don't look so nervous, it's nothing salacious.' He walked back to the canvas, and switched on a small television. 'Ta-da!' he said.

'Look upon my works, ye mortals, and despair!' I said, rather puzzled. 'Raymond, what on earth are you implying? That just having the television on in the background is your entertainment?'

'Ah, but there's far more to it than that. Don't you try to dismiss it with your poetry.'

'But Raymond, it's an Egyptian film. Is this what you were watching? Do you even speak Arabic?'

'Excellent cultural recognition! Yes, it's an Egyptian film. I love them. They are my favourites.'

I shook my head. 'Is this some kind of surrealist joy of yours? Something I will never understand? Are you perhaps drawn to the experience of isolation?'

Raymond smiled. 'I'll make sure you end up writing my obituary. You turn everything to the most marvellous ends. You're not quite right in this case, although you're right about the strange joy. Look : sit down, pour yourself a coffee and just watch this for a while. You will see what I mean.' As I stirred one sugar into the delicate cobalt porcelain cup he had laid out for me, I stared at the grainy image. 'See,' Raymond explained, 'every five minutes I'll show you something wonderful. Look : just there, already. That painting, in the back of the scene, it just fell off the wall.'

'I saw that. But how is that funny? It's just... an odd thing that happened in filming, surely.'

'That's exactly my point. See, the glorious chaos of it? That painting wasn't meant to fall down. They just didn't re-shoot the scene. See, right there, that chair has a broken leg. They couldn't find another chair! They just improvise. Oh, those crazy Egyptians.'

'Wait, how did you see that chair? How did you even notice such a small detail? Have you seen this film before?'

'Of course!' he replied with a laugh. 'I've seen this film many, many times. I taped it months ago. That said, now I wish I had pretended it was just my brilliant artistic eye...'

I couldn't help but laugh. 'You're completely crazy, do you know that?'

'Quite possibly,' he responded without missing a beat. 'I just like to think I have a curious and perceptive mind. Now look at this scene, this is one of my favourites. This is the main character, he's meant to be some sort of smooth playboy. Now look what he's wearing! Green shirt, navy suit jacket, and what are those red trousers? Where do you even buy those? It's like they just raided his sister's closet!'

'I think I'm beginning to understand. Is it the accidental poetry you're drawn to?'

'Yes, I suppose it's something like that. Or something simpler: the chaotic charm of improvisation.'

We continued to watch in silence for a while, before Raymond suddenly clapped his hands together like a child. 'Oh, this is my favourite part,' he said, 'just wait a minute.' I couldn't help but smile at his childish enthusiasm, seeing now how what seemed like a rather odd pastime obviously brought him such intense artistic joy. 'Look,' he said breathlessly, 'everything is improvised, everything is real. See, they're walking through Alexandria, and the man is quoting Emerson, the poem about the beautiful moon reflecting over the lake. And what do you see? The sun, all fifty degrees of high-noon sun burning the people on the dirty Egyptian beaches. That's their idea of romance!'

'You're reading far too much into this,' I said, charmed almost against my will. 'It's just a terrible movie!'

'It's poetry,' he said. 'Real poetry. The poetry of the moon, under the light of the searing hot sun.'

'You're crazy,' I said with affection. 'You're also possibly some kind of genius. I'm not entirely sure. But I can tell you one thing for certain: you haven't painted a single stroke in the last hour.'

'Ah, but that is your fault, you see. I had to show you all the best parts. As my friend, you're to blame if I let my paintbrush dry!'

'Well, I'm confused and charmed. Why don't I finish this coffee and leave you to your work? I'm quite sure this wedding scene will be over soon.'

'You'll miss the bridesmaid dropping her drink in the background, but you can probably imagine that. And the mother forgetting her lines, and improvising this wonderful little speech about love. But if you're leaving, haven't you forgotten something?'

I smiled. 'I hadn't forgotten, Raymond. It's the best lesson you've taught me: always set up your next appointment at the end of your last.'

'Very good,' he smiled. 'How about next Saturday?'

The Charles de Gaulle fresco is still in the lobby of an important French government building, and every time I see it, I think back to my friend Raymond and his strange love of Egyptian films. Then I wonder when our next appointment is scheduled for.

THE EXPECTING NEIGHBOUR

Europe is well-known for its set of sympathetic social care systems. Immigrants from all over the world will flock to Spain or Switzerland in hopes of escaping the more difficult conditions of their home countries, hoping to be caught in the safety of the European support net. For example, in France, Germany or Switzerland, during the winter months, a person cannot be thrown out of their housing if they do not pay the rent. One cannot sequester people's possessions, nor take away the roof over their heads in such inclement weather: it's considered a human rights issue. Europe has an international reputation for taking care of its most vulnerable: the young, the unemployed, and refugees alike are looked after, as are the sick and physically disadvantaged. Thus, a pregnant woman cannot be evicted from her house or deported from a country, even if she is there illegally after her visa has run out, until she has come to term.

However, like any sympathetic system, this network is often taken advantage of. I witnessed this for myself in the case of one of my neighbours, a young woman by the name of Tam Peng. She had come over to Switzerland from China, and was working in a local restaurant as a waitress. She lived at the very top of the office building where our bank was based, probably in what used to be the servant quarters. I would occasionally run into her in the elevator that we shared, on her way down to the restaurant. She was a pretty, petite thing; always polite and well-spoken despite her heavy accent. When she stepped into the elevator in the evening, she sometimes carried with her a light smell of ginger and chilli, but it was hardly unpleasant.

It was a bitter winter in Geneva that year, and everyone went around bundled up in heavy coats and scarves. You couldn't tell if the people around you were skinny or giants: everybody looked like the Michelin man. One day, however, when I was standing side by side in the elevator with Tam Peng, listening to the piped music and trying not to make eye contact, I suddenly noticed that she appeared to be quite a bit larger than could be excused by her coat. In fact, she seemed to be five months pregnant or so. Now, I may not be well-known for my keen observations, but it was a very small elevator, and this was quite a surprise. No matter how big her flowery winter coat was, it could not disguise the undeniable bulge beneath. Furthermore, I knew for a fact that I had seen her not one week before and that she had definitely not been that size. We knew each other by name, and were acquaintances, if not exactly close friends. I was sure I would have noticed the gradual change.

I wondered what rational explanation there could possibly be. Could it be that she had simply been hiding the pregnancy up until then? Could she have been stuffing herself with pizzas and milkshakes for a full week, and doubled in size? No, I reasoned, there must be something stranger afoot. The change was too huge to go unnoticed. About halfway down the building, I had to ask her. 'Nihao, Tam Peng,' I managed; that being the only word I could remember in Chinese. 'Congratulations,' I continued with a smile. 'How far along are you?'

She smiled sneakily. 'Five months,' she replied calmly, resting a hand protectively on her bump. Of course, it would have been impolite to press the issue further, so I simply widened my smile, nodded, and we went back to ignoring each other until the elevator arrived on the ground floor.

Still, the strange encounter rather stayed with me. Did pregnancies really develop in such a dramatic fashion? I couldn't help asking myself somewhat naively. Did this mean that many svelte, petite women around me could be hiding babies for months and months at a time? The mind boggled. The next few times we shared the elevator, I allowed myself to look closely at her. However, as time went by, she did not continue to expand as dramatically as she seemed to have done the first time. In fact, she seemed to say exactly the same size. It was like watching a very peculiar science project that seems to be progressing completely at odds with one's predictions, or against the laws of nature. Perhaps, I reasoned to myself, this was what happened when the pregnancy was so discreet at the beginning. Maybe the weight had just caught up with her all at once, and would not change very much more!

Time went by, and Tam Peng and I continued to be neighbours in the elevator. The weather got warmer and the coats got smaller, until there was no denying the size and shape of her belly. I didn't ask about it again, limiting myself to small talk about the customers at her work, or to polite silence. However, a good five months later, when she was still exactly the same size, I found myself troubled. There was only so long I could attribute her stature to being Chinese and petite. I decided to ask her a few questions.

The next time we were side-by-side in the lift, I smiled politely and launched my attack. 'How are you feeling?' I asked her in my best considerate voice.

'Fine,' she responded a little suspiciously, although with a smile. After a somewhat awkward pause, she added: 'The baby's growing well.' I couldn't really add very much to that, so I had to wait for the next time we crossed paths to try and deepen my investigation. It was frustrating at times, trying to be a polite neighbour!

When we next met, she looked distinctly uncomfortable in her loose summer dress.

'How are you doing today?' I asked solicitously.

She shuffled back up against the wall of the elevator. 'Fine,' she muttered.

'I hope you don't mind me asking,' I continued, 'but have you found out if it's going to be a boy or a girl? Or are you keeping it a surprise?'

Tam Peng shifted from one foot to the other. 'It's going to be a boy,' she finally replied. From her posture, I knew that she was hiding something from me. I decided to push my luck.

'My wife and I are thinking about trying,' I said with my best impression of a shy smile. 'I was wondering if you have a local doctor?'

The girl blinked a few times. 'Yes,' she finally said, before adding, in something of a rush, a Chinese-sounding name. I jotted it down on a piece of paper, thanking her profusely. Of course, I already had several children of my own, but Tam Peng didn't know this.

When I got to work, I asked my secretary to look up the name of the doctor. 'He should be an obstetrician,' I added. After all, Geneva is very small: I figured I could perhaps find out a bit more about this strange condition. For all I knew, maybe women did sometimes have very sudden, extremely extended pregnancies! How was a man to know such things? However, my strongest suspicion was confirmed. There was no doctor by that name, neither anywhere in the city, nor even anywhere in the canton. I shook my head. 'What a mystery!' I told my secretary.

'You're not thinking of having any more children, are you?' she asked me with a bewildered smile.

'Oh no,' I replied with a grin. 'I'm just playing detective.'

The next time I encountered Tam Peng in the elevator, I was prepared. The second the door closed behind us, I cornered her. 'You're hiding something, Tam Peng,' I told her, narrowing my eyes. 'I don't mind a woman having her secrets, but I am terribly intrigued by this one. You've been pregnant for almost a year now. What on earth is going on?'

Tam Peng rolled her eyes and sighed. 'Fine,' she said, straightening her shoulders, 'I give up. I guess it doesn't matter anymore, anyway. I'll tell you the story.' As we stood in the lounge of the office building, she took my hand in hers. 'Here, touch my belly,' she said, holding my hand to her summer dress. 'See, there's nothing there. No pregnancy. It's all cotton wrappers and scarves.'

I couldn't believe it. I patted the soft bump with a strange expression on my face – I wonder what the concierge thought! I had known that something was amiss, but this was almost too strange to believe. 'Wait, so you were *never* pregnant?' I asked, flabbergasted.

She shook her head, abashed. 'I just had to look pregnant. See, I've been living in Geneva for nearly two years now. I love it here. I have a good job, I have a small but happy life. But my visa has expired, and they told me I had to go back to China. I don't want to go. Somebody told me they couldn't evict me if I was pregnant. So at first I thought I should try to get pregnant, but of course it would be so expensive, raising a child, and what if I were to really be deported? That was when I realised I could just pretend. After all, the number of people I see every day is quite small.' She cracked a small smile. 'I didn't know I would be sharing my elevator with a detective.'

'I'm no detective,' I replied. 'I'm just a curious neighbour. This makes much more sense, now. What I don't understand about the ruse, though, is that surely it can only be temporary. I mean, can't the police tell? I mean…' I poked the scarves tentatively with a fingertip. 'Won't they work it out?'

'They haven't yet,' she said quietly. Every time they've come to check on me, I've told them I'm five months pregnant. They send different officers, you see. Of course, there's no reason for them to doubt my story. It has worked already twice. As you can see, I'm still here.' Her shoulders slumped a little. 'It's all coming to an end, though. There's no use in me pretending. I found out last week the restaurant don't need me anymore. I don't know if they found out about my visa, or if they just wanted to fire me. But it looks like I'm going to have to head back to the old country.' She smiled ruefully. 'At least I don't have to carry a fake baby around anymore, though!'

'I have to admit I'm impressed,' I told her. 'Your strategy is a brave one, and it certainly fooled me. But it's not the sort of thing you can keep up forever.'

'Do you want to know something funny?' she asked me quietly. 'When I get home, I would quite like to settle down and have a baby.' She looked down at her bump of scarves with a wry smile. 'A real baby, I mean.'

A month later, I ran into Tam Peng one last time. She was still wearing the bundle of scarves. 'Haven't you had that baby yet?' I asked with a grin.

She smiled back. 'It won't be long now. I'll change the day I get on the plane.' She put her hand protectively on her stomach. 'Until then, I'm five months pregnant.'

I laughed, and motioned for her to step into the elevator. As we stood side by side, watching the numbers flash by, I reflected on the strangeness of our acquaintance. Finally, we stepped out into the lobby.

'I'm not going to say *nihao* anymore,' she said softly. 'I'm going to say *zai jian*.'

I smiled and shook her hand. '*Zai jian*, Tam Peng,' I replied. 'Best of luck with the move, and your upcoming pregnancy.' I winked. She stepped out into the summer sun. And that was the last I saw of Tam Peng, my strange and wonderful Chinese neighbour.

THE FISHERMAN OF
VALRAS PLAGE

In 1972, I was an executive in a big bank and a newly married man, which meant that I was happy, successful and very, very busy. Our holidays as a young couple were few and far between. The committee for the approval of credit, as well as various other executive functions in the bank, relied almost entirely on my authority. It was a fairly high-pressure position, but it was one I truly loved. At this pivotal point in my career, I didn't mind the loss of free time so much, but my young and beautiful wife didn't quite share this driven spirit. Of course she supported me in my work, but she regularly expressed the wish that we could simply have a little more time together. By the time we arrived at our first wedding anniversary, it was clear that it was important for me to do something to prove my dedication to her. After all, surely even bankers need the occasional holiday! I decided to take a full two weeks off to go away with my wife. I felt that I needed to allow myself some time away from work, at least on a few important instances.

Thus, on this occasion, I marked the holiday in my calendar and decided to take my wife away to the South of France. I did some research, and rented a lovely-sounding place on Valras Plage. I had been to various places on the Mediterranean coast often in the past for business and was familiar with the rocky beaches of Antibes and Monte Carlo, but I thought that, for this holiday, I would like to find something a little more special. Valras was reputed to be a much nicer location than the busy resorts of the Côte d'Azur, as well as a somewhat more secluded one. It featured a wide, sandy beach built into a series of sheltered coves, on the edge of a deep, clear stretch of sea. When we arrived, we knew we had chosen the right place.

The house was gorgeous, a modern little bungalow with a white wooden porch out front, with flowering vines climbing up the sides and surrounded by white sand. It looked weathered enough to be charming, but clean enough to obviously be a luxurious place to stay. It had a barbecue outside, as well as a huge American-style fridge. The bedroom was filled with a comfortable king-sized bed, and everything was decorated in a tasteful nautical theme. It was, all in all, a classic beach house, and the perfect choice for an anniversary getaway.

My wife was thrilled, and we settled in quite happily. The first day was a blissful whirl of swimming, walking barefoot in the surf and enjoying big platters of fresh Mediterranean food. We met a rather amusing couple who lived right next door to us in a one-bedroom shack; a pot-bellied man in a blue Hawaiian shirt and his rather large wife, who seemed to be drinking a bottle of red wine at eleven in the morning as they walked down to the water's edge. They were obviously enjoying themselves, and we had a very friendly discussion before parting ways.

'What do you think?' I asked my wife. 'Of the place, I mean, not the neighbours. Not that I have anything against local colour.'

'Oh, it's lovely!' she exclaimed happily, and giggled. 'Maybe we should crack open some cabernet sauvignon ourselves, and join in with the local traditions!'

I laughed. 'Even if I did drink,' I told her, 'I doubt I would be doing that!' I wondered briefly if any of my colleagues or predecessors would have felt differently about the issue. Did some people really just switch off and change temperaments when they left the office? That was emphatically not, I thought to myself, how I conducted my holidays.

For the first time in a long while, I was free of work responsibilities, and although the feeling was rather foreign to me, I tried to enjoy it as best I could. However, I was finding it difficult to switch off.

'Isn't it delightful, just the two of us!' my wife sighed happily, as we gazed out over the waves.

'Yes, my love,' I responded, trying not to sound like I was wondering how our top clients were faring. It is a very difficult thing, it turns out, to move from feeling intensely responsible for an organisation, to hearing nothing from them for a few weeks. Of course, in this day and age, I would probably have been constantly on the phone to the office, or tapping out emails on my iPhone or Blackberry, but this was the seventies, and a holiday was a holiday! When we rented this place, we were given a number to hand out in case of emergencies, and told it belonged to a neighbour. I had given the number of the landline to my colleagues, but had heard nothing from this theoretical neighbour. How odd, I thought. All day at work I found myself wishing for just a few minutes' respite from the responsibilities of a constantly ringing phone. Now, when all I could hear was the cry of seabirds and the contented sighing of my wife, I longed for that loud, important-sounding trilling. I didn't even know where this phone was! How could I be longing for an emergency?

I would not have to wait long, as it turned out. The very next day, as my wife and I were tidying up the crumbs from our breakfast of fresh croissants and preparing a picnic basket to take on a long romantic walk, there was a knock on the door. I opened it to find our neighbours standing there. 'Someone's called for you!' the man said quite happily, without any further introduction. His hair was wet, and he was wearing a red and orange Hawaiian shirt this time. He had huge mutton chop sideburns, as was the fashion of the time. His wife was wearing a loose-fitting white dress with a pattern of flowers. 'I've left the phone off the hook. You should come over and pick up.'

'Oh, it's probably just my mother!' my wife exclaimed merrily. We walked over quickly to the neighbour's shack, and she ran over to pick up without even taking in our surroundings. I looked around. The place quite obviously only had one room, with the bed hidden at the back by a shabby curtain. It didn't have a sea view, as it was right behind our holiday home. The room was quite dark. It smelled strongly of cigarette smoke and faintly of fish guts, although everything was kept very clean.

After a moment, my wife's face fell. 'It's for you,' she said, obviously disappointed. 'Don't be too long, darling, or the midday sun will be out!' I nodded, already holding the phone to my ear, waiting for its precious business tidings.

'Bradley,' the stern, familiar voice said, 'I need your help. It's very urgent.'

A familiar, workday thrill went through me. Something urgent had come up! I was to be in charge again! 'Tell me all about it,' I said at once in my most professional voice. I frowned apologetically at my wife, trying to convey the obvious seriousness of the event. She sighed and dawdled by the side of the battered dining table. Meanwhile, the neighbours hovered in the background, obviously intrigued by the nature of this so-called emergency.

'You remember that report,' my colleague explained. 'The one you were working on when you left?'

'Of course,' I replied.

'Well, it's all gone chaotic. The client called us up today, changed his mind completely. You'll have to do the report all over again, and submit it to the board by the day after tomorrow. And then there are a few new payments waiting for your approval. I just don't know what to do without you here!'

I grinned, then hastily readjusted my features into a mask of concern when I caught my wife's gaze. 'Yes, yes,' I said in my most serious voice. 'Tell me what I need to do.' My wife narrowed her eyes and flounced out of the house, slamming the door behind her.

'We need you back here,' he said. 'Right now, Brad. How fast can you be back in the office?'

My heart sank. It was one thing being reminded of my position of power, quite another being pulled back to it after only one day of holiday. I hesitated. 'Are you sure that's necessary?' I asked, rather timidly. 'I mean, this is my wedding anniversary.' I said this part somewhat louder, in case my wife might still be standing outside the door. I thought I might have heard a little feminine sniff. I tried to think on my feet. If I needed to do this paperwork that quickly, there was really no alternative to a swift journey back to Paris. In those days, there were no faxes; no hastily-scanned email attachments. There was only the postal service, which was incredibly slow. There certainly wasn't anything like DHL or FedEx; not that it would have gone from a small village like ours anyway.

'This is important,' he said apologetically. 'I need you to prioritise.'

'OK,' I replied reluctantly. Then the businessman in me took over, and I added: 'I'll be there by tomorrow afternoon.' After a few more pleasantries and practicalities were exchanged I hung up, slowly. Now for the hard part, I told myself. It was one thing attempting to face down my colleague; quite another facing down my determined young wife.

'But Bradley,' she cried out when I told her, her eyes brimming with tears, 'what about our picnic? What about the villa? We've paid for everything in full!' I guessed she was trying to appeal to my more practical sensibilities, and figured I needed to find a practical solution. 'I know, darling,' I replied. 'We'll have to do something about that.' I wished it was as easy to reassure her as it was to deal with a banking client.

'They'll never reimburse us!' she complained. 'We're already here! Oh Bradley, wouldn't it just be easier to stay and enjoy ourselves a little while longer?'

I had to be firm. 'I can't stay,' I said gently. 'I promise you I would if I could. Look, we'll give away the villa to somebody; some neighbour. Somebody who deserves it. Make sure it doesn't all go to waste. I'll take care of that while you go pack up your things. And next year, I promise, we'll take a proper holiday.'

'You say that every time!' she said, before blowing her nose loudly into her handkerchief.

'It's only our first anniversary,' I reminded her.

'Yes,' she said, 'but that's meant to be for *paper*, not for paperwork!' She turned her back and left the room, slamming the door behind her. I sighed, and decided that my energies would be better expended sorting out the practicalities of my decision, rather than trying to assuage my young wife's hurt feelings. I would make it up to her later, I promised to myself. Maybe I would take her out for a nice meal that very evening. But I just had to get back to work, I told myself. I was important. I was needed. I didn't really have a choice.

After scribbling a few notes and packing up the kitchen, I left the house and stepped out into the bright sun. The first thing I had to do was find a new taker for the house. Should I just give it away to the first person I spoke to? That hardly seemed like a safe option. However, at that very moment, I spied our jolly French neighbours, obviously just coming back from a swim. I waved to them and walked over.

'How was your emergency?' the man asked cheerily. 'Can we make you a strong coffee, or recommend a good place to eat, perhaps?'

Once more, I was struck by how friendly they appeared. I made up my mind almost at once as to what the solution to my dilemma would be. 'I would love a coffee, actually,' I told them. 'I have something of a proposition to make you.'

When I explained the situation to them, it took some time to sink in. At first, we spent some time in idle chit-chat, so I could try to gauge the personalities of these two people I was thinking of entrusting such a nice home to. Were they the kind of people to spill red wine on the immaculate Egyptian cotton bed-sheets? Or would they truly appreciate the loveliness of the sunset from the vast bay windows?

The man had a large pot belly, which he tried to cover up with the large shirts, giving him a rather messy appearance. He had a crew cut, with aviator sunglasses propped on top, and he probably fancied himself some sort of cowboy, although I suspected that if he came anywhere near a horse, he would as likely be trampled on as anything. He worked as a fisherman, he explained, while his wife was a maid. He got up every morning at five to bring the fish to the early morning market, so they had the rest of every day to themselves. They had only moved here recently, hoping to be near the sea, but they couldn't really afford a nice house yet. 'We're saving up, though,' he explained with a toothy grin. 'The seaside part is sorted, now we just need a nice house.'

The wife smiled prettily at me. She was not the most beautiful Frenchwoman I had ever met, being obviously something of a *bonne vivante* with tattoos on her arms, but she was clearly a kind and hardworking person. I couldn't help but take a liking to the odd, messy couple.

'Well,' I said with a smile, 'I might have something that would interest you. It would only be for two weeks, but maybe it would give you a taste of something a little nicer! Not that your house isn't lovely,' I added hastily, hoping I hadn't offended them. I needn't have worried.

'What, this shack? It's a piece of crap,' the husband said in complete good humour. 'But are you suggesting what I think you are? I don't understand.'

'Look,' I said, 'I came here on holiday with my wife, for our first year anniversary.'

'Congratulations! May it be the first of many happy anniversaries,' the wife said sweetly.

'Or the first of many happy wives!' the husband chimed in with a grin. His wife slapped the back of his head playfully.

'However,' I continued, 'as I explained earlier, we have to leave this evening. I have work to do, you see,' I added with the tiniest hint of pride. 'We would like you to stay in our villa.'

'To take your place?' the woman piped up disbelievingly.

'Yes,' I said with a smile.

'We can't possibly afford that,' she exclaimed, blushing.

'We've already paid for everything,' I said with a magnanimous grin. It was hard not to be thrilled by their obvious disbelief.

'For nothing?' the husband repeated blankly.

'For two weeks,' I added. For what must have been about half a minute, both of them just stared at me, open-mouthed. I began to feel almost uncomfortable, and started blushing myself. 'It's not a big deal,' I told them. 'Really. You'll be doing us a favour.'

The couple looked at each other and burst out laughing. 'A holiday!' she exclaimed at once. 'In our own front yard!' The husband simply grinned. 'That's swell,' he said. '*Super*. When can we move in?'

I walked them over to the property, where my wife appeared to be nowhere to be found, and spent a good hour explaining the various appliances. 'I swear that fridge is bigger than our entire kitchen!' the woman exclaimed happily. I refrained from noting that the kitchen was probably bigger than their entire house. I suspect the rent of that place probably cost them their salary for the year. When we parted ways, I left them the keys and the woman gave me a rather un-French hug.

The second the door closed behind them, my wife reappeared behind me, holding all our packed suitcases.

'Do you even know those people?' she asked frostily.

'No,' I replied with a smile, 'but they're our neighbours!'

The ride back to the airport was a rather tear-stained one, but my wife obviously understood there was no going back now. I promised her a nice dinner that night, and that we would go on holiday another time, and by the time we were on the plane home, she seemed to have forgotten her sorrows. As she settled in to read her book, I was free to give my mind over to the business problems that would be awaiting me upon my return. Much as I was sad to leave our lovely holiday behind, I couldn't help but look forward to getting stuck into the job. Meanwhile, I found myself hoping our neighbours would enjoy their surprise luxury stay!

A CHAT WITH NAZLA

When I first settled in France, I had an apartment on the third floor of a building in a lovely area of Paris.

It seemed to be a nice enough place, but there always seemed to be a pervasive odour of smoke coming from upstairs. No matter how tightly we kept our door closed, or how much air freshener we might use, it would not go away. The first time Nazla came to visit us, she not only taught us the origin of the smell, but brought it with her and smoked about ten of the offending cigarettes in our lounge.

Nazla was probably in her sixties, pudgy and tanned, but she seemed quite ancient in a way. You rarely saw her without a cigarette in her mouth. She was a fascinating figure, with what could be described as an almost masculine face: strong cheekbones, and hardly any neck. I believe she was of Italian or Greek origin. She liked to make some of her own clothes, often in dark colours and dramatic cuts. She was a sort of quiet gypsy figure, and I think the smoking formed part of her persona.

My wife Hilary was a very patient person. At this time, she was pregnant, so she was quite happy to have a visitor. Nazla would come downstairs with some strange assortment of cigarettes and cakes, or some dish she had prepared at home, and settle in for a few hours. She never called ahead or made an appointment; just knocked at the door and walked in. I suppose she spent most of her time baking cakes and making clothes for herself. Her visits to our apartment were her social life.

We came to fulfil several essential functions for her. We provided conversation, company, lighters. But we also occasionally provided social entertainment. We ate her cookies, we observed her nice clothes, we provided her with local gossip. She had obviously lived a life of means, but didn't have much of an environment to show off her variety of outfits. Consequently, every time she came to our house she would be wearing a different set of clothes: some nicely tailored suit jacket over a flowered skirt, or perhaps a designer hat with a dress she had made herself, and always a different pair of glasses. I found it very amusing.

Conversation between us was limited, as she was almost completely deaf. She could speak, but not hear any response I made, so I had to work on communicating with my hands through basic sign language. Her lip-reading was also excellent. I began to learn how to speak so she could read my lips more easily. At first I exaggerated every word. Soon, however, I realised she was much quicker than that, and could follow almost any conversation going on around her. It became like a game between us, and both my wife and I became very good at it.

Still, it was not easy to have more than very basic conversation, so we often sat in companionable silence – or else she would simply ask me to light her cigarettes. Often she would come to our apartment without thinking to bring a lighter or matches, so it would be up to me to find her a light. I would either go to the kitchen and light the cigarette with a candle or, if I was feeling more formal, I would fetch the highly decorative lighter we kept in the living room, and use that. Either of these scenes would have appeared quite amusing to any outsider. And there she would sit, clutching the white cylinder of a Gauloise or a Gitane between her lips, sucking deep and then exhaling. At times she was almost completely hidden by cigarette smoke, like some sort of magician appearing on stage through a fog of dry ice, the smell of which never completely left our living room.

With my wife, it was a little different. The two women enjoyed small talk. They never seemed to stop! They appeared to be able to chat for hours about neighbours, the weather, her grandchildren's marriages. It was astounding to me how they were able to come up with nearly endless material. There would be a lot of hand-waving, and lip-reading. In those moments, she appeared more like a mysterious fortune teller, swathed in scarves and wreathed in smoke.

For me, this sort of interaction seemed meaningless, but it was social. Both Nazla and Hilary valued it highly. Nazla, after all, lived alone: she had grown-up children but they had long since moved on in the world. Hilary, at this point in time, was six months pregnant, and spending a lot of time at home. The two women took a great deal of pleasure in each other's company.

One of the funnier aspects of interacting with Nazla was her almost complete inability to stop talking once we had begun. In the early days, I tried the normal subtle tactics. 'Gosh, is that the time?' I would say. 'I really must get going.' This would produce no effect on our guest. I would have to resort to more obvious lines quite quickly. 'I've got to go now, Nazla,' I would say quite clearly. But she would not react, almost as if she had suddenly lost the ability to lip-read at all, and just innocently continue some long story about her childhood, or her daughter's cooking, or her husband's foibles. Eventually I would just have to wave at her or walk away, leaving her to continue talking to my wife, though her strategy was more like talking *at* my wife.

As usual, my wife developed the perfect strategy for coping with this never-ending stream of chatter. She trained Nazla to follow her around the house as she got on with her household tasks. Nazla would watch her cooking, sewing, darning holes in clothes, or preparing clothes for our child who would soon be born. She would look on, chatting away, and occasionally trying to help. I wouldn't say that my wife would have trusted her with party organisation or protocol, but then she had a maid for those things, so she accepted Nazla's bits of help quite happily.

After a time, Nazla essentially became a permanent fixture in our house. When our friends would come and visit us from Ireland, America or France, they came to accept her as a sort of decoration or statue. When anyone else was in the house, she would opt out of talking, knowing she would be an imposition on the flow of conversation. It was only when we were alone with her that she brightened. Still, I believe she enjoyed sitting companionably with us, lip-reading our conversations. I can still imagine her in her chair, chain-smoking, occasionally nodding her head. After a time, although with no recognisable impetus, she would stand up and go round the guests, shaking hands and giving kisses. Then she would walk away, leaving only the smell of smoke behind her.

STRAWBERRIES DAY AND NIGHT

When I lived in Sussex, on the other side of my garden fence was a mysterious figure. A hunched figure, topped with a hat, most often seen carrying a spade. For the longest time, I couldn't quite tell if he was eighty or twenty, as he never even raised his head. After a while, I gleaned from the other neighbours that he was about forty-five, that his name was Mr Kenhurst, and that he was a strawberry farmer.

The strawberry fields stretched down the 500-yard-long length of his garden, covered with clear glass cupolas and watered by automatic sprinklers. They were a rather lovely sight to behold, like a long row of miniature greenhouses. The soft pattering sound of the sprinklers at sunrise and sunset was soothing. He never seemed to water the plants during the day: I think it must have been so the sun didn't wilt the wet leaves. All day long they would soak up the sun through the glass, and then uncover them so they could soak up the water in the evening. There must have been some magic in this technique as it produced the juiciest, most flavoursome berries I have ever tasted.

I know a little bit about strawberries, having grown them myself on a humbler scale. To produce large, red, perfumed strawberries, you need just the right amount of sun and humidity. If one or the other is lacking, the strawberries keep their pale tinge, and have more of an acidic flavour. The berries next door were never pale. I could see them from the windows, those clusters of bright crimson fruits hidden in the dark green leaves. They were exceptionally large, too, and beautifully formed. These were near-perfect strawberries; a true luxury product, but I couldn't help wondering if they were worth the sacrifice of his social life.

Mr Kenhurst, to put it mildly, was a quiet sort of man. In fact, he was almost entirely silent most of the time, roaming the length of his strawberry fields from morning till night every day. I would often try to draw him out, even just with the most basic of greetings, but the simplest 'hello' would never get more than a grunt of acknowledgement from him. At times, I would prepare a whole series of questions to try out across the fence, attempting to coax him out of his silence or even get him to look up, but it was a lost cause.

'Hello!' I would try.

There would be no answer.

'How are the berries today?' I would ask, cheerily.

No answer.

'How are your lovely children?'

No answer.

Or even just: 'Nice weather, isn't it?'

Still no answer. Most of the time, he wouldn't even look up. Sometimes he would deign to raise his battered hat for a fraction of a second, but I never achieved anything approaching eye contact or conversation.

It was more than just being quiet, or even rude. There was an inherent strangeness to the man. I would see him out there in the heavy autumn fog, bent over in the horrid drizzling October rain. He was in his garden in the dead of winter, snowflakes falling all around him, lit by a gaslight. I had never seen winter strawberries, but there they were, kept safe by the low glass domes and their mysterious protector.

At first I assumed he must be the salt of the earth type, an old fashioned sort of gardener who had to raise the plant from seedling to sprout, from blossom to fruit, and could not possibly look away for a single minute. He was certainly out there in his garden from dawn until dusk every day, which is hard not to romanticise, and the fruit was undoubtedly gorgeous enough to warrant it: luscious, huge berries, nurtured to maturity by this caring and dedicated man. There was a certain charm to that vision, but his cantankerous disposition spoiled it quite quickly.

After that, for a very short time (perhaps in an attempt to be charitable) I wondered if he was deaf. The first grunt of acknowledgement, however small, put an end to that theory.

Then I began to wonder if his decision to spend sixteen hours a day outside the house had more to do with avoiding his wife or not taking care of his two children. After all, he didn't seem like the friendliest or the most sociable of people. I mean, how much was there really to do in that strawberry patch? How many bugs or weeds could there be? Perhaps he had come to a point in his life where he wanted to avoid all human interaction, at any cost, I thought to myself.

Something of an answer came when I was discussing him with Mr Thorley, the neighbour who lived on the other side of the strawberry fields, his own garden as daunted as mine by the glorious fruit. Mr Thorley had come over to borrow a rake, and was leaning on the fence in my garden, looking out over the famous berries. Somehow we got onto the topic of their owner.

'He's never even said hello to me,' I said, trying not to sound bitter.

'Oh, I wouldn't take it personally, you know,' he replied. 'It took me months to get even a nod out of him. Even now I don't know his first name.'

'You've lived here for years, though!' I was genuinely surprised, and indeed rather reassured.

'He's a crazy man with a real green thumb. No time for anything else.'

'An obsession, then?' I wondered aloud.

'Oh, he's not just obsessed. There's a sort of method to the madness. He's madly business savvy.' Mr Thorley raised his eyebrows knowingly. 'Grows three seasons of strawberries a year, you know. Only one I've ever heard of who does.'

'Three seasons! Is that even possible?'

And indeed I'd never heard of such a thing. This certainly explained his mysterious night-time activities in the dead of winter. In those days, the kind of plants that gave fruit year round must have been a novelty, certainly in England, although everyone is used to eating all kinds of fresh fruit all year round now.

'But strawberry season is in June! Every child and granny all over Europe knows this, surely! I've lived in Normandy; I've lived in the Alps – no matter how much bright sun and fresh air you get, the season only lasts six weeks.'

The neighbour nodded sympathetically.

'He's a right sort of madman.' He lowered his voice conspiratorially. 'Do you know I've seen him out in the garden past midnight? He goes out there with a flashlight to check on his precious strawberries. You know those old ladies who live with a million cats and dogs? Well he's a bit like that. They're like his babies.' He shook his head. 'I'm pretty sure that's the secret to his success. Sleeping with the berries, curled up between the vines...'

I laughed a little. 'So he must be pretty successful then. Do you think it's worth it?'

'No idea,' he replied, a little grumpily, 'He's never let me taste one, you know. Absolutely rolling in cash, he is, and not a berry to spare. I mean, I obviously refused to pay for the things, but…'

It was fascinating. At that time, there seemed to be no-one else in all of England capable of growing three seasons in a year. Mr Kenhurst had an exceptional green thumb, and it turned out that he seemed to be able to use it to produce green banknotes as well as bright red strawberries!

To understand the extent of his business success, one must realise that, in December of 1975, his strawberries cost £5 a pound. Now, this would have been an outrageously high price at the time, although it may seem less surprising to your modern Waitrose shopper. Winter strawberries would have been a luxury, after all. One has to remember that in those days, an engineer's salary would have been around £20 a week. That would have meant that an engineer would have had to work for a whole week to buy four pounds of Mr Kenhurst's sweet, ripe strawberries, assuming that this engineer shopped at Harrods, Fortnum & Mason or any of the restaurants in London that stocked his precious fruit: the White Tower, the Inn on the Park, and the Connaught.

Yet it was surely no accident that Mr Kenhurst's berries were so exceptional: his dedication to his strawberry fields was unshakeable. One year in the early eighties, the sun barely showed from the summer through the winter. Still he stood in the garden all day, in the drizzle and the darkness, and still he produced his three beautiful crops. It was nothing short of miraculous.

The man must be a magician. So how did he do it? I still have no idea, but certainly the key was spending all day every day in his garden. I found myself wondering whether he ever ate anything. Did his wife slave away indoors at rich crumbles and sweet jams and pies? Or were the crops guarded jealously from all but the highest-bidding buyers?

I never did find out, but I did have the privilege of eating the precious berries, and my, they were an exceptional treat! Sweet, perfumed, still slightly warm from the sun, they needed no sugar or cream. When I brought my first box home I must have eaten a dozen straight from the box, until my fingers were sticky with juice.

Right then, it didn't matter that I had a grumpy neighbour.

I was sure it must all be worth it.

For a time, I lived across the way from one of my physics professors from university. I could open the window from one of the rooms in my apartment and see the interior staircase of the building where he lived.

Kelly was a very fussy professor of mine, who found it hard to snap out of his academic mode even in casual conversation. He must have been about forty years old around the time I knew him, and was a tall, muscular-looking man with red hair and light green eyes. His father was Irish and his mother was probably Mexican, which gave him a rather intriguing face, and a confused but devout sense of Catholicism.

After a time, I began to notice a very strange ritual of his. It was first brought to my attention by an odd noise: an irregular thumping sound. It was most annoying in the morning, although it also seemed to occur in the evening, and it came from the building opposite. I soon realised that Kelly was responsible for this noise: I could see his tell-tale red hair bobbing up and down in time with the sound. After several days of observation, I worked out that he seemed to always go up and down the stairs in his building two or three steps at a time. It was very strange. Doing this on the way up your stairs I suppose I could understand. But doing it on the way down seemed dangerous and unusual. I began to speculate on the possible reasons for this behaviour.

At first, I assumed it must be a special workout routine, some kind of strange cardio. He certainly must have been out of breath by the time he got down or up all four flights of stairs. But although it was the most logical one, this theory did not quite satisfy me. Was it some sort of strange physics experiment?

Some months after I had discovered this habit of his, I ran into him outside the building and stopped him to find out.

'Kelly,' I said, 'first of all, I just have to ask. Why on earth do you jump up and down the stairs? I mean, it's so noisy! Sometimes it distracts me when I'm trying to study! I'm sure everyone in the whole street knows about you and your jumping.'

'Well I'm sorry if it's noisy,' he said, a little haughtily. 'It's just essential.'

'What do you mean, essential? Why don't you jog in town? Or around the stadium? Have you been to the stadium? It's lovely.'

'Why on earth would I do that? I've never done sports in my entire life.'

I was intrigued. This put an end to my first theory, which had seemed to be the most obvious one. However, I then brought out my second idea.

'Oh, I see then. I've been watching you. The irregular pattern of the jumping, the careful way you do it. It's a physics experiment, right? What are you studying, eh? Is it about gravity? Are you practising to go jumping on the moon?'

Kelly's stern expression changed as he cracked a perplexed smile.

'I don't know what you're talking about. What a ridiculous set of questions. Let me ask you something, Bradley.' He had his serious teacher's voice on now. 'Have you seen the condition of our staircase?'

Still half-expecting a physics explanation, I replied that I had not. 'I mean, I suppose it has to do with the angle. I'm just looking across the street. All I can see is your red hair going up and down,' I added. There was a slightly awkward pause.

'It's too clean,' he said simply.

'Sorry?' I had no idea what he was talking about. 'You're complaining because your staircase is too clean?' I repeated. 'You're jumping because your staircase is too clean?'

'It's cleaned every single day by the concierge,' he explained impatiently, as if the explanation was annoyingly obvious. 'That woman gets up at eight every day so she can clean the stairs with a hose like it's the nineteenth century, and she never, ever dries them. So I have to be very careful when I go up and down those stairs. They are wet and slippery, and get dirty very quickly from other people's shoes.'

'You mean you only jump on the dry bits?' I was amused and astounded.

'Yes. Only the dry bits. Firstly,' he explained, 'I do not like to slide. Wet stone steps are a very real security hazard. I have no intention of falling down four flights of steps and breaking my spine.' He paused to adjust his jacket self-righteously. 'Secondly, I do not like to use elevators.' He did not elaborate. 'And thirdly, I do not wish to get my shoes wet. I have a beautiful Isfahan silk carpet in my house and I do not wish to get it dirty. It is my prize possession,' he added proudly.

'You never, ever step on the wet bits?' I still found this hard to believe.

'Never,' he said.

And in all the time he lived next door to me, I believe he never did.

MY NEIGHBOUR AND MY UNCLE

My family has a beautiful palatial dwelling in Istanbul, built of several colours of marble and sandstone, with large arched windows looking over the old town of the city.

The distinguishing feature of this house in my memory is the large stone fountain in the front courtyard. Often, the children and grandchildren of the family would jump into the cool water to refresh themselves. The heat in Turkey in the height of summer can be roasting, and it was a delight for the little ones to sit on the large marble ledge or splash around in the deep water of the fountain. But that was not the house's only charm.

Like most houses of its quality, it was split into family quarters and baths. There were actually twenty-seven rooms and two vast Turkish baths, designed in the traditional fashion inspired by the old Roman set-up, with their frigidaria and caldaria. This meant that they consisted of a series of tiled rooms filled with water of varying temperatures, from steam-hot to nearly ice-cold, so you could progress from one to the other according to ancient cleansing and relaxing rituals.

It was like having a swimming pool, a luxurious bathroom and a bar all rolled into one. The idea was to cleanse oneself in the first hot rooms by sweating out all the impurities, then to progress to other hot water rooms to wash with perfumed soap and, for ladies, to dye one's hair with henna. Then you could relax in the cool water whilst enjoying refreshments. Bathers could thus emerge from one of the hottest rooms and jump into little cool fountains to nibble watermelons, or be handed a cold orange juice drink by a butler dressed entirely in clean white towels.

I would visit there often with a butler and a maid, and loved to use the baths myself, so it was no surprise when I discovered that they were the envy of the neighbourhood. Once, on one of my rare visits from Paris, there was a knock on the front door, and when I opened it I found a woman standing there shyly in the heat. She was middle-aged, with long dark hair and a sweet, roundish face.

'I'm sorry to bother you,' she said in a soft voice, 'but I was just wondering, as I'm your neighbour, if you would perhaps allow us access to your baths? It would be such a kind, generous gesture.'

'What's happened to your bath?' I asked in reply.

'We don't have one,' she said humbly. 'We only go to public baths, probably once every six weeks or so.'

'But how do you wash?'

'Oh, we have a basin. We wipe ourselves clean every morning. That's it.'

'How do you wash your hair?' I found this hard to imagine. It was hard not to feel sympathy for this poor family.

'We wash it in the basin once a week.' She looked at the ground, obviously embarrassed but determined nonetheless. 'We almost never get a full steam bath. It would be so wonderful if we could use yours.'

'What do you mean, 'we'?'

'I have five children, between the ages of two and eleven. Could they come with me?'

I was so taken aback by this woman's request that, somehow, I said yes.

'OK, you can come in. Just go get your children and your towels.'

'Oh,' she grinned, 'we have them already.' She added hastily, 'Just in case...'

Five small children scampered out from round the corner, where, sure enough, they had been waiting with their cases all carefully packed up with towels, shampoo, and a change of clothes. I caught a flash of eager faces and dark hair as they walked right in past me, one after the other, all of them different sizes. It would have been hard not to find them cute, trooping in, all lined up like characters from a Norman Rockwell painting.

I led them to the bath and set it up so it was nice and steamy for them. They all went in together, very politely. I didn't hear a noise from them. Three and a half hours later they all came out together, their faces glowing clean and their cheeks red, dressed very neatly. The mother came out last, ushering them in front of her. Then the entire family walked past me in a line again, saying, 'Thank you, sir.' Suddenly, like a scene from a cartoon, the small children bumped into each other. I looked round to locate the cause of this disturbance, to find that the first and shortest child had stopped suddenly at the feet of my great-uncle, who must have just come home, thus causing the domino disturbance.

My great-uncle was flabbergasted.

'Who are these people?' he asked, as the children scurried out through the door.

'Your neighbours,' I replied with a smile.

'What are they doing here?'

I explained the situation.

'Bradley, Bradley, Bradley,' he said, 'You can't just do things like that around here!'

'So what?' I retorted. 'It's a great neighbourly thing to do. I assumed you'd have told them the same thing.'

'You can't do things like that, or the whole neighbourhood will be waiting at our doors! People normally have to go about three kilometres to the public baths and pay for it. That's just the way it is. Are you going to offer this to everyone you run into?'

'No! But these are your immediate neighbours. They're a lovely set of kids.'

'But you'll get them into the habit, don't you see? What if they come back tomorrow?'

This had not occurred to me. 'I'll talk to her about that. But I don't agree with your broader point. Maybe you *should* be offering it to everybody! Just perhaps not all the time. Why don't you open up the baths once a year or something? It would be nice to share our privilege.'

My great-uncle was silent for a long time. He frowned and brooded and reflected for a good five minutes. Then, all at once, he gave a broad grin and looked at me seriously.

'You're very convincing,' he said, with a touch of pride. 'I'll do that. I'll open it every year, just like they do with the palaces in London. You can tell the neighbours they're very lucky.'

THE PICKLE LADY

We had a guest house in Issy-les-Moulineaux, a modest little house with two bedrooms and a nice reception. We used it to welcome guests of the bank, as it was conveniently placed only a twenty-minute drive from our offices in central Paris. Some stayed for two days, some for a month. I often accompanied our guests there just to share a drink with them and help them settle in.

But every single time I visited the house myself, there would be a knock on the door from one of the neighbours, and the pickle lady would appear. Her name was Antabia. She was a tiny woman, with a dark complexion and a face as wrinkled as a walnut. It was only her slight accent that gave away the fact that she was from North Africa, or perhaps southern Italy, rather than the South of France.

'Hello, Monsieur,' she said.

I asked her what she wanted.

'I am the pickle lady,' she said, with a twinkle in her eye. 'I have been for the past thirty years. I have sold my home-made pickles to every single resident of this house.'

'Oh, but we are hardly residents,' I informed her. 'This house is empty most of the time.'

'Ah, but you are the best targets to buy my pickles! I'm sure you will need some pickles for your guests. The previous owners also used it as a guesthouse, and they bought my pickles almost every month. I'm a widow, you see. My husband used to make the pickles and we made a living selling them exclusively to our neighbours. We never had to sell them to supermarkets or restaurants. Our production was enough to make a living from. Everybody got used to them.' She lowered her voice. 'Everybody got hooked on them!'

'Thank you, Madame,' I said, 'but I'm simply not interested.'

She ignored this protestation, of course. 'Let me tell you about the pickles,' she said. 'I have more kinds of cucumber pickles than you can imagine. I have *cornichons* in all shapes and sizes: big, thick sweet ones and crunchy ones small as almonds. *Cornichons landaise* with mustard seeds and dill, Greek and Turkish cucumbers sliced so thin you could see through them. I've got tiny courgettes and big slabs of beets. Lettuce hearts and full heads of celery half a metre long. Yellow peppers, red peppers, green peppers. Turnips, cabbage and endives. Whole onions and spring onions and garlic and carrots. Tiny white Egyptian onions and miniature Thai eggplants.'

This sounded like a lot of pickles. She reeled this off so fast I had a vision of a house overflowing with greenery.

'And this is not the end of the story!' she added.

My heart sank a little.

'Let me tell you how we flavour these pickles. We use tarragon, jalapeños or small Mexican chillies, thyme. Nothing but the best, fresh herbs from our garden! You must understand, these are nothing like your standard supermarket pickles. These are not pasteurised. There are no chemicals or fixing agents. They are kept in sterilised glass. We never use plastic. Most importantly of all, we never, ever use vinegar. We only use salt and distilled water. The flavours come only from the fresh herbs and spices. You understand? You like this idea?'

I'm quite sure I had not spoken a word.

'Look, Monsieur,' she cooed, suddenly producing several green and shiny containers from her bag. 'I have here with me four glass jars: two jars of pickled *cornichons* and two of green olives with tarragon. Do you want them? They are delicious.'

I looked at the huge jars with some reservations.

'What can I eat this with?' I asked, attempting to defend myself from the daunting quantities.

'You make yourself a rack of lamb and eat the pickles on the side. That is how my husband liked them best. Or why don't you make yourself a vegetable dish, that'll be better for you. Not so much meat. Do you know some of these spices have protein? I can get you some of my black bean pickles! How would you like that? Do you want to know something else?'

I didn't, really, but it would have been rude to say so.

'These pickles are great for your digestion. They kill all the germs in the other food you eat. It's because of the fermentation process that we begin when we seal the jars. They are very healthy!'

I stood there, listening to her babble and watching her count her pickles until I realised there was only one reliable way to get her to stop talking.

'How much?' I asked.

I didn't intend to waste any more time, and I didn't have the heart to slam the door in her face. She was, after all, a fairly inoffensive old neighbour; she was a long-term fixture of the neighbourhood. Also, I was actually rather fond of pickled vegetables.

'Forty francs a jar,' she said; about the equivalent of ten dollars today.

I handed her the cash. 'I do love green olives,' I admitted to her. This pleased her greatly, but was unfortunately taken as encouragement to talk some more.

'There's a secret to these pickles,' she said.

Somehow, I was not surprised.

'You have to make the centre of each of the vegetables absorb all the flavour. You can't have a flavourless core. Here is how you do it: you don't have to inject, or anything complicated. All you do is to slice the skin, very gently, very shallowly. Here is the other secret: don't pickle anything fresh. That's right. Dry out any vegetable you want to pickle. Then it will soak up all the flavours and stay crunchy.'

I figured interrupting might help focus the conversation in a more interesting direction. Besides, being a banker, I couldn't quite resist asking:

'How can you make a living out of this? I mean, vegetables are expensive. This pickling must take up a lot of time, even without considering the weeks you must have to wait before you can sell them. And how about these glass jars, they must cost money.'

'I make a profit of twenty francs on each jar,' she told me. 'I sell about thirty a day, so I make enough of a living that way.'

I worked out that that was about a thousand dollars a week; a comfortable enough living to make just from pickles.

'And it's not very time-consuming,' she added. 'I do the pickling in one big cauldron and then I bottle them. I probably produce around a hundred jars at a time.'

I looked out over her shoulder from the doorway and saw that the line of houses in our alley easily had some fifty or sixty houses on it.

'Well, with your quality of salesmanship,' I said, 'you could easily be selling that in one week in our street.'

I figured she must go further than that, visiting the whole neighbourhood and probably the occasional street market as well. That, or she just had a lot of very faithful clients.

'Do you sell on credit?' I asked her next. I couldn't help but be slightly curious as to her business strategy.

'Oh no,' she replied. 'I have no accounting. It's very simple: I pocket the money and go home.'

It was the first time I had realised that you could capitalise on your neighbourhood relationships. We were a true captive audience, a niche market. And the pickles, after all, were delicious. I decided to contribute to the success of this strategy. I left a note in the guesthouse with my card, which said: *Whenever Antabia passes by to sell you pickles, don't let her leave you in a pickle. Buy a jar, and save yourself ten minutes of precious time!*

THE SMOKY NEIGHBOUR

In the late 1960s, I lived for a short time in Islington, which wasn't always as nice an area of London as it is now. The streets were grimy, the houses were narrow, and the rents were relatively low. Up until the early eighties and Tony Blair's renovation projects, Islington was essentially a slum, with quite a high number of immigrants ending up stacked into high rises. My house was comfortable enough, but it was very close to the neighbours on either side. This meant that, from the small house next door, I could always smell burnt coal, mixed with meat, spices and the delicious scent of baked bread.

I assumed it was a combination of zealous cooking and possession of a coal stove. But one day, towards the end of May 1968, with the sun shining and 25-degree heat outside, I was tempted to investigate why the house had that smoky smell. I knocked on the door, which was opened by a young man with bright eyes and short dark hair. His face was friendly, if a bit sweaty. He introduced himself as Sanjeev. The smoky smell was much stronger inside the house, and it seemed to flood out around him, delicious and exotic all at once. I introduced myself as his neighbour.

'Forgive the intrusion,' I added, 'but I can't help but wonder what the source of that smell is!'

'Oh, we are just cooking tandoori chicken and naan bread,' he replied with a smile.

'But how come there is such a strong smell of smoke? Is there a fireplace? You do know it's almost like summer outside!'

'Ah, it is because we use the old family tandoor.' Seeing my confused expression, he continued, 'A tandoor is a clay oven, in an ancient style. The clay walls absorb the heat from the fire in its base.'

'And it generates smoke?'

'The smoke comes from the coal burning underneath.'

'Ah,' I said, 'so is it similar to the tanoors of Arabic countries?'

'Exactly. The special aspect of cooking in a tandoor is that it takes advantage of the humidity that the food releases while cooking. This way, food stays deliciously moist, and it creates very intense flavours.'

'So what is that delicious smell, again?' I asked, leaning forward as discreetly as I could.

'Spiced chicken skewers and butter naan. Would you like to try some?' He flashed a brilliant salesman's smile.

'What is naan? I have not come across it before.'

'Oh, it's a very simple flatbread. You cook it by slapping the dough to the wall, where it bakes. It's an ancient technique, very straightforward. Here, let me get you some. You must try my butter naan. My friends say it's better than their mothers', and that's saying something!'

He vanished into the kitchen for a time, before reappearing with a steaming plate of flatbreads. He ushered me into his lounge and we sat for a time, talking and munching on the naan. The flatbread was stunning: chewy and moist, with a slightly sweet and smoky flavour.

'Half of my cooking is eaten by my fellow students,' he explained to me. 'The other half goes to my huge family that lives in New Cross. You can get vast Victorian houses there for cheap, which is great for extended families. They have grown to a small community since my grandfather emigrated about ten years ago. Have you ever been to that part of London? It's rather poor.'

'What, poorer than here?' I joked.

Sanjeev laughed. 'Yes, considerably so. I wouldn't recommend a tourist visit. Still, my family seem to have made a good, comfortable life there. But they tell me you can't get decent Indian food there, so I fill that hole in the market!' He flashed that sly smile again.

We talked for a long time, eating the rest of the naan and trying some of the chicken skewers, which he explained to me were 'chicken tandoori', a traditional dish to cook in that sort of oven. I loved them so much that I asked if he could teach me the recipe. He clearly loved this request.

'Of course,' he said enthusiastically. 'Why don't you come round tomorrow evening?'

The first time I made chicken tandoori was great fun. We ground the spice mix by hand, combining fresh ginger, onion, and lemon juice with the fragrant spice mix known as *garam masala*: a combination of pepper, cloves, cinnamon, cumin and cardamom. We then coated the chicken legs in this bright red mix and yoghurt, before baking them in the tandoor. They were absolutely delicious. We ate them together with naan, and talked for a long time about art and politics.

'So tell me,' I asked him, 'what is a smart young man like yourself doing selling bread for a living? Are you training to become a chef?'

'Oh no!' He laughed. 'I'm actually studying art history at University College London. I'd like to become a teacher.'

'How interesting. So the cooking is just a hobby!'

'Yes. A time-consuming hobby, but it generates revenue, too.'

'And what kind of art are you studying?'

'Well, I'm particularly interested in Indian miniatures and wood carvings.'

'So no relation to the arts of cooking and eating at all!'

He laughed. 'I guess not. I can't even think of any miniatures that might feature food. Perhaps naan is not considered a sacred enough topic.'

This was the start of my friendship with Sanjeev, which was to last for the next few months, even after I had moved to Marble Arch. I started coming back regularly for tea, conversation, and the occasional cooking lesson. I learned how to make chicken, and slow-cooked lamb, and four kinds of naan bread.

I also started buying his naan to take home. So, thanks to the strange smell of his oven, he gained both a friend and a loyal customer!

CONSTRUCTION CHAOS

In a quiet and beautiful area of Geneva, I finally found the house of my dreams. After many years and many different properties, at last I was completely at home. Aside from the tranquillity of the surroundings, the house itself was all a person could want. It was large and open, with just the right number of rooms, a large garden, and even a swimming pool and library where one could sit for hours in complete calm.

The central point of the house was undoubtedly the salon, which had been built for the express purpose of entertaining. As I found out, the Swiss used this gorgeously wood-panelled room for parties, and it was indeed perfect for such events.

Quite simply, I was entirely happy with the house, and looked forward to many peaceful years ahead living there.

However, it was not to be.

One morning, I awoke not to the sound of birdsong carried on the breeze, but to a deafening noise that seemed to be coming from somewhere inside the house. It was barely seven in the morning. I leapt out of bed, concerned as to what catastrophe would await me. Was it possible that part of our house had collapsed? A wall fallen in? I searched around the halls and found nothing out of place; not so much as a picture had shifted.

Then I thought to look outside. There, I found the cause of the mayhem.

Our next door neighbours were in possession of a large plot of empty garden, just like ours, and a fair-sized house as well. While I had been on friendly terms with my neighbours, I didn't know much about them. Yet they had always seemed steady and unlikely to make drastic changes. But now, when I looked out of the window I did not find everything the same as it had always been.

Where once the house had stood so proudly there was now a cluster of cranes, giant and monstrous-looking. Currently, they were in the process of demolishing the said house with wrecking balls, smashing it to pieces.

I stared, flabbergasted both by the situation and the damnable noise, hoping in vain that this would somehow pass quickly and leave behind the peace and quiet I already sorely missed.

When I decided to find out what on earth was happening, I discovered that my neighbour had sold his land, house and all, to a speculator promoter, who was in the business of putting up large high-rise buildings. These would then be used by the government to support their subsidised social housing scheme, in an attempt to solve the crisis of the less well-off not having anywhere decent to live. Of course, I supported this idea and thought that the socialist government in Geneva did a marvellous job of keeping the place clean and safe. But their town planning left something to be desired; to my mind, you couldn't just create such an eyesore, a blot on the landscape, in such a beautiful area. It might lessen the burden of the housing problem, but at the same time it seemed a crass thing to do. I later found out that the other neighbours had been petitioning and protesting for twenty years, which meant that the man who wanted to sell to the developer had at least held off for this long. But now he had sold out, there was nothing anybody could do except live with the constant row of arthritic-sounding cranes shattering the idyll.

The following Sunday, I settled myself down to do some reading until dinnertime, preparing myself mentally for another busy week. There is nothing I enjoy more than a solitary reading session in the library, and as I said, the house in Geneva had an impressive one, expansive and filled with favourite books – the perfect place to relax or get on with work.

However, I had barely cracked open my book when the scream of a pneumatic drill smashed my hopes to bits. I sat still for a moment, hoping it would stop.

It did, thankfully, and so I returned to my reading. It was a balmy day, with the sun filtering gently through the leaves that brushed against the window. I could hear the children playing in the garden, enjoying the weather. For a moment, I was back in the idyllic family situation I had envisioned when I bought the house. Everything was peaceful again.

Then the shouting began. One construction worker seemed to be arguing with another over something. Probably something to do with the drill, because in the next instant that started up again and drowned them out entirely. I sighed, and gave up on reading for the day.

My wife was quite phlegmatic about the whole problem.

'It's ridiculous, I know, but we just have to live with it, don't we? Anyway, it'll be over soon enough. They can't keep building forever. What would you like for dinner, by the way? The weather's been so kind, we could have something outside, couldn't we?'

Personally, I couldn't think of anything I would like less than sitting out in the garden, where the noise reached you with even more force than it did inside the house. 'I suppose that might be nice,' I began dubiously, only to be cut off by one of the cranes trying to heft itself about. The machinery seemed as miserable as I was with the entire situation.

My wife waited to reply until there was a break in the chaos. 'Yes, and the children would love it, so I thought...' Her voice was drowned out by the roar of a drill. She threw up her hands and wrote on a piece of paper:

It can't go on much longer, can it?

I shrugged and wrote back: *Who knows?*

Worse, however, than these interruptions to our daily life, was the fact the developer was doing things in a completely illegal manner. We woke up to noise early in the morning, and tried to go to sleep to metallic lullabies late at night. There seemed no end to the madness, and now the children couldn't even play in the garden, thanks to the dust that travelled on the wind from the building site right into our grounds.

I had, naturally, noticed this sort of thing happening before. Promoters often bought land in Geneva with a view to building all over it, only to set about destroying whatever was in their path with no conscience whatsoever. They built tall apartment blocks with no regard for the historic houses they were ripping down in the process. They destroyed all the natural beauty of the environment and appeared to not care in the least.

It hadn't occurred to me, though, that my dream house would be right next door to one of these new developments, and the reality was, quite frankly, a nightmare.

After several weeks of getting barely any sleep and not being able to use our garden or certain rooms in our house where the noise was at its worst, I decided to speak to this new developer. I thought I could at least ask him to start work a little later and finish a little earlier. Aside from our own broken sleep, whenever I saw the men who worked on the site they looked exhausted and miserable, and I often heard them shouting angrily at one another. I hoped that the developer was a man to be reasoned with.

'You must be excited!' he exclaimed, when I told him that I lived next door. 'You could hope to have such an opportunity.'

I looked at him blankly.

'Your land,' he said, and then I understood what he meant at once. That perhaps I, too, would want to sell to him and have my house, the most beautiful house in the world, turned into this bomb site!

I smiled and remained calm. 'I don't think so.'

He looked me over disparagingly. 'Well, I suppose some people like to live in the past, no?' I had him pegged from that comment, and from how I had heard him shrieking at his employees. The way he spoke to me was bordering on insulting, pitying, as though I was missing out on his great vision.

'I only wanted to ask if you might reduce your working hours.'

'Time is money, you know. And I don't have time for this.'

'Oh, I know. It's only that – we're trying to live our lives, you see. And doing that is incredibly challenging with all this noise.' I drew myself up. 'Besides, I believe it's illegal to build so early and so late, isn't it?' I tried to say this as though he might not know, because the state of his French made it clear that he wasn't from around here.

He narrowed his eyes at me. 'The apartments must be built, so you should go home and get used to it.'

'Yes, but I don't think you have been listening. I've been very patient, but it's getting out of hand.'

'Be quiet. You don't understand,' he snapped. 'We're working to a deadline and must get on. So be quiet and go home.'

His rude, unfriendly manner left me almost speechless. 'I think you want to watch your tone.'

'Enough, enough,' he waved me off. 'That's enough.' And then he walked away.

I was furious, but even more so when the construction went on far into the night, and began again even earlier the next morning.

Sadly, this story is still ongoing. God only knows when it will finish, or how much our house value will depreciate next to this monstrous building!

THE DOWNSTAIRS NEIGHBOUR AT
FORT LAUDERDALE

I have never been particularly fond of Florida. I don't like the humidity, I don't like the heat, and I really don't like the vagrant population that seems to emigrate yearly from the frozen north. As far as I can tell, Florida is populated mainly by pale, pudgy Midwesterners, New Englanders, and Canadians, who lounge in the sun with their fruity cocktails like clusters of cold-blooded iguanas.

However, various opinions in my family differed quite strongly from mine on the topic. This became apparent particularly in the form of pressure from my in-laws, who live in the Sunshine State. To cut a long story short, my wife and children somehow persuaded me to take a holiday near Fort Lauderdale instead of, say, Italy or the South of France, which I would have infinitely preferred. I grudgingly agreed to the trip, thinking there would at least be sun, so the whole thing was bound to go fairly quickly.

When we arrived and I saw our accommodation, however, I had to admit I was somewhat mollified. Our apartment was on the seventh floor of a bright, tall building right on the edge of the water. Inside, it was vast and luminous, with breath-taking views of the blue waves and the great ocean liners sailing by in the distance.

Of course, most people staying at Fort Lauderdale seemed to consider the height of entertainment to be eating a plate of waffles and gossiping about fat people in swimsuits whilst drinking four cups of watery coffee, but this didn't mean we were all limited to this approach. We could watch the sunset from the jetty, eat in one of the glamorous beach-side restaurants, or even simply enjoy a walk along the beach. My family and I did all these things; but in the end, the ultimate joy was still being inside the luxurious apartment itself, looking out to sea. The ocean liners didn't always remain in the distance like miniatures. Sometimes, they would cruise right by the beach, their top floors practically at a level with the window of our bedroom! Passengers could probably see us from the windows. The sound of the horn from the passing ships as they floated off into the distance made us feel like we were in an old film. Standing on the balcony with a glass of fresh orange juice in hand, watching the ships leave, was an experience that I would never have again, neither in the Mediterranean, nor anywhere else.

That said, not everything about our apartment was perfectly idyllic. For one thing, the ceilings were very low, which bothered me. This is apparently a typical feature of American buildings, as it facilitates saving money on electricity by creating smaller spaces which require less air conditioning to cool. Furthermore, I wasn't particularly fond of the bathroom. The ceramic tiling was an ugly colour, making the whole room feel old-fashioned and stuffy. I found myself longing for something cooler and more luminous, to fit in with our surroundings. Thus, after much consultation of magazines and a few heated conversations over dinner, we decided to have the tiles and the floor replaced, and redone in marble.

Like anywhere in America, Florida has its fair share of eccentric Italian decorators. I figured we wouldn't have too much trouble finding someone who would understand what we wanted. Sure enough, after a few enquiries, we found a man exceedingly interested in our desire for a vast marble bathtub. I wanted something large and cool, carved out of one block of stone, to be the centrepiece of our bathroom. The man nodded happily when I explained this to him, making his mounds of black curls bounce jerkily.

'*Si, si,*' he kept saying in his thick, rolling accent. 'Yes, that is how they did it in the time of Julius Caesar!' he cried out, gesturing enthusiastically. 'It will be wonderful, the most classical Roman bath you have ever seen.'

His fire for the project reassured me, and I let him proceed with the designs and installation. He tore out all the dreadful orange tiles, making our peaceful holiday apartment into something much more like a dusty, dirty warzone. In just under a week, however, he had worked his magic, leaving with a flourish, a smell of detergent, and an only slightly less than reasonable bill.

My wife and I crept uneasily into the bathroom, and were quite reassured by the sight that met our eyes. In fact, it took our collective breath away. The whole room had been entirely renovated, with the bathtub enthroned in the centre, a vast block of gorgeous marble. Everything was light in colour and sparkling clean, reflecting the sun from outside. I flung open the small window, letting in the ocean breeze.

'Now this,' my wife told me with a smile, 'is more like it.'

'You could practically swim laps in it!'

She giggled. 'The people on the fancy ocean liners are going to get jealous when they look in through the window,' she added.

We decided not to inaugurate the bathtub that evening, as it was already dark, and we were tired. Instead, we went for a celebratory dinner and were in bed before midnight, listening to the seabirds outside.

The next morning, however, I got up bright and early and decided to run a bath in our new bathroom. I marvelled once more at the sheer size of our tub. It must have been close to half a ton of marble! It was a wonder the floor could support such a thing! I smiled and turned the taps on full, then tossed in a handful of bath salts. Whistling, I went back into the kitchen and started making a pot of coffee. I could already smell the soft lavender in the air and imagine the room filling with warm steam. What a joy it would be to start my day just like a Roman emperor, sliding under the bubbles and relaxing all my muscles! If only I had a few lit candles and a silver platter of grapes...

All of a sudden, in the midst of this reverie, there was an almighty crash. I froze, the coffee spoon suspended in my hand. The hairs on the back of my neck rose up. What could possibly have happened? A coconut thrown from a ship's deck? A sudden thunderstorm? A terrorist attack? I set down the spoon carefully and walked across the apartment with a sense of dread to investigate. I opened the door to the bathroom and peeked inside. The water was still running at full steam. However, there was no bath. In fact, there was nothing in the centre of the room but a big, black gaping hole. My mouth fell open. After a moment or so, I leaned gingerly across and switched off the taps. I then peeked down into the abyss, dreading the results. As far as I could tell, there were no bodies, although there was quite a lot of dust and rubble. There was also no furious neighbour peering up; so that was a relief. The marble bathtub seemed to be glaring up at me balefully, though. It was sat smack in the middle of a kingsize bed. Despite most of the water having sloshed out into the room, the tub was entirely unharmed, and even had some water still in it. I sighed deeply, and went indoors to call the caretakers.

'It's about my new bathtub,' I told them. 'It's ended up downstairs.'

'You mean the new tub was delivered to the wrong address?' the woman on the line asked pleasantly.

'I mean it fell through the floor,' I replied.

There was a short silence. 'Right,' she said. 'Well, I hate to say this, but you might just be in real trouble.'

'It's so kind of you to reassure me,' I responded dryly.

'I don't mean to be cruel,' she said, 'but I think you should know who you're going to be dealing with here. Your downstairs neighbour is the biggest lawyer in town. A real hotshot; a famous criminal lawyer. There's not much we can do for you here; you'll just have to talk to him yourself.' There was a cautious pause. 'After all, it's your bathtub. There's nothing we can do for you.'

'Well, isn't that just great,' I muttered.

'We just don't want a lawsuit on our hands,' she added timidly.

'Oh, I'm looking forward to mine,' I said through gritted teeth, before putting down the phone. The anger was mostly frustration: really, I was terrified at the thought of speaking to the man. I had to finish making myself that long-forgotten cup of coffee before making the call.

When I finally picked up the phone, I could hear my nerves in my voice. 'Er, hello,' I said. How on earth did I think I could broach such a subject? I couldn't exactly just say 'my bathtub fell into your apartment,' could I?

'Yes?' the man barked. 'What is it? I'm in the middle of a very important meeting.'

I nearly hung up. 'It's just...' I faltered. 'I'm your upstairs neighbour.'

'Pleased to meet you, I'm sure,' he said shortly, and then waited, expectant.

'There's been an accident.' I cursed myself even as the words left my mouth.

'What's happened?' He sounded worried, now.

'My bathtub fell into your apartment,' I blurted out. I felt myself blushing, and was briefly glad that I was not in the same room as my interlocutor. The silence that followed was excruciating. All at once, though, the man began to laugh. Not politely, not dismissively, but a real belly laugh. I couldn't believe my ears. 'I'm sorry,' I said, slightly confused.

'Your bathtub.... fell? Into my apartment?' he burst out into hysterical laughter again.

'Yes,' I said simply. Because I was not sure what else to say, I added: 'The water probably weighed more than half a ton. It was a marble bathtub, which I know weighed about six hundred kilos. The collective weight –'

'– Is more than a ton!' he crowed. 'Unbelievable! That's the funniest thing that has ever happened in this apartment building, I can tell you that! If you were here with me, I'd clap you on the back and buy you a drink. Listen, though, I'm really sorry, but I've got to get back to this meeting. Can I call you back when I get out? We could get a coffee and talk this over.'

I was flabbergasted. Then found myself laughing as well. 'Are you going to have your snipers take me out?' I joked. 'Surely you don't want to take the man who just wrecked your apartment for coffee?'

He laughed again. 'No snipers, I promise. We'll talk tonight.'

'You're sure you don't want to come and see the situation now?' I asked hesitantly. 'It's quite dramatic. There was a lot of water involved.'

'Oh, don't worry about it,' he said breezily. 'I'll look over the damage tonight; I'm too busy right now. Tell you what; I'll just come over to your place. I like to do my sniping in person,' he added wryly.

Needless to say, by the time this downstairs neighbour turned up at our apartment, I was fairly nervous. I had spent the last two hours trying to keep my children from falling down the pit. It took quite a lot of work convincing them it wouldn't be fun to fall down into the bed. There was no lock on the outside of the door, so it was impossible to keep them out of the room.

When the neighbour arrived, he seemed to feel the same irresistible force as my children, and asked me to take him straight to the scene of the accident. I was surprised to find he was a quite pleasant-looking man with a blonde moustache, dressed in a white t-shirt and jeans. He was tall and quite handsome, probably in his mid-forties, although he could have been younger. He looked neither like a straight-laced film lawyer nor like a scary cop. Nonetheless, as I walked him across the apartment, I was still pretty nervous.

When we walked into the bathroom, he smirked and shook his head. 'I'll be damned,' he said, and started laughing again. 'I bet that's the funniest thing that's ever happened in this whole building.'

Once I had made us both iced coffees, we sat down at the dinner table.

'Aren't you going to sue me?' I asked him timidly.

'Listen, there's no way this is going to be a lawsuit,' he replied at once in a friendly manner. 'Do you know why?' I shook my head. 'Because nobody is going to believe it. The most exciting thing I have ever seen happen in Fort Lauderdale is when someone once thought they saw a shark.' He sipped his iced coffee. 'Simply put: this is not a legal issue, it's an insurance one. There's an easy solution to all this: we both claim, and we both get new rooms. You get a new bathroom; I get a new bedroom. The building owners won't complain as long as they get reimbursed, and that will be the end of it!'

I sighed with relief. We chatted for a long time about other matters, and he took his leave quite amiably a few hours later. He was Florida-born and bred, and he loved the neighbourhood with the sort of bored, conflicted love one has for the places of one's childhood.

'As I said, I really wish you had come here earlier, smashed up some other buildings. It would have made things a bit livelier!'

'You do realise you might have been in that bed if it had happened another time of day?' I asked timidly.

'I'll try not to think about that,' he retorted with a grin.

In the end, we did exactly as the lawyer had advised, and the whole process went smoothly. We had everything cleaned up and repaired, and reinforced the bathroom floor with steel beams. We had a different man come in to design and install the marble bath, making sure to factor in the stress measure of the weight of water!

The lawyer and I became friends, and have stayed in touch over the years. He turned out to be a pleasant, hardworking and very, very funny man. 'I work with murderers and armed robbers a lot,' he told me. 'Nothing really fazes me anymore. When I started work as a lawyer I saw crime and criminals everywhere I looked. Now I hardly notice 'em anymore! I mean, when I send someone to the electric chair, sure, I come home pretty exhausted in the evening, and worry about what to eat. But that's a rare occurrence these days.' He gave that distinctive, barking laugh of his, and I shook my head in wonder.

'And there I was, stressing away, shedding years off my life, no doubt, waiting for this famous criminal lawyer to throw me in jail...'

He smiled. 'Now, don't get me wrong. If you were to shoot a man or anything, that would be different. But if you can get another marble bath to fall into my room, well, I'll just be impressed. Anyway, I learned something from all this: be sure to think about stresses when building anything. Not that I have any real desire for a half-ton bathtub,' he added with a wink.

'You're missing out,' I told him. 'You can probably hear the happy sounds of my family sliding around in there, singing and splashing about. But if you ever hear a cracking noise, make sure you move!'

Of course, the floor below the bathtub never collapsed again, and I never had any trouble with my downstairs neighbour the lawyer. I've visited Fort Lauderdale many times since then, and he and I are still friends to this day.

My first encounter with Clint was a chance one, when I was washing my Corvette in the street outside my fraternity in Texas. I saw a short, blonde boy with red cheeks stumble down the stairs of the fraternity across from mine. He waved at me.

'Hello,' he shouted in a slightly odd voice, stumbling towards me across the lawn. 'I'm Clint Ferguson!'

I was not quite sure what to expect. 'Nice to meet you, Clint,' I replied.

'Can – can I help you wash your car, sir?' Watching him stagger across the road, I felt a little sorry for this boy with the slurred speech and the unsteady walk. He was athletically built, wearing jeans and a chequered shirt. When he got to me, he collapsed into giggles, this time slouching against my car and soaking his jeans through. It was then that I realised that he was incredibly drunk.

'Been celebrating?' I queried.

'Haha!' he laughed with exaggerated sarcasm. Then his face fell into an expression like a Greek tragic mask. 'No, I've been mourning.' He then switched to what is best described as a pout.

'My condolences,' I said, carefully. 'I meant no disrespect. Is it someone in your family?'

Clint leaned forward unsteadily to clap a soapy hand to my shoulder.

'Oh, you can disrespect her all you want. Total floozy,' he said.

He must have seen the horrified expression on my face, for he now proceeded to shake me by the shoulder of my jacket as he explained: 'No, no, not dead! Just jilted. Dumped me.'

He slumped back against the car so hard that he slid slowly to the ground.

'Sandy,' he muttered, frowning.

'Well, I wouldn't say "sandy" was your top risk right now. Probably more likely to be "wet" and "soapy".'

I grabbed the boy by his armpits and hauled him upright. I brushed the dirt from his shirt briskly, and said: 'Why don't you help me clean my car and explain what on earth you're talking about. I'm gathering that you have not in fact lost a close family member, but simply broken up with your girlfriend.'

'S-s-sandy's her *name*,' he said, aggrieved, before reaching out towards me in a flailing motion like a child. 'C'mon, let me do some cleaning. Gimme some water.'

I handed him the hose. He pointed it somewhere about two feet above the top of the car, before readjusting and spraying at the tyres. At this point I was just trying to minimise the damage.

'She, I, uh, told her I was in love with her,' he blubbed. 'And she said she didn't love me back.'

'What a shame,' I said, trying to muster sympathy. 'Had you been together a long time?'

'Oh, we weren't together. I was *in love* with her,' he emphasised, grumpily, as if I were intentionally twisting his words.

I sighed.

'So she wasn't your girlfriend, then,' I said patiently. 'She just rejected your offer.'

'I was in love,' Clint repeated dreamily, spraying water directly onto the car windows so that the full stream bounced back at him.

At this point the hose was starting to lurch alarmingly towards me, so I eased it out of his hands and took over myself.

'Why don't you try the sponge?' I suggested, handing him a bucket of soapy water and a sponge. Clint sniffled a little and started slopping water over the car and himself. Suddenly, without warning, he burst into tears and flung himself into my arms. He was, of course, still holding the bucket and sponge when emotion overcame him, so I found myself completely soaked in water, being hugged by a drunkard.

I sighed.

'What can I *do*?' he howled over my shoulder. 'I love her!'

'No you don't,' I replied, in a tone as friendly as a man covered in soap suds can manage. I pried the boy off me and propped him up against the car again. 'How old are you?'

'Twenty,' he sniffled into my jacket.

'Right,' I said, 'Well it's hardly the end of your love life. Pull yourself together.'

He nodded, but spoiled the impression of listening by sliding off the end of my car.

I sighed again.

'Come on, it's probably about time you got yourself to bed. You can help me clean my car another time.'

This had been intended as an idle offer, but the next weekend I saw Clint come down the stairs of his fraternity again, a little more steadily.

'Hi, Bradley,' he said, a little sheepishly.

I greeted him and shook his hand. 'Feeling a bit better this weekend?'

'Yeah,' he said. 'I'm over her.' He hesitated. 'I'm sorry I was so drunk when I met you. I just…I'm just struggling to cope at the moment.'

There was a pause. Then he started to cry.

'I can see that's going well,' I said quietly. 'Come on, think about something else.' I left the car-washing supplies on the road and sat him on the steps in front of my fraternity. We looked out over the clean-cut lawn and flower bushes until he had pulled himself together.

'Tell me about your family,' I tried.

'Oh, we're from Indiana,' he replied, which made sense of his Midwestern accent. 'Cornfields, nice straight roads, all that. Republicans.'

'And how did you end up so drunk in the middle of the afternoon?'

'Oh, you know, I just like to get a bit tipsy!' He waved his arms vaguely.

This seemed rather an understatement. His shoulders slumped.

'I know it's not good for me. It's just…'

'You seem like a pleasant enough boy. There will be plenty of Sandys in the world! Don't let it get to you.'

'Oh, I know,' he sighed, his head slumping forward. 'It's not just that. I hate school. I don't even know why I'm here. My Dad wants me to be a racing-car driver, so it's a complete waste of my time.'

'Well why don't you quit? If you want to be a racing-car driver there's nothing wrong with that!'

'I hate driving,' he replied glumly. 'I don't even like driving on the freeway, let alone a Formula 1 track. I hate speeding. I'm afraid of being killed,' he added, rather dramatically. I nodded. 'My father

– 98 –

made a fortune as a driver, you see. But for some reason he wants me to go to university, get an education, all that.' He sighed again. 'Say, you don't have a beer, do you?'

I tried not to laugh. 'I'm afraid I don't drink.'

He nodded sadly. 'Typical,' he said sadly. 'I really hate it here,' he added, as if I had just contributed to the general unpleasantness of the state of Texas. I did not feel this required a response.

'I'm on the wrong course,' he continued. 'I'm a musician. I want to play the violin.'

'Really?' This was not quite what I had expected.

'Yeah, really,' he said vaguely, making bowing motions in the air as if to prove his skill to me.

'Well why don't you go to a conservatoire?' I asked.

'Can't,' he said. 'Dad won't let me. He wants me to drive cars, like I said.'

I sighed. 'You're not the only one. Think of all the poets and musicians whose parents forced them into engineering or nursing. And the architects and aspiring doctors who could only get onto liberal arts or humanities courses. One way or another, so many students are on the wrong course. But some of those work hard and make the most of it. You can't just be miserable and drunk. You have to make something out of your life!'

Clint sighed deeply.

I added, as briskly as I could: 'You really ought to stop drinking, you know.'

'But how could I stop,' he muttered, 'with my father breathing down my neck? I hate school, I'm on the wrong course. And I was dumped by my girlfriend.'

'Not your girlfriend,' I reminded him.

'But I want to marry her,' he whined.

'Now,' I said firmly, 'stop all this noise. It sounds like you have plenty of problems. But the best way to start fixing them would be to stop drinking.'

'I just don't understand why everyone told me these would be the best years of my life! I thought I would be working hard, partying hard, meeting a crowd of friends, and my first love on the side!' He laughed bitterly.

'Ah, but what they don't tell you is that you will most likely lose touch with those friends. Your first love might break your heart. The hard partying will ruin your liver and all that hard work probably has nothing to do with the job you'll end up with.'

'And all for just a few tens of thousands of dollars!

I laughed.

That was the second time I met Clint, but far from the last. Every week for nearly six months after that, whenever I washed my car, Clint would come and help me. And every single time, he was drunk. Still, he was an amiable fellow. When he wasn't in a sad mood, he would chatter away, telling jokes or stories about life in Indiana. I grew rather fond of the young man.

After a few months I noticed he was becoming less and less capable of providing this vague 'help.' He was losing weight, and his skin was looking rather yellow. I began to worry about him. One day, he stumbled up to my car looking worse than I'd ever seen him. Unfortunately I was rather in a rush that day, as I had an important class to get to, so I didn't have much patience.

'Hi,' he said, in a weak voice.

I responded as gently as I could.

'Are you OK?' I asked. 'You don't look so well. '

'Mm,' he groaned, 'I don't feel great.'

'You're ruining your health with drink,' I said, as sternly as possible. 'Are you eating?'

'I know,' he said. 'The doctor told me I have to eat but I hate the food in the fraternity. I just can't face it. Could I come eat at your fraternity?'

'Look,' I said, 'you know the rules. You can't just skip around between fraternities.'

I had to leave, so that conversation was cut short.

Later, however, I felt bad, and thought I should probably check in on him. I felt a certain sense of responsibility towards the poor kid. So one day, I went round to his fraternity. Clint hadn't answered the phone when I rang, so I got one of the boys to let me in. I knocked on his door for a long time without an answer, but I could hear noise in the room. I tried the handle. It was unlocked. I found poor Clint sprawled out on his bed weeping, with all his possessions strewn about in boxes.

'Oh God,' he whimpered, 'I'm sorry you have to see me like this.'

'What's happened?' I asked. 'Are you all right?'

'They're threatening to kick me out of school,' he moaned into his pillow.

'Threatening?' I asked. 'Then why are you packing?'

'It's no use,' he said, 'They say I have to see a counsellor and stop drinking, my results are just terrible and I can't, I just can't!' He collapsed into the pillow again.

'Look,' I said. 'Clint. I've said this before and I'll say it again now: you've just got to pull yourself together. Come on. Get dressed. I'll take you to dinner.'

He didn't move.

'It's no use,' he moaned.

'Don't be ridiculous. You're just miserable from drink and weak from not eating. Come on now, what's your favourite dish?'

There was a pause, and a sniffle.

'Steak,' he said.

'I know the best steakhouse in a fifty-mile radius. Come on. I'll meet you outside in twenty minutes.'

We went for dinner. Clint wolfed down his steak, only sniffling a little.

'So what is it you really want to do with your life? If your father wasn't deciding it for you.'

He smiled and took a gulp of ice water.

'If I had ultimate control over my life, and patience, and skill? I'd like to be first violin in one of the great orchestras. I'd like to write symphonies. I'd host great parties and everyone would bring me champagne.' He laughed. 'That's a pretty impossible vision, though.'

'I see you've got a clear idea of what a music career involves,' I replied with a smile. 'Are you playing your violin at all?'

'No,' he replied sadly, 'I just can't really face it.'

'That's a cop-out,' I said, as gently as I could. 'There's no reason why you can't still be a violinist and a racing-car driver.'

'You have to admit that's a pretty ridiculous vision.'

'Well, maybe not both at the same time!'

'I just get back to the frat from my stupid classes, and all I want is to have a beer and watch some TV. I have no motivation.'

'What you're telling me is that you're drinking instead of practising the violin. That's a damn shame.'

We came to a deal: I would take him out to dinner once a week if he promised he would stop drinking. Over thick steaks or *sole meunière*, his two favourites, Clint started to recover. I got to know his story, his background. He started cracking jokes again. He lost that yellow colour. He told me he'd started eating his fraternity's terrible food again, but that he didn't mind so much. He said he'd been practising the violin. And he only ever drank sparkling water with me, although I know he still had the occasional drink on his own.

But one Saturday he came round to my house in the middle of the day. He was sober but he had tears in his eyes. He told me he had been kicked out of school, and that he had to go back to Indiana. His father was enrolling him in racing-car driving training. It seemed that the steaks may have helped with his psychological problems, but not with his test results.

THE MANAGING HOUSEWIFE

For a time I lived in the seventh *arrondissement* of Paris, just over the river, not far from the Italian embassy. My wife and I had a little apartment on the third floor, a modern place in which we raised our first children, all born in the American Hospital over a period or three or four years. Our apartment needed considerable fixing up at the time we moved in, so I spent the first year or so renovating and furnishing to cosy modern standards, sawing, painting and hammering away, even on the weekends. I built nearly all the furniture in that apartment: the tables, desks, chairs, and beds.

Our neighbours were a young couple who had children at about the same time as us. Their apartment was considerably smaller than ours; she was a housewife, and her husband was working as a minor clerk for the French government, so their family had limited means. The wife was called Eugénie. She was a young blonde woman, very friendly but very determined to run their household efficiently and make ends meet. I would often come across her sweeping the stairs in front of her flat, or escorting her small children down the road. She always took the time to speak to me, usually of trivial matters, and our relations were always friendly.

One summer day I ran into Eugénie in the street and, rather than giving me the usual fleeting greeting, she stopped and kissed me on both cheeks.

'*Bonjour, Monsieur Jamieson,*' she said cheerily.

'*Bonjour,*' I replied, tipping my cap to her.

'How are your *bricolage* projects going? Your construction? It has been quiet for a long time now. Not so much of that terrible sawing, crashes waking up the babies...' she gathered herself and smiled brightly. This was not quite the usual kind of neutral topic we stuck to.

'No,' I said, uncertainly, 'our *bricolage* is mostly finished.' I paused. 'I am sorry if the noise has been any problem.'

'*Non-non-non!*' she said brightly, waving her hands forgivingly. 'It is fine!' Seamlessly, she drove the conversation onwards. 'I have seen your children wearing very nice clothes. Where do they get these clothes, is it from your travels?' she asked nonchalantly.

'Yes,' I said, relieved that we had turned away from the guilt of my noisy pastimes. 'I often bring them back from Germany, or England, or America.'

'Ah, I see. Perhaps you can get designer clothes cheaper there?'

'Exactly,' I agreed. 'My wife is rather fond of Ralph Lauren and Chanel.'

'And these clothes,' she said casually, 'do you... give them to charity? Or do you throw them away? I think we usually just throw ours away when they do not fit anyone anymore.' She paused. 'Of course they are mostly from Auchan or Monoprix! So it does not matter so much!'

I could see where this was going.

'Yes,' I admitted, smiling a little, 'we do often throw out the clothes. We just don't have space for all of them.'

'I have seen a Chanel dress on one of your little girls, *non*? A little navy blue thing. My littlest one has something similar although it is only from Monoprix...' She giggled girlishly.

There could no longer be any doubt as to what she was driving at. I decided to get to the point.

'Listen, Eugénie,' I said, 'if you would like, you know, we could hand down the clothes. After all, your children are just a little bit younger than ours.'

Her pretty painted face registered nothing but complete surprise.

'*Mais Monsieur*,' she said, 'that is so kind of you! I could not possibly accept!' She fluttered her eyelashes.

From then on, every time I saw Eugénie, I would bring her a bag of our clothes. It was always a delight to see her little ones wearing our second-hand Chanel and Ralph Lauren as they toddled down the Paris side streets. In fact, I started putting together a sort of trousseau for her as soon as clothes were discarded, collecting our second-hand clothes throughout the year for her. I continued to do this even after I had moved abroad and went on to have more children: once a year, I would send her a box. She always wrote back the most charming notes.

I wonder if I ran into her now, some thirty years on, she would still ask me for clothes. After all, I'm sure her children must be the same size as *me* now!

When I was seventeen and studying engineering in Texas, my English teacher was a most beautiful woman, by the name of Cliona. She was twenty-six, blonde and sporty: a very pretty, cheerful, and energetic young woman who was a joy to be around. Literature was a mandatory subject, even for those of us studying practical or scientific subjects. Stephanie, my English-student girlfriend at the time, and I shared Cliona as a teacher. Cliona was Stephanie's neighbour, and the two young women quickly struck up a friendship that extended outside the classroom.

The only problem with this was that I kept running into my beautiful literature teacher when going to visit my girlfriend. Stephanie seemed almost as enamoured with Cliona as I was, and it seemed like almost every time I was at the house, the day would end with the three of us chatting over freshly baked cookies, or going for long walks around campus. In some ways, these meetings may have had the appearance of a love triangle.

Cliona was a classic Southern belle, with just enough of a Georgia twang for it to be charming without distracting from her opinions, which were endlessly fascinating, and always well-informed, if occasionally very stubborn. She had been educated at Smith and Brown, and was a very intelligent young woman. Though in some ways I suppose that Stephanie was my first love, intellectually she couldn't compete with her literature professor. Cliona and I would go head to head: she was a consistently fiery defender of her opinions!

'How can you not love *Paradise Lost*?' she might begin one of our debates. 'It's such a crucial work of poetry, as well as a radical reinterpretation of some segments of the Bible.'

'It's just so terribly long! I mean, some passages are very exciting, and the characters of both Eve and Satan are wonderfully complex, but I just don't think that the whole of it can be considered one of the best pieces of poetry ever written.'

'Pah! This is just because you weren't taught Milton at an early age. You came to it too late.'

'I don't think anyone should be spoon-fed Milton! Certainly not before the age of sixteen or seventeen. It's far too theologically difficult. Anyway, the same accusation works for you: aren't you interested in world literature at all? What about the French greats, Molière and Rabelais?'

'You know that's not true. I enjoy plenty of what you call "world literature". We'll be studying Racine later this term. It's just that I find Rabelais quite disgusting, irrelevant to modern society, and outdated.'

'And yet you worship Milton, Ben Jonson, and even Chaucer! Chaucer is as outdated as Rabelais, and uses the same bodily humour in places! In fact, Chaucer is a century older than Rabelais!'

'Old is not the same thing as outdated! I mean that Rabelais is irrelevant. All those nauseating passages in *Gargantua* can hardly be considered to be philosophy.'

'That's simply a ridiculous assertion. Of course the disgusting bits are not philosophy. Neither is the bit in *The Canterbury Tales* where someone's arse gets burnt with a poker! Yet Rabelais' ideas played as large a role as Chaucer's in shaping pre-Enlightenment European thought.' I sighed. 'Listen, do you think we could just go and take a walk? It would be nice not to just talk about books all the time. I've already got class with you tomorrow morning! You know we'll end up discussing some of these things over *Paradise Lost*.'

Cliona smiled. 'Alright then. Let's have another of Stephanie's cookies, then we can all go for a walk.' Stephanie herself would alternate between joining in the debates and listening contentedly; but on a few occasions she opted out of the walks, owing to homework, or perhaps another meeting. Cliona and I thus squeezed in a few pleasant wanders around campus, just the two of us, trying not to talk about literature.

On the first of these walks I remember her opening line being: 'Well, here we are. What shall we talk about?'

'That's an awkward way to start a conversation, my dear Cliona!'

'No, I'm serious! I've been thinking about what you said. You're right, we don't always have to talk about literature. Let's talk about something else. Have you been working out lately?'

'Well, yes I have, a bit,' I replied, taken aback.

'You look so muscular,' she said in a teasing voice.

'It's all the reading I do, you know, lifting all those books,' I responded in kind.

She giggled. I could never quite tell if she was flirting with me, but it was an agreeable dynamic. This tension extended into class, where for a term we happened to be studying the story of Phaedra, in both the Euripides and Racine plays.

' "*Je sentis tout mon corps et transir et brûler,*" Phaedra confesses to her nurse. Can anyone translate this line for me?' Cliona asked the class.

I raised my hand. ' "I felt my whole body at once being coursed by a frozen wind, and burning", ' I replied, 'or perhaps "in flames".'

Cliona smiled. 'That's correct, Bradley. And what is the strength of this choice of words?'

'It shows the strong conflict of Phaedra's emotions.'

'Why is Phaedra conflicted?'

'Because she's in love with a younger man,' I replied seriously.

There was just a ghost of a smile on Cliona's lips. 'Hippolytus is also her son-in-law, who has sworn not to love women. But yes, he's also a younger man.'

I believe this particular lesson segued into an impassioned discussion by the whole class regarding the stylistic merits of Racine's prosody, and the moment passed. But this was far from the last time I would wonder if my teacher had as much of a weakness for me as I did for her. Our mix of arguments and flirtation spanned another year and a half, overlapping innocently with two of my girlfriends, until I was nineteen. Did it ever blossom into romance? That's another story…

THE PRINCE AND THE
CAMEL FEAST

The scent of barbecuing meat drifted along the walls.

In our building in the seventh *arrondissement* in Paris, there were many big and beautiful apartments, full of fascinating people I was fortunate enough to know. After all, who wouldn't want to live in such a situation? The building overlooked the Seine, and the rooms were on a large scale; often they played host to government officials, and even foreign monarchs.

In fact, next door to our apartment there lived an Arabian prince. The apartments were fit for royalty: palatial in scale, often more than one thousand square metres, with two hundred of those metres making up the front room alone. They were laid out to have enough space for someone of royal birth and their entire entourage of family and staff.

Having been in many palaces in Saudi Arabia and the Gulf, I knew exactly what sort of lavish entertainment the prince would require and how important this was. During my own time spent with royalty, I had been to feasts where the spread put on was so enormous it looked fit to feed a small country. Stuffed lambs, stuffed camels, food enough for the hundreds of people who then sat around on cushions and rugs on the floor and feasted to their heart's content.

So, essentially, I knew the smell of barbecuing meat when I came across it. I have to say, I was surprised by it. To find that sort of thing in the Gulf was to be expected, but in a posh apartment building on the Quai d'Orsay, right next to the prime minister's private housing? That was quite a different matter, and cause for some curiosity.

I myself was invited to the prince's feasts several times in my position as his personal banker. As I was managing his funds, he wanted me to come along to discuss deals and be introduced to his entourage. The guests at these feasts ate at tables rather than sitting on the floor, as was customary. They gave over to that much Westernisation, as they tucked into their baby camel. I personally had never been very fond of camel meat. I found it too hard and gristly, as though the creatures had been half-starved and marched for miles and miles across the desert before they were cooked, leaving only muscle and sinew, but the prince and his entourage loved it, and seemed to have it prepared for them about once a week.

They would serve up the whole camel in a copper dish a good three metres long, roasted and propped in a sitting position on top of a mountain of rice, pine nuts and almonds, surrounded not only by boiled vegetables but also by about twenty stuffed chickens. The effect was overwhelming. Two big pots on each side of this colossal dish would be filled with ten litres of yoghurt each. Most of the guests ate with knives and forks, but those who followed the Arab tradition pulled and ate the meat off the bones with their fingers. There would be so much sauce that it would dribble down their hands. I found the whole operation quite disgusting. Still, for the prince it was, I suppose, a taste of home.

One day, though, I smelled the familiar scent of seared meat, and I paused to actually think about it in detail, rather than just accepting it as part of the prince's way of life. The practicalities of it, specifically, concerned me. Where on earth were they cooking the camel? Even a baby camel is not a small animal, and this prince lived on the second floor of a Parisian apartment building! Where could they find the space for such an undertaking – there were no expansive gardens, no large kitchens, no open fires to be found anywhere.

I could not for the life of me puzzle it out. When I asked another resident in the building, he just shrugged, as bemused as me.

'I did wonder about the smell,' he said. 'You live next door, right? Does it bother you?'

'Not really. I just can't work out where they would be cooking a camel. Even a small camel.'

My neighbour shrugged. 'Ours is not to reason why, I guess.'

But still I couldn't help but question it. I had always been fond of mysteries, but only when I could figure out the answers in the end.

The next time I went to the prince's apartment to discuss the business of managing his funds, I was also granted permission to have a look around under the guise of seeing how he had decorated his apartment. The decorations were interesting, but they were not my principal concern: I just wanted to find out how he was able to lay on such terrific feasts as though he were still in his palace.

The answer came when I opened the door to one of the bedrooms, only to find that the room had been completely altered.

I was, to put it mildly, horrified.

Instead of finding the usual things one would expect in a bedroom, the place had been transformed into a kitchen, designed purely for barbecuing. The prince had had a chimney built to release the smoke from open fires that burned busily. Members of the prince's staff were currently in the process of roasting a whole lamb with the windows thrown open. Smoke billowed out into the gardens below.

'This is... interesting,' I said, distantly. I was shocked, and sure that this couldn't be legal. barbecuing whole animals over open fires in a second floor apartment? It was so dangerous, an accident waiting to happen. I thought of how I lay in bed just a few hundred feet away, and imagined the whole building being burned to the ground, all to satisfy the prince's desire for the food he knew and loved.

Of course, money can buy a lot of things. I couldn't say a word to criticise the oddity of the situation, because to do so would risk the prince withdrawing his sizeable amount of money from our bank. So I just smiled as though I found the whole thing quite normal and cheerfully attended the next feast I was invited to, all the while knowing exactly what was going on in one of the supposed bedrooms.

I wondered what the owner of the apartment would say when the prince gave up his long lease and left behind a smoke-blackened bedroom, complete with chimney, and forever permeated with the scent of cooking camel flesh. But this was not my concern. I kept my mouth shut and ate what I was offered. The prince kept his account with us for a further twelve years.

Truth be told, however, I was never *quite* comfortable in that apartment again, thinking about the roaring fires that burned far too close for comfort.

LENT IN NEW YORK

I lived in many areas over the twenty years I spent moving in and out of the Big Apple. My apartment in the early seventies had one of the most spectacular views, overlooking the river bordering Brooklyn Heights Promenade.

Our neighbour there was Sabrina Kanjo, a blonde woman in her early thirties who lived with her family. When I met her, I discovered she was rich, beautiful and a devout Catholic. The family owned a chain that distributed food products to supermarkets, and had obviously amassed enough of a fortune to be able to afford an apartment in a gorgeous brownstone high-rise in Brooklyn Heights. Thus, this family had access to fish, meat and vegetables at wholesale prices and, for that matter, in wholesale quantities.

When I first met Sabrina, it happened to be around Lent. Now, New York is not famous for being a dominantly Catholic city, although it has a substantial Catholic population, so I think I can be forgiven for being surprised by our first encounter.

'God I would kill for a steak,' she sighed, waiting next to me for the elevator. She tossed her hair moodily.

I'm sure that was pretty much the first thing she said to me.

'Well why don't you have one? There's a great steakhouse down the road.'

She sighed extravagantly.

'It's Lent, didn't you know, you dummy?' she replied with a bright smile. 'Aren't you practising Lent?'

'Well,' I said. 'I'm Bradley Jamieson, by the way.'

'Sabrina Kanjo,' she replied, sticking out her manicured hand. 'Isn't it wonderful?' she continued. 'Lent, I mean. Just cutting all of that fatty meat out of your system. Makes you feel so purified.'

'I'm sure that's exactly what Jesus had in mind in the desert,' I said dryly. 'So you are praying and giving alms as well as fasting?'

'Oh yes,' she said, 'I give ten dollars every weekend to the... unfortunate man on our front steps. And I always run through my prayers twice, unless there's something very good on TV.'

I decided to leave these statements unchallenged.

'Let's see,' I said, 'So you've been fasting since Ash Wednesday, that's only last week. It can't be that hard just eating fish.'

'Oh no,' she said cheerily, 'I love fish. Good for the heart. Plenty more fasting time to come!'

And she descended the stairs.

The next day, there was a knock at our door. I opened it to find a delivery boy standing there with a small crate of fresh fish. Four silvery mackerel seemed to stare up at me, their black stripes glistening in the hallway light.

'A neighbourly gift,' he said simply, reading off the tag that came with the crate.

I tipped him and stood for a moment on the doorstep, looking at the mackerel, noting that they were so fresh that their eyes weren't even glazed over.

I brought the crate into the kitchen and set it down on the table. It was pretty easy to work out whom we had to thank for this gift.

'Looks like we'll be observing Lent today,' I said to my wife Hilary.

She was overjoyed. 'Look at this beautiful mackerel! I'll grill it up for dinner, with a fresh fennel salad.'

Her enthusiasm was contagious, and the mackerel was indeed gorgeous, but I couldn't help but have a strange feeling about this apparent generosity.

The second day, we were brought a Styrofoam box of sole fillets.

I carried them into the kitchen with a sinking feeling.

'I know how you love *sole meunière* darling,' my wife said softly. 'Why do you look so glum?'

'I'm not sure,' I said, 'I'm happy to have free food, but I'm a little worried about this. I don't understand why she's doing it. Is it going to stop?'

On the third day the delivery boy was already waiting when I came home from work.

'Sorry,' he said, 'it was hard to knock with these things clawing around.'

I looked at what he was holding, and found myself staring at the beady stalks of two very large, very fresh, live crabs.

I walked into the house slowly.

'Guess what's for dinner,' I said.

'Well,' my wife said a little uneasily, 'we were meant to have this lamb yesterday already. I'm a bit worried it's going to go off.'

I sighed, and set the crabs in the sink.

'Look, honey, let's just cook the lamb.'

'There's not really space in the fridge for giant live crabs!'

She had a point. We boiled the crabs and ate them with lemon butter.

By the end of the second week, my wife had stopped buying anything but side dishes like potatoes, rice and vegetables, and we were thoroughly sick of fish. It wasn't that we didn't like it, but eating it for every meal was feeling a little extreme. One day at work I snuck my leftover tuna sandwich in the bin and went out for a guilty steak. That night I brought up the topic at dinner, over free smoked haddock.

'Do you think we should ask her to stop?'

'I don't know. I mean, it's just too much.'

'And *you're* Catholic,' I said with a wry laugh. 'Are you feeling very purified by this fast? It's making me feel guilty.'

Hilary sighed. 'I have found myself thanking Sabrina in my prayers, although I'm not sure I'm very grateful.'

'The thing is,' I pondered, 'it's all very good fresh sea fish. It's probably worth a fortune. Maybe we should start selling it on.'

She smiled.

'I just don't know how to handle this,' I said. 'What if we offend them? We have to live next to them for years. Imagine if they start leaving rotten fish by the door…'

Hilary laughed. 'Don't worry about it,' she said. 'Maybe just talk to Sabrina if you get a chance.'

So I started knocking on their door, but the Kanjos never seemed to be home when we were, although I could swear I once heard the hum of the television in the background. Once I saw her in the street, her golden hair glinting in the sun, but she had already turned the corner by the time I could run after her.

And this was how, in the spring of 1971, my wife and I fasted for Lent without having had any previous intention of doing so. On the Thursday before Easter, the deliveries stopped. And on Easter Monday, I ran into Sabrina in the hall.

'Sabrina!' I said, 'I must thank you for all your generous donations.'

She flashed a big smile.

'So glad you've enjoyed it. Lent is just such an important ritual, you know.'

'We had the biggest roast lamb for Easter,' I said pointedly.

'Oh, how lovely. Yes, it's nice to not be eating fish anymore. You get quite sick of it.'

She laughed. I did not reply. She put her hand on my shoulder.

'Why don't you and your wife come over for dinner tomorrow,' she said kindly. 'We'll have steaks.'

So the fasting was over, and the strange relations too. We went to the Kanjos' for dinner several times, and invited them back as well, but I don't think we ever ate fish together. It was a good month and a half before Hilary could bring herself to cook it again.

ZAHWI, THE CARPET MAN

In my life, I have been to many places where I did not stay long, whether simply passing through on a business trip or staying a few days on holiday. In these cases, neighbours are a more fleeting presence, although, like the places themselves, they sometimes leave cherished, indelible memories behind them. Zahwi in the city of Jeddah was one such passing neighbour.

After 1973, in the throes of the oil euphoria, many bankers rushed to the Middle East in hopes of collecting deposits and enticing the different central banks and governments to keep their money with their particular branch, or to invest it via their offices so they could cash in on the generous commissions. Deposits often accumulated the substantial sum of two percent, though some of the commissions for direct investments and acquisitions went up to eight percent; in those days, an acquisition of a hundred million could make a lucky banker eight million. I was among the first wave of keen foreign investors to get involved. Many of us, for instance, would travel to Jeddah, where the central bank was called the Saudi Arabian Monetary Agency, or SAMA.

Of course, the influx of foreign bankers caused an immediate housing crisis. That said, many of us preferred not to set up there too permanently, choosing instead to stay in one of the city's hotels. The only place really worth anything was called the Kandara Hotel. This boasted an excellent location right in the centre of town, if few other real advantages other than the fact that it wasn't quite as dusty and hot as the other hotels, and that it had been refurbished more recently and to a more modern standard. Still, I stayed in this particular hotel many times during 1973 and 1974 and have many fond memories of it. At that time, Saudi Arabia had no entertainment for its increasingly large number of visitors. There was no cinema and no theatre; the amount of television available was negligible, essentially limited to prayers and the news. Radio was non-existent, and the religious police were quite prevalent on the streets, shadowing or prodding people to make sure they went to prayer the proper five times a day. It was not a place people came to relax, but that did make it difficult to kill time there in between meetings and meals. Conversation was the only real form of entertainment. Once one had exhausted one's business partners for work-related chat, this left only the locals. Luckily, the Kandara Hotel was surrounded by a fairly interesting mix of characters.

Right across the street, for instance, there were a number of carpet merchants. They had presumably been drawn to that particular location by the presence of the hotel, which they imagined (partly correctly) to be full of rich, foreign guests, well-connected to the airport. There was another advantage to this location, which was that they could catch pilgrims as they arrived from all over the Middle and Far East. People entering the country from Turkey, Indonesia, Kenya, Nigeria and Iran all had trouble with foreign exchange, being unable to withdraw cash from abroad.

These pilgrims would emerge, exhausted and heavily laden, from the airport, dragging their possessions and families behind them, without a penny of local currency. The carpet merchants would descend on them like hungry vultures on rodents. They would offer to buy their carpets off them, at a ridiculously low rate. The pilgrims would often accept, as they were strapped for cash, while the merchants would end up with cheap carpets. It was a somewhat symbolic exchange, and certainly an unbalanced one. Some of the pilgrims would get so desperate that they would sell their own prayer rug. In any case, this explained why there were quite so many carpet merchants in this particular location.

They were a ragtag lot, spread out along the dusty pavement all surrounded by crumpled piles of crimson and gold and turquoise carpets. All day long they just stood there with their long beards and robes, hawking all and any that passed by, trying to tell anyone who would listen all about the particular qualities of their wares. Occasionally, I would see them sell a carpet to some hard-nosed old local woman, or to a family of fair-haired and sunburned tourists. Of course the prices would be double for the second type of customer, compared to what they were for the first.

Out of a combination of their handy location and my own boredom, I ended up striking up acquaintances with a few of them, and a particularly memorable meeting was with one by the name of Zahwi. I can't remember how our first conversation came about, but somehow he managed to pique my intellectual interest. I assume Zahwi's domain happened to lie closest to the entry to my hotel, or perhaps he was simply more persistent than his companions. In any case, he was a charming and witty character, and after a rather humorous first encounter in which I made him show me nearly all his rugs without buying any of them, the two of us ended up conversing fairly regularly. He was a tall, thin man, with straight, white teeth, and an especially thick beard. If his claims were to be believed, he had the best and biggest rugs of all the city of Jeddah, although of course I'm sure any of his marketplace companions would have claimed the same thing. He had a pleasant disposition, and a tendency to veer more quickly than necessary onto religious topics. If he wasn't talking my ear off about the benevolence of Allah, he would almost certainly be trying to sell me some carpets. He never gave up; he had a shrewd salesman's instinct, coupled with definite charm that made it nearly impossible to stop talking to him. At first, I felt it would be impolite to tell him to be quiet, but gradually I became genuinely interested in what he had to say. Through this continued interaction, I ended up finding out quite a lot about his profession and passion.

Even though my family owned several Persian carpets, I had never been interested in learning very much about them. Talking to this merchant, I realised just how much there was to know about the numerous aspects of carpet-making: the various thicknesses of threads, the materials, the names of different sizes and patterns, the signs that gave away the levels of quality. Up until my stay in Jeddah, I had only really enjoyed them for the designs, patterns and wonderful colours that characterised these imports. Zahwi, however, taught me how to appreciate them on a much more informed level. He taught me to pay attention to the way the corners were woven or tied, to the design of the central medallion, and to the precise choice of colours. He showed me how to flip a carpet over in order to count the knots per square inch, and how to measure the length and breadth of a piece of fabric using only one's hands. Once we had gone over all these details together, he would tell me the name of the carpet type. It was an impressive exercise, one that demonstrated a real breadth of knowledge on the subject. He could tell the historic period, and even the precise age of a carpet, just by looking at it for a few minutes.

Zahwi loved the idea of teaching a visitor all about the traditions of the Arabian Peninsula, as well as about his carpets and his life. Often, on the way back from a banking meeting, I would end up sitting with Zahwi for hours, drinking sweet tea and listening to his stories. When he had finished trying to sell me carpets, he would often tell me long tales of travels. He loved reminiscing about his tribe and his nomadic origins. Sometimes he would talk to me for so long that I would start to feel like King Shahryar, although Zahwi was certainly no Scheherazade! Nonetheless, he was a fascinating man. He had spent much of his life travelling around, learning various trades before settling on that of carpet merchant. He had then travelled all over the Middle East, especially Iran, buying what he was convinced were the world's very best carpets. Once we got to know each other a little better, he began to tell me about his family, and in particular his many wives and daughters.

'There is a weakness in my family,' he said, 'although it is an attractive one.'

'And what is that?' I asked with a smile, providing the listener's interaction he so obviously sought from his audience.

'I have far too many beautiful daughters,' he said sadly. 'All my beloved wives just keep on producing more female than male children! It is a terrible thing.' He shook his head in mock misery.

'Why is that?' I asked, encouraging him in his story. 'Women, after all, are the origin of humanity! I'm sure your many daughters must be as delightful as your many wives.'

He bowed his head. 'Of course you are right. Be that as it may, I do have a problem: it seems I'm unable to marry them all off to other members of the tribe. There are too many of them.' He sighed. 'This is the burden of a happy father. But look,' he said a little slyly, and I could hear the salesman's tones creeping into his story, 'there is a reason I am telling you this. You are a rich and upstanding young man, fairly successful, yes?'

'Well, I'm hardly rich, but I try to be a good man.'

He laughed. 'That is good enough for me. How about this: I will offer you one or two of my daughters to marry.'

'One or two?' I didn't like the way he said this in exactly the same tone of voice as when he was hawking his carpets. 'That's ridiculous. For a start, I'm already married. Second of all, even if I were not, I could not ever consider marrying more than one woman. Thirdly, do your daughters even speak English? I mean, you obviously learned it when you were selling your carpets, but what do your daughters do with their lives? Are they educated?'

He shrugged, and spread his arms expansively. 'Well, *you* can teach them English! It would be wonderful. For you both, or the three or four of you,' he added hastily, with a wink. 'They are very beautiful.'

'But isn't your family very religious? And what about the dowry?'

'No problem, no problem,' he replied, again sounding suspiciously like a salesman to me. 'For the dowry, you can pay what you want. Five hundred dollars, a thousand dollars, anything you like.'

'You're very funny,' I said, 'but there is no way in the world I am marrying your daughters. Any of them.'

He continued to try this approach with me, although eventually, luckily, he seemed to understand that I was as serious about not marrying any of his daughters as I was about not buying any of his carpets. Our interactions continued as before until the end of my stay in Jeddah, with added jokes about becoming his son-in-law. We parted on amiable terms.

Ten years later, on another banking trip, I came back to visit a very changed Arabia. Jeddah was no longer the centre of financial action: the SAMA had moved to Riyadh, for one thing, and although our branch remained in Jeddah, it was in a minor position. Saudi Arabia had become a banking force of its own, even if no longer propelled by the oil euphoria, and foreign investors no longer played such a key role there.

I came back to stay in the good old Kandara Hotel, which was now surrounded by a smaller and tidier array of carpet sellers. I was relieved to find that, despite appearances, it was not too much changed. After only a few minutes' search, I found Zahwi. There was a little more grey in his beard, but he was otherwise unchanged. When he saw me, his face split into a grin.

'My son-in-law!' he exclaimed. 'Come buy a carpet! Come have some tea!' He poured me a cup of tea with sugar, and launched right back into his old routine of storytelling and carpet-selling. It was pleasantly familiar.

'So what happened to all your beautiful daughters?' I had to ask him.

'Oh, they are all married now,' he replied cheerfully. 'All seventeen of them.'

I stared. He laughed at my expression, then shrugged. 'I may not have managed handsome foreign husbands or generous dowries for all, but they found good men within the tribe. It turns out if you wait long enough, they will get snapped up. Just like carpets: good quality never goes to waste. The right people will always see it.'

I shook my head. 'You're quite the salesman.'

'They all have babies now,' he said proudly. 'They stayed in the tribe, and now I am a grandfather to more than forty children. I can't even count how many I have for sure. They're always running around. Can you imagine that?' He grinned proudly.

'I really can't,' I said. 'You're looking well for a grandfather,' I told him. 'I take it business is going well? You seem to have even more carpets than before, if that's even possible.'

'Oh yes,' he said, 'far more, and of far better quality. It's so nice that we crossed paths now, actually, as I'm expanding in a big way. I'm moving to downtown Riyadh and setting up there. I leave Jeddah in just three months. Just think, if you had come on your business trip at any time after that, we would never have met again.'

'Ah,' I said with a smile, 'but I seem to be too late on one account already. Are you telling me you married away all my future wives? You didn't even wait for me to come back?'

Zahwi laughed, displaying his strong, white teeth. 'You should have agreed when you had the chance. By now, just think! You could have had ten more of my grandkids.' He paused slyly. 'Women are like carpets,' he warned me. 'You wait too long, and all the good ones will have gone.'

THE LIVE-IN GRANDMOTHER

In the 1990s, I was obsessed with the idea of finding a house in Geneva with views over the lake. I was limited in my choices by the fact that I wanted at least ten sizeable bedrooms, a big garden, and room to build a swimming pool, as well as lake views. I also hoped for an elevator, a large reception, a good games room; I wanted a house built out of stone and with some historical character, preferably between the seventeenth and nineteenth centuries. This led to me looking at some sixty places, most of which were immediately eliminated because they didn't qualify for these requirements. It didn't help that the real estate agents simply seemed to show me big houses, without listening to my list of desires and needs, so with many of these houses we would simply have to show up outside for me to dismiss a property out of hand for being too modern or in a less than ideal location.

Even within those properties which seemed to be wonderful, I experienced a series of disappointments, mostly based on the people there who almost became my neighbours.

One such case was a beautiful property right by the lakeside, which seemed to fulfil all of the criteria, and had a particularly lovely garden. At the end of the viewing, I committed in writing, although I didn't pay the agents. In this case this turned out to be a good decision, but it has always been my policy: never give the agents their cut until the deal has actually been signed and confirmed. In any case, I read through the basic contract and found nothing odd in it. I left the viewing contented, sure I had finally found the right place in Geneva. We had to wait two months for the duration of the architectural survey, but I thought nothing of it.

At the end of this period, I turned up at my notary's office to sign the final version of the contract. I read through it carefully, noting that most of it was the same as the first document I had signed. However, right at the end, hidden in the small print in the last paragraph of the document, was a small, mysterious clause, stating that the landlord's grandmother would be able to live in the guesthouse next to the property until she died. I looked up from the document, frowning.

'What on earth is this?'

The notary, concerned, came round to my side of the table and read through the fine print. 'I beg your pardon, Monsieur,' he said, 'the landlord must have added this clause. I was not aware of it.'

'So you're saying he scuttled the sale?'

'He didn't declare this originally, as you well know. So in a sense, yes. I mean, let's not be hasty. How far from the house is the guesthouse? And, not to be crass, but how old is this grandmother? You may wish to consider these elements before you renege on your contract.'

The notary's smooth talking won me over. 'You're right,' I said. 'After all, I do really like this house. Let me go visit this grandmother character. Then we'll talk again.'

I went home and rang the landlord at once.

'You have some serious cheek, writing your own grandmother into the fine print!'

'I see you've read the contract properly,' he observed. I couldn't quite tell from his tone if this was meant as a simple observation or an expression of disappointment.

'Well I should say so! I don't know who you would expect to sign a three-year lease without reading the fine print carefully. You can't just have a surprise housemate!'

'Now, don't exaggerate, my grandmother is nobody's housemate. You're just on the same estate. The same piece of land.'

'Fine, but you're still essentially imposing a very close neighbour on me, without my agreement!'

'Now, don't get grumpy. I fully expected you to read all the terms of the contract, of course.'

'What would you have done if I hadn't read it?' I was trying very hard not to lose my temper, as the reality of what had just happened sank in.

'I can't imagine it would be too terrible a surprise. It's a perfectly respectable clause to put in, as far as I'm concerned.'

'Well, if you really felt like that, and thought it was so respectable, shouldn't you have asked me? For all you know, I wouldn't mind! In fact, I would hope that is what you assumed, rather than intending to trick me into agreeing to something I wouldn't be happy with in the least.' The landlord obviously didn't know what to say next, so I continued: 'Look, I'm having to rethink my interest in this property quite seriously. But before I make any rash decisions, I'd like to meet with your grandmother. Would that be possible?'

'Of course,' he replied. 'Just go over to the house. She doesn't really go out much, I'm sure she'll make you a cup of coffee.'

'I'm not making any decisions until I've spoken to my own family, you understand that? I didn't sign the contract.'

The landlord grumbled, but let the matter be. Meanwhile, I drove to what I had thought was going to be my new house, and walked to the guesthouse to interview the landlord's grandmother. When she appeared in the doorway, any suspicions about her intentions melted away. She was a lovely old woman, aged about ninety, with delicate white hair.

'*Bonjour, Monsieur.*' She greeted me in genteel French with a Swiss accent. 'Do I understand correctly that you are to be my new neighbour?' She let me into her little living room without any trouble. We sat and drank coffee out of flowery china cups, and spoke for a few hours.

This lady, whom I had until then only thought of as an annoying clause that might cause me to lose my house, turned out to be full of jokes and fascinating stories about her life. She really was surprisingly funny, and a gracious host as well. She told me about her childhood, her travels, her interest in poetry, her book collecting, her involvement in charity work, including being a long-standing patron of a local convent. Time flew, and by the time I took my leave and drove home, I had almost forgotten the news I had to break to my family.

'I've just met the loveliest woman,' I told my wife as I walked in the door. Seeing her face, I hastily added: 'She's almost a hundred years old, and she is going to live in the guesthouse behind our new home!'

'I'm sorry?' Seeing my wife's expression of shock reminded me how ridiculous the whole thing had seemed to me only a few hours previously.

'No, no, she's really very nice. I mean, it's a surprise, but it won't be a problem, will it?'

'But I assumed we would have the use of the guesthouse for ourselves!'

'Well, yes, but do we really need it? Anyway, she surely won't be there for very long. It's a temporary arrangement. A service rendered. I can assure you she's a really fascinating old lady. She makes excellent coffee.'

'I can make coffee myself, thank you very much.'

In the subsequent discussion, it quickly became quite clear that my wife was going to prove more intractable on the subject than I had been. 'You really should just meet her,' I implored her. 'She's a sweet old woman. She would just be at the end of the garden!'

'I'm sure she's sweet,' my wife replied. 'It's not the grandmother herself I have issues with. It's the whole business: the secret clause, the attitude. I mean, I'm not sure I'm entirely on board with this surprise guest either, but it all sounds less legal than I'd like.'

'She wouldn't be a guest,' I protested, 'she'd be a neighbour.'

'Same difference. I'm just not OK with buying a house with such strange baggage attached to it!'

'She's not baggage!'

'She's old lady baggage, as far as that contract is concerned.'

'But we both really liked this house!'

'We'll find another one.'

'Look, if this old lady bothers you so much, let me talk to her. Maybe I can convince her to move out.'

'You mean that isn't what you went to do in the first place?'

'Well no,' I answered, rather sheepishly, 'I just went to find out what she was like.'

I went back to the lady's house. This time, she served me a fine English-style tea, with home-made biscuits on the side. She read me some of her poetry, and we talked about literature for several hours: Molière and Voltaire and Rabelais. At the end of this chat, I was reluctant to bring up the subject, but I asked her if she would be willing to move out.

'I would pay for you to take another apartment,' I offered. 'It's not that we mind you being here, but we have kids, and my wife isn't comfortable with the way it has all been handled.' I didn't really want to discuss the secret clause with her, as I wasn't sure how honest her grandson had been about the way she was being introduced to her potential new neighbours.

The lady, however, proved impossible to convince. 'I've lived here, on this land, all my life. The house you are about to move into was my home. Living in this little place seemed bad enough at first, but I've become used to it. I can't imagine having to leave altogether.' She smiled sadly. 'After all, I don't think I'll be bothering you for that much longer.'

I didn't like the idea of pressing the subject with her, so, after promising to return for literary conversation another day, I left.

When I arrived home, I explained the situation to my wife, and we decided to pull out of the contract. It was a shame to lose the house, although I did understand my wife's reservations on the subject. At the time, I was worried we would never find another house as nice as that one, but of course, in the end we did, and it turned out to be wonderful. However, a year later I found out through the notary, who handled the contract for our next house, that the first house was eventually sold for twice the price I had agreed to. Real estate prices in Geneva had changed shortly after we moved on. I also found out that the old lady had passed away a mere eleven months later. A part of me couldn't help but wonder if we couldn't have settled quite happily in that house with the lake views, with the little old grandmother living quietly in the back.

Majilan Matzo was one of the most interesting neighbours I ever had. I certainly never had a neighbour with such nice-smelling wares. Majilan sold all kinds of roasted nuts and seeds: almonds, peanuts, walnuts, pine nuts, pistachios, sunflower seeds, cob nuts, cashews, hazelnuts, even dried beans. He did all this from a small stall near our house in Paris. From our penthouse apartment in the seventeenth *arrondissement*, we were perpetually surrounded by a rich cloud of smells escaping from the hundreds and thousands of nuts roasting.

This sort of establishment is very rare outside of France. I have very rarely seen it in the United States or in London, except when run by an expatriate. In France, however, they are ubiquitous, as common at fairs and festivals as on obscure street corners. There's nothing quite like the rustling of the nuts being stirred around over a hot grill. Children will never lose the sense of wonder that comes from standing on tiptoe near a delicious treat. In this case, the different varieties of nuts, all subtly different shades of gold and brown, were lined up in beautiful glass containers. From a very early age, I would go down to the stand and purchase a hundred grams of one variety or another. I always stood there for a long time, making my decision very carefully. I loved almost every flavour and I am sure that, over the years, I sampled them all. I remember being particularly fond of the pistachios, which have always been my favourite variety of nut. However, the peanuts, of which Majilan offered five different varieties, were also fascinating. He had South American peanuts, Cuban peanuts, Californian peanuts; tiny peanuts from North Africa, huge peanuts from deepest Kenya, inch-long peanuts from Somalia. I tried them all.

Majilan was a marvellous man. He was short, thin, and deeply tanned. Standing in the heat from the grill, with the heat wafting up and making him sweat, he looked half-roasted himself. The heat source was rather like a large, flat wok with curved edges. He would roast one kind of nut at a time. 'You want to eat them when they've just come out,' he would tell me. 'Just not too soon, or you'll burn yourself! Ideally, you wait for the oils to cool off just a little. Then, when you put the nut in your mouth, it will be perfectly hot, crispy, crunchy and perfumed. All the flavours of each individual nut have been released by the heat, you see.'

'I can certainly believe it,' I told him through a mouthful of sunflower seeds.

'Then you must cool the nuts,' he told me, loving the story of his day-to-day work as dearly as if he had just taken up the profession, even though he had been doing it since he was a teenager, helping to run his father's stand. 'You cannot just let the nuts sit in the air, or the temperature shock will be too much for them. Also, if there is wind, they will cool unevenly. So what you have to do is to transfer the nuts into this other pan, and shake them around. This distributes the flavoured oils evenly, and ensures everything cools down a little. They you put them in a paper cone and hand them to your lucky customer,' he concluded triumphantly. 'And the happy customer eats them all before they have time to get cold.'

Majilan believed in simplicity. He liked to let the individual flavours shine through. 'A Californian peanut tastes completely different to a Bolivian one, let alone a Somalian one!' he liked to tell me. 'If you cover them up with butter or sugar or even too much salt, you lose that completely.' Most of his nuts had no flavouring, although he did offer a shake of salt to anyone that wanted it.

Sadly, few values are immune to the law of supply and demand, and few salesmen manage to stick to their principles in the face of change. Slowly, a different nut-based trend had started to creep in during the mid-seventies, from the beaches of the South of France. The plain and salted nuts of my childhood were no longer the tradition. A new craze had started, and it was overtaking the cities at an unstoppable pace, until eventually it arrived on my very doorstep. One day I smelled the tell-tale sweetness wafting through the streets of Paris. Caramel. Nuts covered in caramel. I couldn't even smell the nuts in the street anymore. I ran down to see what had happened, still hoping my suspicions were unfounded. Perhaps someone had started selling candy floss next door! Perhaps there had been a spill of roasted sugar beets from a factory! But this was not the case. Majilan was there, grinning away as happily as ever, stirring the nuts with a big spoon.

'What are you doing, burning down the shop? Making *crème brûlée*?' I asked him.

'No,' he replied gaily, apparently unperturbed. 'I'm cooking nuts, just like I always do.'

I glared at him. I couldn't even tell what kind of nut it was in the pan, either from the smell or shape. They were just big shapeless knobs of caramel. 'You're not cooking nuts. Just look at those lumps! You may as well just be selling sweets,' I lamented. 'You could put anything in there! Cardboard, walnut shells, little bits of wood. No-one will be able to taste anything but the burnt sugar. They'll all walk away with cavities.'

Majilan laughed, wiping his hands on his apron. 'What can I say?' he replied. 'The kids love them this way.' He reached over to shake my hand, with his, large and hot. 'You're not going to abandon me as a customer, are you? You've been one of my most faithful!'

I looked around the stall, appalled. 'This is not what I expected from you, Majilan.'

He patted me on the shoulder. 'Don't worry,' he said, 'I'm planning to bring back in a few varieties of plain nuts, for the old fogies like you who can't learn to change their tastes. Still, you are going to have to learn that the city is a changing place. Nothing lasts forever. You have to roll with the times if you want to stay in the game!'

As he no doubt had predicted, I took this as a sort of challenge. 'Don't be ridiculous,' I sniffed, 'I never said my tastes were set in stone, I just said I was doubtful. Now, let me try a few of these sweets of yours. Then maybe I can give you a more informed opinion on your business tactics.'

Smiling, Majilan carefully composed a handful of walnuts and peanuts for me. They were still crunchy, and deep under the crust of sugar I could just about discern the individual taste of each nut. However, they were nowhere as good as the nuts I remembered, and I told my nut-roasting neighbour as much. 'It's basically criminal,' I said, 'to coat these beautiful perfumed nuts in industrial sugar. You've obliterated all the natural flavours that you taught me so carefully to appreciate. Look, the sugar's even burnt! It's worse than gilding the lily. It's like covering a lily in gaudy paint!'

For a moment my neighbour looked a little pained. Then he shook his head and let loose a hearty laugh.

'My friend,' he said, 'you know I agree with you. Otherwise, I would've been doing this for years, wouldn't I? But this is what people like nowadays. I was losing customers, and I had to find a way to get them back. Kids want sugar more than salt, you see. They're used to eating only commercial sweets all the time. They haven't a taste for simple things.'

'Well, it should be your responsibility to teach them! I swear I almost lost a filling biting into that thing,' I retorted. But on seeing my friend's face, I quickly relented. 'I didn't mean that as an accusation,' I said. 'I understand completely why you've had to make this choice. To be honest, I'm sure you're right about the roast nut market. I must admit it's not one I happen to know intimately.'

Majilan roared with laughter. 'I knew it,' he said. 'I knew you were always faithful to your good old friend Majilan, and you were right to be! My nuts have always been, and always will be, the best roast nuts in the whole city of Paris. In fact, I'll tell you what: I'll always make sure I have a few containers of plain nuts set aside for you, as long as you promise to never give up on coming here.'

'It's a deal,' I replied. 'I look forward to watching the new clients pour in. Although you must know that I secretly hope it will fail. Not because I want you to lose business, but because I want you to go back to the good old ways!'

It turned out that what Majilan had predicted, or even hoped for, was exactly what would happen. I had to admit that Majilan had been right about the current market and young children's tastes. Slowly, the new clients trickled in, arriving with bright eyes, and leaving with sticky hands and sugar-coated teeth. Then they passed the word to their friends and families, and all the people they knew. Over the weeks, the queue in front of Majilan's stall lengthened. With new success, however, came new problems. I kept visiting Majilan, who had started to look a little haggard from all the new work the new customers had required. He was sweating so much that he looked rather like a sugared nut that had been left in the pan a few hours too long. Furthermore, he confided in me that the caramelised nuts didn't store as well as the plain ones.

'Why don't you just go back to the old, classic ways?' I kept asking him. 'You were successful enough! Business was steady.'

But he remained stubborn. 'I want to make more money,' he repeated. 'This is how to do it. I'm changing with the times. It doesn't matter if there's a little waste. It's a better investment overall.'

'What are you talking about? The caramelised nuts are ugly, too,'

I continued in despair. 'They don't keep as well, they don't taste as good, and they don't look as nice. How is this an improvement?'

'The children love them,' he repeated doggedly. 'Just you wait. I'm going to make a fortune with this.'

In the end, his prediction of financial success came true, but it strained his psychological health, and our friendship, quite heavily. After a while, the queues became too long to be worth the wait, and I gave up on the whole operation. Soon after that, Majilan stopped stocking plain nuts at all. That was the end of my relationship with him. From then on, the sickly smell of caramel replaced the beloved aroma of roasted nuts wafting down my street. Nonetheless, I would always remember those perfect roast nuts from my childhood.

THE DEBATING PARTNER

Americans make the friendliest neighbours. It would be difficult to live next to an American without meeting them, and within a student dorm it would be close to impossible.

Wally was my neighbour when I was a student on my first course at Northwestern University. He knocked on the door one day without warning, and I opened the door to a short, stocky, fair-haired man with a big head and a short neck. He had rosy cheeks, light blue eyes, and high cheekbones. He was also completely naked.

He stuck out his hand.

'Hi! I'm Wally!' he said.

'I'm sorry,' I said, 'but you're not wearing any clothes.'

'Dude,' he said. 'Get used to dorm life. We'll be nude all the time.'

I paused. 'Look, this is all strange to me. I'm not used to this casual nudity.'

'You should get used to it,' he says. 'Maybe you should get naked now! If I don't see you nude now, I will see in the shower. People will laugh if you go in a swimsuit.' He raised his eyebrows and grinned.

'Look, I... have a bathrobe.' I shook my head. 'This is beside the point. What do you want from me?'

'OK.' Wally closed the door behind him, and leaned back against it. 'First, I want to know your name. Two, I want to know what you're studying. Three, I would like to see if you can help with my homework. Four, I would like to know how many girls you are dating, if any, and their names. Five, do you want to be introduced to anyone? Six, do you have a driver's license? Seven, do you have a car I can use?'

He paused, and folded his arms, waiting.

I shook my head. 'Look, I can answer all your questions. Come in, sit down, but for the love of God just put on some pants first!'

Wally sauntered out the door, and came back two minutes later in jeans and a tank top. He sat down on the bed and put his elbows on his knees.

'You Americans,' I said. 'Very friendly but my, you're nosy!'

'Yeah, yeah,' he said, 'now answer my seven questions.'

The intensity of his pose made me feel like I was being interviewed, and I laughed.

'I don't remember them all...' Half-joking, I reached for something on my desk. 'Here's my card,' I said, handing it to him. Wally was impressed.

'You already have a card? How old are you, man?' He squinted. 'Bradley.'

'I'm seventeen.'

'Why do you have a card, seventeen-year-old Bradley? Do you have a job?'

'Oh, I have it so I can give it to girls. So they have my number, you see.'

'That's smart,' he replied, nodding. 'Tell you what, I'll get the same card made. We can go hunting as a team.' He flashed a predatory grin. 'Where can I get one made?'

I rather reluctantly gave him the name of the shop.

'So what do you study?' he continued.

'I'm preparing to study engineering.'

'Oh, you're one of those,' he said knowingly. 'I'm studying literature.'

'I can tell from the way you're interviewing me! I'm pretty sure seven questions in less than one minute is impressive journalism, but I don't know who can keep up. Why don't you answer the questions yourself first?'

'You're funny,' he said, 'but no. How about a different question: can I borrow your car?'

I had not expected this.

'I don't usually lend my car,' I said. Seeing his crestfallen face, I added, 'I mean, do you even know how to drive?'

He was incensed. 'What do you mean? I learned how to drive when I was twelve! I'm from North Dakota. Soon as a kid can fit behind the wheel there he can drive. No choice. Cross-country, long-distance, the whole hog. We have a big farm, like a twenty-thousand-acre farm. My dad always let me drive all around the fields.'

'I can't let you drive my car in Chicago when you come from a farm in the Dakotas! I mean, it's not exactly the same level of danger. What are you going to run into in those fields, a hay bale?'

Wally apparently ignored this. 'How much money do you make?'

'How could I be making money?' I asked, 'I'm only seventeen.'

'Well, if you have a car you must have money,' he said, as if I were being stupid.

'My father gave it to me,' I replied, trying not to look smug.

'Oh, you're one of those,' he said again. He pondered this for a moment. 'Guess you'll be moving to a frat in a bit, then?'

'That's exactly what I intend to do.'

He shrugged. 'So what other plans do you have? Do you like to travel?'

'Sure I like to travel. I'd really like to –'

Wally cut me off before I could continue exploring this topic.

'Hey,' he cut in, 'do you want to go with me to my parents' in the Dakotas?'

'Wait, you're inviting me to come stay with your family? After meeting me for ten minutes?'

'Yeah, man, that's America! We can drive next weekend. We can take a day off school.'

'You can't just make me skip school! I'm an engineer. I have important classes.'

'Hey, I have important classes too!' He paused. 'OK, fine, I don't really, but whatever. It's easy. Just steal the notes off someone else.'

'Look, Wally, I've known you for less than half an hour. And you spent about half that time naked. I don't think we're quite at the stage of taking ten-hour car trips together. But why don't we start by having a hamburger instead? I'm starving.'

Wally's face, which had fallen during the first part of this speech, perked up considerably.

'Man, I love hamburgers. Let me just get my jacket.'

So that was how we ended up going to Big Boy and having double-decker hamburgers and thick-cut fries.

'My Dad's a farmer,' Wally said, through a mouthful of sesame bun. 'He sells beef and buffalo meat.'

'That might explain why you're so fond of hamburgers,' I said.

'I sure am. I could happily eat nothing but hamburgers all day. Cheeseburgers, bacon, burgers with relish.' He sighed happily, sending a few crumbs tumbling onto the table.

After a thoughtful pause that was presumably filled with visions of burgers, he moved onto another topic.

'So say, Bradley, I guess you're pretty good at useful science stuff, eh?' he asked casually.

'Well, I hope so. I'm trying to be an engineer…'

'What about humanities subjects? Like, say, sociology? Or comparative religions?'

'Why do I have the feeling I know where this is going? Are you asking for help with your homework?'

'Well…' he grinned sheepishly.

'First the car, now this… Are you just trying to figure out how you can exploit me as much as possible?'

Wally's toothy smile widened. 'Isn't that what friends do?'

I sighed.

'I suppose we've known each other more than an hour, now. So yes, I suppose we can be considered friends.'

'So do you want to come visit my parents?'

I laughed. 'OK,' I said, 'Sure. But it'll have to be on a weekend.'

'Can I drive your car?'

'No!'

That was how I became friends with Wally. Over the next few years, we shared many hamburgers. I eventually answered all his questions and gave him some help with his homework, and later, he introduced me to his beautiful sister, whom I went on to date – but that's another story. The weekend after our first Big Boy burger, we went to visit his parents. I even let him drive my car a few times, but only on the side roads.

THE SILENT NEIGHBOUR

Only in the richest and snobbiest areas of Britain could you possibly expect not to meet your neighbours. In France or Switzerland, where there is less of a culture of small-talk with the people who live nearby, it would come as no surprise to live less than three metres from someone and yet never exchange a word. Of course customs in London are a far cry from, say, America, where any newcomer is welcomed with baskets of home-baked goodies, and no titbit of news goes unshared. But one neighbour of mine kept himself to himself to an extraordinary degree, even by London standards.

During my banking days, I lived for a time in Eaton Square, well known as one of the most beautiful old neighbourhoods of London, with terraced houses in the Classical style, and lush gardens in the centre. It is also renowned as one of the most expensive pieces of real estate in the world. An eight-bedroom house was worth around 17 million pounds; a five-bedroom house might go for 15 million. The square was the haunt of choice for the rich and famous of Britain, from prime ministers and lords to actors and top models, from dukes and musicians to writers like Somerset Maugham. Yet I knew most of my neighbours, and even the richest and most famous of them would usually recognise and greet me if they ran into me. All but one.

Between 1981 and 2002 I was often in Paris and Geneva as well as in the English countryside, but I also spent rather intensive periods in Eaton Square at various points during these twelve years, in a beautiful third-floor flat. Across the landing from me, there lived an attractive young man whom I eventually found out was called Timothy. He was probably in his late twenties; tall, blonde and very aristocratic-looking.

We would often run into each other on the landing, but he never stopped to speak. He would look at me, I would look at him, and before I had time to say 'Hello, I'm Bradley,' he would have disappeared into his apartment. This must have happened a good thirty times over the time I lived there. Sometimes I would see him in the morning, sauntering down the stairs with his hands in his pockets. Sometimes I would run into him in the evening, traipsing down the corridor with a model-esque beauty draped over his arm.

Neither of us extended a hand for a handshake; neither of us had time to offer a coffee or even a greeting. Instead we exchanged a special look which was meant to imply 'I'm sorry, I'm in a hurry. Next time, I promise we'll introduce ourselves.' But we never did. In twelve years as neighbours, we hardly exchanged a word, at least up until one day in 1994.

There were three apartments on our landing, each about 120 square metres. I was tremendously lucky to have acquired a place there, as the waiting list for a purchase or a long-term rental for anything on the square could take twenty or thirty years. The inflation of these apartment prices was somewhere between laughable and horrendous.

One day there came a knock on the door and my unseen neighbour, now almost forty, was standing outside.

'Hello,' he said, 'I'm Timothy. I just wanted to introduce myself.'

'Well, it's about time!' I said, opening the door. 'At last, we meet! Do come in, Timothy. Would you like a coffee?'

The blonde man shook his head gently. 'I'm terribly sorry, but I'm afraid I'm rather in a hurry. I've got to meet my girlfriend.'

'Ah,' I said knowingly, 'if you mean the blonde I've seen a few times, I can quite understand you'd rather have lunch with her than coffee with me!'

Timothy smiled slightly. 'I've an announcement of sorts to make to you.' He paused, delicately. 'I'm moving out.'

I think my jaw must have hung open for a moment, for Timothy laughed in embarrassment.

'Wait.' I shook my head. 'Do you really mean to say you're only introducing yourself to me because you're leaving? What's the point in that?'

Timothy cocked his head to the side and shrugged, apologetically. 'I came to ask if you would be interested in buying my lease. It's a long-term lease. Rather valuable, I reckon.'

'Oh, I'm aware of that,' I responded, my curiosity piqued despite my sense of social rejection.

'I'm willing to offer it for three hundred and twenty-five thousand pounds.'

'I have to admit I'm intrigued,' I responded. 'That sounds exceedingly reasonable. I believe the apartment on the second floor is going for far more than that!'

'Oh yes,' he admitted, 'it's very reasonable.' He did not add anything. I suppose the offer spoke for itself.

I paused, and studied my needs. I didn't really need more space: my family lived comfortably in Paris. I was moving to Geneva. I made my decision quickly.

'That's very kind of you,' I replied, 'but I'm going to say no. I just don't need to add this to my list of properties at the moment.'

Timothy nodded, looking a little disappointed. 'Suit yourself,' he said, 'Don't say I never offered it to you.'

Perhaps I was a little hasty in my decision. Only a few months later I heard he sold his lease for a million pounds. Then I heard that a speculator buyer had resold it only a few months later for two million pounds. In retrospect, this was rather galling. When I had moved in, with my own long-term lease, I had thought I was getting a fantastic deal. Eight years later, when I sold it on, I got back less money than I had spent on it. By that point, there were only four years left on mine: it had become a short-term lease and was far less valuable.

So that was how I missed out on an opportunity worth several million pounds based on a three-minute encounter with a man I had never met. For that offer was the sum total of our interaction: Timothy, of course, moved out within a few weeks, and I never saw him again. I must admit this was a situation where a neighbour was substantially smarter than me.

JOHN AND THE ROAST BEEF

In my early days as a student in London, I rented a three-bedroom house in Addington, Surrey, in a development of pretty little terraced houses surrounding a fountain. In those days, this was very affordable for a student. One of the other houses in this development belonged to my girlfriend's sister, who would soon afterwards become my sister-in-law. She and her husband John had bought this house straight out of college. They intended to live there for the rest of their lives; indeed, they are still there now. I only lived there for around three or four months before moving to Marble Arch in London and then abroad, but it was a pleasant enough place to stay.

Not long after moving in, my wife and I were invited to dinner by John and his wife. We enjoyed a meal of roast beef, Yorkshire pudding, mashed potatoes and peas. It was a fairly uneventful and pleasant event.

They invited us back the next weekend. And the next. And every single time they served us exactly the same meal. By the second month, this had begun to wear a little thin.

'Look,' I said to Hilary, 'why don't we have them over?'

'I think that's a great idea,' she replied. 'Let's just make sure we cook beef. They seem very fond of it.'

That Sunday, John and his wife arrived promptly, shaking the rain out of their hair and coats before settling in at the table. As they sipped their water nervously, John remarked:

'You know I only like my beef rare.'

I cleared my throat. 'Actually, we're eating *boeuf bourguignon*, which has been slow-cooked over eight hours in a red wine sauce with thyme and rosemary.' Seeing his face, I hastily added: 'We even made fries for you, seeing as you love potatoes. In France, it would traditionally be eaten with a nice baguette.'

John kept a very straight face throughout this, but when the stew arrived on the table his expression had turned to one of undeniable disgust.

'How could you butcher this beautiful piece of beef like this?' he burst out.

'John,' his wife said quietly. 'Please.'

'No darling,' he snapped, 'I will not be quiet. We've been invited for a Sunday lunch. I expected a good, English Sunday lunch, just like the five or six we've provided out of the kindness of our hearts! Not some kind of show-offy French nonsense! There aren't even any Yorkshire puddings!'

'It's a traditional *French* Sunday lunch,' I replied, trying to keep my calm.

'It looks rubbish,' he said, sulkily. 'Is that British beef?'

'Yes, it's good Angus Scottish beef,' I replied, thinking this might placate him.

'How could you eat French fries next to this?' he cried out, obviously as anguished as if I had burned the beef to a crisp, or suggested Coca-Cola as an accompaniment.

'John!' his wife pleaded again. 'We've talked about this.'

'I won't stand for this,' he said, ignoring her.

'I made potatoes specifically for *you*, because *you* usually eat potatoes with your beef!' I burst out, angrily.

'They're not even mashed,' he pointed out. 'I can't remember the last Sunday I didn't have mashed potatoes. Or roast beef. Or Yorkshire puddings.'

'Are you kidding?' I stared at him. 'Do you really mean to imply that you eat exactly the same meal every weekend?'

'Don't be daft,' he said, 'we eat it every night.'

'What?'

'Well,' he conceded, 'sometimes we do just get takeaway.'

'Sometimes he likes beef korma on a Wednesday,' his wife piped up in a placating tone.

I was aghast.

'I hope this isn't how Hilary's culinary instincts turn out,' I said. 'Or I'll have to divorce her.'

There was a long silence. Hilary giggled nervously. Her sister looked crestfallen.

'But how are you both so skinny?' I wondered aloud. The sister cheered up a bit.

Hilary answered: 'It's crazy, isn't it? They only eat one meal a day.'

'One nice big meal,' John added proudly. 'Roast beef, Yorkshire puds, mashed potatoes and peas.'

'Goodness me. It's a wonder you're in any kind of healthy state,' I wondered aloud.

'Pah!' said John, going red in the face. 'Says the maker of this greasy-looking French soup!'

'It's *boeuf bourguignon*!' I replied, trying not to get angry.

'I refuse to eat this – whatever it is,' John declared with bombast.

'Look,' I said, 'I don't like to fight with someone who is practically family. But you're a guest in my home, and it is just a piece of beef, for crying out loud. You eat beef korma. That's far more foreign.'

'Yes, but I know exactly what's in my korma, thank you very much. India used to be British, you know. Just because you've been abroad and come back with ridiculous cooking ideas…'

'This is not ridiculous!' I practically roared. 'This is classic French cuisine! Parts of France used to be British! I don't even know why I'm debating this. Now sit down, please, and just eat the bloody meal.'

John stood up all of a sudden and picked up a handful of fries, brandishing them threateningly.

'I will not,' he shouted.

'Don't throw the fries,' his wife intervened.

'Please, can everybody just calm down?' Hilary implored.

John froze.

'Please,' I added.

John sighed, suddenly deflated, and dropped the fries onto his plate.

'Now say you're sorry, darling,' his wife muttered.

'I'm sorry,' he said less-than-repentantly. 'I just don't feel this has been a fair exchange.'

I disagreed wildly with this statement, but didn't want to cause a further fuss, or encourage more food-throwing.

'OK,' I said. 'Don't eat the *bourguignon*. But I don't think I can really invite you back. I don't know how to cook roast beef.' I bit my tongue to keep myself from mentioning his rudeness.

He looked at me with pity.

'Well,' he said with a sneer, 'next time we can just cook it for you. We can just host it at our place. Or bring it over. I don't care.'

'OK,' I said wearily. I was rapidly getting bored of this whole conversation. Frankly, I would have been happy never to see the pair of them again, but I agreed for Hilary's sake.

Later, I confided my frustrations in my wife.

'I even cooked their favourite meat! Think of all the things I could have made! I made the most reasonable, the most boring one possible! English people know *boeuf bourguignon*. I could have made a spicy red Thai curry with coconut milk! I could have made a Szechuan stir-fry with black bean sauce! I could have made the simplest of *steak haché* or *côte de boeuf*! Actually, maybe I should have done that. No! Better yet, I should have sent them to the pub for their silly English pub lunch.'

'It's not their fault they're narrow-minded,' Hilary soothed me. 'Not everybody has had such a cosmopolitan culinary upbringing. You have to accept their views.'

'Well, I have to, since you seem so keen to eat with them. But I don't like it one bit.' The next two weeks we ate at their house, in a rather subdued atmosphere. One day, however, Hilary announced that she had spoken to John, and he had agreed to eat a side of beef.

'What kind of an announcement is that?'

'Hush now,' my wife berated me. 'He's making an effort. Let's have them over this Friday evening.'

So I sighed, and picked up a prime side of beef from the local butcher, and left it with Hilary whilst I went to school in London. I came back that evening to an amusing sight: Hilary was standing the side of beef on its side in the pan, and shouting at it every time it inevitably fell down.

'What on earth are you doing?' I asked her.

'This stupid beef,' she exclaimed, poking it in annoyance, 'refuses to do what it's supposed to.'

'And what are you expecting this beef to do?'

'Well the recipe says to fry the fatty side first, and then turn it over. But that's obviously physically impossible.'

'Hilary, my dear, the fatty side is not the skinny side of the cut. Look here.'

I picked up the beef in its fallen position. 'This is a *côte de boeuf*. What the Americans call prime rib. It's meant to be cut into several steaks. See,' I said, displaying the white veins of fat, 'this is the fatty side.'

Hilary burst out laughing. 'Are you serious? Oh dear. I've just been playing with this damned thing for a good twenty minutes. No wonder!'

'Well it's a good thing our esteemed guests haven't arrived yet, isn't it. Lord knows what opinion they would have had to contribute!'

'Now, now,' Hilary chided me. 'This is my sister we're talking about.'

'Oh, you know damn well it's not your sister we're talking about.'

The pair in question actually showed up quite soon after that, proving their non-Frenchness even more thoroughly by arriving five minutes before the time we had established. No respectable European dinner guest would arrive anything less than twenty minutes after the hour, to make sure they do not surprise the cooks before they are ready. As it was, Hilary and I were still in the kitchen, turning over the beef at the halfway point of its cooking time. As soon as John came in from the front hall, he stomped in as if he intended to take over the kitchen.

'What are you doing to that beef?' he practically shouted. I saw his wife's shoulders slump. 'Don't stick the meat with the fork like that or you'll lose all the juices! And that's not the way to cook it! You have to put it in a three-hundred-degree oven and cut it in thin slices.'

I sighed. I decided this conversation had best be cut short as soon as possible. In my most gracious voice, I replied:

'Hello, John. Nice to see you. Why don't you go sit in the dining room. Hilary will get you a glass of wine.' I caught Hilary's eye. She smiled. I then placed my hands on John's shoulders and steered him carefully out of the kitchen. By the time we served the beef, everyone was in a much better mood, and even if he did poke at the thick steak on his plate and mutter under his breath, he did eat most of it without causing too obvious a fuss. Everyone was much relieved, and the dinner went smoothly.

Thirty years later, Hilary and I still occasionally have dinner with John and his wife, who are still happily married. You can bet that we have roast beef, Yorkshire puddings, mashed potatoes and peas.

THE SORORITY MUSICAL

When I was eighteen, a whirlwind period of my social life began when I was elected the social chairman of my fraternity. There were about forty members in the all-male society, and we used to regularly throw parties where hundreds of external graduates would show up as guests, many of them members of our neighbouring sororities. It was an exciting time, where we would dress in our polo shirts and meet smart, pretty girls in nice dresses every week. We would then spend the evening sipping drinks and nibbling from the buffet or walking in the gardens.

I came up with a few new concepts for parties. The first of these was the 'new faces' party, where members had to bring along someone we had never met before. If one was spoken for, one had to bring along a sister, or perhaps a close friend of the girlfriend or fiancée; with her approval, of course. These would be fairly small gatherings, usually fifteen to twenty of us fraternity boys with our guests, and they were wildly popular. A lot of the boys I knew liked to drink quite a lot, although I never personally drank or witnessed any of the purported excesses that took place in some fraternities: there were no boys running around with their ties around their heads or drinking competitions in my day! There were, however, a lot of pretty blondes and brunettes from good families looking for a nice time, and that we could provide.

The next concept I established was that of 'new stories' parties, where guests were bored or regaled with lengthy shaggy dog stories told by three fraternity brothers. For instance, one of my friends once told a seemingly never-ending story about the first time he went to Bermuda. Again, these were quite intimate events, with mostly close friends attending, and the speaker being quietly joshed about with.

Finally, in my senior year, I got involved in setting up plays and informal concerts. The latter tended to involve quite a lot of country music, this being Texas, but there was a great variety of performances by everyone from pretty young singer-songwriters to a group of moustachioed brothers singing close-harmony.

The plays were something else, though. Usually, these would be fairly classic plays put on by fraternity boys and sorority girls: *A*

Midsummer Night's Dream, perhaps, or, if they felt a bit more modern, something like *A Doll's House*. But in my time as social chairman, I was interested in doing something a little more radical. This was how I decided to write and put on a musical about a political scandal that had recently shaken British politics: the Profumo Affair. Most of our audience would have been fairly unaware of this shocking piece of British news, as few people I know outside my fraternity bothered to real the international papers: most Texan students I knew only kept up to date on the sports and social sections.

The widely-held opinion on the scandal amongst the few who had one in our entourage was that Christine Keeler should be reviled. I remember us having rather heated discussions on the subject, sitting in the front lounge of our fraternity:

'She's just a manipulative call-girl,' a rather annoying friend of mine claimed. 'I mean, just look at those eyebrows. She obviously knows exactly what she wants, and what she wants is an old man with money.'

'She's wreaked havoc among respectable politicians, tarnished their careers, and led to upheaval in – whatever you call your Parliamentary thingy.'

'Now look,' I would find myself interjecting. 'Just because she likes a man with a moustache doesn't mean she's a gold-digger or a prostitute.'

'But it's such a great story if she is! She obviously has no morals.'

'It's the sixties!' one of my close friends replied. 'She's just a free-willed young woman. It doesn't make her a bad person!'

'Oh, you're just soft for her. Brad too.'

'I'm sorry, I can't help but sympathise with her. I think she's been wronged by the media.'

The younger brother of a friend of mine, who had been lounging on the couch until now, interjected: 'I think you're all missing the point, here. I mean, it's just a darn good story. Like that bit where her drug-dealer boyfriend and her doctor pimp have a fight with knives and guns!

'I'm sure most of that has been vastly exaggerated,' I said carefully.

'Everyone likes a good scandal,' the friend on my side agreed.

'I'm going to write a musical about her,' I added at this point.

Our principal challenge, it turned out, was not that we were

writing something somewhat politically controversial. The problem
was finding a girl willing to play a woman thought by most to be a
debauched London good-time-girl. Bearing in mind that our talent
pool consisted mostly of twenty-year-old virgins from respectable
Texan families, this was to be difficult. Luckily, I had contacts,
including the social chairwoman of the neighbouring sorority, who,
by coincidence, happened to have a soft spot for me.

My casting technique consisted of wandering nonchalantly around
the sorority and casually striking up conversation with unsuspecting
young ladies. This had a very low success rate. The girls from
Kansas wouldn't do it. 'What would my family think?' they replied
with wide eyes. The ladies from Boston wouldn't think of it. 'I'm
Catholic,' they explained apologetically. The newest sorority
members wouldn't even consider it. 'I can't risk my reputation,'
they would tell me with fluttering lashes. Three-quarters of the girls
we asked didn't even know how to act. Seeing that I was beginning
to despair, Stephanie, the sorority chairwoman, finally took pity on
me. 'I'll do it,' she said. 'For you,' she added with a mock curtsy. I
had to say I was rather charmed. 'But please, no nudity.' She smiled
coyly.

'Honey,' I replied, shaking my head, 'this is Texas.'

So that was how Stephanie and I ended up sitting down elbow-to-
elbow and writing a musical about the Profumo Affair. We decided
to portray the lead character as 'Christine Feeler,' an aspiring socialite
unfairly maligned by a holier-than-thou British class society, and
Profumo himself as 'Mister Boom-Boom,' the sleazy war secretary.
The song-and-dance numbers included the ensemble piece 'You
Slept With a Russian Spy: So What?', followed by Feeler's cheery
burlesque number 'I've Seen Quite Enough of Eugene Ivanov,'
which involved a feather boa and many jokes about the 'not-so-
Cold-War.' The play then concluded with the mournful 'Everybody
Thinks I'm a Lady of Ill Repute' and the love duet: 'We'll Never
Forget The Cabinet,' which included the memorable line 'All
the things that were forbidden / That we did when we hid out at
Cliveden.' We then managed to find a line of chorus girls and cobble
together a band consisting of a couple of guitars, a bass, a horn, and
a tambourine.

Rehearsals were interesting, with a good first half hour of our initial meeting involving a fairly thorough explanation of British politics. The idea that this scandal had led to the rise of the Labour party, for instance, was almost entirely lost on most of the cast.

'What, was she pregnant?' one said, to everyone's great amusement. 'Are you saying this Keeler woman went into labour at that party?'

I sighed. 'The Labour *party*. The left-wing political party in the United Kingdom. Led by Harold Wilson.'

'The Labour party?' one guitarist said in disbelief. 'What, are you Europeans all Communists?'

The concept of 'lying to the House of Commons' also proved rather baffling. Despite these setbacks, rehearsals went well, and new friendships were forged. After just a month of intense preparation, we were ready to present 'Scandal! The Defamation of Christine Feeler' on our small college stage.

The piece was a complete success. The audience loved it, laughing and crying at all the appropriate moments. Stephanie was triumphant, and won over everyone's sympathy while the weak and corrupt Mister Boom-Boom was booed off stage. 'Christine Feeler' appeared to the gentle strumming of guitars and transformed before the audience's eyes from youthful socialite to martyr, though not without retaining a certain sultriness, particularly in the strapless black gown she wore for her sad solo. Stephanie's lovely singing voice made her the star of the show, although the moment which elicited the most gasps and boos was the appearance of her jealous lover Johnny brandishing a gun. Profumo's character was rather good too, played by one of our fraternity brothers: in his father's pinstriped suit, and with a tiny moustache, he made a convincing British minister. The undercurrent of political tension may have been lost somewhat, but any audience could follow the general drama. They were on the edge of their seats all the way through, and gave us a standing ovation at the end.

Stephanie and I were the toast of both our fraternity and sorority at the dinner and after-party, and it surprised no-one when soon after that our musical collaboration blossomed into romance. Now that I look back I'm amazed that we managed to pull the whole project off without offending anyone, but at the time it was just a lot of fun.

HORSES AND BARBECUES

One of my first trips out of college in Texas was a long weekend I went on with my girlfriend, Monique, who came from a farm in the West of the state. I was just seventeen, and very much bowled over by her gutsy charm. She was a tough, tall, outdoorsy gal with a sweet Southern drawl, who loved nothing more than horse-riding. She decided she wanted to do this with me, and invited me out to stay with her parents.

It was late summer, just turning into a warm and sunny fall as school slowly started up. We drove to the ranch and settled in happily. We spent the first day riding horses up and down her family's fields, surrounded by rolling hills of wheat and corn. Monique's enthusiasm was contagious, although my balance and skill left something to be desired. The weather was stunning, with skylarks flying overhead, and we rode bareback, which I had never done, and found liberating. It was a joy just to get out of the cramped campus. The Texas sky seemed so huge when glimpsed in its entirety rather than between tall concrete buildings. Though I had ridden horses before, I had never gone up to anything approaching a trot, let alone a gallop. I was a little intimidated, but Monique was very encouraging, even if she liked to poke fun at me a little, and her father also gave me some pointers on proper technique. By the end of the day, I was riding quite successfully. I went to bed proud, if a little sore. As I was climbing into bed, wincing a little as I pulled the cool sheets up over my sunburned legs, I heard footsteps in the hallway. Monique came in from her bedroom and sat by my side in her nightie.

'Wasn't it fun?' she whispered gleefully. I nodded in agreement, of course, although my exhaustion must have showed in my face. 'Let's do it again tomorrow!' she said. I tried not to sigh.

'Great!' I said. 'Let's go riding together all day! We could go and talk to Mr Marshall, our next door neighbour. He has the biggest farm in the whole of Texas, it's a good two million acres across!' My eyes widened. At the time, I was sure she was exaggerating, but by the end of the next day, I would not be so sure.

'Are you sure we should ride all day again?' I asked cautiously. 'I caught a little sun today, and I'm not sure how my inner thighs feel about all this chafing.'

Apparently without listening, Monique continued. 'Let's go see Mr Marshall tomorrow. He knows how to barbecue.' Then she paused, looking me over. 'Perhaps you're right, though. Maybe we shouldn't ride all afternoon. We should ride in the morning! I'll wake you up at five thirty.'

I groaned.

The next morning dawned cool and sunny, although the coolness wouldn't last. After a breakfast of waffles with fresh butter and maple syrup, we walked over to Mr Marshall's slightly groggily, leading the horses ahead of us. 'Are you sure he won't mind us coming over this early in the day?' I asked. 'It's not even seven o'clock!'

'Oh no,' she said cheerily. 'I know him well. He's a farmer; he'll be up and around, I'm positive of it.'

Sure enough, when we arrived on the edge of his land, we could see an impressive, toned figure in the fields, chopping wood with an axe. 'Howdy!' he called out when he spotted us. 'And what can I do for you two youngsters this fine morning?'

'Hi, Mr Marshall!' Monique called back. 'We were just wondering if we could borrow your saddles for a few hours!'

He wiped the back of his arm across his tanned and sweaty brow. 'I saw you two riding bareback yesterday. It's a fun way to travel, but I wouldn't want to do it too long myself.' He stroked the muzzle of Monique's horse tenderly. 'No matter how much you love the beast, it's not the most comfortable way to ride! Why don't you go on out back with the horses, I'll bring you the saddles from the barn.' He strode off, his brown leather trousers and cowboy boots creaking in the dust.

The barn was huge and luminous, with dust motes floating all golden in the sunlight, and the smell of hay all around us. 'I used to play here when I was a kid,' Monique told me. 'I've known some of Mr Marshall's horses since they were tiny foals.'

Mr Marshall appeared behind us.

'And she's been riding them pretty much since then, too! I taught her to climb up on the ponies when she was just about the size of a gummy bear. She got the hang of it straight away.'

Monique blushed. 'Well, if you mean hanging on for dear life, then yes!'

'Don't be ridiculous,' he chided her. 'You're a fine rider, and you know it. I'd come with you if I didn't have work to do,' he said in his booming voice. 'But your young man here looks like he'll be good company. You can ride all day in a straight line out there,' he said happily. 'It goes on for acres and acres, not a bend or a turn in sight. It's great for the horses,' he added, patting mine on the flank so that it snorted in what sounded like happy surprise.

'I don't think we'll be riding quite all day,' Monique replied. 'My dear boy here caught a little sun yesterday, and I guess we don't want to spend the whole of our trip on horseback!'

This was an understatement. Really, all I wanted was to be by Monique's side. I couldn't care less about being on top of a horse! I laughed heartily, and said nothing.

Mr Marshall raised an eyebrow then grinned as he dropped the heavy leather saddle onto my horse. 'Well, it doesn't always have to be an all-day pilgrimage. You just make sure you're enjoying yourselves. Don't overdo it, you're on vacation!' he added gently. 'Tell you what: why don't you guys come back here in time for a late lunch? You can make it to the end of the fields and back in a few hours.' He narrowed his eyes in concentration as he hooked the straps in and tightened them. 'I'll throw some steaks on the barbecue for you and make up some coleslaw; maybe a pitcher of fresh lemonade. Does that sound good to you?'

'It sure does,' I said, hastily and gratefully, before Monique could decide that we were better off touring every single one of the two million acres before we left. I needn't have worried. Monique winked at me and smiled at Mr Marshall. 'Yeah, that sounds great!' she agreed.

We rode out into the sun. The fields were not just tidy, cultivated spaces. As soon as Mr Marshall's farm was out of sight, we found ourselves in a vast, hot wilderness. Wild grasses grazed my boots, while the horses had to tiptoe through thorny shrubs. Crickets chirped all around us, and birds of prey circled overhead. Every so often, one of our horses would rear back upon coming across a hare or wild dog, or on hearing a coyote howl in the distance. The way we were going, I would not have been in the least surprised if we had scared out a pack of hungry wolves! In places, the grass was a good metre high.

After a time, luckily, we came upon civilisation, in the form of two tractors lazily crossing the field. 'Nobody's driving them!' I exclaimed in wonder, looking over at Monique. 'What's going on?'

'They're harvesters,' she explained. 'They're gathering up the grain. The harvest takes most of the months of August and September, you see, so during this time, Mr Marshall sets up five tractors. Remember how he said you could ride straight across the fields until you arrived at the edge? Well, it takes the tractors a full two days to do that.'

'You mean the machines really just run on their own?'

She nodded happily.

'But what happens when they reach the edge of the field?'

'Oh, well, see how slowly they're going? He knows pretty much exactly how long it will take them to get to the end. Around the time he figures they'll get to the edge of his land, he goes down there with one of his workers, jumps in and turns them around. They're going so slowly that it's hardly a problem at all.'

We dug our heels into the horses' flanks and approached the clanking machines. Sure enough, they were just crawling along unsupervised. We quickly outstripped them, and found ourselves back out in the wild grasses. Monique and I rode on for a few hours before heading back towards the farm. We crossed the harvesters again on our way back, still trundling along like huge, well-behaved lawnmowers. By this time, I was quite hungry and tired out, as we had done some galloping. I could smell the barbecue smoke, and it made my mouth water. We arrived in Mr Marshall's front yard and carefully dismounted.

Mr Marshall had put on a huge Stetson hat, and he greeted us with two big glasses of iced sweet tea, with fresh pieces of lemon and mint leaves. 'You have a good time?' he asked kindly, looking me up and down. 'Not too worn out?'

I patted my horse on the nose affectionately. 'Well, my legs ache, and I feel a little weak, but I'm a happy man.' I caught Monique smiling shyly at me. 'Riding might be a pretty exhausting sport, but there is just nothing like it to see the countryside. I feel so free!'

'I bet you're hungry – and thirsty, too!'

Nodding in agreement, I gulped the cold, delicious drink gratefully. We watched as he turned steaks the size of dinner plates on the barbecue, which was approximately twice the size of my big office desk! Seeing the direction of my gaze, Mr Marshall laughed aloud. 'You need a serious barbecue if you run a farm, son. Workers like mine need sustenance in the middle of a long day's work. If they're lucky, my wife will make up some cornbread and coleslaw. Of course, sometimes she helps me set up for lost riders, too…' He winked.

When the steaks were cooked, we sat down at a table outdoors. Mr Marshall put his feet up on the wooden table as he gulped down his food. Monique and I ate ravenously, if slightly more slowly, savouring every bite: the creamy, crunchy coleslaw complementing the thick, juicy steaks perfectly. The whole meal was a delight.

'We saw your harvesters,' I told him. 'It's so strange, the way they run automatically! I've never seen anything quite like it.'

'Oh, I actually have two manned ones,' he replied. 'But the rest of them are automatic. You just set them up and set them off! They're only going about two or three miles an hour. It takes them two days to cross from one side to the next when they're doing the harvest. You saw for yourselves that it doesn't normally take that long to get to the end of the fields. Still, it's a good system and it works for me.' He lit a cigar with a smile. The smoke mingled pleasantly with the smell of grilling meat. 'Anyway, how did you kids take to the fields? You think you'll stay and be farmers with me?' He grinned.

'It's tempting, although I'm not sure my legs could take it,' I quipped. 'Is there a lot of horse riding involved?'

Monique put her hand on my shoulder. 'I think I may have worn this one out. Or maybe those coyotes scared him. Don't worry, I'll get him back out here. You could get him stacking logs, picking tomatoes, hoeing the fields…'

Mr Marshall winked at her and laughed. 'You know I'm just kidding,' he said to me. 'I think you young girls and boys are lucky to be out there getting educated. I mean, inheriting this farm was the best thing that happened to me, and I'm happy with the life I've had, but you two have better options. A wider array of choices. You seem like the type of guy who wants to see the world. You'd make a great farmer, I'm sure, but I'm glad you're taking school seriously. I can see you both going far, doing good things. Of course, if you want to come back here and harvest corn with me when you're done, you're more than welcome here!'

I smiled. 'There's a part of me that's tempted. I don't want summer to be over, it's so good being outdoors! It's so strange to think that we'll be back in school tomorrow,' I sighed.

'Do you know,' he added with a smile, 'my youngest son is going away to college next fall. Maybe you'll meet him!'

In a pleasant twist of fate, I did in fact end up meeting Mr Marshall's son. For a time, young Gene Marshall and I were in the same fraternity. He would tell me the news from the West Texas farm even years after Monique and I had parted and gone our separate ways. Even when my legs had long forgotten the strain of riding bareback for hours, I would always remember those fun, wild days, roaming the great American plains with all the confidence of our seventeen years, and I would never forget Monique in the fields.

My family had a beautiful house in Istanbul, near the Bosphorus Delta. One of our neighbours was a lady by the name of Fatima. In my travels in the late sixties, I visited my Turkish relatives there quite often, and got to know Fatima rather well. At the time, she was in her late fifties, and a regular fixture of our household. She was particularly beloved by all for her wonderful baking skills. Every time I saw her, she would offer me some marvellous, freshly-baked treat.

'Would you like to try some of my raisin bread?'

I was not accustomed to accepting the food of strangers, particularly since I knew nothing of her living conditions.

'No thank you,' I said gently the first time, 'I've just had lunch.'

'Oh but you must,' she insisted, as she always did. 'The raisins in Turkey are fantastic, almost as if they have been baked by the sun. They are so long and blonde, with almost no pips; they are perfect for cakes and breads…'

'No, thank you, I don't want raisin bread.'

'Ah, so you don't like raisin bread! Let me get you something else! Let me make something next time you come. What is your favourite dish? I have a rich pistachio cake, or I can make walnut bread, or perhaps you might enjoy little cookies made of dates and rye, they're delicious with coffee…'

It was hard to resist. I accepted a slice of the pistachio cake. It was deliciously sweet and moist, topped with rosewater syrup. I closed my eyes in delight.

'Fatima,' I remarked through a mouthful of crumbs, 'you're a fantastic baker. Your husband must be extremely happy.'

She blushed. 'Oh, Mr Jamieson, don't talk to me about my husband! I'm still a virgin. I am so looking forward to getting married,' she added with a smile that was remarkably girlish for a woman almost old enough to be my grandmother. 'As soon as my younger brother comes back from the States.'

'Do you mean you're engaged?'

'Oh no,' she said, 'I'll wait for my brother's return before I find my husband.'

'What is your brother doing abroad?'

'He's in California. He went there to study but ended up working. He's an engineer. He writes every week to tell us he's coming back. I always have these cakes and breads ready for his return, I can make ten different kinds. I bake them in our clay oven over a wood fire.'

'Wait; when did your brother leave, then?'

'Oh, thirty years ago.'

I processed this as I munched another bite of pistachio cake. 'So you were a young woman when you made this promise?'

'Yes I was,' she said. 'Although I am still young at heart now. I fully intend to keep my word.'

'But what if your brother never comes back?'

'Oh, he'll come back. We made a promise,' she said with such sweet confidence that it was impossible to argue with her.

I saw Fatima nearly every time I visited my family for the next forty years. She was always there in the living room, sharing out her cakes between my aunts and uncles and their visitors. Throughout the years, she was always there to greet me with a smile and some new baked good. 'I've made this new kind of olive bread,' she might tell me one time. Another year, it would be early summer and she would wax lyrical about figs: 'Try my beautiful fig cake. The figs here are like honey; they draw their sweetness from the burning sun and the richness of the earth.' Sometimes we would sit in the sun, sipping cold drinks. Other times, we would sit in the courtyard by the fountain, watching the crescent moon rise.

Each time we had the same conversation about how she was waiting for her brother to come home so she could get married. Her answers to my questions were always the same. Once, when Fatima was in her late sixties, I visited her house. It was a fabulous antique little place built out of black stone, with just three bedrooms. Outside was a small courtyard with cobblestones that probably dated back to Assyrian Babylon. The interior of the house was very clean and tidy. She showed me round the kitchen, which was impeccable, leaning every once in a while on a cane.

'This looks like a wonderfully welcoming place for your husband,' I joked.

She smiled, and replied seriously: 'It's kind of you to say so. I cannot wait for him to see our home.' I never knew how to respond, so I often stayed silent. I did not want to upset her. No matter what we spoke of, the conversations always ended with an offer of bread or cake.

In 2010, I received a letter from my relatives that told the rest of Fatima's story.

Dear Bradley, the letter read, *we write with news of your favourite visitor, Fatima. You will remember how she was always waiting for her brother. A year ago, she told us she would come to the courtyard of our house and dance in the nude for his return. She was 97 years old. She had just become engaged to a 95-year-old man and believed she would be married, at last. We had been joking with her on the matter for months – about her weight, and her virginity, and what a woman her age could wear to get married. She was so full of joy and anticipation. We were all optimistic about the return of her brother. We truly thought he would come. 'It's never too late,' she would remind us. 'My mother lived until 112. Even if I get married at 99, I'll have thirteen full years of happiness ahead. But I will wait for my brother, like I promised him. If he wants me to. And I will dance for his return in the nude in the town square.' She wished that her brother would choose the wedding date for her.*

I'm so sorry to have to tell you, Bradley, that Fatima died yesterday, at the age of 99. Her brother never came home, and she was never married. I cannot really forgive him. I plan to write him a letter to make him realise the extent of the heartbreak he occasioned by his reckless behaviour. I cannot help but think of him as a capitalist bastard, not even willing to come back for a short visit or care that his sister waited her entire life for his return. I believe that California stole his soul, and that he in turn stole his sister's life.

Still, in a time like this we must not only think of the loss and sadness. I feel lucky that we were able to know Fatima, and eat her delicious breads and cakes. She was a wonderful woman and she will be sorely missed, not least by her 95-year-old fiancé. I wish we had told her to get married sooner, but you cannot change someone's beliefs. Up until the moment of her death, Fatima still believed her brother would come back, and there was nothing that could have changed her mind.

THE GREEK NEIGHBOUR
IN CORFU

When I was twenty-two or so, we rented a villa on the Greek island of Corfu. I loved the peace of walking along the beaches, sitting in lovely cafés, looking out over the deep blue sea.

When on holiday in a hot country, one usually feels the need to sleep in in the morning. But on this particular holiday, I was finding this difficult, for every morning around five o'clock, I would be disturbed by a repetitive knocking noise, like a mason building with granite. A strange vision grew in my sleepless mind of an old Roman stonecutter chipping into hunks of marble, creating plaques and statues.

After a few days, romantic vision or not, I had had quite enough of the disturbance. After all, I was on holiday, and this was ruining my peace. I got out of bed, threw on some clothes and stomped over to the house next door. I knocked and waited. A stern-looking Greek man in his mid-forties opened the door, glowering at me.

'What do you want?' he asked rudely, in strongly accented English.

'Look,' I said, not feeling entirely patient myself, 'it's six in the morning and this awful noise has been going for an hour already. If you're constructing something, could you please wait until some decent hour like seven thirty to start the work? I'm quite sure it must be illegal to make this kind of racket this early in the day.'

The Greek man's serious, angry-looking face collapsed all at once in a fit of laughter.

'Sir,' he said with a broad smile, 'please come in. Let me show you something. '

In the background, I could still hear the pounding noises, now accompanied by strange grunts.

I hung back for a second before following him back behind his villa to a kitchen with a stone floor, which seemed to be full of rather primitive-looking equipment. Sitting in front of what appeared to be a large hunk of granite, I found an ancient-looking woman wearing a long, loose skirt in thick jute material. There was no stonemasonry visible, and no recognisable source to the noise. I must say I was a little confused.

'This is my wife,' he gestured proudly. She was extremely muscular and had a deeply wrinkled face, sunburnt to a rich leathery colour. She looked about seventy, although I found out in later conversations with her husband that she was only forty-five! I suppose a lifetime of working hard in the sun and going to the beach had aged her prematurely. I don't know if the couple had any children.

Somewhat embarrassed, I asked the man:

'Sorry, but why have you brought me here?'

He shrugged his shoulders a little and turned to the woman, who had been sitting there in silence, saying something to her in Greek which I assumed must mean 'continue.' He then looked back at me and added: 'You'll see why in just a moment.'

The woman then picked up this huge stone hammer, which seemed to be about forty centimetres long and fifteen centimetres thick as well, wielding it in both her hands. It looked like it must have weighed a good twelve kilos, and she picked it up as easily as if it had been a toothpick. I understood a little better where the muscles came from, but had not quite understood the source of the noise. I then looked a little more closely at the stone hammer in her hand, and suddenly understood it to be a sort of giant pestle. With a noise like rocks falling down a valley, she brought the pestle down into a vast cube, at least half a metre tall, with a hole about twenty centimetres deep, rather like a giant black washbasin. It was filled with great lumps of mince, which by this time she was beating with the pestle like giant volleyballs of meat. Every time she brought down the great hammer with a great smashing sound of stone on stone, she also made a grunting noise rather like a tennis player. The whole thing was quite an astounding sight.

'We sell them to our restaurant in town,' the man explained. 'Every morning we put in fresh beef steaks, and my wife beats them into hamburger, you see? They get made into kebabs and kefta and cooked over the barbecue. But first my wife has to make them soft.'

'It seems like such an antiquated way of doing it,' I marvelled, forgetting my tiredness for a moment.

'Oh, it certainly is,' he answered proudly. 'This is how it was done in Greece and Rome two thousand years ago. You see this piece of granite, right here?' He pointed at the pestle. 'That dates back to 100 B.C.'

'Surely you don't mean 100 years before Christ? Wouldn't it

belong in a museum?'

'I certainly do!' He beamed. 'We are making our meat the same way our ancestors have, for hundreds and hundreds of years. This is far too useful for any museum! You can soften meat for stews and roasts that way too.'

I was amazed. At the time, I'm not quite sure I believed him.

'Look,' I said, 'this culinary history is all fascinating. But I'm only in Corfu for a week. Can't you just take a break? Or start a little later? I'm not getting any sleep.'

He shook his head.

'Unfortunately we have to deliver this meat to my restaurant, and to other restaurants in town, by eight or nine in the morning so they can prepare it for lunch. You see, most restaurants feed their own employees this meat around eleven thirty. So we have to crush at least twenty kilos of meat before you're even contemplating breakfast.'

'What kind of solution can you offer me?' I asked.

The man shrugged regretfully. 'Move to a hotel?' he suggested. Seeing my face, he relented a little. 'But why don't you come down to my restaurant someday. I'll offer you a kebab, on the house. You'll see that all this hard work is worth it.'

So I did. I can't say I slept particularly well on that trip, but I did have one truly excellent kebab: the pitta crisp, the spicy sauce flavourful and the meat exceptionally tender.

There is an epilogue to this story: about a year later, I was travelling in Southern Italy when I saw something which reminded me of this man, and seemed to confirm his story about the age of his pestle and mortar. I was travelling in Pompeii, where I went on a guided tour of the sites that had been destroyed by the volcano. And there I saw one: a giant stone mortar, just like the one in Corfu. I asked the guide:

'Is that what people used to tenderise and grind meat? I've seen modern ones that look just the same.'

'Yes,' he said, 'you're absolutely right. Actually, this one was designed to mill wheat and barley. But most poor families could only afford one instrument for both, grains and meat.'

'That doesn't sound like it would live up to modern health and safety standards,' I said. The guide laughed. 'But on a more serious note: are you telling me that they were eating kebabs in Pompeii?'

'Oh, absolutely. There is a sort of kebab featured in the *Iliad*, and in the works of Aristotle. The ancient diets of the Greeks and Romans were quite similar. The kebab is quite an ancient institution itself!'

Years later, I thought back to this trip when contemplating ancient Greek and Roman recipes. After all, I went home from that trip with the knowledge that I once ate a kebab ground with a pestle and mortar that were over two thousand years old. Even if I did lose a few nights' sleep for it.

THE OLD LADY AND THE
BAG COMPETITION

Being quite a sociable man, I have had very few neighbours with whom I have almost no communication, but two of them happened to live on Eaton Square, in Belgravia. One was an eighty-year old lady. She had inherited her apartment from her husband, a very rich duke who died in the Second World War.

I was thirty-five at the time, and one might perhaps have held the age gap accountable for the fact that the lady and I hardly ever exchanged a word, were it not that I was on very good terms with several of the other old ladies on the square. Whatever the reason might have been, she and I barely spoke for the first few years I lived there.

We had only one thing in common: occasionally, we would both appear on the landing holding black plastic bags. Our eyes might meet for a moment, then we would look guiltily away, dropping the offending bundles onto the landing and vanishing back whence we came, like woodlice scampering back under logs. We never spoke a word. This was our daily rubbish removal ritual. In that particular apartment building, the doorman, who was appointed for life, and took his employment very seriously, would pick the rubbish up four times a week in front of every apartment on every floor. Thus there was no need for the tenants to carry heavy bags down the stairs or wheel unsightly bins to the corner of the road. One simply left one's rubbish in a tidy bag on the landing, and it vanished very quickly thereafter.

Although no words were spoken, the lady's body language was communicative enough. 'What right do you have to be here?' her beady eyes seemed to sneer as they bored into me. 'I've worked all my life. I married a wealthy duke who served as a colonel in the army. How old are you, thirty?' her raised eyebrow seemed to add, and a quick sniff implied: 'How dare you be on my landing?'

If I'm honest, her silences were far preferable to what she actually said the first time she ever spoke to me, which was:

'When did you move in, and when are you moving out?'

'Well,' I responded, as gaily as I could, 'I don't know when I moved in, and I don't know when I'm leaving!'

She narrowed her beady eyes, and dropped her rubbish bag with what seemed like unnecessary vehemence. I smiled at her. 'I really enjoy sharing this little rubbish promenade with you,' I said sweetly.

She scurried back to her doorway, and delivered her next question from the relative safety of the shadows there: 'Do you eat bananas?'

'I'm sorry?'

She glared. 'I said, do you eat bananas?'

'Well, yes. On occasions.' I paused.

'Well, just make sure that you have no bananas in your rubbish because I'm allergic.'

'I'll bear that in mind,' I replied politely.

'And no beef.'

'OK.'

'Or pears. Or garlic. Or peanuts. Or almonds. Do you ever eat almond cake? Almond cake makes me break out in hives,' she barked.

'No almond cake,' I responded with a mock salute.

'Bread makes my throat swell up,' she retorted without smiling.

From then on, we did have a topic of conversation: her allergies. Most of our encounters on the landing were still silent, but they would occasionally be peppered with requests for an inventory of the contents of my rubbish bag.

The strangest thing was that I always seemed to run into her, at least twice a day. One would think that if she had taken such a dislike to me, she would have avoided me. But in fact, I began to suspect the opposite. If I opened the door, hers would creak open immediately afterwards, and our two black bags would appear simultaneously. It was as if she really wanted to compare our bags; as if some sort of strange competition were taking place that she always considered to have won when I admitted there might be any sort of allergen in my rubbish.

It never seemed the right time to point out that she wouldn't be anywhere near the contents of the tightly closed rubbish bag for more than the ten seconds it took to set her own bag next to mine, unless I were to launch it at her in a fit of pique at the incessant and unnecessary questioning.

I once tried to change the dynamic of our relationship by engaging her in conversation about the flowers in the communal garden downstairs.

'Have you seen the lovely peonies this summer?' I asked.

'I don't care about flowers. I care about dogs,' she responded. 'I live with my poodle.'

And that was the end of that conversation.

I only recall one other topic we ever discussed, and that was my jogging.

'I saw you from the window this morning,' she snapped once, as we set our black bags down side by side.

'When I was jogging?' I replied amiably.

'Yes,' she admitted crisply. 'Running. Running up and down Eaton Square, all sweaty. And wearing those baggy, grey trousers! It's improper.'

'You mean my jogging bottoms?'

'If that's what you like to call them. I mean those American horrors that make you look like some sort of homeless person. Someone's bound to throw you a coin one of these days. Or assume you're being chased by the police.'

I laughed. 'I assume you'd prefer it if I ran in a blazer, with a bow tie and gold cufflinks and white shoes?'

She sighed huffily. 'Well at least it would look more respectable.'

'Jogging is an extremely healthy practice, you know. It's an American custom. Great for the heart. My wife is an American triathlete. She'll divorce me if I don't jog.'

'Ha!' the old lady snorted. 'I should have known the Americans were behind it. Well you just be careful, young sir. I daresay you'll be kicked out of the building for improper public behaviour first. Or for your terrible dress code.'

'Well, I would suggest you bring that up with my wife,' I replied politely, 'as she's at the door now.'

The lady peered short-sightedly along the length of the landing, to where Dee had indeed appeared.

'Hello,' my wife said cheerily, giving the old lady a perky American wave. 'Are we arguing about jogging?'

All at once, the little old lady's perpetually grumpy face transformed.

'Hello, madam,' she cooed, in a completely opposite tone of voice to the one she had been using with me.

'Are you trying to talk my husband out of keeping fit?' Dee joked.

'Oh, no!' the old lady said cheerily, waving her hands as if this were some sort of ridiculous accusation. 'Absolutely not! I'm sure it's wonderful.' She looked about ten years younger when she smiled. 'Not that I could imagine such a thing, at my age.'

I was flabbergasted. 'I'm quite sure about ten minutes ago you had never heard of it,' I muttered. The old lady ignored me completely. So did my wife, tactfully.

'So are you from America, then?' the lady continued, walking slowly down the hallway towards Dee. I couldn't believe it. I must have spoken with her fifty times by that point, and I had never seen her even vaguely friendly. At some point, I re-entered our apartment, edging carefully past what was now quite an animated discussion about small dogs.

From then on, our neighbour began a quest to befriend my wife, which amused and annoyed me in equal measure. It provided an interesting counterpoint to our bin-bag discussions which, I'm dismayed to report, became, if anything, more abrupt. It was as if I was judged solely responsible for the poisonous rubbish; appreciated only as an adversary in whatever imaginary bag-competition the old lady imagined was taking place.

More than once, after she was introduced to Dee, she came to knock on our door to say something along the lines of: 'It's been three hours and no-one has taken these bags down. Shall we write a letter and protest?'

Should I have the misfortune of opening the door at that moment, the old lady would only curtly acknowledge my presence, whilst peering over my shoulder for a glance of my wife. 'Oh, it's you,' she used to say, as if I were recognised solely as the man who was not only keeping her away from her new best friend and hindering her important petition business, but who also regularly attempted to assassinate her through the medium of almond cake or banana peel. If Dee did not materialise, the old lady would simply retreat back to her flat, glancing back at me with a dirty look, most likely muttering something about bananas.

JOHN EARLY, THE ARCHITECT

When I transferred to Kent, my wife and I lived in a beautiful old manor house, built in the 1400s and restored in the Elizabethan era. We had a neighbour just down the road who was an architect. His name was John; he was in his late twenties and lived alone. He was half-Irish, and very friendly.

In fact, he was very, *very* friendly. I don't think I've ever had my friendship courted so aggressively. For a time I couldn't decide if it was our antique house that attracted his architect's eye, or my beautiful Irish wife. In any case, I couldn't say I was very interested. He reminded me at times of those little Irish setter puppies who leap on your leg, wagging their tails wildly, leaving paw-prints on your best suits. He would hover casually around the outside of my house around the time of day I got home from work, just so he could say: 'Hi Bradley! How's it going?' Of course I was always perfectly polite to him, but I didn't really have the time or inclination to strike up more of a friendship with him. John, however, had other ideas.

One evening he knocked on the door with a bottle of wine.

'Bradley,' he said jovially, 'fancy a glass with me? I thought there was something a bit American in your accent, so I thought you might like some Californian vino!' He tossed his red hair out of his eyes enthusiastically.

'I'm afraid I don't drink,' I said, as kindly as I could. 'My wife and I were actually just settling in for the night. Maybe another time?' I added this last as a bit of British politeness, and regretted it instantly.

'Your wife, eh?' he said with a grin. I could almost imagine his Irish setter tongue hanging out. 'Is that the red-haired lass I've seen in the garden? She's a gorgeous one,' he added with a raise of the eyebrows. 'Looks just like Grace Kelly.'

'I am well aware of my wife's charms,' I said rather icily. 'Now good evening to you.' I imagined him whimpering, and trotting home with his tail between his legs, and the idea gave me some satisfaction. I had to say I did not like the idea of this rapscallion hanging around to court my wife one bit.

The next time he appeared outside my door was on a Saturday afternoon. This time he was clutching a case of beer.

'Bradley!' he said with a wide grin. 'Fancy a beer?'

'John,' I replied carefully, 'you know I don't drink.'

'What,' he said disbelievingly, 'not even beer?'

'Not even beer,' I answered firmly.

'How about that wife of yours? There's plenty to share!'

'My wife is not interested in drinking with you.'

He sighed, and looked up at me with his big puppy eyes. 'Now look,' he said earnestly, 'I'll be frank with you. I'd like to be friends with you, Bradley.'

'John, I don't mean to reject your friendship,' I said, as gently as I could. 'It's just that I'm very busy with my work at the bank.'

'But we could go to the bars, the pubs. It's not far! We could even just take a walk together. You know we're the same age.'

He put his hand on my shoulder, the equivalent gesture to a dog's paw being placed imploringly on the leg. I decided this was not the time to remind him that I was teetotal.

'You don't know how long my commute takes. I lose more than an hour every morning and evening already not being with my family. There is absolutely nothing that we can do together.'

'Just one drink!' he implored, his eyes wide.

'It's four o'clock!' I said disbelievingly. 'And I *don't drink.*'

'Oh yeah.' He paused. 'Look,' he said almost desperately, 'I know what we have in common. I've heard you build your own furniture.'

'Well, I used to,' I said, a little exasperated. 'I have no time to do that these days. My wife and I just stuck to antiques when we were decorating, to match the house.'

His face lit up. 'Aha,' he said, 'Wait until you hear this. I have an idea. I can build you furniture. Any furniture you want. From Elizabethan or Gothic times; whatever you like.'

'Now you're talking!' I said, intrigued almost against my will.

'Of course,' he said. 'Anything you want. I'm an architect.'

'Well,' I said, suddenly seeing the use this enthusiastic young man might be, but wanting to test him, the way you might wave a stick at a dog, or throw it in the sea to confuse it. 'Here is a puzzle for you. I want a three-ton bed with a wooden frame to be built on the second floor of this house. And I want cupboards underneath so I can store all my sports clothes and underwear in there along with some documents. I want it in the style of Elizabeth I from around 1620, and I want three kinds of lighting integrated.'

John didn't even pause. 'That's easy,' he said. 'No problem at all.'

This was not the response I had expected. 'Wait, how can you do that without having studied it? I just asked you for a three-ton bed. You can't just shrug like that. First of all, why didn't you ask me where the weight comes from, since I only mentioned it would be made of wood?'

'Oh, I can guess,' he replied breezily. 'Instead of a mattress, you obviously want a king-size waterbed. I've seen this very thing in *House and Gardens* magazine. I read it every week.'

I was amazed. 'My god, you really are well-informed! But how did you guess about the waterbed?'

'There is no bed in the world that weighs three tons unless it is made out of gold, or filled with water,' he replied solemnly.

'You must be right,' I said pensively. 'I had a waterbed in Paris, and I intend to transfer it to Kent. The weight of water plus the weight of oak makes up the three tons. I want everything in oak to match this house. I want it aged and stained and sculpted as if it was from 1600.'

'You got it.' He took the beer under one arm and lifted his flatcap as if in farewell.

I was confused, now, as if a dog had brought back a different stick to the one I had thrown, or perhaps a parasol, or a sausage. 'But how will you build the cupboards? You didn't even ask me.'

'Oh, that's easy. I assumed you meant under the bed. So that's, say, 240 cm in length and 220 cm in width. I'll build the cupboards so you can just slide them out if you need them.' He grinned as he thought over the dimensions. 'They'll be massive! You'll be able to put a body inside them!'

'Now let's not get carried away. I'm not sure I like the idea of morgue drawers under my bed…'

'Well, if you really want to feel like Henry VIII…'

'That's quite enough of that, John,' I said. 'First you imply you want to court my wife, and now you think I should kill her!'

He laughed. 'I'm only joking,' he said, 'I'll think of something.'

And he did. He went home, worked away solidly for a couple of months, and presented me with the bed of my dreams. Furthermore, he refused to accept any proper payment for the work, claiming that he only wanted the price of the wood reimbursed. 'It's just a friendly neighbour's gesture,' he said. 'It's what friends do.'

I suppose in this way I accomplished the role of friend that he needed. He went on to build more furniture for me over the next few years, including a gorgeous set of oak kitchen stools that looked as if they could easily be true antiques. I had to admit I had underestimated him when I first met him: he made a few wonderful contributions to our family life. The bed has lasted thirty years so far, and doesn't seem to be going anywhere anytime soon. It's a gorgeous dark oak bed with an Elizabethan awning. It never squeaked or cracked or caused any problem. The sides are beautifully carved, and the drawers underneath are generous, although certainly too small for a body! Every time I go to bed, I feel a little like Henry VIII, and it certainly makes me remember John fondly as an excellent neighbour.

When one lives in a busy neighbourhood, one gets used to seeing things on one's roof: pigeons, lost footballs, the occasional dog toy. What one is less used to is the sudden appearance of children there.

When I lived in Dallas, I lived in a neighbourhood like many others that was characterised by hundreds of almost-identical houses with slanted slate roofs lined up next to one another. Occasionally a larger villa might stand out with a straight roof, but most of the other houses were nestled alongside one another in a row, just as they might be in a suburban sitcom.

One day, sitting in my garden with a newspaper and a cup of coffee, I looked up to see some sort of creature scrambling across the rooftops. Before I could gather my wits to call the pest control services, I blinked and realised that it was in fact a ten-year-old boy. I recognised the boy, who was blonde, thin, and incredibly tall, like a stick insect or perhaps a kind of monkey.

'Nezar,' I shouted up, 'is that you?'

'Yes, sir,' the creature shouted back, before scrambling up to the top of the roof.

'Come down from there at once! You're going to fall!'

In response, Nezar threw himself from my roof to the neighbours', causing my heart to leap into my mouth.

'I'm not on your land anymore,' the cheeky boy called down to me, 'so you can't do anything!'

'Nezar,' I shouted, as sternly as I could, 'you're crazy and you're going to die if you're not careful.'

The boy giggled and ran down the other side of the roof so I could no longer see him.

I marched over at once to his father's house. My neighbour Naz was a very nice man who worked as a chemical engineer. He was quite a large, blonde man.

'Hello, Bradley,' he said, with a sigh. 'Is there something wrong with my car again?'

I should probably mention that the reason I had become acquainted with Naz and his family at all was that he insisted on parking his long Cadillac in a way that blocked our narrow street. But that was beside the point.

'No, no, not at all,' I responded with somewhat forced jollity. 'It's your son I'm worried about this time.'

'Oh dear,' said Naz. 'Is he bothering you? Has he stolen something? Has he damaged your car?'

'No, no, nothing like that. Well, not as far as I know. It's just that he's been climbing on my roof.'

'And he has broken some tiles? Or perhaps he left something up there?'

'No, it's not that. I'm just worried for the boy's safety!'

'That's all? Oh. From your expression, I thought you had something serious to tell me. You had me worried.'

'You mean you know about his climbing antics? You mean he does this often?'

'Oh, yes! It's just a bit of harmless fun. Much better than sitting inside watching T V and eating doughnuts all day, isn't it?'

'Harmless fun? The boy is going to fall and break his neck! What kind of irresponsible parenting do you think this is?'

'Do you always argue with me about everything I choose to do? First you don't like the way I park my car, now you don't like the way my son plays outside. It's really none of your business.'

'Well, I can hardly stand by and watch you allow your ten-year-old to risk his life! Did your parents let you do this sort of thing?'

'Well I'm not exactly the same build, am I?'

Naz was quite a chubby man, being rather fond of Armenian food. 'That's beside the point!'

'Look, Bradley, with all due respect, just let the child be. And I'll try to make sure he doesn't climb on your roof again.'

I marched home rather huffily. The very next Sunday, though, there was a similar apparition on my rooftop. This time the boy was not crouching but walking with his arms stretched out to the sides. I nearly had a heart attack at the sight.

'Nezar,' I shouted up, 'you're not Superman, you know!'

He giggled. 'Oh, I'm better,' he cried out, flapping his arms. 'I'm the jumping man!'

He walked right up to the edge of the gutter and, in front of my horrified eyes, jumped onto the roof of the house next door. I ran into my house as fast as I could and picked up the phone.

'Naz,' I panted, 'this is important. I'm calling about your son. I'm really worried about him. He just jumped off my roof.'

Naz sighed patiently. 'Oh, don't worry. He does that all the time.'

'One day,' I said angrily, 'he'll fall on his head and die.'

'No he won't,' Naz answered calmly. 'He'll land on his feet. He has excellent balance.'

'Well, good luck explaining that you're responsible for your son's untimely death because of your insane misconception that he is in fact a cat.'

I hung up, irritably. I went back outside. The child was still there on the roof, sitting and munching on a snack he'd brought with him. Or maybe he really had gone feral and was eating titbits he had found on the roof. At that point I wouldn't have put it past him.

'Suit yourself,' I shouted up, walking to the other end of my lawn. 'I'm going to sit right here and read.'

The child didn't move.

'Please don't kill yourself, though,' I added hastily.

At this point, Nezar stood up and ambled to the edge of the roof. Then, all of a sudden, his foot went out from under him and he slid off the roof. I gave an almighty yell and ran towards him.

'Oh God, Nezar, are you OK? Can you hear me?' I turned to the neighbour on the other side who had been preparing to mow his lawn. 'Quick, call an ambulance!' I cried. By the time I turned my head back to the scene of what I assumed to be a terrible, possibly fatal accident, the child was nowhere to be seen. I blinked. 'Nezar?' I cried out, wondering if the whole incident had been a mirage caused by too much caffeine.

A small voice came from far away.

'What?' it said, a little sulkily.

I looked up. There he was, totally unhurt, standing by the wall.

'What are you, a cat or something?' I said in a mix of wonder, anger and bewilderment. 'You can't just fall from the top of a house and be fine. That must be a good four yards down onto concrete!'

'Oh, it's fine,' he said breezily. 'I'm used to it. I do lots of gymnastics at school,' he added, with what might be described as condescension.

'No, it's not fine,' I said. 'It's not the same thing as standing on a balance beam. You'll end up in hospital. Then it won't be funny anymore. I'll tell your father.'

'Go ahead and tell my father. He knows. He says it's fine.'

I had to admit the kid was probably right on that account. I did talk to Naz again, but he just shrugged.

'Kid falls down all the time,' he said. 'Nezar's a smart kid. He's always fine.'

And in a sense I suppose he was right, as I never witnessed Nezar getting hurt. I moved out of the house about a year later, but stayed in touch with the father. One day, a good twenty-five years later, I received a phonecall from Naz.

'You'll never guess what Nezar does now,' he told me in a voice full of fatherly pride.

'Well, since you didn't move to New York I assume he's not leaping across skyscrapers, fighting crime?'

Naz laughed. 'Not quite. Actually, he did become a gymnastics instructor for a while, so I suppose his childhood was good practice.'

I declined to comment.

'But you'll like what he's doing now much better. He's become an orthopaedic doctor.'

I laughed in astonishment. 'So you mean he now fixes the bones of other stupid kids who fall of roofs?'

'That's exactly right. And he sends you his best wishes.'

Before moving to the seventh *arrondissement* in Paris I lived for six months in the seventeenth, on Boulevard de Courcelles, looking out over the Parc Monceau. My next door neighbour, Moussantoff, was a very intelligent, rather odd-looking gentleman in his late twenties. He had light blonde hair and pale skin, a goatee and a sharp nose. When he spoke, he was extremely eloquent in French, English and German, although none of these turned out to be his native language.

When he introduced himself to me as a neighbour, he shook my hand and looked at me sharply for what felt like a long time.

'I see you looking at my eyes very closely,' he said, with a delicate accent like one of the smart villains from a James Bond film. 'You must either think that I'm cross-eyed or that I come from another country. Is that not what you're thinking?'

'Sorry, I don't mean to be nosy, but I'm very curious as to your origins,' I said cautiously. 'I couldn't help but notice the shape of your face. Would it be bold to hazard a guess that you might be Finnish or Swedish? Or are you perhaps from one of the Baltic states?'

'No, sir,' he replied rather coldly, 'You are quite mistaken. I was born in Russia; I am Russian. I am a professor here at the university, where I teach Russian.' His expression softened a little with something like pride. 'But I'll tell you what: if you look anywhere in this country, you'll not find anyone like me,' he said as he leaned towards me. 'Can you guess why?'

'Well,' I ventured, 'is it because you speak so many languages? I imagine, as you teach at the university, that you must speak French perfectly, without a single fault in grammar. You might even casually use the *passé simple*, the conditional, the future imperfect… Other foreigners must be jealous of your language skills.'

'You are wrong,' he said. 'Well, you are right about the language skills, but that is the wrong answer.' He frowned, as if I had vexed rather than flattered him. I laughed nervously.

'Do you simply wish me to remark on your no doubt extraordinary intelligence? Becoming a university professor abroad…'

He cut me off almost instantly, this time. 'No,' he said curtly. 'Not that.'

There was a long pause. I resisted the urge to laugh. Moussantoff was obviously taking this line of questioning very seriously, even though I had no idea what he wanted me to say.

'You must be a great culinary expert,' I improvised. 'Just looking, um, at the way you speak and use your lips and tongue I'd imagine you must be either a wine taster or a fantastic reviewer of five star hotels, or perhaps Michelin guide restaurants…?' I trailed off.

Moussantoff was looking at his fingernails. I was getting a little bored of this game, too.

'Since you were born in Russia, are you perhaps a world champion in chess?' I tried.

'You're getting closer,' Moussantoff observed, 'but you are wrong.'

I considered the man again, and tried a different tactic. 'Well, you're thin, you're fairly athletic-looking. Could you be some sort of sports sensation? The 400-metres perhaps. Or the high dive?'

'Wrong again,' said Moussantoff drily. 'I hate sports.' The humour of this dialogue seemed almost entirely lost on him.

'Perhaps you are a polar bear tamer?' I suggested. 'Do the finest Paris zoos only recruit from people who have lived near the Arctic circle?' I was unsure how far I could push the jest. Moussantoff looked a little bit like a man capable of whipping out a revolver. However, I could have rambled on for a while longer. He neither looked angry nor amused. He simply looked bored, and perhaps a bit disappointed.

'No, you're wrong again,' he said, somewhat despondently.

'Look, I'm running out of options,' I said gently, 'You're going to have to tell me at some point, or this will drive me mad for the rest of our stay next to each other. I need to get to know you. I mean, have you lived here a long time? You're not moving out soon, are you?' I tried to keep the hopeful note out of my voice.

'I've been here four or five years. And I don't intend to move out anytime soon,' he said emphatically. 'I know you've just moved in, and I feel rather obliged to be your friend, but you *must* guess what is exceptional about me.'

It would take a proud man indeed to be unruffled by the previous statement regarding this sense of obligation, but I chose to ignore it with an all but audible sigh.

'Well, if we are to be neighbours, I suppose I must persevere with this task. OK. All I know about you is that you are multilingual and extremely intelligent.'

'You're forgetting one thing,' he said drily. 'I am Russian.'

'Perhaps I have been forgetting to factor this into my guesses,' I said, as seriously as I could. To my credit, I swear he looked a little mollified.

'Did you have the best grades in your school?' I suggested. 'Or perhaps the whole of Russia?'

'Now you're getting close,' he said, with a thin-lipped smile.

I decided it was time for extreme tactics. I put on my softest voice and practically wheedled my next question. 'I'm so curious,' I said, as if I were addressing some celebrity. 'Please tell me what is so exceptional about you.'

I had hit gold with this technique. Moussantoff suddenly beamed.

'OK, I'll tell you,' he said coyly. 'I was the top of my class in my high school.' I did my very best to look duly impressed, although I had to fight the urge to burst out laughing. 'I was something of a genius in both maths and languages,' he added, without even a trace of modesty or humour. 'I think they are related: you can be excellent in both,' he mused. 'After all, putting words together is like putting numbers together.' He paused, obviously expecting praise.

'What a nice theory,' I said. 'So why are you here?'

He coughed slightly.

'I was very young when I left to study abroad,' he said, putting his hand to his breast as if he were delivering a speech in Parliament. Or, I added to myself, in a high school auditorium. 'I was given a scholarship by the Russian government. Brezhnev was the first secretary of the Communist party at this time. Afterwards I decided to stay in France. I applied for political asylum and I got it, with the understanding that I would be a professor at the university. I had a contract teaching Russian. But that is not the exceptional part.'

He paused.

'What is the exceptional part?' I asked, duly.

'I'm still a communist,' he said fiercely, then paused for effect. I must have looked rather blank, for he raised his voice to add: 'and I'm still loyal to the Soviet Union!' As an afterthought, he slammed his fist into his palm, which made no sound at all. I wondered if I should salute, or at least applaud. 'I'm very loyal to Brezhnev,' he continued, glaring. 'If you analyse my CV, it could look exactly like I ran away from Siberia to be a spy in good old France.' My brief vision of Moussantoff as Bond villain flashed through my mind. 'But I'm not a spy, they all know that. I qualify to be a spy. I could be a spy, but I think communism is the solution for France. I am a member of the Communist party here; I often give speeches.' This did not surprise me. 'I'm surprised you haven't heard of me before,' he added a little haughtily. 'The Communist party constitutes easily 15% of the French political scene. You'll recognise me when we take over this country one day. We almost did it, after the war,' he finished, in the nostalgic tone usually reserved for very old men.

To be perfectly honest, this speech may have gone on for quite a bit longer than this. I think I tuned out for a while when he started quoting percentages. 'Now the labour movement is very strong,' he added. 'And that's what's exceptional about me. I can't think of any other runaway immigrant from Russia that remained communist. I'm the only one. That's my record.' I had to admit it didn't sound like a common scenario: most Russians who flee the motherland usually give up their communist principles pretty quickly.

I did not voice these views, in hopes of saving the rest of my afternoon, considering that I had been standing by the front door to our building for a good half hour by that point. But escaping this one discussion did not save me. The arrogance of Mr Moussantoff resurfaced every time I ran into him in the corridor or outside the block. I never invited him to my house, nor was I ever invited to his apartment. There was some mix of arrogance and what one might call speechifying in his persona that precluded friendship.

In later years, I came across him in a few articles in major newspapers. His position went on to become more exceptional, as the Communist party's role in Europe proceeded to decline steadily. It is estimated that the party lost almost 80% of its voting power in France between 1935 and the 1990s. I suppose Moussantoff was a true intellectual, preaching the virtues of communism; a man of principles. It was a pity he was so boring.

Neighbours are met and made in the oddest of circumstances. Whether on Earth or the moon, on an island or on a boat, on a freight train or a commercial jet, people will rub shoulders with other people, share armrests and stories, and inevitably become involved in some sort of neighbourly interaction. Some of these brief moments of neighbourliness have no lasting repercussions, whilst others might lead either to lengthy litigation or to lifelong friendship. Most neighbours, after all, are not born, like relatives, nor pre-determined, like classmates, but emerge purely out of coincidental circumstances.

One of the more unusual places I developed a neighbour was a tiny single-engine commercial plane I used to make use of quite regularly in the early to mid-seventies, on my trips from Beauvais, in the Picardie region, to Lyd, in Kent. This was a plane so small that it could take no more than six people, usually only carrying one or two. My flights were usually scheduled by calling the airport, as I was friendly with the pilot and owner of this small plane, who was happy to take me along on his regular France-England flights for a reasonable fee. This was possible due to the fact that, for a plane of that size, the landing fee at Lyd was one pound, as opposed to the £3,000 one might pay at Gatwick. There was not even a terminal, so I usually purchased my ticket on the plane itself, in mid-air. The airports at Beauvais and Lyd were set up in the same fashion: each had one employee, who was customs officer, policeman, passport control and airport guide all in one. The one in Lyd even served coffee and tea and chocolate at the bar. After the first few trips, I didn't need to show passports anymore, and I was on first name terms both with the airport man and the pilot.

In other words, it was not the sort of place you would expect to find yourself accompanied, especially not on a regular basis. Carl was an exception. He was a tall, pleasant, slightly foppish-looking Englishman, who would regularly be the only other passenger on these short-haul flights. At first, I believe we were both somewhat suspicious of the other; after all, one becomes accustomed to feeling a certain luxury associated with the privacy of what is essentially a reserved flight, so the first few times we kept communication to a curt nod and plunged into our respective newspapers. But curiosity proved stronger than any other emotion and, as one is wont to do when thrown together in slightly unusual circumstances, we quickly overcame our initial reluctance and began chatting.

'So,' I said one day, after the flight had stabilised over the Channel, 'we meet again.'

My neighbour smiled slightly and lowered his copy of the *Financial Times*. 'Quite,' he said. He extended a slender hand to me. 'I'm Carl. Pleasure to meet you.'

'Bradley Jamieson.' We shook hands. 'So what brings you to this route?' I asked; 'I must admit I'm curious.'

'I've contemplated the question rather regularly myself, although it seemed rude to intrude.'

'Let's start with your story,' I replied with a smile.

'Very well. Let's see. So I work in Pas-de-Calais, and my wife and children live in Kent. So I suppose in a sense these flights are a sort of commute for me. I try to spend the weekends at home.'

'In that respect, then, we are very much alike. But what brings you to France?'

'Tyres,' he responded. 'I work for one of the major American tyre-manufacturing multinationals.'

'And you're English?' I asked. 'I thought I detected something a little Transatlantic in your accent.'

He smiled. 'Very good, Mr Jamieson. I used to be a fairly major industrialist in the big American factories, before I transferred to their branch north of Paris, then onwards to Pas-de-Calais.'

'Quite an impressive career, then! And please, call me Bradley.'

'Ah, but the tyres are only a part of my career. You haven't asked why I travel back absolutely every weekend – I suppose you think me a very dedicated family man. Of course, I love my wife and kids. But can you guess the real reason I fly back?'

'Let me see. Surely not for the English cuisine.'

He laughed. 'Certainly not. Although I'm not sure how I feel about all this heavy Northern French cooking, all these cream sauces and sausages... But I'd still take them over overcooked beef any day!'

'Alright then, you must have some project that calls you back, and requires your constant attention.'

'That's more like it.' He smiled rather coyly.

'Do you have several families? A mistress, perhaps?'

Carl burst out laughing. 'A good guess, for another man, perhaps. You don't know me very well, and you've never met my wonderful wife, so I won't take offence.'

'OK. You're a writer and you have a novel to return to.'

'Getting colder, my young friend.'

'Young? You can hardly be much older than me!'

'Oh, I was being facetious. Although I'd imagine I'm a few years older than you: I'm thirty-five.'

'Well, I'm twenty-eight myself, so we're not that far off. But let's not get off-topic. A project that requires constant attention… does this mean it's alive?'

'Bingo! I'll fill you in, as I would be surprised if you got this without quite a lot more prodding: I raise sheep. Two gorgeous herds of lambs, ewes and rams.'

'Wow! I must say, that wasn't what I was expecting.'

'Don't I look like the typical farmer type?'

'It was the *FT* which threw me off.'

'Well, I'm only part industrialist. I certainly do care about my companies; in fact I've had to worry about them almost as much as the new-born lambs at the moment, as we're going through some financial trouble, but I won't bore you with the details. I'm the treasurer, you see, so I'm rather too involved with that aspect! But when my wife took me to visit her family in Kent, and we started looking into buying and renovating a farmhouse, well, something about that way of life just really appealed to me. So now I have over two hundred lambs, about thirty sheep, and two dozen rams.'

'I must say I'm impressed. The simple life isn't for every businessman.'

'I think my business skills helped. I ended up with about three hundred acres of fields, and sheep just seemed like the obvious thing to put in them! Do you know something funny though: I actually make quite a bit more money from the sheep than I do from the tyre manufacturing!'

'That's remarkable. Though I suppose I can see your point, actually,' I replied, impressed. 'You see, I come from a family that dealt with tanning and sheep-skins, so I'm not unfamiliar with the whole issue of the economics of the ovine trade! I remember my grandfather discussing the pros and cons of selling meat versus selling skins or wool. I would think an accountant's brain would come in handy in these calculations.'

'Absolutely. And on a much more basic level, mathematics and statistics are rather convenient skills to have when you're dealing with the issue of breeding. I'm particularly interested in lambing, you see; you may have guessed that from the proportion of young ones in my flocks. I actually get my ewes to lamb twice a year, which I believe is quite unusual. A farmer might think it unnatural, but it certainly does wonders for my profits: I lamb twice: once in early spring and once in late summer. It works a treat. And of course, sometimes there are twins, and some of them die at birth; it's quite an operation keeping track of it all!'

'That sounds like a lot of sheep and a lot of work. I don't think I could deal with all the smells and the disease and the droppings!'

'Ah, but it's good for my fields! It keeps the grass green and short as a carpet! Fields in Kent need hardly any maintenance at all. I spent some time in the southern States, and they have to worry so much about pesticides and watering. Here, it just rains all the time, and the sheep fertilise everything naturally. It's wonderful. The sheep make their own food grow! At times, it's like the money just grows out of the ground!'

'But how did you end up with so many sheep? Did you inherit them or something?'

'No, no, this is all my own incentive. I saved up carefully, and bought about thirty sheep. Of course I had all the troubles any new business does; I'll spare you the details of sicknesses and broken fences, but eventually it all worked out, and they soon started breeding. And then I started selling the lambs, and finally I started making some decent money. Now I have two big flocks, and I make pretty decent sums off them.'

'I must say I'm impressed. So you're a sort of self-made farmer! That's a pretty unusual tale.'

'So it is. You must come visit me someday. I mean, our routes already overlap quite considerably; surely you can take a detour sometime to come see my sheep?'

'That would be lovely,' I answered. 'Maybe sometime next month.'

This was how I ended up visiting Carl and his wife and two children in the rolling hills of Kent, only about half an hour's drive from my house. He hadn't been exaggerating about the land; it was a brilliant summer's day, and the three hundred acres of bright green grass dotted with sheep truly were an idyllic vision. We shared a beautiful Sunday lunch, and joked about the lambs' apparent capacity to stand comfortably on a heavily slanted slope.

'Do you think they develop longer front legs?' I mused. 'I mean, it must be so uncomfortable! They must get cramp. How does evolution deal with such an odd landscape?'

He snorted with laughter. 'Maybe they do. Or maybe they just change sides a lot. Although, going along with that logic, surely you and I would have developed some special plane-flying characteristics. It's probably a good thing change doesn't happen that quickly!'

'Well, maybe it would be good for you if the lambs had uneven legs. They might have more meat for cooking!'

'See if you manage to finish the roast we've made before you complain about the size!'

I spent the afternoon with his family, and after that our interactions on the plane were always very friendly. Over the next three years Carl and I continued to be very regular plane neighbours. I probably saw more of this man in travel than anyone else; certainly I never spent quite so much time with the same person aboard planes! Our meeting and the overlap of our commuting routes really was quite a remarkably coincidence. Sadly, I stopped making this commute sometime in the late seventies, when our pilot gave up on renting his plane and moved abroad. Shortly afterwards, Beauvais airport underwent renovation and became more of a major transport centre, so both Carl and I found other ways to travel. We stayed in touch for years afterwards, and eventually I found out that Carl had transferred to the US and sold all his sheep. We lost touch after that, but I do occasionally find myself wondering what his next business hobby turned out to be, and I still tell the joke about the Kentish sheep's uneven legs to many visitors.

THE LONELY PARK AVENUE NEIGHBOUR

Life in New York is the same as life in any big city, but perhaps even more exciting: every week, there is a new restaurant opening, every weekend a new art exhibition to visit. The only thing which can become monotonous about living there is that you get too used to your own luxury apartment, and start to long for change. The space where one settles becomes a limiting factor of the way one lives in the city. Thus, I spent a lot of time trying to figure out which of my three options I should choose: whether I should be living down by Wall Street where I worked, which is why I spent some time in Brooklyn Heights, relocate to the East Side where I lived in my early days as an engineer, or move to the Upper West Side, which was really where I would have liked to settle, overlooking the river and the grand palisades of New Jersey.

When I was about twenty-four, my banking colleagues and I came up with an ingenious system to combat the monotony of living in our beautiful apartments: we set up a system by which we could swap keys, and thus switch apartments when we felt so inclined. This way we could find a little fresh air, a change of atmosphere; what the French call *le dépaysement*. There would be new local restaurants, new coffee shops, new faces to come across on our daily walks, a new library. And there would be new neighbours to meet.

In the course of one of these exchanges, one of my colleagues, Bob Platino, offered me his house on Park Avenue. I was living in Brooklyn at the time, so this seemed like an attractive change of scenery.

'My mother is travelling to Tokyo for three months,' Bob told me. 'She's working on a children's book there. Would you like to take over our house?'

'Ah,' I laughed at the time, 'you would just like to see my beautiful Brooklyn brownstone, no?'

'Of course,' he agreed, 'but I think you'll enjoy my house as well.'

I hadn't realised what I had signed up for until my wife and I arrived at the foot of a grand, towering, 1920s Art Deco apartment block. After emerging from the lengthy elevator ride, we opened the front door of a stunning twelve-thousand-square-foot penthouse. We took off our shoes, and padded around feeling as if we had broken in to a hotel, looking out through the vast glass windows over the parks and skyline of the city. The whole apartment was tastefully decorated with antiques and fine art. It took us forty-five minutes to figure out where we were meant to sleep, as we wandered from reception room to pool room and through the many, many bedrooms. Finally, we chose a nice, modest bedroom with a four-poster oak bed.

After the fourth day of sleeping there and enjoying feeling like we were on holiday in the city we lived in, there came a knock at the door. We were surprised by the fact that the concierge downstairs hadn't signalled the arrival of a guest: the whole building, after all, had very high security. Anyone coming to visit, as a friend of ours found out when trying to come for tea, was subjected to an elaborate show of protocol involving announcing one's full name and having one's picture come up on the intercom. Our friend told us he almost expected to be fingerprinted or escorted upstairs by a security guard.

There had been no protocol here, and yet when we opened the door we found an affable man, who looked to be in his forties, standing on the doorstep. He seemed as surprised to see us as we were to see him.

'I'm coming over for the usual,' he said casually.

'I'm sorry?' It took me a moment to collect myself. 'The usual?' This sounded pretty suspicious.

'I'm Jack!' he said, and waited expectantly.

'Do you usually come for tea with Mrs Platino, perhaps? Or are you a friend of Bob's?'

'Oh, I'm a friend of Mrs Platino's, indeed,' he replied. 'I also know Bob very well.'

'I'm afraid the Platinos are away,' I said pointedly.

There was a long pause.

'Is there something I can do for you?' I added, as he gave no sign of moving on.

'Now don't be silly,' the man said. Jokingly, he tried to elbow past me, but I wasn't having any of it.

'Look, do you want me to call the doorman?'

At this, the man laughed.

'Are you serious? I guess Bob didn't tell you about me, huh?'

'He certainly didn't,' I said, rather ruffled by the continuation of this conversation.

'I'm a neighbour,' he said in a conciliatory tone. 'I live on the next floor, all alone in this big old apartment I inherited. Mrs Platino is pretty much the whole of my social life.' At this point he looked a little embarrassed, and I regretted being a little cold with him. 'She's such a lovely lady. She lets me come sleep over sometimes, you see. I make myself a bed in one of the big bedrooms and just sleep there for a few days. I get anxious if I'm just living by myself all the time.'

This was a little more than I had expected.

'I'm sorry,' I said, 'but I'm finding this hard to believe. This sounds like some kind of elaborate hoax. I don't think I can just let you into this apartment – we're only guests ourselves, you see.'

'Oh, you're one of those exchange guys. I see. Bob told me about this. See, you're just like me in a way. You just need a little change in your life.'

'Be as that may, I'm just not comfortable with this.'

'Look, just give Bob a call,' he said gently. 'Ask the concierge. I promise everybody knows about this arrangement. I'm not pulling your leg.'

'Well I'll be damned. Look, just wait here a moment. I'd better call Bob and ask him.'

I rang my own apartment and, sure enough, Bob knew what I was talking about.

'Oh man,' he said, 'I'm so sorry I forgot to tell you. He has quite the hard-luck story. Was married to this rich heiress, and then she died. So that's how he got the apartment. And now he just lives on his own. So I guess he kind of likes to pretend he lives with us sometimes. It's not like he gets in the way; just makes himself coffee sometimes, watches a bit of TV.'

'You mean he doesn't even socialise?'

'Oh, he does a little, but mostly he just wants to have people around. But listen Bradley, I'm sorry I forgot to tell you about this. If you're uncomfortable with it you can say no, but it'd be nice if you can just let him in. I promise you'll hardly know he's there.'

'But this spoils the idea of this being like our own home,' I said sadly. 'We'll have to be always in our bathrobes, we can't walk around nude or in our pyjamas!'

'Oh,' Bob said cheerfully, 'you'll probably see Jack in his pyjamas. Don't worry, he's very relaxed!'

This was not the objection I had. 'Can you hear what you're saying, Bob? He and my wife haven't even been formally introduced,' I hissed into the phone.

'What's that about your wife? I don't mind.' Hilary piped up from the other side of the room. I sighed.

'OK, well, thanks Bob.'

I hung up, and turned to my wife.

'Hilary, what do you think we should do? I mean, we don't know this man from Adam. He could be a thief! He could be a rapist!'

Hilary, always a tolerant soul, smiled. 'I don't think there's too much risk of that if old Mrs Platino lets him stay with her when she's alone...'

'I suppose you're right. She's not even that old, she's probably about the same age as him! Still, if we end up having a murderer for a roommate, I'm blaming you.'

That was how we ended up having Jack stay with us for three days. It was, as Bob had predicted, a perfectly civilised cohabitation. We hardly saw him apart from a few quick conversations in the kitchen. When he left, he took his dirty laundry and left his bed impeccably made. A month later, Mrs Platino came back from Tokyo, and we moved back to our old apartment.

Some ten years later, I ran into Jack on the street. He had white hair, but I recognised him nonetheless. He seemed pleased to see me.

'How are you doing, Bradley?' He remembered my name. 'What are you up to these days?'

'Oh, banking, same old thing. Still work with Bob. How about you? Still friends with them?'

'Oh yes,' he said, 'I still have my three days' holiday with them once a month. That's how I like to think of it. A social holiday from my big empty apartment.'

'I don't mean to be indiscreet, Jack, but why don't you move out if you don't like the twenty-room apartment?'

'Well, it's hard to give up a place like that, isn't it?' Having seen Bob's place, I was inclined to agree. 'And I have to say I've just got used to it. I'm very fond of Mrs Platino particularly. Ever since Bob moved out I've enjoyed getting to know her a little better.'

'Oh,' I said knowingly, 'it's like that, is it? She's quite a striking woman. Must've been very beautiful in her youth.'

Surprisingly, he blushed a little. 'Now you can't say things like that. Mrs Platino's a very respectable woman.'

I laughed. 'Say, why don't you ask the lady to marry you? Then you two could have a proper palace, and you wouldn't have all this business of moving upstairs and downstairs once a month.'

He shook his head. 'No, it's not like that. I'm fond of my freedom, in the end. Although I suppose if we did move in together we could just ignore each other like some old couples do! I did consider your duplex theory for a time, to be honest, but I decided I'd rather have my own space than an extra twelve thousand square feet.'

DAME AGNES AND HER DOG

It is a well-known fact that most women in the Western world often live a good ten years more than men. Thus, at any given time, a good 70% of the national wealth is in the hands of old ladies who have inherited from their husbands. In consequence, living in the fanciest parts of any city will mean that area will be dominated by old ladies, peeping out from behind lace curtains and walking their minuscule dogs. Eaton Square was no exception. No-one ever seems to leave those houses; they are usually held on to greedily by the inhabitants and their families until the last possible second, then passed down, usually to relatives, or very occasionally to close friends, for a symbolic price. In fact, such was the proliferation of elderly millionaires that I often wondered if some of them didn't help their husbands on their way out of their lives and fortunes!

There is a perpetual crowd of this particular type of woman in Eaton Square, orbiting the gardens in the centre. Each one is a near-perfect carbon copy of her neighbours. An Eaton Old Lady has immaculate silver-grey hair and wears an expensive but tasteful dress in shades of cream, lilac or teal. The most visible difference between them is that some have canes and some don't, but if you look closely you'll discern that some also have slightly different-sized curls in their perms or a slightly different-coloured cameo brooch. They gain respect from each other through age alone, and so those who are a sprightly seventy tend to affect an extra limp to aspire to the coveted status the ninety-year-olds enjoy. The message seems to be that the sicklier they look, the richer they are.

Dame Agnes was amongst the upper echelons of this old-lady conspiracy. She did not have a cane, but she did have a small, very aggressive dog. It was a strange-looking thing, curly-haired but slung low to the ground. It was a pretty pathetic little creature, trotting around on its mistress's heels with a pompous expression on its face.

One day, when I was jogging in Eaton Square, this yapping dust-mite trotted after me and tried to bite me on the foot. It could barely reach my ankle, but its teeth were still sharp. It latched on to the bottom of my trouser leg, getting drool all over it, and I heard the fabric rip. Without thinking, I whipped around in anger and booted the dog with my left leg. There was a yelp.

I used to play football at university. This was no careless shot. My foot carefully picked the dog up by the underbelly, much as you would drop-kick an American football for a field goal, and delicately sent it soaring across the bushes. Had there been soccer goalposts, it would have landed right between them, with the crowd going wild in the background. As it was, the tiny dog flew right across Eaton Square, yapping as it fell. When it hit the ground, it gave up all semblance of being a respectable football and scrambled away as fast as it could, making pathetic sounds. I brushed my trousers off and tried to regain my composure, thinking that would be the end of it, but before I could walk off with whatever dignity I had left, I saw the dog's owner bearing down on me. Dame Agnes' rage could be seen from a great distance; I wouldn't have been surprised if she had actually been emitting steam.

'How dare you!' she shouted as she arrived face-to-face with me. The puppy was huddling behind her skirt, whining. 'What kind of cruel, violent…' She paused as she noted my outfit. 'And what on earth are you wearing!'

'I was jogging,' I answered as calmly as I could. 'And your little pet decided to assault me.'

'Pet?! Assault?! This is a prize hound. And he is always well-behaved.'

If I had needed any defence at this point, the 'hound' in question, having recovered from its journey of shame back across the square, decided it had best assert its tiny self again. It made a noise best described as a squeak and started jumping around my leg again, putting little muddy footprints on my shoes. I nudged it delicately with my toe and said very quietly:

'Could you please remove this… thing from me?'

'Thing!' she practically roared. 'THING!'

Then she bent down with such a look of rage that I couldn't help but worry that she was going to have an aneurysm on the spot. Her hands were trembling so hard with righteous indignation that it took her a very long time to pick up the dog, by which time my annoyance was tempered with amusement and pity.

'Look,' I said, 'I'm sorry I kicked your shih tzu.'

The lady's mouth pursed up and her eyes bulged so hard I thought her entire head might explode, which made me glad I had withheld the joke I had been about to make about practising my jujitsu on her shih tzu. The dog itself seemed to have developed a new terror of me, now that he was level with my arms rather than with the soles of my feet. It started to tremble a little, too.

'*It* is not,' she said, breathing heavily, 'a shih tzu. *He* is a very rare breed, a French poodle crossed with a dachshund. He is entirely of European ancestry. Born and bred.'

'No wonder he's so aggressive,' I commented.

I really thought Dame Agnes might have a heart attack and die in front of me, right there in Eaton Square gardens, which would have been awkward for everyone and difficult to explain. Resisting the urge to laugh at her indignation, I made my expression as sombre as I could, and put my hand on her arm.

'I'm sorry, madam,' I said gently. 'It's just that you're not supposed to have dogs in Eaton Square.'

The blood drained from her face, and she coughed discreetly. She paused, staring at the dog's head for a long time as if gathering herself, then she turned her face up to me. Her expression had been completely transformed into a mask of innocence.

'Is that so?' she cooed. 'I can't really read the signs, you see my eyesight isn't quite what it used to be.' She waved her hands helplessly.

I gave my most genteel smile. 'It's definitely true. I've never seen a dog here before.'

She held the little pup up to me winsomely. 'Surely you can hardly call this a dog?' The dog, if it was indeed a dog, looked absolutely petrified at finding itself this close to me again. 'It's just a little toy! It would fit in my pocket!'

'I must agree that it's hardly a dog,' I said, recoiling a little, 'but I'll accept that it's hardly a football. So I'll let you off. Why don't I accompany you to the gate?' I added, offering her my arm. Dame Agnes appeared vanquished, as she didn't even protest this slight on her so-called prize puppy. She realised she would have to drop the dog to accept my arm, so she did, without ceremony. It squealed and wriggled on the ground a bit, before promptly scampering as far away from me as it could. However, it stopped abruptly when it realised it was in danger of being left behind, and spun around. It gave a comical little ballet of fear and confusion, acting more like a squirrel or a crab than a dog. It ran three steps away from me then two back towards his mistress, doing its utmost to steer clear of me as we walked to the grille. As I opened the gate with my key, I shot the dog the dirtiest look I could muster, and I could have sworn that it cowered.

'So what exactly was that you were doing in the square, young man?' Agnes asked delicately, with a winning smile.

This was not the first time my health habits had puzzled older residents. I resisted the urge to say I was maintaining my college football fitness, instead explaining the concept of jogging to her.

'Well, the dog must have thought you were a thief. He's not used to runners in our square.'

'Yes,' I said, 'I suppose you usually see men walking here in pairs as if they're really intent on admiring the pavement, or too busy discussing how best to restructure Cabinet to actually move very much. But that's because most of them are over ninety. I, on the other hand, need to stay fit. I intend to stay one of the rare living husbands on Eaton Square. My wife is a triathlete, you see. She keeps me fit. I like to jog, and do calisthenics.'

'I see, sir,' she said quietly, in the tone of voice of someone who does not see at all. 'Well I'll just make sure we stay out of your way,' she concluded, smiling. I pretended to tip my hat towards her, adding gallantly: 'I'll make sure I find something else to use as a football in the future.'

THE TANNER'S SON

Sethawa was a neighbour of my grandmother's that I ended up befriending during my various holidays in Konya, Turkey, when we were both rambunctious children with dirty feet and tanned faces. Sethawa's father owned a leather shop, which was a popular trade in the city. His shop had its own well outside, which meant they had an easy supply of the large amounts of running water necessary for the work.

Tanning and selling leather made for a successful business, as many Muslims pass through the city on their Hajj pilgrimages to Mecca, and would often stop to make the ritual sacrifice. The many animal skins this produced would often then be sold to the tanning companies and made into supple leather, in an arrangement beneficial to all parties. In particular during the festive periods, Sethawa's father's shop would be milling with pilgrims, and doing a roaring trade in leather. The operation was a small one, but its owner worked hard and constantly to keep it going, and everyone who visited it left with a strong sense of his competency and kindness.

When I was a child, I loved being around the tannery. The strong smell was a thrill rather than a deterrent to me, and the messiness of the whole operation seemed like great fun. The crackling skins seemed such strange objects, like the shadows of creatures from a play or a dream. The skin of a cow, for instance, is a vast thing. Neither Sethawa nor I had ever been that close to a live cow's face. Here, we could run our fingers through the gritty hair as it lay in the sunny courtyard behind the shop, drying in preparation for the tanning. We were too young at this point to get involved in the actual work, but it was wonderful to watch his father scraping a knife over the skins. He would tell us about the process, quietly, as he worked.

'This is just like what my father did before me, and his father before him. It's an ancient trade, tanning. It is simple and precious, revealing the beautiful leather that hides under every animal's dirty fur and hair. See how it softens when I work it?'

It was quite wonderful, the way he managed to stop us from running around and crowd over his shoulders, peering down at the strange, smelly leather. Another day, we might watch Sethawa's father salting a hide, laying it out in the sun, or washing it in horrid-smelling water and lime. Of course, after ten minutes of relative attentiveness, we would be off again, dashing off into the streets of Konya. But then we were just young boys.

Sethawa and I were the same age, and we cared very little about the differences in our upbringings. Sometimes, Sethawa would chatter at me in incomprehensible Turkish; other times he would communicate in broken English. It didn't really matter: like any children of our age, we just liked to run around in the streets, to cram our faces with whatever food we could find, and to get as muddy and dirty as we possibly could. A tanning shop was the perfect base for such adventures, being, as it was, right in the middle of town.

By the time we were sixteen or seventeen, Sethawa's place in his father's shop had become a somewhat more responsible one. Sethawa's English had improved considerably, and we were able to talk in much more detail about our lives, being the same age in very different cultures. Some of our preoccupations were the same, others were vastly different. Sethawa had a good relationship with his father, and enjoyed helping out in his shop. He took a simple joy in carrying around the stacks of skins he had once jumped on as a child, carefully piling them up so they were easily accessible to his father. They were wholesalers rather than retailers, so there wasn't too much work to be done on presentation; nonetheless, Sethawa really seemed to enjoy presenting the skins in their best light. His father obviously appreciated the genuine effort Sethawa put in, and was kind and encouraging to him in all his endeavours. It was a delight to witness, in a city where many young men had tense relationships with their families. Like many of his contemporaries, nonetheless, Sethawa confessed to me that he felt a certain pull towards the Western world. He worried that his beloved father was expecting him to take over the shop, and for a few weeks he agonised over how to bring the subject up.

'I have these dreams,' he confessed hesitantly, 'of flying across the ocean to America, and never returning. When I wake up, I feel ashamed. What would my family think if they knew this is what I wanted? I could never do this to my father. He would think it was such a betrayal.'

I told him not to worry, and that his father was sure to understand if he did eventually figure out that he wanted to leave Konya. 'Your father is a good man,' I said. 'He will support you no matter what you choose.' The words seemed to reassure Sethawa, and we spoke no more on the subject for the rest of my visit.

That trip to Turkey turned out to be the last I took for a very long time, and I didn't see Sethawa again for almost ten years. When I next visited, I made sure to stop by the shop as soon as I arrived in the city. Sethawa's father was there, his hair only a little greyer, his smile still as kind. 'What can I do for you, old friend?' he asked me. 'Are you looking to buy some nice leather? Or perhaps I can just pour you a nice cup of tea?'

I stepped into the warm darkness of the shop. 'Tea would be lovely, but I really was looking to see my old friend Sethawa. Is he around, your son?'

The father shook his head with a sad smile. 'It's been many years since Sethawa lived here.' Seeing the surprise on my face, he laughed. 'He went the same way as you, you know! He went away to school in California.'

'California?' I was astounded. 'That's wonderful! I mean, he always dreamed of America... but when last I spoke to him, these all sounded like pipe dreams. I had no idea he would actually go.'

His father beamed with pride. 'I managed to get him a student visa, you see.'

'Sethawa told me he was afraid you wouldn't support him in these dreams. I told him he was wrong. I'm so glad to see he was!'

'Yes, I don't know why he worried. I always wanted the best for my son, wherever that might take him. He went to Berkeley, and studied physics and mathematics there. I think he's trying to get into advanced physics. From what I understand, he's interested in satellite design.' He shook his head wistfully. 'My little boy is all grown up!'

'How are you getting on with the shop on your own, then?' I asked.

He shrugged. 'Oh, fine. I ran my shop alone when I was a young man, now I run it alone again. When I need help, I will hire someone. Until then, I am content working on my own. Konya is a growing city, and there is always plenty of business.'

We spoke for a while longer on other matters, until I had to take my leave. Before I left the tannery, however, I asked for contact details for Sethawa. 'Sometimes I pass through California,' I told his father. 'It would be a real pleasure to see my old friend again.'

Truth be told, it would be years before I made it back to California, but when I did, I made sure I drove to Berkeley. Sethawa was no longer living at the university, but I managed to get his address and phone number from a friendly physics professor in the office. I called him up, and we arranged to meet for coffee.

It is a strange thing, meeting a friend from the distant past in a very different setting from the one you shared together. On seeing Sethawa again, even in Western clothing, with a slightly receding hairline and something of a paunch, I was brought straight back to our childhood days playing on the floor of the tannery.

'You've not changed at all,' I told my old friend. 'So tell me, how does it feel, being a Californian?'

Sethawa beamed shyly at me from across the coffee table. 'When I first arrived here, I simply couldn't believe it. Everything was so beautiful: the sky, the palm trees, the pure ocean stretching off into the distance…'

'The women, the good pay?' I added.

Sethawa grinned wryly. 'It was never about that, for me. You must know that wasn't my kind of American dream.'

'Oh, I know. I'm only teasing you. I just couldn't believe it when I heard you'd come here. I was sure you'd take over the shop from your old man, and end up never leaving Konya. He sounds so happy that you've succeeded over here, though!'

'I couldn't believe how kind he was about it. He didn't even get all soppy or anything. He was very straightforward about it. He just told me if I knew what my dream was, I should follow it, and that he would do everything he could to help. So I came over here, studied mathematics, and became involved with the physics department at Cal Tech. Now I'm working in satellite design. Right now, I spend most of my time in the labs, designing satellites that are going to be sent to land on Mars. Can you believe it?'

'The last time I saw you, you were stacking smelly cow hides. You've come a long way!'

'I'm even a US citizen, now! I mean, I guess I had to lose most of my hair in the process, but I made it to where I wanted to be. Look at us right now, successful American men sipping ice-cold soda just ten minutes from the beach. I wish our younger selves could see us now!'

We spoke for a long time, as I had actually studied engineering myself. When I bid him goodbye, we exchanged contact details, and we are still in touch today. As far as I know, Sethawa's father is still running the same business in Konya. If I am ever in either of those places again, I will be sure to drop in on those wonderful old neighbours of mine. I hope their success never diminishes.

MY NEIGHBOUR, THE COBBLER

I have always had my shoes made for me. As a child, my father worked in leather manufacturing, so this was less of a luxury than it might perhaps sound. Not that my father was anything but a generous man: he insisted that my siblings and I should have our shoes carefully made and fitted to our specifications. Thus, every year from the age of six onwards, every six months or so, I would have a new pair of shoes made. I always found it terribly exciting. The shoemaker, one of my father's associates, would sit us down and measure our feet with a length of tape: the length and width of the foot, as well as the circumference of the ankle. Even the toes! We could choose the colour of the leather, the form of the shoe, the height of the sole, the style of the toe; we could determine whether the shoe would have laces or rubber elastics, whether it would be decorated with perforations or tooling, whether it would have leather wingtips or layers of different coloured leather.

Making a traditional shoe is a complicated process. To begin with, the leather must be cut, stained and polished. Then it can be stamped, or brogued with various awls. Holes for shoelaces must also be cut out of the right pieces. The sole and heel must be constructed and glued or hammered together, built up to exactly the right height. Everything is then sewn to the leather body of the shoe. The stitching must be solid, functional and attractive all at once. Then there is the matter of insoles and linings, adjustments to the tongue and shoelaces. Only then can the shoe be fitted and finished.

I have warm childhood memories of having my shoes made by my father's associates and friends. After that, in college, I started having my shoes made by Boston shoemakers; and then I began buying them from Church's in England and Florsheim in the USA. I have sampled many a shoemaker from many a nation. I've never got on with Italian shoes, however, as Italians all seem to have fine, dainty feet. My feet are not thin, but solid: they require a shoe to match. They also have quite high insteps. In any case, the leather the Italians favour is not to my taste.

Thus, since I moved to Switzerland, I had been ordering my shoes from England and America, having new pairs of my old shoes made for me every year or so. I was never lacking in shoes, always having a variety of colours, from dark stained leather to tooled chestnut brogues. I was not really aware of any long-standing tradition of shoemaking in Switzerland. However, one day, as I was walking around the old town of the city, I encountered a man standing in front of shop with a leather apron down to below his knees, smoking a cigarette and looking thoughtful. He was tall, slim, and serious-looking, with wire-framed glasses. His whole being seemed to emanate a smell of leather that drew me right back to my childhood. I stopped for a moment.

'I think I have seen you before,' the stranger said suddenly, peering at me with his sharp eyes.

'Pardon?' I replied. I had no such memory. 'I'm afraid you must be mistaken. I don't think I've ever noticed this shop before.'

The window was full of quite beautiful shoes, gleaming in rows of black, brown, beige and cream beneath their sober posters.

'Ah, but I've noticed you,' he said, dropping his cigarette in the gutter delicately. Obviously he was not a man to stamp out the cinders under his foot. 'I've always admired the shoes you are wearing. In fact,' he said, looking down at my feet, 'you're wearing them right now!'

'I mean, that's possible,' I stammered. 'I do walk down this street quite often. I just don't tend to pay much attention to unfamiliar shop windows.'

'Oh, don't worry,' he replied smoothly. 'Someone wearing good shoes tends to mean they're already catered for by one of our competitors. However, our business has been operating for more than two hundred years, and we're the only people in this city who still make our shoes by hand. I wonder whether you might like to come in and have a look, all the same?'

There was something so friendly and calm about his demeanour that I just couldn't resist. 'My father was a leatherworker,' I found myself telling him.

'So your interest in fine shoes is genetic?' he replied, radiating charm. 'Mine is probably, too. My father was a shoemaker, and his father before him, and so on. We have always worked for this company.'

'I grew up around shoes,' I told him, still feeling this urge both to tell him personal stories and to put him at ease.

'Yet you have such lovely ones!' Seeing my puzzled reaction, the man laughed. 'Have you never heard the French proverb "*le fils de cordonnier est le plus mal chaussé?*" It means the shoemaker's son has the worst shoes of all.'

It was my turn to laugh. 'I hadn't come across that before. Does this mean my father wasn't characteristic of his profession? I always had excellent shoes as a youngster. Comfortable ones, too. When I was young,' I continued enthusiastically, 'my uncle used to come over and break in our shoes for us by hitting them. Our small feet would take a long time to stretch the hard leather, you see.' The man nodded, obviously enthralled. 'Over time, we began to join in this ritual, which was a surprising amount of fun. Shoes and clothes were serious business, to be taken good care of: so to be able to smash them with a stick was incredibly liberating! In fact, over the years, this ritual took on such credence that it became a Christmastime tradition. The whole family would have shoe-beating parties, using an array of baseball bats, planks and sticks.'

'Shoe-beating parties?' the salesman laughed incredulously.

'Oh yes,' I replied. 'We would dance around like some wild tribe, beating up our shoes!'

The man started laughing so hard at the image that he had to wipe a tear from his eye.

'In all my twenty years working in the shoemaking business,' he told me, 'I've never heard such a ridiculous story.'

He led me into the small, dark shop. It felt like stepping into someone's front room rather than a business.

'Now, I truly don't want to pressure you if you just wanted to have a look inside. You're more than welcome to do that. Would you like a cup of coffee, or some sparkling water?'

I declined. There was a pause.

'You may not be interested,' he said delicately, 'but, as a salesman, I cannot help but ask you if you would like to order a shoe.'

I hesitated. I had no real need for new shoes, yet there was something enticing about the offer. 'Why not,' I said, suddenly feeling spontaneous. 'I've not had a new shoe made in the past forty-five years! I'll try you out. After all, the shoes you have in here are lovely.'

The man smiled, and sat me down in a comfortable leather

armchair. He then brought out a box of implements and set about measuring my feet from all angles for a good forty-five minutes, before taking an impression of the whole foot in foam. 'You have truly unusual feet,' he told me after a while, frowning seriously. 'I don't think I've ever seen anything like them. This, of course, is the shoemaker's greatest joy and biggest fear. I think I will have to ask the founder of the company to come and have a look.'

'Is this some relative of yours?' I asked, a little confused.

He laughed. 'Oh no,' he said. 'This is not my family. We simply work here.'

My faith in his whole spiel had worn a little thin, but I agreed. After all, I had already sacrificed most of an hour. It seemed logical to persevere with the operation.

The founder's descendant turned out to be retired and in his mid-eighties, but he was available to come over for this exceptional case. I felt rather like a prince, being treated in this royal fashion. I accepted a strong tea, and sat sipping it, with my feet up on a stool, until the higher consultant could get to us.

Half an hour later, the boss showed up. He was quite an impressive older man, with longish white hair and a heavy chin, which he shook back and forth as he looked over my feet and the measures that we had made. 'These are not the right measures,' he said almost as once. My faith in the assistant had, by this time, slipped away almost to nothing. 'Can't you see this instep? You'll need to make a whole mould of the foot if you want to accomplish anything. It's not just the height of the instep,' he snapped, cutting off the assistant's would-be intervention, 'but the differentiation between the ball of the foot and the heel.' He lowered his voice, taking on a teacher-like intonation. 'See how the anklebone is set quite low? This gentleman will need a full mould made.'

The assistant cowered, and turned back to me ruefully.

'I do apologise,' he said. 'Would you be able to come back in tomorrow morning? I think you need shoes with special compensated heels, to balance out your feet. This would give you better blood circulation.'

I looked down at the floor. The princely feeling was wearing off. This impression obviously came across, as the older man turned up the charm. 'I really am sorry, sir. You see, I believe we can make you the best shoes in the country. I'll bring special equipment tomorrow, from our two hundred-year-old workshop out in the countryside.'

It would have been hard to turn down such an offer, seeing how it sounded more like a plea. 'I'll come back,' I said. 'After all, I don't live so terribly far away.' I was ushered out with many apologies, and much friendly reassurance. As I walked home in my old, perfectly comfortable and, to be honest, relatively expensive shoes, I regretted the decision slightly, but there was no way back. The two men would be waiting for me in the morning. At least it would be over quickly, I thought.

Two hours and forty minutes into the next morning, I began to regret that assumption. One eighty-two-year-old man and one forty-seven-year old managed to spend a full one hundred and sixty minutes essentially just measuring my feet. To be fair, I was sat quite comfortably, with a strong Italian ristretto, and the breeze blowing in from the sunny street. I felt like an artist's model, perhaps being sculpted in the Roman style while sitting at court, probably suffering under the exact same weight of boredom and expectation. To add insult to injury, I then had to wait while this huge, heavy plaster mould chilled and solidified in the fridge. After another long wait only partially relieved by small talk, they made me walk around in a plastic, transparent model of the shoe-to-be, so that they could watch how my feet moved when I walked.

The cast and model fit fine. At the end, they sat back. 'So, when can I pick up my shoe?' I asked, getting up, ready to pay up and head home. The two men looked at each other. 'I'd say about two months,' the elderly gentleman said, while his assistant nodded in the background.

I tried to stop my jaw from dropping to the ground. Two months? 'Alright,' I said hesitantly, realising there was nothing I could do about the situation. Really, I just wanted to get home.

Two months later, the shoe was ready, or so I assumed. Surely, in that much time, they could have sculpted me a shoe out of pure gold? Nonetheless, I was happy enough to finally receive the object I had paid for. I tried the shoes on and found them comfortable enough, and was preparing to walk out of the shop when both men raced to stop me at the door. 'No, no, no, sir,' the younger one admonished me. 'Your shoe is not finished. It is nowhere near perfect! I need you to walk around for me for a few minutes, while I take notes on the imperfections.' The two men then nodded and muttered at each other for a while as I walked back and forth aimlessly, wishing I could just go home. 'We'll need to make him a new insole,' the older man said decisively. 'His instep is higher than we thought in the left foot.' He looked up at me. 'I'm afraid we'll have to keep working a little longer. You could come back tomorrow?' I firmly refused any further delay, so to compromise, I sat down in the middle of the shop and told them I would wait while they finished whatever they had to do. I think my impatience had become noticeable at this point, as the two men scampered off to the back room and started bustling around, knocking things over in their haste.

This part of the proceedings took a good forty-five minutes, but at the end of it, breathless and red-faced, the younger man finished the final adjustments of the shoe, and I stood up in my new footwear one more time.

It was wonderful. They fit perfectly. I don't think I've ever worn such a comfortable shoe. They were beautiful, too, brilliant chestnut leather with delicate tooling along the wingtips. All my annoyance and impatience had vanished, and I grinned at the men with enthusiasm that felt almost childish. 'I love them,' I announced, getting up.

'Oh, wait! I think the *languette* needs to be adjusted,' the older man interjected, leaping up in turn. I felt my shoulders droop.

'No,' I said firmly. 'I don't think so. I know a good shoe when I feel it on my foot.'

'There's half a centimetre more in the back heel than I would like,' the man whined, wringing his hands. 'There might be slippage! The shoe might not take the form of your foot perfectly!'

'I don't care,' I said. 'These shoes are great, and I am leaving.' Triumphantly, I strode out of the shop into the brilliant sunlight. Once outside the shop, I looked around to make sure there were real people around me. If I had found myself alone, I might have wondered if I had in fact been abducted by aliens. What strange men! In all my lengthy visits there, I never saw another person step into the boutique. I myself had been walking by its front door for a good twenty years without seeing it. It was only really the men's beautiful leather apron that had drawn me in. On the walk home, however,

I decided these were some of the best shoes I had ever had, made or bought. In fact, confronted with the sheer luxurious comfort of these shoes, all the troubles of their making seemed to vanish from my mind. I was giddy with it: my legs felt young and sprightly, while my blood seemed to flow freely straight to my brain in a way it didn't usually do so on a simple walk down the road. I decided I would go back to them and ask them to make me a few more pairs, including some for sports. Now that I have owned these shoes for a few months, I'm convinced they have improved my circulation immeasurably. It makes me wonder why people don't always have their shoes made.

For a time, when I lived in New York, my banking colleagues and I would regularly exchange apartments. Like many other people in the 1970s, I took a fancy to the then-fashionable idea of living in Greenwich Village; so I left my lovely brownstone in Brooklyn Heights for one of my colleague's hippie-style houses near Washington Square. In that period, the Village had already expanded quite a bit from its humble beginnings as grungy bohemian backstreet and home of the Beat movement, becoming a hangout for a rather odd mix of hippies in communes and yuppies with families. On one side, my neighbour was a yuppie who used to be a fully-fledged hippie in bellbottoms and dreadlocks. He had spent most of his youth singing and playing instruments and doing drugs at Woodstock, before he turned around and became a Wall Street banker. He kept a few unusual habits from his free-wheeling days. For instance, he would walk from the Village to Wall Street; it took him half an hour.

The other neighbour, Manuel, whom I called Manny, became quite a good friend of mine. Manny was neither a yuppie nor a hippie, but an uneducated man of forty living with his wife and child. He was of Mexican descent, and grew up in quite a conservative family. He had just missed the hippie revolution; he hadn't gone to university, and didn't join any of the movements that were then still active in the University of California at Berkeley. He had narrowly avoided the turmoil of that period, and had lived a fairly contented if uneventful life. He lived in a very plain flat, about thirty square feet, without a single painting or photograph on the wall. When he finished high school, with rather poor results, he had set off to find a job in the traditional way.

I took a liking to the man, and would often sit with him in cafés chatting about his CV and his life to try and help him find the way to success. The first job he found was as a barista in a café called Choc Full of Nuts. He worked there for a good six months, during which time I would often visit, as I was fond of their coffee. Then he went on to KFC for six months, followed by a year at McDonald's. He was hardworking and dedicated, so his employers were always satisfied with him, and it looked as if he might just trundle along in these dead-end jobs for years and years fairly contentedly. But one day, one of his friends took him aside and said: 'Look, Manny, you're twenty-six now. If you're not independent and making your first decent wage by the age of thirty, you will be stuck forever. You will always remain nothing but a server in a cheap restaurant chain, for the rest of your life.' In a way, Manny was insulted by this advice, but it also gave him a much-needed shock. Soon after, he decided he would start his own business with his savings.

One day, when I met him at Choc Full of Nuts, he announced to me that he was starting his own business.

'I've quit my job!' he confided to me in a loud, excited voice, dropping two sugars rather splashily into his cup.

His old manager looked over at us. 'Are you trying to ask for your job back, Manny?' she asked with a grin.

'Oh no,' he replied happily, stirring his cappuccino vigorously. 'I'm starting my own business!'

I raised my eyebrows. 'That's exciting,' I said. 'So what's the business?'

'Well,' Manny said, 'so I was horse-riding with my son this weekend, and I had this great idea. Why don't I buy a horse? I said to myself.'

'A horse? And you're bringing it back to central New York? Have you suddenly inherited a fortune?'

'I'm going to start a taxi company!'

'What on earth are you talking about?'

'Oh hush; let me finish my story. So I bought the horse, then I went on to find an old buggy in an auction. I've started fixing it up. My idea is to start an old-fashioned horse-and-buggy taxi business right here in crowded old central New York! People will pay a fortune to some grumpy old man to sit in a yellow box in traffic for forty-five minutes. Instead, they could be seeing the sights, and feel like they're in a movie on the way to work! And it would be much quicker than walking.'

'I suppose it would certainly appeal to the green anti-pollution crowd in the Village, as well as tourists…'

'Exactly! It would even work for serious commuters. I'm not sure about tourists in our area, but we'll see…'

However, Manny's enthusiasm suffered its first setback quite soon. Having bought the horse and buggy and got them home, he discovered he could not get a taxi license. Now, he had managed remarkably good deals for both investments: the horse was a beautiful stocky thing which would have usually cost around $6,000, but it was nearing the end of its life and headed for the butchers, so it only cost him $500; and the buggy itself was only worth $500. He cleaned and repainted it for another $200, ending up with $1,200 of his savings left over.

Having committed to this business venture, he decided to give his taxi service a go even without a license. He started trying to find commuters in the Village, asking them if they were interested in riding instead of walking to work. 'It'll save you half an hour!' he would shout down, bumbling along the streets in his beat-up buggy with his ageing horse. He made rather a pathetic figure, perpetually stuck in traffic, being honked at by files of angry motorists. He did find a few takers, but unfortunately he kept being stopped by the police. In the end, with all the stopping and starting and traffic and police hassle, it would take him more than half an hour to get to Wall Street, by which time his few customers were more grateful to get out of the buggy than they had been for the ride. The business had almost no repeat customers, apart from one neighbour who used the service because he felt sorry for his friend Manny. The ultimate setback came when the police gave him their final warning: he must get a proper license, or they would take away his horse. Manny understood at last that his taxi plan was doomed.

Over a gloomy coffee, I suggested that he consider the idea of tourism again and forget about taxis. He should think of the horse and buggy they offer in Disneyland, but in New York. It turned out that this was possible, and the city let him set up his horse and buggy in front of the Plaza Hotel, near Central Park South. All of a sudden Manny's luck seemed to change. The beat-up buggy he found at some auction in New Jersey appealed hugely to tourists seeking what felt like an authentic, old-timey American experience. Manny switched entirely to tourism, and became one of only three original horse-and-buggies to offer this service in 1975. Of course, nowadays, there are dozens and dozens.

I was in New York quite recently, so I looked Manny up. We met up for lunch in the Village.

'Well, I guess you made it as an independent businessman!' I said proudly, as he sat down across from me in a suit. 'Remember that silly friend who thought you would give up before you were thirty?'

He smiled. 'Well, I've now been successful for thirty years. You know I've never forgotten that conversation we had, where you told me I should consider tourism. You were a real help to me in those difficult days. Let me offer you a free ride, as a sign of how grateful I am for your advice! Now there's no way I'm taking you to Wall Street,' he added hastily. 'I'm not licensed to go there anymore. But name anywhere else you want. Even the Metropolitan Museum of Art. I seem to remember you were an art man.'

'Well,' I replied, 'as a matter of fact, I had intended to visit the Met at some point on this trip. Shall we say tomorrow?'

'Absolutely!'

When I saw Manny's new buggy, I could not believe my eyes. It was a brightly-painted thing with shiny new leather and brass tacks; the horse was a sprightly young white mare covered in feathers, all strapped up in a gorgeous antique saddle. And there was Manny, wearing a smart dark costume and a top hat, exactly like the nineteenth century coach-and-buggy men of Old New York. Inside, the buggy was incredibly comfortable. I rode around New York for a few hours, feeling like a gentleman even if I looked like a tourist. At the end of the trip, I climbed down in front of the museum steps.

'I can't let you do this for free,' I told Manny, reaching for my wallet.

'Oh yes you will,' he responded at once, hopping down from the buggy. 'I don't need your money. I have a big house in Westfield, New Jersey now. I have a big garage for the buggy. I have a five bedrooms and two acres of land. I feed my horse well. I even have another horse for when my main horse gets tired. Look,' he said, reaching into his own wallet. 'I even have a card! Have a look.'

He handed me his card, which had his name written with elaborate scrolls and a picture of a horse on it. Reluctantly, I put away my wallet.

'Well, I wish you all the best of luck!' I told him.

'Oh, I don't need luck anymore,' he replied. 'I've found success.'

My paternal grandmother got married in her early twenties to a man already well into his fifties. My grandfather was an industrialist, who worked hard all his life running a group of tanneries. He was a very serious man, who began to grow irritable in his later years.

'I'm sure it was just the natural dawning of the andropause,' I told my grandmother with a grin one afternoon, a few months after my grandfather had passed away. 'I can't imagine he would have appreciated that diagnosis, though!'

'Oh, you saw almost nothing of what your grandfather could be like!' she said with a smile.

'You must have had to be so patient,' I mused aloud to her. 'As a young mother with three kids in your early thirties, having not only to look after my father and my two aunts, but also to cook and clean and iron like every other housewife during the Depression... It sounds exhausting!'

She smiled. 'Oh, it was, but it was the same for everyone. In some ways we were lucky, as our family had plenty of resources thanks to your grandfather's hard work. And we did have some lovely moments of peace. Your grandfather would come home for lunch every day; he loved to sit in the courtyard if the weather was nice.'

'I suppose it was a nice break from long days in the office and the factories.'

'Exactly. I would have lunch ready for him...'

'...like a good wife,' I continued with a smile, 'carrying some beautiful, elaborate meal on a nice porcelain dish, on a silver tray, and then enjoying it side by side peacefully. Right?'

My grandmother smiled gently. 'Well, something like that. Perhaps not always peacefully. I'm sure I've told you that your grandfather could be rather difficult about his taste in food. He didn't like anything spicy, and he rarely approved of any sauce of mine that hadn't been stewed for several hours. He was also quite particular about the way his steak or lamb chops were cooked. Oh, he could be quite ridiculous at times, the rogue.' My grandmother shook her head with a sad smile. 'He got into this outlandish habit of showing his disapproval of my cooking by throwing away the entire dish.'

'You mean the plate as well?'

'Oh, yes. If he disagreed with the seasoning, that was the end of our pleasant lunchtime. Up in his hands the porcelain plate would go, and off it would fly, usually into the neighbours' garden. Do you remember the Dahnmanns?'

'Only vaguely. I think I must have met them once or twice.'

'Well they were truly wonderful neighbours, very patient, and keen to make an effort to get along. They were an old couple themselves, and clearly wanted to avoid having difficult relations with us. So they would either clean up the dish if it had survived its fall and bring it back to us, or tidy up the mess if the plate had broken. But one day, something changed.'

'Did the Dahnmanns rebel?'

'Something like that. One day I served your grandfather leftovers of a stew I had made for the rest of the family. You know how your aunties like their spice, so it was a rather hotter stew than I usually made for my husband. I did warn him, but he paid me no heed, and burnt his tongue. He really lost his temper that day, oh my! He stood up and flung the whole dish along with the silver platter into the neighbours' garden, before launching into a long complaint directed at me.'

'And I suppose you reacted by rushing off to the kitchen to make him a new lunch, like the wonderful wife you are?'

'Well, yes,' she admitted. 'But when I got into the kitchen, I heard a loud cry from outside, followed by the sound of your grandfather's laughter. It turns out that the silver platter he had thrown away had come back to hit him in the head.'

'Like some kind of boomerang? But that's impossible!'

'So it seemed to us. But we quickly realised that the real explanation was less to do with bizarre aerodynamics and more with the simple fact that our long-suffering neighbours the Dahnmanns had apparently had enough of us throwing our lunches into their lawn, and had decided to throw it right back! So this huge silver tray, almost two feet long, came flying back, discus-style, and hit my husband squarely in the head. The funniest thing about this story is the way he reacted though. I expected him to really lose his temper when he figured out what had happened. Instead, he sat down quietly, then stood up again, and came to the kitchen door where I was standing. "My dear wife," he said, "I'm so sorry for being inconsiderate about your cooking. This bump on my head, this is a sign from God. This bump is a divine punishment for my ungratefulness and bad temper. I must go and apologise to our poor neighbours. Don't worry about cooking more food. Sit with me afterwards."' My grandmother burst out laughing. 'Of course this benevolent transformation only lasted the rest of the day, in terms of mood. Although, to do your grandfather's memory credit, I must admit that he never threw away his lunch again. That encounter did wonders for our relations with the Dahnmanns, as well.'

'I suppose it must have done them good to get their frustration out of their system just once!'

'That's probably true. They really were wonderfully patient neighbours.'

JAMES BOND IN BELGRAVIA

James Bond has been a universally-recognised figure of adventure and style for the last fifty years, and his iconic mix of fearlessness and debonair charm carried has no less than seven actors to fame. Two of these happened to be my neighbours when I lived in Belgravia: Roger Moore and Sean Connery. As far as I knew, they didn't share the character's propensity for handguns or loose women, although they did both own fast cars. When I met the actors in person, it was quickly obvious that they were a sight less debonair than the legendary secret service member.

I used to see Sean Connery regularly when I was out jogging. We often did that awkward thing where we would be running at about the same pace, and thus would appear to be following each other around Eaton Square. Considering that this was James Bond I was running behind, a man who should be able to jump out of a plane and fight underwater, he didn't seem to be in much better shape than I was. Sometimes he would look back over his shoulder awkwardly, as if to check I wasn't a team of leather-jacketed paparazzi, or to make sure I wasn't gaining too much on him. It was as if we were in a sort of unspoken race. He was always fairly polite to me, although I don't think we were ever properly introduced. We were simply sports partners by coincidence. I have to say I wish I had been better acquainted with him, so I could have told him to get rid of that beard. He was much more elegant before, in his smooth 007 days, although a friend once told me that he had to wear a toupee in all the Bond films as his hairline was already receding. I would probably have also told him that the only decent James Bond film he was involved in was *Goldfinger*, although he made some fabulous other films like *The Untouchables*, *The Medicine Man*, and *Entrapment*.

One conversation we did have involved me jokingly asking if I could buy his Aston Martin 1964 – James Bond's car.

'Do you still have it?' I asked.

Connery laughed. 'It's probably in an auction somewhere,' he replied. 'If you want it, you should look it up.'

Many years later I did in fact come across the famous sports car in an auction, but I decided against purchasing it as I already had an Aston Martin by that time.

My principal experience of Roger Moore was also distinctly different from the movies, and also involved cars: he used to consistently park his Rolls Royce in my designated parking space in front of my house. I would have to drive my blue Daimler Jaguar, which had a bigger engine than his car, around the block to find a space for it, and naturally this bothered me. There was little I could do but glower at his big brown Rolls, as he was frequently out of town and left his car behind. In the few conversations we had when he was in London, I gathered that he had a country house and spent a lot of time in Paris and Hollywood for his films. He usually begrudgingly agreed to move his car, and then never did anything about it. This is how the conversations usually went, if I tried to accost him as he pulled up in front of my building

'Hello, Mr. Moore.'

There would be a long silence while I was studiously ignored.

'Mr Moore, excuse me,' I would say, politely tapping on the window.

'Yes?' he would reply impatiently.

'You've parked your car in my spot,' I would say, figuring cutting to the chase was the best approach.

'What do you want?'

'I said you've parked your car in my spot. In front of my building. Why don't you park in front of your own house?'

'What?' he would snap, without rolling down the window.

'Your car. It's in my spot,' I would repeat loudly.

'Do you want an autograph? Please go away.'

'I want you to move your car. My wife will be home soon and we need the spot.'

'You want a picture of my car?'

'Please. Move. Your. Car,' I ended up almost shouting, so that there was no possible way he could not have heard me.

'Get my driver to move it,' he might mutter, although the driver was still sitting right next to him. Alternatively, if he happened to be in a better mood, he might agree to move it later, although of course he never did. I don't think Roger Moore set much store by good neighbourly behaviour. I suppose most celebrities hardly consider it a priority.

I actually ran into him a few times in the burgundy saloons of the exclusive St James Club, which is in a Parisian château near my house in France. I would see him sitting in the library, surrounded by mahogany and leather, looking incredibly bored as he fended off requests for autographs. He always came across as something of a snob, which was a shame for a man who appeared so charming on screen! I have to say I wasn't particularly fond of Moore's Bond films either, especially when I found out he didn't do any of his own stunts, although he did get the best Bond girls. *The Man with the Golden Gun* I enjoyed slightly because it had one of my friends in it: Hervé Villechaize, , who used to come to my parties when I lived in New York. Furthering my mixed feelings about Roger Moore, around that time, there were rumours running around that his relationships with his successive wives were troubled and occasionally involved physical violence... All of this only served to confirm my conviction that playing James Bond did not help make anyone more of a gentleman.

In the end, Moore sold his Eaton Square place back to the Grosvenor Estate, at which time I contemplated buying it, but the apartment was such a state when my wife and I had a look around that we decided firmly against it.

'James Bond would never have lived in this mess,' she said.

To which I replied: 'Yes, but neither would he have parked in our drive!'

In the 1970s and into the 1980s, the bank for which I worked had an important Japanese partner, which as a young man gave me the chance to travel to many vibrant Japanese cities. I had the privilege of staying at some of the finest five-star hotels: luxury establishments like the Hyatt and the Ritz-Carlton in Tokyo, Osaka, and Kyoto. These were places where one's every want and need was taken care of, which is exactly what you need after a long day. Many of these luxurious hotels were built out of reinforced stone or marble, sturdy structures which looked like they would never shift an inch no matter what the weather threw at them. That being said, some of the hotels were also built in a more locally traditional way, out of pressed wood and cardboard.

While it might have seemed strange to the uninformed eye, these flimsy-looking houses were actually how the Japanese protected themselves against the often extreme weather. I had learned in school that Japan suffered from high winds, earthquakes and terrifying tsunamis, and that in these types of situations the last thing someone needed was a house made of bricks collapsing down on top of them. With the lightweight materials, the residents of these houses could wake up to a scene of devastation and get out before they were harmed.

What I had learned in my sixth grade geography classes served me well when I entered one of these buildings that appeared to be made of only paper and cardboard. I reminded myself that the roof was reinforced with plywood, light yet effective, and that I was completely safe in such a place. Often it was easy to forget within a matter of minutes that one wasn't in a Western-style building.

The houses and hotels were built to accommodate even the fussiest traveller, and often they had Jacuzzis or another source of clean, hot water. Japan is famous for its thermal waters, and houses are often built around natural hot springs in a way that marries man-made structures with the natural world very pleasantly. This was especially true in Kyoto, where there are many chances to get away from the city and enjoy the bathing areas. Indeed there were many intriguing things about my Japanese trips and the places I was able to stay.

The downside of these houses and hotels was the thinness of the walls. It was sometimes possible to hear a fellow traveller coughing or sneezing in the next room. This did not bother me per se – as long as my temporary new neighbours were fairly quiet and kept their voices down, there was no real problem. However, not everybody was quiet and kept their conversations to themselves.

One night in Osaka, I was unfortunate enough to be in a room near a couple who, throughout the evening, went from loud talking to actual shouting. This man and woman became progressively more explosive in their conversation and I was forced to listen to their little drama playing out. It sounded as though they were in the room with me, so loud that I had to lift my head more than once to check that they hadn't accidentally burst through my door! It was a sleepless night indeed, and their argument didn't stop until it was already too late for me to get any rest at all. It was only really on this night that I realised how badly insulated the hotels built of cardboard were. They might have been safe in a natural disaster, but safety didn't help me to sleep well through the storms of other people's problems.

On another trip away to a different part of Japan, I was just preparing myself for bed when I heard another rather noisy disagreement breaking out. Given that I had, at this point, travelled to Japan a fair few times, I recognised the language that the two men were using, yet could understand essentially none of what they were saying. Whatever they were talking about, they were definitely using very harsh words, and their voices rough and angry. So much so, in fact, that it sounded as though the fight might turn physical at any moment.

I waited and hoped that they would either calm down or go out or something that would allow me to get the rest I so desperately needed. However, their fight carried on, and I was moved to action. It wasn't just that I needed to sleep – although, admittedly, that was a large part of it – but that I was genuinely concerned about the violence in their voices. It seemed to me that such arguing could spell real trouble.

I went down to speak to the hotel reception staff, hoping that they could intervene and break up the argument.

'Excuse me,' I said to the man behind the front desk, 'there seems to be... ah, some kind of altercation in the room next to mine. It's becoming quite a nuisance.' I explained my concern about their fight becoming more violent, and asked if the hotel had staff on hand to deal with such a situation.

The man at reception looked at me sceptically.

'A fight? In our hotel?' he asked. I cringed a bit. It sounded as though he didn't believe a word I was saying, and he looked at me as though I might be mad. But then he asked: 'Which room are you in, sir?' in the same voice. He sounded rude and confrontational but slowly, the idea dawned on me that this might simply be how he spoke.

So perhaps this was also how the Japanese men upstairs were speaking. Maybe they weren't fighting at all, but simply having a discussion that sounded raucous to the unaccustomed ear. But it did sound so like somebody who was engaged in a fight. I was used to speaking with soft-spoken Japanese partners, not those who were relaxed and talking in a way that perhaps came more naturally.

'I guess perhaps there's been a mistake,' I said, a little sheepishly. 'But if you could check, I'd appreciate it. Just in case.'

He smiled at me. He was probably used to travellers such as myself assuming the worst when overhearing what to the Japanese were normal conversations.

'I'm sure it's nothing to worry about,' he told me, but he came with me to listen to the argument that was still going on. Whatever he heard, it only made him smile a little more.

'Ah, sir. These are very respectable businessmen, like yourself. They are not fighting, not at all! Only talking business, negotiating terms.'

I stared at him. 'You're sure about that?' It was hard to believe that something which sounded so confrontational could be just a conversation about business. I had heard my fair share of heated discussions in meetings, but not like this, and certainly not in hotel rooms.

But I was heartily reassured that my worry was all for naught. The receptionist reassured me that he knew the two gentlemen in question; he even gave me their names, and I was surprised to find out that I had actually met them earlier that same day. They were the clients of my partner in Japan and, from what I had seen of their behaviour, were not the sort of men who fought. They were quiet, thoughtful, and intelligent.

'It does sound like a disagreement,' I told the receptionist as he saw me into my room, 'doesn't it?'

He shook his head. 'They're only talking, sir!' he assured me cheerfully, still sounding vaguely like he was trying to start an argument himself.

Amazing, I thought, that the accent of the Japanese could be so rough when not moderated. I thanked him and apologised for taking up his time with what had turned out to be a wasted journey.

Nevertheless, I decided in that moment that, safe or not, I rather preferred the hotels made of concrete and marble, because at least you couldn't hear everything that was going on around you. A tsunami seemed a lot less likely than ending up stuck next door to noisy neighbours.

THE INTERMEDIARIES:
PHONEY NEIGHBOURS

In Paris I specialised in oil finance: our bank funded oil and mineral trading, opened letters of credit, and gave guarantees to mine prospectors. It was a fairly powerful and glamorous organisation. Most of the work we did was on the international stage, so we would always have rich clients coming in and out of our bank from producing countries: the Gulf nations, Ecuador, Indonesia, and Malaysia, as well as from the rich Western consumer nations. We were also involved in real estate financing. We had always been an active, profitable set-up, as we specialised in areas that limited our risks and allowed us to have employees that were specialists in their subject.

Our office was in a nice part of Paris. Our neighbours in the next-door building for the first year included a high fashion company, a military complex, a law firm, and a notary's office. Our bank, which was a hub of activity at all times, stood apart in its own building, and our clients would climb out of their limousines and mingle with the ladies in furs and haute couture and the grandfathers checking the time on their Rolexes as they went for another meeting about their wills and testaments with the next-door lawyers. We always maintained friendly relations with the businesses that surrounded us, although we had little cause for interaction.

But after the first year of our success, we started to notice changes occurring around us. First the fashion company closed, so suddenly that we wondered if there had been a death in the management, or perhaps if the offices had suffered some terrible cockroach infestation and had to be evacuated at once. We were not so far off with the latter theory: all of a sudden, we realised that the building had been practically completely taken over by real estate agents. Shortly after that, the lawyers and notaries, who traditionally inherit their practice from their parents or grandparents along with the clients, vanished in their turn.

This time the plague that came to replace them was one of oil traders and brokers, some of whom had represented our old clients. It was a huge and unexpected change. These newcomers must have offered substantial amounts of key money and paid outrageous prices just to be able to kick out these long-term tenants and move in at once. It was as if the entire block had suddenly become infested with insects or pests that had forced all the other respectable inhabitants to flee. These traders swarmed outside the building and seemed to spin webs outside the door of my bank. At first, I assumed it was our clients they were after. Their shiny vitrines were quickly filled with pictures of outrageously expensive apartments in Paris or the Bahamas. The oil traders slipped brochures under our doors almost daily, obviously hoping we might pass them on to our clients. But one day I understood what they were really after: me.

When I came to work, all of a sudden I was treated as if I were some sort of pop star; a King Midas, or Croesus: 'Can you give me any tips on the oil trading today?' they buzzed. 'Can I give you this cake my wife made, or this expensive bottle of wine?' they wheedled. 'Oh, and can you help me finance my project?' they whined. 'Hey Brad, can I borrow five million? I have this shipment of fuel oil that has to leave from Bulgaria in the morning.' All of them seemed to have tried to make it appear as though they had just run into me, but they all seemed to have had the same idea at once, so the overwhelming effect was as comical as it was annoying. I had to literally elbow them aside to get through to the front door.

'For God's sake just let me have my coffee!' I had to roar, swatting them away. 'Do I need to get mosquito netting installed? Just because you are my neighbours doesn't mean you're immediately entitled to these ridiculous privileges.'

'Would you like to advertise our new apartment blocks to your clients?' they cried. 'Will you come to lunch with me and my partner tomorrow?' 'Can I borrow a million pounds? I'll repay you within a month, I swear. It's for this Russian deal…'

'Why on earth would annoying me like this make me want to help you? Are you crazy? Go away! I have work to do!'

'But that's why we moved in!' one of the younger traders piped up, pretending this was a joke. 'My wife even made you some muffins!'

'I don't want muffins!' I cried out. 'I want to go to work in peace! Go away! I have no interest in your stupid projects!'

'But I'm your neighbour!' one particularly persistent man continued.

'You don't lend to your relatives; you don't lend to your

neighbours,' I replied as patiently as I could. 'And do you know what the funny thing is? If you people had lived somewhere else and approached me in a more respectful way, maybe I could have done great business with you! But the assumption that you have these privileges automatically bestowed upon you because you suddenly, suspiciously, come to live less than fifty metres from my desk is just ridiculous! Now I just see you as obnoxious neighbours, as opposed to potential partners. Also, I really hope the previous occupants made you pay a lot of money.'

'But you see, we're potential partners. We work in the same line of business!'

'No, *you* appear to work in *my* line of business. Trading companies, oil companies, real estate financing: that was all *our* business. You traders, you're good for nothing. We don't need you. You're just a bunch of charming pimps with two telephones. Look at you, with your cakes and your stupid loan requests. Why does real estate even exist? Just to charm you into believing things are better than they are. I'd be perfectly capable of choosing a house on my own, thank you very much. You haven't got a chance of working with me: I don't trust any of you.'

'But I'm your neighbour!' one of them protested.

'Well, you're welcome to mow my lawn or borrow a cup of sugar. But there is no way in hell you are going to get five million dollars off me before I've had my first cup of coffee.'

HERSHEY BAR DRAMA

For a time I had the privilege of working in a very nice office at the top of 30 Rock, which is one of the most impressive Art Deco buildings in the Rockefeller Center complex that fills the area between Fifth and Sixth Avenues. This was in a rather successful period in the late 1970s and early 1980s. In one part of our company, we did trading; in the other, we offered investment advice. My own office was a spacious and modern one, with big glass windows looking out over the New York skyline. I had a large desk, a potted plant, and easy access to several of my favourite landmarks. However, one of the best things about working in 30 Rock was the kiosk in the front lobby.

I liked to take the occasional snack break. When I felt a craving for a chocolate bar, or some salted nuts, all I had to do was take the elevator down and walk across the beautiful marble mosaic in the lobby, stopping just short of the revolving front door. The kiosk stood right next to the bank of elevators; all ten glass boxes lined up expectantly. The small shop happened to stock tobacco and newspapers, as well as my very favourite chocolate bar, the Hershey bar with almonds. This made it an excellent neighbour. Perhaps unusually, my interest in this particular candy bar was the almonds rather than the chocolate. I have always found American almonds to be far tastier than any you can find in Africa or the Far East: they tend to be small, perfectly shaped, and sweet in flavour. I far preferred them to the chocolate they were encased in; in fact, on days when I was feeling particular impatient, I would sometimes pick off the milk chocolate, and just eat the little American almonds.

I also liked Mars bars, which were an American novelty to me at the time, with their sweet, chewy centres. Not that I was always going for snacks: I usually just walked outside to pick up a newspaper. In those days, newspapers in New York were incredibly bulky because of the advertisements inside, which always seemed to take up hundreds of pages. This meant that they were rarely stocked in a rack inside a building lobby, as they are now, but were usually sold from shops.

Whatever it was I happened to be buying, the little news kiosk served the same purpose to me as I would imagine a local pub would to a working Englishman. I had the same kind of complicated relationship with the kiosk's owners as one might to a cantankerous bar manager: they might provide the things one needs on a daily basis, but I didn't necessarily get on with them. There is usually a kind of recognition, but few shared topics of conversation beyond the weather. These service providers form their own special brand of neighbours, both entirely necessary and, at times, managing to be difficult or annoying despite the fact that they were essentially strangers. In the case of the kiosk, this wasn't helped by the fact that there seemed to be a new owner every year or so. When I first started working at 30 Rock, the kiosk outside was run by a friendly old American man in his seventies. In fact, the next two or three owners fit exactly the same type, each as stooped and white-haired as his predecessor; to the point that I began to wonder whether they simply passed the business on between friends or relatives. After that, however, it was taken over by a series of immigrants: an Italian, followed by an Egyptian, then a tall Indian man.

I didn't know these later owners as well, as by that time I was living in Europe and only coming back to my old office on the occasional business trip. This pattern would continue for a good fifteen years. However, I did have a few memorable encounters with the Indian owner, one of which still bothers me to this day. What happened was this: one day, on one of these business trips, I arrived on a sunny morning, straight from the airport. I was a little peckish, and decided to stop for an almond Hershey bar on my way into the building. In those days, a chocolate bar cost less than a dollar; in fact, closer to twenty-five cents. I picked up a Hershey bar and handed it over to the kiosk owner. Reaching into my pocket, I discovered that I had no change, only large bills. I realised then that I had just taken money out at the airport, having come over from Europe less than an hour earlier. Well, I figured he could deal with it. After all, working on the front doorstep of 30 Rock, I imagined the kiosk owner would have more than enough change to give me.

I handed over the hundred-dollar bill with an apologetic shrug. He handed me a bunch of coins, which I put into my pocket with a smile. As I was turning to walk back into work, it suddenly struck me that I should have been receiving far more cash than that. I drew the coins back out of my pocket, and counted out nine dollars. I walked back swiftly to the kiosk.

'I'm terribly sorry,' I said, 'but I believe you've short-changed me.'

The man cocked his head to the side. 'But sir,' he replied, 'you gave me ten dollars.'

'No,' I explained patiently, 'I've just come back from the bank. I only had hundred-dollar bills in my pocket. See?' I reached into my pocket and drew out another, as proof.

The man shook his head slowly, as if in complete disbelief. 'Sir,' he said, 'you gave me ten. Ten dollars. I gave you nine dollars back. That is the correct amount of change.'

'I gave you one hundred dollars!' I raised my voice, but tried not to lose my temper.

The man shook his head. 'Sir, I don't like this lying. Are you trying to rob me? I don't have that much money in my till.' Slyly, he pulled the drawer out and motioned for me to look over the counter. 'See? Nothing but tens and twenties. Most people pay in change,' he added pointedly, as if lecturing me on my behaviour; 'No-one has ever given me a hundred dollar bill, sir. Not even you.'

I was enraged to see that, of course, there was no trace of the hundred dollar bill in the drawer. 'Don't be ridiculous,' I said, 'you've obviously just hidden it under your desk, or put it in your pocket. You've just stolen from me!' I added.

'You're the one trying to steal from me,' he said calmly.

'I just *gave* you a hundred dollars!'

'Try and prove it,' he said. 'Now, if you'll excuse me, there are customers waiting in line behind you.'

I exhaled loudly. Looking behind me, I saw that it was true. In that moment, it seemed as if the man might have won: perhaps there was indeed no way to prove it. I had a meeting to get to, and I really didn't have the energy for a big fight that soon after a long transatlantic journey. Of course, there had never been any doubt in my mind as to whether it had been a hundred dollar note; there was no question that I had been robbed. To this day, the episode makes me angry when I remember it. I wish I had climbed over the counter and ransacked the drawers, or simply shaken the man by his collar until he gave up and admitted the truth. But at the time, none of it seemed worth the hassle. By the time I arrived back in my office, the almond Hershey's bar tasted like sawdust. In one sense, however, the joke was on him: from that day onwards, I always walked all the way to the other entrance of the Rockefeller Centre and bought my Hershey bars from a different kiosk. And I made sure he never got any custom from my colleagues, either!

A LONG TRIP WITH AIR FRANCE

I generally like going to the airport quite late, so as to save on waiting time; in the United States, I was often able to catch planes just ten minutes before their take-off. However, those golden days are long past. Security measures have become draconian all over the world. Nonetheless, I try to aim to get to the airport just an hour before take-off, at least for flights within Europe, but in recent years, I've started having a little trouble reading the computer screens that indicate the flight details. All the traditional boards with those big white, spinning, clicking letters and numbers seem to have been replaced with tiny computer screens, which they place high up. Needless to say, this is a little difficult for me with my eyesight. Consequently, this year, I asked for assistance. I didn't need someone to push me around in a wheelchair, or even really give any support, except to help me read the screens and then point me in the right direction so I could get to the gate on my own.

Considering that this was a new development for me, I decided to leave a good two and a half hours between my arrival at the airport and the supposed departure of the plane, which was at 7.45 pm. I was intending to fly to London City Airport, in order to celebrate an important birthday with a family member. I had managed to coordinate all my children so that we could meet up for the evening celebration. I was travelling with my six youngest children from Geneva via Paris, and the others would meet us in the U K.

However, a series of events conspired to make us somewhat later than I had planned. For one thing, my daughters love to shop at the airport, so we spent a little time looking around all the fancy shops. Secondly, our boarding passes had a very curious code for the terminal, so we mistakenly headed to Orly South instead of Orly West. Delays notwithstanding, by the time we arrived at Orly West, we still had a good hour and a half before the flight was meant to take off. I assumed we had nothing to worry about. As we had no luggage, we were immediately handed boarding passes. At this point, the girl by the check-in asked us to sit for a moment and wait for the assistance to come and find me. We complied quite happily, thinking we still had plenty of time.

The girl who had given us our passes was a slight, blonde girl who couldn't have been a day over twenty-three. She had elaborately styled blonde hair, heavy makeup and glittering fingernails. She was assisted in her position by another three young women, one of whom was filing her nails, and the other two of whom were chatting about their respective hairstyles. There were admittedly few other people travelling on the flight, but it still seemed like they must have had something better to do! Still, we were quite relaxed and had time to kill, so I didn't really mind at the time. I chatted to the blonde girl for a long time about what it was like working for Air France, where she had travelled to, and other neutral topics to pass the time. She didn't have any particularly interesting insights, but it was a good excuse to keep her attention. Every few minutes, I would ask her if she knew where our assistance was.

'Don't worry,' she would say every time. 'It's all here in the computer. They must be on their way right now. They usually arrive within ten minutes.'

Over an hour later, however, I was starting to worry.

'Look,' I told the girl, 'are you really sure they're coming? Shouldn't we just go to the gate on our own?'

'Oh, that won't be necessary. It'll only be a minute longer.'

She smiled brightly and went back to chewing her gum. A few minutes later, she started packing her things into her satchel.

'Where are you going?' I asked worriedly.

'I've finished my shift,' she explained blankly. 'Don't worry! Someone will replace me.' She flounced off, and a tall man stepped into her place. 'There's no problem,' he assured me at once. 'Assistance will be on its way at once. It says so right here on the computer.'

'I know the gate,' I told him, increasingly impatiently. 'I can just walk there on my own. There's not much time before take-off!'

'Oh no,' he said. 'You requested assistance; you must wait for it.'

Just ten minutes before the plane was due to depart, I lost patience completely. Ignoring the protestations of the tall man, I herded my children through customs and security. The whole process only took about five minutes; we had no trouble. The gate turned out to be just the other side of security. We rushed over to the gate with our passports and boarding passes, only to have the woman manning it shake her head.

'Oh, you're here,' she said with a little roll of her eyes. 'Where have you been?'

'We didn't get the assistance,' I explained, slightly out of breath. 'It never came. But we're here now, we have everything.' I waited expectantly.

'I'm sorry, sir,' she said in a blasé tone, looking down at her fingernails. 'Boarding is closed.'

'Closed? Well open it up!' I demanded. 'We have a flight to catch!'

'I can't do that.'

'We've been waiting hours for your assistance! This is completely unfair! This is your mistake, not ours!' I tried to explain.

'The gate is closed, and the plane has already taken off,' she explained. 'You're late,' she added unhelpfully.

I took a deep breath. 'I have been waiting just fifty yards away for almost two hours,' I told her. 'With your silly blonde co-workers chatting about their hair and their nails while my children and I waited and waited and waited. This is completely ridiculous.'

She gave a little shrug. 'You requested help. You had to wait for help. There's nothing we can do about it.'

'Yes, there is. You can find me another flight, as fast as possible. We're tired, and we're hungry, and we absolutely must be in London tonight for this birthday.'

'There's really nothing I can do. My manager will deal with that,' she replied without a smile. 'Now, first off, you'll have to go back through security.'

I sighed, realising there was little I could accomplish here. I assembled my children, and went back through the rigmarole of security, before trying to find someone who could assist me. Everyone I asked seemed to be vapidly chewing gum, without a clue of what was going on. It was enough to drive anyone crazy. Luckily, the manager, an older woman with a pencil skirt and a tight bun, finally made an appearance. I was relieved to see someone who looked a little more serious and severe, but, although she was a little more sympathetic, it turned out she had little help to offer us either. I had to threaten the company with a lawsuit before she made much of an effort to organise us another flight, and she still went away for almost an hour before reporting back.

The news she brought back then was even worse. 'I'm afraid there are no more flights.' I looked up at her, dejected. By this time, it was long past the younger children's bedtime. 'Don't worry,' she added with a somewhat more solicitous air, 'we'll give you vouchers for a hotel.'

'A hotel? It's not even nine o'clock! How are there no more flights?'

'Well, there is one more flight to London, but it's with BA, so you would have to pay the full, last minute price. The next Air France flight isn't until the morning.' She cast her eyes over her watch. 'In fact, even that BA flight would be rather tight at this point. It's leaving from Charles de Gaulle airport, which is a good fifty minutes away from here. I'm sorry, but I don't think you'll be out of here before tomorrow morning.'

After a long debate, the manager offered to give us vouchers to get Eurostar tickets. Desperate to try to arrive that night, I agreed, and travelled across some truly disreputable parts of the city to get us to the terminal at Gare du Nord. No matter how much we hurried, we arrived to find that we had missed the last train. I could hardly believe our bad luck. I could even see the empty Eurostar carriages sitting there like duds, unused. All the ticket offices were closed: the place was like a ghost station. Nobody was there at all except a few suspicious men, most of whom looked either like drug addicts or Mafiosi. There was no apparent police force or security around, so we hurried out of there as quickly as we could.

At this point, I realised our options were pretty limited. In a single moment of luck, I realised I had the keys to our Paris apartment in my pocket. I don't usually carry them around, but happened to have left them in my jacket. I reassured my children that we would get some rest, then set out again in the morning.

Unfortunately, we then were stuck in a roadblock on the *périphérique* for nearly three hours. By this time, the children were very hungry and starting to cry. I wasn't in a particularly light mood myself. But I invented some games for them to play, and tried to keep everyone calm until we arrived at the house. All of us were so tired by that point that we collapsed without eating or cleaning our teeth. We slept barely three hours before setting out again for the airport.

The next morning, tired but determined, we arrived at the airport with more than two hours to spare before our 7.15 flight – I wasn't taking any chances. We found our favourite Air France neighbour, the blonde girl with the chewing gum, sitting at her desk giggling with her friends. When I told her our miserable story, however, she was quite apologetic, as was her boss, who turned up a few minutes later.

'We had a computer breakdown,' he explained. 'All the messages told us assistance was on the way, so it was the proper policy to keep you waiting. However, the people at assistance never received a message at all. They didn't know anybody needed them.'

'Well, that's ridiculous. Someone should have sent me through. All I was waiting for was a man in a yellow jacket to walk fifty yards with me! Because of this, I missed a very important family birthday. Neither I, nor any of my young children have had a wink of sleep. It's been incredibly stressful. We've been travelling for nigh on eighteen hours, and I'm still not even on a plane!'

'I really am sorry,' the blonde girl said, with an insincere simper.

The manager looked at her sternly, then kindly at me. 'We'll investigate as soon as we have all the details.'

'You'll still be hearing from my lawyers,' I replied firmly.

Meanwhile, surrounded by my children and waiting for assistance once more, I determined that I would wait only fifteen minutes, and set off if nobody had turned up within an hour of the flight's departure. I was taking no chances this time; there was no way on earth I intended to be anywhere but on that plane to London when it took off. I took the time to commit a few small acts of revenge upon the airport and its inhabitants. First of all, I told the security people that there was a severe strain of chicken flu in Paris that day that was probably being passed on by every single boarding card they handled. Next, in duty free, I paid for my six Euros of chocolate with a hundred-Euro note, and told the clerk that all the bills in circulation were covered in killer germs. 'Don't you have a washing machine for Euros?' I asked her in mock horror. 'That's terrible! You're putting us all in danger, yourself first!' Finally, I convinced a devout Muslim man working in a coffee shop that the milk he was serving came in cases made from pork. I'm quite sure he nearly quit on the spot!

At last, the man in the yellow jacket appeared.

'I was beginning to think you were a myth!' I told him wryly, and he laughed.

'Ah, so you're the man who had the nightmare yesterday. I'm so sorry! You've suffered the worst kind of collateral damage. If it's any comfort, you're not alone. You see, the assistance service has just been outsourced to a private company. The transition has been complete chaos. Back in the day, we just used walkie-talkies, and we never had a problem. But the last month and a half has been a mess.'

'I hope they've been inundated with lawsuits.'

'Oh, absolutely,' he said cheerily. 'Feel free to contribute!'

I had to laugh. 'Well, I do wish you'd found me yesterday. Everything would have been much less horrible.'

'I really am sorry,' he said sincerely. 'The whole thing is a shambles, really. I'm thinking about quitting myself.'

'They should really change the slogan to *Air France, take your chance*,' I commented, before slipping him twenty Euros.

Finally, we arrived at the gate and boarded the plane. Although we made it to London in the end, we missed the birthday party. I still intend to sue Air France: I won't win, but I might damage their reputation. It's a real shame to see how the company has gone down the drain. I certainly hope the girl at the check-in desk gets in trouble for her incompetence, even if it was made up for by the assistance man when he finally did find me. Like in any situation in life, I try to see the good sides: in the end, after all, we made it to our destination, and I even think the terrible journey might have brought me closer to my children. We looked after one another and jollied each other through the whole thing, making it just about bearable. Perhaps the key here is that the only truly good neighbours are one's own family!

FIXING THE ROAD

In the early seventies I lived in a country house in Kent, a region which is truly the garden of England. It was a charming and calm area, with a few lakes and rivers running through the rolling countryside. Our house was built in 1410 and extended in 1620, as part of a vast country estate which consisted of two big houses, an orangery, two gatehouses, a coach house and a converted church. These wonderful old buildings were surrounded by three and a half acres of beautifully maintained woodland, vegetable gardens, and flowerbeds. These were approached by a road.

Over hundreds of years, this approach between the gatehouses down to the other buildings had been worn down by the coming and going of horses, carts, early automobiles, tractors, removal vans and taxis. In the process it had developed a series of increasingly deep ruts and potholes.

In 1975, the bills for car repairs were racking up, and I had had just about enough of having to clean the mud off my car every time we had visitors. I was rather proud of my cars, and I liked to look after them. Fixing the road was the obvious place to start. Recently, one of the neighbours' tyres had exploded, and I had no intention of putting my own cars in any such danger. So, that summer, I had a workman come in to have a look; he wandered up and down for a few minutes before giving me an estimate of one hundred and forty pounds for the repair of the road.

I sent a handwritten, softly-worded letter on Florentine paper to each of my six neighbours.

Dear neighbour,

The state of the road is a problem for all of us. We are a community, and we must look after our common property together. I am happy to organise the repair of the road, and the cost will be £20 each, which I'm sure you'll agree is substantially less than the cost of the damage to our cars.

Yours, Bradley Jamieson.

My neighbours were not poor people. These people probably regularly lost £20 notes in the washing machine and thought nothing of it. They were a retired couple, a very successful artist, a lawyer, a farmer who owned thousands of acres of land, his newlywed daughter, and an investor in precious and exotic woods, who lived with his young son. Yet I did not receive a single response to my letter. One month went by, then two and three. I would run into my neighbours occasionally when they walked their dogs pottered around in their gardens. Not a single one of them ever mentioned the state of the road, or offered me the twenty pounds.

'Hello,' I might say to the lawyer as he hurried by in his Mercedes, despite noticing that he had hastily begun to roll his windows up when he saw me. 'And how's your car?' I asked pointedly.

'Oh, it's fine, thanks for asking,' he replied breezily. Its new tyres were very muddy.

I could not resist adding: 'You know you could have avoided those expensive repairs by simply giving me twenty pounds?'

'Don't be silly, it had absolutely nothing to do with the road.'

'Your tyres exploded,' I reminded him.

'They were old,' he said defensively.

'Suit yourself!' I said, as loudly as I could whilst staying polite.

Another time, in October, I saw the artist walking her Labrador in the drizzle.

'Hello!' I called out to her.

'Oh, hello there, Mr Jamieson,' she said reluctantly.

'You don't happen to have those twenty pounds, do you?' I had to admit I was becoming rather impatient.

'Oh, I'm terribly sorry; I don't have a penny on me.' She did not offer to bring it over on a later date, but instead added a little snottily: 'The road's fine, you know. Just a few bumps.'

Her dog splattered happily through the mud.

'Just a few bumps?' I shouted. 'It's like a World War I trench!'

'Don't be silly,' she replied, pulling her dog along the mangled road.

The final straw was witnessing the wood-dealer's son falling over on his bicycle, then running away from me when I came out of my house to help. I realised they were all not just being lazy: they were now consciously avoiding me so as not to have to deal with the issue. All for a measly twenty pounds!

At this point, I composed another letter, which my wife talked me out of sending.

Dear neighbour,

Please put an end to this foolishness. This is your chance to prove that you are not lazy, incompetent, or as generally useless as you have been appearing as a community over the last eight months. I now understand that an Englishman's house really is his castle: a place where he can hide and not contribute to the community in the least. Where is your spirit of cooperation? Where is your love of your neighbours? Don't you see this would actually be to your financial advantage?

This is hardly an outrageous expense. You probably spend £20 on a briefcase. If you will not fix the road, let it fall to pieces. I hope all your dogs fall into potholes and all your tyres explode.

Yours, Bradley Jamieson.

I tore up the letter. Then I paid for the repairs. The road was fixed within a week. Not one of the neighbours ever mentioned the improvement; and I never received a single letter of thanks or comments in reply. It seems that sometimes, being a good neighbour is a thankless task.

Some neighbours are such an invisible presence in our lives that we don't really realise how crucial they are until we reflect on them, years later. Then we might see how often they surfaced in our lives; how seemingly insignificant meetings with them might have been more important than we first thought, or given weight to pivotal moments in the trajectory of our personal history.

Hamisch was one such presence. He was a neighbour of my family's house in Istanbul, so I would see him every time I went to Turkey on holiday. This happened often when I was a child, then more sporadically as I grew up. Hamisch worked in his family's shop, surrounded by large jute sacks of wheat that he bought wholesale, threshed and cleaned, then sold on to the village housewives and husbands. It was a self-contained operation, handed down from father to son over decades and decades. They bought the grain and dried it in the sun, then Hamisch would thresh it by hand himself with a flail, and package it before selling it on. The shop was filled with stacks and stacks of threshed wheat, the grain bundled up, ready to be carried off. He would sell it in large quantities, the smallest bag weighing a good ten kilos. The biggest size was forty or fifty kilos, which required a porter from across the street to be called in to help. The porter would then haul a bag over his brawny shoulders, and bring the wheat to a horse-drawn carriage or truck for the customer to take home.

When I first met him, Hamisch was a tall, strong, wide-shouldered man in his late twenties, with a swagger like Popeye and big, brown, almond-shaped eyes. He had long, thick hair that he shook when he was hot, and he worked incredibly hard every day of his life. As far as I can remember, he almost never stopped threshing with a hand-held wooden flail, and he almost never stopped talking. He was a fascinating figure who liked the company of children and seemed to rely on my rapt attention, as if I were the only spectator to the great sport of threshing he spent all day practising. I thought of him as a sort of Olympic athlete in his field. He was strong enough to throw ten kilos of grain into the air, then raise his stick and bring it down over and over on sheaves of harvested wheat. When I was a child, of course, I did not truly understand the logic of his act. The whole thing just looked like great fun! I used to love to sit on the floor of his shop, with the occasional customers going in and out around me. As I grew older, he patiently explained his trade to me.

'You see, boy,' he told me with a young man's grin, 'grains come with all these parts we don't want. We cannot eat everything. When you harvest wheat from the fields, it comes surrounded by dry sheaths, covered in dirt and all stuck together, with little mice in the bottom of the bag.' He waggled his dark eyebrows; I giggled. 'So after we buy it in bags all rough and ready, we let it dry in the sun until everything is nice and clean and rattles around when you move it. Then, what I must do is hit it with my magic stick and shake and shake it to separate out the grains that we'll be able to sell. Once everything is nice and dry, the grains fall out of their own accord, while the chaff and the mice go flying!'

'That's a strong kind of stick,' my inquisitive younger self commented. 'And you're a strong kind of man.'

Hamisch smiled, pleased at my interest. 'You're quite right. It's actually two sticks, as you can see, held together by a metal chain. I made this flail myself. See, I hold this one and swing the other around. It hits the pile of grain, loosens the husks, and all the delicious wheat falls out, ready to be sold, or cooked, or ground down into flour.'

'Can you eat the grains?' I asked, popping one into my mouth.

Hamisch shook his head gently, just as I found out the answer for myself. I spat out the hard grain, and he laughed. 'So impetuous,' he sighed. 'No, you cannot really eat the dry grains. If you pick them young from the stem in the field though, you can chew them.'

'Can I try the stick?' I asked, not to be discouraged.

'Maybe when you're a little older,' Hamisch replied. 'It's quite heavy, and can be dangerous. In fact, the flail has often been used as a weapon by peasants when they had nothing else to fight with! If you swing it hard and fast enough, it will break more than just grains.' Seeing my face light up with childish glee, he held the flail higher in the air, away from my hands. 'When you're older, I'll let you try.'

Day after day, I would sit there on the warm floor, surrounded by the sweet, dusty smell of wheat. Sometimes I would watch him work hard for hours and hours, until beads of sweat stood out on his brow. He would often tell stories as he worked, enjoying the captive audience I provided him with. Stories of his childhood, stories of his family, stories he had heard on the street. Sometimes I would bring a young friend or two with me, or one of my cousins would wander over from the house, but most times it was just the two of us between adult customers. I liked to think that Hamisch considered me a friend, although it's more likely that he was simply grateful for the company and the distraction. Still, he was kind, and paid close attention to me, which was all I needed. Often, he would stop for a long time to chat to a customer and sell some bags of wheat, but he would always remember where our conversation had been paused in order to come back to it.

In the end, I don't think I ever did wield the flail myself. As I grew older, I became far more interested in the business aspects of Hamisch's life than in the act of threshing; the way the shop was run as a family, with all the work conducted within one room. By the time I had become an adult myself, however, Hamisch began to open up to me more and more about the less idyllic aspects of running a small shop. 'I get so tired,' he confided in me one day, setting down the flail to sit down next to me on the floor. 'All my muscles just ache and ache.'

'The day is almost over,' I tried to comfort him. 'Soon you can go home and have a nice meal with your children.'

He grimaced. 'Don't get me wrong, I love my children, but they're pretty exhausting themselves. I just wish I could plant a big garden and spend my time there in peace. I'd love to grow my own potatoes, courgettes and strawberries. Maybe some grape vines. Just think what a joy it would be! Instead, I stand in this dark shop, threshing for seven hours a day. I've been doing the same thing all my life, now. It's no way to live. It's ageing me faster than I like.'

I looked closely at him. It was true, he had aged considerably in the five or six years since I had last seen him. His hair had gone white, and his face was marred by deep wrinkles. He looked a good fifteen years older than he was.

'Maybe you should take a holiday,' I suggested gently, suddenly acutely aware of my immaculate suit, and of the tears in his linen trousers.

'I can't,' he said. 'I have eight kids to feed. My kids exhaust me. My wife exhausts me. Everyone around me is complaining all the time. Oh god, and now I am too!' He gave a great barking laugh that instantly made him look five years younger.

I thought perhaps a more philosophical take might bring him comfort. 'Perhaps you just need to look for solace in your hard work: after all, there must be a pleasing simplicity to it, repeating the same task, completing it every day? It's a thousand times more satisfying than being a bureaucrat behind a desk, where nothing is ever done, and it's endlessly boring and frustrating. When I sit for hours and hours, how I wish I could be punching sheaves of wheat with a stick!'

Hamisch laughed bitterly. 'If you could feel what it's like to have hands as calloused as mine, you would think differently. I would love to sit still in a suit for ten hours on end, sipping coffee. It would be wonderful.'

'But you only have to work seven hours a day,' I tried to argue. 'Think of the variety of your work!'

'Now I have to work ten hours a day so I can feed my kids. My wife is pregnant again, too.'

I had to smile and shrug. 'I guess the grass is always greener on your neighbour's side of the fence. I'm sorry you're dissatisfied, though.' It was then that I realised how much I had grown in the time I had known Hamisch. Although we hadn't witnessed each other's ageing in anything but bursts, we had somehow formed a completely different relationship than the one we had when I was young. All of a sudden, I had realised that a man whom I once fervently admired had started to envy my life! We talked for a long time after that, sharing memories of the past, and dreams of our futures. It's in moments like these, in contact with the people and neighbours who pass through one's life, that one really comes to value one's growth and understand a little more of where one has come from.

RHONDA AND ROWAN

Some of the most difficult neighbours are those one knows best. Who hasn't lived with, or next to, someone very dear to their heart, who nonetheless managed at times to be the most infuriating person in the world? Who hasn't been driven mad by someone they still love sincerely? The love-hate relationship is a well-documented one: we have all experienced its complicated thrill. Spouses and children are in no way exempt from this rule, and neither are siblings.

My own children Rhonda and Rowan were a particularly fine example of this sort of love-hate neighbourly relationship. As a ten-year-old girl and a twelve-year-old boy respectively, it was hardly surprising that they would have the occasional squabble, but the two of them managed to turn it into a kind of fine art. The balance of power was quite something to witness; the rules and skills honed so finely they seemed more like war generals than pre-teens. So fine was their craft that I was unaware of their rivalry for the first five years of it. According to their version of family history, the feud began when they were just five and seven years old.

Rhonda and Rowan were quite exceptional children. Rhonda was the witty one, as charming as she was clever. She was sporty and artistic as well; as excellent at ballet as she was at breakdancing. She could win you over and cut you down in the space of a single minute, without losing her peppy smile. From a very young age, she was known for the elaborate practical jokes she orchestrated at the expense of her siblings; but there was a real spirit of fair play about her that kept these games from ever becoming unpleasant. Rowan, on the other hand, was a serious child most of the time, except when he became excited about a subject, and his enthusiasm bloomed almost visibly. He was the sensitive type, and he intended to be an actor, studying drama from a very young age. Tall and blonde, he was also an excellent basketball player. What he brought to the tradition of practical jokes was a combination of enthusiasm and quiet determination that was hard to rival. Just by comparing these two profiles one can easily see why the two siblings were so close and yet such fierce rivals: their personalities, like those of many brothers and sisters, were contradictory in some aspects, and complementary in others.

Many of their recurring fights had as their source the proximity of their bedrooms, as the children lived on a corridor right across from one another. For instance, Rowan, being quite an intense young man, sometimes liked to listen to his music rather loudly. If Rhonda was trying to study, or play a game, she would quickly get frustrated with this and decide she had to intervene. So the second he left the room to get a snack from the kitchen or even just to go to the bathroom, she would sneak into his bedroom and put chewing-gum over his light switch. This was a clever ploy, as it meant that he wouldn't notice it straight away. It would only be when he was getting ready for bed that he would realise he was unable to turn the light off.

Rowan did not fight back at once. Being a thoughtful child, he obviously had to find the perfect, discreet way to respond. In military terms, this would be the equivalent of staying up all night in his tent with his closest advisors, pushing little figurines around a map with a wooden ruler. At last, he came upon a solution. He snuck into his sister's room in the morning, when she was out playing in the garden, and painted her light switch the same pale green colour as the walls. This was the French, flat sort of light switch, so once it had changed colour, it was very nearly impossible to find it. The result was much the same as Rhonda's original prank, although it was somewhat more subtle, and a little more permanent.

Now, I don't allow my children to possess or even access the keys to their rooms, for security reasons: to avoid fire hazards, children locking themselves in, and hassle for the cleaners, amongst other things. This meant that the kids could go into each other's rooms essentially as they pleased. Of course, being well-brought-up, they were mostly respectful of each other's privacy, but this easy access did have the unfortunate side effect of facilitating their pranks. Imagine if all neighbours who squabbled could get into each other's private property so easily! The consequences would be interesting, to say the least.

Nonetheless, discreet tricks were the children's favourites for years and years. One time, Rowan decided to sneak into his sister's room and mix up all the stickers she had on the walls. Like many ten-year-old girls, Rhonda had spent a lot of time creating a mosaic of stars, butterflies and other small decorations across the wallpaper to personalise the bedroom a little. Rowan had something of an eye for interventions that weren't noticeable straight away, but still caused quite an uproar as soon as they were worked out. Luckily, moving the stickers back didn't spoil the decoration, and Rhonda eventually decided that she preferred the new arrangement. That was key to these little pranks: they were not intended to have permanent or damaging effects, but they still managed to be annoying when they were discovered! Most importantly, of course, none of these tricks were isolated. Retaliation was always as swift as it was inevitable.

As in a war in the traditional sense, a set of rules became established. The two developed a veritable art out of exacting equivalent revenges. In the case of the stickers, I remember finding out that Rhonda's response had been to sneak into her brother's bedroom and mix up all his clothes. As Rowan went to a different school, it was particularly easy for her to find these opportunities. For instance, he was absent on Wednesday mornings, while she was at home with all the time in the world to cause mischief if she was so inclined. Mixing up Rowan's clothes was particularly crafty, as it didn't sound that bad in theory, thus making it difficult to punish her. However, to anyone who knew Rowan's temperament, it would have been immediately obvious how annoying this must have been, as he was very orderly, and had labelled all his drawers, from his suits to his socks. Coming home from school to find all his socks mismatched and all his underwear thrown in haphazardly with his shirts would have driven him mad!

His revenge, the very next evening, was to take away all the frames of her paintings. This left no damage, but it did achieve its aim of annoying Rhonda greatly, as her room looked rather odd with all the unframed canvases hanging on the walls. Furthermore, Rowan hid the frames at the back of his closet, so she could not get them back for days. For some reason, this marked a real turning point in this particular feud. Perhaps Rhonda was stressed from school; perhaps she was just growing impatient with this never-ending pettiness.

Whatever the reason, in revenge, she managed to steal the key to her brother's room from the butler and lock him in from the corridor. No-one had ever done this in my house (to my knowledge, at least), and we only found out from the sound of his yelling. Luckily, Rowan's room had a balcony, so he could simply go outside and

vent his emotions to the winds, where he was quickly overheard by
the gardener and rescued. Again, the prank was fairly short-lived
and ultimately harmless, although it accomplished its purpose, but it
seemed to me to mark a turn for the threatening that didn't exactly
put me at ease.

After that, not all the pranks were so discreet or innocuous.
Everyone who has been involved in petty feuds will know how it
happens. Arguments escalate, and grievances no longer feel as though
they can be satisfied by small and reversible attacks. For instance, on
one occasion, Rowan crept into his sister's room in the early hours
of the morning when she was out at a sports lesson, carrying a drill.
Methodically, he sat down and started drilling straight into her
electrical plug. Of course, he electrified himself a little in the process,
but probably saw this as little more than a small sacrifice for a greater
cause, much like a general who lets the first lines of his infantry die
in hopes of glorious victory. Sadly, in this case, General Rowan
misjudged his attack, and he blew out the electricity for the entire
house. Perhaps an analogy with a nuclear conflict might have been
more appropriate here! At this point, I could no longer avoid direct
intervention. It's difficult to conduct a secret war when it is affecting
the lives of civilians! I gave my children serious talks on the subject
of practical jokes, and assumed the matter was at an end. Of course,
it wasn't.

'He drives me mad,' Rhonda sulked, putting on her best pre-
adolescent pout.

'She drives me mad,' Rowan brooded, with his best grown-up
frown.

I sighed, in what I suppose is a typical fatherly reaction. There was
nothing I could do but wait and hope it all blew over.

The next move was Rhonda's. She waited over a week before
doing anything, which was just long enough for all bystanders
to forget about the feud entirely. However, her next strike was
ruthless: she found her brother's lovely wooden bowling pins,
and threw them from the balcony down into the garden. One fell
onto the marble terrace and broke; the others landed in the mud.
Of course, he didn't discover this until the evening, by which time
they had been rained upon as well, adding insult to injury. I found
out about this episode purely from the sound of his shouting. I made

Rhonda collect the pieces, wash them, and give them back, but from Rowan's frosty countenance I doubted anything resembling peace had been brokered. I began to keep a closer eye on these difficult neighbours of mine, trying to watch out for their next move. It was hopeless, though. I could be on neither of their sides, so there was no way I would ever be privy to their battle plans.

I didn't have long to wait, though. One Sunday morning, I was woken up by wailing from Rhonda's bedroom. I came in to find her sitting on the floor, cradling her favourite doll. When I saw what Rowan had done, it was hard to repress a smile, although at the same time I understood that he had hit her in one of her weak points. She had owned this baby doll, which she called Amazone, since the age of two. She had loved to play with her, dress her up, and push her around the garden in a little chair. Today, however, Amazone was much transformed. Rowan had obviously found some paint in his sister's room and covered the doll's face in a mockery of makeup. Her eyes were blackened, her nose was purple, and she even had a little red bellybutton. I consoled Rhonda and helped her clean Amazone up as good as new, but I knew I had to intervene somehow, before this game became too much to handle.

That night, I went to see Rowan in his room.

'I'm not angry,' I told him, 'but I'm worried about this fight you are having with your sister. It seems to me this thing has escalated beyond the point where it's very much fun for either of you.'

Rowan looked a little confused. 'It's just a doll,' he replied.

I had to smile. 'I don't mean the doll,' I said, 'I mean your little feud. Your series of pranks. What I have to suggest is very simple: if the two of you find it so difficult to live side by side, would one of you like to move to another floor?' I suggested this as a landlord and peacekeeper, as well as a father.

He looked at me in surprise. 'I don't want to move!' he said at once. 'I like living next to Rhonda. I mean, she's annoying, but it's just a game. It's fun!'

I shook my head in wonder and left him to get on with his work. Later, I had a similar exchange with Rhonda.

'No way!' she said. 'I don't want to move! It would be so boring.'

That evening at dinner, I watched the two little neighbours more attentively. Sure enough, they were sitting next to each other and chatting away happily, despite the doll incident having only happened the previous night, and the bowling pin episode the week before. Though the game might have appeared warlike to an outsider, there was obviously absolutely no malice to it. I reflected on my own relationships with my siblings, and recognised the same mix of competition and affection. Of course children might play tricks on each other for entertainment, and even get into patterns of baiting and revenge. It didn't mean they weren't close, and even good friends! I smiled as I looked around at my children, eating together, squabbling and conversing away happily. Neighbourly conflicts within a loving family, I reflected, were a natural part of our lives, and really not something to worry about!

In our family library, we have a rather large travel section that we have expanded over the years. The books in the collection span the years of world exploration from the sixteenth century to the early twentieth. Many of these travellers risked their lives on foot, on horseback, and occasionally by boat or train, to expand the borders of the mind. Some went to further academic research projects on manuscripts or religious customs; some went looking for anthropological or sociological research on foreign cultures; some went for medical research, planning to investigate surgical knowledge abroad. And some simply went on a quest for adventure, venturing out into the unknown with no planned destination in mind.

Recently, I have become very interested in women travellers. I had heard that within the four-hundred-year period our collection spanned, the family library featured about twenty-five women travellers, which already seemed quite impressive, since as far as I knew most adventurers throughout history were men. To my great surprise, as I began my research, I found that, in our library alone, there were various accounts of over four hundred women travellers. During that time, I became particularly interested in one in particular, who turned out to be a sort of neighbour of mine from a different era: Lady Stanhope, who was born and raised in Kent. Various brave women disregarded social convention and fled the strict confines of Georgian or Victorian society, but few did it with quite as much panache as this one. Lady Hester Lucy Stanhope was a British socialite and adventurer who travelled to the Holy Land at the start of the nineteenth century, at the age of thirty-three. In a decisive act that was especially unusual for her era, she never returned.

Lady Hester Stanhope had a rather wild life, despite her quiet beginnings in the Kent countryside. She was born and spent her early childhood years in Chevening, a beautiful Elizabethan mansion in the south-east of England, designed by Inigo Jones and considered by many to have been the inspiration for one of the houses in Jane Austen's *Pride and Prejudice*. Chevening is the historical place of lodging for the British Foreign Secretary, and is quite an impressive house just a short drive from my house in Kent, so I suppose that was one of the reasons I first became particularly interested in Lady Stanhope.

Hester Stanhope was the child of the eccentric Lord Charles, 3rd Earl of Stanhope, who rebelled violently against his own nobility, destroying his own coat-of-arms wherever he found it, doing manual labour, and renaming their family home Democracy Hall. Lord Charles gave away his fortune out of support for the French revolution of 1789, leaving his twenty-seven-year-old daughter Hester impoverished. Soon after that, he passed away, leaving his only daughter orphaned. Tall, slender, dark-haired Lady Stanhope then became the official hostess for her uncle William Pitt, the Prime Minister of Britain, thanks to her charm and success in society. This gave her considerable clout, and gave her the time and funds to pursue her research interests in the Middle-East: she quickly became an extremely well-read and passionate Orientalist. After a series of crushing disappointments in her love-life, however, she started yearning for something more. Seemingly an impulsive woman in terms of temperament, she decided to make a change in her lifestyle and pursue the interest she was most passionate about: the East. She set off for the Mediterranean in the company of her private physician, Dr Charles Meryon, who would become her biographer, and a twenty-year-old by the name of Michael Bruce, who would become her lover.

Headed for Egypt, the trip took almost two months, with significant delays incurred when the crew were shipwrecked during a storm off the coast of Rhodes. At the time, Rhodes was a Muslim centre of the Ottoman Empire, with beautiful mosques and a famous Turkish-language library, which might seem surprising to the modern traveller, since Rhodes is now a thoroughly Catholic part of Greece. There, whilst hiding and awaiting rescue in an old windmill full of rats, she changed into the warm, dry clothes of a Turkish youth: comfortable trousers, a loose shirt and a turban. Her transformation had begun; she would never go back to wearing Western dress. In 1812, the party arrived in Alexandria, where Lady Stanhope learned Arabic and Turkish. She then set about travelling widely: now a masculine figure who smoked a hookah pipe and journeyed with a wide entourage of camels, mules and slaves. She was welcomed in the desert and mountain cities of Lebanon, Syria and Egypt, where the locals were both bemused and charmed by her. She quickly acquired a reputation as a royal figure, visiting the courts of many important people, including the Pasha, the local governor, whose court she entered riding on horseback and without a veil: two acts which were forbidden for a Christian and a woman, respectively. Later, she was crowned 'queen of the desert' by the locals in the ruined city of Palmyra. Her reputation grew, so that she became involved in several local political skirmishes.

For a time, treasure-hunting became her new obsession: she became convinced that a map she had come into possession of would lead to a horde of three million gold coins. This led to the first archaeological excavation in the Holy Land, but did not unearth any gold. Instead, they found a seven-foot headless marble statue, which she ordered to be destroyed and thrown into the sea, fearing that she would get into trouble for grave-robbing or the theft of antiquities.

After a few years, having gained favour with many local leaders, she converted to Islam, and began establishing a reputation as a sort of strange Western wise-woman, whom travellers would seek out for wisdom. She shaved her head and began offering sanctuary to victims of intra-clan violence in the region. She studied alchemy and astrology, and got into trouble for some of her political involvements. Her eccentricities grew alongside her popularity. Many believe that her delusions of power were responsible for her increasingly extravagant lifestyle; some suggest she may have been insane. For instance, she kept her horse in a constantly-lit stable, and fed it sherbet and exotic fruit. Gradually, she retreated to her house in the Lebanese mountains, surrounded by olive trees and flower gardens, and fell further and further into debt. She became something of a recluse, only accepting visits from various European travellers; receiving them after dark and entirely hidden, showing only her face and hands. This image of holiness did not keep her safe, though: she eventually died in isolation within her crumbling palace walls, its doors locked against her hordes of creditors. Apart from the poverty, it was probably the end she would have wished for: in her last years, she became particularly vocal about her disenchantment with the West. She loved the adventure, the fairly influential role she had come to play in the East, and the friends she made there. To this day, there is a shrine to Lady Stanhope in Damascus, where she was revered for her wisdom and bravery.

Dr Charles Meryon eventually published her biography in three volumes, and it is a fascinating read : both for the portrait it paints of the brave and radical woman Lady Stanhope was, and for its insights into the cultures she explored.

THE BOY FROM INDIANA

I've known a surprising number of smart country boys who were forced into getting an education in a subject that did not interest them by families anxious to make sure they had the best possible futures. John Murphy was one such boy. He was my neighbour in the fraternity house I was a member of in Texas. He was eighteen, from a modest background in Indiana, and he never quite got used to the Deep South; the accent, the cowboy hats, the chewing tobacco, and especially his major itself all stayed as completely foreign to him as if he were from Taiwan or Togo.

He had trouble in fluid mechanics and chemistry, which were the engineering courses I shared with him, and which happened to be crucial to his degree. I did fairly well in these subjects, so John would often come to me with requests to help him solve a problem, by which he meant giving him the solution to a problem, or to ask me to help him achieve at least a B or a C on some piece of homework. He was not a particularly ambitious boy; he just wanted to get through the courses. He would show up at my door in a state of agitation, running his hands through his messy red hair, so often that I came to predict his arrivals as regularly as clockwork.

'Oh Brad,' he would moan, 'I don't know the first thing about the fluid mechanics in a hydraulic pump on an aeroplane. I can't calculate them. I hardly even know what the question means! For all I know a hydraulic pump is something you find in a gym. I'm going to go mad!'

'Look, Murphy,' I would say, 'sit down.' Then I would do my best to give him the lesson, carefully explaining the problem in simple terms in the hope that he would come to the solution himself. He would laugh, as if the fact that I was doing his homework were some elaborate game. I don't think he ever understood even the tiniest part of what I was talking about, but as soon as he was off the hook and didn't think he was going to fail, he instantly stopped caring. This happened around three or four times during the term. At the end, he came to me with his final chemistry assignment.

'Look,' he began, 'I know this is a ridiculous thing to ask. But could you just do this for me? I haven't the faintest idea how to start, let alone finish this thing.'

'Murphy,' I said, 'I'm happy to give you a hand in this. But you really need to stop and think about what you're doing. You're failing chemistry and fluid mechanics. You're not that good at operations research or at the study of electricity. What happens if you have an oral exam? I mean, think about what happens if you do graduate, and you start job interviews. You're not going to get anywhere on this course, are you?'

John sighed. 'Not really.'

'Why don't you just sit down and have a good think about your options? I mean, you could change careers completely, become a lawyer, a dancer, a salesman, or anything you want. Look at you; you're a nice, good-looking guy. You've got really straight teeth. You're very charming. You're perfectly intelligent, but admit it: you're not cut out to be an engineer.'

'But I always thought I would be an engineer! My parents invested so much in this course. It means the world to them.'

'You're terrible at engineering. I'm sorry, but it's true. Your parents won't be proud of you staying in a degree that doesn't make you happy – or that you fail!'

'Oh, it's true all right. You and my teachers know that better than anyone. Maybe you're right. But what else can I do? I've got no other qualifications.'

'You're a smart guy. You've got charm. You could do anything. You could walk across campus and sign up on a completely different course. What about law?'

'Too difficult.'

'Something in the liberal arts?'

'Reading is boring.'

I sighed. 'Do you even want to do a long university course? I mean, have you thought about going straight into a job? In sales, for instance?'

'My dad always said working in sales was for losers.'

'What does your dad do?'

'He's a used-car salesman.' John grinned and paused, thinking this over. 'I guess he didn't want me to end up like him. But I reckon my dad turned out all right.'

'There's nothing wrong with selling used cars! In my opinion, your charm would get you far in that career!'

'Do you really think so?'

'Of course!'

'Well, I'm on this course now and it's costing my family a fortune, so I won't think about it now. I'm just going to try and get through it.'

'OK. Would you like to go through this paper with me now?'

'Oh, heck no. Let's go for a hamburger!'

By the end of that term, John was getting Ds and Fs on any bit of work I hadn't been able to help with. Eventually, he was sent a warning by the school, informing him that if he didn't improve his grades in the second semester, he would be thrown out of school altogether. In April of the second semester, John came to see me without any homework in his hands, which was an unusual sight.

'Yeah, I know, no homework for you today. I've come to say goodbye,' he said with a sheepish expression. 'I'm going back to Indiana. I'm going to work for my dad in his used-car lot.' He gave me a small, sad smile; 'I'm not sure how I should feel about this,' he confessed.'

'Don't look so glum,' I replied, 'this is a really good decision for you. Engineering just isn't your thing. Maybe used-car sales will work out for you!'

Indeed it did. Murphy wrote me long, funny Christmas letters for many years after that. He got on famously at his job, and ended up making a great living. He now owns a villa in Wisconsin looking out over Lake Michigan, where he lives with his wife and three children. Every once in a while he likes to tell me that he wished he'd listened to my advice earlier, as he realised in retrospect that he truly had been dreadful at engineering, and it turned out that he loved doing a hands-on job.

CUSTOMISED HUMMUS

When I first moved to Paris, there was little in the way of international cuisine to be found. France has such a long history of priding itself on its food that it took a long time for the country to open its arms to more adventurous tastes, whether ginger and chilli, avocado and coriander, or tahini. Of course, there were exceptions. Paris always had a few excellent Italian restaurants, and maybe one fancy Chinese place next to the more down-market ones. In the nineteenth and twentieth *arrondissements*, as well as in the fifth, you would always find a good selection of North African food. The smell of rich meat stews with tomato and harissa always wafted through the streets of the Latin Quarter, just as you might catch the distinctive aroma of a barbecued *méchoui* lamb.

Lebanese cuisine, however, took a little while longer to carve out its place in the French capital. In the early-to-mid 1970s, the combination of the oil euphoria and the Lebanese War brought about a great deal of immigration to the West. Paris saw its fair share of new arrivals, including the culinary variety. All of a sudden, Lebanese restaurants and bars started opening up, serving everything from falafel sandwiches to deep-fried lamb kibbeh balls with fresh mint; from platters of marinated seafood with herbs to juicy chicken shawarma with pickled vegetables; from hot black tea and coffee with cardamom to strong Arak liqueur. Suddenly, these foods that would once have seemed unimaginable to the classic Parisian palate became incredibly popular in their exoticness: spices other than salt and pepper! Meat that wasn't beef steak medallion! Desserts and sauces without cream! The restaurants moved from the fringes towards the town centre and crept right into the golden triangle of Paris: the popular, luxurious area of the city bordered on its three sides by the Champs-Élysées, Avenue George V and Avenue Montaigne. Next to the stuffed, crimson-carpeted brasseries, all at once there appeared cosy, luminous spaces with cushions and indigo tiles. In place of the traditional Parisian cafés, one might stumble across an intimate meze bar.

Around this time, I had an office in this area, so I witnessed this development first-hand. I had always had a taste for Middle Eastern food, which was inspired by my grandmother, who had travelled all over the region, collecting recipes. I became a regular patron of an establishment known as Shamus's Bar, run by a short, blond Lebanese man called Shamus White. Shamus was a friendly young man, who appreciated my interest in his fresh produce and daily changing menu.

Our initial conversations were mostly about the history of Lebanese food in Europe, and the rise of interest for it in France.

'I'd never seen a Lebanese restaurant in Paris until recently,' I confessed. 'Why do you think it has become so popular? Your restaurant always seems to be full! It can't just be the décor...'

'Well, the increase in Lebanese immigration at the moment has a lot to do with it. I mean, Paris has always been a hugely multicultural city! It's just been too caught up with its own cuisine to notice the possibilities. But now, I think that is changing. There is a big influx of cooks from the old colonies in particular: from Senegal to Cambodia and Tunisia to Vietnam. So perhaps Lebanese food has simply claimed its rightful place in enriching the delicious multicultural atmosphere of the new French city.' He paused for a moment. 'And another thing – meze are really not so different to Spanish tapas, so it's not going to seem that unfamiliar to your modern diner. In fact, it is a widely received theory that Spanish tapas originated in the Middle East, and were brought over the Mediterranean in the Umayyad invasion, in the eighth century!'

'Is that so! How interesting. That might go some way to explaining how easily European audiences convert to Middle Eastern cuisine, once they discover it... you just need to highlight the historical convergence!'

'I think it's easier to convert a hungry man with a plateful of chicken and vegetables than with a history lesson.'

'And that is why you are the chef!'

After a few visits and friendly conversations, Shamus took me back into his small but immaculate kitchen and introduced me to a variety of wonderful dishes. 'We make every meze dish fresh in the morning!' he told me enthusiastically, peeking under lids and stirring small dishes of sauces, pickles and spices. 'If I'm not too busy, I like to be in the kitchen myself.' He tipped dried *za'atar* and paprika into saucers.

'I'm glad to hear it,' I replied. 'Most of the big-name chefs here rarely make it into their own kitchens. They just plan elaborate menus and shout at people down the phone.'

'I can't really imagine that,' Shamus said with a laugh. 'What if the cooks started taking liberties? I heard of a chef back home in Beirut whose sous-chef started putting sun-dried tomatoes and olives in the flatbreads. Can you imagine? Such a thing would never happen if you were right there, looking over everyone's shoulder.'

As Shamus moved around his kitchen, he detailed his personal meze preferences. 'Of course, everything must be doused in pools of the finest, golden olive oil. Tabbouleh must be made with several handfuls of fresh parsley. Any other kind of tabbouleh is not truly Lebanese.'

'Not even with mint and raisins?'

'Oh, it can have anything you like in it. Tomatoes, mint, spring onions, whatever takes your fancy. But in this bar, at least, you will never find it without lots of chopped parsley.'

'I'll bear that in mind! So what else does your classic Lebanese meze podium contain?'

'Well, of course we must have a classic *baba ghanouj*, a rich aubergine spread with tahini. I also make an excellent homemade *labneh*, which is a sort of thick, creamy yoghurt cheese. I like to have a few fried aubergines as well. Add a few nuts and pickles for variety, maybe a few fresh salads: something like *fatoush*, perhaps, served with pitta chips and pomegranate molasses. Then you get down to business. Do you know of *awarma*?'

'Is that a lamb dish? I think I have come across that before.'

'Very good. It is in fact a salted, fatty *confit*, which the French are always thrilled to recognise. What have I left out? Ah yes, of course. How could I forget? You must have a large bowl of hummus.'

I was particularly interested in finding out what his recipe for hummus was, as this beloved Middle-Eastern dish has as many variants as it does makers. On this slow Saturday morning, Shamus and I had quite an involved debate about this.

'So tell me,' I began, 'as the first Lebanese chef I've met in Paris: do you have your own special recipe for hummus?'

'Of course I have a special recipe,' he told me with a sly smile and a slight roll of his eyes. 'Do you know any chef that doesn't? Unless they have inherited it from their mother or grandmother unchanged, nobody makes hummus without a special approach of their own. Anyone caught with a recipe book would be recognized as an imposter.' He wiped his hands on his apron and opened the vast fridge to lift out a vat of chickpeas. 'These have been soaking overnight, for a start. Nothing else will do. You need a good teaspoon of bicarbonate of soda, too. Some people over here use canned chickpeas, which is of course a terrible aberration. I, personally, think you require a pressure cooker to achieve the creamy texture I like. I don't like it grainy, and I don't like it to feel like a mousse.' A little self-consciously, he started siphoning chickpeas from one pan into another.

'That's fair enough,' I replied. 'You're a chef. You need to be in control of your hummus. I personally like my chickpeas extremely well cooked and blended twice over.'

He looked up, tossing his hair out of his eyes, checking I wasn't joking. When he saw I was being serious, he grinned. 'I do love to make all the decisions in my kitchen, particularly where hummus is concerned. But as a professional chef, you actually end up with slightly less control than you would like. For instance, I personally like my hummus heavy on the lemon and light on the garlic, but my customers think otherwise. Thus, I may have developed what I consider the perfect hummus recipe, but I only really get to make it at home.'

'Light on the garlic, you say? I think you may be a man after my own heart. I make my hummus with no garlic at all!' I told him.

Shamus threw up his hands in mock horror. 'No garlic! Now this, I have never tried.' A glint appeared in his eyes. 'Show me,' he said. 'The restaurant is almost empty; my sous-chef can handle everything. Come on, make me a small bowl of your hummus. It might be useful to know!'

Laughing at his serious interest, I made up a small bowl for him with my preferred set of flavourings, opting for a large squeeze of fresh lemon juice, a generous tablespoon of tahini, and foregoing the chopped raw garlic entirely. 'Now, your chickpeas are a little less cooked than I like mine, but if I blend them a little longer, the final result shouldn't be too different.' I finished off the serving with a generous dollop of extra virgin olive oil and presented it to him. Shamus leaned over and pulled two fresh flatbreads out of an oven, bouncing them up and down to stop them from burning his hands. He then tore off generous pieces of the bread, scooped up my special hummus, and ate it in silence. We sat for a time, happily eating the bowl of hummus without comment. At the end, Shamus wiped his face with the back of his hand and nodded a few times. 'Not bad,' he said. 'I still think you need garlic.'

I laughed. 'It's a minority position, I understand.'

'Still,' he said, 'now that I know what you like best, I will make sure to always offer your special recipe.'

The conclusion of this conversation ended up sealing our friendship, and my status as a faithful customer to Shamus's Bar. From then on, whenever I came by, true to his word, Shamus would run back into the kitchen and make up a special bowl of hummus for me, ladling the hot chickpeas fresh from the pressure cooker and creaming them with tahini and lemon. Jamieson's Special Hummus, as he jokingly liked to call it, was slightly more liquid in texture than Shamus's traditional version, and required a little more salt, but I loved it. Shamus Bar became a place of pilgrimage for me, whenever I wanted hummus or fresh, hot flatbread. Shamus and I are still friends, and when I am in the city, I always make sure to stop by.

THE THIRD-FLOOR
NEIGHBOUR'S TROUBLES

In the early 1980s, when I lived on Eaton Square, my daughter Rouena and I would often take long walks. If the weather was nice, she would sometimes take a book with her and sit in the shade of the trees to read peacefully. Even in the coldest temperatures, we would sometimes take a jog together. So it was no surprise when one day Rouena came into the house flushed and out of breath. It was, however, a surprise when she told me angrily that someone had tried to arrest her.

'I'm sorry?' I said. This was rather hard to believe. My daughter had always been incredibly well-behaved, and she had certainly never been in any trouble with the law. Furthermore, as far as I knew, she had just been out for a walk in Eaton Square which was hardly a criminal offence.

'Someone just tried to arrest me,' she explained, 'because of the way I was dressed.'

'What?' I raised an eyebrow as I looked her outfit up and down. My lovely young daughter always dressed respectably: today she was wearing a lovely designer silk blouse and a demure black cardigan over Diesel jeans. 'What's wrong with your outfit?'

'Jeans,' she said, and for a moment I thought she might burst into tears. 'Apparently you can't wear jeans on Eaton Square. That's not true, is it?'

'Of course not!' I said, trying not to get too angry myself. 'What a ridiculous idea.'

'Well some lady called the police.'

I sighed. 'This is just some ridiculous Belgravia thing. I'm sure they just came to appease the old creature. This would never happen anywhere they have actual crime to worry about, like Brixton.'

'The worst thing was he was some kind of special Belgravia policeman! And even then he was quite apologetic and perhaps a bit confused, actually; he kept on saying 'I am just delegated to protect the property!' But he seemed to think this might be legitimate; I had to tell him these were cotton trousers, not jeans. For some crazy reason he seemed to believe whoever this woman is!'

'Look, darling, there's no way jeans can be illegal. Or cotton trousers, for that matter. There's no dress code just for being in Eaton Square. I'd understand, perhaps, if you were wearing some sort of torn-up punk outfit covered in safety pins, but that's simply not the case. I'm sure this policeman just felt that since he had taken the trouble to turn up, he had to do what he'd come for.'

'I'm not like that; you know that. I wouldn't look out of place serving her tea,' Rouena added ruefully.

I put my hand on her shoulder. 'Sweetheart, please pay her no heed. I'm sure she's just a bitter old woman. She probably never got used to the idea of women wearing trousers in the first place. You know in France it's still technically illegal under Napoleonic law?'

She laughed. 'She's probably that old, isn't she.'

'To be fair, she probably has Alzheimer's,' I added gently.

'Don't find excuses for your crazy old neighbours,' Rouena berated me. 'There's no excuse for calling the police on me! I mean, the whole thing is insane. What would they say if Sean Connery was jogging in shorts? Are we supposed to be in black tie or evening dress all the time?'

'Look, Rouena, please just forget about this whole thing.'

She sighed. 'OK, Dad,' she said, 'I guess it's not important.'

Unfortunately, that was not the end of it. I witnessed the truth of my daughter's sad tale only three or four days later: not that I had doubted her word, but it was hard to imagine there being such a nasty side to the classy Eaton Square neighbourhood! This time, Rouena and I had taken advantage of a bright, cold autumn morning to go for a small jog around the garden together. As there was no-one around, we were quite surprised when we heard a voice shouting from the window of one of the houses.

'What are you doing here again, little missy! I thought I told you lot to stay well away from me!'

I saw Rouena's shoulders slump, and straightened my own in response.

'What on earth are you talking about?' I shouted back up, as sternly as I could. 'That's my daughter you're talking about! She has as much right as anyone to live here!'

'Who's that?' came the voice, slightly more quavering now. 'Show yourself!'

I stomped out of the square and stood below her window, with my arms crossed. 'Here I am,' I said. 'And this is my daughter Rouena.' I called back to my daughter to come and stand next to me. 'She lives with me. In our family home. Which we happen to own. We have more of a right to be here than the rest of you renters! She's a permanent resident! She goes to the local school!'

'Well that's very nice of you to say, Mr Jamieson,' the little old lady replied, 'but you don't have to defend these youngsters and tramps. You and your heart of gold would scoop any horrid youth off the streets.'

'You're crazy,' I muttered, before raising my voice again. 'Are you implying I'm pretending this is my daughter? This is my daughter! Her name is Rouena! Look at our noses! She's my flesh and blood!'

'Yes, that's all very nice, dear,' the old lady said rather vaguely, waving her hand. 'Just make sure she stays away from my house.'

I was so outraged that this time my daughter was the one who had to calm me down. 'Don't worry, Dad,' she said soothingly. 'Thanks for defending me. She sounds like some crazy old woman.'

'You have so much more of a right to be here than her,' I muttered; 'She's only here because she married some rich old man who almost certainly died in the war.'

'Please don't fret,' Rouena said again. 'You know I love living here. I can put up with a crazy person or two!'

Still, our neighbourly troubles were not yet over. About a week later Rouena was fuming again. This time, I guessed a little quicker what might be bothering her. My daughter lost no time in explaining.

'It's that old bat!' she very nearly shouted. 'This time she just kept shouting at me herself! From the window!'

'Calm down, darling,' I said, 'surely it's an improvement on the police?' I paused for a moment. 'But what can she possibly have been complaining about, this time?' Rouena was wearing a white chiffon dress, as it was a pleasant summer's day.

'She kept shouting at me from the window; she was starting to disturb the other walkers in the square, so of course I went over to see what was wrong, or if I could help her. I didn't immediately figure out who it was until she yelled "Oh it's you again!" as if I was some sort of burglar!'

'Did you point out that you weren't wearing jeans, and also, incidentally, that wearing jeans isn't illegal?'

'No. She sort of took me by surprise. She asked me if I had keys to our flat. I said yes, of course, so she barked: "Do you have them on you? Show me!" So I answered that I didn't, but that my father was at home and could get them, but I had to ask, why did she need them? Then of course she started shouting again, like a mad person, I really wonder if there is something wrong with her... It would have been funny if it wasn't so horrible! "The youth of today" she kept yelling, and shaking her fist in the air, "taking over our nice homes and walking around with their stupid inheritance money and being young!" Well, OK, she didn't exactly say that, but that was the spirit of the thing.'

'I suppose a lot of the older folk around here must resent the intrusion of nouveaux riches and foreigners... But we're hardly either. I mean, we own our place!'

'I know! That's exactly what I told her. She replied: "What are you, fourteen? You don't own anything!" which was, of course, fairly insulting as I'm obviously older than that. But she wouldn't hear anything of it. Eventually someone came up behind her in the room and asked her to be quiet, I guess. Then she disappeared.'

'Dear Rouena,' I told her, 'you mustn't worry about these people. You know we have as much of a right as anyone to be here.'

'Oh, I know that,' she replied with a small shrug.

'Sometimes you have strange and difficult neighbours,' I said. 'And it's not always the ones you expect!'

I have many fond childhood memories of visiting my grandmother at her holiday home in Konya, and one of the sweetest of these is the thought of Ahood Labana's shop. Mr Labana's bakery was just down the road from my grandmother's house in Turkey, and it was a sweet-toothed child's paradise. When I was eight or nine, I loved nothing in the world more than to stand outside, pressing my nose against the windows and staring at the mounds and stacks of baked goods. The glass windows showed off what seemed like an endless variety of cakes and sugary delights, gleaming in the sunlight that streamed through the display case. There was every sort of cake you could imagine: from American classics like sticky pineapple upside-down cake and bright green Key Lime pie to beautiful Lebanese *kinaffa* made of wheat, honey and ground walnuts; from towering icing-laced cheesecakes worthy of a wedding to odd little cream-filled *pâtisseries* from Austria; from rich chocolate truffle gâteaux with three tiers of ganache to the simplest little lemon pound cake.

I used to walk by the shop window every day, staring greedily, as if I hoped to consume everything with my eyes. I would always be tugged along swiftly by my grandmother's arm. 'It'll rot your teeth right out of your head,' she would say, not in an unfriendly way. 'It'll taste good for less than a minute, and then you'll have to get your teeth pulled because of all the cavities.' I would let myself be led away, reluctantly, if without protest, torturing myself by keeping my eyes on the wondrous cakes until the last possible moment. Of course, at last there came a glorious day where I was allowed to go in and buy myself a treat. I knew just what to buy. I had honed my decision for months and months. There was one cake hidden away to the far left of the window display, a heavy-looking brown cake that glistened with nuts and crystallised sugar syrup. When I whispered to Mr Labana that I would like to try a piece of it, he laughed a deep belly laugh. 'Ah, so you have seen my famous Wet Bottomed cake! The boy has a good eye,' he added with a wink to my grandmother, who was not amused. 'Can you guess why it's called that?'

'Is it because it has a wet bottom?' I ventured timidly.

'Why yes, my little man, it is indeed! This particular pecan pie of mine has so much treacle and butter and sugar put into it that it soaks right through the crust. It's a real delight.' Here, he went to the window and cut me a generous slice, the size of which made my grandmother tut. I handed over my coins and stared at my prize. It was almost too beautiful to eat! Of course, I only waited four seconds or so before devouring it in its delicious entirety, cramming my mouth with the sweet, crunchy, sticky pecan nuts. Even just thinking about it now, many years later, makes my mouth water a little. The taste sticks in my mind just like the nuts stuck in my teeth that day! I'm quite sure it was the single best slice of pie I have eaten in my entire life. Even if I also have a soft spot for Mr Labana's paper-thin apple pie, which has a crackling, golden crust under its delicate topping of fruit.

Every day of my holiday, I would walk by the shop. The days when I was allowed a treat were exceptional ones, but I was filled with joy from the experience even on the days I wasn't. I am quite sure I sampled most of the cakes in that bakery over the years I visited Turkey. When I was sixteen, I came back to Labana's to find that the shop had expanded considerably. It still had the same tantalising front window display, but next to all the cakes I had loved and drooled over my whole life, there were now slabs of chocolate full of hazelnuts and almonds, and little delicate truffles, and crystallised ginger and orange peel. Mr Labana was thrilled to see me, as it gave him an occasion to show off his new offerings. 'See,' he said excitedly, holding up one round dark chocolate, 'this is a walnut cream. It has a praline ganache made with fresh walnuts, and a whole walnut on top. The walnuts come from my own garden at home! Try one!'

I popped it into my mouth, and was overwhelmed by the sweet and slightly bitter taste of the nut. It was exceptionally delicious. 'Labana,' I said, wiping my hand over my mouth, 'you've outdone yourself. I think you may well be as good a chocolatier as you are a baker!'

He told me all about his expansion, and his further plans. It seemed that business in Turkey had gone so well that they were thinking of taking it abroad. In fact, twenty years later, when I was walking down the street in Paris, I came by chance across a beautiful patisserie that turned out to be called Labana! I stopped in awe and looked in the window. Sure enough, I knew at once that this shop was related to the one from my childhood. They seemed to have specialised in the Middle Eastern pastries, but they also still had a version of my old favourite Wet Bottomed pie. I walked in and chatted to the shop assistants for a while. They told me that the first branches had opened up abroad in 1985, and that business had been excellent since. It seemed there was a real market for this kind of international baking in a cosmopolitan metropolis like Paris. 'Labana himself stills works in the shop, you know,' the assistant told me. 'He's actually just on the other side of the city.'

I could not believe my luck, and took a taxi to this other shop at once. Ahood Labana was an old man, but when I walked in the door his face cracked into a smile thirty years younger. 'Bradley!' he exclaimed. 'You haven't changed a bit!' I had probably been sixteen years old the last time I saw him. 'Come in, come in. Pick any dessert you like. It's a gift for you.' I couldn't help but smile. Somehow, being in this shop, I was as excited about choosing a pastry as I had been as a child. Even with no grandmother to tug on my arm and make me walk away, there was a certain forbidden thrill about being allowed to choose from this endless array of beautiful, delicious things; in fact, many more choices than even in my childhood. Still, I decided to return to classics, and requested a small piece of Wet Bottomed pie. Labana obviously took great pleasure in cutting me the slice and giving it away for free.

'For a generous man,' I told him, 'you've been incredibly successful!'

'I have always stuck to my principles,' he replied. 'I never changed my recipes, and I always remember my faithful clients. Extra cakes, extra shops, and new customers are all a bonus.'

This attitude obviously served my old neighbour well. Labana's pastry shops quickly became an institution in the Middle East and Europe. From that little shop that I remember in my childhood, he started a business that made him an international billionaire! His children have followed in his footsteps, creating new *pâtisseries* every week and preparing to take over the business. It is always a joy to walk into a shop and see the same delicious cakes I recall from when I was eight years old.

MY LONELY NEIGHBOUR

In my engineering days, I had the busy life of an ambitious career man, but, like most hard workers, I nonetheless usually managed to get home in time to relax a little bit before dinner, and enjoy the sunset in summer. When I was twenty-two, I lived in a big house which I shared with a few of my engineering colleagues in a pleasant part of New Jersey, not far away from Princeton. We had a beautiful two-acre garden, and were surrounded by fields and streams perfect for kayaking, fishing, and horse riding.

My next-door neighbour was a high-powered executive who lived with his two daughters. At the time I had been an engineer for just under a year and a half; my neighbour was probably in his mid-fifties. He was a tall man with salt-and-pepper hair.

One sunny Saturday afternoon, he looked over the fence and grinned at me. 'Hey, Brad,' he said, 'I've just been barbecuing some ribs. Got lots left over! You want a couple?' He wiped his hands on his apron. 'Prime Chicago beef. I have a private supplier who hangs his meat for twenty-eight days. It's the best beef money can buy!'

I smiled, set down my newspaper and walked over to the fence. 'Well, what a lovely neighbourly gesture! I must say I'm rather fond of ribs.'

'Well hop on over,' he said. 'The gate's right over there.'

That was how I ended up in my neighbour's garden, eating a delicious prime rib sandwich with mustard and pickles. We introduced ourselves and chatted amiably about local life and various parties we had attended in the community. After a while, there came a voice from an upstairs window: 'Daddy?' A pretty face appeared, with long blonde hair hanging down. My neighbour looked at me earnestly and said, 'I'd like you to meet someone. My daughter Heather, who is visiting from university. She studies in Boston, you see, but she always makes sure she comes home at the holidays to enjoy my beef sandwiches!'

The girl materialised in the garden, tall and lithe in a white summer dress. She was very pretty, and very chatty, having just finished a course with the debating society, which she was the head of. I found her very charming, and we got on wonderfully, but after just half an hour or so she ran back into the house, as she explained that she had some homework to finish. Another woman appeared in the doorway, whom I assumed at first to be her mother.

My neighbour beamed, and quickly made me glad I hadn't greeted this apparition by saying 'And is this your wife?'

'And this is my other daughter, Colleen!' he said jovially. 'She's just turned thirty,' he added pointedly in an aside to me. The woman in question definitely looked a good ten years older than thirty. The skin under her eyes was saggy, her hair was dishevelled and greasy, and her clothes were out of fashion. She looked tired and thin, although she had nice bright eyes. 'I married young, you see,' her father continued under his breath, as she approached us from across the lawn. I didn't quite know how to respond to this, so I just waited uncomfortably for Colleen to arrive. She stood by my side, clearly as ill-at-ease as I was. Her father pushed the limping conversation along, encouraging us when we flagged. Eventually, he got to the crux of his intervention. 'Hey, Brad,' he said casually, 'why don't you two go out to dinner sometime?'

I froze. 'Oh, um,' I stuttered, 'sure. I'll see.' I couldn't help but hesitate, looking at this woman who appeared to be twice my age. I was beginning to feel like I had been tricked, drawn in with the rib sandwich and the pretty sibling as bait, only to be trapped like a lobster. I tried to think on my feet, to figure out a tactful escape from this situation. Unfortunately, these were my neighbours. I would be stuck with them for as long as I lived in that area, and I was quite fond of our house. The hedges were small. I couldn't hide. So I plastered on my shiniest diplomatic smile and replied to Colleen, 'I'm awfully sorry, but I'm quite busy with work at the moment. Maybe we can go for a drink sometime.' Her eyes widened and she seemed unable to reply. I was utterly incapable of thinking of a way to react to this. After what felt like the most awkward thirty seconds of my life, however, her father prompted her with a ridiculously unsubtle display of eyebrow waggling, and she muttered something which sounded like an acceptance, before creeping away from the barbecue back towards the house. I made my hurried excuses and walked home as briskly as I could. The sandwich was sitting oddly in my stomach. I wasn't quite sure it had been worth it.

A few weeks later, my suspicions were confirmed. My neighbour grinned in a way that was almost too friendly, as I got caught in the garden.

'Hey, Brad,' he said, 'have you gone out with my daughter yet?'

My stomach sank.

'She really likes you,' he pursued, without any attempt at small talk. 'She's really upset that she never gets to leave the house. Why don't you take her for a drink?'

I sighed inwardly. 'I'd love to,' I replied, as convincingly as I could.

'I mean, it's a bit early for a drink. And anyway she doesn't drink,' he added hastily, confusing me further. 'Why don't you have her over for a coffee?'

'I don't drink either,' I replied cautiously. 'But she's more than welcome to come over for coffee. I actually have some cookies in the oven. Why doesn't she come out and speak to me herself?'

The father laughed heartily, in the manner of a man who can't help but be a bit panicked by such a suggestion, before positively yelling his daughter's name back towards the house. There was an awkward silence, before she came running across the lawn. I mean this quite literally: by the time she arrived next to us, her hair was a mess, and she was panting. 'Brad!' she said. 'Hello!'

I smiled nervously. 'Your father has just suggested I have you over for a drink. Would you like a coffee?'

She smiled, and for a moment her features were less pinched. 'Let me just go brush my hair,' she said, returning to glumness. 'I'll be right over.'

'Come sit in the garden with me,' I offered.

We sat on my terrace with two strong coffees and a plate of cookies. Colleen combed her greasy hair out of her eyes and smiled awkwardly. I panicked, and decided flattery was the best course of action.

'So how come somebody as pretty as you wasn't snapped up at an early age?'

She sighed, apparently unaffected by the implied compliment: perhaps she had learned how to ward off false praise.

'Well, I just don't know where to start.' She looked at me quickly, as though deciding whether she could trust me, before continuing: 'I was married for twelve years to a very violent man. When I fell in love with him I was young and foolish. He abused me physically and emotionally, cheated on me, and beat me. I finally decided to break free when my father threatened to take him to criminal court. I left him and got a divorce.' She took a long drink of coffee, her gaze settled firmly on the table. 'Now I don't really know what I'm doing. I don't know why my father wants me to go out with you; I'm sorry if this coffee is an imposition. You seem like a really nice boy and I appreciate it; I'm just not sure which direction to go. I think I'm afraid of men.'

'I'm not surprised,' I replied, 'it sounds like you've had a bad experience. We can be a violent race. On behalf of our species, I must apologise.'

She gave a sad little smile. 'Oh, I'm sure there are good men out there. I just don't know how to find them. And my father thinks he's helping by trapping any half-decent man who so much as walks by the house… no offence, of course.'

'None taken. I can understand this must be a difficult situation for you.'

'I mean, I love my father, and I know he's just trying to do the best thing for me, trying to help. I had a happy childhood, you know, our family was very close. But these days it's becoming more difficult to be comfortable at home. Father brings his colleagues to dinner, he flags down men on the street, he even tries to advertise me to nice old men we meet – my dentist, for instance. He organises these huge neighbourhood barbecues; he takes me out to dinner. It's terribly embarrassing. I can see they're not interested. I mean, I don't know why. It's not like I'm damaged goods.' Here, to my horror, she started to cry. 'Or maybe I am.'

'Don't say that,' I tried to comfort her. 'Why on earth would you think that? You're still a nice young woman.'

'I'm hideous,' Colleen wailed. 'I'm depressed. I've been suicidal for years.'

'Why don't you see a counsellor? There are ways to get better, you know. I mean, do you have friends you can talk to?'

She shook her head vehemently. 'Oh, I could never go to a doctor. For one thing, my father would try to get him to marry me.'

'You could go to a female psychologist.'

'It would just be too embarrassing. I don't think I could take it. You know, there's nothing wrong with me!' she cried out. 'There's no reason to be so unhappy.'

'That's not how unhappiness works,' I said gently. 'I mean, there are plenty of things that have affected your state of mind. The end of your marriage, a tense home life...'

'I'm jealous of my sister,' she acknowledged. I held back from saying I could understand why! Instead, I replied:

'She's no different from you. She's just a little more naïve and more relaxed about her life. All you need to do to be as attractive as her would be to put on ten kilos, and buy a couple of nice dresses. Maybe wear your hair up from time to time.'

Colleen smiled sadly and combed her hand through her dirty hair. 'I could make more of an effort, I suppose.'

'Look,' I said, getting into the spirit of this pep talk, 'life is short. You have to enjoy it while you can. You're still a beautiful young woman. You're single. You have a loving family who look after you, and know how to make damn fine ribs!'

'I know I'm too skinny,' she said reluctantly. 'I just don't ever feel like eating. I think it's the depression.'

'Maybe it's just that there's not enough good food around for you! If you like, sometimes I could send over some dishes our cook makes when he visits. He makes great American classics – the juiciest meatloaf, the best spicy sloppy joes, sometimes something fancier like a nice prime cut of beef with pepper sauce. See, I can tell from the twinkle in your eye that your mouth is watering already. You've just had a rough patch. Everybody has them.' I put my hand on hers comfortingly, and she smiled. I withdrew it quickly, lest she got the wrong idea of my intentions, and she laughed.

'Don't worry,' she said, 'I won't try to marry you. I could do with a friend right now.'

I grinned a little sheepishly at being caught out. 'It's just that I'm seeing someone else at the moment,' I added awkwardly.

She laughed. 'Look,' she said, 'we have almost a ten-year difference in age. I know you won't fall in love with me; we're in very different places in our lives. I'm not very educated, I married young, and ended up with a miserable life. It's fine. I'm not looking to be your girlfriend. But I wouldn't mind having nice conversations!'

And that was how I became friends with Colleen. There was never any flirtation implied in our relationship: I became something more akin to a psychological counsellor to her. I began sending food round to the place regularly, and a week after that first cup of coffee, I bought her a self-help book. A little while after that, we went out to a restaurant together. Often, we would end up having long conversations when we were both in the garden, leaning over the fence like a very platonic Romeo and Juliet.

Slowly, I watched my new friend pull herself together and work on creating a new life. She would tell me about her unsuccessful dates, and I would reassure her that there would be many better ones to come; she would ask for my opinion on her new outfits, or a new haircut she was contemplating. Sometimes she would cry, or talk about her depression, and I would try to help. We stayed close for another two years, until I moved away. I never discovered if she found the right man; but I was happy to be her friend in the meantime. And a few times, I got to go round to her family house and enjoy her father's delicious barbecue again!

THE GARDENING BARON

When I lived in Belgravia, in central London, I owned a key to the garden reserved for residents, and would often walk there. It's a beautiful garden, with dozens of different kinds of flowering shrubs, and trees hundreds of years old. Often, I would wander there alone, enjoying the dappled sunshine through the leaves, or sheltering from the rain. Other times, I would run into one of the ubiquitous old ladies, or young men discussing what to do with their vast inheritances or where to take their equally rich girlfriends on holiday. And sometimes I would run into Baron Graham Digby.

Baron Digby had inherited his title. He was thirty-two, the same age as me. We were both bankers. He worked for a noted private bank in the city, a position he had presumably obtained thanks to his relations and his aristocratic heritage. Often when I ran into him in Eaton or Belgrave Square, I would greet him. 'Hello,' he would reply, in his soft, plummy voice, without looking up, 'How are we today, Bradley?' Other times he would be so engrossed in studying the shrubbery that he wouldn't even hear me. I wasn't convinced he was a very talented banker: gardening was obviously his true passion.

'I'm fine, thank you,' I would reply. 'I'm just heading off for my jog. What are you up to?'

I remember one fine spring morning when he replied rather curtly:

'I'm inspecting the shrubs,' as if this were both perfectly obvious and an acceptable reply to a friendly greeting. I must admit I was piqued.

'Tell me, Graham,' I said, wandering nonchalantly up to where he was kneeling in the grass, 'What's the difference between lilies, calla lilies and orchids?'

Baron Digby sighed, and continued pawing at the little plants. 'I'm actually in the middle of something,' he muttered, in as polite a tone as one can muster between gritted teeth.

'I always get confused,' I continued with a smile, 'I have them in my country house in Kent, and my wife is just as obsessed as you are with gardening. You English seem to have it in your blood, this rummaging around in the dirt. If you're not going out to sea in boats or invading somewhere in Africa or Asia, you just have your faces in the green grass. Don't you miss human contact?'

Baron Digby sat up straight. 'Are you criticising the English?' he asked, very politely.

'I'm just making an observation,' I said gently. 'Why aren't you engaged in conversation with me? Am I truly so dull that you'd rather stare in silence at your shrubs? That's all I'm asking. Also, I'm interested in lilies. I was trying to engage you on a topic you'd be well-informed on.'

Digby regarded me thoughtfully. 'I do apologise,' he said. 'I didn't mean to be rude. I just get very involved with my plants.'

'That's quite alright,' I said. 'I didn't mean to disturb you. I understand. I mean, I don't really understand the appeal of gardening, to be honest. When my wife does it for hours at a time, it's usually because she's trying to avoid me.'

He laughed a little. 'I take it you're a cynical soul, then,' he said quietly. 'But there's something incredibly therapeutic about gardening. There's a real joy in bringing these things to life, helping them sprout, encouraging them to flower. It's primitive; it's wonderful.'

'You sound like a farmer,' I couldn't help saying. 'Why would primitive things have such an appeal to a successful banker from a good family?'

'I suppose I'm rather torn,' he said, with a slightly crooked smile. 'My parents always had such high aspirations for me. I do believe if I'd had the choice I would've become a farmer.'

'Ah, but I bet you'd think differently if you were raised a farmer! You would be scrabbling in the dirt and eating porridge and bacon. But now you're a banker raised on tea in bone china and your grandmother's pastries.'

'Now you're just sounding cynical again. But you must have some kind of interest in botanicals yourself. What was your question again?'

'Oh, I was just wondering what the differences between lilies, calla lies and orchids were. It seems like something a posh botanist might know about!'

He smiled, and replied softly: 'Well, you might just be right about that. To be sure, the three flower types do have a lot in common: the soft, thick petals, for instance. But lilies tend to be trumpet or bell shaped, while calla lilies will have that distinctive funnel or horn shape. Orchids have a more complicated form, because they tend to develop close relationships with their pollinators.'

'You mean with specific birds and bees?'

'Yes, exactly. Whereas pretty much anything can pollinate lilies. The other difference is that orchids come from roots, while lilies and calla lilies come from bulbs. Orchids also prefer the shade, while both kinds of lilies can live in full sun.'

'And you usually keep orchids indoors?'

'Indeed. That's about all I can tell you. Oh, one more thing: there are around thirty thousand species of orchid, about a hundred kinds of lily, and only eight kinds of calla lily.'

After discussing gardening in general for a while, we left on good terms, and from then on Graham Digby always made sure he greeted me when he saw me in the garden. We became friends. One day I came across him emptying boxes from his station wagon in the square.

'Let me help,' I offered.

'Oh, thank you, Bradley,' he huffed and puffed over a tower of boxes. 'I'm just putting all of these into storage; I need to keep them dry. On Friday I'm driving down to Wiltshire, where I have a farm; that's where I do most of my gardening. I have an orchard there too. Some of the plants need constant looking after, you know.'

The next few weekends I saw him packing many of his gardening items into his car on the Friday evening, presumably as soon as he came back from work. Sometimes he wouldn't be back until early Monday morning. I helped him carry the big, dewy plants and boxes of seeds from the square to his apartment. In return for my assistance, and to compensate for my smart cream shoes being completely covered in black dirt, he invited me to his home for tea.

When I entered his apartment, I couldn't believe my eyes: it was like walking into a fragrant jungle. The whole place was filled with plants: trees standing in the corners, vines draped from the bookshelves, flowers hanging in baskets. He even had small orange and lemon trees sitting on the balcony. 'I have to try and make sure they get enough sun,' he explained. 'I'll plant them in the garden as soon as I get to Wiltshire.'

'Why don't you just move there?' I asked him, as we sipped tea and nibbled on ginger biscuits. 'I've now lived next to you for three years, and you are always going back and forth with your plants. I don't believe you have any other entertainment in the city. Most fervent gardeners end up moving when they've had enough of these urban parts.'

'People don't just give up apartments on Eaton Square,' he sighed. 'Besides, I have my job. It would be much too far to commute.'

'But what about your wife? Don't you miss having a family life?'

'My wife loves gardening even more than I do. She wouldn't survive in central London. Besides, there's far too much to do in the country: weeding, cutting grass, pruning the trees. September is the busiest time, and it's also the prime period for banking after the holidays, as you well know. I'm working until eight or nine every night, and then I have to rush off at the weekend to pick the apples and pears. Then of course you have the final strawberry season, the last peaches and cherries, before the walnuts and quinces are ready.'

'You have quince trees? I'm rather fond of quince. I make a great quince jam; my grandmother taught me the recipe.'

'My wife makes a marvellous quince jelly,' he said.

'Ah, but this is different. Have you ever tried what the Spanish call *dulce de membrillo*? Well this is quite similar. It's like thick quince jam you can cut in squares to eat like a sweet, or with fine cheese.'

'That sounds most unusual! I've worked with fruit and vegetables all my life, but I've never come across such a thing.'

'If you give me some quinces I will make you some. All you have to do is stabilise the sugar so it doesn't crystallise.'

At the end of the next weekend, I saw him pull up in the square in the pouring rain and begin to lug crate after crate of apples, pears and quinces up the stairs. I walked across to give him a hand, and in less than an hour we had filled every surface in his apartment with the fruit, and made the entire building smell like autumn in the country. When we had carried the last crate into the entry hallway, and stood there, dripping wet, he said: 'These quinces are for you!'

'What, all of them?'

'There aren't that many this year! Anyway, I have plenty of apples and pears to work with. Just have me round for some of that jam thing you were going to make.'

That weekend, we prepared the quince paste in my kitchen,

grating the quince finely and cooking it down with sugar and lemon zest until it turned bright red.

'So in a sense it's just like marmalade,' Baron Digby said as he stirred the preparation.

'It's funny you should say that,' I replied, 'as the word "marmalade" actually comes from the Portuguese word for quinces! My grandmother also taught me that.'

'I will have to write down the recipe,' he added. 'It's starting to smell delightful.' When the cooking was done, we had a good ten kilos of chunky jam. I gave five of them to him as a gift. Eventually, Baron Digby did move back to Wiltshire to be with his wife and fruit trees, but he would write to me every Christmas, and he once told me that he had made quince jam himself. He became extremely popular with the neighbours for distributing well-packed jars of jam to them.

Sometimes, a great holiday can be spoiled by the smallest of incidents: a sick child, a long traffic jam, an insurance claim, or a spate of bad weather. Even the most beautiful of locations can hide secret trouble.

Deauville, in Normandy, was no exception. I often had business there when I was a banker in Paris, and as my wife loved the French coast, we would often travel there together. The town was something of a resort, popular amongst rich English, Dutch and Spanish families who enjoyed the wide beaches of soft sand, great for swimming, sailing, and long walks. We used to go on long horseback rides at sunset, with the surf lapping at the horse's hooves: it was a blissful setting.

Some of the other tourists, however, came for slightly less relaxing entertainment: many of the hotels in Deauville were built following the success of the rare allotment of a gambling licence to a casino there. Many would sail in on their yachts, or drive down from Paris in their Aston Martins and Jaguars and spend their hard-earned money (or inheritance) at the felt-topped tables. Gambling was of no interest either to Hilary or to me, but it was difficult to ignore, as our favourite hotel in Deauville, the famous Hotel Normandy, happened to look out over the gorgeously lit casino itself.

This particular holiday was the first time we had stayed there. It was late spring, and we had a lovely first night in the hotel when we arrived late on Friday. Our room had half-timbering, elaborate toile-de-Jouy wallpaper, and a china tea-set: we felt rather like we were staying in an English country house. Hilary and I spent a delightful weekend in twenty-three degree weather, riding horses in the morning, playing tennis in the afternoon, and finishing off the day with an evening drink in the rose garden and a lovely meal in the hotel. As we settled into bed, we planned to start the day off early on Sunday so we could get in a jog and a swim before lunchtime. We drifted into a peaceful sleep.

At midnight, there was a loud knock on the door. I started awake, and got up to put on my bathrobe. 'Who is it?' I asked, as I clambered across the room, but when I opened the door, there was no-one there. Hearing voices from the room next door, I realised that the knock hadn't been intended for me.

'What's going on?' Hilary asked sleepily from the bed.

'Nothing, darling,' I answered. At this point there were a series of stumbling noises, followed by a crash.

'Is he drunk?'

'I suppose that might be the case,' I admitted. 'We are right next to the casino, after all.'

'Who gambles drunk?' my wife muttered, at which point the shouting next door began.

First, there came a loud woman's voice, in southern-accented French. 'How dare you come back here at this time, stinking of wine!'

This was followed by a distinctly blurred and thus fairly difficult to make out man's voice: 'Oh, it's you,' he said. 'Go away.'

It was obvious that the woman had been waiting up for the man and preparing this tirade.

'Go away? Go away?' the wife responded. 'This was meant to be a holiday! Just you and me! What if the kids had been here?'

'The kids aren't here. That's the point. I'm just having a bit of fun.' There were some muffled sounds, and then the noise of stumbling footsteps.

'What are they saying?' Hilary asked, sitting up in bed and switching the light on. Hilary's only French was left over from her school days, and the couple had quite thick Marseille accents as well. 'Is it exciting?'

I sighed. It was obvious that we would not be getting any sleep. 'She's just angry that he's home late.'

'You idiot!' came the woman's voice again. 'Our kids, they're ten and twelve, and already smoking...' I couldn't make out what came next, until the man shouted: 'Well, I'll just find another woman, then.'

'With all the money you have?' the wife responded. I began to suspect this marriage had been on the rocks before this holiday to Normandy. These sounded like well-rehearsed arguments. Next door, the woman's voice softened, and the next thing we heard was her wailing: 'Is there someone else? Don't you love me anymore?'

'Are they fighting?' Hilary murmured. 'How is this so loud?' Her faint smile of amusement had quickly turned into an expression of disgust. Other people's family dramas apparently became much less interesting after about ten minutes.

'We have a joint balcony,' I explained. 'One of those wonderfully stupid turn-of-the-century designs. I'm really sorry about this, honey.'

There must have been some quiet venom exchanged, as the next thing we heard was the French woman insulting her husband in colourful language.

'*Ta gueule!* Shut up!' the Frenchman shouted. 'Shut up or I'll leave! I'll leave you soon anyway, you're getting so fat.'

'As if I'd want to stay with you, you crazy old drunk! I don't know why I married you in the first place, or why I stayed after you slept with the secretary!'

'What are they saying?' Hilary asked again, her eyes wide.

'He's angry, um, because he's not had good luck gambling.' I didn't want to translate this vile fight and ruin our vacation. 'Look, let's maybe just switch the TV on for a bit. I'm sure it'll quiet down in a minute, then we can get some sleep.'

Slightly shaken, my wife and I proceeded to half-watch a documentary about shepherding. In the background, the fight continued for some time, covering the husband's troubled childhood, alcoholism, gambling problems, and lack of care for his wife. I also learned far more than I would have liked to know about his extramarital affairs. I hoped most of this was flying over Hilary's head, but the tone of the argument was hard to ignore.

'Should we go over and talk to them?' she suggested timidly.

'I don't think that's such a good idea,' I replied.

'Well maybe we should speak to the hotel manager? I'm worried.'

At this point there was a tremendous thump against the wall that made both of us jump. There was more incoherent shouting, then silence.

'Is he beating his wife? That's inhuman. Please, let's just leave. This is horrible.'

'I'm sure they're just packing. They decided to leave earlier to, um, go back home. They probably have a really early flight.' There was another thump from next door, and I laughed nervously. 'He's probably just throwing the luggage around.'

Hilary narrowed her eyes. 'Can you *please* call the manager?' she said, louder than before. 'This is unacceptable. I'm worried for the poor woman.'

'How do you know it's the woman we should be worried for?' I muttered, but I was already halfway across the room. I picked up the telephone and rang the lobby.

'Yes, hello, I'm sorry to wake you this late.'

'That's alright,' the manager replied sleepily. 'What can I do for you?'

'There's a couple next door, fighting.' I lowered my voice. 'I'm worried there may be physical violence involved.' Hilary coughed.

The manager sighed. 'I'm afraid I doubt we'll be able to do anything. It's their private room, you see. It's their private business. French law, you know,' he added vaguely. 'I'm sorry for you, *Monsieur*.'

'Packing, eh,' was all Hilary said when I put down the phone, but she looked unconvinced. After a few hours the couple fell silent, and we managed to get to sleep. When we woke up the next morning, the fighting was over: we didn't know if either of them had left, or both, or whether they had just blown off steam and fallen asleep side by side. But within an hour or so, any illusions we might have had about the couple's reconciliation were shattered when we heard the fighting start up again. It escalated quickly, and Hilary and I decided we'd best get up at once to escape from it. About twenty minutes later, we heard a door slam, followed by total silence.

'Do you think that was him?' Hilary whispered.

'I have no idea.' I shook my head. 'Come on, darling, let's get out of here.'

'The thing I can't get over,' she continued, as if she hadn't heard me, 'is how much we could hear! I mean, what if things had become physical?'

I laughed, and Hilary blushed. 'These nineteenth-century buildings are completely ridiculous,' I added as reassuringly as I could. 'I'm looking forward to going back to a country where they have sound insulation!'

AN UNEXPECTED NEIGHBOUR
AT THE PLAZA

When I was working in Washington, I had the occasion to stay in a lot of glamorous hotels, as I was often flying to Paris, London, and New York for business. In the Big Apple particularly, I was lucky enough to stay in some of the best in the world, including the St Regis, the Plaza, the Regency, and the Waldorf Astoria. But one thing I noticed about nearly all of the hotels, with the possible exception of the St Regis, was that they exerted very little control over the comings and goings of their clientele. I suppose it had to do with abiding by the American constitution and its rigid concept of individual liberty, and was intended to make the powerful and privileged guests feel comfortable, but it did let some rather odd types infiltrate the fancy air-conditioned lobbies.

The Plaza has always been one of my favourite hotels, with nearly all of my stays there being enjoyable from the moment I set foot on the red-carpeted front stairs, and was escorted through the golden revolving doors by their footmen. I would often use my lodgings there as both personal and business spaces, as I stayed in one of the larger suites on behalf of the bank, and could receive clients in the conference room to promote investments and acquisition and other Wall Street business. This way, I could comfortably have serious business meetings at imposing glass tables with vases of orchids, as nice as in any European office, while being within walking distance of my luxurious bedroom. All of this with commanding views of the Manhattan skyline.

Thus, it was not surprising for me to receive knocks on the door in the middle of the day or even in the early evening, with some client coming in to close a deal, or a secretary arriving to have letters and contracts dictated to her. But one day, the knock was not followed by the entry of any of my business partners. When I opened the door, a beautiful woman was standing there. 'Hello,' she murmured sensuously.

'I'm sorry, who are you?' I responded, stepping back a little. The apparition was dressed in very tight, black clothes that stuck to her like cling-film without being exactly revealing. Her cleavage was covered in sheer material, which did a terrible job of hiding it. She smelled very strongly of perfume, which seemed to emanate from the silk scarf she had wrapped around her. She didn't look like a typical client, but of course you never know.

'Bradley,' she said very gently, extending her hand, 'how lovely to meet you.'

'I'm sorry,' I said, 'I don't think I'm expecting anyone but my secretary, and unless she's dyed her hair and grown a foot taller in the last hour, you're not her.' I held back from making a comment about her skimpy clothing. 'All my meetings finished a good hour ago. I was just having a quick nap.' This was a lie, in hopes that she would take the hint and leave me alone.

Instead, she smiled coyly. 'That sounds nice,' she said invitingly. I paused. This conversation was obviously not going the way either of us had been expecting. 'Can I invite you to dinner?' she asked next. 'I'm your neighbour,' she added flirtatiously. 'I'm staying next door.'

'How do you know my name?' I asked, a little more firmly.

'Oh, I have my ways.'

'Well that's very nice,' I said shortly. I was quickly losing patience with this infuriating creature and her air of mystery. 'What do you want? Are you involved in marketing? Business? Are you part of the hotel management!'

She laughed, a tinkling little laugh which was meant to be inviting, but I merely found it annoying. 'I'm your neighbour!' she repeated.

'Well, what are you selling, then?'

'I'm not selling anything!' she exclaimed innocently. 'I'd just like to have dinner with you.' She lowered her voice. 'I'd like to get to know you.' Seeing that this was having no effect on me, she pouted a little. This whole act was beginning to look rather cheap.

'I don't really have dinner with strangers,' I replied curtly. 'Unless there's a very specific purpose, arranged by my bank. Or my mother. Besides, I'm busy tonight.'

She paused, apparently undisturbed by this rejection. 'Can I come in?' she purred. I thought I detected a hint of a Russian accent.

'Well, you can come in for five minutes if you want a glass of water, but I'm expecting someone. I have to dictate a long report to my secretary before I go meet a friend.'

This threw her slightly. 'Never mind,' she said, waving her hand. 'Let me just tell you a few things about myself. If you can't have dinner with me tonight I can meet you afterwards.' Here she paused, suggestively, and edged a little way into the room. I was on to her now, and distinctly uninterested.

'For what?' I said, deciding to play her game.

'Whatever your hobbies are,' she said coyly. As I did not respond, she continued, slightly awkwardly: 'We can go walking, um, go to a disco…' she recovered confidence. 'I can do anything you want.'

'What does that even mean?' I said, my face completely blank.

'Anything you want,' she repeated, with emphasis on the first word. She took a step closer.

'Well that's not very nice,' I said in as innocent a voice as I could muster. 'I mean, somebody I don't know; why would they do what I want? Why aren't you doing what you want?' I was rather hoping to annoy her and make her snap out of her little act.

'Well…' she said, then trailed off. Clearly deciding more clarity was needed, she shrugged her little scarf off her shoulders, exposing her cleavage, which I pointedly ignored.

'Maybe,' she cajoled, 'you might change your mind after a couple glasses of wine?'

'I don't drink, and I'm not interested,' I said firmly. 'Now if you'll excuse me, I have to get back to work.' I put one hand on her waist and pushed her distinctly away.

'I'll see you later, then,' she said uncertainly, as I propelled her gently to the door.

'No, you won't,' I said decisively, and closed the door behind her. I could have sworn I heard her say 'I'll be back,' but this seemed more comical than threatening at the time. At this very moment, my secretary arrived from her room down the hall and obviously met the girl on her way out. My secretary gave me a wink.

'What the hell do you mean by that?' I said, insulted.

My secretary blushed, and apologised so quickly that I regretted my sharpness, and explained the whole story. At the end, she simply said: 'Be careful, this is New York. You could be robbed three times in a day without even noticing.'

'Oh, don't worry,' I replied, 'I saw right through her little act. The only things of value are quite safely in my little dresser over there,' I confided, gesturing towards the bedroom.

'Surely you don't keep too much cash there?' my secretary said in a worried voice.

'Oh, it's rather a bad habit of mine,' I said jovially. 'I like to keep a good stash available so I can save time when I'm out and about. I don't like to wait in restaurants for my credit card to clear, for example.'

'Please just don't take too many risks,' she said quietly. At the time I thought nothing of it. I left the office, locked it, and went to dinner. When I came back several hours later, however, I had a bad feeling as soon as I entered the room, when I noticed a lingering smell of perfume. Seized with worry, I dashed across to the dresser. When I opened the drawer, my worst fears were confirmed: the several hundred dollars I knew had been there only hours before had vanished without a trace, along with the beautiful gold Certina watch my father had given me when I was twelve.

I ran downstairs to the lobby to report the theft.

'I've been robbed!' I shouted. 'Has anybody suspicious been in the building? Do you have cameras? Call the police!'

'I'm afraid we don't, sir,' the concierge said calmly. 'Some of our clients want to retain their privacy.'

'Yes, well, I'd have quite liked to retain my gold watch,' I snapped. 'Can you call the police?'

'Sir, it would be no good. The contents of your room are your own responsibility.'

'That's ridiculous!' I paused, remembering something. 'Wait, what if I think I know who it is? A tall woman with long dark hair. Scantily clad. High heels.'

The concierge raised an eyebrow with a knowing smile.

'Oh, don't be a fool,' I said impatiently, 'I mean that this woman came to see me this afternoon.'

'I see, sir.' The eyebrow raised higher.

'She stood outside my door,' I added pointedly. 'And did not come in. She tried to get me to go to dinner, some such nonsense. I don't know how she could have got back in, but I'm sure it was her. She said she was my neighbour. Can you tell me who's staying next door?' I pleaded.

He sighed. 'Well, I'm not supposed to tell you that, but I feel bad when these things happen on my watch. Here, let me have a look.' He hauled up the big leather register and flicked through it. After a time, he said: 'Well, your neighbour is a family with children.'

'How about the other side?'

'It's empty. Sir, I'm afraid you've been had. This person must not be staying here.'

'And yet you allow these... low-lives to walk the hallways?'

'Well, the clients usually invite them in, *sir*,' he responded pointedly. 'There's nothing we can do about that. As I said, such matters are your own responsibility.'

'I daresay I hope you're not implying what I think,' I said, as sternly as I could.

The concierge withered under my glare. 'All I'm thinking,' he replied timidly, 'is that this person must have stolen your key. It's one thing to have people in the corridors, but they shouldn't be able to get in. If what you're saying is true, and I don't doubt it is,' he added hastily, 'this... person must've just gone to find out when you were going to be out, and had some accomplices who broke in.'

'She must've seen I had no interest in what she was peddling, and figured theft was the only way to get money from me...' I paused. 'I wonder if the same thing would have happened if I had accepted her offer of dinner!'

The concierge looked at me with a sad smile. 'Sir, I truly meant you no insult. I just would suggest you keep your valuables better hidden, or in a safe from now on.'

'Oh, I will. I don't think I'll let anything out of my sight! I'll take them with me in the shower! But it's the watch I'm most disappointed about,' I said sadly. 'It was a treasured gift from my father. I don't want to think about who will wear it now.'

The concierge nodded sadly. 'The important thing is that it's not your fault. This person was obviously organised and had done their research.'

'I mean, how did she know my name?'

'I have no idea, sir. It must be a sort of inside job. I very much doubt there was any chance this lady was really your neighbour.'

'And I was supposed to just figure this out?'

'Of course not. It wasn't your fault.'

'Well,' I said wryly, 'I would like to respond that it is in fact *your* fault, but really it's just a shame.'

'I guess you can't choose your neighbours,' he said meekly.

'Sometimes your neighbours choose you!' I added.

A DISPUTE OVER HELIPADS

In the eighties, my family and I bought a house in St Tropez. It was a classic brick house, with two swimming pools and beautiful gardens, and a jetty and beach out back. It was not overly luxurious, but it was certainly enviable both in looks and in location. This was the heyday of my banking career, so I was always a very busy man. Spending a day or a weekend at that house was an excellent way to get to spend time with my family, lounging by the poolside or gathered around the oak dining table. The trouble with St Tropez in general, however, is getting there. For a popular holiday destination, parts of it remain fairly inaccessible by many means of transport, which, I suppose, some might consider part of its charm, but not if one has a busy schedule! The roads are small, and if one lands in Nice or Toulon, which are the closest airports, the drive by car can take up to two and a half hours. However, if one has a helicopter, it only takes ten to fifteen minutes or so, as one can just zip across the bay instead of having to navigate around it on the tiny coastal roads. The short helicopter ride wasn't even that expensive, especially if four people were sharing the cost, which would bring the price to around that of a rail ticket. Besides, there is a certain thrill to a helicopter ride: it makes the common travelling banker feel like MacGyver or James Bond.

But there was one crucial issue with travelling by helicopter: where to land? I thought I had struck gold when I found out that my neighbour had a heliport on his vast tracts of land. Yet no matter how close to him I managed to get, or how friendly I was to him as a neighbour, he simply refused to let me land there. I had to use one of my other friends' heliports, which was a good half an hour drive away, where my next door neighbour's would have been just a minute-long walk from our front door.

My neighbour was a strange and difficult man. He was an ageing businessman long past his prime, his face wrinkled by too many sunbeds and his eyes reddened from too many late nights. He was renowned in the neighbourhood as a fairly shady character, but he was tolerated because of the huge parties he threw. He was a somewhat extravagant man, with a taste for the more visible luxuries in life. He liked to dress in flashy designer clothing: sharply tailored Gucci suits, Lacoste shirts in bright colours, Rolex watches, and always a big pair of the latest Ray Ban sunglasses. Every weekend, he seemed to have a huge cocktail party, either on his lawn by the swimming pool, or in his vast marble-arched entry hallway, where his rich and famous guests would mill up and down the red-carpeted stairs in floor-length evening gowns and tuxedos. Everything had to be wildly over the top. Often he would have theme parties: the Roaring Twenties, for instance, when all the guests would turn up with feather boas and flapper dresses and long cigarette holders, and sip strong cocktails late into the night. Or something more ironic, like his Hippie party, which was worth attending just to get a taste of what the rich and famous imagined bohemian clothing looked like: a cream Dior shirt with a ruff, perhaps, or two buttons undone instead of one; an Hermès silk scarf covered in bright flowers. How this particular neighbour made his money was always something of a mystery to me; he seemed to rarely leave his house.

In any case, he was not a man particularly interested in helping out his fellow neighbour. 'I'm a busy man,' he would say, with a false sort of heartiness. 'I can only give seven minutes of my time to any one person. So fire away!'

I found this sort of bluster somewhat annoying. My neighbour was a single man and pretended to have many friends, even though I wasn't too sure about the quality of those acquaintances and associates of his. To be perfectly honest, I didn't like going to his parties so much myself; I presumed many of the other guests were just as bored as I was.

Nonetheless, I needed something from him, so I tried to be as charming as possible. 'It won't take a minute,' I told him. 'I'll cut to the chase, and spare your precious time. It's just a small request – you see, I often fly into St Tropez by helicopter…'

'All the best people do, my good man,' he said, drinking deeply from his martini and looking over my shoulder, as if already bored.

'It would really be convenient if I could land on your helipad,' I finished swiftly.

'That's ridiculous,' he scoffed, completely unapologetically. 'This is my land! I mean,' he added, 'I'm quite happy to have you all here for my parties, and I wouldn't like to cause a scene, but I'm afraid that's more of a favour than I'm willing to offer. Sorry, old man!' He clapped me on the shoulder, and put on a more serious expression:

'If I say yes to you,' he said, 'I'm saying yes to everyone.' Without waiting for an answer to this statement, he then walked back into the crowd of guests.

After several unpleasant variants of this conversation, I decided there was no hope of him relenting and letting me use his heliport. I applied to the city for permission to build one of my own in our garden. But because of the configuration of the borders, I was informed that this would only be possible if my neighbour gave me permission to fly over his land on the way to mine. My shoulders slumped when I received the official piece of mail, as I knew I had little hope of getting through to my neighbour's sense of sympathy. Nonetheless, I squared my shoulders and prepared my speech for the next party we attended. It would only have been a question of flying across a few of my neighbour's acres of land, a portion which was basically a field anyway, but of course he refused outright.

'I can't have all my acquaintances flying across my land. If I say yes to you, I'm saying yes to everyone!'

'Because all your friends have helicopters?' I retorted in exasperation.

'Well, some of the good ones do,' he said sarcastically, before turning his back on me and rudely ending the conversation.

It really was incredibly frustrating, as the only alternative would have been approaching my own property from the sea, which would have made it near-impossible to land without cutting down half the trees in our garden!

My neighbour was a rather strange character, and I never fully understood why he wouldn't give in to any of my suggestions. Perhaps it was a point of pride not to let another man's helicopter fly across his garden? Perhaps he wanted to have the only helipad in the neighbourhood? In any case, the whole thing was a terrible shame.

This argument went on for eight years, and no matter how much I tried to bribe him by inviting him to our parties and making overtures of friendship, the only thing he would do for me in return was invite me back to his parties. Every time I went, it was for the sole purpose of asking him if I could land in his heliport, or build my own, and every time, no matter what kind of mood he was in, how many drinks he had finished, or how well we had been getting on, he would say no. He really was a most unhelpful neighbour.

ROSIE, LUCY, AND SHIVERS

In my days as a student at the London School of Economics, I decided to take an apartment in Paddington. It was an easy decision on my part – I wished only to be closer to my girlfriend of the time, Lucy, whose friend had suggested a place just down the hall from her own apartment which had become available. I leapt at the chance to live in such a convenient location.

I found London to be something of a culture shock after the clean, promising streets of America. If America offered wide open spaces and adventure, London seemed only to consist of a constant, gnawing cold, and pollution. In October, the city already seemed to be in the depths of winter, the roads icy as the temperature dropped as low as four degrees on the worst days. And, although I was quite a wealthy student, my desire for proximity to Lucy won out over how unimpressed I was with the new home she helped me to find.

As far as I could tell, the place seemed to have come straight out of a Dickens novel. The stairs up to my apartment were rickety and winding, with paint and old wallpaper peeling from the walls around me as I ascended flight after flight of steps. The carpeting on the floor was shabby and worn, and I could only imagine how many thousands of shoes had trodden dirt into it before mine. The landlord appeared to be completely uninterested in updating the place, although I did comment that most apartment buildings in America now had elevators so that one didn't have to undergo the Herculean task of climbing hundreds of steps.

However, the idea of change seemed not to have touched England at all. It was almost as though the country was stagnating, stuck in the mentality of the Second World War. Even outside of my rather depressing dwelling, a sense of gloom pervaded the grey streets and fog-filled skies. The pollution was quite terrible, and on some days I could barely see my hand in front of my own face for the thickness of the smog that hung across the city like an ugly blanket.

To make this worse, so many people smoked in those days. In America, many people were already more health conscious after the Surgeon-General report in 1963, but in London nearly every adult seemed to smoke away their troubles. It didn't seem to be something anyone enjoyed particularly, so much as just something to do, to keep their hands busy and the cold at bay. Even the most cheerful thing about the city, the famous big red London buses that dotted the roads like bright spots on cloudy days, were filled with people smoking.

Personally, I found this a little hard to take. When I was sitting on a bus, I didn't want my lungs filled with someone else's smoke, yet here I was, surrounded by Londoners in their thick coats, coughing and smoking to their heart's content. It was quite an unpleasant experience, and mostly I tried instead to drive my Aston Martin, though it was difficult to find parking in the city even then, especially on wet days, when people drove all the more to keep out of the rain.

Perhaps it was the dispiriting nature of the weather and the lack of clean fuel that kept Londoners so caught up in the past. More than once, I found myself queuing behind older people who seemed to still think that they needed to ration their butter and tea, and that the grocer was indeed a very important man to know. They chattered about how decimated their own towns and villages had been by the war, how destroyed London itself had been, as though the whole affair had taken place only a couple of days before. How they had, a few years previously, had to queue up for hours to get so much as a pint of milk or a loaf of bread in Yorkshire or Sussex.

I almost wanted to point out that now, in the sixties, in London of all places, it was perhaps safe to not worry so much about events that had mainly taken place almost twenty years before. The past was very much in the past as far as I was concerned, yet England was reluctant to move forward, still feeling the aftershocks of such events with raw clarity.

In fairness, the war had left a lot of London feeling as though we were all living a century in the past. Because of the terrible bombings, many buildings were pieced back together quickly and shabbily, with only the cheap materials available at the time, or else left partly derelict. Even the London Underground stations were left with wooden escalators, as though time had stopped still at a certain point. Many of the buildings that escaped the bombings mostly unscathed were relics from a Victorian heyday, ornate and towering, but crumbling to bits when you looked past the façade.

My apartment in Paddington was something like this. It was a complete shock to me, to go from the LSE, which was in the intellectual heart of London where people actually took pride in their properties and surroundings, to Paddington, where many of the houses were like mine, falling to pieces with nobody to care. Oftentimes, I felt my heart begin to sink as I approached my building, because I knew exactly what I was in for.

The electricity was one thing. It was patchy at best, flickering on and off without any notice, rhyme or reason behind its caprices. I might be sitting reading or making myself something to eat, and suddenly I would be plunged into complete darkness, and have to wait, in whatever position I found myself, until the lights came back on. There weren't many streetlights, even, to cast a glow into my rooms and it was almost a game, to work out when the electricity might cut off. I decided eventually that it was at certain peak times of usage when it turned off, such as when everybody was cooking their dinner, although sometimes it would just be off for an age and I had no clue why.

The cold was the other thing. I was not used to cold weather such as I experienced it in London. Up until then, and in fact for the last twenty years, I had been used to central heating, and my tolerance of cold weather was rather limited.

So it was rather a shock to find that even the heating system in the building was like something entirely Dickensian. One operated it by feeding a meter found out on the common landing with coins. I learned early on how the English monetary system of the time worked, mainly through having to put shillings into this damnable meter. This was pre-decimal British currency, so there were twenty shillings to the pound, and twelve pennies to a shilling. It wasn't a difficulty to get hold of an endless supply of shillings, but if you were ever caught short the meter wouldn't take anything else.

Being quite organised, I was soon keeping on hand as many shillings as were necessary to keep myself warm. I worked out that if I went to bed at ten, putting two shillings in the meter just before, I could be warm and sleep soundly the whole night through. Otherwise the cold would wake me and I would be forced out to feed the meter in the blackness of night. If I didn't plan like this, it would have been a ridiculous system which revolved around dancing through the freezing air onto the landing and constantly giving the meter more and more money.

One person who never seemed to organise her coins was Rosie, my girlfriend's friend, who had helped me to find the apartment in the first place. Not long into my stay, I was woken at two in the morning to a little rap at my door. When I got out of bed to open it, Rosie was standing there in her dressing gown, an imploring expression on her face.

Rosie was a very small and pretty blonde, the sort of girl who knew how to ask for things so that she got what she wanted. I had seen her around the LSE on more than one occasion, and thought she was quite striking. She smiled at me winningly.

'I'm so sorry to wake you. It's just... would you happen to have a shilling for the meter? My place is freezing!'

I stared at her somewhat blankly. 'Don't you have money?'

'I don't have a penny to my name. I'm broke.' She widened her eyes and bit her lip, as though she were truly embarrassed by the situation. 'I'm really sorry to ask, but it's so cold, and I can give you it back tomorrow. Please?'

It felt something like rescuing a damsel in distress, so I gave her a couple of shillings. She smiled at me and ran to put one in the meter, and I returned to bed, hoping that would be the last of it and that she would give me back my money the next day.

And yet the next night, I heard the same little tapping on my door at two o'clock in the morning, and got up to find that it was Rosie again.

'I feel just awful,' she announced, hugging herself and rubbing her arms, 'but I completely forgot to get any money today. How cold is it tonight?! Do you think you could help me out?'

This time, I went out into the cold air and put the shilling in the meter for her. She touched my arm as I walked back to my room.

'Thanks, you're so kind. I really appreciate it. I'll give you it all back as soon as I can.' She smiled, and I got the feeling she was being a bit flirtatious with me. Rosie was the sort of girl who intrigued me, scatter-brained and yet very clever with it, but she was, after all, Lucy's friend. Flattered though I was by the possibility, I simply shrugged it off, and gave her a few shillings for the morning and the next night.

Goodness knows what she did with them, because I never saw that money again, either. Rosie kept coming to my door at odd hours, in her nightdress or dressing gown, asking favours of shillings another few times before I had to finally suggest she organise herself better, that I hadn't got any spare change lying around. Rosie looked a bit perturbed, but after that she didn't ask again, and I continued to sleep warmly through every night.

I didn't stay in the Paddington apartment building for a moment longer than I needed to. After six weeks I'd had it with the archaic heating and electricity situation, and moved into a much nicer house share, with pleasant people. However, I did keep in touch with Rosie and still saw her at the LSE. I could never work out whether she had really been scatty enough to forget her shillings, or if she was poorer than I thought, or if she had really been flirting with me.

Whatever the case, I learned years later that she had gone on to become a famous judge in the British appeal courts. It was difficult to reconcile the image of the slender girl in her night clothes, standing out on the dark landing, with a high-powered legal figure, but then she had always been quite intelligent, diligent, and driven, as her approach to getting the shillings off me proved.

As for me, I was more than happy to move on to other adventures, though the memories of my difficult first few weeks in that freezing Paddington hovel remain with me to this day.

OUR NEIGHBOUR IN ETRETAT

Etretat, a beautiful old coastal town looking out over the Atlantic coast and Normandy hills, is considered by many to be the Antibes of the north of France. It's famous for its dramatic cliffs and glorious nineteenth-century houses, and has been hugely popular with English tourists for the last two hundred years thanks to its location, including Churchill, Montgomery, and a smattering of royals. Etretat tends to be thought of as a base for secondary homes rather than for hotels, attracting visitors looking for that homey experience rather than the luxury of maid service and Jacuzzis. There were, of course, more temporary sources of accommodation available, most of them bed-and-breakfasts established in the old turn-of-the-century townhouses originally set up as tuberculosis recovery centres in the mid-nineteenth and twentieth centuries.

When I was twenty-five and newly-married, my wife and I went to visit a family friend there and stayed in a B&B on the beach. It was a gorgeous place, run by a slightly grumpy old French lady, furnished impeccably with lace curtains and a comfortable leather sofa. We stayed on the second floor, which would have been delightful had there not been an almost constant squeaking noise coming from upstairs.

Now, I was raised in a family of ten. I could read in an armchair while my brothers and sisters played tag around, over and under me. I could do homework while someone practised dribbling a basketball over my head. I could have long conversations about literature on the phone while the radio announcer was explaining the news loudly in the background. I could understand exactly what my mother was scolding my younger sister for whilst I myself was discussing sports with my school friends. I can also block out the sound of London traffic passing by my window, or the jazz or disco music my neighbours sometimes play, and I can sleep through the shouts of lovers fighting in the street. But there was just something different about this squeaking. Something slightly uneven and swiftly becoming impossible to ignore.

'*Why* is the upstairs floor so squeaky?' I asked my wife. 'The floor in our room isn't. The floor next door isn't.'

'I don't know, darling,' Hilary responded calmly. 'It simply doesn't really bother me.'

Well, it bothered me. It started driving me mad. I couldn't sleep; I couldn't maintain a serious conversation with my wife or the family friends when they came to visit us in the hotel. The funny thing was no-one else seemed to care.

'Are you OK, Brad?' our friends asked me. 'Is there something wrong with the B&B?'

'No,' I said, then, somewhat desperately, 'I mean, it's just the floor. Creaking. Can you hear it?'

They paused expectantly. The floor creaked. The friends shrugged.

'Sure,' the wife said, 'it's a little creaky. Do you really mind that much?'

'Look, I'm sorry,' I sighed. 'I know you've booked us this wonderful place. But can you please intervene? Nothing drastic,' I added hastily. 'I don't want to cut our holiday short. But I wondered if you could perhaps ask the manager if we can change rooms? Or otherwise perhaps we can go to another hotel? I don't know. All I know is it's driving me mad.'

Our friends were very sympathetic and tried their best to remedy the situation. Unfortunately, all the rooms were booked; we couldn't move within the B&B. Furthermore, all the other hotels in the vicinity were booked, due to there being a sailing race in the port that weekend. Our only choice was to drive back to London, or stick it out with the squeaky floors. I did not intend to ruin our holiday: I decided to grin and bear it.

Lying awake in bed that night I knew I would regret this decision. I tried to read; I tried to watch television quietly so as not to wake my wife. But nothing I did could cover the sound of that squeaky floor. In fact, it seemed to be getting worse.

'Hilary, I've been thinking,' I said to her after we'd been there a week or so. 'What I don't understand is why someone is making this noise. I mean, it must be someone; it must be a person. It's too irregular to be anything inanimate, and it's too big to be any kind of animal.'

'I hope not,' my wife answered with a small smile. 'I think it's quite obviously the sound of someone walking around upstairs.'

'Exactly!' I said, banging my fist on the table. 'It must be a person pacing. But why? They must walk a good ten kilometres a day just back and forth in that tiny room. They can't be waiting for something to cook. There are no kitchens, I know, I asked downstairs.'

'You asked downstairs?'

'Yes. I'm taking this seriously, you know. But I was wrong. It couldn't be cooking. Perhaps, though, he could be eating standing up. It's a cheap enough hotel to not have tables in every room. Maybe he's pacing to cool down his spaghetti?'

'Darling, if there's no kitchen, it seems unlikely he would have any food to cool.'

'It could be takeaway!'

'I suppose so.'

'You can carry food, you know. Anyway, that's beside the point. I think it's far more likely that he's some sort of thinker. A politician, working out his next speech. A policeman, pondering evidence. A man getting divorced, thinking about his case in court.'

'Or a divorce lawyer,' she contributed helpfully. 'Thinking about the wife's case.'

'He could be.' I narrowed my eyes, unsure if she was making fun of me, but she maintained a sweet smile.

'He could be a sportsman, doing exercises to keep limber,' she suggested.

'Or recovering from some terrible injury!'

Suddenly, I too saw the fun in this dialogue and forgot to worry about the squeaking, which continued unabated above us.

'Maybe he's taking his new girlfriend on a tour of the attic, arm-in-arm!'

'Maybe he's counting the tiles on the floor!'

'Maybe there's a terrible wrinkle in the carpet that he's embarrassed about and he keeps trying to iron it out.'

'He could be waxing the floor,' Hilary suggested impishly. 'You know, some people wear socks over their shoes to polish.'

'Or he could be insane.' We paused, having run out of ideas. The squeaking noise continued, obvious now.

'Or a ghost,' Hilary added, sending us back into fits of giggles.

Once the laughter had calmed, we heard the squeaking again.

'Look,' Hilary said, wiping a tear of laughter from her eye, 'there's one obvious solution we've been neglecting. Let's just go up and ask him.'

I stopped in my tracks. 'Obviously, sleep deprivation has addled my brain. My darling Hilary,' I replied, 'this is clearly why I married you.'

She smiled, and we ran up the stairs as excitedly as children on Christmas morning. We knocked on the door and waited, listening to the creaking beyond. The noise ceased. We knocked again. For a moment, I remembered the less amusing thoughts I had had about this room in the middle of my sleepless nights. What if it *was* a ghost? Then the door was opened by a tall, middle-aged man with a thin moustache.

'*Bonjour,*' he said, slightly confusedly.

'Hello,' I replied in French. 'Um, we are staying below you.'

'Oh, *d'accord*! What can I do for you?' he said with a friendly smile.

'Well, the thing is...' I began, then hesitated. All of a sudden it seemed rather ridiculous.

Hilary added gently: 'It's just that the floors in your room are rather squeaky. We can hear you walking around.'

'Really?' the Frenchman said in surprise.

'Yes,' I said. 'We've been trying to figure out what the noise is for days.'

Suddenly, he let out a laugh. 'You must think I'm some sort of madman!'

'Well, that was one of our options,' I confessed.

'I'm a philosophy professor,' he continued. 'At the Sorbonne. I was just working on my next class on Plato's *Symposium*. I tend to pace when I'm thinking. It had never occurred to me that it might disturb my neighbours!'

'A philosophy professor!' I repeated. 'To think, Hilary, that didn't even occur to us!'

'To think!' she responded dryly.

'I'm terribly sorry,' he said. 'It's just that I tend to stride back and forth on the stage when I am lecturing, so I find it difficult to think without pacing! But I have an idea: I could swap rooms with you if you like?'

I thought about this for a moment. Hilary looked at me in surprise. 'Actually, I don't think that will be necessary,' I responded. Now that I know what the source of the noise is, I don't think it will bother me that much.'

'Well look, I am really sorry,' the professor added. 'I'm actually working on a book at the moment, so it's probably worse than usual. I have another idea: let me give you some of my books! If nothing else, they'll help you get to sleep,' he added with a grin.

THE BABATA BROTHERS: JED,
THE JACKAL HUNTER

When I was in my early twenties, I spent some time in Konya, Turkey, visiting my grandmother at her holiday home. There wasn't a lot to do in the city once I had wandered the dusty streets, gazed up at the blue and white minarets and eaten my fill of lamb and bulgur. Thus, over the course of many quiet afternoons, I found myself striking up a few interesting friendships with our neighbours, including the three Babata brothers.

Jed was the middle brother, being in his mid-thirties and thus a good ten years older than me. He was a quiet and serious type, who liked to spend most of his time outdoors. He made a living by taking tourists and locals out into the surrounding countryside and showing them where the best hunting was to be found. His brothers told me he had made a reputation for himself as a serious but extremely taciturn guide. Foreign tourists seemed to like this, as it meant they didn't have to make uneasy conversation.

Jed and I were the least predisposed of his family to be friends, having nearly nothing in common. However, one day, when I was rather bored, I found myself chatting to him in the shade by the side of a market stall. We agreed on some minor point of discussion, which Jed contributed to mostly with movements of his hands and fierce nods of his head.

'Would you like to go hunting with me?' he asked all at once, rather abruptly.

I was taken aback, but intrigued. Jed and I were hardly friends, but there was a part of me that couldn't help but be curious about his occupation. 'Why not?' I replied. 'I've got no plans for the afternoon. What do you hunt around here?'

The taciturn Jed nodded. 'I'll show you,' he said. 'Just come with me.'

I assumed we would be hunting some sort of bird, as that seemed to be the fashion in these regions. I had met a few other casual hunters around here before, and assumed the selection of prey would be fairly limited. We walked out of the market, stopping by Jed's office to collect two shotguns. This 'office' turned out to be a bare white room, with a battered old desk sitting on a scuffed wooden floor.

A string hung forlornly from a nail on the wall, as a reminder that a painting or photograph once adorned it, but there was no colour anywhere. There weren't even any magazines for the people who might sit in the three mismatched chairs, presumably waiting their turn. Behind the desk, there was nothing but a row of guns, stacked up against the wall. 'Have you shot one of these before?' he asked me as he unhooked two, his tone giving little away as to his assumptions or intentions.

'Yes, I have, actually,' I assured him. 'I lived in Texas for a while. I fancy myself a pretty decent shot. I mean, mostly I just shot at snakes, squirrels and the occasional tree, but, you know… I have a little bit of practice.'

The attempted humour was lost on Jed. He gave another of his mysterious nods. 'Good,' he said. 'You'll be shooting bigger things today.'

We drove out of the city until we found ourselves on bumpy roads, surrounded only by the dry, dusty earth, low bushes, and a few rocks. When we pulled the dirty 4x4 over, I looked back to Konya and saw the city stretching into the distance, glimmering flat and white in the late afternoon sun. Jed climbed out and fetched two rifles out of the back of his car, along with a handful of shells, and an enormous flashlight. 'These are Remingtons,' he told me with a hint of pride. 'American. Expensive.'

'They're very nice,' I replied uncertainly. 'What's the flashlight for? It's three in the afternoon. We won't be gone that long, will we?'

Jed ignored my question. 'We'll be hunting for foxes and wolves, principally,' he said, shading his eyes with his hand. 'Maybe sometimes we'll come across a deer or a hare, you never know. But the little carnivorous ones are what we're interested in.' He removed the bolt, checking the breach. Then he began to load the magazine, one round at a time.

'Wolves?' I asked. This hadn't been quite what I was expecting.

Jed nodded. He grabbed the rifle and tapped it against a rock to settle the bullets, then slammed the bolt back into the breach. There was a pause as he made these final adjustments to our equipment; I eventually realised he wasn't going to volunteer any more information. Then he stood up and straightened his shoulders.

'We should get going,' he said, snapping on the safety catch. 'We wouldn't want it to get dark.'

We walked for a long time in complete silence, with the only sound being the scuffing of our boots and the rustling of the dry grass. All at once, a shot rang out: the first time Jed shot at something, it was so quick I was startled by the noise. The attack must have operated like a reflex, deeply ingrained: he obviously saw something move in the distance, and had the barrel on his shoulder and his finger on the trigger without having to think at all. Something flopped in the dust in the distance.

'Nice shot,' I said. Jed nodded, already walking towards the animal. 'What is it?' I called after him.

'It's a jackal!' he called back disinterestedly, so quietly that I had to strain to hear him. He picked up the dead animal by the fur on the scruff of its neck.

'Congratulations!' I shouted, unsure if that was an appropriate response.

Jed shrugged. 'Maybe a deer next time,' he answered, trudging up the hill. 'Or a wolf.'

We walked for a while longer, as the heat lessened a little.

'Have you been hunting here for a long time?' I asked him, struggling a little with this total absence of conversation.

'Yes,' he replied. After a few minutes of walking in silence, he obviously realised this might seem a little rude, and added: 'I came here with my father when I was a child. I learned to shoot in these very hills, although there were more animals in those days.' I smiled, but the effort had obviously exhausted him, and he lapsed back into silence.

I couldn't help but get rather bored of this after a while. 'What is it you're hoping to shoot?' I eventually asked.

'Deer would be good,' he replied evenly. 'We can eat deer.' He obviously continued thinking on the question for a while as we walked on, before adding: 'Hyenas are good, too. They are dangerous and quite exciting to hunt.'

'Dangerous?' I asked.

'Yes,' he said. 'They are basically half lion, half dog. They could kill you with a single bite to the throat, if they wanted, but it's much more likely they would pick at your carcass when you are dead.'

Unexpectedly, he grinned, exposing his blackened teeth. The topic obviously excited him far more than anything I had mentioned before. I shivered involuntarily, thinking to myself that I would rather not meet any of these creatures.

As we walked on and on, the sun started to sink close to the horizon line rather faster than I had expected it to. 'It's getting rather dark,' I eventually mentioned, trying to keep my tone of voice conversational. 'Shouldn't we be heading back to the car?'

'We haven't shot anything but one jackal,' he replied stubbornly.

'Won't it be dangerous, what with the hyenas around and everything?'

'We'll be fine,' he answered shortly.

'It's dark,' I said, realising as the words left my mouth how childish they sounded.

'I have a flashlight,' he reminded me.

'What if we get lost?'

'We won't get lost. We'll walk back to the car.'

'What if we're chased by a hyena?' I asked, only half in jest.

'We run.'

That was the end of that conversation.

At some point, without saying a word, Jed produced a compass. We kept on walking in nearly complete silence, watching the darkness pool in the bushes. Eventually, the sprawl of the city reappeared between the hills, with the lights flickering on. Once I had this objective, my heart stopped beating so hard, and I let myself relax into walking, almost forgetting I had come here to hunt. All at once, there was a rustle in the grass and I felt Jed's hand grab my shoulder. The idea of Jed being frightened scared me more than any sound around us could have, and I gasped. Then I saw it: the wolf in the grass, staring right at us, not ten feet away. All day we had been looking for a creature like this, and now one had taken us by surprise. I felt my pulse begin to race with panic, but it didn't even occur to me to grab my rifle. For a moment, everything was frozen in place. Then the wolf turned to the side and vanished into the grass with hardly a rustle. Jed and I stood for a while, listening to each other breathe.

Eventually, we started walking again. 'He wouldn't have killed us,' Jed eventually volunteered. 'I could have shone the flashlight in his eyes.'

I did not reply for a while. 'I'm glad we didn't have to find out,' I said at last.

When we arrived back in Konya, we parted brusquely, barely exchanging a word. I never went hunting with Jed again, and I can't say I would recommend the experience!

THE BABATA BROTHERS: FERO, THE
SANDWICH MAKER

The youngest Babata brother, Fero, was very different to the taciturn Jed. In fact, the contrast between them was so strong as to be nearly overwhelming. There were two important things to know about Fero. First of all, he ran the family sandwich shop, and made a modest living from it. Secondly, he never stopped talking. The man seemed to have a nearly endless array of stories, true or false, to entertain any audience for hours on end.

The sandwich shop was just across the street from my grandmother's house. From her balcony, in fact, I could actually watch him cutting up bread and spreading sandwich fillings, all whilst carrying on several conversations at once with his customers and passers-by. He usually wore big, loose shirts that made all his gestures dramatic and showed off his smooth, olive skin. In the back of his shop he made his own cheese, which was pungent and salty.

Fero's most distinctive trait, apart from the fact that he never stopped talking, was his penchant for exaggeration. I could never tell what was true and what was pure invention: where he had travelled and what had happened to him in his life, the sorts of people he had sold sandwiches to, and how many people he had poisoned with his cheese. 'I've sold sandwiches to ministers and given them away to beggars,' he liked to tell his audience. 'I gave a practising Hindu a pastrami sandwich so delicious he didn't even notice it was meat, let alone beef. A famous Turkish actress loved my cheese so much she used to break into my shop at night to fill her handbag with it. I once saw a child grow ten centimetres after finishing a glass of water in my shop. I swear to you, incredible things happen in the streets of Konya! You just have to look out for them.' I would shake my head, but most people listened to his stories with rapt attention. 'I always make sure to put small insects in sandwiches I make for people I don't like. I also have a tin of fresh cheese that I spit in every morning for the same purpose.'

'And nobody ever catches you?' I asked dubiously.

'Oh no,' he replied cheerfully. 'Everything is so delicious that they would never notice. A cockroach looks quite a lot like an olive if you're not paying too much attention... Then again, I have snuck all sorts of things into my sandwiches. Spiders, lemon peel, and powdered sugar have been some of my most successful. In fact, the combination of lemon peel with my own cheese was so delicious that I've started advertising it in the shop!'

'But you used preserved lemon for this, didn't you?'

'Of course, of course. What difference does it make?'

Fero's enthusiasm was unstoppable and highly contagious. As my grandmother lived so close, I would sometimes come down to visit Fero in her company. Now, my grandmother famously hated sandwiches, and Fero knew this. Nonetheless, every single time he saw her, he would try to convert her. 'Ah, Bradley's darling grandmother!' he would exclaim. 'I have just the treat for you!'

My grandmother was not a woman to mince her words. 'I don't like sandwiches,' she would remind him at once, sharply, though with a smile.

'Ah, but that is because you haven't yet tried all the varieties I have to offer you.'

'It's a very strange thing, putting two slices of bread around meat and cheese. It's not natural. If you're going to eat portable food, why not make it something hot and spicy? A classic kebab, for instance, without too much of that greasy sauce.'

'A kebab is basically a sandwich, though,' Fero pleaded. 'I can make very healthy sandwiches. All the owners of kebab shops in the city of Konya prefer to eat my sandwiches than their own kebabs, it's a well-known fact!' I rolled my eyes, but he continued blithely. 'The ministers come down here on their lunch breaks and order their favourite meats. I can put any spices you like. I can invent a new kind of cheese for you, if you want, dear lady!'

My grandmother was charmed by Fero, completely against her will. Nonetheless, she continued to refuse to eat his sandwiches. 'You mustn't be offended,' she told him. 'I am not hungry.'

Fero was unfazed. 'You are never hungry! Someday, though,' he would say. 'Someday, I will make you the perfect sandwich and I will change your mind. A tightrope walker from a circus once came here. She didn't like sandwiches. I made her a sandwich in an extra-long, thin French baguette and – ta da! – she was converted. Then of course there was the lion tamer, whom I had to find fresh lion meat for. He wouldn't eat anything else, of course. That was his life. It had to be grilled, too, and it smelled to high heaven. Very gamey. Kind of a yellow colour, too.'

My grandmother would tire of Fero's inventions long before I did. 'We must be going,' she would say briskly. 'It's nice to see you, Fero, but I can't stand here talking all day.'

'Are you sure, sure, sure you won't have a sandwich? Even a teeny tiny one?' Fero tried, with his best salesman's smile. 'I can make a sandwich as small as a coin and still put four fillings inside.'

Of course, my grandmother had to have the last word, too. She was a humorous poet, given to spontaneous verse-making, and in this imaginative man she saw a perfect match for the barb of her skill.

'Fero,' she said:
'Even if you cry and sing and beg me on your knees
I'll never eat a sandwich or your awful homemade cheese.
You could fry a golden apple or put lion on the grill
But you'll never be a cook with half a penny's worth of skill!'

Fero, of course, doubled over with laughter. He seized my grandmother and pretended to kiss her cheek. 'Never have I been turned down so prettily,' he replied, 'or insulted in such daring verse. You have failed, however, as I will never stop trying. Just wait until you see the new soft cheese I am making in the Italian style. It is soft as cream, with a crunchy top like a meringue. You've never seen anything like it.'

I laughed as I guided my grandmother away. 'Yes,' I said, 'I'm sure you've made it out of pure clouds and rainwater. You probably don't even need milk for your magical cheese!'

Fero's cheese was the backbone of his boutique. Interestingly, he didn't have his own animals. 'Is it that you prefer to import the milk?' I asked him one day.

'Oh no,' he said. 'It's because my cows were stolen by a troupe of masked bandits. Oh, except for the one who ran away to live with a beautiful woman. I couldn't really resist her when she asked, even though it was my very last cow. She had such lovely sad eyes.'

I grinned. 'OK, so you import your milk.'

'Yes,' he said. 'But I do everything else myself.'

This, to do Fero credit, was true. He never hired anyone to work in the shop with him, preferring to rise at dawn and slice all the vegetables himself, mixing the sauces and laying out the spices. He lined up his many varieties of cheese and sliced meat, from cured beef to roast chicken slices. 'I never, ever use lettuce,' he liked to say. 'It spoils a sandwich completely. Everything gets limp and soaking wet. The meat is slimy, the bread falls to pieces, it is a complete sandwich disaster for everyone involved. No, a nice, fresh slice of tomato is the best thing to add, especially when they are ripe at the height of summer. Sometimes I get a man to bring them directly from Italy.'

Of course, not all his stories were pure invention. Sometimes, he liked to gossip about his clients. Much like a local barber, he would listen carefully as the clients aired their grievances to him, and then report the news around the neighbourhood. No secret was safe with Fero, unless of course you were counting on it being so warped by his powers of exaggeration that no-one would ever believe it! I was never sure how much Fero had really travelled, but he had a deep interest in world cuisine that coloured his sandwiches. Sometimes, I think he pushed the limits of his clientele. I don't think the inhabitants of the backstreets of Konya were really prepared for his garlic pesto, or his pastrami and pineapple roll. 'It's all the rage in Hawaii!' he would tell passers-by, waving his dubious creation. Even if no-one but a few teenagers bought it, though, he would be content in the knowledge that he was being creative in his line of work. In the end, he did this for pleasure. He had inherited the shop and loved working there, but it would never make him rich. He made just pennies on every sandwich sold; just enough to survive with his wife and three young children who lived just above the shop. 'They live off nothing but my sandwiches, you know,' he once told me with a twinkle in his eye. 'When they're let out into the real world, they're going to be so disappointed. It's why my wife will never leave me: I never taught her how to make sandwiches for herself. She loves them so much she would die if she couldn't have them.'

There was a childish inventiveness to Fero's style that had obviously been inspired by the tales of his youth. 'My grandmother was a lot like yours,' he once told me with a sad smile. 'I only knew her when I was very young, but she made up brilliant poems and she told so many wonderful stories.'

'I suppose you've inherited her talents, then,' I told him with a smile.

Fero narrowed his eyes, as if insulted. 'Except, of course, I always tell the truth.'

THE BABATA BROTHERS: BOB,
THE CARRIAGE DRIVER

Bob was the eldest Babata, and as such the role he played for me was much more that of a family friend or distant uncle than of a buddy, as his younger brothers were. Like Jed and Fero, he lived just down the road from my grandmother's house in Konya. Whenever I was in Turkey, I would catch up with the three men. When I was young, I use to call Bob 'Mister Babata'. Being more than twenty years older than me, I suppose he must have seemed very adult to my youthful eyes. Even in the 1960s and 1970s, when I came through Turkey regularly on business, Bob always seemed like a figure of calm and authority, despite his entertaining profession.

This neighbour ran an old-fashioned horse and carriage business, taking tourists around the bumpy, dusty backstreets of the city in a rickety wooden buggy. The horses were old, but their manes were braided with ribbons and flowers. The carriage had been bought at a junk stall from a travelling market, but it had been repainted a flamboyant red and adorned with a leather fringe. The cushions inside were comfortable. His trade was popular in the spring, when the streets were wet with rainwater and the bougainvillea was in fragrant bloom.

Bob's name wasn't Bob, of course, but probably something like Abdul. The sobriquet 'Bob,' however, had obviously been designed for the good of his European clients. He must have become so used to hearing it all day that it eventually came to be the way he thought of himself. Bob loved Konya, and knew the city better than almost anyone I met there. When I first met him I was just a young boy scout, and he took me on adventurous rides around the city with my friends, telling tales of ancient glory.

'You must always have one white horse and one black horse,' he told us, gesturing at his ageing rides. 'It is essential to the magic of the carriage ride.' While he didn't quite have the imaginative madness of his brother Fero, he still managed to capture the attention of every passenger I saw him with. Everything became imbued with magic: the clattering of the tramway, the spires of the mosques. Many of Bob's stories were old, traditional bits of Turkish folklore. 'Do you know that some grandmothers believe if a baby is sick, they can cure it by putting it on a wooden spoon and lifting it to the moon? They also say that if a child cannot walk, you must tie its feet with a lace, and then cut the lace.' Through his lively telling, these tales seemed incredibly fascinating and exotic to me.

Furthermore, Bob was incredibly knowledgeable about details of the history of the city. Or so I thought, at least, when I was young. When I was a little older and savvier, I began to question the veracity of his assertions. 'The city of Konya had its heyday during the Ottoman Empire,' he narrated. 'Of course, that is how old this very carriage is. The skins this leather is made of might have been sat on by emperors and foreign princes!' To a boy of eight, of course, this was the most exciting fact in the world. Its truthfulness mattered little. The titbits of historical fact only helped to anchor the madder tales in my mind as truths.

'The name of the city comes from "Iconum", which is Latin for "icon". Do you know the legend of how the city was built? They say that Perseus came here, holding the head of Medusa, which turned all his enemies to stone. Once everyone was gone, he took over the city for himself and reigned for a hundred years. See for yourselves how everything is made of white stone? Almost every building you see has been there for over three thousand years.'

Of course, the carriage itself probably dated from the 1930s, and many of the buildings we drove past were high rises from the 50s. Still, there was a real charm to Bob's storytelling. I have wonderful memories of those trips around the city, as Bob travelled the same routes over and over tirelessly, always coming up with new anecdotes and historical facts or fictions to entertain us. Markets, the stalls of carpet sellers, and famous landmarks all became imbued with magic. 'The city was founded during the Copper Age,' he would say. 'It is said that there are vast treasures of copper outside the old city walls. Every year, someone is reputed to be digging for it. Maybe this year, it can be you!'

When the weather was cold, he would have a wool blanket embroidered by his mother to throw over our knees. On some lucky days, he might pass around a plate of spiced date or apple cookies, fragrant with cardamom and nutmeg.

When I was a little older, I often came to see Bob on my own. Outside the tourist season, when his business was slow, he would offer to drive me to destinations that seemed outlandish, even exotic: the Syrian border, or the beach in the North of the country, several hundred kilometres away. I always refused, not wanting to make an imposition, but I appreciated his spirit of adventure and his generosity.

Even for an adult, it was a wonderful little space, the inside of that carriage; full of magic stories and suspended, as if separated from the world outside. I assumed that such an institution would last forever, somehow preserved from the passing of time. However, on one of my visits in the late 1970s, I arrived at the corner of the street where Bob's carriage usually sat, only to find it missing. I assumed he had simply gone on one of his tourist tours, although this was unusual in the evening, but it was still not there the next morning. Instead, as I was buying a sandwich from his brother Fero, I suddenly spied Bob Babata at the wheel of a battered old Mercedes with 'taxi' painted in flaking letters on the side. I ran up to the window.

'Bob!' I said. 'What on earth happened to your carriage? Come have a coffee with me!'

Bob shrugged with a resigned smile. 'Such is life,' he said. 'I've been ill.' Looking at his face, I saw now that the wrinkles around his eyes and mouth had deepened. He must have been over fifty by then, and his curly black hair was starting to grey in places. 'I'll take an hour off to talk with you,' he told me. 'Let me just park this old thing.'

Fero made us both coffees with milk and left us to talk in the shade of his booth.

'Are you alright?' I asked my old friend and neighbour with concern.

'Oh, I'm fine,' he replied dismissively. 'I just ended up with a stone in my kidney. Had to go to the hospital, it was all rather painful and expensive. In the end, I had to sell the carriage. Couldn't keep looking after those horses.'

'You mean they weren't magical after all?'

He cracked a smile. 'I don't know. They're someone else's horses now.'

'So you're a taxi driver now,' I said.

'Well, I've always been a taxi driver in a way!' he replied. 'There's just slightly less demand for fantastical stories and Konya history.'

'And you're still earning enough?'

'To be perfectly honest,' Bob leaned in, 'I don't even really need the money any more. I've made plenty with my horse and carriage business. It's just a little extra income. I'm really just doing this to amuse myself. I spent my whole life going around and around the city of Konya. I would miss it if I couldn't do so any more.'

That was the last time I saw my neighbour Bob Babata, but I'm sure he spent the rest of his life in Konya, driving his taxi down the same old streets and telling the same old stories.

In the mid-sixties, I lived briefly in Stanford. After I had finished engineering school in Texas, I contemplated the idea of doing graduate studies in California. However, I was quickly offered a fabulous job in engineering, and decided against continuing graduate school at the time. Nonetheless, I did have some curious experiences in my brief time there, particularly in the house I rented from a colleague.

Howie was a tall and bearded redhead, who was studying for a PhD in economics and finance. He was an affable man, of French descent, whose company had always been pleasant and discreet. I agreed to rent a floor of his house quite happily. The building itself was a typical bit of campus housing from the early 1900s: fairly staid, with a few Art Nouveau flourishes. We each had our own bedroom and dining room, and so we saw fairly little of each other.

One day as we ran into each other by the front door, Howie said: 'Hey, how come you never come to my parties?'

'Parties? I didn't know you had parties?'

'Of course!' he replied in surprise. 'I have a party every Saturday.'

'I've never seen you have a party here,' I said. 'I mean, I suppose I've not been here many Saturdays,' I added as a conciliatory afterthought. 'I spend a fair amount of time out East, or back down in Texas.'

'Well I party here every weekend,' Howie replied. 'It's a whole lot of fun. A few of the professors usually turn up, I think you'd find it interesting. You should come along!'

So that weekend, as I was planning to stay home in any case, I awaited this famous party. I wandered around the house in the late afternoon and into the evening, wondering if I had misunderstood some crucial piece of information, like the location, or the date. I tried the lounge downstairs and Howie's room on the second floor: silence. Howie and his theoretical party were nowhere to be found. But as I walked back up the stairs, Howie suddenly appeared from the shadows above me, as if materialising from thin air. He was dressed in a long, brown Arabian robe with silken buttons and a high neck, embroidered all over with strange designs. Balanced on top of his wild red hair was also a small hat. It was an outrageous sight.

'What are you, some kind of Arab sheikh?' I laughed aloud. 'Or no, are you a Chinese magician? Wait, is that a Jewish kippah?'

'No, no, my friend,' he said, very slowly, 'I'm American. Of French descent, you know, man!'

'You're crazy,' I replied.

'Sure, man,' he responded, in the same leisurely drawl. 'Now come to my party!' I wondered if he was drunk.

'I've been here an hour,' I said, 'just wandering around. There's no noise and I haven't seen a single soul. Is this party just you and me?'

Howie laughed. 'You're looking for fun in all the wrong places, man! Come on, I'll show you.'

We went up the stairs to his floor, which I had already checked twice for any signs of fun.

'Is this some kind of joke?' I asked.

Howie smiled mysteriously. 'The party is right here!' He gestured up at the ceiling. I wondered briefly if he had gone mad, before realising what I had apparently missed was a sort of manhole in the ceiling of his bedroom.

'Here it is,' Howie announced, pulling on a piece of string which unfolded a ladder. 'My party. Come on up!'

I gaped up, completely taken aback, then ascended gingerly. The attic turned out to be quite a pleasant space, although it smelled rather strange. There was a radio playing softly, and seven or eight people sitting around cross-legged on the floor in a sort of circle. They were all wearing these colourful robes and crazy hats and scarves, drinking beers and smoking. In fact, the whole place smelled quite strongly of smoke.

'Hey man!' one of them greeted me. 'Come chill!' He then burst into a fit of giggles.

Gingerly, I stepped out of the square hole in the ground and stood up.

Howie put his hand on my shoulder. 'Sit down and enjoy yourself,' he said.

'But who are these people?' I asked, still a little uneasy.

'Well, let's see. Mostly students, but two of them are my professors.' One of the men he had vaguely designated, who was wearing an outrageous orange beanie hat, waved his hand.

I hovered slightly awkwardly at the edge of the party, feeling rather out of place in my suit.

'Relax,' Howie said, 'Do you smoke green tobacco?' He pulled out a large rolled cigarette.

In those days I was still a smoker, but I was a little suspicious. 'No,' I said, 'I only smoke Marlboros.'

'Ah, but this is something very special,' he said pointedly, wiggling his eyebrows in a ridiculous fashion.

'I'm not really into rolled cigarettes. I prefer a filter, you know.'

He laughed for a long time, until the laugh turned into a cough. 'You don't get it!'

'Be cool, man,' the man on with the orange beanie chimed in. He had a ridiculous scruffy-looking beard. 'You and your suit should, like, hang loose.'

'This is silly,' I said as sternly as I could. 'What is this?'

Howie laughed again, uproariously. 'It's pot, man!' And the other people sitting on the floor burst into howls of laughter.

'No thank you,' I said politely, attempting to ignore the men on the floor, 'I don't do drugs.'

'It's the weekend, man! You'll recover in two hours. Then you can go back to your work.'

'I can't,' I explained. 'Not only is it against my principles, but I would never start taking something addictive.'

'It's just like a cigarette!' the professor chimed in again, in his annoying voice. 'All you do is inhale and you're off to heaven!'

'It's bad enough that I smoke Marlboros! And aren't you afraid of being arrested? You could end up in jail! What about your tenure?'

I felt as if everyone were looking at me askance, so I was quiet. I looked around, trying to find an escape, but I could no longer find the trapdoor. Thus, I ended up sitting down awkwardly on the outside of this circle of potheads, trying to conduct a conversation with a man incapable of stringing words together without giggling. It was awful. The smoke alone was making me feel dizzy and slowly giving me a headache. I didn't get high; I just felt nauseous. After what felt like an eternity of odd, stilted conversation, I finally got up unsteadily to find my flatmate.

'Howie,' I said, 'I've got to get out of here.'

'Come on man,' he wheedled, 'you've only been here, like, ten minutes.'

'Howie,' I said, 'if you don't let me out of here I will end my lease. Can't you see I'm going insane?'

Eventually, he took pity on me and let me down. Soon after, I moved back East to start my new job, and I never had to go to another one of Howie's pot-smoking parties.

When I first started at LSE, I lived quite a long commute away, in a small, dirty flat in Paddington. The area was poor and smothered in smog; there was never any parking near the school. In short, it was not a pleasant time. Quite quickly, I clubbed together with a few colleagues who I figured out were in similar situations, and we went hunting for a new place to live. I started scouring the newspapers and advertisements placed on the billboards in the corridors at school.

My flathunting partners were three of my friends: one Canadian, one American, and one British, walking into a series of apartments… It was the perfect set-up for a joke! As it was, the joke seemed to be that we would fail to find a place to live, as we started out having very little success in our mission. But finally, our luck seemed to turn: we found a fabulous old building between Hyde Park and Sussex Garden, with a classic staircase at the entrance and a vast reception lobby.

'Welcome,' said the manager, spreading his arms. We gaped, open-mouthed.

'This place is gorgeous!' I exclaimed.

'There's no way we can afford this,' the Canadian muttered. He came from an old Quebecois family, and had been extremely successful in his studies; in fact, he would end up working for the government in Ottawa, but that's another story. At this point, he was a reasonably well-off student, and the fact that he was still daunted by the rental of this place was not a good sign.

I cleared my throat and turned to the manager. 'OK, let's get it over with. How much is the rent?'

The man smiled coyly and clasped his hands. 'Twelve pounds a week,' he said.

'Oh, then somebody else must've already grabbed it,' said the Englishman. 'Or there's some kind of scam. There's no way a place as grand as this would still be on the market at that price!' He was the youngest of us: an eighteen-year-old student of economics, but he was extremely sharp, and would go on to be an executive of a large multinational company in London

'No, no, I can assure you, there's no scam,' the manager said hastily. 'There's been quite a lot of interest, granted, but for some reason nobody comes back to actually rent the place.'

'Well they must be mad!' the American said. 'This place is amazing! What do you guys say we take the place now, huh?' The American was the weakest link in this group: the rest of us had been friends for some time, whereas this PhD student in international affairs was slightly older, and had sort of tagged along with us at the last minute. He tended to be fairly glum, even sulky, when any of us had professed any interest in the places we had seen before, so to see this display of glee was hard to resist.

I raised my palms in surrender. 'Should we?'

The Englishman frowned. 'Seriously, what's the catch?'

'There's no catch,' the manager assured us.

'OK,' I said, thrilled and awed at our good luck. 'Where do we sign?'

We moved in within a week. Each of us had big rooms, and I was allocated the biggest of all for finding the apartment in the first place. All the rooms were fully furnished in a glamorous style, with thick carpets and gilded mirrors: we felt like we were living together in a palace! Furthermore, it was an incredibly spacious place for four students, where each of us had our own bathroom. There was even a guest room. All in all we were pretty thrilled with the place. I did think my room was a bit gaudily decorated, but I put this down to indulgent English post-war taste. The walls were covered in rich Bordeaux velvet hangings, while the floor was all thick shag carpet, probably made of lambswool or some other indulgent material. Everything was decorated with silk, velvet and gilt. We felt like lords of the manor, sipping tea in our leather armchairs in the heart of London, and were, altogether, pretty happy about our investment.

That is, until we got a knock on the door, and opened it to find an older gentleman standing there with a strange grin on his face.

'Hello, I'm Lord Anglais,' he said, 'I'm your next-door neighbour,' he explained. 'So, you're the lucky tenants. Or not-so-lucky, as the case may be...'

I was suspicious. 'What do you mean?'

'I mean... Well, why don't you invite me in and I'll explain.'

I apologised for not having asked him in at once, clarifying that we were simply taken by surprise. At the time, the American and I had been having tea in the sitting room, so we took our neighbour back there with us and poured him a cup.

'I don't want to give you youngsters a hard time,' Lord Anglais began. 'But have you ever wondered why this apartment hasn't been rented for a good three years now?'

My stomach sank. 'I must admit it seemed too good to be true.'

'Yeah,' the American chimed in, 'I mean, we're surrounded by lords and pop stars and city brokers! We're hardly the target audience here!'

'But this is such a nice place,' I added sadly, expecting some terrible news about the property itself. 'Is it going to be demolished? Is there an infestation we haven't discovered?'

The gentleman laughed. 'No, no, nothing like that. It's not that there's anything wrong with the building... It's just that there's a certain stigma attached to it.'

'What, like a murder?' The American looked concerned. 'Don't tell me there's a ghost here we didn't know about!'

Our neighbour shook his head with a smile. 'No, it's more of a political stigma. Does either of you two gentlemen know who Christine Keeler is?'

The American frowned and shook his head, whilst the pieces of the puzzle suddenly started to click into place in my head.

'Oh God,' I said. 'Did this use to be her house?'

'It did indeed.' Lord Anglais then turned to my colleague. 'Christine Keeler is a figure of some disrepute in British politics... She was, or is, a call-girl; one who got involved with a member of the British cabinet and a Russian spy at the same time. This was Cold War stuff, very nasty; it was a huge scandal. Ended up bringing down the Tory government. Not,' he nodded at me, acknowledging my understanding of the political situation in the posh parts of London, 'very popular with the crew who live around here.'

'Tories are your Republicans, right?' the American squinted slightly, trying to make sense of this story. 'So you're saying you Brits steer clear of this house basically just because some hooker shacked up with a politician here?'

'That's exactly right.'

'But that's crazy!' he continued. 'I mean, that's cool! In the States, that would probably add to the value of the house!'

'The British don't feel that way,' Lord Anglais explained. 'They're ashamed of this part of their history. The building was used for illicit purposes, after all. One of your very rooms was probably the place where the scandal played out.'

'I have to admit,' I replied, 'that I'm personally rather thrilled by this discovery. I mean, it makes a lot of sense of the décor in the bedroom, particularly the mirror over my bed.'

The gentleman appeared extremely flustered at this point, and did not seem to know what to say. 'I mean, I got the whole place cleaned thoroughly,' I added hastily. 'Don't get me wrong, I just thought it was rather overzealous redecorating. But now that I know the truth, well, I find it rather charming to be living in this piece of history.'

'You wouldn't feel tainted by it?' he pursued, his greying brows furrowed. 'And don't you think your flatmates will want to know? Won't they be upset?'

'Not really,' I had to admit. 'Let me explain: almost none of us are British, and the one Brit among us is pretty much a socialist. I think when they find out they'll react in much the same way that I have. To be perfectly honest, I suspect my American colleague here would have paid a premium had he known about this sordid side. I think it's rather fascinating!' Seeing the older man's face, I continued: 'But please don't think any less of us for it. I understand that you just wanted us to be aware of the situation; that's very kind of you. Tell me a bit more about yourself!'

'Oh, don't worry! I'm surprised, but also in a sense relieved. I just didn't like the idea of you boys living in here without knowing anything about it. If you're fine with it, that's marvellous news all round. As for myself, well, I used to be a colonel. Then I went on to work in the City as an advisor. Now I'm pretty much retired. Plenty of time to poke around in other people's affairs!'

I smiled. 'Well, I guarantee we'll do our best to keep the political scandal to a minimum in this house from now on.'

About thirty-five years later, when I had become a fairly successful banker, the Englishman and I ran into each other by chance in London. We started joking about old times, and went for a cup of coffee to catch up on each other's lives. When I mentioned our old apartment in Hyde Park, though, his face turned bright red, and he got so embarrassed I thought he might just get up and walk away! What was always a subject of great amusement to me and the North American flatmates had remained a source of shame for the Englishman.

DOORMEN AND DUKES

It is often said that the Duke of Westminster is the richest man in Europe; for twenty years he was certainly the top of every list of the highest incomes. However, after a time it was decided that sovereigns would no longer be taken into account when determining the richest people in the world, since, although the vast estates are in their name, if they weren't heads of states they wouldn't be in possession of them in the first place. After all, sovereigns inherit without taxation, which rather skews the scale. For that reason, on an international level, the sultan of Brunei was disqualified from being named the richest man in the world, despite owning the whole country, including his own luxurious palaces and a famous international chain of hotels.

At this point, the Duke of Westminster's status was hotly contested. However, as he was not actually a sovereign, and did in fact own many of the most luxurious parts of central London, it was finally decided that he would keep his position as richest man in Europe. During the time of this debate, I found myself wondering how a man like him could end up with such riches amassed. Of course, his family and origins would have a lot to do with it. But could it also be because he employed cheap labour? Because I had lived on Eaton Square, one of the parts of his considerable estate, I had seen some of the people employed there, and I mean no disrespect when I say the level of staff quality was not high. After all, very few properties in London have doormen, so there would be little opportunity for comparison or complaint. But I believed then as I do today that really, a good doorman should be like a butler, impeccably dressed and almost obsequiously polite. These were far more likely to be rude, drunk and rather sweaty. But then again, the buildings in Belgravia were hardly manor houses: just big townhouses built out of brick, covered in stucco and painted with masses of whitewash. I suppose it was hardly the place to look for excellent service. In any case, the place was swarming with interns and trainees, who must have been on considerably lower salaries than their glamorous positions would have seemed to imply.

In my experience, all of the Duke of Westminster's domestic employees, doormen and security guards seemed to have the same profile: dour, somewhat shabbily-dressed, perpetually seeming to smell of garlic, complaining because of their low pay. Perhaps the garlic smells were limited to the doorman I was the most accustomed to dealing with, but no doubt one can imagine the picture nonetheless! Several of the doormen I met were trying to pull off some shady deal on the side, involving trying to overcharge for every small service. None of these elements seemed to me to indicate that they were furnished with generous pay. Every single one I spoke to seemed to be housed in dank basements that grew stuffy in summer and freezing in winter. These underground flats usually only had two rooms, even if they had to house a couple with a child, or even some employees' elderly parents. The conditions were far from luxurious. This was a widespread situation: every building on the estate had a doorman, who specialised in picking up the garbage, giving out information, and had very little else to do. Many of these doormen, including the one in my building, seemed to be rarely sober and always ready to gossip. After all, if any tasks needed doing, like cleaning or showing guests around, they could easily be carried out by one of the many underlings or trainees.

The doorman of my building was of Portuguese origin, which would explain the obsession with garlic in his cuisine. He had moved to the UK with his large family of small children, and must have been constantly producing vats of spicy fish or meat stew. He seemed to spend most of his time complaining about the weather and the social system in Great Britain, and the rest of it drinking red wine. The man would be perfectly sober in the daytime but completely drunk in the evening. Occasionally he would get loud and abusive, and yet he managed to keep his job for almost three years. After a few complaints from the inhabitants of the building, however, he was replaced by a sixty-year-old Irishman who turned out to be fairly drunk in the daytime, but completely sober in the evening.

'Now don't get me wrong,' he told us in his thick Galway brogue, 'this isn't how we do it back home. But I got a sore telling-off in my last job for the drinkin', and this seems like a good way to get around it.'

'Well as long as you're discreet about it,' I said begrudgingly, 'I'm sure we'll all get on.'

'Oh, I'm discreet. As discreet as they come,' he assured me. 'But you know who's not quite so discreet?' And he proceeded to recount several lengthy and juicy bits of gossip about our various illustrious neighbours which he had managed to pick up in his first two days on the job. From then on, I got on quite well with him, and was exceedingly well-furnished with knowledge concerning the lives of the other inhabitants of Eaton and Belgrave Square, from members of parliament to writers and sculptors. The Irish doorman stayed for seven years before retiring back to Ireland.

From conversations with the Irishman, with whom I became fairly close, I estimated that the duke was paying his doormen about half what he should have been, or what he would have had to if he employed people who were used to living and working in London. In my opinion, that must be the secret to his fortune.

THE BARBECUE ON THE HILL

When my Irish wife and I were first married we often used to visit her uncle, Father O'Brien, who was a priest living in the gorgeous countryside surrounding Cork. These would be fairly uneventful escapades, as there is little to do in the peaceful valleys and hills of County Cork other than horse riding and salmon fishing. I quite enjoyed angling in the wild rivers there, so on many a drizzly holiday morning, Father O'Brien and I would pull on our rubber fishing trousers and stumble upstream before the sun even rose. After we had caught a few salmon and cleaned up at my in-laws' house, Father O'Brien once suggested we head over to visit Paddy, who would be organising a lamb grill on top of the hill.

Paddy was my wife's second cousin, and thus a sort of distant relative of mine. In the time-honoured Irish way, however, he had invited me into his home as part of his family. Arriving at Paddy's house was like a very Irish version of a scene from *The Sound of Music*: we got there by clambering up the emerald slopes to the little stone home at the top. By the time we arrived at the edge of the garden and could smell the enticing scent of smoke and meat and rosemary, we would be swamped by blonde, rosy-cheeked youngsters. Paddy had thirteen children between the ages of two and nineteen, each more charming than the last. It was a sort of overwhelming pastoral vision, and for a moment I must confess I wondered if I had mistakenly ended up at some sort of Mormon festival.

I looked over at my companion nervously and cleared my throat, but Father O'Brien obviously thought I was just intimidated by such a crowd of young children. 'Don't worry,' he whispered. 'There will be baked potatoes and grilled lamb shanks in just a minute. You can ignore it all. They're a perfectly pleasant family.' Slightly worried, I looked around for any sign of polygamy, and felt my heart sink as two women appeared in the doorway. Just like Utah, I thought to myself. Wondering how my Catholic friend made space in his heart for this sort of lifestyle, I approached with some trepidation, warding off the small children with their incomprehensible babbling. They certainly seemed like such an innocent family! I wouldn't have been in the least surprised if they had been capable of staging a musical in matching dresses. At this point, however, they were more interested in telling me all about their lives.

'I gotta slug,' another small child chanted, holding his hands behind his back. 'Wanna see?'

'We've been for a walk!' one of the teenage sisters chimed in proudly. 'All over the hills! We wanted to find you and Daddy fishing and bring you snacks!'

'But then we ate the snacks,' the first boy confessed.

'And then we played leapfrog!' a little girl added. 'It was fun.'

'That all sounds lovely,' I said, which unfortunately encouraged each of the children to continue incoherently chattering, recounting their stories, all speaking at once whilst swarming around my legs.

'Mister, mister, what's your name?' said one boy who must have been about ten years old, tugging on the back of my shirt.

'Bradley,' I said, in as friendly a manner as I could, although I was feeling a little overwhelmed.

'Bradley and Paddy! Daddy Paddy!'

The children jumped around chanting this as I stumbled through the fields towards the house.

At last, I made it through the crowd. I was ushered inside by Paddy and offered a cool glass of lemonade. 'This is my wife,' he said, gesturing at the lovely red-haired lady with the pitcher of cool drink, and then added 'and this is our delightful maid.'

The other lady, who I now realised was wearing a pinafore, dipped her knees slightly and smiled. I sighed inwardly with relief, and grinned more enthusiastically than was entirely necessary. The maid vanished into the kitchen. The wife said gently, 'I hope you weren't too overwhelmed by the masses of children. It's school holidays, you know.'

'Oh they're very amusing. Although it's hard to sort their stories out!'

'Don't worry, it gets easier,' the wife said encouragingly.

'Just ignore most of them,' Father O'Brien added, 'and nod a lot in a friendly manner.'

'That sounds about right,' Paddy grinned. 'Now why don't we go back out and join them? The lamb will be ready soon. Now, would you like some more lemonade?'

'Thanks,' I replied. 'Do you know,' I added pensively, 'I think you're one of the only Irish people I've met who doesn't drink. It must be because you're too busy making babies!'

Friendly neighbours, in this book and in my life overall, have been so rare as to occasionally arouse suspicion. For instance, I have never had any trouble with my neighbour Annabella, and for many years I could not understand why this was. Now, this may sound surprising to the reader. Annabella is a tall, good-looking , friendly woman in her mid-thirties. She lives next door to our family house in Kent. Her areas of expertise are horse-racing, breeding, and teaching sports. She is charming, polite, and she always has a kind word for my children, who happen to get along brilliantly with her own offspring. She often invited us over for cake for no apparent reason and, forgetting that I don't drink, would regularly grab a bottle of champagne from the fridge when I was in her kitchen.

Why would this surprise me? Well, our land was side by side, which often spells trouble. We lived at close quarters in an isolated community! We shared hedges and a few metres of access road, which is another sure-fire recipe for less than pleasant run-ins. Yet no, we never disagreed about anything. So I repeat my question: why? Either Annabella was simply the world's most pleasant woman, or there was something fishy going on.

Once, my son borrowed a horse of Annabella's to ride for the day, and tried an ambitious jump over a fence, in which the horse's leg was quite badly hurt. Ashen-faced, I knocked on her doorway to explain and apologise. She opened the door with a radiant smile.

'There's been an accident,' I began. 'I shouldn't have let my son go out riding alone, I'm so sorry.'

Her face didn't fall a bit during my apologetic explanation. 'Oh, Bradley! Never mind. These things happen,' she said breezily. 'Come on in, I've just made cake. It was meant to be for my sister's visit tomorrow, but never mind. I fancy a nice big slice right now.'

Another time, our gardener had left a rake of his in the middle of the road after finishing tidying up the autumn leaves. Of course, if someone had run into it without seeing, they might have been hurt badly. I blanched when Annabella appeared at my door, holding the sharp-looking tool.

'Hi Bradley!' she said brightly. 'I think your gardener might have forgotten this outside! Wouldn't want these things to rust, would we. I nearly ran it over with my car. Wouldn't that have been a shame!'

I blinked. 'I'm so, so sorry,' I began. 'I have no idea what came over him. He's usually very conscientious.'

She waved away my apology. 'Oh, no matter, no matter. So, tell me how things are going in your life? Would you and perhaps your gardener like to come over for dinner this weekend? I could make a chocolate cake.'

Now, I might not have been so suspicious if this had happened in rural America, or even in some parts of Germany or France, where neighbours often get along well. The English, however, are another matter altogether: I have met neighbours there who disliked each other simply because one preferred cricket and the other football. This sort of unstoppable kindness and inexplicable generosity was simply unheard-of.

'Derek,' I said thoughtfully one day, 'why do you think Annabella is so nice?'

Derek was our family secretary, who also looked after various general services. He was an Englishman himself, and not prone to beating around the bush. Derek did not seem to think this was an odd question. 'Well, sir, I don't know,' he said tactfully.

'She is nice about parking. She lets us borrow her horses. She is even nice to the children. What is she hiding from us? What's her secret? I want to know.'

I was being facetious, of course, but there was a serious undertone to this line of questioning. I usually have a sort of sixth sense about these matters, and have been proven right time and time again in terms of odd intuitions regarding people's character.

Derek paused thoughtfully for a while, then cleared his throat. 'Well, sir,' he said, 'I might suggest that she has every reason to be nice to you.' There was a pause, and Derek allowed himself a small smile. He took after me, this man; I could tell. I was intrigued. 'If you don't mind me saying, sir,' he continued, 'the woman simply has to be friendly towards you all the time. What's more, it's really in your best interests to be nice to her in return. It's rather as if you are married to each other,' he concluded slyly.

I was no longer amused. 'What the hell are you talking about, Derek? Annabella may indeed be single, but you know perfectly well I have a wife. I don't like what you're implying one bit, if I even understand it correctly. It makes no sense.'

'With all due respect, sir,' Derek replied, 'that wasn't what I meant in the least. I simply believe there is an obvious, longstanding and perfectly straightforward reason why your neighbour Annabella has found it in her best interests to maintain amicable relations.'

'And that reason is?' I asked, intrigued and annoyed in equal measures. It is one thing to have a vague pet theory; quite another to have it taken over by a somewhat arrogant secretary.

'Let me explain,' Derek said hastily. 'It's very simple. Annabella's sewage goes under your house – this house. We take it in turns to pay the city council for the sewage treatment. At the end of each year, we receive a bill that summarises all the sewage costs. Your accountant and I divide the costs, so there is a balance: either you reimburse her, or she reimburses you.'

'Why did I not know about this?' I snapped, feeling rather peeved.

'We didn't presume that you'd want to be involved in such a petty affair,' he replied tactfully.

He was right, but I was also quite disappointed to find that my guess had been correct, and for such mundane reasons! I found myself wishing I had stayed in blissful ignorance, imagining that Annabella could simply be a friendly, easy-going woman. 'Harumph,' I said, or something to that effect. 'I don't really like the sound of this. Is there no way out of it? I like to have my independence on these matters. This sounds unpleasantly like reliance to me. What if something goes wrong?'

Derek shook his head. 'I'm afraid there's no easy way out, sir. You and Annabella are partners in sewage. There's no easy to way to undo that relationship, unless you should divert all the sewage away from both your properties, which would be both time-consuming and expensive. Believe me, we've thought it through before. It would be far worse for her, but it would still be a great deal of trouble for you. By the way, you should probably know that this applies to water as well. We set this all up to save everyone money. In the case of the water pipes, to get a better deal, we decided on a mutually beneficial solution involving slightly bigger pipes in slightly less space. More volume, less cost. They lie right on the border. There's no way out.'

'Those bills are shared out yearly, as well?'

'Yes,' he admitted.

'Well, you're going to have to do something about this. I don't care for this solution one bit. I want it over. If normal, slightly conflictive relations will ensue, I don't mind. That's what English neighbours are for.'

'Sir,' Derek interjected, 'if you don't mind me saying, I'm afraid that this will be the equivalent of asking for a divorce. This arrangement has been in place for years, benefitting both parties equally. If we try to separate, it will mean quite a lot of expensive work has to be done on both sides of the land. On top of that, Annabella is likely to be angry and cause trouble for us legally. To be perfectly honest, sir, I think it would be in your best interests to continue your role of friendly neighbour. Why don't we just calm down and accept this marriage of water and sewage? It's the easiest thing to do, and the best thing for everyone. With all due respect, sir, you're trapped.'

'Now I see why you called it a marriage,' I grumbled. 'Alright then. So be it. Marriage by sewage! Who'd have thought it.'

In the end, or at least to this day, we didn't change anything. I let Derek and Annabella continue muddling through whatever their dubious financial arrangement was, simply hoping that nothing would go wrong in this set of shared responsibilities. Annabella has remained an extremely friendly neighbour, but she is no longer a usual or mysterious case. Although, now that I think of it, she hasn't offered me cake in quite some time.

THE BEST BAGUETTE

Hemingway famously believed that Paris was the best city in which to be starving because of the sheer quality and abundance of the food. In *A Moveable Feast*, he writes:

'You got very hungry when you did not eat enough in Paris because all the bakery shops had such good things in the windows and people ate outside at tables on the sidewalk so that you saw and smelled the food.'

Of course, in Hemingway's time you could eat for a week off one dollar! Nonetheless, this atmosphere of culinary glory and enticement was very much my personal experience of the city, a good half century on. Paris is a place where one is constantly walking by shops full of mouth-watering food. The butchers' windows show off succulent cuts of fresh meat, the markets are full of fresh vegetables still muddy from countryside gardens, and the bakeries are overflowing with beautiful baguettes. I swear the food in Paris is better than almost anywhere in the world, and I don't just mean the luxury items at the fanciest cafés or restaurants. Even the *plat du jour* at a brasserie or the simplest olive in the humblest grocery store is an art in France.

Consider, for instance, the humble baguette. I don't think I have ever had as excellent a hunk of fresh bread as I did when I lived just down the street from a small bakery in the heart of the seventh *arrondissement*. At this point in time, I was twenty-seven and a successful banker, with a young family and a sprawling apartment on Rue de Cornell. Even though I had known Paris as a child, it was a new experience to me to be living there as a young professional with excellent resources, in one of the fanciest areas of the city.

Part of France's culinary strength is rooted firmly in its history as an agricultural country. A Frenchman once told me that because they have the most temperate climate, the richest earth, the best sun and the purest waters, they can grow the best wheat, and therefore produce the best bread.

'The best sun?' I remember asking, looking up in disbelief at the grey, rainy skies that are ubiquitous above Paris from September to March. 'You must be joking!'

'Not at all,' my friend replied. 'In the hottest and sunniest countries, it is much harder to control a crop of wheat. The earth can dry out; there is often insufficient or dirty water. In the French countryside, there may not be too much unclouded sun, but there is the perfect balance of sun and rain.'

My friend's argument was simple. He believed that France knew better than anyone how to make great, simple food. Bread, of course, is the easiest benchmark of any Western country's culinary greatness. The English make dull, square loaves with no flavour, which is an excellent indication of their cuisine overall. The French, on the other hand, are famous the world over for their baguettes. A baguette is distinguished from other loaves of bread by the fact that it is baked in an oven full of steam, which is how it gets its distinctive combination of a fluffy centre and a crisp crust. Now, I have always believed firmly in following the nicer local traditions of whatever city I happen to be living in. When in Rome, do as the Romans do; when in Paris, buy baguettes. Ask almost any Frenchman where he gets his bread, and he will tell you either that he gets it delivered daily to his front door or, more likely, that he walks down to the boulangerie to get it before breakfast, or sometimes before dinner, particularly if there is to be a cheese course. My two-year-old daughter and I participated in this ritual wholeheartedly. As the sun rose over the city, Rouena and I would go for what I liked to call a finger-walk, where my daughter would toddle along holding on to my finger. We would walk just around the block, to the nearest boulangerie. We would pick up a baton of warm bread, and come straight back home. Sometimes I would give Rouena a small piece of the soft centre to chew on. Few pleasures beat tearing open a new baguette and eating it with jam and butter, other than perhaps the steaming cup of strong coffee I would have on the side.

There was an element of luck involved in our family being so close to such an excellent source of baguettes. I would argue that in Paris they are all very good, but each resident will have their own local place that seems to them particularly exceptional. The baguette from the boulangerie I frequented would always be hot and freshly-baked, with a thin, crisp crust and soft, warm *mie*. On the days when I didn't manage the pre-breakfast ritual, I would be so taunted by the smell on the way to work that I would end up having to pick one up for my lunch.

This boulangerie had its own wood-fired clay oven, and baked every single loaf they sold in a room behind the counter. The bakery was unusual in its miniscule size, and in the fact that it was run by two sisters in their seventies. Annette and Gillette were two wizened old ladies in hats, who looked as if they had been baked in their own ovens. They were more toasted than the baguettes! Every inch of their skin was saggy and brown, from their cheeks to their stubby fingers. Both women were thin and short, with long, wrinkled necks hunched between very narrow shoulders, which made them look rather like tortoises. Annette and Gillette could have been twins, even though I never actually found out if this was the case. After knowing them for three years, I did manage to ask them, but received no response other than an uncharacteristic giggle. This, of course, could have been acquiescence as easily as it could have been acknowledging the cheek of the question. The sisters were extremely serious and constantly busy, and they very rarely chatted to their clients. I figured that the reasons they didn't do much talking could have been double: either they wanted to avoid having to give the bread away to their acquaintances and friends for free; or they didn't want to waste time, as there would always be a line of people waiting to buy the baguettes, and probably a freshly baked load to be taken out of the oven.

The boulangerie was so small that it seemed to me they must produce no more than three types of bread: the baguette, the white loaf and the *pain de campagne* or wholegrain bread. On rare occasions, they might also produce a special cereal or sesame bread. I was very fond of this sesame loaf, which had a richer taste than their white breads, and I would always buy it when I saw it in the window. After a few of my visits, I realised that if they had this bread, the sisters would give it to me without asking. With their eagle eyes, they noted that I liked this particular bread, and the few times they had baked this loaf that they now knew to be my favourite, I knew it was for me. This, to me, was the ultimate proof of how excellent they were at their job, no matter how quiet they might like to stay. It made me feel like a valued customer.

Annette and Gillette were not unfriendly, but they wasted no time on small talk. In any case, they had very small mouths with lips like buttons or hazelnuts, designed to be pursed in concentration rather than chattering or grinning. In fact, the only time I saw them open their mouths was to indicate the price to a new customer. Regular customers, of course, knew the price of their usual loaf by heart; passers-by and foreigners needed to be told. It was a mark of recognition to be one of the clients the sisters only nodded to. Annette and Gillette were supremely economical in gesture. Sometimes they shook their head in recognition of a client they hadn't seen for a long time, or nodded at someone who might have been an old friend, but mostly, everything they did fell into simple patterns. They handed over the bread, took the money, and gave the change back immediately. In those days, the baguette cost only about ten centimes!

I loved visiting that bakery, standing in line surrounded by the warm scent of freshly baked bread. Sometimes I tried to chat to the sisters. They never seemed to mind the occasional passing comment: 'Oh, it's cold outside today!' or 'It's not too busy, this afternoon!' They simply chose not to answer. Somehow, perhaps miraculously, they never came across as unfriendly. They were just as taciturn as turtles. I suspect they would have retracted their heads if they could have, in order to better concentrate on the baking.

Whatever the oddities of their personalities, the sisters made some of the best bread I have ever tasted. I visited them nearly every day for the three years I lived in Paris, up until we moved apartments upon the birth of my son. Though I had moved several miles away to the sixteenth *arrondissement*, if I had time, I would sometimes drive across the river just to stop by Gillette and Annette's to say hello. I wasn't expecting a response, just a shake of their long necks and elongated faces. Nonetheless, just stepping into the shop and purchasing a nice warm baguette would always bring me the same simple joy. Even after two years, they would smile when I came in, and remember to offer me that delicious sesame loaf, if they had any.

Even after leaving the country in the late seventies, I still had many occasions to make business trips over to Paris. Still the happy memories and great smells of wood-oven baking would draw me back to that very same boulangerie. Between banking meetings, I would dash over in a taxi just to buy one of those special baguettes. It smelled so good that I would often have nearly finished it before getting back to the bank or to my hotel. There was a part of me that hoped that this particular boulangerie would last forever, unchanged even as Paris became more and more modern around it. I saw it as a sweet-smelling island, governed by these two immortal figures. I must admit I hoped I could always stop by, whenever I ended up, like Hemingway, hungry in Paris.

Sadly, like all good things, this too came to an end. One day in the late 1980s, on one of my business trips, I jumped out of a taxi in search of my customary breakfast loaf only to find the bakery had disappeared. In the space of two months, it had been replaced by a boutique selling off *prêt-à-porter* clothes. Their shiny display window made me feel almost ill with nostalgia. I found myself wishing I had witnessed the front being boarded up, which would have marked the event of the bakery's passing in a more symbolic way. Instead, I went into the clothes shop and asked if they knew what had happened to the sisters. The clerk was sympathetic, having eaten their glorious bread herself in the past. She told me that both sisters had died that very same year, within the space of only two months. Annette and Gillette were no more. Just like that, my baguette adventure in the seventh *arrondissement* came to an end. I have never found bread anywhere as nice as theirs, and certainly not in such a charming setting. Nowadays, even in France, everything seems to be made with artificial yeast, and flour from all over the world. My friend's vision of wheat grown in French soil under French sun, watered with French rain, may sadly be no more, and it is a rare thing to find a wood-fired bread oven, even in Paris. Nonetheless, even now, if I wake up particularly hungry, I find myself dreaming of those baguettes!

MY VERY LOYAL NEIGHBOUR

I used to take holidays in Ireland about three times a year to visit my in-laws and friends, and also to pursue various investments my companies had in Dublin. There is not a lot else to do in Ireland. I enjoyed going to see my in-laws, but once I had caught up with their latest news, we quickly got bored of each other's small talk. However, there were a few things that kept me coming back. For one thing, I was interested in horse racing, and Ireland was a great place to attend the races, sitting in the stands and trying to keep out of the rain, and pick the best yearlings. Of course, I enjoyed riding the horses as well. The riding in Dublin is not challenging: it's all flat grassy land, at least to the east of the city, not far from Kilkenny, where I had my house. Many of the horses are of excellent breeds, which suited me as I was only interested in buying thoroughbred horses, which were usually raised on horse farms. But horses were not the only cause of my interest in Ireland.

Above all else I loved walking in the green fields near my in-laws' house, enjoying the lush emerald grass the isle is famous for, pondering the day's events, or planning the next story I would write. Ever since I was a young child, I particularly loved walking in the fields with a good book, meandering with my nose in the pages until I found a place to sit down and read for hours, perhaps by a rocky brook or in the shade of a leafy tree. Sometimes I would walk to the pub and back, even though I don't drink, just to give a little structure to my hikes. Mostly I walked alone, and often for miles at a time, but sometimes I did let someone accompany me. I was particularly fond of inviting my neighbour, who lived just behind my house: her name was Susy.

Being a quiet sort, Susy was the perfect companion on my reading escapades. She had a rather sizeable head, her skin a soft, sandy brown colour, and her eyes were big with long lashes. She was a somewhat strange, if affectionate friend to have around. She would often come and lie on the ground next to me as I read, or nuzzle my head. She was quite large, easily weighing four hundred pounds, and she had a tendency to breathe quite loudly, but we would settle into a fairly pleasant state where neither was disturbing the other. She spent a lot of the time snacking, which I would tell her off for, but she always ignored me.

'Oh Susy,' I would say, 'you really should watch your weight, my darling.'

She would not respond, but keep munching away. She had a very large tongue, which for some reason she loved to show me, often wetting her lips when I looked into her eyes.

'You mustn't flirt so, Susy,' I would say, 'a much older man!'

But she would say nothing. Sometimes, if I was in a solitary mood, I would let her follow me at a distance, very discreetly, from ten or fifteen yards away. We became very close, although we spoke very little.

Yes, Susy almost became like a pet to me. She really was my favourite cow. She had bright black hooves and a bell like those of the Swiss cows, so I always knew when she was nearby. It was a long-lasting friendship: we met holiday after holiday, month after month, for a good five years, and I always looked forward to seeing her whenever I visited the Emerald Isle.

AN UNEXPECTED SALESMAN

Between 1976 and 1990, I used to visit Deauville annually, and often enjoyed staying in the glamorous yet homely Normandy Hotel with my wife Hilary. Being near to the sandy beaches, the many racecourses, and of course the famous casino, the place tended to attract a considerable number of rich English tourists. Many actors flocked to the town too, as since 1975 it has played host to the famous American Film Festival, which takes places over ten days every September and aims to showcase new, more adventurous films that might not have made the big Hollywood cut. The red carpet was slightly shorter than the one in Cannes, and the champagne perhaps slightly less expensive than it would be in Venice, but the dresses were still glamorous, and the paparazzi and admirers still flocked there in droves.

Altogether, this made up the six principal reasons why the English came to Deauville: drinking, eating, horse riding, going to the beach, gambling, and attending the festival. I myself had little interest in most of these. I didn't mind horse riding or spending a nice day at the beach; in fact the two combined rather well, and of course I was fond of some of the excellent restaurants in the city, but I didn't drink or gamble, and I probably wouldn't have recognised Danny De Vito or Tom Hanks if I'd run into them on the street. At the time, I was actually in the process of buying a house in the rolling countryside just outside Deauville, so we were really only in town to eat and sleep! We did enjoy our stays in the Normandy Hotel, though, and managed to feel like we were on holiday even when we were actually in the country for dull bureaucratic tasks.

One autumn day in the late 1970s, when my wife and I had retired to our hotel room after dinner, there was a knock on the door and a stranger appeared. He was short, with immaculately combed blond hair. Despite the fact that he was standing in a heated, dark hotel corridor not too far from midnight, he was wearing a pinstripe suit, tie, and bowler hat. He also had the tell-tale sunburned nose of a sailor. It would have been near-impossible to assume he was anything but a purebred Englishman.

'Hullo,' he said, with the clipped precision of a man who has attended either Eton or Oxbridge, and probably both. 'I'm Bovis.

I'm terribly sorry to interrupt, but I couldn't help but overhear you speaking English the other day when you were taking your tea in the courtyard, and again this evening at dinner.'

'Hello,' I said cautiously. 'I'm Bradley. Bradley Jamieson. What can I do for you, Bovis?' I wasn't disinclined to trust this man, but it was past eleven in the evening, and I was hardly in the mood for company, having already changed into my pyjamas.

'I really don't mean to intrude,' he added. 'It's just that I think we should become better acquainted. I'm staying right next door to you, you see. I'm actually intending to stay in this hotel, oh, probably another few weeks or so at least. I'd imagine I could make quite a lot of money. You seem like the sort of man who can respect such aims. I know a good businessman when I see him.'

I smiled, my pride stoked slightly against my will. 'What, in my bathrobe?' He smiled slightly sheepishly and seemed prepared to apologise, but I cut him off as graciously as I could. 'Well, go on then. If you're going to stand there, you may as well explain your intentions.'

Bovis coughed discreetly, and produced the closest thing to a grin a man of impeccable upbringing can make.

'Well, alright then,' he said, 'I won't take up much of your time, you have my word. You're probably aware that this place is swarming with Englishmen. You're also no doubt conscious of the fact that this includes a great number of rich people looking for a good bargain abroad to carry back home along with their triumphant casino money, or to spend the last of their francs on.' He leaned on the side of my doorway with false nonchalance, and moved in to deliver the heart of his pitch. 'You might not know, however, that this includes a great number of salesmen, in the business of what the French call "*brocante*" and antiquities particularly. This means ones who didn't quite make it in Pimlico or on the King's Road or even on the Portobello antiques market. Well, I was one of these. It's just too difficult a crowd to sell to, you know? Too busy with their little London lives, their banking deals and their pub lunches. But once you get them over here, out of their raincoats and Wellingtons and into their Lacoste polo shirts and Ray Bans, they're much more relaxed. They're far more likely to make an impulsive purchase to impress their new rich friends or their new young mistress, for instance. I realised this on one of my sailing trips, so I sold my shop to a friend who wanted to open a restaurant, and I've come to set myself up in Deauville. What you're witnessing is the first stage, in which I try to find where the potential buyers might be hiding.'

Surprisingly, I had to admit I was rather won over by his irresistible combination of candidness and salesman's charm. 'You know you're not supposed to pitch to clients before they've had their first morning coffee, or after their last after-dinner one…' I chided him gently.

'I'm so sorry,' he said, in a tone of genuine mortification. 'I don't think I realised quite how late it was. I just overheard you and your charming wife leaving the restaurant, and I knew you were staying in the room right next to mine, and, well…' His voice trailed off uncertainly, although his eyes stayed bright. He ran a hand through his impeccable blond hair.

'That's quite alright,' I said. 'It's just that Englishmen aren't usually so big on hard salesmanship! But I've lived in America. It's perhaps not so surprising to me. In fact, there's something rather impressive about your dedication and directness. So please do go on. Finish your pitch. Let's see if we can close some kind of deal before the last coffee starts to wear off and I get sleepy.'

Bovis smiled happily. 'Well, that's just dandy. So, as I said, I'm in the antique business. Furniture, particularly. You'd be surprised at how many Englishmen like to buy English furniture abroad.'

'Wait,' I replied, 'you have furniture for sale in your room? Does the hotel let you get away with that?'

'Well, it's just a temporary arrangement. So far I've had no complaints.' He smiled smoothly. 'I intend to rent a warehouse in the near future, so I can set up shop more permanently there.'

'You're lucky I'm unruffled by this possible illegality,' I replied wryly. 'But as it so happens, my wife and I are just in the process of buying a big country house not so far away, and we were just getting to the stage where we were contemplating the question of how to furnish the place. This could just be a lucky chance meeting for both of us! So tell me, then, do you have any Georgian furniture?'

'I must confess,' he said ruefully, 'I don't actually have any with me at the moment. Oh, you should have seen my shop on Portobello road!' he added wistfully. 'So much varnished mahogany, a bunch of lovely little bookcases and side-tables and, overall, more intricate woodwork than you could possible hope for. I'm particularly fond of the claw-foot tables. In any case,' he said, resuming his business-like pose, 'I can easily source some for you. Tell me more about what you're looking for.'

At this point, we realised the transaction was unlikely to be accomplished that very night.

'Look, Bovis,' I said, 'I'm obviously very interested in what you have to offer here. But I'm tired, it's late, and it's looking like we're not going to be able to shake hands on anything right this minute. Why don't we meet for lunch tomorrow?'

'That sounds perfect,' he replied.

My first impression of Bovis's friendly disposition was confirmed over Caesar salads on the sunny Normandy Hotel terrace. Furthermore, he brought along his black bulldog, named Churchill, who won over my wife, so all in all it was a very pleasant meeting. Despite having had no intention to do so only two days previously, I quickly agreed to order a considerable number of pieces from him. Over the course of our acquaintance, he ended up furnishing several rooms of our Normandy house. I even made him aware of the growing popularity of furniture from the Arts and Crafts movements, and he ended up making a fortune selling some of these antiquities at double the price they were worth to American and German visitors. Eventually, Bovis became one of my top suppliers of English furniture, and we stayed friends for many years.

Throughout my life, both in work and in my social circles, I have found many a useful acquaintance. Friends who can help you when you most need it, colleagues who can give you insider information and good ideas; neighbours who have combined the best of both these worlds.

When my wife and I lived in Kent, we thought we had found such a person in Mr Van Bayier. He lived close by with his own wife, and was a great entrepreneur. Van Bayier's main interest was in building, and he bragged to me that he had almost built his own house from the ground up, through a lot of innovative ideas and the hard graft of renovation.

'One thing you can say for the Dutch,' he told me confidentially, 'is that we are never afraid of hard work, not at all.' And though Van Bayier was Dutch, and looked every inch of it, he had lived in England, with his young English bride, for so many years that there was hardly a trace of an accent in his voice. In spite of his pale good looks and chummy disposition, he was well established in England by the time we knew him and, at the age of thirty-five, had enjoyed some moderate success with his entrepreneurial endeavours. He had a way of making you feel like you were his best friend, which was what made him such a good salesman.

'We're looking to extend,' I said to him one day, 'but it's so expensive, isn't it?'

'Oh, no. No, not at all. Improving your home needn't be expensive, my friend!' He smiled at me. There was something harmless about him. He was quite short and very rotund, with gin blossoms in his cheeks that made him look strangely boyish. Anyway, he seemed the sort of man one could trust – he gave an impression of utmost openness, almost a lack of guile that belied the steely determination that lay underneath. 'What do you have in mind?'

'Well, the stables...'

'Yes, of course! The stables. I could convert them for you into the most charming apartments. It would be no problem at all. And not so expensive. Do you know, I take issue with these big companies, always trying to rip us off.' Van Bayier shook his head as though a big construction company was the worst thing in the world.

'They hire too many people who just sit around doing nothing all day, never show up on time, and don't know the first thing about building. That's why the prices are so high! You're paying for them to slack off and eat sandwiches.'

I wasn't so sure of this myself. The companies I had already spoken to about extending my property had explained the pricing to me, and it appeared fair, if on the dear side.

'You hire me, on the other hand,' he went on, 'and I can deliver you a building that will be beautiful and functional! You won't believe your eyes when you see how quickly I can work. And I am one man, with a very small company of trusted, talented builders. Geniuses! We can sink part of the swimming pool and put in a nice, big living room. I know the area, the ground, you know. And it'll all be heated, of course, that's only right. No problem, no problem at all. Why hire an architect when you can hire a friend?'

I hesitated. He was so good at selling the idea to me that something put me off. 'I'll have to talk to my wife about it,' I finally told him, hoping this would settle things until I came to some sort of decision.

'Yes, naturally! I'll look forward to hearing from you. I hope you will let me bring your vision to life.'

At this time, I was travelling a lot for work, and so my wife Hilary took over the duty of extending our house. In the end, it was her choice who she hired, and we decided that Van Bayier was as good as anyone. Also, since we knew him already, it wouldn't feel so intrusive having him in and around our home. Besides, you couldn't argue with his prices, nor his heartfelt promises of giving us an amazing home in a short space of time. It was something of a dream come true to know such a reliable sort of fellow who would be true to his word. He was just the kind of man you could trust, always eager to make friends with us, bringing flowers for Hilary, and inviting us out to dinner with him and his twenty-four year old wife: a quiet, pleasant woman we got on with very well.

While I was away for a long period of time, Hilary asked Van Bayier to come round and talk about the specifics of his plan for our property. Even though our building was protected, he told her it wasn't a problem to get the necessary permission from the local council to extend it and give it modern heating. Hilary was pleased with how he took charge of things and took up a contract with him confidently, looking forward to how wonderful our improved home would be.

Van Bayier held up his end of the deal admirably. Within a month we had converted stables, all heated, and even little lights in our alley, which made the whole place feel brighter and more comfortable. When I returned home, I was quite taken aback with the speed and expertise of his building work. The pool was wonderful, the plumbing all worked perfectly in the new stable apartments, and there was really nothing I could fault him for.

Of course, that was before the council phoned.

We hadn't had two full weeks to enjoy the changes before I received an accusatory phone call.

'We've seen that you have extended and drastically altered the character of a listed building,' the woman on the other end of the line said, before adding: 'without planning permission.'

For a moment, I couldn't think what she was talking about. 'I've done no such thing.'

She asked my name and address and I told her. 'Then you should know,' she said impatiently, 'that you live in a house of historical significance and any alterations have to be applied for in writing and approved by a governing body.'

'Our contractor did that for us.'

'It's not on our records.'

I paused as realisation set in. 'He never got permission?'

'No. And because of this oversight on your part, I'm afraid the additions to your property will have to be demolished. What you have at the moment is an illegal dwelling, and we can't allow it.'

It seemed a rather brutal conclusion, but the council were as good as their word. They tore out the indoor plumbing, the pool was filled in, and the garden was cluttered with the debris of our shattered home. They took the bathtub and put it in front of our house like an inverted dome, in a sad echo of war victors scattering upturned helmets. They did the same thing with the toilet, putting it upside down right in the middle of our garden. Ironically, they kept the washbasin open in the destroyed extension. They left it filled with water and placed a paper sign floating in it, reading 'out of action.'

Van Bayier seemed not to notice this when he arrived later in the week to collect the last part of his payment, but I angrily sent him away. I couldn't believe that we had been so foolish as to blindly trust someone who had made such outrageous promises! The worst part was that we had already paid him most of his £35,000 fee, with only £5,000 left to give him.

I thought that, out of common decency, he would stop coming over and asking for this last bit of money once he saw what a deplorable mess our house was now in. But Van Bayier was unconcerned by the state of things and claimed that the council had got it wrong. Every day he crossed the alley from his house to ours and asked for the £5,000 we owed him, a considerable amount of money in 1975. Otherwise, he told us, he would have to take legal action against us. All of this said in the same calm, promising manner in which he had offered to build us our dream home.

In the end, I gave him £3,000 and told him to be grateful for it. I had neither the time nor the patience for a lengthy legal battle, and it would have only caused more trouble in the neighbourhood. So I paid him off, after a fashion, which seemed to be the best thing to do at the time. At least it got him out of our house for good.

We never spoke to Van Bayier again, but made sure to tell others what a snake in the grass he really was. If anyone told us they had received an offer of building work from him, we made sure they turned it down, and so his fortunes were reversed. It must have been either this, or his overall bad character, that caused his wife to leave him in the end. We remained friends with her, and bonded over how none of us could believe how dreadful he really was.

After this experience, I decided to always choose the pricier and more realistic route when it came to buildings, and have never had any problems like it since, in any other country in the world. So I suppose you might say that I learned my lesson, and that you get what you pay for, thanks to Mr Van Bayier and his unscrupulous dealings. But it was a very expensive lesson indeed.

A MYSTERIOUS NEIGHBOUR

Our secondary family home in the South of France was always St Tropez, and for a time we rented in Antibes, but I always had a soft spot for our guest apartment in Cannes. Nestled at the foot of the vast, glamorous apartment complex known as Super-Cannes, we were right on the edge of prime real estate, looking out over the cresting waves of the bay and with the Alps in the distance. But just minutes away from our guest house, if one went for a walk, as I often did, one would quickly come across the rather perturbing sight of a line of guards in full uniform standing in front of a pair of barricaded gates, looking menacing as they held what looked suspiciously like old-school hunting rifles to their chests; big black guns with pumps that look like they were meant for hunting lions or elephants. I knew that French law would not have allowed private ownership of any such machine guns, but the effect was menacing all the same.

There is not a great deal to do in Cannes, other than wandering aimlessly down the streets, if you are not a big sunbather or a drinker. Coming up with theories about one's mysterious neighbours becomes a sort of pastime when one walks up and down these streets, where so many walls hide actors, politicians and Mafiosi, counting their millions in bank notes or having affairs with each other's wives. It's hardly surprising that Cannes has a lot of theft: criminals prowl the backstreets looking for big jewels in bedrooms, or breaking into basement safes. In a way, I was prowling too; but what I wanted was neither jewels nor scandal, but simply information with regards to my neighbours' identity.

I found it hard to get the place, and the questions it occasioned, out of my mind. I was usually in Cannes for business reasons, but in between meetings with clients, out of a mix of boredom and a desire for fresh air, I would often go for a walk around the back of our building. This neighbourhood route of mine led straight past the high walls of this particularly mysterious house: they were whitewashed and topped with glass and barbed wire, which gave a disconcerting impression of both luxury and menace. In front of the gate, through which one could see part of a courtyard with a fountain, and the wall of what appeared to be a classic villa beyond, I would come across these bodyguards, chatting away to each other in French and chain-smoking.

Eventually my curiosity got the better of me, and I approached one of the guards.

'Excuse me,' I said as politely as I could, 'I know I'm probably not supposed to ask, but are you able to tell me who lives here? Why are there all these guards?'

The guard coughed, and looked over at his colleague, who shook his head. The first guard sighed a little. 'We are sworn to secrecy, *monsieur*,' he said sternly.

'Surely you must see something,' I coaxed him.

'Nothing,' he replied.

I hung around for a bit, asking a few questions and trying to encourage him to give me any titbits of information. But I must have been a little bit too insistent in my interrogation, for the man suddenly pumped his gun as if he was going to shoot. I thought he might just do it out of stupidity, to prove a point or just get rid of me! I wasn't sure if the gun was loaded, or if that sort of hunting rifle could kill a man at close range, but I certainly didn't feel like sticking around to find out.

I walked away, and I decided I had to be less direct in my approach. The next time, I took my walk at a slightly different time, so as to make sure I crossed paths with a different set of guards. This time, I tried a slightly more oblique tactic.

'What a lovely place this is! He's a lucky man indeed. Tell me, is he in at the moment?'

The man narrowed his eyes a little. 'I'm not sure,' he replied.

I could tell he was already on his guard. I tried a different approach: 'What, don't you know who you work for?' I gave my best impression of a sneer.

In reply, the man gave one of those distinctly Gallic shrugs. 'They say he's a dictator,' he said, in a thick southern accent. 'We're just hired to do a job. They don't tell us who we work for.' He lit a cigarette. 'One of my colleagues thinks he saw him in the armoured car,' he said, obviously keen to show off what knowledge he had. I congratulated myself silently on my approach. 'I think he's some kind of Arab. Or African.'

I sighed. Clearly these guards were not actually given much information. 'Maybe it's someone like Gaddafi,' I said, by way of keeping the conversation going. 'Although he'd probably have a huge entourage. I don't think he's very discreet. It would be all over the papers.'

The guard shrugged again, possibly in agreement. 'Lots of people come in and out but we don't know who they are,' he said next. 'Maybe it's a woman,' he added, rather archly. I gave up at this point, and headed back to the office. For a time, I abandoned my quest to find out more about the mysterious walled villa.

But one day, a few months later, I had an unexpected stroke of luck. I happened to be passing by when I noticed that the gates were closing, obviously having just let in one of the big black armoured cars. There was only one guard by the gate, a short, wiry man standing on his own. Unable to contain my curiosity, I approached the man.

'Do you know what they're doing?' I asked, pushing my luck a little, but this man seemed to be of a different temperament to his colleagues, and his natural curiosity obviously showed.

'I often ask myself that,' he said, leaning in a little conspiratorially. 'I mean, how do these guys make their fortune? They're always coming in the cars with the black windows, with their sunglasses and big briefcases. There must be some kind of business going on in there. Which is why I don't think it's a politician, you see.'

I smiled, a little taken aback. 'Yes, I've wondered that myself. So do you think it's someone in business?'

'Well, I don't know,' he replied thoughtfully. 'I mean, it's a little high-security, unless they're a really paranoid millionaire.'

'You seem to have thought about this a lot!' I said with a smile. 'I must admit, I've tried to ask some of your colleagues these sorts of questions, and I may as well be asking the stone columns. If the columns were holding hunting rifles.'

'Oh, most of us are muscle-heads,' he said with a grin. 'They hire us to be bodyguards, but really we're just bodies. Huge bodies, all pumped up with testosterone and the occasional steroid. Sometimes I think they hire us to be stupid, too. Then I look at my colleagues and I can see why: the way they talk, I wonder if their heads are filled with foam!' I laughed. 'I mean, I'll be honest with you: I don't know who we work for either, but at least I think about it! Sometimes one of them acts all tough because he thinks he's got some information, but I get a different story every time. Often he's a dictator, sometimes he's an Arab, sometimes he's Iranian, once someone told me he was from the Caribbean, like some sort of deposed South American dictator.'

'St Tropez is full of these mysterious figures,' I said. 'Unless you ever see them, you'll probably never know who it is. It drives me crazy!' I laughed. 'But I hadn't heard the South American theory before. I mean, why would he be in Cannes and not in Spain or something?'

'Maybe he likes the sea. The temperate climate,' my interlocutor suggested. I laughed. 'Still, it's a fairly exciting job. That's what I like about it. It can be a bit boring at times, just standing around looking tough. I like to try and pick up bits of information. For instance, I once overheard one of the men in suits talking to another about the fact that they had to go to the bank to cash in fifty thousand dollars.'

'So the security isn't all that great, is it,' I wondered aloud. 'Why on earth would some difficult, reclusive dictator come to this tourist trap of a neighbourhood?'

'Have you seen the villa?' the man commented. 'It's huge. It's absolutely gorgeous. At least ten bedrooms, and all these gardens... If I were a dictator, I'd definitely stick around here.'

The strange bodyguard and I continued to chat for a while, until he was joined by a few of his beefier companions, and indicated to me that he could no longer speak so freely. I took my leave in a friendly fashion.

But this was not the end of the mystery. I must admit ahead of time that I never found out who actually lived there, although I made several fairly well-informed guesses. I did have one more informer, though: the gardener, whom I once met by chance on one of my walks. As I saw him coming out through the gates, between the bodyguards, I caught up with him around the block and asked him a few questions. He was an affable enough man, although he freely admitted that he didn't have any better idea of his employer's identity than any of the bodyguards did. 'He stays inside most of the time,' he sighed. 'At least I assume he does. He certainly doesn't spend a lot of time sunbathing on the lawn or smelling the flowers... I have seen him, though, you know.'

'Really?' I asked in surprise. 'I didn't think people knew what he looked like. I guess this definitely removes the theory that it could be a woman!'

The gardener laughed. 'Oh, it's definitely a man. My impression of him, based on a few glances from a distance, is of a very old retired African with white hair. As I said, he rarely leaves the villa, although he has many advisors that come from all over the world, Africans, Arabs, maybe even Japanese.'

'What's his name?' I asked, unable to contain my curiosity.

'I'm afraid I don't know.' He shook his head ruefully. 'It's a great mystery to everyone who lives here.'

'That includes me,' I said with a laugh. 'I think I will have to stop thinking about it, or it'll drive me crazy!'

In the end, in the twenty years I spent occasionally visiting St Tropez, I never figured it out. Maybe some day, by chance, in a newspaper or on television, I will recognise those gates, and see a known figure exiting from them! Meanwhile, it will remain one of the best mysteries I never solved.

It all began with the daffodils.

Our country house in Kent backed onto a forest, with only a stretch of track separating us from the wider wilderness. For the first few months of our living there in the late 1980s, this track remained rather barren and uninspiring. Though it didn't bother us particularly, the spring months brought with them a wonderful surprise.

Wild daffodils, a bright yellow and orange blaze of them. Thousands of them seemed to spring up overnight, much to our delight. They were exceptional flowers, with the tallest of them growing a foot and a half of verdant stem, the cheerful flower exploding magnificently out at us from the top.

'Aren't they beautiful?' my wife exclaimed, as we stood marvelling over the burst of nature that had quite abruptly come to life on our patch of land. It certainly made a nice change from the dreary mud of winter. 'It's like a greetings card!'

Three hundred yards of cheerful flowers now welcomed us whenever we came home, waving in the breeze like dozens upon dozens of little faces smiling and saying hello. We even took pictures of them, astounded by their size and the sheer rate of their growth. They had appeared with so little warning that we were always a bit surprised to see them still there, their presence like something otherworldly and entirely lovely at the same time. Daffodils are one of those flowers that perk you up if you feel low, and that's just what they did. They made our whole house feel lighter and more like home.

Essentially, our house was the only one on the track and the road itself belonged to us, with the forest beyond being public land. However, the forested area was used primarily by our nearest neighbour, a woodcutter by trade, who had this great forest at his disposal to make his own living. We had never had any trouble with him before, and in fact had never given him or the forest much thought. We had only talked occasionally about how nice it was to be so close to nature, to have all those trees on our doorstep, and how lucky we were to live here, with little trouble or interruption from the outside world.

Yet one day shortly after the daffodils had appeared, we made our neighbour's acquaintance in quite a less pleasant manner. A letter landed on our doormat and I opened it, since it was addressed to neither me nor my wife but simply 'The Occupants'. Upon opening the letter, I wished that I hadn't.

To whom it may concern,

I have noticed that you are growing an army of daffodils in the alley bordering my forest. Please remedy this situation immediately. I am a reasonable man, but those flowers are eating into my forest, and I cannot allow them on my property.

I trust you will find a way to dispose of them at your earliest convenience. Many thanks and have a pleasant day.

I stared at the letter, somewhat in shock over it. The whole thing was just too extraordinary and too petty to be believed.

'What is it?' My wife came up behind me and peered over my shoulder before breaking out into laughter. 'Oh! It's a joke.'

'I don't think it's a joke.'

'Come on. Nobody could really mind a few daffodils.' She took the letter from me to give it a proper read.

I frowned. 'It certainly seems that he does.'

'But they're so lovely. And besides, I don't think he actually owns the forest, does he?'

'No more than we do. It's public land, I believe. And the road is ours alone.'

'Well then,' she said, 'he has no right to complain about our flowers.'

'I'd best write back to him, though. Just to smooth things over.'

She seemed to be finished with the whole affair, and I couldn't blame her. It seemed like such a silly thing for someone to be upset about, not to mention wildly unfounded. 'Suit yourself.'

Dear Sir, I wrote,

First, allow me to thank you for your concern over the recent growth of wild daffodils on my property. However, let me make it clear that this is indeed _my_ property. The road that runs between my home and the forest does not belong to you. And I have it on good authority that you don't own the forest, either. I think it would do you good to find something else to worry about, other than a few flimsy flowers that won't live longer than a couple of weeks.

Have a good day.

There, I thought to myself, all sorted out. How naive I was. Just as I thought that might be the end of it, I was confronted with yet another letter not two days after I had delivered mine to his house.

To whom it may concern,

You are confused over boundary issues. That's quite all right, since you're new. I'll explain it to you. The forest is mine and your daffodils are across the border. You cannot grow anything outside the grounds of your house. If you don't do something about this hazardous situation, then I will be forced to take action.

I look forward to a clear road as soon as possible.

'This is ridiculous,' my wife said when I showed her the latest letter. 'This is complete neighbours' nonsense. I don't think you should even reply. He's not right in the head.'

'If I don't, then he'll probably be over here shouting the place down.'

She paused. 'All right. But be polite, would you?'

Dear Sir,

It's my road, and therefore I can grow what I like there. You cannot dictate what grows beyond your own property, even if the forest belonged to you. Which it quite clearly doesn't. So please stop wasting my time with your stupid concerns.

All my best!

It took him a little while to come back at me with anything else, but he predictably replied with the worst and most explosive letter yet, one that contained no illusion of neighbourly niceties whatsoever.

Look, it's a simple enough matter. If you don't get rid of the vile plague that is spilling into my forest, I'll tear them up by the roots and salt the earth and that will be that. So it's up to you. Pull them up immediately or else.

'Does that look like a threat to you?' I asked my wife, showing her the letter.

She sighed. 'Oh dear. What *did* you say to him?'

'Nothing to provoke that!' I insisted, though I had to admit if only to myself that I perhaps hadn't helped the situation. But that wasn't really the point. The man was so very clearly in the wrong, his claims incorrect, and worse than that, plainly stupid. 'That's it. I'm phoning the lawyer.'

'About flowers. You're going to phone our lawyer about some

wildflowers.'

'It's the only way to get any of this settled.'

I honestly believed that by getting a letter from our lawyer we could straighten the whole mess out and perhaps even be civil again. So I got hold of a letter from our very old-fashioned lawyer at Markby's, stating where our boundaries began and ended, and explaining that if our woodcutting friend dared to touch anything that lay on our property, it would constitute trespassing and criminal damage, and he would be taken to court over it.

'That'll set him straight,' I said smugly.

My wife only shook her head, and her doubts were proven quite correct when we received yet another letter.

I understand that you believe you are in the right but there are really no two ways about this. You have to pull out the daffodils.

I replied straight away.

Dear Sir,

Please reread the letter from my lawyer and trust that he is a professional. You should listen to his advice, and please leave us alone. If you pull them up, you will suffer the consequences of your actions.

'Is that a bit extreme?' my wife asked.

'Not at all,' I told her.

The next letter was delivered by hand from the woodcutter to me, though we didn't speak and there were very few words on the paper he gave me.

I am putting you on notice. In one week I will pull up the daffodils.

'That's it!' I said, slamming the front door. 'I've had enough. He's mad. He is completely barking mad if he thinks we're going to let him come onto our land and destroy our things. It's illegal and ridiculous and I won't stand for it.'

Dear Sir,

I don't think you quite grasp the gravity of what you plan to do. I am warning you, as a friendly neighbour. If you pull them up, you will have to grow them again. Aside from that, we will sue you if you set foot on our land. So think about that before you decide what to do. If you doubt for a second that the land you tread on is ours, I suggest you hire a surveyor. I have listed below the contact number and pricing of a very fine one, though if you do this you will also incur the cost of his fee.

Please never set foot on my property again.

In all honesty, I did not expect that to be what finished it. He was so determined to get me to back down that I thought he would contact anyone he had to in order to prove his point, although he was completely in the wrong.

However, after my last letter, things went very quiet. The daffodils remained.

I learned later, from another nearby neighbour, that the woodcutter did not want to pay for a surveyor, and had decided to leave it be for the time being.

However, it turned out that our neighbour was persistent in this matter on more than just a personal level – he actually went so far as to involve my own lawyer's offices, engaging with them in a slew of letters. Still, I was most startled to receive a letter in the post from Markby's. Since he had disclosed my name and address, apparently hoping that the proper authorities would somehow force me to uproot the daffodils, I had been copied in to this correspondence.

His letter to them was as odd and insulting as his letters to me had been.

To whom it may concern,
I am writing to express my distress concerning an ongoing property dispute with my neighbour. His property borders mine, and he insists upon growing an unacceptable amount of daffodils which spread onto my land. Please advise him to stop this behaviour and dispose of the flowers.

Markby's had rightly sent a rather short and unsympathetic reply, their standard response in matters they did not want to take on.

We are sorry to hear of your domestic troubles, but do not believe that this sort of issue warrants our intervention. We wish you luck in solving your problem.

After that, it seemed that almost every other day I received a copy of his correspondence with Markby's and, just as he had with me, my neighbour became increasingly threatening and unreasonable, until eventually I felt that I had no choice but to intervene again.

I couldn't help but feel it did not reflect well on me to have this ridiculous incident dragged out in the law offices of London, and Markby's were more than clear with him that they preferred not to enter into discussions without his having hired his own lawyer. Although, thankfully, they in no way suggested this as a recommended course of action, and it seemed he was too cheap to do so.

Eventually, I wrote my neighbour one final letter, in a short attempt to close the book on this drama once and for all.

Good afternoon,

I have been copied in on your exchange with Markby's, and would suggest that you give up your discussions with them. You would do better to save the money you have spent on stamps and envelopes. You will be pleased to know, if you venture a peek out of your window, that the daffodils have withered and died for this year, and so won't be bothering you anymore.

I wish you all the best.

The following year, as the daffodils pushed their way out of the earth once more, I waited with bated breath for a letter to land on my doormat, once again demanding their destruction.

None came.

The daffodils bloomed and flourished and have done every year since, filling our alley with bright colours and good cheer, growing taller and stronger and no doubt driving our neighbour entirely insane with their very existence. It makes me laugh to think of him not being able to do a thing about it, while we get pleasure from the beauty each and every time.

'Do you know?' I said to my wife one year, seeing the woodcutter grimace towards our flowers as he made his way into the forest. 'Daffodils might be my favourite flower.'

She just smiled.

NICK AND THE HALVA

As a child, I sometimes went to stay with my family in their house in Istanbul. We visited the city many times, and so over the years I ended up making a few acquaintances. One of them was a boy called Nick, who was my age. When we first met, I was a studious sixteen year-old with visions of studying in America. Nick was a hardworking boy employed in his father's sweetshop, who dreamed of taking over the shop at some point down the line. Despite the differences in our upbringings and dreams, we had a good relationship.

The shop specialised in a type of Turkish sweet known as halva. Halva is found in various forms all over the world, from Greece and Estonia to Zanzibar and Bangladesh. The form made with sesame is particularly popular in the Middle East, Poland, and the Balkans; and this was the principal creation of Nick Senior's shop. 'Everyone claims they invented halva,' Nick's father told me. He liked to wax lyrical about his product. 'The Russians are particularly loud about it. But I believe in the Turkish claim, perhaps with a little connection to the Aleppine cuisine in Syria. It's a different substance to what you might find at an Indian wedding or in the mountains of the Oural. The keys to our kind of halva,' he continued, 'are two special ingredients: *tahini*, which is a fine sesame paste, and *natef*. Now, *natef* is a strange substance made from the soapwort root. Soapwort is known as *'erq al halaweh* in Arabic, because of this, but, as the English name indicates, it is also used to make soap!'

'You use a kind of soap in the halva?' I asked, making a face.

Nick smiled. 'Let me finish my story. You can use this root, which is sometimes called Bois de Panama, to make all sorts of things. To understand halva, however, you only really need to know about *natef*. You see this root?' he asked, rustling around in a drawer and producing a small piece of wood the colour of cinnamon. 'Usually, we import it from South America. See how it smells like tea?' I held the piece of wood in my hands and marvelled at its capacity to produce such delicious desserts. 'It has many more flavours hidden inside, if you only boil it up with a few cups of sugar, maybe add a splash of orange flower or rosewater. It will eventually turn a light red colour. Then all you have to do is let it cool, and beat it with a whisk until it's fluffy and white. Then, of course, you add in all the ground sesame, and whatever else you want to flavour your halva: pistachios, chocolate, vanilla, or chocolate. I prefer mine simple, with nuts. What about you boys?'

'I like the pistachios the best,' I admitted shyly, and was rewarded for my interest with a sticky chunk of the sweet.

Nick Senior was a little bit of a raconteur, but I only really got excited about the process when his son snuck me into the little factory behind the shop. 'See those big tanks?' he whispered. 'That's where they make the foamy *natef*. It's delicious, like a very soft molasses, or marshmallow. Sometimes when no-one is looking I steal a little.' We peered over the steel rims, watching the automatic paddles frothing the syrup in a centrifugal motion. 'This is still quite liquid, which means they haven't added much sugar. It gets stiffer then.'

'And after that they add the nuts?'

'Well, first the tahini. Then the nuts, if any are going in that particular batch. You and your pistachios!' he laughed. 'Then there's the best bit, I love to watch it. My father scoops the mix out, which is now thick and pliable, and stretches it. It really looks like candy then. He kneads it into a soft white dough. Then he fits it into various moulds, and packs it, and sells it. That's it.'

The excitement on young Nick's face was contagious. 'Does your father let you help out back here?'

'Sometimes. But he's never let me do the final part, he says it's too messy and dangerous. I guess there's a lot of hot, melted sugar involved. When I'm a little older, though, I will know how to produce all the stages. I will make my own shapes and packaging.' He seemed so thrilled at the prospect.

Later that day, we sat on the floor of the shop eating chunks of the halva with black olives and cheese, which was Nick's slightly unusual favourite combination, and I found myself appreciating the sweet even more now that I understood the process of its formation.

Every year I visited, I brought back boxes of halva as a gift to my family in Paris or London. In fact, to this day, I prefer to import the sweet directly from Turkey. There's just something about that touch of sesame that I find an irresistible foil to that cloying sweetness. Add a few perfumed Turkish pistachio nuts and you will find me a happy man.

This story has a somewhat bittersweet ending, though. There was a point when I did not return to Turkey for ten years. When I did, I went to the halva store as soon as I could. I was in my mid-twenties, and was looking forward to catching up with my old friend. I assumed I would find him running the shop. However, I was greeted by Nick, Senior, who opened the door with a wary expression. I shook his hand happily, unsure of the source of his unease. 'How is business? How is your family?' I asked him enthusiastically.

He only shook his head softly and let me into the shop, locking the door and turning over the 'open' sign as he did so. The sweet smell of halva surrounded me, reminding me of my childhood. 'Things have changed,' he told me sadly, as we stood in the darkened room. 'I am happy to see you, believe me, but I must tell you some sad news. My son is no longer alive.'

I froze. I could hardly believe my ears. 'I don't know what to say,' I replied. 'I'm so sorry for your loss. What happened?'

'Our dear Nick is no more of this world.' He repeated the tragic fact as if it might make it sound more real. 'There was an explosion. An accident. A fuel tank somewhere outside of town.'

'Oh my god,' I exclaimed. 'How terrible. How sad.'

I looked away as Nick's father wiped a tear from his eye discreetly. 'It's strange,' he said, 'seeing you again. I mean, it's wonderful. It reminds me how he would have been in his mid-twenties by now, too.'

'He always talked about talking over the shop,' I said.

He smiled sadly. 'Yes, he did. Now, there's no-one to take his place. I will run this place myself until I can't manage anymore. Then I will have to sell it and move on.'

I looked at him, aghast. 'But you have the best halva in all of Turkey!'

This couldn't help but bring a smile to his face. He bustled back into the shop, obviously trying to move away from this conversation. 'I'm glad to hear you say that. You were one of our most faithful customers. Do you know, I never forgot, in all these years, what your favourite was.' He rustled around in a pile of cardboard boxes, then stood up. He smiled proudly, although his eyes were still a little red. 'Here you go. Pistachio halva. On the house.'

I accepted gratefully, then laid a hand on his shoulder. Nick stood like that for a moment, then drew me in for an uncharacteristic hug.

After a few seconds, he let go and stood back up, but the expression on his face was a happy one, now. 'I'm so happy to see you,' he said. 'It reminds me that life goes on. People may come in and out of your life, but you never forget your good neighbours.'

VAN GOGH, A NEIGHBOUR IN SPIRIT

Kent has always been considered a particularly picturesque part of Britain; the garden of England, as it is known, embodies a classic pastoral vision of the country, all rolling fields and lovely seaside. Consequently, the region has bred quite a number of Romantic painters, including Thomas Sidney Cooper, Samuel Palmer and J W Turner, the 'painter of light', who once called the skies over the Kent coast 'the loveliest in all Europe'. From the Thames estuary to the distant, misty London skyline, Kent was rendered over and over by realists and impressionists alike; all drawn to that soft country quality.

When I first moved into our ancient house near Canterbury, I found myself discussing the local history with one of my neighbours, who was an artist. Our house had been built in 1410 and renovated in 1620, so I was curious to find out a little more about its past and the heritage of the surrounding region. But one topic that came up took me by surprise.

'Did you know that Van Gogh used to live in Margate?' she asked me one day, as we were out in the garden, enjoying a bright spring sun.

'No, I'd never heard that. I always thought of him as a completely Dutch painter,' I replied in surprise.

'Of course,' she nodded, 'but he also spent some time around here in his early twenties. This was three or four years before he started painting full-time, at the age of twenty-seven. He came over to teach.'

'How fascinating. Did you say he was in Margate? I can certainly imagine the seaside would have been inspiring for any artist of his generation. I know T.S. Eliot used to go there.'

She smiled. 'It's funny you should say that. It was actually Eliot who first introduced Van Gogh to the region. The poet had come to Margate to recover from a sort of nervous breakdown, and the painter came to visit him there and partake of the good seaside air by his side. I suppose Kent must have made a good impression on him, for he came back shortly after.'

'And so he was teaching in Margate,' I marvelled. 'How interesting!'

'Yes, staying in Ramsgate, actually, on the coast. I read a lot about this when I first moved here,' my neighbour confessed. 'It's fascinating. I think there's something in this region that's particularly attractive to artists and writers: it seems to draw interesting people. Something about the wide open spaces, maybe.'

'It's certainly in a great position to attract people from the other parts of Europe, being so close to the sea... I mean, the tip of Kent could almost be French soil!' I joked. 'It's no surprise the northern continental countries all want to escape across the Channel to come here.'

'They must not know about the weather!' she joked in return. 'Although, saying that, now I recall that Van Gogh was actually quite fond of the British skies himself.'

'I suppose they would have the same appeal to a Dutchman as they had to someone like Turner... Besides, everyone knows that the English Romantic painters were very much inspired by the Golden Age of Dutch art. So there's an old connection between the Netherlands and Britain...'

'Yes, that makes sense. Of course, Victoria and Albert were big sponsors of Dutch painters. In fact, the biggest private collection of Dutch paintings in the world is still in the royal family.'

'And the royals themselves loved this county! I know they used to hunt around here with their falcons and hounds, throughout the ages.'

'So the English love the Dutch painters, and the Dutch painters love the English landscapes, and everyone loves Kent! I remember one of Van Gogh's letters to his brother Theo, where he discusses how much he enjoys the light in Kent, and the sea mists. He talks about what a happy, peaceful time he had there, teaching at the school and making friends with the pupils and other teachers.'

'When was this, then? In the 1880s?'

'Yes, something like that.'

I grinned. 'That means that if Van Gogh had stayed around, and if we had moved here, he would have been a contemporary of my grandmother! She was born in 1884, you see.'

My neighbour laughed. 'I like that idea very much. I mean, that makes you and old Vincent practically neighbours!'

'I must say I do love Van Gogh, especially his early work. Some of the darker, more realistic of his early paintings are really very moving, even if they are not as well-known as his brighter work.'

'I always thought the influence of Gauguin transformed his painting,' my neighbour mused in agreement.

'Well, and his life!' I added with a laugh. 'And not always in a good way.' I shook my head. 'Still, I often wonder if such genius is genetic. I mean, influences and teachers are one thing, but think of child prodigies like Mozart! But then training must be essential too, in something so technical. You have to learn the rules before you break them, right?'

'I'm rather inclined to think there is something genetic in it. Something to do with talent, or inspiration, or something. I don't think just anyone could become a painter!'

'And I suppose you would know,' I replied with a smile.

'But as a painter myself, I can certainly say that this place inspires me.'

'Yes,' I agreed, 'we're very lucky to live in Kent. But I don't think it will make me a painter. At least that means I get to keep both my ears!'

Hospitals are consistently one of the most interesting places to meet neighbours, as there is even more of a lottery element to the neighbour acquisition process than usual!

In this particular case, in the spring of 2002, I was sent in to the Geneva University Hospital by my GP. The doctor was worried about an increase in my heart rate, which had gone up from its usual steady pulse of sixty beats per minute to the somewhat more alarming frequency of a hundred and ten beats per minute. Neither of us had any idea how this might have happened, so he thought it best to get it checked out.

Coming into the emergency ward is never a calming experience, especially when it happens to be particularly busy. It was unnerving to sit there quietly while an old woman was lying on the floor in pain next to her children, and a young man with a sallow face coughed incessantly. Then a man in handcuffs was led in by the police, wounded and bleeding from the head. This character was admitted immediately, as he was obviously in a critical condition. The rest of us less dramatic cases looked on in silence. I began to wonder how many hours I would have to wait before being admitted! I started to get a little anxious, and became very conscious of my heart beating, still quite fast, under my shirt.

After another twenty stressful minutes had passed, with the woman writhing and the man coughing and my heart hammering, I decided I had better take some kind of action. I went up to the front desk and explained the urgency of my situation, after which the secretary somewhat reluctantly admitted me into a special ward.

There was only one other patient in the heart section; an elderly man who was on two portable phones when I came in, as well as the fixed phone from his bedside table. He did not look like he was relaxing to take good care of his heart. He was sitting up in his hospital bed, straining from the exertion. After a moment, I noticed with amusement that he appeared to have pulled a pinstripe suit jacket over his hospital gown. 'No, no,' he was shouting, 'sell off the gold. Gold is going down! Don't you have any decent contacts out there?' After a short pause, he cried out: 'Japanese? No, that's nonsense, get it from Argentina! The stocks are great now. Buy them now. Buy them all up. And make sure this is all in dollars, OK?' Then he hung up with a satisfied grin. Only then did he appear to notice my presence.

'Who are you?' he barked. 'Another intern? Go away and tell them I want to see a real doctor. I'm probably in a critical condition.'

'I'm not an intern,' I replied.

'Oh, sorry. You don't look like a doctor...' he said dubiously.

'I'm not a doctor. I'm a patient.'

'Oh.' He said. Then his face split into a grin. 'How's your heart doing, then?'

I smiled back, relieved. 'It's just a little fast.'

'Well, they'll be sending in some sort of pimply-faced intern in a minute to check on you, I'm sure of it. Now, if you'll excuse me, I'm going to have to make a few phone calls.'

As if on cue, both phones started ringing. He picked both up at once, with a dexterity that belied his apparent situation. 'Diamonds? How many diamonds?' he barked. 'Get Paris on the line. Tell me what the price is per barrel! Yen? Don't do it in yen! What's the spot rate? No, you idiot, it's a communist government!' It was bewildering. Not only could I not follow the separate strands of the deals he appeared to be involved in, I couldn't even figure out how many conversations were going on at once! After about three minutes of rapid-fire exchange and a bit of swearing, he hung up again and turned to me with a calm smile. 'Now, where were we? Ah, yes. Introductions, I presume. Well, I am Ari Betoyan. As you can probably tell from the inevitable eavesdropping that these rooms produce, I am a businessman.' One phone rang, and he held up an apologetic finger with a smile as he picked up. There was a short silence, then he bellowed: 'You work for me, Paul!' and slammed the receiver down. Calmly, he turned to me again. 'Sorry. What were we saying?'

'I'm Bradley,' I said. 'Sorry, I've forgotten your name.'

'Ari,' he said. 'It's Armenian. I'm a businessman, like I said.'

'I can see that!' I replied. 'So what is wrong with your heart, then? I mean, you just closed about ten deals in a row! How bad can it be?'

'Oh,' he said, 'maybe it's just that I can't survive without doing a deal a minute. It's in my nature, you see. I was born that way. I was a nervous child, always very intense. This translated quite handily into an ability to do business deals. That's how I made my fortune, and that's how I can afford this suite. How about you?'

'Insurance,' I replied.

'No, I mean, what's wrong with you? Why are you in this hospital at all?'

'I'm not sure,' I told him frankly. 'I guess I'm in here to find out!'

'Let me tell you something,' Ari added. 'I'm eighty-five years old. I'm turning eighty-six tomorrow. Maybe I've got to keep doing all these deals because if I stop, I'm going to die.' He looked at me seriously. I wasn't sure how to react.

'Congratulations!' I tried, smiling cautiously.

This seemed to be appropriate. He broke out into a grin. 'All my family will be coming! I have an advanced case of diabetes, you see. I am here for a series of tests.' At this point, his two mobile phones rang at once. 'Paul?' he barked. 'Silver? Check the statistics. What do you mean, expensive? Corn is out of fashion. Don't you read the newspapers?' I stopped paying attention as the exchanges grew more complicated. At the end, he hung up both phones at the simultaneously with that same satisfied smile. 'I don't know how I would live without it,' he confided in me.

'But isn't it bad for your heart, all the stress of these deals?'

'Oh, it doesn't really matter anymore, does it? I've written my will. All my affairs are in order. If a businessman can't do a little gambling at the age of eighty-six, when can he?'

I had to admit there was some wisdom to the position. At this point, our conversation was interrupted by the intervention of the doctor. When he came in, Ari winked at me. 'Ah, you're lucky. They've brought you a real doctor!'

The doctor smiled patiently at him, then turned back to me. 'Well, I looked at your medical history, and I must say I haven't quite figured out why you're here. We'll have to run a series of tests.'

'Wait, do you mean everything seems fine? Can I just go home?'

'Well, it's not quite as simple as that. Your heart is still fast, but it is stable and consistent in its beat. We can't rule out any explanations at this stage. You need to stay here a few days for observation.'

I tried to argue, but the doctor was adamant, and eventually I gave up. I unpacked my small bag, and settled into my bed. The whole time I did this, Ari Betoyan did not stop making phone calls, with his three phones clutched any which way.

In a pause in his transactions, as we were being served our evening meal, I asked him: 'So what are you trading?'

His face lit up at this opportunity to show off. 'Oh, anything, really. Whatever is doing well on the market. Right now, let me see... Wheat, corn, cotton, copper, iron, silver, gold...' he reeled off.

'All the classics, then,' I replied with a friendly manner.

'Are you making fun of me?' he asked suspiciously.

'Oh no,' I said hastily. 'It's just that I used to be a banker myself. I know a little about trade. I couldn't help but notice you've essentially traded half the earth's worth of materials! Why don't you mix it up a little? Maybe get involved in selling pork bellies. It's a volatile market and you will make money on the ups and downs!'

'How disgusting,' he grimaced. 'That has absolutely no attraction for me.'

'Or you could do something else a little cleaner but still more exciting, like soy for example. That's a little more modern. You might make a buck or two.'

'I don't know anything about soy,' he admitted a little unwillingly. 'Say, you don't have any tips for me, do you? Any contacts still in the industry?' he asked, brightening a little.

'Of course! They're no use to me now, you may as well. I'll put you in touch.' At this point, my neighbour's phone rang, but he didn't answer it, instead listening intently as I continued. 'I'll tell you what else is worth investing in right now: the euro. It's just gone up from .82 to nearly one dollar. The dollar is weakening, it's inevitable, while the euro is set to go up and up.'

Ari grinned. 'OK,' he said, 'I'm a gambling man and I'm dying soon. I'll do it. How much should I speculate on?'

'I don't know, a couple of million?'

'I like your style, Bradley,' he said. 'I know I've only just met you, but I can imagine us doing business together in a past life. Better late than never!'

He then picked up the phone, called his broker, and bought two million dollars' worth of euros. Although I eventually drifted off to sleep, I'm quite sure he kept talking and dealing throughout the night.

The next morning, while he was ringing other people on his other two phones to gloat about his new investment, the doctor re-entered the room. He took my pulse and shook his head with a smile. 'We've run some analyses,' he said, 'and we just can't find anything wrong with you. Now it seems your pulse has gone right back down to its usual sixty. It's strange, this situation. I think we'll have to keep you overnight, in case it comes back without explanation.'

I was astounded. 'You mean it's gone back to normal even with my neighbour here doing deals all day and night?'

'I know,' said the doctor. 'It's quite strange.'

'Surely my heartbeat should be going up not down in these circumstances!' I turned towards Ari's bed to make sure he had not taken offence, but he was deep in conversation with at least three people on his phones.

'I know,' he said again with a shrug, 'but there's nothing else for us to check. All we can do is keep you here for observation. Meanwhile, I'll just run you through a few questions. For instance, what did you eat before coming here?'

'Nothing special.'

'Any stimulants? Coffee?'

'Only my usual eighteen cups a day.'

He glanced up to check if I was joking. 'And you do this every day?'

'Oh yes,' I assured him. 'Ever since I was sixteen. Some days I only drink about twelve.'

The doctor noted this all down without comment. 'Are you taking any medicine?'

'Some vitamins,' I said. 'Nothing special.'

'What kind of vitamins?'

'Um, a fish oil pill. Some herbal remedies. And, come to think of it, a different kind of vitamin C. Our nanny at home gave it to me.'

'Can you tell me the brand? If it's the only thing you can think of that was different about yesterday, it might be relevant.'

'I have no idea,' I admitted. 'But I can call home and find out.' I dialled the nanny. 'Can you tell me what kind of vitamin C you gave me?'

'Ah yes,' she said. 'Well, you see, we had run out of your usual kind, so I gave you some vitamin C my father found. He gives it to his horses. He's a farmer.'

I relayed this information to my doctor, who raised an eyebrow. 'How much?'

'How much?' I asked her.

'I'm not sure,' she said breezily. 'It's a big pill, the fizzy kind. I put it in water for you, don't you remember?'

I thanked her and hung up.

'Well,' the doctor said, 'you'll definitely have to stay for observation now! I'm quite sure medication meant for horses is not usually good for humans. It will probably pass through your system naturally, but it could also be quite dangerous.'

I sighed and resigned myself to having to spend another day watching my Armenian neighbour do deals.

Luckily, it turned out to be quite an exciting day. By that night, two particularly exceptional things had happened. First of all, the euro went up nearly five percent from its parity level. Thanks to my tip, my new friend made thousands of euros overnight. 'What a great birthday gift!' he crowed. Secondly, Ari's entire extended family seemed to have managed to materialise in our ward. Old women, little children, grown men with wives; all came in with gifts, flowers, chocolate, and boxes of Armenian food. I was fed baklava, halva, and Turkish delight, and tiny cups of coffee. In fact, I was handed so many snacks that I started hiding them in my pockets when I got too full to eat any more.

'Are you sure this is good for your diabetes?' I asked him at one point.

He shrugged joyously. 'I'm eighty-six!' he said. 'What do I care? I'm a born gambler! And this baklava is exceptionally tasty.'

Someone pinned a rose to the pinstripe jacked that Ari still wore over his hospital gown; someone sang happy birthday. All in all, it was a wonderful day, and Ari hardly did any new trading at all. He only took about fifteen phone calls, and half of those were birthday wishes.

Despite this happy atmosphere, by the next morning, I had grown quite tired of my stay there. When the nurse came in in the morning, I told her at once. 'I'm ready to leave,' I said. 'I have to get to a board meeting!'

The nurse looked at the board on the foot of my bed. 'I'm sorry, sir,' she said, 'but it says here we have to keep you for observation.

You'll have to ask the doctor personally, only he's not here today. He'll be back tomorrow.'

'Tomorrow is too late,' I replied through gritted teeth.

'Trouble?' Ari asked me. 'Too much coffee at my party yesterday?'

I had to laugh. 'As long as none of your relatives put vitamin C in their baklava…' I joked. 'No, everything is fine. In fact, completely fine. My health is, at least. I have a board meeting to get to. I just can't stand to stay in bed another day.'

He grinned broadly. 'Why don't you stay here another day and give me some more tips?'

I shook my head. 'I'll happily give you my phone number, but I am just going to have to leave. In fact, you may want to fall asleep for a while, as I am about to do something almost criminal.'

'Oh, we're no longer young men,' he replied. 'We can take risks. We know the score. Best of luck with your escape!'

'And best of luck with your deals!'

Mimicking him, I pulled my pinstripe jacket over the hospital gown. Then I decided that wasn't enough, and changed into my full suit. I slipped two cushions under the sheet, and walked right out of the hospital. It was blissfully easy. It was only when I arrived home that I realised I had forgotten to give Ari my telephone number. Then again, I decided I had already given him the tip of a lifetime. We would both keep fond memories of each other, even if we didn't keep in touch. And I still had some baklava in my pocket.

In France, most big executives seem to be hired for life. The combination of the social security system and the union system allows a kind of job security that is a nightmare for employers and a dream for employees. Once they make it to the top, that's where they stay. Thus, in my days as a banker in France, I saw cases where the presidents of banks were fired for total negligence, and immediately reappointed as presidents of even bigger government banks. Most continue in this way until they are sixty-five and hit retirement age.

One of my neighbours in St Tropez, Monsieur Bartonée, was a major executive in a multinational company. He handled the treasury and the acquisition strategy of his company, where he had worked for almost ten years. The salaries of executives in France were only about $150,000 a year in those days, and according to the location, the house he owned must have been worth a good $8 million. Either he had big bonuses or another mysterious source of funds, but Bartonée certainly seemed to have nearly endless disposable income. He was slick, tall, and spoke perfect English, and he appeared to live by the theory that one's earnings and savings were meant to be spent on social events, parties, and pretty women. His wife was a charming model, and the couple seemed to have parties every weekend with hundreds of guests, usually including a handful of glitterati, luxury drinks, and generous buffets. I became friends with both of them as we were living next door to each other; we often met for lunches and dinners together on the beach. I attended some of their extravagant parties, doing my best to muster the superficial small talk expected at a gathering of this sort in St Tropez. This is not the place one might meet intellectuals, artists or travellers who tell long, illuminating stories or discuss literature. Most of the discussions have to do with sailing, dating, drinking and dancing, if they manage to get off the topics of the weather, and what everyone is wearing.

However, this particular neighbour, Mr Bartonée, was something of an exceptional case. Not only did he want to flaunt his riches and glamorous wife at his many parties, but he also had to show off his Rolls Royce everywhere he went. Thus, he drove his Rolls Royce on any possible occasion, on the tiny roads around St Tropez that could hardly take its width, or on the port that was always so crowded that he could hardly move. In fact, I believe he actually enjoyed these traffic jams, since everyone had to move so slowly that they would inevitably gawp at his extraordinary vehicle. I sometimes wondered if he purposefully drove into traffic at busy times to engineer this situation. One day, I ran into him on just one such occasion, when we had both been stuck in traffic for a good quarter hour and were barely inching forward, surrounded by angry Frenchmen and frustrated tourists on all sides. We drove side by side until it seemed rude not to greet him.

'Hello!' I shouted from my open window.

'Hello!' he said back, waving. 'No, not the Senegalese,' he shouted next. 'Their prices are ridiculous.'

'I'm sorry, what?'

'Keep the stock another week or so,' he responded. 'No, I'm not talking to you,' he said, but before I had time to be reassured, he added: 'Get me Texas on the line, straight away! The merger is going through.'

I was completely flabbergasted until I realised that Bartonée had a mobile phone in his hand. Craning my neck a little, I realised he actually had a phone in each hand!

'One is my car phone,' Bartonée shouted out the window.

'Are you talking to me?' I called back with a grin.

'Yes, yes, Bradley, I'm in the middle of some important deals,' he yelled back. 'Sorry Paul,' he added, almost in the same breath, 'Yes, add another million! No, not the salmon ones. Yes, I mean the Japanese acquisition.'

As I laughed at this extraordinary transition, he started shouting about Japanese clients, and I realised he had plunged right back into whatever multiple deals he had been handling, as well as what sounded like preparations for some party. It was like listening to some sort of strange modern play. Shaking my head, I pulled away into traffic, wondering why on earth he chose to conduct business from his chauffeured car when he could as easily have been sitting at home with his beautiful wife, or could have afforded a nice quiet office with a sea view. I couldn't believe that he would carry out what sounded like such a serious deal in this ridiculous manner. The whole concept struck me as flippant and rather childish. But over the eight or so years that we were neighbours, I watched him continue to do business this way, whether in the height of summer or even at Christmas, and I had to conclude that he must have known what he was up to.

Around 1993, we ran into each other on one of the rare occasions where he was doing his deals on foot. He was just hanging up the phone when we ran into each other, on the way back from the famous Pampelonne Beach.

'So, not in your car, then?'

He laughed. 'I just finished an acquisition deal with Thailand. It's all in their hands now. I thought I'd get the chauffeur to drive back so I could get a little fresh air. I'm just headed to the car now.'

'Well, it's a rare thing we get to have this kind of neighbourly chat, when you're not being driven or surrounded by party guests.'

'Indeed,' he replied. 'Will you walk with me?'

'With pleasure!' We settled agreeably into step. 'So I must ask you something.' I began, 'do you ever go to work? I mean, do you have an office? Every time I'm here in St Tropez I seem to run into you constantly!'

'I mostly work in my car,' he admitted. 'I mean, I'm always at work! It's comfortable. It gives me a sense of power. And it has a phone installed. It's like a perfect travelling office!'

'I have to admit it's hard to see the flaws in that idea, apart from the petrol consumption, perhaps. So how is your lovely wife?'

'Oh,' he waved his hand, 'she's a thing of the past, I'm afraid. We're getting divorced.'

'A thing of the past? She can hardly have been a day past thirty!'

'Thirty-three,' he said. 'My new girlfriend is twenty one.'

I shook my head. 'At your age – what, fifty?'

'Fifty-five. But that's how it goes in St Tropez.' He shrugged. 'Such is life. *C'est la vie!*'

We walked along the beach for a while, during which time I discovered the somewhat disturbing fact that the new girlfriend was in fact the daughter of a friend of mine. As we neared the road, I slowly realised that the car we were headed towards was not one I recognised. It was indeed a Rolls Royce, but a brand new one, and a convertible at that: the streamlined Corniche, in a daring Bordeaux red colour.

'My, my, dear friend,' I found myself saying. 'So it's not just the new girlfriend, it's the pretty young car as well? Does this have to do with the profits of your new Thai acquisition? Or is it some kind of mid-life crisis?'

He slapped me on the back affectionately.

'No, it's just a simply renewal,' he explained. 'I change Rolls-Royce every four years.'

'Your poor women!' I said jokingly. 'Do they know about this policy? That's a pretty short expiration date!'

'Oh, they love the cars,' he replied, pretending not to have understood my insinuation, although I could tell from his roguish grin that he knew perfectly well what I meant. I wonder if he ever settled down in a proper office, and how many years he continued his high turnover of cars and girlfriends.

Once, many years ago, I stayed with a Saudi prince in Yemen. Unsurprisingly, his house was beautiful and rather stately, lying as it did near the border of Saudi Arabia. He was a very welcoming man, eager to see to my comfort and enjoyment during my stay. Every need was catered for and every whim indulged. It is the way over there to treat a visitor almost as family. As soon as I arrived, I was instantly swept along into one of those notoriously fabulous and decadent Arabian meals. These great dinners often last for hours and are full of highly calorific and deliciously greasy food. All participants sit around on the floor, eating stuffed lamb and camel over enormous servings of gooey rice. The atmosphere at this particular dinner was jovial and relaxed. It was a real party, everybody evidently enjoying the prince's wonderful hospitality and generosity.

Of course, the one sticking point to all this luxury and eating was the extreme heat. Already a hot and unpleasantly dry part of the world, this was only made more uncomfortably by the massive swell of heat generated from cooking all these luxury foods. It could reach upwards of fifty degrees in such conditions, and I found it most uncomfortable to sit around eating and sweating. Everyone was enjoying themselves, but it was clear that they were also rather pushed to their limits in the heat. Even the prince himself appeared to struggle in such conditions.

After our meal was completed, several hours later, our host took pity on us and clapped his hands.

'We should clean ourselves and then go and enjoy some nice cold air,' he declared, looking pleased with his decision. None of us could argue with such an offer. We all went to the many bathrooms in the beautiful house and washed our hands and faces and cleaned our teeth, to make ourselves presentable for the rest of the evening. Then we followed the prince's lead.

Unexpectedly, though, we did not stay in his house. Instead we went up to his neighbour's property where, the prince assured us, we would be most welcome and comfortable. The neighbour's house was markedly older than the prince's. It looked as though it had stood on the very same spot for thousands of years, and the prince told us that our presence would not be an intrusion.

'My neighbour welcomes me like family,' he said, waving away any uncertain looks, 'and you'll appreciate the change in climate, I'm sure.'

Our host's neighbour was indeed as hospitable and pleased to see us as though we were his own guests, welcoming us into his home and urging us to enjoy it. It was beautiful and we were served coffee and tea to enjoy at our leisure.

The change in temperature was completely astounding, and nobody could quite work out how it was possible that such an old house was so beautifully cool. It made the prince's house and the outside world feel like an oven by comparison.

This old house was full of small windows on the topmost part of the structure, places where the sun could not reach to fill the house with such unbearable heat. Whoever had designed such a house had surely created a miracle in the arid landscape that surrounded it. These air ducts at the higher parts of the house delivered cold air down into its lower rooms, where we were to be seated. This natural air conditioning system was quite fascinating to me. Though outside the sun blazed all day and created forty-degree temperatures, within the prince's neighbour's house the temperature remained a more than tolerable twenty degrees. It felt positively arctic after our overheated, five thousand calorie dinner. After being around that sort of intense cooking heat, we all welcomed the sudden relative coolness.

None of us could quite believe that such an archaic aeration system worked, however.

'You mean,' I found myself asking the prince, 'there's no electrical fan system? Air conditioning?' It was quite improbable to me that such a system could actually be so effective. It was the most comfortable I had been since I had arrived in Yemen and I had no desire to go back out into the scorching moonscape beyond the doors.

He simply laughed and clapped his hands again, thrilled with our scepticism and fascination with the house. 'No, no, friends. It's all design and nature. Exceptional, isn't it?'

And exceptional it was. There were truly no fans or electrics, no water-cooling set-up. This was just an incredibly old system that predated all modern ways of keeping a property cold in such boiling conditions and had been successful for thousands of years. Newer houses, like the prince's own, had not been so well equipped and so we imposed upon his neighbour's hospitality to continue our evening.

This was, I found, typical of Arabian generosity. The prince provided us with an exceptional meal and then his neighbour was glad to welcome us into his own home so that we might continue to enjoy each other's company.

It was one of the most pleasurable evenings I had ever spent in that part of the world, and one which I shall never forget.

SHERWOOD THE HUNTER

I had some truly lovely times in my country property in Kent as a student. I rented a beautiful four-bedroom house for £12 a week, deep in the countryside near Cousley Wood. I was lucky to have a place where I could retreat to study for my PhD and get some work done in peace, usually over the weekend, surrounded by the rolling hills and quiet fields.

My neighbour there was a young man by the name of Sherwood, who worked in the orchards under his father's supervision. Sherwood could have been an attractive man in another activity: tall and clean-shaven, with long dark hair and brown eyes, he might have cut the dashing figure of a farmer out of a nineteenth-century novel. In truth he was a dishevelled, miserable creature with hunched shoulders from spending all day picking fruit, and he had a ghastly temper to match.

I think Sherwood resented his isolated country life deeply. After all, he was young: he craved human contact. His father was very strict and wanted his son to be a farmer like him, so he made him start work at the age of ten. There were few young people in that area of the countryside, and once he had dropped out of school, I don't think the boy had much of a social life at all. You might imagine that such a sense of isolation would make a young man happy to make contact with the people he did run into. Yet I would see him in the morning, and greet him across the fence, but he would never answer.

I gradually started to realise that his silence went further than lack of politeness. For instance, I started to notice him skulking around the garden when I had company round. You see, I used to entertain occasionally up at the house. We would have the most wonderful barbecues in the summer, with a mix of students and professors milling around the garden, enjoying the sun and sipping cool drinks, talking of current affairs, music, philosophy, and the occasional bit of student gossip. Presumably, having left school unwillingly at the age of ten, he must have resented the spectacle of a bunch of academics enjoying themselves and conversing. I suppose the smell of my barbecue must have drifted over his land as well. God knows what he was eating; I can't imagine his father looked after him very well. Whatever the reason, whenever I had friends round, he always seemed to materialise across the fence, carrying his father's shotgun for no discernible reason and scowling like a grumpy old sailor.

Watching him climb the ladders and hunch up into the trees like some sort of strange monkey, it seemed as if work had deformed him, not just physically, but also psychologically. He seemed from a distance to be perpetually upset or angry, and I learned quite quickly that he was no easier to understand from close up.

One day, I was out by the fence, getting ready to cut the hedge, when I saw Sherwood coming at me with a shotgun. He walked determinately to the edge of the fence, and stopped, with the gun pointed straight at me.

'If you touch our side of the fence I will shoot you,' he said.

It was the first time I had ever heard him speak.

'Good morning, Sherwood,' I said, keeping my voice as amiable as possible.

He just stood there with the shotgun under his arms.

'Don't say good morning,' he spat, 'I'm mad at you.'

'Why are you mad at me?' I asked very calmly.

'Because you're my neighbour,' he answered, as if this were obvious.

'And because I am your neighbour I am your enemy?' I asked.

'Yes,' he said, a little sulkily. I remembered that he was barely more than a teenager. Still, there was a wild look in his eyes, which made me a little nervous. Mostly, though, he inspired a great deal of pity in me. He was obviously a very disturbed young man.

'Is it like this everywhere in England?' I asked next, trying to draw him into civilised conversation.

'Yes,' he said. Conversation was obviously not his forte.

'Would you like to come over for a barbecue next Sunday?' I tried.

'I don't want your meat. I don't want your fish. I don't want your vegetables. I don't want anything to do with you.'

'How did you deal with the previous tenants in this lovely house?' I pondered aloud, trying to keep the conversation calm.

'I tried to kill them,' he said very calmly. 'I tried to kill them but it didn't work.'

There was a silence.

'How's your father?' I asked.

'I hate my father,' he replied.

'Are we going to be able to improve our relations in any way?'

He narrowed his eyes, and suddenly grabbed the fence to shove his face closer to mine.

'I don't want any kind of relation with you. Don't come near my fence.'

'At some point in the future,' I said in my calmest voice, hoping to draw on his farmer's sense, or perhaps some primitive logic, 'we're going to need to repair the fence at the bottom of the garden. We'll need to pass through your orchard.'

His eyes were almost popping from his head, but he was still almost not moving. The effect would have been comical under different circumstances, but at that particular moment it was rather disturbing.

'I have the right under English law to kill you. As long as your head falls on my property.'

I was silent. There wasn't very much I could say to that.

'Even if your head doesn't fall on our property I will kill you and drag you onto our property before the police come.'

This seemed like an unnecessary addition.

'Well you're a very cheerful neighbour,' I said. He didn't seem to find this funny.

'Don't come near us,' he said, glowering at me like a threatened animal. 'Don't talk to us.'

'OK,' I said, raising my hands as if in surrender. 'OK.'

I turned around, quite slowly and deliberately, and walked away, trying not to think of the barrel of that shotgun.

This conversation would be repeated in various forms approximately once a month for the next two years. I learned to live with the threatening presence next door as you might, perhaps, with a particularly grumpy grizzly bear.

One day, however, as I was enjoying a quiet breakfast on the terrace, I heard the noise of an engine, followed by a series of shots. I ran out to the back of the house to see Sherwood waving his gun in the air and shooting because there was a garbage truck going by his property. The people in the truck were yelling, Sherwood was yelling, the whole scene was terribly chaotic. At last the truck drove off, presumably as fast as the driver could, and Sherwood stomped back home, glaring. I retreated to my breakfast, although the coffee had gone cold and the whole thing had rather lost its peaceful appeal.

I decided to go speak to the father, in hopes of understanding the situation a bit better. Perhaps, I thought, we could come to a better solution for dealing with our proximity. The father was not a great deal more loquacious than the son, and although he was slightly more pleasant, this wasn't saying much.

'Sherwood is mad,' the father said. 'Don't go near him.'

'But surely he's just a troubled soul?'

'He's not troubled,' the father said briskly. 'He's just barking mad.'

'If he's mad, why don't you send him to a hospital? It might be better for him.'

'Oh, he's not *insane*,' he said with a sort of offended emphasis, as if shooting at garbage men was a normal if slightly odd pastime for a young man. 'I need him to pick the fruit.'

I wasn't quite sure how to handle this change of tack. 'Well,' I said at last, 'what do you suggest I should do about the situation?'

'Avoid him,' he answered at once. 'He's mad.'

And that was the end of that conversation.

For the next few years I spent at that house, nothing changed. I once saw Sherwood chase two squirrels around the orchard for three hours, waving the gun at them. There was obviously something quite seriously wrong with him, but his father refused to deal with it as he wanted the free labour. I always thought it was a terrible shame, even though I was never quite sure what kind of madness drove him. It seemed like the boy might have had a better life if he'd had an education, or been sent to someplace he could be looked after.

I never did find out what happened to the boy. Perhaps he's still there, thirty-five years later, terrifying the squirrels and the bin men.

STEINMITZER THE AUSTRIAN

My family house was one of the oldest and largest in a cluster of beautiful old houses in St Tropez. The area was redolent with local history, attracting many prestigious visitors from among the regular crowd of actors, businessmen, and politicians who frequented St Tropez as their principal holiday destination. The residences around ours varied in size, some being only two-bedroom houses, more in the style of a gatehouse than a mansion.

In the 1980s, one of our neighbours, Steinmitzer, a man of Austrian origin, was the ambitious head of a multinational company who had just come into an unexpected fortune, probably through a series of acquisitions in the USA. Much of his work involved speculating with various Wall Street banks, dealing with asset stripping and acquisitions. Although we lived only a few hundred yards away from each other, we hardly spoke, so I didn't know much more about his interests or personality. But one day, without prior warning, he knocked on my door and said, without any further introduction: 'Bradley! I'm ready to buy your house.' He stood there, in his pinstriped suit, looking for all the world as if he were concluding a deal which had been set up months before, between two close friends. 'I'm ready to buy for cash,' he added. Seeing that I was not reacting, he prompted me again, with a grin. 'So, will you sell it to me?'

I was still rather flabbergasted. 'Do you know who I am?' I replied cautiously. 'I mean, how do you know my name?'

'Well, I'm your neighbour!' he responded, in a tone of voice that implied that this explained everything. Seeing this interpretation was not reflected in my expression, he added, somewhat sheepishly: 'I'm Steinmitzer. I've been to one of your parties. In the summer. With those brokers from Japan. Don't you remember?'

'I must admit I do recognise you vaguely, and I could tell you your name and occupation. You obviously already know who I am. But this doesn't quite explain this unexpected visit, and it certainly doesn't explain your demand. Particularly the part where you seem to be implying that it's been settled in advance.' I didn't mean to be rude, but I did fully intend to clarify the situation. I couldn't help but feel that this was a rather ridiculous conversation to be having at all!

'Oh, it's not a demand,' he said hastily, loosening his shirt collar. 'It's an offer. I'll make you a good offer!' He flashed another bright smile.

'You have that little gatehouse down the road, don't you?' I asked him, then paused, struck by a thought. 'How could you afford to buy this sixteen bedroom house?'

'Ah, but that's the thing, isn't it?' he said in what he obviously thought was a mysterious tone of voice, incidentally not answering my question. 'I want this to be a great investment. I'm looking to upgrade, and I absolutely love your house. I just fell for it completely when I came to your party! I would like to have parties like yours. Better ones, even!' He winked rather rogueishly. 'I'd like to run my business from this house. I want a large swimming pool like yours.'

'Look, perhaps I haven't made myself sufficiently clear. But this house is absolutely, categorically, not for sale. It belongs to our family, and we have never expressed any interest in moving anywhere else.'

'I'd give you a great price,' he wheedled.

'I think you're being very presumptuous to assume we need the money. We're not selling,' I replied curtly.

'Well,' he said with a little shrug, 'if you ever reconsider, just let me know.'

'You're wasting your time,' I told him, as gently as I could, and closed the door.

Twice he came back, twice we had stilted conversations, and twice more I gave him the same answer: we had absolutely no interest in selling. At last, he seemed to understand that my decision was final, and he stopped coming round. I assumed this was the end of the story, and gave it no further thought.

But several months later, my family and I received an invitation to visit a house down the road. Figuring this was a sign of Steinmitzer extending the hand of friendship in hopes of making up for our rather more tense moments, we set off. At the address given, however, we stopped and gaped, open-mouthed. I checked the cream paper the invitation had come on: there was no doubt we were in the right place. I realised I had severely underestimated both Steinmitzer's real estate ambitions and his financial resources. The house was a grand old white thing, with an alley of palm trees and a Classical-style colonnade out front. It was without a doubt one of the biggest ones in the neighbourhood, with a sea view, and probably three times as much land as we had stretching out around it.

Steinmitzer was behind the house, where about fifty guests were milling around in sundresses and suits. He himself was wearing a pair of oversized sunglasses, and grinning as he sipped from his martini glass. 'Bradley, my old friend,' he greeted me without a hint of sarcasm. 'Lemme get you a drink.' I left my family to sample the trays of canapés, which I discovered to be Austrian-themed: little sausages and potato dumplings, and stacks of cream-filled and chocolate-covered pastries, which seemed a little heavy for such a warm summer's day! I helped myself to a glass of sparkling water with lemon and let Steinmitzer guide me around his admittedly vast property.

'The gardener keeps these lawns impeccable, doesn't he? I love what he's done with the roses and pansies and whatever you call those big tropical blossoms. I'm thinking of getting a little Japanese-style garden put in, you know, with fountains and rivulets and all that.' He nattered on, seemingly impervious to my disinterest. As we wandered along the side of the huge outdoor swimming pool, he said casually: 'I have to say, Brad, I'm actually glad you didn't sell to me. I mean, your house is about, what, a third of this size? I don't think I would've been able to have this many guests out there.' He laughed heartily. Before I could respond, he continued, almost as if he were impervious to my presence. 'And I mean, have you seen the swimming pool? It's Olympic-sized, you know. We had it custom-made so you can swim and look out to sea. Can you see the little turquoise mosaic tiles? They're based on an ancient Greek design from Athens. Come on, admit you're a little jealous!'

'No, not at all,' I replied calmly. 'I mean, this looks like a great house. I hope you'll be very happy.'

'Have you seen the indoors? You must see all the great furniture I've had brought in.' Reluctantly, I let Steinmitzer propel me across the lawn and through the vast, glass front door. 'See, how do you like my designer chairs? The Philippe Starck dining table? We also have a Jacuzzi. We wanted to keep it all very modern on the inside, but still absolutely classic. Nothing urban or clashing. All cream and beige. Do you like this shag carpet?'

'It all looks lovely,' I said, smiling a little at the game. I couldn't help but feel a bit sorry for Steinmitzer in his obvious need to show off. I wondered how much of his savings had gone into flaunting his victory over me. We toured the entire upstairs, with vast bathtubs and big glass windows looking out over the sea, and impeccable rooms done up to look up like hotel suites. It was all very beautiful and of course to the highest standard of luxury, but I couldn't help but feel that it lacked soul. Eventually, I managed to find my wife and children and get us all home. I had to admit that evening that I was glad to be back in our own comfortable lounge.

'You're just jealous,' my wife teased me.

'Oh, no,' I said, 'trust me. It's a beautiful house, and I'm sure he'll be very happy there, but there's just no place like home.' I paused, reflecting. 'Even when you have many homes!' My wife smiled.

Over the next few years of us being neighbours, Steinmitzer continued to invite me, even though I wasn't really a regular visitor to St Tropez. His principal interest was obviously in finding the thing that would finally make me admit to being jealous. Every time, he seemed to have made some extravagant change, installing some ridiculous feature our house lacked –and, I should add, didn't need: a massive kitchen with stainless-steel counters, an antique oak dining table that could comfortably seat twenty-four guests, a Swedish-style sauna, a landing site for his helicopter. Every time he made me do this grand tour, I would say the same thing, wishing him all the best. I suspect he was rather frustrated that I never provided the envy he so obviously craved, and after a while these forced visits became very boring. He eventually stopped asking me round, and soon after this we lost touch. I suppose he felt he had proved whatever he thought his point was to me, and had no further need to show off!

THE BINGO FARMER

During the early days of my first marriage, I could quite often be found visiting my in-laws. They were a loud, welcoming brood of typical Irish stock, Kilkenny-born and bred, who owned many farms in the area. However, as times moved on and work became more focused on industry and the office, they had largely migrated to London for better business opportunities. Yet they kept a second home in Kilkenny, and were there as much as time allowed.

Whenever I went over with my wife, we had a house all to ourselves, which gave us the privacy that a young married couple needs while still allowing us to be close to her family when they were in their house. More often than not, we would arrange our holidays to coincide with theirs, during Easter and the summer. The layout of the area was slightly strange. Behind the house that my wife and I stayed in was a lovely view of the rolling, lush Tipperary hills, dotted with the large Irish cows that belonged to the farmer whose house sat behind ours, next door to my in-laws. It was a triangular neighbourhood of only three houses and I think that this fostered an increased sense of community between me and my new neighbours.

Because, if truth be told, all the peaceful, beautiful scenery was really home to neighbours who were rather loud and boisterous. The Irish have strong family values which extend out to newcomers who are willing to embrace their culture. For example, the Irish never drink alone, only socially with friends and family. Although I didn't really drink, I was welcomed under their collective wing.

My father-in-law was an exceptionally sociable man, who preferred drinking down at the local pub to staying in, but the nearest neighbours, the O'Tooles, did not share his philosophy. They preferred it when the neighbourhood got together to have a little private party, and my father-in-law was always keen not to offend them.

'You can never be too careful with your neighbours,' he told me on one of my very first visits, 'especially that lot. Oh, they're all sweetness and light when you're rubbing along alright. But bear in mind, they can turn nasty. Put a few drinks in them and it could all get very dangerous.'

This was unfamiliar territory for me. I simply wasn't used to the idea that not sharing a drink with your neighbours could lead to any sort of altercation – the worst I knew was the coolness of English neighbours or the occasional disinterested rudeness of French farmers. As for my father-in-law's drinking habits, and how they varied from the neighbours' more insular attitude, I think that he simply liked to have a large group of people to talk to, but the neighbours liked to be the centre of attention. They were, as I previously said, quite raucous, always keen to crack jokes and share their alcohol with us when we were there.

It was at my in-laws' house that I first saw coffee being spiked with whiskey. When I said no to his offer of a large glass of Guinness (which was always the first thing he gave to visitors he liked), my father-in-law winked at me and asked if I'd like some Irish in my coffee. I declined. When they came around to welcome me to the family, as it were, the neighbours proved to be even more adventurous with their drinking choices. They offered me orange juice, which I accepted gratefully, and then went on to try and add their favourite Jameson whiskey to it.

'No, thank you,' I said, quickly taking my drink.

'Ah, it's nice. You'll like it. Just give it a good go.' The farmer himself, Sean O'Toole, was red-faced and drank a fair amount, but was always generous with his tipples, quick to want everyone to feel as good and merry as he did after a few pints. 'Whiskey and orange juice go together like Paddy and Mick. Go and try it and tell me it doesn't.'

'I'm all right with just the orange juice, thanks. I don't really drink.'

The farmer regarded me somewhat shiftily and then burst out laughing, clapping me on the back. 'Clever lad. You know what they say about drinking. Terrible evil. Terrible sin, of course. It'll make you throw a punch at your dearest pain-in-the-backside neighbour... and miss.'

The whole family roared with laughter. They were forever telling little quips like that, about how to make an Irish stew and so forth. Sean said that for a proper Irish stew all you needed was some potatoes, carrots, meat, and a lot of whiskey. Pour in the whiskey and forget all about the stew. I truly did enjoy their humour, it was always very good-natured and, like most of the nights we spent in their company, full of alcohol.

One evening, when we had become friendlier and more familiar with the neighbours, Sean brought us some drinks around and invited us down out to play bingo. I was dubious to say the least.

'Isn't bingo a game for women?' I asked. In my experience, this had always been the case, though of course I had never had any encounters with Irish bingo.

The men all looked fairly offended, but the farmer laughed. 'Oh, oh well. If you think it's a woman's game, I can bring a woman along. I'll bring my lovely wife.' Having seen his wife, I doubted she was much for going out. She worked with him on the farm and was only fifty years old, but looked far older than her years. I'd originally thought she was over seventy until my wife's mother's corrected me and clucked that she'd 'had a hard life, poor dear'.

I quickly interrupted with, 'No, no, that's okay. But my in-laws will be very upset if I don't invite them along, if that's alright?'

'More the merrier! But come on and hurry up, it starts in a little bit.'

It wasn't quite true that my wife's family would have been upset if I had left them out of the bingo arrangements; I'm not sure it was exactly their cup of tea. But they were a tough lot, much like the neighbours, and frankly I felt a lot safer with their moral support and backing. Half the time I wasn't entirely sure what the farmer was talking about. He loved to tell good Irish jokes, but if he segued into more serious conversation – as he sometimes did while drinking – I found myself floundering a bit, at a loss for the right thing to say.

The bingo trip turned into quite the family outing. A huge group of us convened at the bingo hall, most of our party being the loud, drunken extended family and friends of our farmer neighbour. We took up a lot of space and I learned something new about the Irish – they can be fiercely competitive when the moment calls for it. In fact, I wouldn't have thought it was possible for one to care so much about bingo, but the farmer was incredibly impassioned. As we sat around, most of our party getting more and more inebriated from a constant flow of Guinness and whiskey, many of the neighbours' family seemed to forget the rules, or become deeply frustrated that they weren't winning every time somebody else got a full house.

When the man at the next table won twice in a row, that was when things became rather heated.

'You're cheating, aren't you?' Sean suddenly asked him.

He stared back, struck momentarily dumb by this accusation. 'I swear on my life, I've never cheated at anything!' Whereas I would have perhaps answered in a slightly appeasing tone, the man rose to his feet. 'Who'd you think you are, spreading lies about me?'

I sat back silently. I wanted to point out that nobody was exactly spreading lies, but our farmer friend was already out of his chair, red faced and angry. 'You're a cheater!'

'I'm having a lucky streak.'

'Lucky cheat,' the farmer shouted.

Perhaps anybody else who didn't come from such an environment would have been shocked or even frightened, but I had quickly become accustomed to the way the Irish, or at least the ones I had met so far, handled their emotions. In my opinion, it was in many ways healthier than the English way of repressing any bad feelings. At least in this way, with all the shouting and grandstanding between two drunken men, they were airing their grievances and therefore letting them go that much quicker.

That was how it worked this evening, anyway.

'I'm no cheat,' the other man said, 'maybe you're just not very good at bingo. Did you go to school? Do you know all your numbers?' By this point, the argument could have erupted into physical violence, but the man who kept winning was smiling a bit, easing the situation, and eliciting one of the farmer's booming laughs.

'Just a bad night for our lot, I suppose,' he said loudly, 'you lucky so and so. You'll have to buy us all a drink with your winnings, won't you?'

By the end of that night, I was fully initiated into the ways of the Irish. How a man you might argue with early in the evening could be a friend for life come its end. And I could see that, loud and pushy as they could sometimes be, Irish neighbours are among the best in the world. They are sociable and welcoming, always ready to share with you what they have and as quickly as they might be drawn into a fight, they are willing to make peace just as easily.

Few people know exactly where the North Sea is. If pressed, they would probably respond with images of polar expeditions, glaciers or grizzly bears. When I tell people at parties that our family house in Kent is only twenty minutes away from the North Sea, they don't usually believe me. But I do: in fact, it's only an hour away from London. One would only need to drive straight east, to the Thames estuary, and lo and behold, there it is: a cold body of water, admittedly, but hardly an Arctic waste. I often used to drive there from my country house, to wander along the beautiful sand, stone and grass beaches.

The seafood that came from those icy waters was of truly incredibly quality. The North Sea produces beautiful oysters, mussels, clams and cockles. Sometimes, I have been lucky enough to come across them in the wild there, simply washed up on the rocks and beaches! Even when bought from the fishermen who set up stands on the beaches in the summer, near the small villages of Kent, they are almost without exception large, fresh and juicy. I particularly enjoy them with a white wine and shallot vinaigrette, or rich home-made mayonnaise, or just a squeeze of fresh lemon juice to bring out the complex, briny flavours. Towards the end of summer, however, when the cold sea winds began to blow in off the waves, our family retreated indoors to the candlelit seaside restaurants or simply to our own kitchen table. Then, without a doubt, my favourite dish was a rich clam chowder, sweetened with corn, thickened with Kentish cream and flavoured with pepper. There are few seaside joys as simple as a big bowlful of clam chowder, mopped up with a hunk of good country bread.

One day, I had been discussing my love of seafood with a neighbour, who turned out to be a fisherman by trade himself.

'Well, I daresay you sound like a real seafarer! Do you ever do any fishing yourself?'

'I have to admit I'm not really a fisherman. My only hunter-gatherer's instincts are go into picking up the occasional shellfish on the rocks!'

'Well, would you like to try it sometime? I'd be happy to have some company on one of my trips out. It's starting to get cold, after all, it'd be something to take my mind off the boredom of it!'

'It would be my pleasure,' I told him happily. 'It sounds like quite an adventure! Heading out onto the North Sea…'

'Now, you know there are no polar bears or anything like that?'

I laughed. 'What, no fjords either? Don't worry, I'm prepared.'

'That reminds me: don't forget to wrap up warm,' he added. 'It gets fairly windy out there.'

He wasn't joking. Despite only having met me a few times, he was after all my neighbour, and determined to do me this favour. The morning of our expedition dawned grey, windy and bitterly cold. Over the top of my woollen scarf, I looked out across the sea, which stretched into the distance, seemingly never-ending. 'It looks a bit threatening,' I said hesitantly. 'Is it always like this?'

'Are you asking me if it's safe?' The fisherman smiled broadly at me from under the hood of his oil slicker. 'Well, no safer than any other sea voyage… But certainly safe enough.' We clambered into the boat, which was no more than five metres long. The waves splashed about us threateningly as we sped across the harbour, with the small engine sputtering along, until we hit the high sea. There, surprisingly, everything actually felt calmer, as we were now bobbing on the back of the vast swells, rather than feeling the small waves break against the hull of the boat. We travelled on for a few nautical miles. 'I reckon the weather will have quieted right down within an hour or so,' the fisherman said pensively. 'What do you think of it so far?'

'It's not exactly the Bahamas,' I muttered into my scarf.

My companion laughed a great barking laugh. 'Well, let me take your mind off it by teaching you a few things. First off, you need to learn to hook some bait.'

'Yes, I know that,' I said impatiently. 'What do you think boys do with their childhood?'

He laughed again. 'My, you're turning out to be a cantankerous sort! Maybe the life of the salty sea dog would suit you better than I thought when I met you in your nice coat and leather shoes!'

I had to crack a smile. 'One trip to sea and I've become some sort of Hemingway character! This doesn't bode well for a life anywhere near the coast.'

He taught me how to cast a line, angling through the strong waves.

I had my doubts, assuming that the fish would stay deep in the water, far from these mad waves. I was wrong: our lines were long, and the bites were quick in coming. Within twenty minutes I had picked up two sea bass and a monkfish! My new friend couldn't help but be a little disgruntled, seeing as how he, as the professional, had only managed to find two small monkfish.

'Beginners' luck,' I assured him, holding back a satisfied smile with difficulty.

'Don't look so smug,' he responded. 'We're only twenty minutes in.'

We sat quietly in the middle of the sea, watching the winds clear away the clouds. My apparent early proficiency seemed to desert me after the half-hour, and I sat without a bite for a time, while my new friend hauled in a few huge sea bass. I didn't mind: the views were incredible, and after all I already had a fairly respectable catch. 'This,' he said with something like glee, 'is how it should be,' as he toppled a third large, silvery fish into the bottom of the boat.

'I wouldn't be so gleeful,' I said confidently, half-joking. 'Three's a charm, you know. I don't think that beginner's luck has deserted me quite yet. Look, the sun has come out and everything.'

At this point, with excellent timing, something tugged at my line. I reeled it in carefully, and pulled it over the side of the boat. When it fell at our feet, the fisherman let out a long, low whistle. 'What a catch!' he said, genuinely impressed. 'You lucky bastard!' The fish was large and flat, a mottled yellow colour. It was flat overall, with bizarre spiky fins and a strangely-shaped mouth that hung open.

'What a creature!' I exclaimed. 'It looks completely prehistoric.'

'It's funny you should say that,' the fisherman replied, his voice still touched with awe. 'This species of fish has swum in these waters for twenty or thirty million years. That is not the most exciting thing about it, though: it's the most delicious fish in the North Sea. Do you know what it is?'

'I must admit I don't! It looks sort of familiar, but I don't know the name.'

My neighbour looked pleased to be able to share his knowledge on the topic. 'It's a John Dory. Quite a beast, isn't it?'

'Oh!' I said. 'I've had that in a restaurant. It is in fact delicious. Actually, now that I think about it, I think I've been served it in

France, as well, called a St Pierre. It makes a great fillet; truly a fantastic fish. Of course I've only encountered it on a plate, with a rich butter and lemon sauce. Not pulled alive and flapping from the depths of the ocean!'

'Now, don't get all Hemingway on me again. It's only water.' He cracked a smile, though. 'I must admit I'm very jealous. John Dory is my absolute favourite fish.'

'Well, if you like we could share it when we get back. Grill it up.'

'You know you're supposed to be helping me earn money with a good catch, yeah?' He laughed. 'I'm only joking. Of course we should eat at least one of these. Do you know how to make one of those nice French sauces you were mentioning earlier? That got my mouth watering.'

'I certainly do. It's very easy. Anyway, surely you've got nothing to complain about: sea bass must fetch a good price!'

'Oh, don't get me wrong, it certainly does. It's also delicious. It's just that there's a sort of special thrill to catching a John Dory. It's a fairly rare event.'

When we got home, we took the fish back to his house, where we grilled it up and shared it with lemon butter sauce.

'So, what did you think of your great North Sea expedition?' he asked me through a mouthful of tender, flaky fish.

'Cold,' I said at once. 'But worth freezing to death for. I don't regret it for a minute.'

'If you get some warmer clothing, maybe you should contemplate a career change. You could make the most of that beginner's luck! Do you know that if we had simply taken a net with us, we could have picked up hundreds of oysters as well?'

'Well, if this banking business ever stops being so lucrative, maybe I'll contemplate being a fisherman. Until then, I'll just enjoy the fruits of your trade!'

I never went out to sea with my neighbour again, but I kept excellent memories of our successful trip. It also meant that I could always impress gullible friends with my tales of sailing on the North Sea.

When we lived in our seventeenth-century house in Surrey, our land was surrounded by a vast, lovely forest that had been growing for hundreds and hundreds of years. It was more than a little wood such as you often find in the English countryside – this was a stately cathedral of trees, stretching over hundreds of acres and full of ancient oaks and alders that creaked in the wind and whose shade bustled with local wildlife, from deer and boars to mice and magpies.

This forest belonged to our neighbour, Mr Brill, who used this beautiful local wilderness as a sort of personal stockpile for his firewood: every three years, he would cut down the young ash, cedar and oak trees. He would axe down trees barely twenty years old, even though oak should really be left to grow for a hundred years, if one wishes to obtain the highest-quality wood. But Mr Brill was ruthlessly efficient, and intended any property of his to be productive; cutting and selling this wood was how he made a living. He sold some of the wood simply for local farmer's fireplaces, but mostly he aimed to have nice cuts to sell to furniture makers and the occasional sculptor.

'Wood is my business,' he explained to me. 'The forest is my land.'

In front of our house, we had three hundred acres of land on which Mr Brill grew crops of rapeseed that filled our eyes with glorious yellow flowers and made us sneeze in summer. At the bottom of these golden fields, there was a river, where I loved to fish for trout. The trouble was, the best way to get to the edge of the water would have been to cut across the field and the edge of the forest beyond; except that this was Mr Brill's land, and Mr Brill did not approve of trespassers. Most days I hardly saw him at all, except when he came back from the woods with a tractor piled high with felled trees. He was usually swaddled in an oversized Barbour jacket and wearing Hunter wellingtons. On occasion, he would have a Remington rifle slung over his shoulder; at first I imagined he must simply have it in case he occasionally found a small animal to hunt when patrolling his woods. Later, I suspected he kept it mainly to ward off trespassers.

In the early days of living there, I brought up the topic of crossing his land casually, not imagining it could be a problem. We were talking about how we both enjoyed angling for trout, and about the best times of year for a big catch, and which bend of the river we liked to stand on. 'I love the bend by the edge of the forest,' I said nonchalantly, 'but it's rather a long walk from our front door. Would you mind very much if I cut across your land to get there?' In my mind, this question was almost rhetorical; a mere question of politeness, a pleasantry exchanged.

'What, you mean walk across my forest? That's ridiculous. Of course not,' he snapped back, as if I had suggested driving through it in a race-car, or had requested to cut down a hundred trees for a bonfire.

I tried not to let my shock show, although in truth I felt rather as if I had told an acquaintance, 'Oh, we should meet up for a drink sometime!' only to have them reply, 'What a preposterous idea!'

'Do you even walk there?' I responded cautiously.

'Nonsense. I'm an outdoorsman. Do you think I have time for aimless wanders? I don't want anything or anybody strolling in and around my wood. And what are you implying, that I don't know how to use my own land properly? That's outrageous.'

I backpedalled as hard as I could, sensing the situation might get out of hand. 'No, no, not in the least! I was simply alluding to the fact that I could save a good awkward twenty-minute walk if I were just able to cut across the field.'

'What, ploughing it up with your boots? Leaving your scent everywhere for the animals? Likely as not, I'd shoot you on sight if you tried it!' He laughed then, as if trying to cover up the threat, but I could tell he was not joking. He was being deadly serious. I felt my stomach sinking.

'Look, don't be ridiculous,' I tried to cajole him. 'It's just a fifteen minute walk. I wouldn't trample anything. I've crossed fields before!'

The man, however, remained completely inflexible, and our neighbourly conversations, which up until that point had been fairly friendly, diminished sharply. Mr Brill obviously considered himself an old-fashioned English country gentleman, for whom his house was his castle and his land was his dominion. For the rest of that summer, I decided not to deal with the issue, and continued to take the completely unnecessary twenty-minute detour around the woods every single time I went fishing. Once the weather started to get cold and this began to get frustrating, however, I happened upon a new plan.

I approached my neighbour one day when he came home from the fields.

'Look,' I said, after all the usual introductory pleasantries had been exchanged, 'I know you're not happy with the idea of me walking across your land. But there's a different solution to this problem; one we've not contemplated yet. Would you be willing to sell me two or three acres? Just in a thin strip, so I can walk straight to the river without crossing your property. I would be very happy to pay for this, and we can avoid any trouble with trespassing!'

'Absolutely not,' he replied, barely letting me finish. 'I can't split my land. Selling it to you would have exactly the same result. You'd still be tromping all over my property.' He crossed his arms.

'And you still won't consider letting me walk through the field? Even when it's empty, in the dead of winter?'

'You go fishing in winter?'

'It's a rhetorical point,' I said in desperation.

'It's my land,' he said gruffly. 'That's all there is to it.'

I repeated different forms of these two demands fairly regularly for the next twenty years we lived side by side. Every single time, he would turn me down. About ten years ago, he passed away and his son took over the land. My wife and I went over about a year after the sad event to try to bring up the age-old topic with the son. We were disappointed, however, to find that Mr Brill Junior turned out to be no more talkative than his father, and seemed to have just as much of a temper.

'I thought you might bring this up,' he said with something approaching a glare. 'Though to be honest, I was rather hoping you weren't going to.'

'Look,' I said, cutting to the chase, 'we mean no disrespect to your father. It's just that this whole thing seems a bit ridiculous. It's such a small piece of land! You have four hundred acres! What difference do two or three make?'

'Ah, but you don't think the way we do. We are old-school landowners, you see.' He did not seem inclined to pursue the topic.

'Yes,' I said rather bitterly, 'this truly is a sort of medieval conflict!'

'You don't understand family pride,' he replied almost angrily.

'With all due respect, this land belonged to my great-grandfather. It now belongs to me. Every single acre of it. And it's going to stay that way.'

That was the end of the discussion. It turned out the son was as inflexible as his father. Not only did he not give in to our demands, he actually appeared to be quiet upset about them, and we hardly spoke very much afterwards. And as long as we lived in that house, I continued to take the long way around the forest to go fishing.

In the many years I lived in Britain, I encountered this motif again and again: an Englishman's house is his castle, and his land is not to be trespassed upon. May this story remind many English people of their neighbours!

THE TWO FACES OF GUS MAJARO

Gus Majaro was a frightening man. He was tall and blonde, unusually so for a Muslim man. He had light green eyes and a sharp nose. I believe his family was originally from Serbia; there was certainly a sort of Eastern European tidiness to his appearance, with his buzz-cut hairstyle and toned muscles. Outside the classroom, I don't think he would have been too intimidating a figure, being a sporty and quite amusing character. He was a friend of my uncle's, I had met him at home before I met him at school, and he had made a pleasant impression, telling jokes and lounging easily on the sofa.

In the chemistry lab or the sports field, between which he split his career, however, it was quite a different story. The first time I met Gus Majaro as a teacher, I didn't recognise the family friend I had so briefly and pleasantly met. In our chemistry class, he was one of the strictest teachers I had come across, barking all his instructions with a steely glare, and never a hint of a smile crossing his face. His methods were severe, requiring that we memorise all the formulae in class by heart and occasionally stand in front of all our classmates to recite them. He never let anyone mess around in any capacity: anyone gossiping with their neighbour was sent out of class; anyone taking liberties with any of the chemicals to be found in the room went straight to the head of the school for punishment. Majaro took chemistry seriously, and reminded us every day of just how dangerous the various fluids and powders we had access to were.

'It would only take a second's slip to kill yourself and all of your comrades,' he repeated, with what seemed like a manic glint in his eye. 'So don't mess around. Or, mark my word, I will.'

He was intransigent on the question of wearing proper attire in the course of experiments, from gloves and lab coats down to ridiculous goggles. This was not to say that he was squeamish about using the dangerous chemicals himself. If anyone tried to joke or play around in the laboratory, Majaro would grab a few choice chemicals and make them blow up as a warning.

'Oh,' he might sneer, grabbing a seemingly random bottle off the shelf and dumping a large amount of it into a Petri dish. 'You think you can just hurl chemicals together that way, without careful measuring? Well, see what might happen if you had chosen these elements!' Here, he would throw in a sprinkle of some kind of powder, producing some hideous reaction or other.

It was a remarkably effective tactic. We were all scared of him all the time. The first explosion we might have been amused by, but over time his interventions became increasingly threatening. Some of his experiments produced black smoke, or a deafening explosion, or a proliferation of invisible gas that made us all cough for hours. Some of them boiled like witches' brews, or foamed up like a disease. One day he spent time showing us all the various colours of metal heated up to explosive temperatures so that sparks flew everywhere, allegedly in order to explain fireworks. 'Barium chloride: green! Aluminium: white! Copper chloride: blue! Sodium: orange!' he shouted, throwing the salts by the handful into the flame of the Bunsen burner, and watching the whole class cower back as they burst into coloured flame. Once, he gleefully stuck a whole leg of lamb into acid so that we could see the whole thing disappear, both meat and bone having melted right into the vicious liquid in the bowl.

After that one, there were no student pranks for quite a few weeks. Majaro's approach to maintaining discipline in the laboratory was akin to an army commander maintaining control by regularly firing a gun near his soldiers' heads, making them all jump out of their skins. No-one was ever harmed, of course. Gus Majaro knew what he was doing. But it certainly made for a less than relaxing learning atmosphere. I found this constant tension anything but conducive to hard work, and more beneficial to stomach ulcers. Pressure never suited me as a child; I wasn't always good at working to deadlines. I was too much of a perfectionist. Trying to learn in an atmosphere of constant fear meant that I became a mediocre student at a subject I had once enjoyed. I began to think of Majaro's chemistry classes with nothing but fear, and I would have done my best to avoid the man if I had happened to run into him in the corridors or outside the school.

In the gymnasium, at least, he was a little more sedate, if just as strict. Here, he appeared a more relaxed, and it was here that all at once I recognised my uncle's friend, although I mentioned nothing of it. What difference did it make, that we had once crossed paths outside the school? He was still, as far as I was concerned, a terrifying man who happened to be capable of destroying me, physically as well as academically. Nonetheless, stripped down from his lab coat and cartoon villain's goggles and clad instead in loose shorts and brightly coloured tank top, he looked a lot younger. Which is not to stay he wasn't still a fairly severe trainer, making us run for hours on end in training for track and field, and do endless military-style push-ups. 'Come on, you wimps!' he would howl. 'Twenty-five more for the road!' I wasn't really interested in this aspect of training, much preferring team sports like volleyball that privileged agility over muscle. Majaro needed to maintain his Soviet-style fitness, I guess, and what better way to do this than by leading a bunch of teenagers? For the rest of us, it was exhausting.

Thus, on the one hand, we had the terrifying chemistry teacher; on the other hand, the gruelling P.E. one. However, one Saturday I went to my uncle's house, only to happen to encounter Majaro leaving. The two of them were laughing together, obviously very close. I hardly recognised Majaro, what with him looking so relaxed and happy. He was clearly partway through telling a story to his chum, and I overheard his conclusion: 'This student, he put a piece of magnesium near the dry ice! I mean, can you imagine? BOOM! Smoke everywhere. I mean, it would have been amazing, but it could have been so destructive. These kids have no idea!' At this point, he caught sight of me. 'Oh, hi, Bradley!' he said cheerfully.

I blinked. 'Er, hello, Mr. Majaro!' I called back, after a panicked pause. Was I going to be in trouble for catching him outside of school?

On the contrary. 'So how have you been getting on?' he asked me, leaving my uncle aside for a second to accost me in a friendly fashion. I hesitated. I had been struggling in his class of late, partly out of sheer terror. He smiled encouragingly. 'Your uncle says I'm too hard on you and your classmates,' he said gently. 'Do you think he's right?'

Again, I hesitated. He seemed to be genuinely concerned! 'You can be quite frightening at times,' I admitted at last.

To my amazement, he sighed. 'Oh no,' he said. 'I had no idea I was being taken so seriously! You see, a young teacher has to make so much more of an effort to come across as impressive. I had some real trouble with maintaining discipline in my early days, but perhaps I've gone overboard. I noticed your results have gone down considerably since last year. Please don't tell me I've been part of the problem?' he asked kindly. I lowered my head. He put his hand on my shoulder, which encouraged me.

I looked up at him: so tall, so blonde, so brawny, but smiling sadly now, rather than glaring. I realised I was no longer frightened of him. 'The thing is,' I told him, 'we all know you could break all our bones with a baseball bat or dissolve us in clouds of smoke. If you're shy like me, that really puts a dampener on your performance. I'm not saying you need to be a nice guy all the time, and you should definitely continue to stop us from blowing our arms off in chemistry class, but perhaps you could just give a little encouragement, too.'

My uncle shook his head. 'I can't believe it, Gus,' he said with a laugh. 'Scaring the kiddies. Who would have thought you had it in you?'

From that day onwards, Mr. Majaro became just a tad friendlier towards our whole class, and a lot more smiley towards me. No-one noticed much of a change, being preoccupied as they were with not blowing up the laboratory and still managing to pass their end of year exams, but it boosted my confidence tremendously. By the end of the year, I had straight As in chemistry! Which goes to show that, in teaching, fear may be an effective technique for maintaining order, but a little encouraging smile goes a long way.

LUXURY BANKING

In the mid-1970s my New York bank had a branch in Egypt, which I used to visit a few times a year. This branch would turn out not to have been a totally successful investment, having made only mild profits until it was closed down just a few years after its opening. I always wondered what had been responsible for this failure. The state of the economy, the quality of the clientele, a set of badly-kept balance sheets or incompetent employees? It was not a particularly unusual or noteworthy failure, so a combination of all of the above was probably responsible for the lack of success, with some emphasis on the first of the three. Whatever the reasons, though, the bank branch made a series of loans that turned out to be a loss. It wasn't for this failure that I remember the branch, however, but for its rather strange banking neighbour, who had a much more interesting approach to failing than we did.

On the street next to ours, there was an offshoot of a fairly well-known French bank. The building it was housed in was quite an impressive one. They had somehow managed to acquire and set up in one of the old royal residences, which had probably been used as guest houses or gambling casinos in the past by old King Farouk. Now, King Farouk was not a man known for his sensible tastes. He was reputed to eat six hundred oysters a week, owned two of the world's biggest cut diamonds, and regularly went on shopping sprees in the capital cities of Europe. This may explain the luxurious nature of this building somewhat, although the people who currently lived there didn't have quite such expensive tastes. The branch was run by an amiable young German man by the name of Helmut. At first, they seemed like very friendly banking neighbours, often inviting me over to have tea or to eat hummus and red bean salad with flatbread. We had plenty of business chat to share in those days, and it was a nice change to discuss these things outside the atmosphere of competition that reigned in a conference room. The ambiance in their office was lovely, and we would often sit downstairs chatting in French for hours in the hot afternoon. They had a cook from Paris, which further reinforced the impression of château-like luxury given by sitting in wingback leather chairs. In many ways, it felt much more like having afternoon tea with a good friend than meeting with a banking acquaintance. In fact, the house didn't feel like a bank at all.

The place had been built in the nineteenth century and done up less in the style of Napoleon and more in that of Louis XVI, at least in terms of the architecture and interior décor. Inside, the vast staircases and balconies gave everything a stately and classical air. The walls were panelled with wood, and everything was painted in rich, muted colours. The overall effect was rather like stepping inside a French take on an Ottoman palace, quite gaudy but pleasant all the same. Most of the furnishings were in the Imperial style, swathed in oak carvings of leaves and ribbons and covered in gold leaf.

Rather overwhelmed, I once asked for a tour of the place. Helmut obliged quite happily, dismissing my concerns that I was keeping him from his work with a wave of the hand. Around this time, I had begun to wonder when and where the actual banking took place, but I was more interested in finding out what was hidden away in the rest of the building. We toured the more practical sections first, so I experienced the remarkably quiet layout of the bank itself, where a few backroom employees and accountants appeared to be crammed into a couple of rooms, chatting away across their messy desks. I assumed this was only a small part of the operation, and paid little attention. Leaving behind this section of the building, however, everything became much more interesting. We climbed a marvellously regal marble staircase, decorated with mosaics and gilded bronze, up onto a landing. Here, basing my guesses on the layout of our own neighbouring bank, I had assumed I would find a dozen important rooms serving as offices for the higher-ranking workers of the bank, as well as perhaps a few conference rooms. I was right about the conference part, or at least, the first room fulfilled this role. It was empty but for a well-worn table, and so we moved on quickly. Beyond that, however, where I had expected to find offices full of busy board members and executives, we walked into a large bedroom. This was luxurious, with more oak panelling and silk curtains around the bed; not a place where any banking work was likely to be conducted! I wasn't quite sure what to say, so I followed Helmut silently through another two bedrooms, before we emerged into a dining room and kitchen. I had found all my suspicions confirmed. 'On the other side of the landing,' Helmut explained, 'if you follow the staircase, which is in the image of the one we just came up, you will find the private quarters where my wife and I live.'

'Are you saying these aren't private quarters?' I asked. 'I'm sorry, I don't understand. Isn't this supposed to be a bank?'

Helmut laughed. 'Well, it used to be a palace, you know. We didn't want to lose too much of that feeling.'

'But how do clients feel when they see this? Don't they feel like they've accidentally stumbled into someone's house, or perhaps into a museum? It doesn't feel like a banking sort of atmosphere at all!'

'Ah, you see, you're assuming this would be dissuasive, but in fact we actually attract clients with this atmosphere you refer to. It adds a sort of almost touristic dimension to any meeting, a relaxed approach. We like our clients to enjoy the décor, and sip tea while they do business with us. This is our way of marketing the bank.'

'Are you trying to tell me you're making profits despite this exaggerated opulence?'

He waved a hand dismissively. 'Well, we've only been set up here for a couple of years. As you well know, you don't make a profit for the first five years in any kind of banking institution.'

I had to keep my mouth firmly shut not to react to that ludicrous comment. Our own branch had been in Egypt for less than half the time of Helmut's, and we were making steady if not exceptional returns. Then again, we obviously weren't spending our budget on luxury tea leaves and silk bed-sheets. I shook my head gently. 'Well, I guess at least you're living like a king!'

He smiled. 'What can I say? We get to enjoy the beautiful weather, we're practically on the banks of the Nile, and we're not failing. In fact, we're attracting new clients every day. Why should we change our strategy? Anyway, I consider myself a lucky man. After all, who would expect a French bank to hire a German?'

I had to agree with this in theory, although of course I protested: 'Don't be ridiculous, you have exactly the right combination of languages and charm for them. There are too many rich Frenchmen in Egypt already.'

'I'm a lucky man,' Helmut said again, 'and I intend to enjoy the privileges this job has offered me. What new banker gets to live like King Farouk?'

'Well, I must say I wish you all the best of luck. Maybe if you keep away from the oysters, you'll be safe.' Even as the words left my mouth, I realised that it was impossible to imagine Helmut wouldn't be regularly holding opulent parties in this house, with trays of oysters and champagne everywhere. Why wouldn't he? He was obviously proud of the place. If his office was a palace, he obviously had no intention of it feeling like a bank. 'In any case,' I finished, 'I hope your strategy pays off.'

'You'll see,' he said confidently.

Of course, I did see, but not in the way that he had hoped: time would tell that this was in fact, of course, a deeply flawed approach. Three years later, the bank still wasn't making any profit, and Helmut had been fired. He had to move out of his palace almost overnight, leaving behind his chef and all the luxury furnishings. Shortly after that, our own bank left Egypt, and I never found out what became of the poor man. I suppose he must have gone back to Germany, where he probably works in some dusty cubicle, dreaming of his days as a banker king on the Nile.

A SHORT HOLIDAY

In the summer of 1974, my wife Hilary and I were looking to rent a house for a month in the English countryside of East Sussex. We had been looking for a quiet break with lots of long walks and peaceful evenings, and thought we might have found the perfect place when we came across a secluded farmhouse in a holiday brochure.

Over the phone, the agent painted a completely idyllic portrait of the East Grinstead area: 'You've got Ashdown Forest to wander in for walks, which is supposed to be the home of Winnie the Pooh,' she nattered. 'The other cultural highlight is probably the home of the man who composed the Christmas carol 'Good King Wenceslas', although that might be less relevant in the summer. But you can drive into the city and explore the High Street in town. It's a beautiful little place: all fifteenth-century timber houses and quaint tea-shops. I'm sure you'll love it!'

Somewhat overwhelmed by the sheer onslaught of irrelevant information, I paused for a while before asking cautiously: 'What's the house like?'

The agent tittered. 'The house is the best part. It's been refurbished to palatial standards, with a gorgeous drawing room full of Edwardian furniture and wooden panelled walls. There's a little stream just outside the front door, and a beautiful garden which is looked after by a local gardener. It should be overflowing with roses this time of year.'

'And you're saying the location is quiet?'

'Oh, it's absolutely lovely. You won't be disturbed.'

Hilary and I were sold. I checked quickly on a map to find out how far the place was from roads and railways, and once we were satisfied that we would have complete rural peace, we booked.

When at last the holiday arrived, and we turned our car into the long driveway, we were thrilled. The countryside was indeed beautiful, with rolling green hills all around and the edge of the forest not far away. The house itself was even bigger than we had thought it would be, and was an impressive sight, its classical façade climbing with ivy, and the rose garden off to the side. We climbed out of the car and looked around happily.

'What a glorious month this will be!' Hilary sighed.

I smiled and put my arm around her shoulders. 'Exactly what we hoped for!'

We moved in and set about exploring the area. For the next week, we enjoyed a blissful holiday together, going for long walks in our wellies and filling the kitchen with flowers. We cooked beautiful meals together and stayed up late reading in the wingback leather armchairs by the fireplace. At the end of this romantic week, we were enjoying a lovely Sunday lunch of roast chicken with rosemary potatoes, when the most atrocious smell filled the kitchen.

'Did you leave something in the oven?' Hilary asked in a concerned voice.

I laughed uneasily. 'I don't think anything I cook could produce a stench like that. It must come from outside.'

'Maybe it's a tractor driving by with fertiliser?' she reasoned.

'That could be,' I said, 'although it's pretty overwhelming for that. Maybe they've dumped it right outside our house. I'll have to have a word.'

But there was nothing outside the house, nor was there anything in sight that I could imagine might produce such an effect on the pure country air. Standing outside the door, I thought I could hear some frantic animal noises, and wondered suddenly if we might not be as isolated as we had hoped. I walked towards what seemed to be the source of the smell, which happened to be a direction we had not yet had time to explore on our long rambling walks. I headed west and discovered that the strange noises were becoming louder. All at once, I stumbled into a clearing and found myself looking out over a vast, muddy pig farm. The smell was overwhelming. The huge, dirty pigs were rooting about in vast troughs: I could have sworn I could hear them chewing and gulping. The whole scene was impressively disgusting. As I stood, staring down, a farmer approached me from across the field.

'Can I help you, sir?' he asked in a thick southern accent.

'I suppose you're not used to seeing many visitors around here,' I said rather glumly.

'No, we're not – you must be staying at the big house, then.'

'Yes, we are. Or we were. I'm not sure we can stand the smell. What on earth is it? How come it wasn't so bad before today?'

The farmer laughed, a deep belly laugh. 'Oh, you city types,' he said, 'you're all the same. Can't handle a little pig scent in the air!'

'Well we were quite fine until today. What on earth has happened?'

'We've started them on a new sort of fermented feed. It's meant to do wonders for their health. Made with fermented grains and milk whey. Sure, it smells like hell, but we're pretty used to that sort of thing. I mean, surely you must have been around fertilised fields before?'

'Yes, I have,' I said defensively. 'It wasn't anywhere as bad as this! This is just horrific! I mean, in the south of France they sometimes use rank seaweed as fertiliser and even that doesn't smell as awful as this does!'

He shrugged. 'Well, what can I say? I'm sorry for the inconvenience. But I should warn you it's not going to get any better. This will happen every day now. Sorry.'

I walked home glumly. Hilary was waiting by the door, which she had cautiously closed to try and keep some of the smell out.

'It's a pig farm,' I declared without waiting. 'They've gone into some kind of horrible feeding frenzy. The farmer's feeding them with some new fermented thing.'

'Oh, that's disgusting,' Hilary said quietly. 'Is it just today? Surely the wind will clear it up?'

'I'm afraid not. I ran into the farmer and he told me it would be like this every day. I don't think we should stay here much longer.'

Hilary sighed. 'You're right. It was all too good to be true, wasn't it?'

Within two days, we had packed and driven off, deciding we would pay for a few nights in a hotel than have to eat another meal with that awful stench in our nostrils.

Upon arriving home, we rang up the agent immediately and demanded compensation.

'It's complete misrepresentation,' I said sternly. 'You can't just tell us all these stories about Winnie the Pooh and idyllic countryside and conveniently apparently forget to mention the giant pig farm down the road. It smells horrible there. It's uninhabitable.'

Luckily, the agent was sympathetic: it turned out that when they had visited the property to assess it, they hadn't been able to smell anything, and we were some of the first people to stay there. They admitted to having known there was a farm in the vicinity, but hadn't contemplated the disturbance it could cause from such a distance. They agreed to compensate us completely, which was a happy enough ending to a sad story.

We continued to work with the agents for years afterwards, and occasionally laughed over the story of this ill-fated holiday. They told us that after our unfortunate stay, they stopped representing it to their clients. The house had a 'for sale' sign on its door for over two years after that. Later, rather amusingly, they passed on the news that it had been bought by a major American bank.

'Perhaps bankers are immune to terrible smells,' the agent joked.

'Maybe they'll rename their house the Piggy Bank!' I replied.

THE POETIC NEIGHBOUR

In my early university days, when I was on a course in Georgetown, Washington D.C., I lived in one of the larger student dormitories. My course was essentially a preparatory course for the college degree I intended to continue in Texas, and it only lasted a few months, but I managed to meet some interesting neighbours nonetheless. Nicholas was one of the more memorable ones. Almost every week I would hear a knock on the door, and open it to find Nicholas standing there with a piece of paper in his hand. He was a tall, thin man, with a thick crop of messy hair and a crooked grin. He had bright green eyes and a sharp nose, and looked for all the world like a Romantic poet.

'I'm so sorry,' he would say, with a completely unapologetic smile, 'but could I borrow a cup of sugar?'

Sometimes it was sugar, sometimes it was salt; sometimes it was some completely ridiculous item, like a paper towel or some tea. Nicholas, I quickly realised, was a poet, and he enjoyed turning his requests into little verses:

'I don't intend your friend to nag
But I would die for a teabag!'

Or perhaps:

'I have no cash, it must be free,
But may I steal a cup of tea?'

Or yet again:

'I'd like to bake but I've no flour
Could I come into your student tower?'

Many of these were fairly lame, and made up on the spot, but they could be pretty amusing. He was a friendly enough fellow, and we didn't mind loaning him the items, even when we quickly realised that they would never be returned. Nicholas was actually an assistant professor, lecturing in poetry and English Literature at the university, so his company was never dull. He obviously enjoyed the friendship of undergraduates, and came to our dormitory mainly in hope of intelligent and stimulating discussion. Sometimes, his offerings were slightly more elaborate:

I stand here at your door to beg
The loaning of a humble egg!
My housemates have eaten them all;
I have no friends on whom to call,
And so, lest I forget to dine,
Oh kindly, humble neighbours mine,
I ask you this small, humble loan
So my soup won't be made of stone.

I clapped slowly. 'It's very nice, I said.' My flatmate craned his neck from the kitchen to see over my shoulder.

'I don't get the bit about the stone,' he shouted over. 'Why would you be eating stones? That's gross.'

Nicholas laughed. 'You're right, that's one of the weaker lines. It's the old tale of stone soup.'

'Oh, I get it!' I said. 'Of course. The man who was so hungry that he tricked other people into contributing to his pot of soup, claiming he would be making delicious stone soup. Of course the soup was delicious, but only because of the ingredients added.'

'I don't get it,' my flatmate grumbled from the background.

'Never mind,' said Nicholas. 'It's appropriate here, but not particularly strong, poetically.'

'I think it's quite a funny reference.'

'He can have an egg anyway,' my flatmate added apologetically. Nicholas laughed.

'I don't know how to thank you or repay you,' he would tell us every time we provided whatever he had come looking for. 'I don't happen to have any cash with me.' (He never did.) 'Perhaps I can read you a poem of mine, as a sort of sign of my appreciation?' The opinion in our corridors was somewhat divided as to the quality of these poems. I myself found them rather amusing, but they did rather go on and on at times. My flatmate thought them pretentious and annoying, and tended to scurry off and busy himself in the kitchen, or pretend he had urgent work to be getting on with. I don't think

Nicholas ever noticed; really, he just wanted some people to read aloud to. He cleared his throat dramatically. 'This is a poem about love,' he said:

> This eve, I saw a girl drift through
> The dusty library
> I hardly knew what I could do
> This happens so rarely.

> Her hair was blonde, her eyes were blue,
> She held a book of Yeats
> The dusty stacks she wandered through
> As if guided by the fates.

> My breath was short, I clutched my chest,
> I hid behind the stacks.
> I could not think – I felt so blessed –
> A single thing to ask.

'You used "dusty" twice,' my flatmate commented. 'And "ask" doesn't rhyme with "stacks."'

'Well, I disagree with the former,' Nicholas said amiably, 'as it was meant to be poetic repetition. But you're probably right about the latter. Nothing really rhymes with stacks, does it.'

'Backs?' I suggested. 'Anyway, please let him finish. Let's find out if he gets the girl.' Nicholas nodded, pleased, and continued:

> She rose; I thought that she might leave,
> I saw my moment pass
> I knew I must be by her side,
> This bonnie bookish lass.

> I gently took her by the hand
> With nerves most abysmal
> And asked her: 'Do you understand
> the Dewey Decimal?'

> 'Oh pardon me?' the virgin sighed

'I know it oh so well.'
'Then how,' I quoth, 'am I to find
some Yeats, oh pray do tell?'

She took me to the poet's corner,
Showed me all the verse
And love descended on me
Like the dawning of a curse.

But then she waved and walked away
Never did she come back
And yet until this very day
I haunt that very stack.

He cleared his throat again. 'I'm hoping it might inspire some of
my more reticent students, particularly the male ones.'

'Yeah, I'm sure it'll work great,' my flatmate grinned.

I was quite charmed with the man, especially the first few times
he visited. I was only seventeen, and I enjoyed the company of this
thirty-year-old. He obviously appreciated my listening to him.
After a few weeks of this rigmarole, we ended up inviting him for
dinner, figuring he must be short on cash if he had to keep borrowing
food items. This may have been something of a mistake, as we were
suddenly exposed to the full breadth of his poetic composition.
Nicholas, it seemed, had a taste for pseudo-classical epic verse, which
was amusing only in short segments. I should have guessed with the
library poem, but nothing had prepared me for the sheer lengthiness
of that recital at dinner. My flatmate, who was an excellent cook,
had prepared for us a leg of lamb in a spicy sauce, with rich mashed
potatoes on the side, and a green salad. It was a delightful meal, and
was all ready to eat by the time we sat down. Everything was freshly
cooked, hot and steaming.

Before we could sit down to eat, however, Nicholas staggered
upright. 'Let us have a toast!' he said rather loudly. I suspected he
had had a few glasses of wine already. Without any encouragement,
and while we all eyed the food hungrily, he began to recite:

I sing the praise of Arlington the green

Where engineers and poets lay their scene
Beside the lawyers, doctors and the rest
Who come to read and write and fest.
We dine tonight on roasted lamb and corn
We'll drink good wine and praise that we were born
To come to Georgetown University
Together in this American city!

I will spare you the rest of the tale, but suffice to say that the food was fairly cool by the time we ate it. My flatmate, unsurprisingly, was rather angry about the whole incident, and we didn't invite Nicholas back. Still, he continued to come around to borrow various small items. In fact, a few times, I actually went for a walk with him around campus, partly to get him away from my flatmate. If the weather was nice, Georgetown was actually a lovely place to wander. Nicholas used me as a sort of sounding board for his poems, or talked about his latest conquest: as a poet, he was always falling in love with pretty young girls. I don't think he ever achieved the fame he hoped for, but he certainly kept our dormitory entertained.

THE DANGERS OF PARKING

In Essex, on the drive back to my Wivenhoe house from work one evening, I decided to stop at a movie. This was not an indulgence I often had time for, but I happened to be in the mood for some entertainment, with a side of popcorn. I drove towards Colchester in my beautiful Spitfire car, intending to go and see *For a Few Dollars More*, a classic Clint Eastwood film, before heading home to study: I quite enjoyed the occasional over-the-top spaghetti western, and it was raining heavily.

I drove into Colchester: it had started to get dark, and I was not in the mood for a lengthy wander in the downpour. The Spitfire was a brand new sports car of mine: big, shiny and bright red, it was a recent and much-beloved purchase. I enjoyed zooming it up and down the skinny English roads, its streamlined, classic shape earning us nods and the occasional wave from appreciative motorists. I parked the car on a street not too far from the cinema, considering myself lucky to have found a parking space, then dashed towards the cinema without worrying too much. Medium-sized English towns are not usually places I consider crime spots, and I figured locking the car was safety enough.

After the film, which was enjoyable in a sort of ridiculous way, I found the car easily and drove away, intending to get home in time for dinner. The rain was still pouring down, in that determinedly grim way that British rain pours. However, the drive down the dual carriageway was a fairly peaceful one, until all at once the motor stopped. I was right in the middle of the road when it happened, but luckily I managed to steer over to the side and pull over. It was fortunate the road was fairly quiet at that time of the early evening, as I would have been in serious danger of having an accident on the slippery tarmac. Once I had stopped safely and calmed down, I realised I would have to find help. Of course, there were no mobile phones in those days, nor had they installed those handy emergency phones on the side of the road. Cursing the English weather, I climbed out of the car and into the rain. I dashed across the road, jumped over the railing and cut through the fields, looking for a light. It was not a pleasant walk: my trousers were soaked with rain, and my shoes covered in mud. At last, however, I spied a glimmer of lamplight, and followed it to the front door of an isolated farmhouse.

When I knocked, the door was opened by a kind-looking old woman with white hair and an apron. 'I'm so sorry to bother you,' I said. 'I've just had an accident. My car stalled in the middle of the road. Would it be possible to use your phone?'

'You poor thing!' she said. 'Come into the warmth!'

We walked along the cosy, dark corridors to the tiled kitchen. Her husband was by the table when I entered reluctantly in my damp socks and dirty clothes. 'Well well,' he said jovially. 'Look what the cat dragged in. Can I make you a cup of tea?'

I accepted gratefully, and sat for a while by their roaring fireplace, warming my hands around a cup of strong black tea. The farmer's wife had made a chocolate cake that day, and we shared a rich slice of it as I explained my situation to her.

'Why don't you call Ernie?' the wife said to her husband, after I had thawed and dried out somewhat. 'Ernie's our local garage man,' she explained to me. 'He can fix anything.'

Ernie was called, and turned up within half an hour with his battered tow truck. We drove out into the rain, now in almost total darkness. Luckily, my sense of direction was fairly strong, and I knew the area quite well. I directed him to the approximate spot without too much difficulty. We picked up the car and drove to the garage. By the time we were there, it was nearly one in the morning. I stayed up all night with the mechanic; fiddling with the car, trying to figure out what had gone wrong.

'I just don't understand,' I told him in frustration. 'It's a perfectly new car. I can't imagine what would have gone wrong.'

'Spitfires are meant to be reliable too,' Ernie agreed. 'Are you sure you haven't been on the German Autobahn, or speeding on back roads?'

'I mean, I'm not exactly a slow driver, but I've been perfectly careful. I certainly haven't done anything worthy of burning out an engine like this!'

After a few more hours of adding oil and black grease to my already muddy clothes, I heard Ernie utter a low sigh. 'What is it?' I asked, concerned.

'Well,' he said mournfully, 'I'm sorry I ever doubted you. The trouble has nothing to do with your driving. Nor, I suspect, with you. See, look in here.' He pointed with a grimy finger. 'The tubes are completely caramelised from the inside. Somebody put sugar in your engine. About four pounds, I reckon.'

'Why would anybody do such a thing?' I replied, flabbergasted.

'It destroys your car. It's a dreadful thing to do. The car runs fine for a little while, but then the petrol and sugar begin to combust, and coat the piston and inside of the engine completely in a thick crust of hot sugar. It's almost impossible to remove.'

'Are you telling me that there's no way to fix this?'

'I'm afraid not,' he replied regretfully. 'I hope you've got insurance. You're going to need a new car.'

Angry and somewhat upset, I thanked Ernie, and got myself a cab home. Luckily I had insurance, and I was able to make a claim and get the car replaced. I got myself another Spitfire, just as nice as the first, but I couldn't quite move on from the incident. I decided to head back to the spot where it was parked: I just had to try to solve the mystery. I knocked on the door closest to the place I knew I had left the car. It was opened by an extremely tall, nasty-looking old woman who glared at me over the top of her reading glasses.

'What do you want?' she snapped, pursing her lips. She had frizzy hair and a little moustache on her upper lip. All at once she snapped her short fingers, which were pudgy like a garden-gnome's. 'You're the bastard who parked in my space!' she said loudly. 'I recognise you. I watched you walk away.'

I gawped open-mouthed a few moments as I realised what must have happened, before retorting: 'Do you have any idea how much damage you've caused?'

'Well, I see your car all shiny and fine, so it can't have been that bad!'

'This is a new car!' I said. 'I can't believe the cheek; that you can stand here in front of me not only admitting to your crime, but apparently proud of it!'

'You parked in my space,' she said obstinately, with a little sneer.

'What do you mean?' I replied as calmly as I could. 'It's the street! Anybody can park anywhere they like! It was raining! I was only there about two hours!' I was trying my best not to lose my temper, but the woman wouldn't relent.

'Nobody parks in my space,' she said ominously. 'I put sugar in your tank and I'm disappointed you didn't grill to death.'

I just stared at her, feeling as if my jaw would drop off. 'You are one of the nastiest people I've ever met,' I said, extremely quietly. 'You could have killed me. I could easily have you sued. But I'm not the same kind of person as you. I'm not going to punish you for your crime. You will be punished enough by the lonely, miserable life you have ahead of you. Your conscience will caramelise you from the inside just like you caramelised my engine.'

She just glared at me. Without waiting for her to add anything else, I took my leave and got back in the car. I suppose there are nasty neighbours everywhere, even if they are only neighbours to one's local cinema! It really was a rather horrible episode: I guess she was just a very destructive person. That, or perhaps she was just *very* attached to her parking space.

THE INTERIOR DECORATOR

In my Californian banking days, we had a guesthouse in San Francisco, on the edge of the Palisades area. It was a beautiful part of the city, not far from the Golden Gate Bridge, with stunning views out over the ocean. Much like the Finistère region of France, this place felt like the end of the world. Standing by the coast there was like setting foot on the last bastion of the continental USA: every time I went there, I felt as if I was about to fall off the cliff into the sea! Indeed, one can't go any further on American land in that direction without getting in a boat and heading to Hawaii. I enjoyed the place thoroughly, as it had fine weather and mild temperatures almost all year round.

Ours was a four-bedroom terraced house, a beautiful, stately place built in the old Dutch tradition, painted in bright colours that shone in the sunlight. Like much of California, it was a multi-coloured reflection of America's multicultural heritage, propped on a hill heading straight down to the ocean. The bright red shutters were reminiscent of a ski resort in Austria, while the yellow columns, green palm trees, and blue and pink exotic flowers wouldn't have looked out of place on a Portuguese villa. The effect was somewhat psychedelic, and certainly extremely Californian.

I always enjoyed being in San Francisco for a few days at a time when visiting clients. I usually travelled across the States with an employee of our bank, so we could share whatever business we were engaged in. The area was quite calm, and our work was spread out over a few days, so the two of us had plenty of time to walk down the narrow, hilly streets and explore the odd selection of second-hand shops, dim sum restaurants, and manicure places that dominated the scene in San Francisco. Just down the road from us, they even had one of those places where you could get one of those weird pedicures where fish nibble at your feet in a tank of warm water! It truly was a wonderful place to visit. The only touches of unpleasantness I ever experienced were the occasional high winds blowing in from the desert or the high seas, and the threatening look of the island prison of Alcatraz. California is not a scary place, yet I can think of one occasion I did end up rather frightened.

I had come over to San Francisco with a junior credit officer. We were visiting the bank of America in order to line up some important syndication deal. It had been an extremely busy day, so we were just sitting on the large couch in my bedroom, talking about business and having a quiet cup of tea, when there was a strange, sharp thump. I nearly dropped my mug in surprise.

'Did you hear that noise?' I asked in concern.

'Well yes... It's probably just the neighbours.' The junior credit officer's eyes were a little wide.

'Listen,' I said, 'I don't want to alarm you, but is there something strange in our tea?'

'What do you mean?' he asked, puzzled. 'I mean, it's no English cuppa, but I don't think there's anything unusual about it...'

'I mean, no-one could have dropped pills or anything in, could they?'

'What are you talking about? Are you feeling quite alright?'

'Yes, yes,' I said hastily. 'It's just... Will you just look behind you?'

'Brad,' he said solicitously, 'do you need to go to bed?'

'There's nothing wrong with me. At least I think not. You can tell me in about ten seconds. Just look at the wall behind you.'

Obligingly, my partner turned his head and looked behind him.

'Can you see it?'

'See what? It's just a wall... Oh!'

At that moment, there had been another loud thump. We both clearly saw a large black spike appear in the middle of it. Obviously, there was something about sitting in a big, dark, empty flat at night in a fairly unknown city that would unsettle the strongest of characters.

'See? Can you see it?' I said a little frantically. 'What's going on? Are we safe here?'

'I'm sure there's a perfectly rational explanation,' he said, a little shakily.

'I don't like it,' I said firmly. 'I feel like I'm in a low-budget horror film.' I stood up, pulling my bathrobe tight around me, and walked over to the wall. 'Well,' I said unsteadily, 'someone is hammering nails into our wall. Is this normal in California?'

'They're right over your bed,' he replied, which was not reassuring.

'Maybe there's something wrong with the construction,' I said, as confidently as I could, before the solution suddenly appeared to me. I suddenly laughed out loud, making my partner jump. 'We're fools,'

I said. 'It's so obvious. Someone is simply trying to put up pictures next door. They've just underestimated the thickness of the wall.'

'Yes, well, that's a rather inconsiderate thing to do, isn't it,' he said huffily. 'Particularly at this time of night.'

'With massive nails,' I added. 'Look, I think this has rattled us quite enough for one night. Why don't we just go speak to him? Californians are fairly friendly. I'm sure we can make him understand. All we need is for him to stop for the night so we can get some sleep. Saving the wall would just be a bonus. It's not our house, after all.'

My partner agreed. This is how we found ourselves heading out into the street in our pyjamas in the dead of night, and knocking on a stranger's bright pink door. It opened after a pause and some small crashing noises in the background. An extremely tall, skinny, muscular man appeared, wearing very tight black jeans and an open white shirt.

'Oh hello!' he said brightly. 'To what do I owe this... delightful surprise?'

The combination of his exposed stomach and the fact that he was holding a hammer in his hand was rather unnerving.

'Uh, hi,' I said. There was a pause. 'We're sorry to disturb you this late. It's just... you don't happen to be currently nailing things to your wall, do you?'

'He's holding a hammer,' my partner muttered under his breath.

The man laughed rather flamboyantly, tossing his long hair back. 'I sure am. You're not telling me those nails are going through the wall, are you? That's just awful!' He rolled his eyes and shook his head primly. 'I truly am sorry about all that. I'm Kim, by the way.' He held out a slender, manicured hand, which we shook in turn. 'Do come in!' he added, motioning inside extremely gracefully.

'You don't mind us coming in in our pyjamas?' I asked hesitantly.

'Oh no,' he said, 'I'd love it. You look really cute. You just come right on in.' He raised an eyebrow with a grin, before disappearing into the house. As we somewhat hesitantly followed his ridiculously tiny waist and toned legs into the lounge, he explained to us that he had moved in the week before, and had just started the process of hanging up all his pictures. At this point, he gestured around the room. 'I'm just nailing, nailing, nailing them up. Didn't even think what I could be hitting!' We had arrived in the lounge, and were now surrounded by a collection of some of the most provocative art I have ever seen. Kim seemed to possess an extensive collection of very modern, sensual photographs and paintings, some of them bordering on obscenity.

'These are great,' I said casually, not looking too closely. 'Look, I really don't want to intrude on your interior decoration or anything. It's just that the banging is keeping us up.'

'Also, the nails are coming straight through into our bedroom,' my colleague added.

'Oh dear,' Kim said. 'I'm really very sorry about that. I'll have to do something about it. Maybe I can find some smaller nails. These huge ones were the only thing I could find and, well, I do like big nails!' He tittered.

'Well, that's very kind of you,' I said. 'I mean, you can do anything you like in your flat of course, as long as it doesn't damage the wall too much!'

'Don't you worry your pretty face,' he said. 'The matter is closed. There will be no more nailing in your bedroom. Now, can I tempt either of you gentlemen with a nice drink? I made this fabulous carrot and mango juice this afternoon, you simply must try it...'

We agreed to stay for a drink, and chatted for a little while longer in his ultramodern kitchen, which was full of glass furnishings, black marble work surfaces, and modern art. Kim actually offered to come over and repair the damage from the nails himself, but I was a little distrustful of his obvious keenness to see my bedroom. However, he was so apologetic and charming that the incident itself was quickly forgotten. We talked for a time about art, Californian living, and the mysteries of banking, before agreeing to call it a night. I only saw him a few times after that, as we only kept that particular guesthouse for another three years or so, and I was only in California about four times a year, but it's nice to have a memory of a pleasant and understanding neighbour, even if his taste in art was a little unconventional.

The house was magnificent. America is known for making cars, houses, and roads on a larger scale and over the top, but even by American standards the house in New Jersey was a behemoth.

It was in the more refined and upper class northern suburbs of New Jersey, near Short Hills, and a wonderful find. I couldn't believe the scale of it. Fourteen bedrooms spread over three levels, and an enormous attic besides. It was perfect. At the time I was house-hunting with a few engineering friends, seeking a comfortable houseshare.

We were also fortunate enough to have very welcoming neighbours. They really believed in offering their own brand of hospitality, and as soon as we had settled they were bringing us little gifts for our new home and asking us to dinner and barbecues in their more than generous stretch of back garden. Eager to become more at home in our surroundings, we of course leapt at the chance to get to know the people who lived next door.

Naturally, in America things work slightly differently than in most European countries. One might have just met somebody, but this doesn't seem to be a conversational barrier. Quite the opposite, if our new neighbours were anything to go by. We attended a barbecue they were hosting one warm summer's day and were instantly subject to a round of questioning that, if not asked with a jovial and friendly nature, some would find intrusive.

I had become something of an old hand at discussing my personal business with interested Americans, and took little issue with divulging where I had attended school, what I had studied, and how this had led me to my current career path. I was a bit more reticent on the subject of how much I earned in a year, and how on earth I had paid for the house.

'It wasn't that bad a price,' I said, slightly cagey.

My host smiled at me. 'Oh, come on. Who was selling it again? There aren't many real estate agents who give you a fair price, are there? They're all only out for themselves.'

I shrugged. 'I didn't have any problems. It all went quite smoothly.' This was true enough. 'Very well indeed, actually.'

They were invariably thrilled with my openness. 'Seems like you'll fit right in around here. These houses are a lot to take on, aren't they? But worth it. So roomy. You could have a whole other family living in your attic and never even know it, couldn't you?'

'Hopefully not,' I said, raising a laugh.

'And they must have told you about the poor lady, mustn't they? Very sad business, that.' My neighbour's wife affected a look of sympathetic sorrow. 'You'll have noticed for yourself. The changes they made after it happened.'

For a moment, I considered pretending to know what they were referring to, but decided it was safer to be honest in my confusion. 'What sad business is this, exactly?' I asked. I had found all of the houses in my new street to have the same cheerful family feeling as each other, with no hint of tragedy.

'Oh, you don't know.' My host looked a strange mixture of surprised and pleased. I only realised afterwards that he had been eager to tell the story all along. 'It's a strange thing, for sure. The way fate catches up with people.'

Over our dinner, I was accordingly regaled with the tale of the widow who had lived in the house.

She was, my neighbour began, a lovely woman. Beautiful and kind. She had married quite young and loved her husband more than anything in the whole world. They were apparently an inseparable couple, happy and successful.

However, in 1958 her husband was flying out to Cuba on business, while she remained behind. This had been during the Cuban Revolution and of all the dangers in that country at the time, the least statistically likely tragedy befell him. There was some technical fault with the plane and it dropped from the sky like a felled bird, crashing into the depths of the Caribbean, with no survivors. Her husband was only forty-five at the time, and his wife was left alone in the world with only her two sons, who had already left home at this point.

The widow was brought low by grief. She was fractured into pieces by the loss of her husband, and although she was financially secure, thanks to a hefty payout from a life insurance policy and her own inheritance, life lost all its savour. She moved into the large house near Short Hills, presumably to escape the family home where she and her late husband had lived together.

But such a large house was too much for a single woman and she
had lost the inclination to fill it with family and friends, to decorate
it with pretty pictures and nice possessions. It was as if a light had
gone out in her and it quickly became obvious that most of the house
wasn't getting used at all.

'You'd notice the lights weren't on,' my neighbour's wife said,
nodding ominously, 'it would be completely dark in there. Except
in the attic.'

I turned and looked at the top floor of the house, imagining it lit
up like a lighthouse, the only point of brightness on top of a dark
mountain of rooms. It seemed extraordinary to me, so much of such
a beautiful house going to waste, falling into disuse and disrepair.

She would, my host told me at length, stay inside, writing and
playing music and living what seemed to be a life of leisure, but
was really an extended period of intense and suffocating mourning.
Eventually it became obvious that she didn't ever leave the house.
She would go out into the garden and see to the plants and wave and
smile at the neighbours, but she never went further. She had a maid
who looked after the house for her, the parts she didn't use, and this
same maid would go out and shop for her.

Her whole life was lived between the garden and the attic, a little
world she created just for herself, a safer world to live in. Somewhere
with no random occurrences, nothing left to chance.

'It's crazy to think, but she didn't get the train or drive a car.
Not to the city. If you asked her about it, she'd say the world was a
dangerous place. I guess she was right. Every day in the news there's
some tragedy, isn't there? Something new to be afraid of. But she
was afraid of *everything*. It was like she just turned into a hermit.'

I shook my head, trying to show my empathy for the woman
while wondering why I was being told all this. It was a sad story, yes,
but I couldn't see how this affected the house. 'So, what happened to
her, then? Why did she leave?'

'Oh, she didn't leave. Not exactly...'

After six long years of solitude in this reclusive existence, the
widow was at home in her attic, sitting quietly by herself, when a
single engine plane lost control and crashed into the house.

I gawped, doubtful over the whole story now it had reached its
rather shocking conclusion. It sounded like something straight out

of a film, not the sort of thing that happened in real life. 'Are you serious?'

He nodded, clearly a little pleased by how horrified I was. 'It was unbelievable. Right into the attic, killed her straight away and destroyed the whole top floor. If you look at it now,' he gestured to the house, 'her kids did very well with it. But you can tell it's not Victorian, if you know anything about architecture. It's brand new. They stuck to the old style, but there's only so much you can do...'

When I thought about the straightness and cleanness of the attic floor, the refurbishment was more obvious. 'That's incredible!' I meant the entire tale. It was amazing and sad to consider the strange twists and turns a quiet life could take. That someone afraid to ride the bus into Newark would have such a tragic end.

'The sons didn't really want to have the house hanging around their lives, I suppose. They didn't want to live in it. That's why they sold it on. It must have been difficult for them.' He joined me in staring at the house, as though thinking about it properly for the first time in a while. 'Imagine. All those years in between, being alone, and then that. She could have been out and about, getting on with her life, and it'd have never happened. She would still be alive now.'

I looked at the house in a whole new light. It wasn't only a place for a new family to claim as their own and put their mark on; it had stories and secrets of its own. It was its own lesson in how fate really does catch up to a person, no matter how we try to hide. Of course, I'm not personally psychologically affected by these things. It was a good house. Despite its history we enjoyed living in it for three years, before selling it on.

A MISLEADING OFFER

When I was at NYU, I met a French artist by the name of Jean through my literature professor. Jean was a very interesting man, half tortured artist and half canny businessman, whom I took a liking to from the minute I met him. I suspect that, at first, his principal object in my acquaintance was to try to sell me his art, but we began to socialise regularly and became great friends. His paintings weren't really to my taste – vast, depressing murals in the style of much French painting at the time – but I let myself be talked into picking up a few, as a friend. They turned out to be so large I couldn't find anywhere to hang them in any of our family's houses, or even in our bank, but that's another story! Perhaps everything that Jean offered me had some kind of unpredictable twist.

Jean's most memorable contribution to my life was actually an offer of accommodation. I was considering taking over the management of my old bank in Paris, and as I was already travelling over to Europe rather regularly to see my wife Hilary in England, I decided to combine the two objectives. I asked Hilary if she would like to accompany me to Paris, in order to study the new environment, while I also went in to talk to some people I would be working with there, as I hadn't managed to find much time to fly back to the old world in the few preceding months. When I mentioned this plan to Jean, he was overjoyed that I was heading back to France.

'Brad, you absolutely must go to St Etienne when you're there. I know it's not on Paris's doorstep, but if you're looking for a romantic getaway with your beloved, I can't think of a better place.'

'Is that where you come from?'

'Yes, I know the region like the back of my hand. And I have a place you can stay, for free. The perfect countryside hideaway for you. You can explore St Etienne, and the museums in Lyon, and of course the historical locations of the Vienne countryside, full of Roman ruins, and of course the wonderful mosaics. And if you get bored with all that, the local football team plays just down the road.' He winked.

'I must say I like the idea of turning a humble business trip into something a little bit more like a holiday,' I admitted. 'We can pretend to be tourists. You say you still have a place there?'

'Oh yes,' he said. 'My father's old farmhouse. It's a beautiful place, classic, you'll love it. Here, let me give you the address. Run this all past your *madame*, of course, but I guarantee you'll be thrilled.'

I smiled. 'I can't imagine she'd want to turn down your offer of fabulous country accommodation…'

I was right about that, of course. Hilary was thrilled at the prospect of combining an exciting little jaunt to Paris with a relaxing break in the Vienne countryside. We prepared for the trip for the next few weeks, and were practically bubbling over with excitement by the time we got into Paris. The first leg of the trip went extremely smoothly, with the weather in Paris being lovely, and all of my talks with the bank going well. We drove south-east quite blithely, looking forward to relaxing after the bustle of the big city. Our moods began to wear a little thin when we got lost, and clouds started to gather on the horizon. We went up and down country lanes for what felt like hours under a steady drizzle. As the sun set and it began to look increasingly unlikely that we would find the place before nightfall, we truly began to worry. But all at once, on the other side of a small forest that had hidden another turn in the road up until that point, the house appeared. Behind it, rolling hills stretched off into the dusk, with only one other farmhouse faintly visible among the curtains of rain.

'Thank God, this must be it,' my wife sighed in relief. 'See, those are the neighbours Jean mentioned.'

'What, over there in that field?' I squinted. 'I guess you must be right. They look pretty far away, though. Must be a good two kilometres.'

'I'm sure this will all look lovely in the morning when the storm clears,' Hilary said in her most soothing voice. 'Then we can maybe go say hello, after we've had a bit of rest.'

'You're right,' I replied as we walked to the door. 'Let's open up the shutters and then get our suitcases.'

The front door was locked. My wife and I looked at each other in dismay under our umbrellas, trying to figure out whether to burst out laughing or burst into tears. It was now raining quite hard. We somehow managed to stay calm, despite being exhausted by the long day, and reasoned that the key must be with the neighbours. We clambered back into the car.

'You know when Jean said we should go say hello...' I said pensively, as we drove down the bumpy country lane, 'I wonder if this is what he meant.'

'Surely not,' Hilary said, appalled at the suggestion. 'He would have told us. Wouldn't he?'

'He must have assumed it was clear. Or he asked these people to open up for us and they just forgot. We'll find out in a minute in any case; I'm sure there's some harmless explanation.'

'Harmless' was not the first word that would come into either of our minds when we first set eyes on the neighbour. For one thing, he was about six feet tall, with dishevelled brown hair, a bushy beard and yellowing teeth. He smelled quite strongly of sweat and alcohol. He was also clutching a shotgun.

'Hello,' I said hesitantly, rain streaming down my face, but too hesitant to advance onto the porch. 'We're sorry to bother you this late. We were just wondering if we could possibly have the key to Jean's house?'

'Who the hell is Jean?' the man barked. At this point, I noticed his wife standing behind him, hunched over in a dirty white nightie like a creature from a classic horror film.

'You mean Paul's son?' she croaked, showing her missing teeth.

'Maybe...' I said hesitantly. I had no idea what Jean's father's name might be, or indeed what his relation to the house was. 'We were given the address by my friend Jean,' I tried to explain. 'A colleague of mine, in America.'

'America?' the neighbour growled suspiciously.

'I mean, he's French,' I explained hastily. 'He told me this was his house.' Even as I spoke, I could hear how suspicious the story sounded. I tried to joke: 'Surely I wouldn't make this up just to try to break into a strange house? How would I have been able to find you?' I could almost hear Hilary worrying about the impact of this, but the old man only grunted. Backstory and logic would obviously have only a limited impact on this man's assessment of us. I smiled uneasily. 'Would you mind if we just stood out of the rain?' The man didn't answer, but he didn't try to stop us as we scurried into the front hall.

'We haven't seen Paul in about three years, have we?' he asked his wife. 'What the hell happened to him?'

'Maybe he's dead,' she replied, completely dead-pan. 'Maybe he does have a son.' She shrugged. 'America,' she added vaguely. 'How bizarre.'

'What does it matter, anyway,' he muttered with a Gallic shrug. 'We may as well let them into that old house. It's only the rats that'll mind. Go fetch them the key.'

His wife scurried off into a backroom. I hoped he was joking about the rats. We listened to the noise of drawers scraping and small objects falling to the ground for an uncomfortably long period of time before she reappeared. Her husband barely moved the whole time, only once readjusting his hold on the gun and coughing, loudly.

'Here it is,' she said, presenting the key awkwardly. As I took it from her grubby hand, she clutched at me. 'See, there's this note,' she croaked. 'You have to return the key to us every day.'

'Did Paul leave the note?' I asked cautiously.

'Well, probably,' her husband replied grumpily. 'We haven't seen Paul in years. I still think he's probably dead.'

'We'll return the key to you tomorrow morning,' Hilary said hastily. 'Then we can work out how to organise the rest of our stay.'

'Stay?' the man barked.

'We're on holiday for a few days,' I said hesitantly.

'Holiday!' He laughed, a wild drunkard's laugh. 'I hope you have an amusing time,' he said sarcastically, before escorting us to the door and slamming it shut behind us.

A little shaken, Hilary and I drove back to the house with the precious key. The door gave after a bit of wiggling, and creaked open. My heart sank. We walked into the front room slowly. The place was filthy. The windows were crusted over with grit, the floor was thick with dust; the beams were strung with cobwebs. I suspected something might be nesting under the stairs.

'This has obviously remained completely untouched for a long time,' Hilary said in wonder.

'About three years, I'd say,' I added bitterly. 'What a mess.' There was a leak in the kitchen, through which dirty rainwater dripped down onto the floor.

'We can't stay here,' Hilary said anxiously. 'Can we? This house is made of broken rocks and full of dust,' she added with a little laugh.

Much as she tried to make light of the situation, I could tell she was quite worried.

'I'm not sure we really have a choice,' I replied reluctantly. 'Come on, let's go and see how bad the state of the bedroom is.'

Luckily, the bedroom was ever so slightly less disgusting. The tightly-closed door had obviously helped keep out some of the dirt that had infiltrated the rest of the house. The bed was one of those old, high fixtures with wooden legs that had a certain provincial charm but was bound to be terrifically uncomfortable. The floor, like the rest of the house, was made out of huge slabs of stone, which were impressive but cold underfoot. All around us, the house seemed to creak, as if it was swaying in the winds of the storm, which was now raging outside.

Hilary seemed to gather her forces. 'You're right, we don't really have a choice. It's not like we can stay with... those people. To be honest, I'd rather sleep in a dirty bed than in the same house as a drunkard with a shotgun.'

I laughed. 'Come on, let's just do some basic cleaning. Then we can get some rest. We can even sleep in in the morning.'

'Or we can get up at dawn and drive right out of here!'

We swept and mopped and dusted for a good two hours before we felt the house was in any state worth sleeping in. Nonetheless, with some of the more visible dirt removed and with the lights on, the place did regain some of what was no doubt its original quaint charm. Finally, we climbed into our high bed, fitted out with some moth-eaten sheets, and fell into a deep sleep.

In the morning, the weather had cleared, and we felt a great deal better about the place. There was still the matter of the kitchen to see to, but we decided we had earned an escapade first. We breakfasted on supplies we had brought with us in the car, then headed over to our neighbours' house to drop off the key on our way into Lyon.

When we arrived at the neighbour's house, the wife was inside, up to her elbows in washing up gloves that smelled a little odd when she came and stood at the door. Surprisingly, the whole scene was only made a little bit less threatening in broad daylight. She hardly spoke to us, but went out through a back door and shouted her husband's name across the fields. An awkward quarter of an hour later, he appeared, sweaty and covered in dirt. Offering no apology or explanation for the state he was in, he simply held out a filthy hand for the key. 'You just getting up?' he grunted. I bristled, considering that it was before ten in the morning, and that we had been up well past midnight cleaning, but decided not to say anything.

'We'll be back this evening,' I responded stiffly.

'What for?' he snapped.

I was flummoxed. 'To... go to bed?' I volunteered. 'To continue cleaning?'

This failed to elicit a laugh. 'You'll still be here?' he said in complete disbelief.

'We don't really have anywhere else to go!' I burst out. 'I mean, the place is a compete nightmare. It's disgusting. The plumbing doesn't work. We're going to have to buy lightbulbs, and probably rewire some of the lighting.'

The farmer barked with laughter. 'You city folk, you're ridiculous. You're young. You should be used to this sort of thing.'

'We're not,' I said shortly. 'Anyway, we're staying.' I paused, unsure what to say next. The farmer guffawed, and went back into the house.

'Tourists,' I heard him mutter distinctly.

Notwithstanding, we had a lovely day in the city, and forgot about all our troubles to the extent that we ended up staying out quite late. We found a perfect little bistro, and ended up settling in for a delightful three-course meal. By the time we got back to the muddy country lanes, it was past ten o'clock at night. We had not been looking forward to this part in the least, but it turned out the farmer had been looking forward to it even less so: he had obviously completely forgotten about us and gone to bed. He must have been roused from his drunken farmer's slumber by the sound of our car pulling up, for he arrived at the door in his dressing gown, once again brandishing his gun. This time, however, he shot it into the air without waiting for an introduction. 'Stop!' I shouted, as I got out of the car. 'Please! We just want the key!'

'You again!' he roared. 'Why are you here again? Get off my land!'

'We just need the key,' I pleaded.

He vanished into the house, slamming the door behind him, and for a time we feared that he might not come back. 'Our luggage is in the house,' Hilary whispered. 'What are we going to do?' Luckily, he reappeared after a few tense minutes, and flung the key down into the mud.

'Look,' I said in as conciliatory a voice as I could manage, 'why don't we just keep the key for the next two days? We can just bring it when we leave.'

'You could just leave now,' he replied menacingly.

'We'll bring the key in the morning,' I replied reluctantly.

'You do as I say,' he growled. 'As Paul said.'

'Paul is dead,' the wife's voice added eerily from the background. Peering into the darkness of the house, I could just make out her nightie.

'Jean should have told us about this,' I said as firmly as I could. 'This is ridiculous.'

'Who the hell is Jean?' the farmer asked again, his eyes bulging wildly.

'Never mind,' I said, 'I'll see you in the morning. Goodnight,' I added faintly, scuttling back to my car.

We spent an uneasy night in the house, and a slightly subdued day exploring the Roman ruins after leaving the key on the porch, not quite having it in us to face the enemy any more than was entirely necessary. The third night, even though we got back around six in the evening, the same shouting match occurred. This time, the gun wasn't fired, but the scene was quite frightening nonetheless. Hilary was shaking by the time I got back in the car with the key.

'Darling,' she said faintly, 'can we please leave? I know we were meant to stay a few more days. But I simply can't stand it. Surely it's not worth it?'

I put my arm around her and kissed the top of her head. 'I'm so sorry this has been stressful. Look, why don't we just go check into a hotel? We'll find somwhere nice, and spend a few more days here. Let's just forget about Jean's place.'

'For all we know it isn't even Jean's house at all!' Hilary added with a small smile. I laughed. 'I hope you have a strong word with him when you get home!' she added.

I smiled. 'I certainly will.'

The rest of our holiday was fairly uneventful, which we were unreasonably thankful for. The soft, downy bed in the luminous hotel room was a complete joy after the horrors of that farmhouse, and Hilary and I managed to get an enjoyable holiday out of the second half of our trip at least. We toured the Roman ruins, and the Gothic cathedrals in neighbouring villages, and the art museums. We enjoyed the beautiful local beef, and a special walnut-flavoured variety of macaroon. Most of all, we enjoyed the peace of being entirely responsible for all of our own circumstances!

It was a valuable lesson to learn, though: one of the many mistakes I made in my youth, and learned something from. One cannot simply turn up at someone's house without knowing anything about it. There could have been snakes! The water could have been poisoned! The roof could have fallen in on our heads. Anything could happen: in some ways, we got off easily with dust and bad lighting. From then on, I never went on holiday unprepared again.

Our bank had a guesthouse in Cannes, which we rented there in order to receive various clients. It was a lovely place, in an excellent location right at the base of the glamorous Super-Cannes hillside development, with three bedrooms and a large garden where we could enjoy the sunlight. In the early-to-mid-eighties, Hilary and I used to love to go there on holidays with the children. The clients followed much the same strategy, combining their own personal trips to their villas and yachts with their banking business, so the summers we spent there were both busy and fun. We had many enjoyable meals in the trendy seaside restaurants, and relaxed in the shops. But above all, it was a great place to bring children, as it was close to the beach. The weather in Cannes is beautiful nearly all year round, but particularly in high summer, where the sun shines hot from cloudless skies for most of three months. My children, who in 1985 were three, eight, and ten years old, played outside all day long. The played badminton, long rounds of tag, and hide-and-seek. They played ping-pong, with my eight-year-old screaming his head off at every point lost. And they set up lengthy, noisy games of football, where the ball almost inevitably ended up kicked into the next-door neighbour's garden.

Most neighbours are used to this sort of occurrence, but Stéphane was not most neighbours. Stéphane was an old man, retired, and did not have a high tolerance for other people's children. He had a small head, white hair, and a long nose, over which he peered with beady eyes. He liked to wear a three-piece-suit and a gold watch at all times, and he spoke with the upper accent one can only acquire from having gone to the prestigious École Normale Supérieure. He lived alone in his villa, despite the fact that it had at least eight massive bedrooms, and a vast garden.

Stéphane didn't like the idea of kids crying, or shouting, or making any sort of noise. In fact, he absolutely couldn't stand it. Every time my children were being a little bit loud or rambunctious in the garden, Stéphane would either shout at them in French, sometimes using swearwords, or downright threaten to call the police! Of course, I would shout back that this was completely unacceptable, and encourage my children to carry on as they cared to, but when I tried to go over and discuss the matter in a grown-up way, Stéphane would just vanish inside his house, slamming the door behind him. Finally, after a particularly vituperative outburst, I managed to corner him by the fence.

'Look,' I said, 'this is completely unacceptable. They are only children. Children play. Sometimes, they will play loudly. You must stop threatening them!'

'This is my home,' he snarled. 'I came here to retire in peace. You should just get your idiotic children to behave! They're your responsibility.'

'So are you renting here in Cannes?' I smiled brightly.

Stéphane bristled. 'I'm the owner, of course. *Bien sûr!* That's just an insult. You're absolutely ridiculous.' He folded his arms across his chest.

'Where is your money from, then?' I challenged him. I felt, obscurely, that by annoying him I was siding with my children. The feeling was rather satisfying. 'A villa in Super-Cannes is no small expense.'

'That's absolutely none of your business,' he said haughtily.

'Alright,' I said in a conciliatory tone. 'It was just a question. All I mean is: what do you do in life? I'm trying to understand your character.'

'My character is none of your business either,' he said with a huff, before relenting somewhat. '*My* business, however, I don't mind telling you about. I'm a bureaucrat. *Un haut fonctionnaire,*' he said. 'I work for the French government.'

'Well that's respectable,' I said, 'at least most of the time. I hope there are not too many brown paper bags under your desk!' I was referring, of course, to the well-known high commissions that occur in these jobs, but he ignored the jibe, presumably assuming I was accusing him of corruption. 'Anyway, just because you've been a bureaucrat, you think you have the right to tell people off? You're not in a position of authority anymore,' I said firmly. 'We're equals. We're neighbours.'

'Yes, we're neighbours,' he scoffed. 'And you're a neighbour with really annoying children.'

It was my turn to be offended. I moved on to my principal line of enquiry: 'Don't you have any children?'

'I had them,' he replied shortly. 'A long time ago. I have washed my hands of them. They are now forty.' He paused, delicately. 'I hate children,' he added in a conversational tone. 'Especially the small ones. All that crying, and vomiting, and no sleep – ugh! It's enough to make a man sick.' He produced a particularly oily smile. I must admit I was finding this character increasingly repulsive, the longer I talked to him.

'That's too bad,' I said carefully. 'You don't know what you're missing.' My stomach was boiling, completely against my will. 'You must not be a very tolerant person,' I went ont, as casually as I could, trying not to lose my temper. 'I mean, I hope you're not sick. With your big stomach, you seem to be all full of hot air. The way you scream at my poor children, I sometimes worry you'll explode in a puff of gas.'

'My health is excellent, *Monsieur*,' he replied snidely.

'Long may it stay that way,' I said as sarcastically as possible. 'I'm going to play football with my children.'

Stéphane didn't exactly transform overnight after this altercation, but he certainly became a lot quieter. I suppose he simply couldn't be bothered, once he realised we would not be changing our fun-loving ways as a family.

At a number of points in my work as a banker and in the oil trade, my presence was requested at various seminars. These were serious events, often necessitating international travel, and led by specialists in their fields. They usually went on for several days, and featured unusually fine refreshments as well as a great deal of hobnobbing and exchanging of business cards. These summits, of varying size and intended impact, tended to centre on a more or less ambitious theme in the domain of economics or finance, tied in with politics and sociology. In the late 1990s, one such seminar I participated in involved a dialogue between Western economists and specialists from developing countries of the East. It was organised and led by China and included delegations from Indonesia, Malaysia, the Philippines and Thailand, as well as a number of Western participants. The theme was, broadly, Chinese development: both its models and its impact. The seminar was held in Shanghai, the most populous city in China, which sprawls across the delta of the Yangtze River.

When we arrived, the weather was nice enough, if a little heavy, and the pollution was not too bad, which left most participants in a good mood. On the first day of the seminar, a tall Chinese girl in her late twenties sat down next to me. She flashed me a smile, and I noticed her small, white teeth. Studiously, she adjusted her pencil skirt and pulled on a headset; most of the seminar was intended to take place in English, so she obviously needed an interpretation into Chinese. From her demeanour, and subsequent contributions, I quickly worked out that she was obviously a fairly important player in this seminar, wielding a great degree of charm and intellect. She asked a lot of good questions and presented a multiplicity of insights, particularly on the issues linking political and economic development, which were obviously rather red-hot topics in a communist country with capitalist aspirations like China.

In her first intervention, she introduced herself as Tuni Kitty and argued very persuasively for the need to instigate more aggressive trade with international markets. Before most of the Western men there had finished gulping coffee and wiping their bleary eyes, Kitty had sat down, having delivered the core argument of that entire leg of the seminar. It was barely quarter past nine. After this, I paid a little closer attention to this strange creature. She could not have been older than twenty-eight, with pale skin and dark, fiery eyes. She was remarkably thin. Later, at the buffet lunch, I would notice she put away plate after plate of noodles, fried spring rolls, beef in black bean sauce and steamed vegetables, as if she had been starving for months. Maybe she spent too much time working to eat properly, or perhaps she just felt she had to get the most out of every aspect of this sponsored seminar. Over this lunch, she sat down next to me again, obviously having taken a liking to me, or perhaps noticed my interest in the points she had made earlier that day.

I smiled at her. 'That was an interesting parallel between the Chinese and Japanese models you drew this morning. Very enlightening. I couldn't have said it better myself.'

She bowed her head and her elegant neck. 'Thank you. Of course, in many ways, Japan has simply imitated the American model of research and development. It has established a system for the assembly of manufactured goods at a small unit cost, on a grand scale. Everything else, it has just copied the West for.' This was obviously not a woman who ever took a break for small talk. 'I believe China has a further advantage over Japan, though, if it can follow this lead, because it has such cheap labour and hardworking population which has been used to working overtime for its survival.'

'I'll believe that,' I replied with a smile. 'I have visited China before. Indeed, I've rarely met such driven people. The Chinese ability to copy Western manufactured goods, especially luxury ones, and sell them at less than a tenth of the price, is really quite impressive.'

Kitty nodded seriously. 'In that respect,' she said, 'China was simply imitating Japan, imitating America. It's not just Rolex watches and Gucci scarves, either,' she continued, cracking a small smile. 'We can make a Nike shoes for ten cents, and a television for ten dollars. That way, we don't even need to do any marketing. People just want cheap products that seem somehow familiar to them. For instance, here in China, we seem to love luggage. Again, it's all about looking American, I suppose, but it's also that we have a history of travelling long distances. A piece of Samsonite luggage somehow plays into both of those cultural needs.'

'Surely this admiration for raw capitalism is completely at odds with Communist ideals, though?'

She nodded sadly. 'As you can imagine, the government hasn't put a penny towards this seminar. It's entirely sponsored by our company.'

I smiled. 'You're a very driven woman from a very driven country!' I told her.

Her economic theory was strong, if fairly limited to this idea of copying at a lower price. There was little originality to it, but a stubbornness which did her credit. Of course, this apparently simplistic idea of hers of using lower prices to raid and dominate international markets was little different to the ideas on the theory of price that had won George Stigler the Nobel Prize!

There was only one flaw to Kitty's participation in the seminar, which was her impenetrably thick accent. Every argument she made was fascinating and straight to the point, but one had to pay serious attention to latch onto it. For some reason, I seemed to have better luck than most of the other participants in understanding what she was trying to say. The more excited she became about the ideas she was trying to get across, the more garbled her speech became. Her incisive questions often had to be repeated more than once, and I often had to step in and actually explain to the master of ceremonies or the other seminar participants what she really meant. I believe I simply had the knack of understanding her logic rather than her accent, either because her views aligned quite well with mine, or because we ended up spending so much time together even outside the conference room. Kitty really seemed to have latched onto me. In every coffee break, as well as at every buffet lunch and dinner, she would come and talk only to me. I didn't really mind, as the only other people I knew in attendance were old, dull business acquaintances of mine, but as the seminar continued, I started to become a little uneasy at this assumed friendliness.

At the end of the third day of our meetings, we were having a quiet coffee before heading back to our hotels. I was relieved to find that Kitty wasn't keeping up her usual stream of commercial and political chatter, as our last meeting had been rather draining. However, after a few minutes of silence, Kitty suddenly piped up on an uncharacteristic theme: 'Can I come travel with you?' she asked simply. For a moment, I wondered if I had misunderstood her.

'Travel? Where? I'm only flying back to France for work.'

She smiled. 'I have a visa, I can enter France,' she said enthusiastically. 'I would like to travel with you. I would like to work on my accent, you see. I would like to see Europe. Understand its business models better, from the inside. You could give me insight. You could show me around.'

I had absolutely no idea how to respond. 'Kitty,' I said gently, 'I must go back to work. I cannot just be your tour guide.'

'Then take me to work with you!' she said brightly. 'I like you!' I sighed quietly. I had absolutely no intention of going along with her scheme. For one thing, I really was beginning to have had enough of her accent, her incessant questions, and her strange emphasis on copying the Western world. Her character was difficult for me to understand. I had had to recognise that even though I have dealt with many Chinese people, Kitty truly represented the most serious part of the Chinese character. There was no humour in our conversations, no small talk, no jokes. Everything I said she took completely seriously. I could not imagine travelling with her, even just for the length of the plane journey home : it would have been exhausting!

'Kitty, I simply cannot do that,' I explained. 'I'm a busy man.' She didn't seem to take the rejection badly, only nodding, pausing briefly as if to compute the information, and moving back to talking about business. Our time spent together, however, showed no sign of decreasing, and I began to quite look forward to the seminar's end, just so I could escape.

My trepidation turned out to have a good source. On the last day, after a leisurely lunch, Kitty and I were walking in the garden. It was a lovely day. The magnolias were in bloom, there were fish in the pond, and I was quite looking forward to heading back to my regular Western life. I was only half-listening, therefore, when Kitty veered off our usual topic of cheap labour and started to explain to me how much she wanted to find a way to claim political asylum outside of China. She was hoping to spend time in Europe, she said, and America, in order to study the commercial systems better. 'Another way to achieve this,' she said conversationally, 'would be to manage to obtain some kind of permanent visa. For instance, I could get married to anyone in the West.' She paused. At this point, I began seriously to start paying attention again. Kitty turned to me quite seriously. 'Would you marry me?' she asked, completely deadpan and without any kind of preamble. I felt my blood freeze. 'Or, you know, perhaps you could find me some other method of political asylum,' she added, in the same tone of voice.

If I hadn't been so shocked, I might have burst out laughing. 'That's an odd way of proposing to a man,' I said, forgetting for a moment her inability to understand humour. She blinked. 'What I mean is no,' I said hastily. 'No. Please don't take offence, but I just don't think that's a good idea.'

'Is it because of the cost?' she asked at once. 'I would cover everything. You wouldn't have to pay a dowry or anything. We wouldn't even have to tell my family, if you don't want. It would be a business arrangement, unless you wanted more, of course.' She added this last in a matter-of-fact way, without affection. The whole situation was fast becoming completely surreal. I resisted the urge to put my head in my hands and groan.

'Kitty,' I said as firmly as I could manage, 'we are not getting married. We hardly know each other. Tomorrow, I am getting on a plane home.'

'It would be so easy!' she said, apparently unfazed by my lack of enthusiasm. 'I could come too!'

'I am getting on a plane alone,' I said. I resisted adding that I would never be coming back.

After this, I left the garden as hastily as I could. As I walked back up to my hotel room, strangely disturbed by this episode, I realised that our four previous days of excellent neighbourly relations obviously had an ulterior motive. I was a little hurt that she hadn't simply chosen me as a neighbour because of my excellent understanding of her arguments and accent. In a way, it was a shame I felt no attachment or attraction to her. She would have been a charming enough young woman if she hadn't been so serious. Notwithstanding, I was glad to see the end of that seminar. Kitty and I parted ways amiably enough, without bringing the subject of marriage up again, and without making any plans to stay in touch.

Nonetheless, fifteen years later, I received an email from Kitty. Despite never leaving China, her life appeared to have turned out incredibly successfully. With the economic development of China, she had started working for a PR company, which she had climbed the ranks of and now owned. She was responsible for two factories that made luggage, and also three skyscrapers. I smiled when I read the email: ambitious Kitty had obviously obtained everything she wanted, despite the fact that I hadn't been able to get her into the West. Perhaps, in fact, my refusal had hardened her resolve to be successful on her own territory!

THE SWIMMING POOL

In my early days as an engineer, I lived and worked for a time between New York and New Jersey. I lived with a club of similarly-employed friends, so the atmosphere in our house could occasionally take a rather technical turn. Our conversation involved a fair amount of practical discussion, mathematical game-playing, and problem-solving. Not that our interactions were without humour, but it did establish a special sort of bond between us. That said, we did occasionally manage to make some friends with different interests and backgrounds! One of the newer neighbourhood boys to become friends with our group was called Gus. He was still living with his family, just down the road from us, so he occasionally liked to ask us over to his home for an afternoon drink or a home-cooked meal. Once, at a time when the two of us were getting along rather well, he asked if I would like to come along for a big barbecue by the poolside. Now, I was still only twenty-two, and the idea of such a glamorous event was hard to refuse. Most of the exercise I got in my daily routine was limited to jogging and the occasional bicycle ride around town, so I rejoiced at the rare opportunity to swim some laps. The day for the excursion dawned bright and sunny, and we were in an excellent mood as we walked the short distance to the house.

Gus's parents were generous in their estimations of young men's appetites, as only Americans can be. Between the two of us, my friend and I must have managed to consume a good five pounds of beef fried up into thick, greasy burgers. Along with this, we ate a good six baked potatoes and masses of sour cream with chives, all of this washed down with a few big glasses of coke. At the time, I was not aware of the fact that you cannot just burn off five thousand calories immediately after consuming them: it has taken me a good forty years to learn this. Consequently, Gus and I took the young American male's standard approach in those days of immediately jumping into an intense bout of postprandial sports. We swam quite hard for a few hours, with me doing steady laps in crawl and breaststroke, while Gus, who was a slender, acrobatic type, practised a series of impressive jumps and dives. It was quite something to watch: he would leap up in the air, flip and seamlessly end up underwater. It splashed the side of the pool rather a lot, but it did look rather fun. It was enviable, but nothing I was tempted to try. Gus's parents, however, obviously felt differently on the matter.

'Hey Brad,' the father called out in that jovial way parents sometimes adapt with the children's friends, half friendly, half teasing. 'You seen what my son can do? Why don't you show us what you've got?' He was obviously quite proud of his son's achievements.

'Oh, I'm not as talented as Gus in that department, I'm afraid,' I called up from the pool.

'Come now,' the mother chimed in. 'Surely someone as muscular as yourself must be able to do some jumps for us!'

'I'm not a dancing monkey,' I joked. 'There's only room for one of them in this pool!'

'Well, you should practice, then!' she added. 'Isn't this the perfect time and place? Look, the diving board isn't even that high or anything!'

'He's just embarrassed,' the father said with a grin. 'He knows he's not as good as our Gus!'

I swam over to the edge of the pool and pulled myself up. 'Look,' I said, 'it's not that easy. I just don't have that much elasticity and strength! I do, however have one skill: I can dive. A good, classic dive.'

The mother clapped her hands prettily. 'Well show us that, then! Come on!'

'Come on, guys, leave him alone,' Gus said from the other end of the pool.

'Don't worry,' I reassured him. 'I'll just do a quick dive. An easy one. No acrobatics!'

I walked around the pool and climbed up on the springboard. I looked out over the turquoise water, glinting in the bright sun, flexed my legs and dove off.

The next thing I knew, I opened my eyes in bright white light, and found myself staring at a hospital ceiling. My back and head were pounding with pain, and my vision was rather blurry. I tried to focus. I heard Gus's mother's voice first: 'Oh my God,' she said in tones of great relief, 'he's awake!'

'What happened?' I croaked. 'My brain hurts.'

'You… Oh, I'm so glad you're OK!' She buried herself awkwardly in my shoulder, in the closest thing to a hug she could manage from her position and my bandages. 'Oh,' she sobbed, 'it's all my fault, I'm so sorry, we just didn't think to warn you, of course you wouldn't have been used to it, how could you know?'

'Mom,' Gus cut in calmly, before explaining. 'Brad, you dived straight down. You hit your head on the bottom of the pool.'

'You were in a coma,' his mother burst in again. 'We were so scared.' Her voice trembled, and for a moment I thought that she might start crying again.

'It's only three and a half feet deep, you see. It's not meant for proper diving,' the father added, all his bravado gone. 'We're so sorry. We shouldn't have encouraged you.'

'You just floated up to the surface,' Gus added soberly. 'It was really scary.'

'So we brought you straight to hospital.'

I tried to smile. 'That's really nice of you. Really, it's nobody's fault but my own.' Gus's mother burst into tears again.

Luckily, it turned out I didn't have a concussion, just some rather nasty bumps and bruises. I was discharged after two hours, and was able to go home immediately. Gus's parents drove me home. It was a very quiet car journey, with everyone scrambling over each other to apologise at the end. It was a shame, as it had been a nice afternoon, but the whole thing was rather ruined in everyone's memory. I never went back to Gus's house, and I think his guilt stopped him from coming around to our place quite so often for a while afterwards. Nonetheless, this was a valuable lesson to learn, which I would think of often, especially years later when I had children of my own. I always measure the depths of any pool we go to before I let anyone practice their diving there!

The countryside surrounding our country house in the North of France goes on uninterrupted for miles and miles. In the appropriate footwear, one can walk for hours and not come across another house. Perhaps one might glimpse a farm, and eventually one would be able to see the sea, but one would be unlikely to cross anyone else's path except on a very sunny holiday. From the windows of our house, there is nothing to see but an expanse of more or less bright green grass, rippling in the wind, under miles of blue sky. In the distance, one might see the line of a forest; above, one might glimpse the silhouette of a hawk.

Now, imagine the most unlikely thing to appear in this scene. A tiger, perhaps. An army of monkeys in suits. A tall oil rig. Well, the first two may never happen (unless a local zookeeper loses his keys!) but the last was very nearly a reality, at least in the mind of one crazy neighbour of mine, a man by the name of Philippe.

Philippe had always struck me as a quiet and reliable man. He had worked for close to twenty-six years as a manager in a local bank. However, one day I saw him pacing around in the fields outside our house. I gave it no notice until I heard a roar of machinery. When I looked out the window again, I saw three people gathered around a kind of digger. I ran down the stairs to investigate, shivering as the cold Normandy wind hit me in the face.

'What on earth is going on?' I roared over the noise of the engine. 'Are you digging for gold? Have you lost your minds?'

The men looked up at me inquisitively. After a moment, Philippe motioned to the man at the wheel of the machine to switch it off. 'What is wrong?' he asked me. 'Are we disturbing you with the noise? It's quite late in the morning, and this is my land, you know!' he added, cocking his chin upwards somewhat defensively.

Philippe was not a friendly-looking man, and he had not proved himself to be a very good neighbour to me. He was in his mid-fifties and of medium height, red-faced and scrawny. His skin looked like it had been blasted daily with wind and sun, like some sort of polar explorer. I suppose just being an outdoorsman in Normandy produces this effect. Our relations had been tense if not unpleasant before this encounter: he always seemed to be worried about something, complaining about trees, fences, hedges, shade; anything he could think of. Once, he even came to complain to me about wild deer jumping over the fence between our properties. Of course, there was nothing I could do about the wild animals, but he tried to blame me for it! He was obviously wary now, expecting me to come to him in return with a complaint.

I smiled as amiably as I could. 'Oh, I'm aware it's your land, don't worry.' Philippe had probably inherited the land, which was a scaled-down version of a much larger farm from the 1950s. There must have been ten hectares of grass surrounding his farmhouse. 'I've been awake for hours. I was just curious as to what was going on,' I continued. 'What are you digging for?'

'Oil, of course! Well, we are looking for gas first. Then, we suspect, we will come across the oil.'

'There's oil here?' I asked, frowning a little.

'We believe so. We haven't found it yet, but we are searching. We are confident we will come across it soon.'

'What, you mean just by luck?' I was astounded.

'Well, we have a suspicion there is a gas field here. After all, that's the only way to look for oil, historically!'

'A suspicion? I can understand that the Chinese, the Babylonians or the Egyptians looked for oil this way. But this is the twenty-first century!'

'We read about it in a history book,' he snapped at me. 'What do you know about it anyway?'

'I used to work in the oil business.'

'What, you mean digging yourself?' he sneered.

'No,' I replied patiently, 'but I know what my men were looking for. I often was involved in research. I know you need certain types of geographical conditions, and there is usually some kind of historic trace of them, even if they are not well-known! You need pockets of bedrock, for instance, or highly compacted sand. This field is nothing but mud.'

'You find oil in all sorts of unexpected places,' Philippe retorted, a little uncertainly.

'First you might look at a satellite image, or an aerial photograph,' I continued. 'You think about seismic lines. Have you done a seismic study?'

'Don't be stupid,' he muttered. 'We're just a few guys, doing this all with our own means.'

'After the seismic study,' I pursued, ignoring him, 'you inspect the area carefully with scientists. Then, and only then, do you think about drilling. I cannot help but think that you have skipped straight to the last stage!'

'Look, we've just got a feeling about this, ok? There's a huge crude oil field somewhere near here. We'll find it. Then we'll bottle it all up and sell it. We'll be millionaires, and you'll regret this conversation then!'

'Yes,' I replied sarcastically, 'when I look out over the field of drills bobbing up and down, pumping up gallons and gallons of crude Normandy oil, I will regret it.'

Philippe ran his hand through his hair. 'Look, I'm not a fool,' he said. 'I know about the oil business too. We're wildcatters! There's always a lot of luck involved. Sometimes you just have to dig, and find out. Sure, you end up filling in many of these rank wildcats. We have the cement right here. But you'll never be sure whether there is oil or gas around unless you look for it!' I got the distinct feeling he was convincing himself as well as me. Or perhaps he was speaking for the benefit of his cold and bedraggled companions, who were waiting impatiently to turn their machine back on. God knows how much they must have spent to hire it!

'I didn't mean to be inconsiderate,' I told him gently, 'I just wanted to make sure you were aware of the facts. I lived in Texas for a long time. Even if you do find any oil, there's an 85% chance it'll dry out in a few days or weeks. That happens even right in the heart of oil-country, in Texas or Alaska!'

Philippe sighed, and didn't respond. The men shuffled their feet.

'Look,' I explained, 'I realise I'm butting in on something that is eminently not my business. But I'm just trying to be a good neighbour. In one of my books, I have a true story about some crooks who sell an oil field in Bordeaux to an uninformed Arab Sheik who was visiting Paris and was taken for a ride. Of course, the field he bought was empty. There is no oil in South West France. There is no oil in Normandy either,' I repeated.

'You don't know that,' he said again, bullheadedly. 'France is a country rich in resources. It has a glorious past, and untapped riches to be found. It's filled with thousands of hectares dedicated to agriculture. Why couldn't we French have more than this? We used to have colonies; French used to be the main language spoken all over the world. Why would the Arabs have all the oil, while America has all the industry, and we have nothing at all? It's just not fair. It's just not possible.' The bitterness in his voice was toxic; I suspected this was a rant he had aired many times before. 'I wish you would stop treating this as if it were some sort of joke,' he concluded. 'To me and my countrymen, it's very serious.'

As he said this, a light bulb went on my in my head. I got my diary out of my pocket. 'Look at this,' I said, flicking quickly through the pages. 'I promise I am not patronising you. Just look at the date today. It's April 1st. Who have you been talking to?'

'I know it's April the first,' he positively spat out, although his eyes darted around nervously to his companions. Noticing his embarrassment, I put an arm on his shoulder and tried to guide him a little ways away from his group. 'Stop it!' he said, shrugging my hand off like a teenage boy. 'No-one is trying to embarrass me except you. There is no joke here. It is not a *"poisson d'Avril."* There is no fishy business here. There are just a couple of aspiring businessmen being distracted from their hard work by an annoying neighbour on a very cold morning!' He turned his back on me sulkily and stomped back towards the machine. After a moment, the engine was switched back on. None of the other men even looked at me.

'Have fun digging!' I called after their backs. 'Mark my words, you'll just dig and dig!'

There was no response.

I shrugged and walked back towards the house, shaking my head. I left them digging away in the mud, absolutely certain they wouldn't find even a drop of oil to write home about. The whole thing was as tragic as it was comical. Later that day, still wondering about my neighbours, I read the newspapers and did some research online, including studying an oil journal. I concluded that my suspicions had been correct, and that there was absolutely no possibility of finding natural gas or crude oil in Normandy. I guess the men would just have to find out for themselves, though. Some people just aren't willing to believe in good neighbourly advice!

THE HOUSE ON THE HILL

Our house near Canterbury always held something of a mystery for me. It was a wonderful property in all the ways that mattered, however one thing about it grated on me, and left me questioning the logic of whoever had built it.

Its position.

There was no way for me to fathom why, when the structure was erected in 1620, it had been decided that the house itself should be placed on top of a hill, with the garden to be found at the base. It seemed like a lot of extra effort for both those who had built the property and for its subsequent inhabitants, who were forced to walk or drive up the hill to reach the main part of the house.

Then there was the structure of the house itself. It was a two storey house, built entirely of heavy stone, with at least forty tons of wooden beams used to support the whole structure. It seemed a kind of madness, thinking of people dragging the necessary materials up the hill in order to put the house together. After all, houses that were built long after my own property, from the early 1900s up to as recently as the mid-1950s, could be found at the end of my few acres of gardens, in the little valley that ran beneath our house.

I suppose it was only a matter of time until I discovered that there was rather a good reason indeed for the positioning of our house.

It was December 1999 and there had been severe weather warnings for a couple of days, but near Canterbury we had yet to see any real ill effects. I certainly felt rather safe and away from it all in my house. It rained a lot, but that was simply the sort of thing one was used to. Nothing to be concerned about. We certainly didn't take the warnings very seriously.

My wife even made a joke about battening down the hatches, and I laughed and said we'd be safe and sound. We were just going about our daily business, unconcerned as to what the weather was deciding to do. It was as if we were ignoring a poorly behaved child, not expecting anything truly awful to happen as a result.

It did seem, though, as this particular day went on, that the rain became more of a punishing beat against the rooftop. I could hear it lashing against the windows as the howling wind drove it down. After a while of this harsh weather, I became concerned for my home and my own safety. No house is built to withstand great storms and our place was old and had been built and rebuilt so many times. I wondered how the old stonework would hold up to the challenge.

'It's getting worse,' my wife said, peering out of the window behind me. 'Oh. You should come and see this!'

Looking out of the window, I could see trees swaying in the distance as though great hands were trying to drag them from the ground, roots and all. It was quite a sight, seen through the blur of constant rain that splashed against the windows so violently that it seemed it could break them entirely. Branches flew past us, as big as my arm, as though they were nothing but leaves, lighter than air.

The land around my house, what I could see of it from my vantage point on top of the hill, was quickly becoming submerged in a layer of water, so it seemed as though I were in a castle surrounded by a shallow moat.

The shrubs and even the trees in my own terraced garden remained unaffected by the gale force winds; they were sturdy oaks as old and solid as the house itself. Yet even as I watched in horror, trees on neighbouring properties were crashing to the ground as if they were nothing more than a flimsy flower or two.

My wife became worried and I couldn't argue with her. There was no telling how bad the storm might get, how it might affect us. 'The roof's so terribly old, I hope it doesn't cave in. Oh, dear. Do you think we'll be all right up here?'

I nodded. 'I'm sure we will. No need to worry. We're well out of the water.' I was still trying to make it funny, as though it wasn't serious, but looking out at the destruction taking place, it was terrifying. Who knew that mild and predictable English weather could turn so dark and violent in a matter of hours?

After a while, thunder began to crack the sky and my windows shook with it, the deep grey skies blackened with cloud cover, only to be illuminated with powerful flashes of lightning. It was like looking at an angry god, seeing all the devastation that occurred just minutes away from my house. I gasped to see it.

Of course, a storm like that only has so much momentum, but it lasted for a good few hours, the hammering rain, the terrifying wind that sounded like a human voice echoing and booming. By the evening, we were through the worst of it and, though leaves and twigs scattered our garden, nothing was broken, nothing lost.

The following day, when I ventured down to see if my neighbours had weathered the storm as well as I had, I was met with scenes of chaos and destruction that shook me.

At the base of the hill, the flood waters had risen far higher than I had imagined they could, fetid water filling the houses of my neighbours. One particularly unlucky family had been flooded and had a tree fall on their roof, smashing it in quite dramatically and rendering their whole house basically unliveable in. They weren't the only ones to lose trees, leaving gaping holes or splintered trunks in the ground around us, wrecking the natural beauty of the area.

It was almost as if the end of the world had come and, to some of the people around me, it must have felt as if it truly had. Neighbours, those I knew well and those I didn't, were wading through the flood water, coming in and out of their houses and shaking their heads like all was lost.

'What will you do?' I asked one of my neighbours. It seemed a hopeless situation to me, losing one's home in such a manner, even if just for a temporary period of time.

He shook his head mournfully, still looking shell-shocked and perplexed by the whole ugly business. 'Try and claim it on the insurance, I suppose. It's whether they call it an act of God or not, but we'll give it a go. It's difficult to get insured when you live here.'

I didn't completely understand what he meant by that until I had spoken with a few of the other affected parties. Then I realised that the whole area under my house was a flood plain, which put it in extreme danger whenever there was heavy rain and severe storms. To the people who lived down in the valley, it was a rare thing to see a storm so bad that it ruined so many houses and flooded the land completely, so the risks were worth it.

However, for the first time I very much appreciated the clever builder who had decided to place the house I lived in out of harm's way, safe on top of the hill, on a solid foundation of stone. I had experienced no flooding whatsoever, in spite of the rain that had sloshed and beaten against my doors and windows. My house remained watertight and stable, though my neighbours were missing huge chunks of their roofs and many of their windows had been smashed in by the wind.

Even those who had not been so badly damaged by it had sodden carpets and ruined furniture to contend with, from where the rain had slid in through unexpected nooks and crannies. It was remarkable how many people the bad weather had hurt.

This whole event and the aftermath of watching my neighbours trying to put their homes back together, gave me a keen eye for what to look for in a property. A lesson which I have since imparted to my children, and in fact to anyone I know who is tempted to look for convenience or attractiveness over safety. The most important thing to look for in a house is a good foundation of rock that will not shift or slide in bad weather, and will not crumble over the years. And it is necessary, before you commit yourself to a place, to find out whether it will be able to remain in the face of the rougher times, as well as the sunny days.

As with anything we experience in life, a house must be able to weather any storm that comes its way and still be standing strong after the bad weather has passed.

A CHANGE OF SCHEDULE

When I was studying at NYU, and when I got my first engineering job after that, I lived on the Eastern seaboard of the United States for one or two years in a fraternity house that I shared with some of my engineering friends. It was a vast, creaky old house from 1810, with thirty rooms, four of which formed my comfortable suite on the first floor. We had a lovely time living there.

Malcolm had become friends with us as he originally worked as an engineer in the aerospace industry. He was fun, sporty, and good-looking, and after successfully completing his studies he now worked for Delta airlines. Like all pilots, he always seemed to have a dozen girlfriends, each prettier than the last. It must be something to do with those natty navy suits, or perhaps the little caps they wear! He also always seemed to have strings of stories about flights to tell us. We would sit by the fire in the winter, listening to his tales of charming air hostesses, unreliable co-pilots, drunken passengers, and emergency landings on obscure Indonesian islands. Malcolm flew all over the USA, with many of his routes seeming to focus on California and Florida, and all over the world as well, criss-crossing the world's oceans and landmasses in his Boeings 727, 707, and 737. As this was the late 1960s, no-one had yet heard of Airbus! Malcolm was a very accomplished and serious pilot, yet he always knew how to keep us entertained.

'So this one time,' his story might go, 'there we were, heading right smack towards the middle of the Pacific Ocean, sun bright in my eyes, and I start to feel a little woozy... And I realise right then that the Russian pilot, that friendly Russian pilot, hadn't just been making me coffee: he had been putting shots of vodka in! I had been so busy socialising with him and then preparing for take-off that I hadn't even noticed!'

'So what did you do?'

'I pulled myself together, man, and had another coffee!'

Many of his tales had to do with bravado in flight, but there was something quite charming about his confidence. Of course, many of his stories turned into jokes or one-liners, one of his favourites being the story of a plane which was grounded for several hours before take-off.

'As the flight attendants come round with drinks,' Malcolm would narrate, sitting back in his leather armchair with a stiff whiskey or a cup of tea, 'one of the passengers asked why it had taken them so long to get into the air. 'Oh,' the flight attendant explained, 'the pilot was bothered by a noise he heard in the engine. It took us a while to find a new pilot.' And Malcolm would laugh uproariously and slap his thigh at the hilariousness of his own story.

But he was not only a funny, bon vivant type; he also enjoyed a nice quiet afternoon or evening in. He and I particularly bonded whilst we were sharing this house and came to develop a habit, which was that I would read the *New York Times* aloud to him: as he used his eyes so intensively twelve hours a day, he didn't have it in him to squint and focus on the fine print, but he still wanted desperately to stay on top of current events. I quite enjoyed reading aloud, and in Malcolm's company especially, so these news sessions became a regular feature of our life together. All in all, we three engineers got along famously with Malcolm, and we lived quite contentedly together in New York for almost a year with no trouble.

But one day, I was awoken at four in the morning by this repetitive creaking noise from upstairs, which I quickly figured out had to come from someone pacing. As I wondered what on earth could be going on, the noise continued, repeating and beginning to fall into an irregular pattern. Eventually, I could take it no longer. I hauled myself out of my warm bed and out onto the freezing landing, where I went to find our concierge, who did our cooking, cleaning and also served as a guardian to the building.

'I'm so sorry to wake you,' I began, 'but there is this terrible creaking noise upstairs, and I just can't figure out what it can be.'

'Well, surely it must just be one of your housemates?' she responded a little grumpily. 'It's not exactly a big deal to have a bit of insomnia…'

'Not a big deal? It's four in the morning! We all have to go to work in a few hours! I'm going to be exhausted!'

'So am I,' she remarked.

'Look, I'm sorry. Could you maybe just investigate this tomorrow?'

'Investigate? It doesn't take a Sherlock Holmes to figure out what's going on here. Clearly, whoever sleeps immediately above you is having some trouble doing so.'

'Malcolm? But he sleeps like a log!'

'Well, maybe he's got someone up there with him!' she snapped, and closed the door in my face. I wandered back upstairs somewhat despondently. I decided to leave the matter until the morning and speak to Malcolm about it directly.

I intended to lose no time. However, the next day at breakfast, as I sat sipping a stronger coffee than usual, Malcolm did not turn up, so I had to wait until evening to bring the matter up. I went to work rather troubled, and was rather curt with several employees. I was grateful to get home that evening, but Malcolm was still nowhere to be found. At last, when I was sitting in the lounge with the *Times*, the mysterious pilot appeared. I decided to cut to the chase.

'Hello. Did you sleep well last night, Malcolm?' I asked.

He raised his eyebrows. 'Well, I suppose I did. Not a very long night's sleep, but yes.' He appeared rather surprised by my line of questioning.

'Did you have a guest? Some troubled flight attendant, perhaps? Or was it a pair of drunken air hostesses?'

'What on earth are you talking about? I very definitely slept alone!'

'Look, someone was pacing in your room at four this morning. Are you having some kind of troubles with insomnia? Do we need to send you to a counsellor for some psychoanalysis?'

Malcolm laughed, and rubbed his eyes rather sleepily. 'Oh dear. I see what's gone on here,' he said. 'The reality is much simpler. You see, I'm shaving.'

'Shaving? At four a.m.? What are you, insane?'

'Yes,' Malcolm drawled dryly, 'I enjoy shaving in the middle of the night. Of course not, you maniac.'

'But shaving only takes five minutes,' I added, deciding to leave the previous sarcasm unchallenged if unexplained. 'I swear you were making the floor creak above my head for a good forty-five minutes.'

'Ah, but you see, then I have to jump into my pants.' Malcolm seemed to be finding this conversation rather droll. I was unamused.

'You jump in your pants? What are you, some kind of child?'

'It's part of my exercise,' he explained. 'I can't just slip them on, you see.'

'OK,' I responded, shaking my head. 'Let's just pretend this whole conversation isn't getting weirder and weirder, and assume that it's normal to be doing any of these things before the sun has even thought about rising. Putting your pants on only accounts for probably another two minutes. That leaves 42 still to go.'

'Well, let's see,' Malcolm responded, with the air of a man taking something very seriously. 'It takes me another two minutes for my belt. Then I put on my shirt. I have a special way of running to put on my jacket, you see. Keeps the creases out.' I honestly couldn't tell if he was joking or if he had lost his mind. 'It takes five minutes to put on my tie,' he continued. 'And out of frustration for all these mundane tasks I find myself walking back and forth across my suite, from one mirror to another. I'm terrible at tying ties, you see. It's been a real weakness of mine since I was a teenager. Hey, did I tell you one of my flight attendants once caught a couple trying to mess around on the plane, and when she asked them what they were doing the wife replied, "Oh, just straightening my husband's belt"?'

'Very funny, Malcolm,' I responded dryly. 'But I'm not joking here. How do you get your underwear on?'

'Oh, I jump into it, of course. But straight out of bed.'

'OK,' I said, 'I can play this game as long as you can. Explain to me, please, the terrible thump that occurred around 4.45.'

Malcolm grinned. 'Oh, that would be my pilot's case. It's a very serious item of luggage, full of legal documents in case we go to court, and catalogues of all the different airplanes I have to fly.'

I sighed. 'I guess I'm at least starting to have a clear image of what on earth you get up to in that suite of yours. Remind me never to walk in in the morning. But seriously, you haven't answered my most important question. Why on earth are you doing all these clothing calisthenics at four am?'

Malcolm laughed. 'OK, I give in,' he said. 'Sorry for messing you around, old friend. It's just kind of irresistible when you look this grumpy. I guarantee it's all 100% true. But I'm really sorry if I have kept you awake. The reason is very simple: my airline schedule has changed. I used to be able to leave the house around eight in the morning to go to JFK or La Guardia airport, in order to make my first flight around ten. But now my take-off time has changed to six o'clock at JFK. I barely make it if I get up at four.'

'That's terrible, man,' I said. 'I have a lot of sympathy for you. But it's going to be a problem. I'm not a very deep sleeper. If I feel the way I did today at work, I'm going to end up firing my entire staff or at least getting very addicted to caffeine. How long is this going to last?'

'It's only supposed to be for two months. But I really don't want to be a pain. Maybe I should just go stay somewhere else for the duration.'

'I don't want to kick you out,' I said. 'I didn't mean that.' Suddenly, I had an idea. 'Wait a minute. Who's sleeping in the corner room on the second floor?'

'The one with no view?'

'Yes, that one. I mean, I know it has no view, but I don't think it's directly above anybody. Do you catch my drift?'

He smiled. 'I see what you're getting at. That room does happen to look out over two trash cans and a brick wall, but to be honest I can live with that for two months if it means you'll be in an acceptable mood!'

I grinned and narrowed my eyes. 'When am I not? On that note, I'm going to bed.'

The room-switching theory worked a treat, and for the next two months of Malcolm's terrible work schedule, he did make a lot of jokes about the view, but at least the rest of us living in that house managed to get some sleep.

When I was a twenty-three-year-old engineer, I went on a management course at Princeton University. I found a small terraced house that looked out over a very nice square, with a lovely park outside. It was a lucky find, as Princeton is famous for its parks and historic houses, and affordable too, considering that the house was built in 1650! My next door neighbour was a graduate student, who went to Princeton as well: I had seen him a few times on campus. I often saw him going in and out of his front door with a beautiful girl. I met them once on the lawn we shared in front of our terraced houses. We introduced ourselves, and chatted over a shared plate of cookies the man had with him.

'You must be my neighbour,' he said with a charming smile. 'I'm Callum. Would you like a cookie? They're chocolate chip. Fresh from the oven.'

Callum was six foot five, with small eyes and a big mouth that was most often fixed in a movie-star grin. He had a sharp nose, like Charlton Heston, and was wearing a navy pinstripe suit. He struck me as a pleasant, easy-going man.

'I wouldn't say no,' I said, picking a large one, crunching into it and finding it still warm. 'I'm Bradley Jamieson, by the way,' I added through a mouthful of crumbs.

'Pleased to meet you. I'm a student and occasional lecturer in the social sciences,' he explained. 'I moved in just a few months ago. It's nice to meet someone who lives so close by!' He went on to detail his work interests to me. We ate a few cookies each, and moved on to the topics of winter sports and European travels, which were interests we both shared. I also found out he was from Indiana, and that his beautiful girlfriend was called Pat. That was the sum total of our interaction. After a while, it started to get chilly, and we both moved back inside.

A few days later, we happened to cross paths again, and had a pleasant conversation about some paper he was writing. It happened to be on a topic I was fairly well acquainted with, so we stopped and chatted for a few minutes. As the conversation drew to its natural end quite quickly, Callum suddenly laid his hand on my arm and looked at me earnestly.

'Can I ask you something a bit unusual?' he inquired casually.

'Of course! Anything at all.'

'Will you be the best man at my wedding?'

The question came completely out of the blue, and stunned me. Callum smiled, and I just stood for a few seconds, blinking. After a pause, I managed to reply: 'We've only known each other a few days! We've spoken twice!' I stopped, a little bit awkwardly. After all, I didn't want to ask anything which might come across as rude, such as 'Why me?' or 'Don't you have any closer friends?' I coughed. 'I'm sorry, it's not that I'm not rather charmed... But what does your girlfriend think of this? We haven't even met! I mean, for all she knows, I could be a serial killer!'

Callum laughed. 'Well, this would be a good time to let me know. As for Pat, she doesn't mind at all. We discussed it over breakfast yesterday. You see, we organised this wedding rather hastily. It's all a bit last minute. We were just so caught up in the passion of it, you know. It's sort of like we're eloping, but on home territory!'

'And you really want me to be the best man?'

'Why not? I don't have any siblings, my close male friends are few and out of state. Pat has as many bridesmaids as she wants, and that's the important thing. Participants are just a passing detail, if you're forgive the turn of phrase. We've got great caterers lined up, a lovely last-minute venue... We're getting married in the Methodist church just down the road. You know the one?'

'Yes,' I said hesitantly, still a bit flabbergasted. 'I know the place.'

'You're my neighbour,' he added brightly. 'It'll all be so convenient!'

I had to laugh. 'Fine,' I said with a shrug. 'OK. I'll do it! What are my expected duties?'

'It'll be simple,' Callum assured me. 'I'm sure you've seen the movies. Just sit there for a while, then stand up and hand over the ring. Then we'll all go out together and have rose petals thrown over us. That's pretty much it. It'll be over quickly. Obviously, I'm looking forward to it hugely,' he added hastily.

'Alright,' I said. 'I'm in.'

The day of the wedding was bright and sunny, and the church was busy but not packed. I assumed they had kept the number of invitations to their nearest and dearest. The ceremony was a fairly classic one, if relaxed, and I managed to pull off my minor role in the ceremony without too much trouble. I didn't forget the ring, or trip, or cough at any inappropriate moments. During the ceremony itself, I saw why it didn't really matter who played the side parts and incidental roles: after all, this was Callum and Pat's moment. Pat was resplendent in a long white gown trimmed with lace, and Callum was grinning like a man who still couldn't quite believe his luck. When all was said and done, we walked out into the bright sun and found ourselves showered with rice. I found myself thinking I was quite glad to be in the middle of such a happy, emotional time for these nice people.

We walked down the road in convoy to get to the reception, which was held in a tastefully-decorated marquee on the lawn. Again, everything was on quite a small scale, but the effect was lovely. We sat down at the long tables, which were covered in white tablecloths and strewn with vines and blue flowers. I had just settled in happily to relax and wait for the food, when someone pinged a knife against a glass. 'Oh, of course,' I thought to myself, 'there will be embarrassing speeches now. Poor guests. Poor groom!' Then, all at once, I realised many faces seemed to be looking at me. Only then did it dawn on me with an awful sinking feeling that I was in fact the best man. The only person who could make an embarrassing speech at this point was me! I looked over at the groom with a mixture of surprise and desperation. He shrugged. He obviously didn't mind about this any more than he had the other 'passing details' of the ceremony. I sighed. I had two choices: make a fuss and refuse to give a speech, which was bound to ruin the atmosphere, or stand up and give it my best shot. I was not a man to give up easily.

I smiled, straightened my tie and stood up. There was scattered applause: I worked out that most guests were probably already on their second flute of champagne, and therefore unlikely to give me too much trouble. 'Ladies and gentlemen,' I began, then paused to clear my throat. 'Most of you will probably not recognise me. I have no shame in admitting to being rather a last minute recruit to this fine wedding. I'm sure Callum won't mind me saying this.' I looked over at my friend for reassurance. He grinned quite happily. 'I'm as late an addition to this wedding as that baggy suit he bought for twenty bucks at Robert Hall! He probably just ran down the street to buy it between classes.' There was scattered laughter from the guests. Obviously this personality trait of Callum's was fairly well-known. 'But from my short acquaintance with Callum, I can tell you one decision he made without hastiness: his choice of bride. Pat is a wonderful young woman, and from the short amount of time I've spent with them planning this wedding – very short,' I emphasised, to more laughter from the hall, 'I can tell this is no last minute, charity shop wedding. The trimmings and trappings are just passing details, as Callum told me himself. Callum is witty, smart and driven. He's charming enough to get a near-stranger to agree to not only be the best man at his wedding but even improvise a speech without warning!' The groom grinned apologetically. 'And Pat, well I've only met her once before today, so the way he talks about her, I assume she must be some sort of royalty. I look forward to getting Christmas cards from the happy couple, and then from their dozen children, who will all no doubt be millionaires. I won't bore you any longer: let's all raise our glasses to the happy couple.' After everyone had toasted the couple, however, I found myself adding: 'Wait, I've forgotten something! It's not a best man's speech without some bad jokes. Seeing as how I don't know any embarrassing stories about the groom's past, I shall have to leave you with the following. Do you know the one about the two peanuts who were in love? Well, they were walking down along the Princeton River, hand in hand, and then one of them got assaulted.' I sat down to a mix of laughter and puzzled applause, and caught a grateful wink from Pat.

I have to admit I was glad at this point to sit down and enjoy my three-course dinner. After the cake, everyone milled around for a while before the final event: the throwing of the garter.

This event was originally more often a part of European weddings than American ones, but as Callum's origins were partly Irish, the couple had obviously decided to embrace it. The groom removes a highly decorative, ceremonial garter, usually made of frilly white lace, from his bride's leg, and tosses it into the crowd. Allegedly, the man to catch it will be the first to marry. Thus, this tradition is the mirror-image of the bride's bouquet-throwing, which features in most traditional Western weddings. Now, I had been a volleyball player between the ages of sixteen and twenty-one, and I still had the ability to jump more than a metre and a half in the air. My record had been one hundred and seventy-two centimetres at the high jump, and I could definitely still manage a hundred and sixty easily. Callum untied the garter from his blushing wife's leg and tossed it into the air. I leapt enthusiastically and happened to catch it, a gesture which was met with roars of approval by all. 'You're next in line!' Callum congratulated me. 'Just you wait! You'll be the happiest man alive soon!'

I moved away only a few months later but, amusingly, I actually did happen to get married less than a year after the day of Callum and Pat's wedding. I even invited Callum, although he couldn't come as he was on a business trip. But thirty-five years later, I received an unexpected email from my old neighbour. It turned out that as I had once been on the board of a large company, and this being after the advent of the internet, my old friend and neighbour had managed to look me up using only my name.

Dear Brad, the email said, *I hope you'll remember your old neighbour. After all, you were by my side on the happiest day of my life! I have some sad news to pass on, and also some exciting. The first thing I have to tell you is that my beloved Pat passed away last year. We spent many happy years side by side, but I now live alone. I'm now a businessman, and I would love to catch up with you, which brings me to the second thing I wanted to share. I've heard of an exciting deal. I'm now in Michigan, working in the oil business (I know, it's a big change from lecturing in the social sciences!), and I remembered that was what you ended up doing. If you'd like to meet up sometime, just let me know! Remember that I'm the man who essentially arranged your happy marriage by throwing you that garter...*

Best wishes,
Callum.

I was happy to hear from him, and wrote back at once:

Dear Callum,

It's wonderful to hear from you. First off, I must give you my most sincere condolences. I had only met Pat briefly, but she seemed like a wonderful woman, and you were certainly very happy together. Unfortunately, I will have to disappoint you on the business front, as I am no longer in business: I have recently made the decision to focus on my writing. I'm currently working on a volume of short stories! I hope you might forgive me this, as I feel like I was involved in the biggest deal of your life: your marriage. If you're ever in Geneva, do let me know, it would be great to catch up. And if you're ever lucky enough to remarry, just let me know. I'll be happy to be your best man!'

A NEIGHBOUR FOR THE SCOUTS

When I was fourteen, I went on a trip to Eastern Europe with my Boy Scout troop. We were a fairly honourable, if chaotic bunch, who got along well most of the time, and only squabbled as much as might be expected of boys our age. We travelled often as a group, which meant that I got to see some interesting parts of Europe in fascinating periods of history. For instance, this particular trip took us to Belgrade, Rome, Trieste and Sofia, all on one ridiculously busy ten-day trip. We saw classical temples and communist statues all in less than two weeks!

Of course, many of the landmarks we completely missed: first of all because as fourteen-year-old boys, they were hardly our first point of interest, and second of all because we were scouts, and therefore above all focused on camping, hiking and exploring the outdoors. Still, Eastern Europe had a lot to offer. The weather was freezing the whole time, but there was a certain charm to the long stomps through the foggy woods, the campfires at dusk and crawling into our sleeping-bags at night for well-earned rest. We set up a vast camp of tents in the forest, and every day at dawn, we would set out on some adventure in the surrounding countryside. The first day, we went hunting in the forest, which was incredibly exciting. None of us actually managed to shoot a single living thing, but it was thrilling to feel like men, shuffling through the undergrowth in our big coats, seeing our breath turn to steam in the air. We dined on baked beans and sausages heated up over a small fire, and stayed up late sharing ghost stories. The second day was uneventful and exhausting, spent in a vast, wandering hike, where we got lost for about two hours in the middle, and we retired to bed gratefully.

But that night, just as we were about to fall asleep, a figure appeared outside the tent I was staying in. One of the boys gasped, and we all shuffled back against the wall, trying to hide from what we imagined must have been some sort of terrible nightmare. The laces that kept the tent shut made a loud noise as they came undone, and a man tottered into the tent, singing to himself and clutching a big blue bottle. 'Don't be scared,' he said in strongly accented, broken English. 'I am your neighbour!' He then proceeded to collapse over some of the boys, and immediately fall asleep, snoring loudly. Torn between giggles and shock, we convened and decided that the solution was to speak to an authority figure. I pulled on my coat and went over to speak to the camp manager.

'I'm sorry to come see you so late,' I said a little shyly, 'but there's a man in our tent.'

The camp manager's face registered intense shock. 'Dear god,' he said. 'Are you alright? Is he asking you questions? What does he seem to want?' But all of a sudden a knowing look came into his eyes, and he squinted a little. 'Wait a minute,' he said. 'Does this man look about fifty or sixty years old?'

'Yes,' I replied confidently.

'Does he have white hair?'

'Yes,' I said. 'Well, it might be considered white if he ever washed it.' I was feeling braver after seeing the manager's apparently relaxed reaction. There was certainly no urgency to this questioning, just a sort of amusement.

'Does he have a red face?'

'Yes.'

'Does he have very wrinkly skin?'

'Yes.' I was getting a little bit bored of this. 'And he smells terrible. He's holding a bottle.'

The camp manager shook his head. 'I'm surprised you hadn't met him yet,' he said with a strange smile. 'This man is indeed your neighbour, as he said.'

'What is he, some kind of local drunk?' I was becoming impatient, and consequently a little brave, in the way that teenagers can be.

The camp manager laughed loudly. 'Oh, well he is something like that. He also happens to be the guardian of the camp.'

'This camp? You mean this drunkard is meant to be responsible for us?' I couldn't quite believe it.

'Yes,' the manager replied thoughtfully, apparently unoffended by my tone. 'He's an old capitalist, you see, who was totally depressed with the arrival of communism. He hates everything about it. The regime, the laws, everything. So he believes that excuse is sufficient reason to get drunk every night.'

'But that's pathetic,' I said indignantly.

The camp manger shrugged. 'He thinks you boys come from rich countries, you see. I think he hopes you will be his salvation. He just wants to talk to you, talk to everybody, anybody who embodies the vision of the life he's missing out on.' He sighed expansively. I began to wonder if my camp manager hadn't had a sip from the blue bottle himself.

'This is a security issue!' I said as sternly as I could, although I hesitated a little even as the words left my mouth. 'Surely it isn't safe that this complete crazy drunk has just fallen over in our tent? Can't we at least kick him out?'

The camp manager appeared to be thinking out loud. 'I see your point, Jamieson,' he said thoughtfully, 'but I can't do anything about it. The man essentially manages the camp, you see! He's my superior. I think you can probably get away with rolling him out of your tent, though, if he's as drunk as you are implying. As for the next two nights, well, you'll just have to improvise. Why don't you just have a chat with him? He's an interesting enough man. Just don't promise him anything. It'll only make him miserable.'

'What do you mean? What on earth would we promise him?'

'Well, every year there's some foolish kid who promises to send him things when he gets home. Things you can't get in communist countries: food, or music recordings. But of course when kids get home they completely forget about it. And then he's miserable for days, and drinks even more than usual.'

'I'll bear that in mind,' I said hesitantly, then bid the camp master goodnight and walked back to the tent. I wouldn't have said I felt particularly reassured by this conversation, but I guess it was better to know what strange man we were facing! When I got back, I explained the situation to the other boys, who displayed a combination of confusement, bemusement and amusement. Some of the older boys had already taken it upon themselves to confiscate the suspicious blue bottle, and had managed to get so drunk that one of them was being sick in the woods.

We found out later, thanks to the camp master, that like many poor communist peasants at the time, our visitor was actually drinking some horrible form of homemade moonshine. The blue bottle was originally used to store white spirits, which were then distilled with fruit and whatever else was available in order to make rather dubious liquor. I was glad I was not interested in drinking: seeing the faces of those older boys the next morning certainly would have put me off the idea even if I had been! The camp master also told us, with a laugh, that the boys needn't have worried about stealing the bottle, although they really should steer clear of the poisonous stuff in the future. Some years, the man actually came into tents earlier in the evening hoping to share his moonshine! Apparently, the conversation of teenage Americans was worth sacrificing some of his precious alcohol to.

Us younger, virtuous scouts were rather put off by this story, as it demonstrated what I had begun to suspect, that our camp manager himself was not exactly a pillar of virtue! Still, it did mean we worried less about being caught sneaking out on walks in the morning, climbing trees on hikes, or poking at the fire. It was a good thing we were sensible or we might have got ourselves into trouble! Nonetheless, after that nightly visit, we secured our tent as best we could against the drunken intruder. We were less afraid of wolves or bears attacking us during the night than of being looked after by an irresponsible adult!

In the late seventies, our family rented a house in the rolling hills of the Burgundy countryside. We stayed in a leisure development at Clairis, which had a golf course and a swimming pool, along with a cinema and a racecourse nearby. It was a lovely place, between Auxerre and Vézelay, although the quality of the restaurants on site was deplorable. My wife and I often drove down there in a camper and spent a few weeks enjoying the sun and activities. I was interested in this region because of its historical overtones: this was, after all, where a large contingent of the first crusade left from. Thus, this region was also connected to my ancestors, the Jamiesons. Furthermore, I had several friends in Auxerre, including the mayor, from my banking days.

I also had a friend and neighbour there, Roberto Sanbart, who owned a tannery and a dye factory nearby: 'the *tannerie* and the *teinturerie*,' he would say with a laugh. This joint business strategy meant that he was responsible both for treating the animal skin to transform it into leather and for colouring it so it could be sold and used for shoes, suitcases and wallets. Sanbart was a man with shiny black eyes and a smart moustache who always had a story to tell, preferably with a lot of hand gestures which betrayed his Italian origins. I would often go over to his house for dinner, alone or with my wife and my daughter Rouena; in the summer we always had huge barbecues, with course after course of meat, and sometimes a pasta dish first. This usually involved a considerable quantity of chicken, as he raised free-range *poulets*.

'Italians, they speak with their hands,' he would say. 'They put their fingers together so they can shake their hands at you. Chickens just put their beaks together and shake their heads downward.' And he would laugh uproariously, brandishing a barbecued chicken thigh at me for emphasis.

Sanbart was a strong man, and he enjoyed showing this off. One of his favourite tricks was to pick up the skin of a cow he had just tanned, lift it up over his head and throw it about three yards away onto the pavement. The thing probably weighed about twenty-five kilos. His children and my little girl loved the trick and would often beg their papa to perform this after dinner, to everyone's amusement.

The hides would then lie in the sun to dry, until they were ready to go on to be dyed.

This always looked rather impressive: Sanbart was a muscular type, and he looked like some sort of prehistoric man, hauling dead animals around over his shoulder. He often wore a black leather jacket, which would have made this impression more threatening, had Sanbart not been one of the nicest Italian men I have ever met, and a real family man, too.

'You look pretty strong,' I told him once. 'How on earth are you in the leather-tanning business and not the mafia? And why on earth do you live in the middle of Burgundy?'

Sanbart laughed. 'It's a good question. Most of the tanneries of France are in Lyon or Le Havre, actually, so they can use the water of the Loire or the Seine. Tanneries need huge quantities of water to function. But of course there's the river here, so my father established his business in this countryside that he loved.'

'So did you always plan to work in the tannery? Maybe it's because you come from a country shaped like a boot that you became a leather worker.'

Sanbart laughed. 'Actually, I used to be a wrestler in my youth. You know, with greased-back hair like an Italian gangster in some movie. But my father told me I had to quit wrestling and work for him.'

'So you never went to college?'

'No, but I was always perfectly content with my life. I kept on playing sports on the side, and the longer I worked for my father, the more I ended up developing a love for the job and the industry. Then I met my wife; now I have my kids and I'm a happy man. You see, if he hadn't made me work there, I would probably have ended up being a wrestler or some sort of criminal on the streets.'

'I have to say I wouldn't want to fight you!'

He shrugged. 'I could take you. But instead, here I am, a fairly respectable *tanneur-teinturier*. The most violent thing I might do is throw a hide at you! Or make you eat some more of this chicken *cacciatore*!'

Sanbart was passionate about his business, and enjoyed taking us on tours to look around the works. I used to take Rouena with me, who was four at the time; she was always fascinated, although his thorough explanations were probably more interesting to me than to the kids.

'Tanning is a magical process, a transformation,' he would begin. 'What you're doing is fundamentally changing the structure of the protein, of the skin. You cannot make leather back into skin. So you remove all the flesh and fat and hairs; in the old days you just did this by scraping with a knife.'

'Like the Indians in those cowboy movies?' one of Sanbart's boys piped up. 'When they kill the moose?'

'That's right. Except there are not so many moose in Burgundy. Anyway, when the hide is clean, you cover it in salt. This acts as a preservative, and helps to dry it. You let it dry. Then you soak it in different solutions, water and lime, to remove all impurities and soften the leather. It takes a lot of water; that's why we need the river.'

'And that's the smelly part!' the other boy added proudly.

His father smiled indulgently. 'Well, all of the process is rather smelly, if I'm honest. You're drying a bit of dead animal and then soaking it in several poisonous solutions! But you're probably remembering the tanning itself, which is the more complicated part. In the old days they used solutions of tree bark. Now it's usually a chemical or mineral bath. The acid solution soaks into the skin. Then you let it dry in the sun again. And ta-da!'

Rouena looked a little blank.

'All of papa's jobs are smelly,' the boy added. 'The chickens are too!'

My daughter wrinkled her nose.

'You know your great-grandfather was a tanner?' I asked her. 'It's a noble profession!'

'Yes, papa,' she sing-songed dutifully.

Sanbart laughed his big Italian laugh. 'Come on, little girl, if this is boring, I will show you the *teinturerie*. That is something a little more fun than all these skins lying around.'

He took us to the factory, where we looked out over a lot full of barely-covered baths bubbling like witches' brew. The dye works consisted of a series of well-aerated tubs covered with tin roofs. We watched from a platform as the machines pulled out swathes of cotton and wool and big pieces of leather and transferred them from one bath to the other.

'That's so you can get the perfect colour. The longer you leave it in, the more intense the dye gets. You move it from one bath to the other to mix the shade you want.'

It was quite mesmerising, watching the bright indigo and burgundy and ochre cloths carried around and splashing in the baths.

'Can they make pink?' Rouena piped up.

'Oh yes,' Sanbart said. 'I can make a thousand different shades of pink. If you brought me all your clothes I could dye them all.'

I shot him a warning look. Luckily the concept of a thousand shades of pink was too magical for Rouena to latch onto anything else.

'Now, now, be careful, little one or I will tan YOU!' he shouted suddenly, jumping at her, laughing. Rouena squealed and ran away. Sanbart looked up at me and smiled: 'You see, business can be entertaining, even for small children!'

As a banker, I have had the good fortune to travel to many exotic and interesting locations. I always found the Far East to be a particularly fascinating area. We had Japanese partners in our bank, and often on my trips I made a stop in South Korea.

South Korea is very much a world apart from North Korea, but it was possible to go and stand near the border that divided the two countries and observe the frontier guards who kept them apart. It was truly eye-opening, to see how little separated South Korea from its neighbour.

At this time, in the early 1980s, South Korea was just getting on the right track to becoming a real player on the world stage. These serious, studious people were committed to bettering themselves and becoming as important as the Japanese, who dominated the technological market. My clients included conglomerates like Hyundai, and many up and coming construction and engineering companies. I could see how the people of South Korea could push themselves and become as great as their Japanese competition.

The people in South Korea were especially intriguing to me. One day, I was alone in my hotel room when there came a knock on the door. I was preparing for an appointment and had no plans to meet with anybody before that.

Nevertheless, I answered the door and found a rather voluptuous Korean woman in her forties. I hadn't met her in any of my previous meetings and didn't think she worked with or for our clients, and my first thought was that she was perhaps looking for company of another kind.

'Hello,' I said, trying to mask my surprise and impatience, 'how may I help you? I'm not looking for any company just now.'

She stared at me for a moment and shook her head expressively, waving her hands as if to illustrate the words she was trying to speak. 'No! No, I am next door. Room 407. You are 406.'

I have something of a talent for understanding accents, but even for me it was a struggle. She spoke with such a thick Korean accent that it was almost impossible for me to work out what she was trying to say. From what I could tell, her English was also very fragmented, broken up with quick pauses as she searched for the right words.

'You speak good English,' she eventually said.

I nodded. 'Yours isn't bad.' It was somewhat less than true, but I hoped that a well-placed compliment would persuade her to leave rather than offer me anything else. She was looking at me with such interest that I was sure she was about to ask me to take her out at least.

'I can pay you,' she said.

I was stunned by her forwardness. 'Pay me... pay me for what, exactly?'

'If I pay you fifty dollars, will you speak English with me for one hour?' She gave me the most appealing, hopeful look.

'Hang on a minute. That's what you want? For me to speak English with you?' I couldn't help but feel let down by her odd intentions. 'You don't want to go for dinner? Or drinks?' Finally, I realised she could not be a streetwalker, as I had originally assumed, and I took note of her formal style of clothing. She was dressed as if for a meeting herself. 'What are you doing here, then? At this hotel?'

She peered at me as if it should have been obvious. 'I am on a business trip. But my English... it is not good. I need to speak to clients. I need more business, and you can only make money with good English, can't you? Get a better start at things.' She nodded, as though agreeing with herself. 'Can you speak with me? One hour. It's best to speak, face to face.'

I laughed, still taken aback. 'I doubt you could afford me. It'd be more like three hundred dollars an hour for my services.' It was only a joke, designed to lighten the mood and get her to see that I couldn't take her seriously. I was no teacher. It seemed ludicrous that a stranger would expect me to teach her English in my very few spare moments.

'Oh.' She apparently didn't take it as a joke at all, and looked crestfallen. 'That is a Korean salary for a whole month. I cannot afford... my room was only seventy dollars for my whole stay and I thought...'

'Listen, I'm really sorry, madam. But even if you could afford it, I can't spare an hour to talk English with you. I can talk with you for ten minutes if you like, free of charge. It would be my pleasure.' I paused and thought about all the people I had known who learned English for business purposes. 'Have you heard of Berlitz? They do a wonderful course through books, if you don't have time to attend proper lessons.'

She raised her hand to stop me from proceeding with my advice. 'Lessons, courses. This is all very expensive. I don't have the money for those things.'

I was, I admit, growing slightly more than impatient with her. I wanted to be left alone to prepare for my meetings. 'You could always watch English television. That's a good way to learn.'

'We don't have English television programmes in Korea. I learn English so far by stopping tourists. Young people, students, they are very cheap but they don't talk business. I pay them ten dollars for an hour. But you are a businessman, very important, and you know more. I pay you fifty.'

'You could use the fifty dollars to buy some books and tapes. They're really quite useful.'

'I have many, many. I learn at home. But they don't help when you want to have a conversation. There is no… no give, no take. I need to know how to talk face to face with people.' She crossed her arms and looked at me sharply. 'Fifty dollars, sir. Please?'

At this point, I actually began to somewhat admire her tenacity. She was completely determined to have me teach her and I almost wished that I had the time. For me, she represented the atmosphere of the country at the time, the feeling of forward motion. I had seen many companies making cars and electronics, silks and clothes. It was starting to become a master of production.

'Look, you are very much on the right track. Korea is lucky to have people like you. From what I've seen, you're making great strides already. I appreciate your generous offer. I bought a suitcase here yesterday for only eight dollars, I know that fifty is a lot for you to give.'

She seemed relieved that I knew this. 'Yes,' she sounded saddened, 'yes, it is a lot.'

'But I really can't help you. I really am sorry, my hours are very important and when I have a spare one, I have to rest.'

'If you could only…'

'I'm sorry, the answer is no.'

After this, she did leave me to myself, apologising for my lost time. Her limited English was a problem, no question, but she had a quality that could not be learned. She was driven and dedicated to what she wanted, and I was sure that she would find somebody who would teach her what she needed to know and that she would become a great success, entirely without my help.

A SPIRITUAL NEIGHBOUR

Simone Weil is another one of my neighbours in spirit, as she is buried in Ashford, Kent, where I lived for a long time, and is also connected to France, where I spent many years. She is a fascinating Frenchwoman and anglophile, political activist and Christian mystic, pacifist and soldier. Weil is remembered mostly for her philosophical writings, her particular blend of strength and weakness, and her death at the young age of thirty-four.

Weil was born in Paris in 1909 to a middle-class family, and very quickly developed the intense sympathy for the miserable and suffering that she would become famous for. Thus, at the age of just six years old, she refused to eat sugar after finding out that soldiers in the trenches of World War I were deprived of it.

She was an incredibly intelligent girl. By the age of twelve, she was proficient in Ancient Greek, to which she would add Sanskrit a few years later, when she began to study the world religions. Although not raised in a religious environment, she gradually became more and more drawn to the teachings of Christianity. She ended up writing extensively on the subject, and is considered by many an expert in the field of mysticism.

Simone Weil grew into a beautiful, slender young woman with short, dark hair and intense eyes. In her disregard for material things and physical pleasure, however, she decided not to have any love affairs. She usually dressed in baggy clothing, and almost never wore makeup.

She studied philosophy at the elite École Normale Supérieure, along with literature, history, political theory, and mathematics. After completing her education, Weil became a school teacher and professor, although she took time off at various points, both for health reasons, and to devote herself to political activism. For instance, in 1934, she took a year out in order to work as an anonymous labourer in two different factories, with the intention of getting to better understand the working class. She also participated in some of the principal French general strikes, protesting unemployment, wage cuts and unfair working conditions.

Over this time, her left-leaning political side grew. She read Marx and Engels voraciously, and began to write her own tracts on the worker's conditions. She got into several intellectual arguments with Trotsky, who treated her as a fool at first, but eventually came to admire her determination and even incorporate some of her arguments into his own discourse.

Politics essentially dominated this phase of her life. In 1936, despite being a pacifist, she ran away to fight in the Spanish Civil War on the Republican side. Unfortunately, soldiering was not exactly her most successful venture. She was myopic and somewhat clumsy, and consequently did not have very good aim. This meant that she was unpopular in missions and allegedly only shot a gun twice the whole time she was deployed. She did, however, come home with some interesting scars, from when she was burned in a kitchen fire.

Upon her return, she headed over to London to join the French Resistance during the Second World War. She intended to train as a spy and code-breaker, but her weak health got the better of her. She contracted tuberculosis soon after her arrival. Her recovery was hampered by the fact that she refused to eat more than what she believed soldiers in occupied France were allowed. The illness got progressively worse, and she transferred to a sanatorium in Ashford, where she died soon after.

Simone Weil is buried in Ashford, and there is a small memorial to her not so very far from my house. There is also a section of the A28 road named after her. She was obviously a headstrong and intelligent woman, who believed so strongly in her principles that she would happily die for them.

A RUSSIAN IN ROME

In 1992, I happened to be staying in a famous hotel in Rome. For once, I was on a cultural rather than a business trip, visiting the Vatican Library and the Vatican Museum, which are two of my favourite locations in the world. I love manuscripts, and could happily spend hours at a time looking over obscure and fascinating documents. Spending a day poring over papers and coming away enriched with knowledge is like going into a jewellery shop and getting all the jewels as a gift for free. In these two places, some of the manuscripts date as far back as to the ninth century, although most of them are medieval. When I felt like taking a break from enjoying these manuscripts in Latin, Greek, German, and French, I would move on to the Museum. There, I could feast my eyes whilst resting my brain a little, enjoying the most magnificent statues spanning almost all of Western culture, from the birth of Christ all the way to the dawn of industrialism. A day spent like this would be, in essence, a perfect holiday for me. After one such blissful day, I walked back across town to the sound of church bells, feeling like I was on top of the world. I watched the sun set from a terrace café, where I enjoyed my favourite Italian dish of pasta Alfredo, with its distinctive cream sauce and just a touch of nutmeg. I twirled the strands of sweet, Parmesan-sprinkled papardelle around my fork as I thought back over the day's intellectual and spiritual discoveries. After a last glass of cold San Pellegrino, I headed back to my hotel with a full stomach and a calm mind. I wrote down some of my thoughts in my notebook, then retired to bed fairly early and fell into a deep, contented sleep.

I was awoken in the dead at night by a heavy, insistent knock on the door. I sat up in a fright in the pitch darkness, with my heart pounding. I switched the lamp on my bedside table on, and remembered my settings. I glanced at the digital alarm clock and saw that it was around five in the morning. The knock came again, louder than before, and accompanied by a loud Italian voice. 'I'm coming,' I shouted back, before throwing on my bathrobe and scrambling across the room. I opened the door to find three policemen in intense discussion. The tallest and blondest of them turned to me sternly, and said something in Russian. 'I'm so sorry,' I said, flabbergasted.

'What?' The other two policemen, who were obviously Italian, turned to each other and frowned.

'You're under arrest,' the blonde policeman added in a heavy Russian accent.

'There must be some mistake,' I replied hastily.

'I'm looking for Mr Kowzowski,' the Russian added.

'You've got the wrong man,' I responded, as politely as possible. 'I'm Bradley Jamieson.' The Italians looked rather relieved. 'I can get my ID if you like,' I added.

'That won't be necessary,' one of the other policemen cut in. 'We must just have the wrong room. Do you know Mr Kowzowski?'

'I'm afraid I don't,' I replied reluctantly.

'Could you show us some ID all the same?' the Russian asked.

'It's standard procedure,' the other Italian explained apologetically.

'That's fine, just give me one minute.'

I went back into the room to find my passport. Meanwhile, outside, I could hear the policemen discussing what to do next. In the time it took me to find my passport and walk back, they checked their documents and realised that Kowzowski was in fact in the room next door, probably deeply asleep. As I reappeared with my identity document clutched in my hand, they ignored me and knocked on my neighbour's door. I hesitated: was I to stay and watch the arrest? Would this be dangerous? Or should I retreat to my room, at the risk of appearing to ignore their order? I decided to stay for a moment, in order to better judge the situation. The door was opened, but I didn't see a face. A pronounced smell of cigarette smoke came from the dark room, and the three policemen entered and began interrogating whoever was inside quite heavily. 'I certainly hope they have the right person this time,' I muttered under my breath, pacing up and down in my bathrobe. The voices in the room escalated, and the door slammed shut.

I was about to head back into my bedroom to try and recover my lost slumber, but just a moment later the door flew open again. The three policemen reappeared, dragging with them a very tall, very muscular blonde man with a crew cut. His hands were behind his back and handcuffed. The man – Kowzowski, I presumed – struggled a bit at first, then appeared to give in to his arrest. I backed into the wall as he went past me, a pronounced reek of cigarettes and sweat emanating from him. I didn't really care to be accidental collateral damage in this man's arrest! They continued down the corridor quietly and vanished.

I breathed a quiet sigh of relief and walked back into my room, closing the door carefully. I threw off my robe and crawled back under the covers. I was just drifting off to sleep when there came another knock on the door, this one far more tentative. Rather grumpily, but resigned all the same, I rolled out of bed and grabbed my passport from the bedside table. I opened the door fully expecting to see the three policemen, but in fact discovered the concierge standing there sheepishly, clutching a bottle of Pinot Grigio and a packet of lemon biscuits.

'I'm so sorry,' he said at once, proffering the obviously hastily-procured gifts. 'Those thugs; I had no idea they would disturb our customers. But you see, we have to cooperate with the arrest. Please, take these small tokens of our remorse.'

'That's quite all right,' I said sleepily.

'Please, please, you must take then!'

'I don't drink,' I said vaguely. 'But I'll take the biscuits.'

'Oh, I'll keep the Pinot, then,' he replied, rather confused. 'Fine. It's quality Italian wine, you're missing out.'

There was a short pause, in which I tried to convey a sort of polite fatigue. It was only a few seconds, however, before the concierge burst into speech again, obviously unable to hold back. 'This Kowzowski, you see,' he continued excitedly, 'is apparently some kind of big deal in Russia. We've just witnessed a sort of historical arrest: he's a well-known car smuggler. He's part of some vast Russian deal, you see, a tremendous criminal conspiracy that took over the country after the fall of communism. The crime rate must have tripled after 1990. You see, the fall of the Marxist-Leninist economies meant the collapse of all the infrastructures and safety nets. People were poor and desperate, and people wanted a taste of the West, in any way they could get it. The market opened up chaotically, and unregulated. There was, of course, huge capital flight and low foreign investment. That's how you get a sharp rise in crime: I'm talking about drugs, arms, and car theft. A whole lot of car theft. It's true James Bond stuff: payoffs, and checkpoints, briefcases of money, spies. So this Kowzowski, what he does is smuggle luxury cars. They have Mercedes, they have BMWs, they have all the cars folks like us can only dream of. I think it would make a great movie.'

He paused. I couldn't really think of a response that didn't involve going off into a discussion about either luxury cars or the fall of communism, neither of which, quite frankly, I could face at six in the morning. The concierge still looked no closer to curtailing his monologue. 'Apparently, all these Russians make big money this way,' he continued conversationally. 'Some of them are big businessmen already, you see, oilmen and bankers and politicians. They all work together to get a cut. They have other jobs, they just do it on the side in order to double their profits,' he added somewhat unnecessarily. 'Everyone is doing it. They're smuggling Dior, Hermès, anything that smacks of luxury, capitalism, all the forbidden, foreign ideals. The Russians aren't buying Russian, you see. On a small scale, what they do is to drive brand new cars that they buy in Italy all the way to Ukraine and Russia, where they sell them at a higher price than they would fetch here.' He mimed pushing a toy car across a map. 'They smuggle the cars straight through the borders, pretending they are just their own cars, you know? Everyone is stealing a cut of the profits, you see. Sometimes, the big guys, they actually just ship a load of cars across the border. Kowzowski's been keeping a low profile lately, but it didn't save him. No wonder these days we're always used to reading in the papers about this and that man getting killed!' His chaotic, enthusiastic rambling trailed off.

'Yes,' I said, rubbing my eyes as obviously as I could manage. 'I do see,' I added with a trace of irony.

'You sure had the wrong neighbour tonight,' he added, completely oblivious to my tone. He smiled and rubbed his hands together. 'Are you enjoying your time in Rome?'

I blinked slowly. 'I was,' I respond carefully.

The concierge grinned brightly. 'I'm glad to hear it. Have you seen the museums?'

'I have,' I said quietly. I then yawned as conspicuously as I could. After another long pause, the concierge got the message, or just went off to talk to someone else. In any case, he finally bid me goodnight and left the room. I got back into bed as quickly as I could, and pulled the sheets up under my neck. As I tried to clear my head of the chaos of having almost been arrested, and then bored to death, I thought back to my precious manuscripts. How long ago, it seemed, I had been at peace with the world, worried only about medieval script, wandering streets and eating creamy papardelle! I spared a thought for the mysterious Kowzowski. Not only was he going to spend the night in a hard cell; he would presumably also never know the joy of deciphering ninth-century Latin script. Just before I fell asleep, I found myself thinking how lucky I was, in the end.

THE FRIGHTENED NEIGHBOUR

In the early 1990s, one of my favourite hotels in New York City, aside from the Plaza and the St Regis, was the Helmsley Hotel. Standing just down the road from the Rockefeller centre, the Helmsley towers over the very heart of Manhattan. Its location is superbly convenient, within walking distance of MoMA and St Patrick's Cathedral. Some visitors might enjoy the view from the top of the 30 Rock building itself, whilst others might look forward to a glamorous shopping binge at Saks Fifth Avenue. One of my preferred features of the neighbourhood, however, was slightly less well-known: it was, in fact, my favourite Chinese restaurant in New York. The Tsian Yang was famous for their Cantonese sea bass, steamed with ginger and shiitake mushrooms, and for their thin strips of caramelised beef, sweet and sticky with soy sauce and honey. They also had one of the best incarnations of the traditional Peking duck that I have ever encountered.

On one of my regular visits to New York for banking reasons, I was assigned a lovely suite on one of the top floors. From my window on the forty-second of forty-six floors, I could look down over the city skyline and Central Park. An interesting feature of the building was its structure, which curved outwards from the summit towards the base, so that if one looked down from above, the building sloped towards the pavement. Architecturally, it was a fantastic structure; as a hotel, it could hardly be more comfortable. On this particular night, like any other, after a gorgeous dinner at Tsian Yang, I climbed in under the goose-feather duvet, read my book for a while and settled into a deep sleep.

My dreams, for one reason or another, were troubled. Perhaps the Cantonese sea bass hadn't agreed with my system. In the middle of the night, in any case, I was abruptly awakened by a wailing alarm, overlaid with a strangely calm voice which seemed to fill the room. It took me a few seconds to realise that this was in fact the fire alarm. 'Keep calm,' the announcement was saying, on a haunting loop, 'This is not a drill.' If any words could be calculated to have a less calming effect on the human mind, I cannot imagine what they are. 'Stay in your rooms. Do not open the doors. Do not move through the corridors. Do not use the stairs. Do not attempt to use the elevators.

Do not panic.' I found my watch and squinted at the dial in the light from my bedside table lamp. It was just after two in the morning. I sighed, as a vision of the next day's work floated unbidden into my head. It was going to be a tough morning.

At this point, there was a sharp knock on the door. Assuming this was a part of the drill, possibly a planned evacuation, I moved towards it at once. I assumed, of course, that it would present me with a calm concierge; a be-suited employee, come to usher me down the smoky corridors. 'Do not open the doors,' the looping announcement said again, with eerie timing. I froze. I stood for a moment in shock, listening to the haunting voice of the announcement. I was still more bemused than I was frightened, but I was unsure how I was expected to deal with this situation. What if I opened the door, and it killed me? This time, I paid attention to the content of the whole warning: 'Keep calm,' it began again, 'This is not a drill. Stay in your rooms. Go to the bathroom. Wrap your head in a towel. Lie face down in the bathtub. Do not open the doors. Do not panic.' The voice was severe, rather glum, like an obituary might sound read out of the radio. It felt as though I was being told off by a rather stern American professor. This unnerved me, and I began to feel a creeping of fear in my stomach. Surely they wouldn't announce to us that this wasn't a drill if it were anything but a real and terrible threat?

The knock on the door came again, and I found myself paralysed with indecision. 'Please,' a very small voice came from outside. 'Open the door.' This, coupled with the strangely calm tone of the announcement, started to make me more than a little anxious. I was alone in my suite, and growing increasingly scared of opening the door. What if the corridor was full of fumes? I thought. I had learned from reading that more people die in fires from breathing carbon dioxide than from being burned. Surely I didn't want to contribute to such an awful statistic? What if the hotel had already descended into smoky chaos, and people were trying to find refuge in my room? What if people were looting? I should go to the bathroom, I reasoned. I should follow the instructions, and start to calm down. Despite being very placid in tone, the announcement was quite loud. If the volume, coupled with the threat of death, weren't enough to quickly drive a person mad, the looping certainly would.

The bangs on the door became louder and louder. The squeaking voice became slightly clearer. 'Open the door,' it said in panicky tones. 'I'm your neighbour! I'm scared! I need to hide! Please,' it repeated in a very broken voice. I couldn't bear the thought of not helping this person. 'To hell with it,' I thought, 'bring it on, fate. If this person has survived this long and is still able to talk, he's obviously not been fumigated to death.' I disregarded the recording and, in what felt like a dashing show of bravura, opened the door.

No looter appeared before me, nor a be-suited concierge; nor were there any clouds of smoke visible. Instead, there appeared a very small, very old Japanese man. He was wearing a bathrobe and looked completely terrified. 'Oh sir,' he said in a small, squeaky voice, heavily accented: 'Thank you so much. I'm scared. Can you help me?'

'I'm Bradley,' I said, trying to make light of the situation, although I had to admit the man's fear was contagious. 'Don't open the door,' the announcement continued repeating in the background. 'Do be quiet,' I said in the general direction of the ceiling.

'I'm Tasch,' he said slightly panicky, obviously unsure how to react. He hesitated for a moment, bouncing up and down nervously in his hotel-room slippers. 'Please, may I come in?'

'Of course,' I said at once, stepping back to let the small Japanese man into my room. He stood inside, quivering in pure terror. He truly was shaking from the crown of his snow-white hair to the tips of his slippered feet. The announcement continued to loop in the background.

'You really should not have been in the corridor,' I said, taking on a sort of avuncular personality in the face of his obvious distress.

'I know, sir,' he croaked, 'I'm so frightened. I just forgot what to do.'

'This old man,' I said, gesturing in the general direction of the speakers which continued to repeat the message, 'is giving you fairly straightforward instructions.'

'I don't want to be trapped all alone in my tiny room, on the forty-second floor!' he squeaked. 'What a terrible way to die! I want to get out,' he said, in a panicky voice, 'but some people wouldn't let me use the stairs. So I came here.'

'There's no way out,' I said, trying not to panic myself at the thought. 'But surely in Japan you must be used to catastrophes!

What would you do if this had been an earthquake?'

'Get out,' he answered at once. 'That's the problem. I've never been in a big skyscraper like this. Hotels in Japan can be dangerous, yes, but they are not high. You can always run away. Here, my options are: die alone in the fire; die in collapsing skyscraper; die jumping from building.'

This was not a particularly heartening thought. 'Or,' I added as jovially as I could, 'just wait the thing out, and have champagne when we're rescued.'

'I don't drink,' he said despondently, and a little confused by my apparent glibness. 'Can we hide now?'

'Look,' I said, 'why don't you take the bathtub? Follow the instructions. Wrap up your head in a wet towel and lie in there. I'll sit in here with my book. Perhaps I'll develop a meditation technique to shut out that dastardly announcement.'

'Oh, sir, I couldn't possibly let you sacrifice yourself like that.'

'Please,' I said, 'stop talking like we're going to die.'

'We're going to die,' he said absolutely calmly. 'We're trapped in the top floor of a burning skyscraper. There are not many options.'

'Well you're a jolly companion for the end of days,' I observed. Panic was really starting to get to me at this point. I tried to recapture the feelings I had had at first: exasperation at the announcement, annoyance at the thought of working tired the next morning. But the negative thoughts were hard to get rid of: what if there was no next morning? If Tasch thought we were going to die, who was I to tell him otherwise?

'Do not leave your rooms,' the announcement repeated for the seventieth time or so. I felt a sort of adrenaline flood through me.

'Tasch, listen to me. We're going to get through this,' I said with what I felt was a sort of bravura, like a Shakespearean captain preparing his troops for battle, even in the face of certain defeat. 'There's room in the bathtub for two. We'll get a towel each and huddle in the bath.' Inspiration seized me all at once: 'If the fire comes into the room,' I continued, 'we'll break the window and jump out. The side of the building is curved, after all. We'll just slide down! Then we can just brush ourselves off and walk down the road to my favourite Chinese restaurant. It'll be grand, you'll see.'

I think fear really had begun to addle my brain at this point. Less than ten minutes later, I found myself sitting in the large Jacuzzi bathtub with a complete stranger, helping him to wrap his head in a wet towel. Amusingly, now that I was reduced to little more than a gibbering wreck, Tasch seemed to regain some common sense. 'I think you're crazy,' he said conversationally. 'We're forty floors up. If we jump, we won't be eating any Chinese food. We'll be squashed to a pulp.'

'But there's no other way,' I said glumly. 'We're trapped.'

'I think it's better to die in the smoke,' he said cheerfully. 'But still,' he added, apparently trying to comfort me now! 'If we did jump, and go to the Chinese restaurant, what would you order?'

'The sea bass,' I said sadly, in the tone of one who imagined he would never taste such a dish again. 'Steamed in ginger and scallions with just a bit of black bean sauce,' I muttered, slipping into a culinary reverie. Tasch could probably barely hear me over the sound of the still-repeating announcement, but he nodded calmly. Eventually, both of us found some sort of peace sitting in that bathtub. We mostly sat in companionable silence, listening to the drone of the announcement, for a good hour and a half longer. Occasionally, one of us would get up to stretch our legs, then come back to sit. We also talked a little: about the Japanese village Tasch grew up in; about my banking work in New York; about our favourite Chinese and Japanese dishes.

All at once, however, the announcement stopped. We stared at each other, blinking in stunned silence. The room suddenly seemed very empty: it was as if we were all at once released from a strange trance. The speakers crackled back to life, this time with a live voice. 'Ladies and gentlemen,' we heard in a voice I recognised as that of the general manager, whom I had met only the preceding morning. How long ago that seemed now! 'We would like to apologise for any undue alarm caused. This was in fact a false alarm. The recording was set off accidentally. You can all go back to bed now.' Tasch stared at me. 'You mean it wasn't true? There wasn't even the possibility of a fire?'

I bristled. 'This is ridiculous!' I leapt from the bath. Our mutual friendship, founded on a now-baseless fear, seemed all at once hollow and laughable. I removed the towel from my head hastily. Tasch was just as bemused and embarrassed as I was, presumably at the thought of having had to expose his innermost fears to a stranger for no apparent reason. We bid each other fairly curt, if polite, goodbyes, and headed to our respective beds. Despite the stress, however, I found myself being grateful for Tasch's entry into my room: after all, had he not come over, the evening would have been very different. Although I would probably not have spent it huddling in the bathtub with a towel over my head in the company of a strange Japanese man, I also would probably not have had the deep experience of feeling so close to death that I planned my last meal. There was a certain strange peace in it, and I certainly found myself appreciating New York the more for it, the next day, as I wandered around in a caffeinated haze. Which is not to say I didn't write the hotel an exceedingly sternly-worded letter on the matter!

ESCAPING LANZAROTE

My bank had an investment in Lanzarote, an island I've been fond of for a long time despite its somewhat forbidding climate and appearance. However, because it is a beautiful place, I do have a tendency to forget too easily just how boring it is in reality. My reasoning, in preparing for my trips, is always along the lines of 'it must be better than London!' Of course, at least aesthetically, or geographically, it is. Of all the Canary Islands, it is the most windswept and dramatic; a chunk of volcanic rock rising from the sea. It is a striking place, covered in impressive natural rock sculptures and coated in a thick, sandy coating of ash. In fact, in nearly any part of the island, the visitor can dig only four inches into the dust, set an egg in the hole and cook it in seven minutes. You can't do that on the beaches of the Côte d'Azur! Because the island is completely composed of volcanic rock, the temperature stays relatively stable day and night. This is because the basalt rock absorbs sunlight during the day, and emits the heat during the night. Altogether, it is a strange and impressive place to stay and, although there is little to do on the island, I always do enjoy my visits there - at least for the first two hours or so.

Our bank invested in a housing development there, in partnership with a German company and a major Spanish multinational. Everything proceeded in the typically languid Spanish way, with hours and hours just spend waiting around between appointments. All we had to do was discuss the acquisition and collect a few signatures, but somehow these simple tasks dragged on for days. Such was the level of nonchalance, I was almost surprised they didn't just provide us with lounge chairs and pitchers with sangria. There really wasn't very much to do on Lanzarote, once one had gone to a few of the rocky beaches. Once I had chatted with a few of the other businessmen on their cigarette breaks, eaten a bit of seafood and done a little online shopping, I had pretty much exhausted the limited resources of the place. After pacing up and down the rocks, nearly falling into the steaming rock pools, I found myself wondering if I should buy some eggs to test the ash–cooking story. At this point, I decided some sort of holiday intervention was needed. After all, I was away from grey, rainy London, even if it was only for work. I was supposed to be enjoying this trip! I had brought sunscreen and everything!

I decided that the solution to my problems was not to cook a bunch of eggs, or wreck my shoes on these rocks a minute longer. I would rent a helicopter and go across the sea to Morocco, I reasoned. Agadir was only an hour and a quarter away. I would escape the rocky tedium of the Canaries for a night and sample the familiar delights of Northern Africa. Upon arriving in Agadir, of course, I remembered why I did not spend more time in Morocco in the first place. Like Lanzarote, it did have its delights, but they were somewhat quickly exhausted. For one thing, the temperature was absolutely sweltering. I had forgotten just how hot it could get there. In Agadir, one could probably have boiled an egg just by leaving it outside for a while. In fact, the two main memorable features of Agadir are the scorching sun, which gives the visitor a tan within a day, and the absolutely ubiquitous poverty. As one of the biggest cities of south-western Morocco, Agadir had made huge efforts to modernise after being mostly destroyed by a terrible earthquake in 1960, but had succeeded only in becoming a rather bland resort city. I realised I would have to make the most of yet another less than ideal holiday destination. I found a hotel where the rooms were a series of villas on the beach, overlooking the somewhat dirty waves. My small, private villa was lovely enough if a bit rickety.

There was a market near the coast, although it was not anywhere near as interesting as I imagined the historic Casbah would have been. I quickly found that my immediate neighbour on the beach was actually a snake charmer who worked there. He was a young, swarthy local man with curly, greasy black hair and a pimply face. There was something sleazy about him, but, being as bored as I was, I was also a little curious. Moroccan markets are always full of snake charmers, as they are very skilled at attracting creatures and charming them with clever tricks. I mean tourists, of course. A snake charmer's best skill is magicking money away from an unsuspecting audience. The snakes themselves always look as if they have been drugged, swaying back and forth like drunken youths on a dancefloor. It is hard not to feel a little sorry for them. I once read that modern charmers often remove the venom glands and teeth or even sew the mouths shut, which really took away any fascination I might have had with the ancient act. It simply struck me as barbaric and stupid. Even so, this particular snake charmer did not strike me as being particularly skilled at his craft. He sat well out of the way of the snake as it wriggled around on its rug, and played the flute with far less musical talent than my youngest children. One day, he had a miserable-looking young companion banging on a drum, but he seemed to do most of his 'work' alone. None of this was particularly impressive or entertaining.

Still, I had cause to observe this particular snake charmer closely, as he kept walking in front of my front door on his way back and forth between his own shack and the market beyond. One day, however, I had the occasion to see him from much closer, as, without any warning, he came and knocked on my door. I was a little taken aback, but opened the door to him – again, mostly out of boredom. He smiled, displaying rows of dirty brown teeth. He really did look like quite a shady character. I couldn't help but feel a little bit apprehensive. 'Hello, sir,' he said, nodding his head a little in a strange way, looking for all the world as if he was trying to hypnotise me.

'Hello there,' I said a little hesitantly. 'What can I do for you?' I noticed that he had a sort of shabby, dirty white cloth in his hands. As he held it out towards me, I saw that there was a soft, elongated object wrapped inside. I recoiled. 'Is that a snake?' I asked. 'Is that safe? Is it moving?' He man laughed raucously.

'It is not poisonous, sir,' he said. I edged away from the doorstep, trying to get back within the safety of my house without this strange man noticing. At this point, however, he realised he was quickly losing the advantage of a private audience, and explained. 'I'm bringing you a fresh fish I just caught,' he said. 'Maybe you would like to buy it?' He gave a smile so wide I was worried his jaw might drop off.

'What on earth would I want with a fresh fish?' I asked him. 'I can have a nice meal at the hotel.'

He nodded enthusiastically. 'Yes, a very nice meal! With this fish. You can eat it!' he said. 'Send it to the hotel kitchen and they will cook it for you! They will fry it and boil it and serve it with rice!' His enthusiasm for this theoretical simple meal was rather charming.

I cocked my head to the side pensively, estimating the size of the fish in the cloth. After all, perhaps this was just a peculiar facet of the city's local charm. I was staying on the coast, and I did love to eat fish. Maybe this event wasn't as inappropriate as it seemed, even if it did smell as if this man hadn't washed for at least a week. If a man, however strange and dirty, was to deliver freshly-caught fish to my very doorstep, who was I to refuse?

'It's fresh fish,' he said, as if guessing my one worry, 'of a very rare variety. You can't get this anywhere else.' He unwrapped the top corner delicately. The cloth seemed to stick suspiciously to the fish inside. 'See,' he said hastily, 'look at the silver scales! You can only find this type of fish in the South Atlantic.' He gave me its local name. I looked at the fish. Its eye was completely dull, and its scales didn't look quite as wet or shiny as it seemed to me that they should. I reached over swiftly, noticing the man's impulse to recoil, and removed the white cloth from the fish completely. The fish was a strange colour, bent at a weird angle, and the stench was overwhelming. 'That's a rotten fish,' I sighed, hardly able to believe the situation I found myself in. 'You may as well have brought me a snake,' I said dryly. 'There's no way on earth I'm eating that thing.'

'No, no,' the man assured me with something akin to desperation, 'it's freshly caught! I went fishing out to sea, I caught it yesterday!'

'Are you quite sure? It smells like you caught it five days ago, and then kept it in the sun. Are you really trying to tell me this isn't just something your snakes dragged in?'

'It's just like a marinade!' he said as brightly as he could. 'All natural! I hung it up after I gutted it so it would taste better.'

'I'm sure you've achieved that,' I replied. 'I'm sure it tastes just like guts. Do you even have a fridge in your little shack?'

He looked at me blankly. 'I keep many snakes,' he said hopefully. 'Maybe you would like to see some snakes, sir?'

'No thank you,' I said, 'I'm going back to London.'

THE BOAT NEIGHBOUR

Whatever F. Scott Fitzgerald or Hemingway might have led you to believe, Cannes can be a rather dull place to stay. It's beautiful, of course, but what exactly is there to do? Kipling describes the port in summer as being 'like the third act of a music-hall revue,' with its 'pink and white houses, blinding sun, blinding green vegetation, roses, wisteria, irises, judas trees, even hydrangeas and rhododendrons all out together.' I would be inclined to add that most of one's time in Cannes feels rather more like a lengthy intermission; one in a crowded theatre where the ushers have run out of ice creams. After one has walked up and down the Croisette a few times, and toured the nicer shops, its appeal is essentially used up. To be perfectly honest, I find one can be bored of the Croisette by the time one gets to the end of it the first time round. Once one has seen one sea view, one has really seen them all! After a week or ten days in Cannes, I would usually get to a state where I was actually looking forward to getting in to work and doing business in the morning. Like everyone, I enjoy the occasional lazy morning, but I would much rather read the paper and have a quick espresso before heading off to be productive!

It wasn't that our guest house wasn't pleasant, or that its location was anything but charming. It was simply that a sort of Provençal languor permeated the area, making stays there feel more like a long holiday in the sun than like a true business trip. Once the weather started to cool off, the atmosphere became much worse, as even the feeble pretence of holidaymakers' excitement faded away, and only a few disgruntled locals remained. After two weeks in Cannes in the autumn, even a trip to a client's house, or a short tour of the chilly bay in their yacht started to look like a welcome bit of excitement. Of course, once on the actual boat, it would be nothing to write home about: a falsely chatty aperitif, some predictable canapés of smoked salmon or, if the client felt like showing off, a couple of Arcachon oysters.

Still, after one particularly adventurous day out, I found myself longing for those slow mornings and identical evenings. In this particular case, I was invited by a particular minister from the Gulf to spend the day on his boat in the port of Cannes. After the oil crisis of 1973, many of the Arabian ministers, whether they were involved with housing, commerce, oil or health, seemed to suddenly become rather rich, and began to gravitate to the luxurious beaches of Cannes. They were a welcome addition to our client base, and they certainly brought a certain excitement to the predictable shores of the South of France. We were working on a rather important banking deal, although I suspected that most of the day would be spent in pleasantries. By this time, it was November, and I was down on a short business trip from Paris. The weather in the city was horrible this time of year: there are few things less agreeable than walking down the dirty streets with one's coat clutched around oneself, being whipped with gales that feel like they have blown in straight from the Siberian steppes! A trip to the Côte d'Azur had seemed like a welcome break. Of course, once on the scene, the familiar boredom had descended quite quickly, not helped by the fact that the weather in the South of France was only marginally warmer than in the Ile-de-France.

I set out to the client's yacht, bracing against the cold, wet wind that blew in off the Mediterranean. It wasn't far above zero degrees centigrade out, and the breeze felt as if it had swept part of the sea with it in order to fling itself under my scarf and between my coat buttons. When I finally spied the boat, I was reminded of Maupassant's description of his yacht at Cannes as a 'great white bird:' it was a vast and impressive creature, bright white, shrouded in fog from its engines. It was a great relief, at first, to step onto the minister's warm boat. The boat itself was luxurious: forty metres long and with a lovely polished mahogany and brass interior. The client welcomed me as if he were an Arabian sheikh, except of course that he was wearing cargo shorts and a Filipino-looking printed shirt in bright colours. The contrast between us was amusing: I must have looked like some sort of dishevelled seafarer, just come in from the perilous journey across the wintry port – I probably had frost in my hair! – while my host looked as if he had just recently been sipping cocktails on a Hawaiian beach, surrounded by hula girls. In fact, his hair looked oddly sweaty, as if his headscarf had been recently removed. I quickly understood why: the interior of the boat was positively steaming. It must have been eighteen or twenty degrees in there. I wouldn't have been surprised if my client had been sunburned!

As soon as we sat down to discuss our business, I began to feel nauseated. The shock of humid heat coming straight on the heels of the bitter wind was excessive: I felt rather like one of those travellers in the Sahara who, coming upon cold water at the end of a long, burning trip on camelback, drink it too fast and make themselves terribly ill. It was not, however, just a question of a temperature shock that my organism was having trouble handling, but an increasingly horrible smell: the whole yacht smelled of diesel fumes. The engine was running, which in itself would not have been surprising had we been anything but firmly docked and moored in the port. Thus, we sat on the upper deck of the yacht, pretending to have great fun discussing business, while the fumes wound up from the belly of the ship and filled the room. The smell was nauseating, sweet and vile all at once. I began to sweat heavily. My host, however, did not seem to be troubled. He sat back easily in his shorts and t-shirt, nattering on and on about whatever project we were working on. It occurred to me that this must be how he always received people on his boat: that motor had probably been running for months now! I began to feel slightly faint. It wasn't just the smell of fuel that was starting to disturb me, but the uneven up-and-down movement of the boat in the port. Every time a boat came in or headed out, it made a series of waves that sent us tilting left and right. Even the large size of the boat didn't compensate for this.

Noting that I must have turned a slightly greenish tinge, my host offered me some tea. I accepted gratefully, imagining perhaps a cool cup of ice tea with a sliver of lemon, which might have helped with what was starting to feel like seasickness. Instead, what I was presented with was a glass of hot tea so syrupy it left sticky marks on the pitcher. The shock of sweet tea was just too reminiscent of the cloying stench of the engine fumes, and after just one gulp I had to excuse myself to be sick over the railings. Clinging to the side of the boat, I breathed in the miserable cold air of the port gratefully. Even the strange sea stench seemed comforting after that sickening sweetness.

I found myself wondering why my host was on a boat at all. If he wanted to be in the warmth by the side of the water, surely he could just have found a nice house on the side of the port! I understand why one would love to have a boat to travel the seas from Cannes to Corsica, Sardinia, Venice, even North Africa, but why would one want to have a boat just to sit in? Shaking my head, I went back inside and finished off the deal with my client as swiftly as I could. I confessed to feeling rather queasy, in response to which he was sympathetic, if a bit surprised.

He didn't quite seem to understand the situation, though, as for months afterwards, he would continually beg for me to come to his boat again. He was obviously proud of it, thinking of it as a delightfully comfortable place of luxury, rather than the poisonous, seasickness-inducing sauna it really was. I couldn't admit the whole thing had made me feel sick, being rather embarrassed at what felt like an admission of weakness. Therefore, I ended up having to invent a series of increasingly unlikely excuses to avoid these invitations: doctor's appointments, trips to Paris or London, visits from sickly relatives. The awful thing was that it probably ended up looking like I was just trying to avoid the man himself, when really it was just his boat that I feared.

Amusingly, a few years after we had lost contact, I made an interesting discovery from one of my colleagues who still worked with him.

'Oh, it's awful, that boat, isn't it!' he began when I mentioned my unpleasant memories of that whole time.

'Just atrocious. I never went back. I suppose I probably lost us a good client by not spending enough time buttering him up, but I couldn't stand the thought of ever being on that horrible yacht again.'

'Ah, but do you know the reason why he was so adamant that visits should be on his boats?'

'You mean there's some logic to it?'

'Well, something like that. The thing is, the man's house is actually a dirty, undecorated shambles. I was once invited there when the boat was taken for repairs, and, to be honest, it may be hard to believe but the house was even hotter and smellier than the boat! The carpets were dirty, the whole place looked really badly maintained. He knew it too; you could tell he was ashamed. I think he actually spent much of his own time avoiding his home. He probably spent all his money and time keeping the boat nice.'

'If the boat seems nice in comparison to the other, I'm glad I never had to see the house!'

It turned out I had been doubly lucky, then: to avoid ever having to go back on that boat, and to have never seen the house. The experience also made me grateful for the humdrum business of the Côte d'Azur, and the usual aperitif meetings with clients. It may be a well-known saying that 'familiarity breeds contempt,' but familiarity also breeds comfort. I may have become blasé about Cannes over my many visits there, but, after that incident, I never took its peaceful charm for granted again.

KEN AND BILL, THE RACING BROTHERS

As a student of engineering at Daytona in the 1960s, I became involved with open-wheeled formula racing as a hobby. There is just nothing quite like the thrill of speeding around a circuit in the bright Florida sun with little more than a flimsy, brilliant little piece of metal between one's body and the road. I got quite good at it in those days, racing every few weekends and even getting involved in Formula Three. My neighbour Ken was also a racer, although a marginally more successful one than I, so we often headed off together, sometimes spending whole weekends down at the track, zooming around like the irresponsible young men that we were.

Formula Three, although not as well-known as the high-class Formula One, is nonetheless an internationally-recognised championship that has been around since the 1950s. Many participants in Formula Three go on to get involved in Formula One racing: in fact, almost all Formula One hopefuls feel that their careers are getting serious by the point at which they start racing at this level. Now, I had no intention of getting involved in Formula One. I valued my life, for one thing, and besides I had the promise of other, less death-defying career options ahead of me. Nonetheless, I did enjoy it tremendously, although I never quite won the races. I was young, of course. Later in life, I came to recognise formula racing as one of the stupidest sports that humanity has created, being as how it consists of flinging instruments of death at high speed across asphalt. Besides, I have seen too many accidents to either enjoy or participate in it anymore. But in those days, it absolutely thrilled me, and even when I wasn't racing, I ended up getting involved in it in some way. For instance, even when I wasn't at the wheel, my neighbour Ken liked to take me along to the Daytona International Speedway to go and cheer him on, often in the company of his brother Bill. Bill didn't race himself, but he was a car mechanic, and although he occasionally enjoyed watching the race with a beer in hand, what he truly loved was to be on the side of the track, fixing up the cars as they sped on their way.

One day, Ken rang my doorbell on a Sunday morning. 'Want to do something exciting with your weekend?' he greeted me with a grin.

I blinked a little in the bright sun, my first coffee of the day having barely kicked in. 'Well, that depends. What are you suggesting? I was finding my quiet read-through of the *Sunday Times* over freshly-brewed coffee pretty exciting, myself.'

'Not quite as exciting as racing,' he replied, with a glint in his eye.

'You know I'm not racing at the moment,' I said, a little confused.

'Ah, but I am.' Seeing my face, Ken laughed. 'Now, hear me out. I'm not just coming around to your house at the crack of dawn to drum up some spectators. I know you come and watch me often enough, and don't think I don't appreciate it every single time. But I've got a slightly different favour to ask you this time. Bill's working the pit stop this afternoon, at the race, and his partner has dropped out at the last minute. I was wondering if you would mind helping him out?'

'I've never worked at the pit stop, you know,' I replied cautiously.

'That's no problem. Bill knows you, and he knows you're a keen racer yourself. You know the cars and the parts, you know how to refuel, and you can change a tyre. Any odd mechanical problems Bill can sort out. He just needs the extra manpower!'

'Well, I'm not sure how much manpower I can offer before my second cup of coffee,' I replied. Then again, it is a gorgeous day. And it's not *exactly* the crack of dawn.' I paused briefly, then gave in. After all, why not? It seemed like an experience worth having, and it's always hard to turn a friendly neighbour down. 'Why don't you come in for a cup of coffee, and then we can head on over.'

'Thanks a million,' Ken beamed. 'You're the best.'

Less than an hour later, we were at the track, preparing for the day's races. The Daytona International Speedway is a huge race track with multiple layouts, most famous for hosting NASCAR, as it was set up by that organism's founder in the late 1950s. On a summer's day it was a crazy, exciting place, heady with the fumes of petrol and the shouts of the spectators. Working in the pit stop was a great combination for me of being both a mechanic and a spectator. We set up and lay in wait, with all our resources within easy reach. The tension was at its highest the moment we heard the first cars start up, with that distinctive zooming sound that never ceased to surprise me with its shrillness.

'They're off!' Bill said cheerily. From the flush in his cheeks I could see that, even after years of doing this, the start of a race still absolutely thrilled him. 'Better get ready,' I answered, wiping the sweat from my brow. After just two laps, the cars started pulling off abruptly at the side of the track. Our first customer needed to be refuelled, probably due to some kind of minor leak. The next two needed tyres changed: I had to acquire the skill of changing tyres as fast as physically possible! Luckily, I had a knack for it, but it was both incredibly stressful and terribly hard work. I can solemnly declare that since 1968 I have never changed a tyre again, in any car! The next car to screech to a halt by us had something wrong with its engine, which Bill managed to fix in less than two and a half minutes using only a screwdriver. I had to marvel at the skill of it, and at the obvious enthusiasm that he had for the job.

I could tell, too, that he was watching for his brother and grinning every time Ken's souped-up Triumph zipped past us. His excitement warmed my heart – although perhaps the boiling midday sun had something to do with that! About two thirds of the way through the race time, Ken pulled up at our pit stop. 'There's something wrong with my engine,' he panted. 'God, it's so damn hot out there!' Ken pulled off his helmet with a sigh, and knelt down next to his brother. 'Can you see what's wrong?'

'Well, your seat's come loose, for one thing. If you hand me that screwdriver I can tighten it, it'll only take a second.' Once he looked under the hood of the car, though, he frowned a little. 'There's something wrong with the spark plug. We probably don't have time to fix this,' he muttered under his breath. 'Brad, would you get my little brother a fresh helmet while I cobble this together?'

'Just the quickest thing you can do,' Ken said quietly. 'I need to get out there!'

'Don't worry, bro!' Bill said, already elbow-deep in the body of the car. 'I'll have this sorted in no time.' The sound of the competitors' cars speeding past gave the whole scene a terrible urgency. I could feel sweat trickling down my brow. At last, Bill shook his head and slammed the hood shut. 'Go, now. This should hold you through til the end.' He slapped his brother on the back affectionately as he climbed back into the front seat. Then he sped off, and within four seconds he was around the corner and invisible to us once more. Bill wiped the back of his hand across his forehead, leaving a grimy mark behind. Ten minutes later, there came a roar from the crowd, and the engine noise gradually died down. Over the loudspeakers, we heard the sound of Ken's name. 'He won!' Bill shouted gleefully. 'My little brother won!' He then grabbed me in an excessively oily and sweaty bear-hug. I felt pride swelling in my breast. There was something special about feeling involved in the win, even if it just meant standing by the sidelines and changing tyres. We had contributed in a tangible way to my friend and neighbour Ken's victory, and that was a wonderful thing to know.

Incidentally, this would turn out to be the last race that Ken won, which added to the glamour I felt in being involved with it. Of course, he continued to risk his life in the high-adrenaline world of racing for years, but that was his last big tournament win. I like to believe my presence in some way contributed to the atmosphere that led to that victory!

Stephanie was very much alone. She lived in my building in Paddington, when I was attending the London School of Economics. During my time living there, we often passed each other on the landing, her in her fluffy dressing gown going down to get the post, me off to the LSE to work on my PhD.

She was a pretty woman of Irish heritage, about ten years older than me, and rather shy and quiet. She would say hello and not much else, and I never saw a friend come in to visit her, or caught her husband on the stairs. I could hardly imagine two people living in her tiny flat, but she had once told me that her husband worked away, that he was always selling this and that, toothpaste and mouthwash and a various assortment of things, in Manchester or Doncaster, northern places that she seemed to think were incredibly far away.

Aside from these little titbits, it wasn't really until the day she came knocking on my door than I knew anything about her at all.

It was the middle of the day and I didn't have any classes to attend. I wasn't expecting anyone, but I answered the rather frantic knocking all the same. Stephanie was there, wrapped in her dressing gown, her face streaked with tears.

Without even so much as a good afternoon, she burst out with, 'I think my baby's coming!'

I blinked. 'You're pregnant?' I said, a bit disbelieving.

She nodded. 'It's early, but. Oh.' She reached out a gripped my arm. 'Please, please could you take me to the hospital? Or phone me an ambulance? Anything, *oh...*' She looked as though she might faint at any moment, so I did as she asked and called for an ambulance. I had no idea what to do with her except sit her down and fetch her a glass of cold water. At twenty-three years old I hadn't really had any experiences of women having babies and the whole thing was a dreadful shock.

'Sit with me?' she asked pitifully, and so I did until the ambulance arrived to take her to hospital.

I expected that that would be the end of it and thought that the next time I would see Stephanie, she'd have a baby in her arms and hopefully her husband would be home to take care of her.

However, it was barely an hour later that Stephanie was once again knocking on my door, a blush inching up her neck.

I peered around her as though she might be concealing a newborn behind her back. 'Did you have the baby?'

She burst into nervous laughter and I could feel her embarrassment. 'Oh, no. About that. I'm so sorry. It seems it was a false alarm. But... thank you for being so good.'

'Um... you're welcome.'

The entire event left me bemused. How could she think she was having a baby when she wasn't? And why wasn't her husband there? Surely his work wasn't so important that he'd leave his wife to rely on the good will of her neighbours.

Apparently, that was the case, though.

A few days later, I met Stephanie in the hallway. This time she was wearing a dress and I still couldn't really tell that she was pregnant. Her face, though, was white.

'I was just coming to find you!'

'I'm on my way out...'

'This time it's definitely it. Would you mind?' She was a little conciliatory, perhaps ashamed to have to ask me again. I looked at her with a slightly critical eye. She practically begged me: 'Please! This time it's true! I can feel kicks in my stomach. The labour pains are terrible!'

Again, I phoned for an ambulance and waited with her on the stairs while she moaned and clutched at my hand and complained about her husband being away.

'It's just so far,' she said, panting a bit, 'and he doesn't have a phone where he is.'

'It's not that far,' I mumbled, but she drowned me out with a groan of pain.

But by the time the ambulance arrived, the pains had subsided and Stephanie had to admit that again, this was not the day her baby was going to be born.

'You should wait a bit,' I said, 'if this happens again.'

'Wait a bit! What? And drop it out on the pavement?' She shook her head. 'I don't think so. My friend's friend had a baby in the bath. In the *bath*. Can you imagine? Awful. Better safe than sorry, don't you think?'

Frankly, I didn't know what to think. I had heard stories about women just suddenly giving birth in the backs of taxis or at the theatre, but had no idea if they held any truth. At the age of thirty-five, Stephanie was no more educated on the subject than I was, and rather nervous on top of that.

The third time she knocked on my door, it was early evening and I had just sat down to eat my dinner.

I sighed when I saw her.

She shook her head and clutched her stomach. 'Please?' she asked, meek. 'Please come with me? I'm terribly frightened.'

So this time I ended up riding in the ambulance with her. The paramedics believed I was her husband and I had to set them straight on that, just as I did the staff at the hospital.

'It should be a quick labour, she's quite far along. She must have waited,' a nurse said, as I sat in the waiting area, 'what a brave woman your wife is!'

'She's not my wife.'

She frowned a touch. 'Girlfriend, then.'

'Neighbour, actually,' I corrected, and she quickly moved away.

Thankfully, this turned out to be the real deal, and I was the first person to see little Patrick. It made me smile when Stephanie said, 'My little Paddy.' I couldn't help but visit her again as she recovered, tease her lightly about Paddy from Paddington, which she admitted she hadn't even thought of. She appreciated my company and I found that I didn't mind seeing her, suddenly calm and content as she was. And when, two days after the birth, her husband arrived back from his business trip, their family was finally complete.

MY MOST FAMOUS NEIGHBOUR

For a long time, when I lived and worked in Texas, I got into the habit of frequenting the Houstonian Club for its state-of-the-art sports facilities. Attached to the glamorous Houstonian Hotel, it showcased the best of Texas style in a modern setting. As the hotel was quite close to the offices of the oil companies I was dealing with on a day-to-day basis, I often made use of their gym after work. I also occasionally enjoyed a trip to the sunny tennis court and three heated swimming pools, shaded with palms trees. The Houstonian Hotel, however, is known less for its gym facilities or even its swanky restaurant than for the fact that for a long segment in the 1980s, it served as the official residence of President George Bush, Sr.. George Herbert Walker Bush, the father of George Walker Bush, was vice-president from 1981 to 1989 and then president from 1989 to 1993.

Despite the fact that he actually spent most of his time outside the state of his origins, in 1985 the state government of Texas permitted George Bush to use the Houstonian as his official voting residence. There was only was condition to this unusual allowance: that he should promise to build his retirement home in the city of Houston. Thus, the official voting residence of George and Barbara Bush became Suite 271 at the Houstonian. Of course, they didn't live there full time, and they only paid for the room on nights they actually spent there, at the very favourable rate of approximately $250 per day, instead of the regular rate of approximately $800 per day! One of the employees once told me that, every time the Bushes were due to show up, the staff had to put up their family photographs on the walls. His sons Jeb and George Junior would often stay there with him, or perhaps come to meet up for a meal in the hotel's Oak Room restaurant, where Bush Sr. often reputedly went to eat pasta.

I had met George Bush a few times in the early 1980s, when he was a big investor in Zapata, a large and successful company which owned and leased out rigs for offshore oil drilling. Bush Sr. was an oil man in a big way, and so successful in his investments that he ended up a millionaire by the age of forty. We used to run into each other at meetings with the stakeholders, although we never exchanged much more than business chat and occasional small talk.

I also once attended an event at the Houstonian where he was giving out prizes for the best local athlete. As I used to play a lot of tennis at the Houstonian Club, I would sometimes see him on the courts there, where he was a keen player and obviously in excellent shape for his age.

Many of our bank's clients lived not far from River Oaks. Many stayed at the Houstonian itself, or in the other hotels near there, like the Inn on the Park or the Remington. I personally favoured the Houstonian, and often stayed on the second floor. This meant that I quite regularly ended up in the suite immediately next to George Bush's. Very occasionally, I would have a friendly run-in with his security which, to do him some credit, was fairly discreet. This was possibly due to the fact that he was still only vice-president to Ronald Reagan, at least in the early years of our very passing acquaintance. But even when he was president, he remained a fairly approachable man. I remember he once gave me a tip regarding the best local restaurant to go to for a steak! This was certainly one of my more famous neighbours, even if we only crossed paths two or three times in the years I spent in Texas.

FRENCH-STYLE RETIREMENT

Nearly all old French men have the same daily rituals: they drink coffee, go for walks, shop at the markets, nap in the afternoon, eat large dinners, go to bed early. The specifics vary from one man to another, but the basic patterns are the same. This is something I don't understand about the French: they spend all their time wanting to retire, but when they finally get there, they have nothing to do! Now, these are not just the daily activities of the retired farmers or schoolteachers, but also of men who were once powerful businessmen, bankers, brokers and politicians, as well as painters, librarians and chauffeurs. They all have the same fate. All of a sudden, as if overnight, they become nothing but coffee-drinkers, gossips, avid newspaper readers, and personal shoppers for their wives' vegetables.

In Paris, one often runs into men who once closed million-dollar deals before breakfast spending half an hour picking out the best potatoes from a muddy basket. I have seen men who used to reduce an entire parliament to silence with their speeches spending a whole morning haggling over the price of salad and chatting to the barmaid in a café. I had several employees who started talking about retirement planning by the age of twenty, as if it were all that counted! Of course, there are a few additions to the schedule of the rich and retired, such as attending their private clubs, but overall, it is the same for all of them.

Philippe Giscard d'Estaing was one such neighbour. A well-educated relative of the president of France, he quickly rose through the ranks of his peers to become a successful businessman. He was an extremely powerful acquaintance of mine: a tall, good-looking man about fifteen years my senior. I met him through shared business circles, as he was involved with various oil and multinational companies. He was the chairman of Thomson, one of the three biggest companies in Europe, and was also sat on various boards for important multinationals, including one that I happened to chair. Giscard was a charming man, and we became good friends. Every time I met him in meetings, or over lunch, he seemed to represent all the good things about a classic upbringing in the powerful circles of France: he had excellent government connections, a fantastic knowledge of politics, and a great sense of business understanding as well. On top of our shared work connections, Philippe Giscard d'Estaing also happened to be my neighbour in the Avenue Foch area of Paris, less than a hundred yards from my house.

Another neighbour I met in his heyday, and again when he was retired, was Camille, another senior executive of a major multinational company with whom I regularly did business. He was involved in oil refining, finance, and industry, making his way quickly to the top of the business ladder through the usual channels: good education, good connections, education at ENA. Of course, it is a well-known aspect of French society that the graduates of the École Normale Supérieure, known as '*énarques*,' essentially run the country. They make all the decisions in finance, industry, foreign and interior policy! We sat on each other's boards through the years, and, as I mentioned, for a time we were neighbours on Avenue Foch.

Camille and Giscard, to me, seemed to follow similar patterns. They were both tall, educated and incredibly successful businessmen. Through hard luck and good connections, they made it to the very highest echelons of French society. They actually happened to know each other, through similar business relations, but the three of us never tended to socialise together. Still, we passed on news of each other when we did meet up, and thus stayed connected in one way or another through the years.

Camille retired early, at the age of sixty, which is not in any way unusual in France. Mr Philippe retired at the somewhat more conventional sixty-five. From that moment onwards, I watched them slip into the patterns of French retirement almost from day to day. Not that I didn't enjoy joining them in some of their pastimes! For instance, although I continued working, I began to enjoy visits to the local markets. Even though our family, by this time, had a cook and a butler, I liked carrying my vegetables those two hundred yards back from the beautiful market at the end of Rousse-Pontigny in the sixteenth *arrondissement*, or from rue de Bellefeuille. If I was adventurous, I might even shop at the market on Place de Passy. I loved choosing my tomatoes, which were plentiful in summer in Paris: big, fresh Italian ones that could be used for sauces or eaten raw! I was particularly fond of the big coeur de boeuf varieties. I liked picking out thin spring onions and choosing my own cuts of meat. I particularly enjoyed my visits to the butcher who specialised in free range fowl, or what I used to call 'runner chickens': coquelets, poussins, chickens and ducks. In these small, daily decisions, it was much more interesting to get involved myself than to rely on the family cook.

To my surprise, at least once a month, and sometimes more, I would run into Philippe or Camille on these shopping excursions. I would say to them jokingly, 'What are you guys doing these days?' They would always reply something along the lines of: 'Oh, picking out the best onions,' or 'buying a kilo of beefsteaks.' How domestic our lives had grown! Where once, only a few years previously, we would have been discussing stock markets, interbank rates and trading deals, now we discuss only the price and weight of potatoes and onions and beef! We would often walk together for a time when we saw each other at these markets, talking of passing details of our daily lives as if we had all forgotten our high-powered business careers. The transformation was strange to witness.

It truly was a remarkable change: how someone could wield power for forty-odd years, rubbing shoulders with the high and mighty and accumulating millions, and then, all of a sudden, the minute they retire, their lives boil down to a walk to the market, a good book and a film on TV. This is the essence of French retirement! All these high-powered men spend their whole lives waiting for it, and when it comes, it is completely boring. The solution I have picked to this problem? Never retire completely: instead, carry on leading a busy life! In this fashion, one can continue to be involved in business − and still pick out one's own vegetables at the market.

Dentists are rather formidable people, and Dr Randeau was the most formidable of them I have ever encountered. He was my family's dentist for years in Geneva, where he had moved after a successful career in Paris. He worked at the Swiss university as a dental surgeon, and also managed to run a lucrative private surgery on the side. This happened to be conveniently situated near our house, which had rather contradictory effects. On the one hand, it facilitated unpleasant trips to the dentist by removing the long journey there. But on the other hand, it did have the side effect that my children would occasionally run into a man who was essentially a figure of horror for them, no matter how pleasantly he greeted us as neighbours.

I myself had excellent relations with the man. In the ten minutes before I opened my mouth to be poked and prodded with metal sticks, or rinsed with foul-tasting blue fluid, I squeezed in a short, enjoyable chat about politics or economics. Dr Randeau was a well-educated man, always on top of the latest news, and as such would have been the ideal man in whose company to spend an hour or so, were it not for the incidental fact that he had to make one wince, groan, and occasionally bleed. He was quite an overpowering character: after all, I was completely at his mercy in that room! He could have done anything to my mouth. It didn't matter that I would have destroyed him in the subsequent litigation, and probably lived richly off the spoils of the trial, once my face had recovered. For a very short space of time, a man with strong arms and a variety of pointy-looking tools had complete power over me. He could as easily have deformed my teeth as repaired them! I always looked at him with awe and fear, and respected his power.

All in all, Dr Randeau was a good dentist, and he looked after my wife and children as well as me for many years. One day, he announced that he was taking early retirement. I transferred to a friend of his, with whom I developed good relations, and Dr Randeau slowly slipped into the vague regions of memory reserved for acquaintances and torturers. When I took a trip to Venice with my younger children a good five years later, our old dentist was the furthest thing from our minds. Wandering and getting increasingly lost in the narrow cobbled streets, stopping for coffees on the plazas, or admiring the churches in the warm spring sunshine, Venice worked its magic on me and my family.

We were staying at the Gritti Palace, which is one of the best hotels in the world and certainly the best in the city. Built in 1525 as part of the Doge's private residences, it is a glamorous and artistically decorated hotel, glowing with gold trim, crimson hangings and Murano glass details. From the windows of our hotel room we could look out over the green and blue waters of the Grand Canal as it winds its way across the Jewel of Italy, or sip espressos on the balcony to the sound of the bells of the cathedral of Santa Maria delle Salute. It was close enough to the heart of the city to be conveniently located for almost any destination we chose, whilst still being private enough to be peaceful. I had come here mostly in order to dictate my latest novel to my literary assistant, and the first few days of our stay were spent pleasantly enough working and enjoying our surroundings. The children played with their nurse and went up and down the canals with their mother; the weather was beautiful; all the food we ate was wonderful, fresh and seasonal. We were having a wonderful time in the Gritti Palace Hotel, which seemed to me to embody Baudelaire's ideal values of '*luxe, calme, beauté et volupté*,' luxury, calm, beauty and voluptuousness.

One morning, at breakfast, however, this idyll was rudely disturbed. We were padding down the carpeted corridor to take breakfast in the restaurant room, when whom did we run into but Dr Randeau! He had just emerged from his suite and was locking his door behind him, impervious to the shock of worlds. 'Hello,' I said, as pleasantly as I could manage in my state of relative shock. 'What a surprise, seeing you here!'

He rearranged his expression of surprise into a more agreeable one. 'Well hello,' he said, shaking his head a little in obvious bewilderment. 'It is indeed a surprise.'

'I suppose you're here on holiday?' It was hard not to feel as though this person was intruding on our relaxing territory, a million miles from the day-to-day concerns of working life, and I could tell from the doctor's face that he felt rather the same. This was confirmed in his next reply.

'Actually,' he said, 'I've been here for about four months. I'm retired, you must remember. This has been my home for a while now.' He bowed a little, as if welcoming us into his home. I decided not to rise to this bait. He turned to my littlest girl, Rhonda, who was hiding behind my legs. 'Been brushing your teeth twice a day, little girl?' he asked her, with a wide grin. I remembered that he really did have the best teeth I have ever seen. Poor Rhonda did not see the humour in this question, and merely retreated behind my leg. The doctor shrugged. Having seen the expressions on my children's faces, I was reluctant to continue on the subject of his prior profession. Thus, after a few more slightly terse exchanges, we made our separate ways down to breakfast. It was obvious that we would sit on opposite sides of the dining room, although the arrangement felt a little ludicrous. As soon as we sat down, my little ones started babbling, their eyes wide.

'Papa, what is that man doing here? He is not nice!'

'Well, I guess this is what you get if you charge as much as he does for his surgery sessions! Or at least, as much as he did. I wonder if he ever does dentistry anymore?' I thought aloud.

My wife shook her head. 'It's a disgrace,' she said. 'He can't be a day older than fifty-five!'

But our thoughts on our old neighbour's fortunes were cut short by the children's questions. Little Rhonda was frowning at me. 'Did you ask the nasty man to come here?' she asked me.

I laughed. 'Goodness, no. Why would you think such a thing?'

My wife sat Rhonda on her lap and comforted her. 'Don't worry, little one. We would never do such a thing. I promise you won't have to go see the dentist on this trip.'

'But do I have to brush my teeth?' she asked, her eyes wide with fear.

'No, darling,' I said. 'Well, at least not any more than usual.'

We ran into Dr Randeau practically every day after that for the next five or six days of our stay, but we never talked again after the first encounter. I suppose he needed to feel he was retired, just as we needed to feel we were on holiday! Of course, I'd imagine the situation was far from ideal for the doctor himself: trying to enjoy his quiet retirement in a lovely, expensive hotel, hundreds of miles from his previous life, and all of a sudden being confronted with the faces of seven of his old clients. Still, it was a rather unpleasant encounter. My advice to the reader is to do your best to avoid this problem: never run into your dentist on holiday!

ROBERTO THE COWARD

My family had a farmhouse in the countryside near Pisa. It was a beautiful old country mansion, tucked away in the rolling hills of Tuscany a short distance from the beaches of the Tyrrhenian Sea. 'Right at the top of the boot,' my father used to say, 'no mud here!' Our family had a preference for the temperate, historically rich north of the country, at least for our own holidays. I was particularly fond of the countryside surrounding Florence, and loved the occasional day-trip to that fine city, strolling along the ancient stone bridges and enjoying the local gelato. It was always a pleasure to roll down the winding Tuscan roads, in the shade of the cypress and olive trees, whether heading out for a day of museum visits or returning for a family dinner in the evening. The house itself was built of large, local stones, decorated with beautiful Roman-style mosaics and wonderful paintings. Even the ceiling had frescoes, like the classical villas. Whenever we entertained there, it was easy to imagine ourselves hosting an antique style of banquet, two thousand years ago: all it took to perfect the picture would be a basket of grapes, a pitcher of water and a few loaves of bread. We could have been Renaissance bourgeois or Roman fourth-century centurions, feasting with our friends.

Of course, like every family endeavour, visiting the house had its complications. As we would usually fly in to the airport in Florence from France, England or the USA, we would arrive into the local airport without any local transportation. Thus, on one of my visits down in the company of both my parents, we were preparing to get on a bus, when we ran into our neighbour Roberto. As he lived next to us, he offered us a ride. Our Italian neighbour would not hear of any objections. In fact, he was absolutely adamant that we could not possibly pay for a bus when he was headed in the same direction himself. We were reluctant, partly out of not wanting to inconvenience our neighbour, partly out of a knowledge of the local driving style. Still, in the end we agreed. The Italians are a very helpful people: they pride themselves on being happy to go out of their way to do a neighbour a service. It is very difficult to turn them down. However, occasionally these kind offers do not turn out quite the way they were intended.

The weather on the drive was bright and sunny. Roberto was in an effusive mood. We managed to cram all of our luggage into his tiny Italian car and started out on the road home in good time. The drive back to ours took a good two and a half hours, and went along the hilly roads. My father in particular loved that drive, as he could stick his head out the window like an enthusiastic puppy and breathe in the fresh air. He would lean his head on the door, and rest his arm on the open window. 'We're here!' he would sigh, usually amusing our taxi driver, who would be completely blasé to the charms of his native roads after years of ferrying tourists along them. 'You can smell Italy in the air!' Roberto was also charmed by this, but did not take into account that my father's somewhat eccentric position might not be best suited to the narrow, winding roads. Like most Italians I have met, Roberto drove with a love of speed and little regard for the rules. He positively flung the little car around the bends and curves, zooming along as if he believed he was in the Grand Prix. My mother protested a little, but we didn't want to offend. Sadly, we had rather underestimated the amount of risk Roberto was willing to take. Going a good sixty or seventy miles per hour around a long bend in the road, Roberto decided it would be wise to overtake the car in front of us. If luck had been on our side, this would merely have been a little dangerous. But as timing would have it, there just happened to be an oncoming car right at that particular moment. The driver saw us at exactly the same time as we saw him, which was nearly too late to avoid a grave accident. Roberto slammed on the brakes, which may have stopped us from running straight into the other car, but also crashed my poor father's head right into the metal window-frame. We screeched to a halt and sat, panting, in the backseat.

My mother, sitting next to me, was the first to speak. 'Is everybody alright?'

Roberto craned across the seats to look over his passengers. His face grew pale when he saw my father. '*Mamma mia!*' he said.

'Oh, god,' my mother said in turn, when she could look into the front of the car. 'He wasn't wearing a seatbelt.' There was a deep gash in my father's forehead, which was bleeding profusely. My mother got out of the back of the car and came to the front to have a look at his injuries.

'He might have a concussion,' she said at once. 'Call an ambulance.'

'Yes,' I said as sternly as I could, before Roberto could even think of volunteering to drive, 'I think an ambulance would be best.'

'Well,' my mother said wearily, 'it looks like that's our only option in any case. Our friendly neighbour seems to have disappeared.' I looked around: it was true. I couldn't believe it: the cowardly Italian had run away.

'He probably thinks we'll have him arrested for negligent driving. Well, he certainly deserves it, causing this accident then abandoning us on the side of the road!'

'We'll worry about that later,' my mother said calmly. 'Let's focus on getting your father to safety.' We found a telephone not far away in a roadside café, and the ambulance arrived quickly. Nobody else had been hurt, which was miraculous, although my father appeared to be in rather bad shape.

I must admit I had a few moments of real panic. With the blood pouring down his face, and nearly fainting from the concussion he turned out to have suffered, he did not look like a man who had suffered a small accident. He hardly looked like a man who had survived a car crash. He did not respond to our questions, or move at all. When we arrived at the hospital, in fact, they took him for dead. Luckily, I kept my head and requested they call a doctor friend of mine, whom I knew was a professor at the University of Rome, and a visiting lecturer at Pisa's famous school of medicine. He came at once, which reassured my mother and me hugely, and set to work straight away. It turned out that my father's head had to undergo surgery, which took several hours. They also stopped the bleeding and ran a series of tests to check for brain damage. My mother and I spent a few terrifyingly tense hours in the waiting rooms, the bright Italian sunshine outside bringing little comfort. It seemed so terrifically unfair that this charming, childish habit of my father's had turned out to be so dangerous, through no fault of his own. I resolved at once never again to accept a ride from an Italian.

When we were allowed in to see my father, he looked much less bloody, and we were told his brain has suffered no damage. Nonetheless, he was in a coma for three whole days, through which my mother and I stayed by his side. My friend, the doctor from Rome, whose name was Giovanni, spent some time with us to explain the situation.

When I saw him after the operation, I shook his hand warmly. 'Giovanni, I can't thank you enough for your timely intervention. Is my father going to be OK?'

Giovanni nodded calmly. 'His life is safe, now. I must warn you about something, though. He has lost his adult memory. Now, don't worry, this is a common feature of head trauma. It will return, but it will take some time.'

'What do you mean? He has lost his memory?'

'No, no, nothing that bad,' Giovanni assured me. 'Your father still has an incredible childhood memory, you see, so his brain is obviously working fine. He remembers nursery rhymes, religious choir songs, and details of long stories he must have been told by his mother when he was young. With just a bit of training and a few athletic sessions, I believe everything will be restored. He just needs time.'

'Does this mean additional surgery?' I asked.

'I don't think so. It will be a long process, but I think your father is over the worst of it now.'

In truth, it took my father two years to recover his full memory, and to start telling stories from his adult time. Later, he would relish telling us his version of the accident story: how he had been napping, dozing off to sleep in the Italian air, and had been jolted awake by this rude Italian's driving. 'My eye almost flew right out of my head!' he would say; never a man to leave out the dramatic aspects of a situation. 'If my head had been any further out of the window, it would have been snapped clean off!' This recovery of memory and personality is apparently near-miraculous, and very rare in men of my father's age. It turns out we were incredibly lucky to have called on Giovanni, who I now know is one of the most expert doctors in the world on the subjects of brain haemorrhage and concussions. He saved my father's life. Thus, one friendly Italian saved my father from another friendly Italian! Or: a brave man saved him from a coward. The latter is probably a better representation of the truth, although less amusing, for the other neighbour, Roberto, turned out to be a real coward indeed. Not only did he fail to visit in hospital, but he didn't even come round to the house afterwards to apologise or check in on my father's recovery. He was afraid of his liability, and probably assumed we were going to give him trouble for what had happened, but it didn't excuse the lack of basic human courtesy. Of course, his crimes were far worse than that: I firmly believe that he deserved to spend time in jail, but I don't have time to deal with cowards. Our family decided against having any further involvement with Roberto. We simply pretended he no longer was our neighbour, and never spoke to him again. I hope that small act of exclusion was enough punishment to encourage him to repent for the destructive stupidity of his acts.

Instead of dealing with Roberto directly, which would have been really like closing the barn doors after the cows have escaped, I focused on making sure everyone around me would be safe from men like him. Punishing a man for one accident seemed less important than protecting from any future accidents. Thus, from that time on, I absolutely insisted that every member of my family wear seat-belts at all times. Sticking one's head out of the window was strictly forbidden, no matter how fresh the air. And most importantly of all, I taught my family never to accept rides from a stranger, no matter how friendly he may seem.

THE COVETOUS NEIGHBOUR

The 1948 Humber Super Snipe remains one of the most beautiful cars I've ever owned. It looks like an aspiring Rolls Royce, or perhaps a little like the vintage phantom of one. In the old days, when a poor man would get married, he would say to his wife: 'I can't afford a Rolls Royce, but I can afford a Humber Super Snipe!' As a student at LSE, studying for my PhD age twenty-three, I was lucky enough to already have an Aston Martin which had been bought and paid for by my parents. However, my eager, young man's eyes wanted more, and when I saw my heart's desire at a garage sale, I couldn't resist. So I dipped into my savings account and pursued my dreams, and drove back to my dorm at the wheel of a fabulous second-hand Humber Super Snipe. It was big and black, like the car a government official might drive, or that the Queen might wave from the window of in some national procession. It was bulky enough to be impressive but sleek and sophisticated to attract a lady's eye, too. I absolutely loved it.

I had many adventures in that car. I might go away for the weekend with my student friends to drive the country lanes of England. I might drive to a field and barbecue a whole cow. I might travel to Wivenhoe for a party in our rented house, picking up a few friends on the way. I might take my girlfriend to Hampstead for a lovely meal of roast pheasant. Any one of these expeditions was bound to be made more pleasant by the fact that it took place in such a wonderful vehicle. I won't pretend there wasn't a certain element of what was known in the current slang as 'coasting,' or showing off. It was, after all, quite an impressive car. There is a specific thrill attached to the possession of a truly impressive car that little in the world can top. When I parked it in front of the school, in my own designated parking space, it drew quite the audience! Groups of girls stopped and tittered, boys slowed their pace as they walked by or whistled admiringly.

All the attention the Super Snipe gathered, however, was not entirely positive. One of my neighbours, David Hanso, was exceedingly jealous. He was a Canadian student who lived in my dorm. We were not exactly friends, but, as neighbours do, we occasionally interacted. I knew enough about him to gather that:

he had an incredibly obnoxious temperament; he was not doing well at school; and he was very, very jealous of my Humber Super Snipe. He was a tall, blonde, thin, Canadian with no charm and no sense of humour. His main pursuits seemed to be chain-smoking and complaining.

David used to skulk around the halls looking miserable, bothering me and my neighbours. Almost every time I ran into him, he seemed to be whining about wanting to borrow my car. It wasn't that I minded lending my car in general, to friends or girlfriends, but I didn't like the idea of giving the keys to someone I just happened to live next to, despite the fact that we were barely friends! I always got the impression David was far more interested in trying to get my car off me than in actually making friends, which, as anyone will tell you, is not the way to get into someone's good books. I didn't feel particularly inclined to help this difficult person get lucky with women! It wasn't that our relations were bad: I remember once bringing him back a hamburger from Wimpy's, so we must have got along at least some of the time. Overall, though, we could hardly have been considered close.

As the year went on, David became more difficult. Work was going badly for him, and one of his friends told me he was worried about being kicked out of school if his grades didn't improve. He spent more and more time in his room, and the only time we ran into each other was when he was grumbling late at night in the kitchen. One day, I happened to cross paths with him when he seemed to be in a particularly foul mood, clutching a beer bottle in his fist as he stomped down the corridor. 'Come on, Brad,' he wheedled when he saw me, breathing air heavy with beer and cigarette smoke into my face, 'why don't you just let me take your car for a drive? Just a little ride round the campus to cheer me up.'

'I'm sorry, David,' I told him, 'I just can't do that.' I looked pointedly at the bottle in his hand.

He growled. 'What do you care, anyway. You've got another car!'

'What, so you can crash one and I won't care?' I bristled a little. 'That doesn't mean they're not precious to me! I take good care of my cars,' I said. 'I'm a responsible driver.

'Whatever,' he muttered threateningly. 'If you don't lend it to me, I'll find a way to take it anyway. I know how to hotwire an engine,' he added boastfully. 'It's so easy in these old cars. So it really doesn't matter if you don't give me the car. I'll just go and take it myself.'

With this parting threat, he took a swig from the beer bottle and stomped off back to his room. At the time, I gave the incident little thought. He was obviously in a bad mood and stressed about his results, so I assumed it was nothing but an idle threat. The story went stale for a few months: up until our final exams, I hardly saw David at all. But that summer, I was taking a holiday in France with one of my friends. We decided to drive down in the Aston Martin, as it was a smaller car and better-suited to long distances. I left the Humber Super Snipe in its parking place outside the school, where I figured it would be fairly safe and well-supervised.

I was wrong. I came back after just one week in France, and my Humber had disappeared. There is nothing like the terrible sinking feeling I felt in the pit of my stomach when I turned up to pick it up, and it was nowhere to be seen. I was terribly upset. I went around asking everybody I could think of. My friends, co-workers, and colleagues; every girlfriend who had borrowed the car at any point, and all my dorm neighbours. Almost everybody knew the car; but nobody knew anything about what might have happened to it. Although the car had not been a huge investment, I had no insurance, so it was a rather crushing loss with no hope of compensation. Insurance for students in those days was negligible, and in any case didn't cover theft.

There were, however, some resources left to me. I called the police and reported the theft. On the phone, the men were very helpful and assured me they would do everything within their power to help me out. Within days, two policemen came to see me in the dormitory. My friends on the corridor were astounded: it really was quite an impressive sight, these two grown men in their bulky jackets and hats, with their badges and guns quite plainly visible, walking up to my room! People must have thought I was some sort of high-powered criminal. At the time, I was just glad to see some reinforcements. I talked them through the details of what had happened; at least, the little I knew for sure.

'It's a strange case,' the older policeman said to me. 'Why would anybody want to steal an antique? It's not tremendously valuable. It's got to be either a great collector, or an aficionado. Unless ulterior motives were involved. Can you think of anyone with any reason to steal something of yours?'

I paused. 'I'm not sure,' I said hesitantly.

The policeman smiled reassuringly. 'Any information you can give us will help us try to find your car.'

'Well,' I sighed, 'there was one conversation I had a few months ago…' I told them about David, while they scribbled notes furiously. I felt a little guilty, but my interest in finding out what happened to my car, and the hope of getting it back, were stronger than any compulsion to protect David, whom I must admit I couldn't help but rather suspect at the time.

As the case progressed, however, I began to have doubts about this hunch. After two full interviews with me, the police informed me that they considered the case too complicated to be dealt with under their jurisdiction alone. They explained that they were going to refer it to Scotland Yard. At first, I was impressed with this, imagining men equipped with deerstalkers and perhaps a team of bloodhounds, but my enthusiasm wore thin very quickly once I actually met them.

The first time the policemen came into the student hall, they caused quite a stir. We were all sitting around drinking coffee and reading the newspapers as we did in our spare time. There was a couple of students kissing in front of the television. Into this calm student scene strode two policemen, looking to interrogate David. They didn't even take him outside, or drive him to the station, but sat down awkwardly on one of the couches and launched into their spiel right then and there. He stubbed his cigarette out as quickly as possible, and hastily straightened his hair. I had to say I felt a little bad for him, watching the blood drain from his face. It was a completely surreal scene, David looking both anxious and bull-headed, sitting with policemen as they played through their no doubt well-rehearsed 'good cop, bad cop' routine. This happened two more times within the next month. The intrusion of policemen into halls was perhaps a little thrilling at first, but the fun of it quickly wore thin. I began to wonder if I should call the whole thing off. If my car hadn't reappeared after eight months, I reasoned, why would it do so now?

The situation slowly got worse, despite no progress being made on the case. For months and months on end, I had officers from Scotland Yard turning up to ask me questions about a theft which I hadn't witnessed, had happened almost half a year previously, and which, to be honest, I had pretty much entirely recovered from at that point. After the first scene, the humour of David's interrogations started to wear thin, and I felt a little bad at having been responsible for his being hounded by policemen. David didn't speak to me, only occasionally glared at me in the corridors, but I didn't think his behaviour came across at that of a guilty man. Of course, he had brought this upon himself with his empty threat, but it still felt a little unfair.

In September of the next year, almost two years after the theft, I moved out of halls in order to take an apartment on Edgware Road. Still Scotland Yard did not give up the case, but kept calling me with news of an inquisition which seemed to make absolutely no progress. I began to wonder if they had some sort of vested interest in the case: I had never heard of anything being pursued over such a long time! By this time, there was absolutely no chance of me getting the car back. I finally rang them up and told them the whole business was consuming too much of my time, and offered to give up the claim. 'You'll have to come into our office, sir,' they replied. 'There's some paperwork to be done before a case can be closed.' Filling in a lot of paperwork did not particularly appeal to me, so I put off the visit for as long as I could. The calls diminished in volume, and as I never saw David anymore, I essentially forgot about the whole business. Eventually, I moved to New York.

Just two weeks after I had arrived in the city, I was flabbergasted to receive a call from Scotland Yard. 'We're just calling to let you know we haven't made any progress,' a policewoman told me, completely deadpan.

'Are you kidding? You are making this transatlantic phone call, almost three years after a theft, to let me know you still don't know anything?'

'It's just procedure, sir.'

'Look,' I said, as calmly as I could, 'I paid less than a hundred pounds for that car. Will you please just forget the whole thing?'

After going through the usual rigmarole of resistance, the policewoman seemed to finally get the message. 'Just give us your address,' she told me. 'We'll send you the papers, you sign the release and send it back to us. As soon as we receive us the case will be closed.'

'I won't hear from you again?'

'You won't hear from us again,' she replied, not without humour.

That was the end of the story. No-one ever found my beloved Humber Super Snipe, I never saw David Hanso again, and I stopped receiving regular calls from Scotland Yard. It was not the last car that would be stolen from me, but that's a story for another book…

THE OLYMPICS TRIP

When I was at graduate school at New York University, I briefly shared an advanced aeronautical engineering class with another student by the name of Bob. The two of us got along well, and talked a lot about sports, which were one of our common interests. We became particularly close when we were assigned a project together. Bob was particularly into winter sports: snowboarding, skiing, and anything else that involved racing down a snowy slope at top speeds. I shared some of his enthusiasm, although I didn't have as much experience attending these events as he did. Bob seemed to manage to attend any local events, many international events, and even a few winter Olympics in his time. 'In fact,' he boasted to me early on in our acquaintance, 'my father has got me tickets to the Olympics this winter. I'm so excited.'

'I'm sure you are... You're a lucky man,' I told him without resentment or jealousy.

'These are going to be really interesting Olympics, you know. Two of the big hopes have died in training: an Australian alpine skier and a British luge slider.'

'Goodness, that's dreadful. Does this sort of thing happen a lot?'

'Well, these are all fairly dangerous activities, of course. Accidents on track are fairly common. But these games have a sort of dark cloud hanging over them. You heard about the figure skating team, of course?'

'The Americans? I remember seeing something on television about it a few years ago, about some kind of tragedy.'

'You're sure right about that. They died in a plane crash.'

'What, all of them? God, that's awful. Now that I think about it, I feel like I have a vague memory of the president issuing a statement on the subject.'

'They were all travelling together, of course, heading straight to the World Championships in Prague. The plane crashed over Brussels, killing the entire team and a few accompanying officials. All of them. Men and women, teams of partners, reigning champions, gold-medallists, the best in the world. It was utterly devastating for the sport.'

'Am I right in recalling the president commenting on the incident?'

'Oh, yes, absolutely. I mean, this was an international tragedy, but on top of that, the Kennedys were close friends with one of the skaters who died. He probably would have sent messages to the grieving families anyway, but this made it even more poignant.'

'They cancelled the World Championship, right? I seem to recall that.'

'That's right. The sport's never been the same since. It will be very interesting to see how the new team are holding up in face of the pressure a few years on.'

I was at Bob's house one evening, working on our project, when Bob received a phone call. It was just three days before the winter Olympics, and he had been buzzing with excitement about this for the last few days. I shared in it vicariously, looking forward to his tales upon his return. I had to admit I was beginning to wish I had managed to get myself a ticket. I was sitting in his messy student room, with papers strewn everywhere. It was cosy, if small, and incredibly badly lit: Bob seemed to find this charming. Bob returned from the other room with an ashen face.

'What's wrong?' I asked, concerned.

'I've got to go home at once,' he said quietly. 'I... It's just family business. My grandmother is ill. My father wants me home straight away.'

'My god,' I said. 'I'm so sorry. I hope everything is ok.'

Bob appeared a little disorientated. An incredibly organised man, his mind obviously started going through the list of things to do before his departure. I wouldn't have been surprised if his suitcase was already half packed in his mind. 'The project,' he said first, a little vaguely.

'We're nearly finished,' I replied at once. 'I can finish it and present. Absolutely no problem.'

'I should leave tomorrow morning,' he said, as if to himself. I nodded.

'The tickets,' he said.

'You can get them at the airport tomorrow?' I replied, assuming that was what he had meant. 'It's midweek, you should have too much trouble getting space on a national flight.'

'No, no,' he said, 'the Olympic tickets. I need to sell them at once. It's the day after tomorrow! How can I do that? They were a big investment from my father, a gift. I can't let them go to waste. He'll be sure to worry about them.' Then his face lit up as the solution presented itself to him. 'Brad, would you do me a huge favour? Will you go in my place?' I grinned. 'That's hardly a favour, Bob! That's actually incredibly generous of you. And yes, I'd love to go.'

'Oh, thank you so much. That's a load off my mind. Now if you'll forgive me, I have to pack. Why don't you take all the project notes away with you now? Oh, and the tickets. The tickets, of course. They're right here on my desk.' He gestured at the chaotic pile of papers. I walked over and assembled the stack of our work, gathering everything surrounding it just to be sure I had it all. The ticket was lying on top of it all, a small cream rectangle with stylish crimson type. *Olympische Winterspiele, Innsbruck 1964*, it read, and I felt my heart leap. I picked it up and stared at it for a moment. 'You're a lucky man, Brad,' my friend said light-heartedly. 'I'll expect all the details when I come back.' He hugged me, rather uncharacteristically, then showed me the door.

When the Olympic weekend arrived, I left from Idlewild airport, which has now become JFK airport. It was a familiar place to me, so I went through the checks without worrying too much, reading the day's newspaper. It was full of Olympic news and predictions, and filled me with anticipation. My briefcase was full of the presentation I was hoping to finish up in a moment of spare time. Of course, the little cream rectangle with its beguiling German type was tucked in as well. The journey went smoothly, and we landed in Frankfurt a little early. I left the airport in good time, and stepped out into the cold air. I got the train to Innsbruck, and sat down next to a German gentleman in a black coat. 'It's chilly, isn't it?' I said, rubbing my hands together.

'Yes, it is,' my neighbour responded politely. 'And a good thing too. Are you headed to the Games?'

'Yes, I am indeed. Do you mean the weather's a good thing for the Olympics?'

'I do! They were worried, you know. Innsbruck is usually covered in snow by this time of year, but it's been an unseasonally warm winter.'

'It's not very snowy now,' I replied, looking out over the distant mountains. 'What are they going to do?'

'Oh, you haven't heard? This is a great story. They've called in the Austrian army to carve out more than twenty thousand ice bricks from the mountains, and carried them to the bobsled and luge locations. They also carried forty thousand cubic metres of snow to the ski slopes.'

'That's insane!'

'But completely true. They ran magnificent photographs from it in the daily newspapers. Pictures of hundreds of butch army men packing down snow with their hands and feet.'

'That's Germanic efficiency for you!' I said with a nod to the gentleman, who smiled.

At this point, I reached into my briefcase to pull out something to read, and a passport fell onto the table. My neighbour, since we had established a fairly friendly rapport at this stage, picked it up, presumably to look through my visa stamps out of curiosity, or perhaps to laugh at my picture. But when he opened the passport, he looked over at me with a worried expression. 'Um,' he hesitated, 'is this you?'

'I'm sorry?' I said, rather offended. 'What do you mean?' I looked down at the passport, and to my complete shock, saw my friend Bob's face looking up at me. 'Oh my god,' I said. My train neighbour shuffled away from me a little, obviously now believing me to be some criminal he had accidentally caught red-handed. 'It's not like that,' I said hastily. 'This is my friend. I must have mistakenly taken his passport.' The neighbour nodded, although I don't think he believed me, as we spent the rest of the journey in awkward silence. He scurried off the train quite quickly when we got to Innsbruck, and I never saw him again. Still, one strange man thinking I was some kind of criminal was nothing compared to the worry I was feeling at the thought of having accidentally stolen my friend's passport after he had done me such a huge favour.

I was so worried I completely forgot to look forward to the Olympic Games themselves, and nearly missed the train's stop in Innsbruck. What was I going to tell Bob? Had I just stopped him from being able to fly home to see his ailing grandmother? How had I managed to steal his passport? It dawned on me, then, that in his phenomenal organisation, Bob had probably carefully set out the passport right next to the ticket, which had been on top of the pile of notes. I must have picked it all up at once. By the time

I found a phone in the Innsbruck train station, I was something of a nervous wreck. I rang Bob's apartment, but of course he didn't pick up, having already left for home. This should have reassured me, as I would have realised that he'd been perfectly able to travel, but it didn't. I remembered, luckily, that he had left me his family's number as well, in case I had any questions when I was writing up our project. I rang the second number, and after a few moments with my heart in my throat, Bob himself picked up.

'Brad!' he said. 'It's great to hear from you. How is it? What have you seen so far?' He paused. 'Wait, surely the opening ceremony hasn't even happened yet! What's up?'

'I'm so sorry,' I blurted out. 'I stole your passport. I mean, I didn't steal your passport, obviously, but I have it with me, in my bag. It was an accident.' Bob burst out laughing. This wasn't quite the reaction I had been expecting, so I didn't quite know what to say. When, finally, his laughter calmed, he said: 'You haven't stolen my passport, Brad. You've actually found my passport.'

'What?'

'You found my passport! I'd lost it in my room. Of course, it's useless, the one you have. I ordered another a few days ago; I picked it up in plenty of time.'

'You mean this one is useless?' Relief flooded through me, and I joined in the laughter. 'Oh, I was so worried I'd accidentally trapped you at university!'

'No, no, nothing like that.'

In those days, of course, you could order a new passport and receive it within an hour or so at the passport office. There was none of the modern business of applying, and form-filling-in, and waiting in endless queues in hallways. Bob and I chatted for a little bit longer, and when we were both reassured that all was well, I headed off to the Games in peace, and enjoyed the opening ceremony concert of Beethoven and Mozart less than an hour after the passport panic. Still, I found myself wondering later on what might have happened if I had accidentally produced Bob's passport in the airport, rather than in the train. I'd imagine I would have got in quite a lot more trouble than worrying a single German train neighbour! From then on, I determined to pay much more careful attention to the contents of my bags when travelling abroad on short notice.

Scotland is not the most interesting place to stay. For a time, I used to say that Scotland is so boring, there's nothing to do but create religions and raise sheep! However, every once in a while, I found this was far from the case, with more or less agreeable consequences.

My wife Hilary and I once stayed in a small hotel near Aberdeen. This was in the early 1970s, before the great oil boom had hit Scotland, and the village we were staying in still had every mark of relative poverty and isolation. It was not without its charms, of course, including a pub with a nice fireplace and a rather lovely little local church, but overall it was not the sort of place one would voluntarily pick for a holiday. My wife was devoutly Catholic, so we attended the local church service every Sunday. Her uncle in Ireland was actually a friend of the priest there, so he recommended we try and talk to him before or after the service. 'He's an interesting fellow,' he told us. 'Very knowledgeable on the topic of the history of the church in Scotland.'

As the church was just a short walk from our hotel, getting to the service early in the morning was hardly a complication. As it happened, we arrived into town on a Saturday night, so this outing was our first on the trip. The priest who held Sunday mass did indeed appear to be a pleasant man, who gave an interesting, witty and mercifully short service. Afterwards, as planned, we stopped to talk to him. He was a man in his mid-forties, perhaps surprisingly slim for a man of the cloth. He's actually one of the few Catholic priests I've met who was not only far from overweight, but actually quite thin! In my experience, they tend to indulge every small vice that is permitted to them, and a few of the ones that aren't! But this one was rather different. He didn't drink, and he didn't look as if he ate very much either. He had quite a caustic sense of humour, but he knew vast amounts about the local history, and obviously was very fond of his congregation.

'I love my work,' he said to us. 'I don't know how I couldn't.'

'What, every aspect of it? I can tell from your figure you don't indulge in a lot of vices, but don't you mind the celibacy?'

'Oh, no,' he said, not without humour. 'I wouldn't really have time for anything else. I give a service at eleven and another at six every day of the week, as well as the Sunday service.'

'And people come to these services?'

'Well...' he hesitated. 'Sometimes. On occasions, we have a congregation of two or three. But those that do come are very faithful.'

'So there's a large Catholic population in Scotland? I wasn't really aware of that. I always thought most of Britain was Protestant in one way or another.'

'Ah, you're wrong about that. The Reformation may have worked hard and bloodily to stamp out any trace of it, but it doesn't mean there's not a dedicated core of Scottish Catholics. It's known as the Catholic Kirk, of course,' he said, with the glimmer of a smile.

'I suppose I had forgotten about Mary Queen of Scots.'

'Yes, she was as Catholic as they come. But even in modern-day Scotland, there's still a good following. There's an archbishop in Glasgow, for instance.'

'Don't be offended by this question, but don't you don't find Catholicism outdated? You seem like a sensible man. Don't you get tired of all the ridiculous outfits, and swinging the incense, and all that?'

'I'm quite fond of the pomp and circumstance, actually. The little old ladies really go in for that stuff.'

'Well, I will say that you were far less boring than some Catholic priests I've met. If this was my local church, I wouldn't mind attending regularly.'

'See, I'm glad to hear that. It's terribly sad,' he told us, 'the church is losing even the most loyal of its members. People are just losing interest in modern society. They're not looking out for each other.'

'Christian values are hardly a priority in today's society,' I had to agree with him. 'Do you get youth in the congregation?'

'Oh, sure. People come with their families. But once they leave, they don't tend to come back. The church isn't hip, it isn't cutting edge. It doesn't encourage people to make vast amounts of money or drive fast cars or shoot criminals, the way most of our culture and advertising does!'

'You mean the message of the church is at odds with the one modern society projects?'

'Yes, exactly. And yet, conversely, it has all the more relevance in a corrupt society. I suspect these troubled souls will come flocking back. What I'm worried about is: will there be a church waiting for them, when they do?'

'You really think the church is in trouble?'

'Oh, deeply so. Churches are being sold off. There's a church right in the centre of Edinburgh that's been turned into some sort of bar. People love that.'

'What a strange concept!'

'It certainly is. Sometimes I wonder what would happen if I started giving a service from the middle of the room. I'd probably get thrown out by security.' He gave a sharp laugh, without bitterness. 'But what can I do. It's my calling. I'd probably start trying to make a drunkard see the error of his ways and get punched in the face! I'm rather attached to our poor old Catholic institutions.'

'I'm interested in what you're saying in the contract with the values of modern society, though. Are you implying that the church is a sort of bastion of resistance, which could serve as a refuge from these corrupting influences?'

He sighed. 'I'm not sure I am that idealistic anymore. But I do certainly believe a refuge is offered, if anyone needs it. The Catholic church is one of the only sources of salvation for the poor, the unemployed, the hungry and the sick in this country. I don't even mean salvation in the sense of the soul! Although that, too, still has an important draw for people: just look how many people want to have their funeral in the church, or be buried in our churchyard, even if they've never attended a service in their life! I believe that those people, too, can be saved.'

'You're saying that your church is a popular funeral venue.'

He laughed. 'Yes, that's exactly what I'm saying. God, that's a worrying thought. Is the Catholic church more popular with the dying than it is with the living?'

'Well, your service was popular with a few more people today,' I assured him, and we parted on friendly terms.

The very next morning, as Hilary and I were sipping coffees in the small hotel's dining room, the headline of the local paper caught my eye. 'Local Priest Killed in Cemetery,' it read. 'Look at this, Hilary!' I pointed it out to her. 'The criminal influence of Glasgow seems to be extending into the countryside!'

'Goodness me,' she said at once, having picked up the paper, 'look at the picture. It's that nice man we were talking to yesterday!'

I couldn't believe it. I snatched the paper back and skimmed the article as fast as I could. It was indeed the man we had met just the day before: according to the newspaper, he had been strangled in the cemetery just outside his beloved church, by none other than one of the beggars who slept there.

'Why on earth would anyone do such a thing?' I wondered aloud.

My wife shook her head. 'We'll never know. Perhaps he wanted to steal the collection. Perhaps he was just crazy.'

It was such a terrible shame, considering how much this priest obviously cared for the poor and needy in his community. What an ironic twist of fate for him, to be killed by those he hoped to help!

For a time, we rented a house in Jeddah, Saudi Arabia, for clients of our bank. My wife and I knew I would probably stay there on a lot of long business trips, so we paid special attention to the choice of this guesthouse. The one we found was situated near the coast of the Red Sea and had a large garden and a terrace. These were the features that drew me to the property; in fact, I would go so far as to say they were specifically why I rented it. The sight of green grass or leafy trees was a rare thing in that part of the world in the early seventies, certainly in a city where, in some neighbourhoods, it was impossible to get a glass of cold water from a tap, and the idea of a shower was an unimaginable luxury. This property not only offered all of these attractions; trees, grass, filtered drinking water and showers, but a few flowers as well.

Like everywhere in Arabia, the heat evaporated any kind of liquid almost instantly, which made the consumption of fresh water very expensive. Summers in Jeddah could have temperatures in the mid-forty degrees Celsius. Most households kept their use to a minimum, due to the constraints of the price. If insufficiently watered, plants in Saudi Arabia often wilt and die in a day! However, I had an English wife, who was completely obsessed with gardening. She particularly enjoyed looking after flowers. So the guesthouse in Saudi Arabia, despite being in what was essentially a desert climate, had to have its tidy little garden and a few overflowing flowerbeds. To her credit, when we stayed there, my wife had real green thumbs even faced with the dry, chalky Gulf soil. I brought my family with me on many of my visits, especially when I had to be gone for more than a week. Much as my wife and I enjoyed our trips to Paris and London, there was a certain special attraction to that house in Jeddah.

Furthermore, Jeddah has a certain historical charm, being the location where T.E. Lawrence met King Hussein in the early twentieth century and agreed to help him try to carry out his dream of uniting the Arab states into one kingdom. These agreements led to a series of bloody battles against the Turks, and the ultimate failure of King Hussein's plans, but Jeddah, for me, still retains some of that hopeful sense that Lawrence of Arabia must have felt here. 'It was indeed a remarkable town,' Lawrence wrote in his *Seven Pillars of Wisdom.'*

We signed on for a three-year rental lease, paying the rather high deposit without second thoughts. We settled in comfortably, buying some antique furniture for the guests and planting some flowers in the garden. But after just one month's rental, we had something of a surprise. One Thursday evening, my wife and I came back from a daytrip to find our landlord, a slim, tanned man in his early forties, standing in our garden. He had his own keys to the outside garden, so it was no surprise in itself that he was able to get into our property. The part which was harder to believe was that he was not only quite solidly settled in, with tea and coffee set up on a small table, but that he was surrounded by a large group of other people, all sitting on our terrace in the sun. 'Hello,' he said, 'we are just about to pray.' Flabbergasted, my wife and I moved into the house without much comment. This group of more than twenty people sat together in our garden for another fifteen minutes or so, after which they shared tea and coffee. The whole scene was a little too intimidating to approach, but we stared at them open-mouthed from the kitchen windows. When they finally left, I went to speak to my landlord.

'I'm sorry,' I said, 'but what are you doing here?' I noted that he was as scruffily dressed as the other few times I had met him, and that his hands were dirty. Not exactly what one would expect from a landlord, I thought with a sniff.

'You don't mind, do you?' he said, graciously. 'It's just an old tradition. This is my grandmother's old house, you see,' he explained. 'We've always done this.'

'What is this?' I asked.

'Prayer,' he said with a little pious bow. 'And a barbecue,' he added.

I couldn't really think of much to answer to this. As he was so obviously ready to pack up and move on, and had tidied everything up after him, I didn't really press the matter or ask for further explanations. I assumed that the event was a one-off that had been planned for a long time before the house was sold. However, the next month, when I came back after a trip to Paris, I found out that he had done the very same thing the next Thursday, and the Thursday after that. Our gardener and housekeeper explained this to me: this was before the days when international calls were easily available. We didn't even have a landline in this guesthouse! Thus, we only found out about these repeated prayer events after they had gone on for several weeks. 'The third time,' the gardener explained reluctantly, 'he was actually using the kitchen as well!' This was too much for me.

I went to my landlord's house to confront him. He appeared, smiling and wiping his hands on his robes, from the doorway of what seemed to be a very small kitchen. 'You're going to have some serious explaining to do,' I said to him, with no preamble or pleasantries. 'How could you not even ask my permission to bring twenty people to our house, four times a month? It's ridiculous. A complete invasion of privacy.'

'I'm sorry,' he said, appearing genuinely ashamed. 'I didn't know you would feel this way.'

'I just cannot tolerate this. If it was your intention to have these regular events there, on my property, you should have told me before you let me sign a three-year lease!'

'It's an old tradition,' he said. 'Since my great-great-grandfather's time! We always have a party on the holy day! We have discussions, prayers and a barbecue.'

'Every week? And you really didn't think to tell me this? Can't you see that this is completely unfair! It shouldn't work this way.'

'Well, yes it should. At least I believe that it should,' he bristled, putting on a wounded air. 'That's our family tradition. I didn't think you would mind.'

'You clearly have no modern notions of liberty, or privacy! This is completely ridiculous.'

The man was silent for a time. 'I, too, think that this is ridiculous. We cannot break the rule of our tradition in our family. We are going to break your lease.'

I was rather taken aback. I had been about to suggest this, as a threat, but he had rather stolen my thunder. I felt a little like someone who had turned up to break off an engagement to his fiancée, only to be jilted.

'Well,' I said, as angrily as I could, 'OK. We will break the lease. You will have to reimburse us everything since the start of our tenancy. We will leave the property at once.' We had, after all, already paid several months advance rent as well as the deposit.

To my surprise, he said: 'OK, we'll do that straight away.' He paused, and smiled calmly. 'I really am sorry about all this. To prove this, I will pay the deposit on your next house, as a gesture of goodwill. After all, since you are agreeing to leave, you are actually doing us a favour, as I can now continue our family meetings. I am sure we will be able to find another tenant easily,' he added smoothly, 'and I don't want any further trouble.'

'Alright,' I said, my mind still reeling, 'it sounds like going our separate ways is in everybody's best interests.' Little did I know to what extent! We shook hands on our agreement, breaking the lease. We packed and moved out within a few weeks, and found another house nearby very easily. As promised, the landlord gave us the money for the deposit on the new guest house. I left with no ill-will.

However, several years later, when we had moved to Riyadh, as the business centre migrated there anyway, we heard news of our old landlord. Far from being a quiet man devoted to prayer, we actually found out that he had become one of the richest men in that part of the world. And far from being a kind man who let us out of our lease and paid our deposit as a gesture of kindness, we found out he had immediately knocked down the house in Jeddah and built a skyscraper in its place! It was remarkably sneaky, and deeply manipulative. The prayer meetings, the apologies, all had been an elaborate scheme to get us to want to get out of our three-year lease, as he had received a better offer. All he had wanted all along was for us to move off his land so he could get on board with the trend of developing Arabia. I was completely stunned when I found this out. We had been completely fooled by his strategy. He was certainly one of my sneakiest neighbours!

When I was seventeen years old and studying engineering in Texas, the neighbour in one of the rooms next to mine in the state court dormitory was a boy by the name of Steve. The building was a huge, comfortable five-story affair, with about twenty rooms on each floor. Each of these had their own desk, cupboard and shower: fairly minimal, but comfortable enough for student life. Steve was from Oklahoma, and had come to Texas to study liberal arts.

Steve was not an unattractive young man, with bright green eyes and an aquiline nose, but he had very little success with the ladies in the time I knew him. He was not very tall, and a little bit on the chubby side whilst I, on the other hand, was enjoying a period of popularity, as I played volleyball, football and basketball at the time. This contrast, added to the fact that I was two years older than him, meant that Steve liked to come to me for advice.

'Oh Brad,' he would sigh forlornly. 'How do you do it?'

I did not enjoy this sort of obvious admiration any more than I liked to brag about my achievements, so I sometimes found these conversations a little bit awkward, although it was hard not to feel sorry for the boy.

'The sorority girls won't even have a hamburger with me in the cafeteria,' he would continue, 'while you could date any one of them you chose.'

'Now you know that's not true. Everybody gets rejected sometimes. Everybody gets lucky sometimes, too. You've just got to wait your turn,' I tried to reassure him.

'But I'm so fat,' he whined. 'Who would want to date someone like me?'

'The answer to your problems is right there in the way you're thinking, Steve! Can't you see? If you feel so insecure about yourself, make some changes! Do some sport! You don't have to become a full-time athlete to feel a little more comfortable in your body. Are there any activities you enjoy? Any sport you could take up as a hobby?'

'Well, I quite like swimming, but I don't think that's what I need. What I need is more muscle. I need to look manlier, you know?'

'There's a gym here where you can work out, if you want. Do you want to do some weights with me sometime?'

'Oh no, I couldn't do that. I'm sure everyone would laugh at me. They'd probably come in just to laugh at flabby old Steve.'

I tried to assure him that this was a ridiculous approach, but it was no use. The boy's self-esteem issues were deeply entrenched, and there was nothing a slightly-older boy like me could do to help out. I think he blamed some of his insecurities on his modest background and the fact that his parents had put all their revenue into his education. This sort of high expectation bred a deep guilt in him, and I believe it had a profound effect on his personality, particularly when he found himself not doing as well as he had hoped in most of his classes. It wasn't that he didn't work, although he did have his moments of laziness. It was just that his results didn't quite live up to his expectations.

'Well, maybe just start with some small changes,' I suggested. 'Go for a small jog in the morning. Or do some sit-ups. Maybe do some cardio exercises: they'll improve your circulation, which might help you stay concentrated when you do your homework.'

Steve just sighed despondently.

'It's not concentration that's the problem. It's the work itself. You wouldn't understand. You engineers are all so smart; you're good at figures and inventions and all sorts of things. We liberal arts students are only supposed to be good with words. I don't know why they require us to do all this other stuff.'

I hated the thought, but sometimes I worried that Steve was just lazy. However, something came up soon after that which challenged at least this one assumption. Steve often came to my room in the evening to ask for help with his homework and/or life, so this in itself was not a surprise. He had been away for four days or so on holiday, so I was pleased to hear the knock. However, I could not refrain from gasping when he opened the door. Steve's face was entirely wrapped up in white gauze, and his leg was in a cast.

'Hi!' said Steve, with what was presumably a grin, although it was hard to tell with his head wrapped up like some kind of Egyptian mummy. 'Can I get some help with this homework?'

'What on earth happened to you?'

'Well, my nose is broken. And my leg too. I had to go to the hospital twice.'

'What, were you mugged? Did you get into a fight?'

Steve giggled. 'Oh no, nothing like that. I went skiing.'

'And then got mugged on the slopes? Did you get run over by a snow plough?'

'Nope. Just... Clumsy.'

'That's some impressive clumsiness, my dear friend.'

'It was the first time I went skiing. Went to Aspen, in Colorado; I heard that was the cool place to go. And it was fun, it was great fun... until the injuries. So, for about two hours.'

'Wow, that sounds like terrible luck... or a bad instructor.'

'Instructor? You can get skiing instructors?'

'Did you seriously not know this, or are you pulling my leg? You can't just race out onto the slopes without any preparation! That's so dangerous!'

'I honestly had no idea.'

'Wait, were you just trying to save money?' I added, struck by the thought that I might be being unfair on Steve.

'Oh, this is sheer ignorance,' he replied glumly. 'Anyway, so first I broke my nose by falling over. My skis came off and hit me in the face. It was pretty funny, I guess. But then I had to go to the hospital.'

'Are you telling me that these were separate incidents?'

'Oh, yes. So after I got discharged with my new mummy face, I went straight back on the slopes. I managed to ski until the end of that day without anything else going wrong, so that was a relief. But about ten minutes into it the next morning I ran into a tree and broke my leg. So that was that.'

'This sounds like some kind of outrageous comedy skit.'

'Trust me, it wasn't funny.'

'Did you go back to the same hospital? Did they recognise you?'

'No, we were on a different part of the slopes. I had to be taken off in a stretcher to a special hospital that deals with leg injuries.'

'Wait, was the first one just for noses?'

Steve rolled his eyes and grinned. 'Of course not. Anyway,' he continued, 'that's the story of how I'm all broken. I don't think I'll be trying that again. No girls are interested in boys who can't ski.'

'What, you're saying they don't all come over and help you get up? Check on you when you're down?'

'Nope. They just laugh.'

'And you're forgetting the nurses. There must have been cute nurses.'

'If there were, I was on too many painkilling drugs to notice.'

I could tell that this conversation track was making Steve a bit glum, so I changed tactics.

'Well, congratulations in any case,' I said. 'You've got your first skiing accidents out of the way. As soon as you're healed you can get back out on the slopes! Practice is the only way to get better.'

'I don't know. I'm worried about my nose... What if it never heals? They didn't do cosmetic surgery or anything. Just wrapped it up. What if I just turn into some fat, limping kid who can't ski?'

'Oh Steve, don't get into this kind of self-pity. Listen, we'll go skiing together sometime, ok?'

Over the months that followed, Steve continued to put on weight and did not, I'm sorry to say, improve his standing with the fairer sex very much. His nose healed badly and was always a bit crooked, and I think he limped a little when he walked, although he denied there was anything wrong with his leg. Still, he stayed cheery, and eventually started to talk about getting back on the slopes.

'Look, why don't you come with me this winter,' I suggested about a year after the accident. 'I'll get you a proper teacher if you can't afford one. We'll go out together; I'll make sure you don't fall down.'

We went back to Aspen, and I watched Steve improve slowly but surely under the watchful eye of the tutor I found and paid for. By the end of our trip he was able to go almost as fast as I could, although admittedly mostly in a sort of snowplough formation. Still, he enjoyed himself, and managed not to break anything, so I considered the outing a definite success. At the end, I helped him find some better, shorter, skis and an outfit that didn't look twenty years out of fashion, and Steve's sporting outlook seemed far more promising than it had a year earlier.

Steve never exactly became a ladies' man, although he did eventually meet the woman of his dreams. He graduated two years after me and went on to become the head of marketing for a big company on Madison Avenue in New York City. We continued to exchange Christmas cards for the next fifteen years. He continued to ski for a few years, but he ended up marrying a lovely young woman with no interest in sports whatsoever, so after a while he wrote to tell me his skiing days were behind him. I couldn't help but reply that this was probably a good idea.

A ROOM WITHOUT A VIEW

When moving to Geneva in 1992 with my wife and children, I looked at over sixty different locations to try and find the perfect house. There were quite a few criteria to fulfil, some of them more unusual than others. For instance, ours was, by this point, a large family, with ten children and multiple aunts and uncles. I eliminated the houses that were not near good shopping areas. Schools were very important too, as was nearness to the town centre and to good public transport links. However, through this rather arduous process of elimination, I ended up with a house that seemed perfect: a building in a wonderful location, that had the architectural structure of an 18th century palladium, the right number of bedrooms, and a beautiful garden, as well as excellent location. Best of all, the property had an incredible view out over Lake Geneva.

The price was reasonable, so I committed to the purchase on the spot. However, it turned out it would take four months to get the paperwork done properly. I agreed to this delay with some reluctance, but it seemed to be intractable. Overall, though, I was mostly pleased with the find. However, just a week or so later, as we were drawing up part of the contract, I noticed that construction seemed to have begun in the garden. I didn't ask any questions, as I assumed it was just a passing project, something to do with local road-works perhaps, or general engineering going on in the area. Perhaps, I thought idly, they were simply putting new plumbing in the surroundings buildings and had to dig through the garden to set it up. Whatever my reasoning, I gave the matter no more consideration. Over the next four months, I didn't visit. I simply waited for the lawyers and notaries to do their work, whilst making the first preparations for the move and looking forward to moving into our new home overlooking the lake.

However, this peaceful mood was short-lived. On the day we came to the signing, we had the rather rude shock of finding out that not only had a piece of the garden been sold without my knowledge, but that works had been begun to build another villa there.

'This is ridiculous!' I said. 'You can't do this! This wasn't in the terms of the sale!'

'What do you mean, *Monsieur?*' The landlord shrugged, feigning innocence. 'It has nothing to do with your agreement. It's a completely separate plot of land. Your neighbour can do what he wants with it.'

'It's right next to the house! You didn't tell us anything about a construction project.'

'It was already underway. I thought you would be aware of it!' he protested, unconvincingly.

'This is ridiculous. This is not correct procedure,' I informed him as firmly as I could.

The man sighed. 'Look, *Monsieur*, this is none of my business. It concerns only you and your neighbour. I am simply selling the land to you.'

'It is entirely my business if you are building things right in my back garden!' I paused. 'It's right between the house and the lake, this project.'

'Look,' the landlord said, 'I'll lower the price of the house.'

This hasty capitulation worried me more than the preceding argument. 'Wait a minute,' I said, 'I'm not sure about all this. Why would you have to do that?'

'Well, we could keep the old price,' he replied huffily.

'You know perfectly well that's not what I mean. We can discuss the price later. I'm more interested in talking to this new neighbour of mine, actually.'

'I'm afraid there's no reason why I should allow this. As I said before, it's none of your business what your neighbours are planning to build.'

'Well, that comment alone makes me retract my previous questions. I should let you know that I'm very seriously contemplating cancelling our contract and looking elsewhere,' I threatened in earnest.

'Alright then,' he agreed begrudgingly, 'I'll arrange a meeting.'

My soon-to-be neighbour and I met for coffee a few days later. He turned out to be a passing acquaintance of mine, from a major family in Lausanne, and one of the richest men in Geneva. This in itself did not put me off, but it did worry me as to the scale of his possible plans.

'So,' he began, 'are you my new neighbour-to-be?'

'Well, I might be,' I said, in as friendly a manner as I could manage.

'Did you have a safe journey?'

'Look, please don't take offense, but I didn't come here for small talk. I'd like to sort out my family's future before this espresso has gone cold.' My interlocutor nodded and smiled, obviously used to business-like interactions. 'Now. Can you please tell me, quite simply, what your building plans are for the garden.'

He evaded my questions as long as possible, giving only vague answers and trying to weasel his way out of responding using his charm. Nonetheless, he eventually sighed and gave in. 'If you really must know, we're building a villa. A lovely villa. Now can we move on from this conversation?'

'A villa. How big is this villa?'

'Villa-sized.'

'Don't be funny with me. Can you show me the plans?'

He sighed. 'I don't have the plans.'

Another long conversation ensued in which he tried to avoid giving me the plans. Finally, however, I wore him down. He buckled and gave me his architect's name and address. I drove straight to his office, where he showed me the plans for the villa. 'It's a villa in name only,' he explained. 'Really, it's a set of apartments with lake views.'

'OK,' I said cautiously, 'that doesn't sound too bad. The way he was avoiding my questions, I thought he might be building a whole bunch of council flats, or turning the flower beds into a parking lot!' Then what had just been said sunk in. Lake views? In front of my building? 'How high are these apartments?' I asked casually.

'Oh, about twenty metres,' the architect replied. My stomach sank.

The house I had committed to buy was only about fifteen metres high. 'Oh,' I said quietly. The best feature of that house had been its lake view, which I now realised was incredibly unlikely to survive the construction of this villa. The master bedroom had directly overlooked the blue waters: this had been my favourite fact about it. 'Thank you very much for your assistance,' I told the architect. I got back into my car and called my lawyer. Then I drove back to the property and told the landlord I wasn't going to buy the property.

'I've changed my mind,' I said firmly. 'There's no way I can buy this house. I'm sorry.'

The landlord, of course, nearly lost his temper, and tried to argue that I was in breach of contract, but when I told him I had seen the architect's plans, he went quiet. 'You never mentioned any of this to me when we set up the contract. You're the one in breach of contract. You knew perfectly well that the lake view was the principal reason we favoured this place over the others. We've lost the privacy, the peace and quiet, and the views of the lake. There's absolutely no reason for us to go ahead with the sale.' As he was about to start arguing, I added: 'Any objections you have, you can address directly to my lawyer. I'm going home to tell my family the news.'

The seller eventually admitted he was in the wrong, making me glad I had taken the time to speak to the new neighbour and his architect directly. After all, I had been one signature away from moving into a house which no longer possessed the feature I had chosen it for! In the end, however, I forgot this house quite quickly, as the next property we found turned out to be even more perfect. It was closer to town and shopping, and had more interesting historical features. So in the end, we moved into a house without the precious views of Lake Geneva, but which quickly turned out to be a wonderful old family house. We have certainly been happy there since then, and there have been no difficult neighbours building in our garden. Perhaps it was fate, after all, that we were discouraged from moving into the first place!

Cannes is one of the most beautiful cities of the French coast. In the shade of the Alps, and looking out over the warm waters of the Mediterranean, it stays gorgeous in all four seasons. Many wonderful hotels, like the Martinez, the Grey d'Albion and the Carlton, were installed on its famous *Croisette*, right on the edge of the glamorous beaches; but in the last thirty years there have also been a whole lot of slick, modern apartments built, no less glamorous and somewhat more affordable in the long term. My bank owned one, which we used to house occasional clients of the bank. In the heyday of banking that was the early 1980s, we had a particularly high number of clients who enjoyed coming over to conclude deals with us: Swedes and Finns mostly, as we had a major Scandinavian partner, but also a variety of clients of Arabic, Japanese, and American origins. Many of these would come down intending to rent apartments in Cannes or Antibes, or boats off the shore of Monte Carlo, to soak up the sun and do a little tourism whilst carrying out their business transactions. Nonetheless, we found it expedient to have a guest house in Cannes to cater for many of them. After all, who would turn down the offer of an apartment near the glamorous hill of Super-Cannes, overlooking the bay and the low mountain peaks?

Our guest apartment was a modest but lovely place, only about 120 square metres in size, but including a very nice living room where we received clients, and a balcony with a sea view. Our clients loved waking up and looking out over the curve of the city, the white sand beaches and the rolling turquoise waves. But the guests were not our only clients. In fact, some of our neighbours were too! Immediately next to us, there was a five-hundred-square-metre apartment that belonged to one of the richest Arabs I have ever met. He was one of the lucky desert millionaires who came into their money after the 1973 euphoria of oil price increases, when men were elevated from paupers to tycoons overnight.

My neighbour's apartment was modern and slightly gaudy in terms of décor, with leather sofas and brightly coloured wall hangings: but, after all, one would be hard-pressed to make any apartment on the Croisette ugly. I occasionally visited this next-door neighbour, as we got on rather well, and he would usually cook us some kind of feast: a spiced stew that had been bubbling on the stove for hours, or a tajine of roasted vegetables served with a selection of herbed flatbreads. Once, he spit-roasted an entire lamb with herbs and spices, right in the middle of his vast kitchen, so we could share a veritable North African *méchoui*. The kitchen alone must have been about eighty square metres, a ridiculously sharp and modern room fitted out in chrome and glass, and these antiquated dishes seemed somewhat out of place there, but they were always delicious nonetheless. My neighbour was certainly nothing short of adventurous in his cooking!

One day, however, he called me up at home suggesting that we go out for dinner. 'Let's have something different for once,' he said. 'I know we both love Lebanese food, and the occasional big Arabian spread, but I think we need to sample some other kinds of cuisine.'

'Sure,' I said. 'What are you thinking? A classic French bouillabaisse, maybe? Or a good steak with pepper sauce?' I must admit the idea of eating in a restaurant didn't sound too bad on an uneventful Thursday evening.

'No, no, something even simpler. I'm in the mood for some real junk food. I would like a nice, big Italian pizza.'

'Why not?' I replied. 'We'll just go next door, they have one of the best wood-burning pizza ovens.'

'I have a much better idea. Just come with me, you'll have a surprise.'

I sighed inwardly and hung up. I am not particularly fond of pizza, as I don't really enjoy hot cheese: one may as well be eating a particularly stringy ball of melted plastic! However, I wanted to maintain good relations with my neighbour, and I figured he must have something interesting in mind. I was not disappointed. When I arrived at his front door, I was greeted by four beautiful air hostesses dressed in smart, navy outfits. 'The Rolls Royce is waiting downstairs,' one of them said, tossing her long blonde hair. 'It's taking us to the airport.' She smiled.

'I thought we were going out for a nice dinner,' I said, a trifle confused. 'The pizza at the airport is definitely not better than the pizza here!'

My host materialised in the background, in a smart linen suit. 'Don't worry, my friend,' he said expansively, 'we're getting takeout! From Milano.'

My jaw dropped. 'OK, I've heard of some extravagant meal plans,' I said, 'but this is something else! Isn't it a bit... excessive? I mean, how good can these pizzas be?'

He grinned, obviously thrilled at my reaction. 'Just wait, it's only about twenty-five minute flight. You'll see,' he said with something like a giggle. 'You'll enjoy it.'

We arrived at the airport, and embarked on his vast DC9-50 aeroplane, a McDonnell-Douglas twin-engine private jet, which he kept parked in Nice. When I stepped inside, I couldn't believe the luxury it was fitted out in: it was just like stepping into a strangely-shaped hotel room, with a large bed right in the middle of the plane's body, and a magnificent bathroom complete with mosaics and a Jacuzzi. The plane also featured at least twenty comfortable leather seats and a saloon area.

Two captains and an engineer were waiting for us. We took off within minutes, watched the sun set as we soared along the coast and across the plains of Italy, and landed barely twenty minutes later. Another Rolls Royce was waiting for us, and took us straight to a well-known pizza shop called Chez Paolo, where the pizzas were already waiting, packed in insulated boxes. On the drive back to the plane, they filled the Rolls Royce with the rich steam of rosemary and olive oil. We flew straight back home, and I must admit that his theory had no flaws in a practical sense: by the time we ate them, back on the terrace in Cannes, they were neither too hot nor too cold. I embraced the junk-food spirit and had a can of Coca-Cola on the side. To me this was excessive, but it was a sacrifice that I made both to my relations with the client and to the expedition: after all, I thought it would make a good story to tell my family later on! It was certainly one of the most extravagant excursions for food I've ever been involved with, and I have known a lot of people with a taste for excess. The fuel alone must have cost about $20,000 or so, without counting the fees for the pilot, the two Rolls Royces, the air hostesses and, of course, the pizza itself!

THE FRATERNITY COVER-UP

As a young student in the 1960s, I was in a fraternity with many interesting people I called my friends. It was a great experience of communal living, and mostly we all rubbed shoulders quite happily, all hoping to achieve excellence in our chosen fields.

Yet, as one might expect, not all of them shared my exact outlook on life. Even at a young age, I considered myself to be a conservative sort of person who looked forward to building my own family based on the good old fashioned morals that I had been raised with. I had very little time for indulgences of any sort, and mostly committed myself to working hard in order to reach my goals.

Daniel Guess, a fraternity brother who lived on my floor, was not of the same mindset at all. He was more committed to the ideals of the 1960s than anything else. He wore his hair long, and spent his nights drinking and having fun. To me, he seemed quite rebellious, but I appreciated his sharp sense of humour.

It quickly became apparent to me that Dan fancied himself as something of a playboy, while in no way having the financial backing to achieve this ambition. While he dreamed of dining out in the finest restaurants and travelling to stay in fancy hotels in exotic locations, he was trapped largely by a lack of funds. He certainly didn't have the money to buy jewellery or expensive clothes for the girls he met at our fraternity parties, who he was desperate to impress.

Dan felt that this was the great unfairness of his life. He saw himself as destined to become an important, free-loving libertine, and yet could only get so far with what he had.

He more than made up for this with his charm, though. He was the kind of person who could wrap other people around his little finger. I should have known that he was trouble the moment I set eyes on him. He was handsome and muscular, with film-star good looks. He wore a mischievous grin on his strong features and was forever draping his tall frame across the furniture, lazy and self-indulgent. He had that naughty look about him, like a little boy who had stolen something.

Naturally, this made him ever so popular with girls, as did his careless dismissal of the fraternity rules.

I found the fraternity rules strict but fair, and most of all common sense. They didn't impinge on my own plans at all. We were permitted to have parties in the fraternity and could have girls over for them or to dinner, as long as it was all done out in the open. We were not, under any circumstances, allowed to have girls over to sleep at night, or to stay up late with us in our rooms.

Predictably, Dan found this rule completely unfair. It didn't fit with his own ideals at all, and he went out of his way to rebel against it.

'Don't you think the rules are stupid?' he asked me on more than one occasion. 'I mean, who even came up with them? We're adults. We should be allowed to make our own choices. Don't you believe in personal freedom? Aren't we meant to be living in a democracy?'

I mostly thought he was getting ideas above his station. Dan thought of himself in such grand terms and I just wanted to carry on with my day to day life. The rules were there for a reason.

'I don't mind so much. They're not difficult to live with.'

'Not difficult to live with! You think so? I'm like a tiger in a cage.'

I laughed at that, but he wasn't entirely joking. And it was only a matter of time until I got tangled up in Dan's schemes.

The first time Dan came and asked me if I would cover for him, I was surprised. I was quiet and studious, and hardly the obvious candidate to support the sort of deception he wanted to carry out. He had a girl he was interested in and wanted her to have dinner with him in his room.

'You want me to lie for you?' I asked dubiously. 'I'm not sure...' I wasn't a good liar and didn't believe in it. I thought I would inevitably be caught out if I attempted a deception, even a small one.

'Just say I'm busy if the frat president comes around, all right?' Dan asked me. He smiled, sure I would do as he wanted. He was like that. 'It's not a big deal. You don't have to stress out about it.'

All I could think was that he was breaking not one but two rules. As I said, we weren't allowed to have girls in our rooms, but we were also banned from eating our meals there. This was one of the rules that I accepted entirely without protest, since it was all in the name of hygiene. Students are notoriously messy and nobody wanted dirty plates littered all about the place. By having a designated dining area, we neatly avoided this. It also allowed us to socialise more easily.

And Dan just had no regard for the rules or the reasons behind them.

I liked Dan. He was a lot of fun and we always laughed together. But I also had great respect for the rules of the fraternity and didn't want to get in trouble for lying. Still, I didn't want to lose Dan's friendship by refusing his request outright.

'Okay,' I said after a moment, 'but I don't want to lie. If anyone asks, I'll tell them you're asleep. So why don't you go to sleep for a bit, lock your door. That way I'm not lying, not exactly.'

He sort of smirked at my plan. 'Good plan, genius. Thanks. I owe you one.'

Little did I know that he would come to owe me more than one favour over the coming months.

My cover story for him was all well and good, and it worked. Nobody suspected that Dan was taking food into his bedroom for a girl. It was just ridiculous. But it wasn't just the one time. Dan kept on locking himself in his room with a girl.

It was bad enough when I thought he had a single girlfriend who he wanted to keep seeing. But it quickly became obvious that it wasn't always the same girl. In fact, it was a string of them, a different one almost every night, which made me enormously uncomfortable. He did seem to have a steady girlfriend: there was one girl who showed up more often than the others, and she was always friendly and nice when she saw me.

But that didn't stop him from having a lot of other girls on the go, too.

I knew that this could only end in disaster.

'Don't you ever worry?' I asked Dan one morning after he saw a girl out who I didn't recognise.

He shrugged, leaning against the wall of our kitchen. 'Not really. Come on. You're only young once. What's the point in worrying about things? If you were worrying all the time you'd never do anything.'

'But you've got a girlfriend,' I pointed out to him, 'and anyway, you could get kicked out of the frat for this.'

'Not with you on my side.'

I sighed. 'Look, I'd rather give you twenty dollars and you could go and get a motel room. That way you'd have more privacy and you wouldn't have to think about getting caught.'

'Yeah, that's a good idea. But then I wouldn't have the dinner, would I?'

I couldn't believe his flagrant disregard for authority, but there wasn't much I could do. He was, after all, my friend. I certainly didn't want to turn him into an enemy just because we had a different view of life, opposing ideas of right and wrong.

'You'll get old before your time, always thinking about the worst thing that could happen,' he told me. 'You need to relax. Take a day off or something.'

'But if you get found out, they'll know I've been covering for you,' I said desperately. Dan was hardly subtle.

'No, I'd never tell anyone about that. What are friends for?' Dan winked at me, and went on much the same as ever. I tried not to let myself think about what would happen if he got caught.

We were friends, yes, but that would be his problem.

For the rest of the time we lived together, Dan carried on seeing several girls every week, keeping the spirit of the 1960s going in his own way, preaching about free love and the importance of living a life of pleasure, a life free from any regret.

I don't know what happened to Dan in the end, after we had stopped living together. I can only assume that he grew up and out of his rebellious phase, that he saw sense and, much like me, settled down to have a family of his own.

NEIGHBOURING CHILDREN:
THE BARRIER GAME

The children were at it again.

I found that the noise didn't bother me. I had fully committed myself to living a life of countryside idyll, and felt that the noise of schoolchildren laughing and shouting didn't concern me at all. My house lay in a small lane with a barrier which they would jump over on their way back from school, giddy with freedom and fearless with youth. The youngest of them was ten, the oldest around fourteen, and I couldn't really begrudge them their fun and games.

It quite cheered me to hear them, though they were of course trampling across my land on their way home to their own apartment buildings, using the way as an adventurous shortcut and enjoying themselves immensely doing so.

My butler Gotham, on the other hand, had no such fond feelings for them. After only a short time of the children swinging over the barrier, it broke fairly badly and needed replacing. The expense of it – no small sum – was more of a mild irritation than anything else to me.

'But it's a terrible inconvenience,' Gotham said to me. 'You do realise that they're just going to continue doing this?'

I shrugged. 'They're young.'

He sighed at me. 'They're foolish. They think they can destroy other people's property and get away with it. You could phone the police!'

'I don't think that's necessary.'

'It *feels* necessary. They're delinquents,' he muttered, but left it at that. It was true that these children were behaving in rather a poor manner, and that I would never allow my own children to do such things. But I chalked it up to the high spirits of youth. Besides, my children went to a lovely, if strict, school quite a distance away. These children were from local schools, where perhaps the discipline was not so important.

Gotham would chase the children off if he caught them loitering about by the barrier. It made for quite entertaining viewing. First Gotham would walk up to them and shout at them to move off. Unafraid, of course, they laughed at him. He was fifty-five, an old man to such young children, and they never got nervous until he broke into a run, waving his fist at them. Then they screamed and ran off, calling rude things back at him as they left. I couldn't condone their accidental vandalism, but it did make me smile.

That is, until one day Gotham was running after them and suffered a mild heart attack. I was always joking about how he was going to do himself a mischief, chasing about like a teenager, but when he did it was anything but funny. It didn't break his spirit, though.

'While I get back on my feet,' he said firmly to me, 'I expect you to do something about those troublemakers. People will think you don't care about your house. They'll think you're soft.'

One doesn't argue with a man who has just had a heart attack, so I was forced to agree with Gotham that I would set to and do something about the problem children. If nothing else, to stop him running after them and causing himself any more damage.

The last thing I wanted was a dead butler.

Still, I gave myself a couple of days listening to the children play around my land... until they broke the barrier again, and I had to pay out another substantial sum of money. Even if they were enjoying their game, I decided it was becoming a bit too costly and decided to install a camera. I thought that perhaps if they saw a security camera watching their every move, they might think twice before playing quite so roughly on the barrier. After all, if they simply jumped over it, there shouldn't be any problem, and I did like the idea of them having the way as a shortcut home, for lunchtime and at the end of the day.

It was just the sort of game I had liked to play as a boy, adventuring across a forbidden place and making it home in no time at all.

The camera proved to have little effect. The children still played on the barrier, still broke it, and even though I came out of the house a few times to tell them off when I caught them, it changed nothing. They didn't seem to take it very seriously, and so I decided it was time to install a thicker barrier, one which had a key and so appeared more official and imposing.

It made no difference.

Even the installation of a so-called unbreakable electronic barrier proved to be something of a non-starter. For the first few days, the children passed over it without cause for concern, but after almost no time at all, even this piece of improved technology was left shattered.

By this point, it was quite clear that the children were doing this on purpose, baiting me the more I tried to protect my barrier. While I took no personal offense, it was becoming far too costly a game and after repairing the barrier yet again, I employed a security guard to watch when the children passed by four times a day.

'There's a definite improvement,' my wife said cheerfully, 'no more noise, either!'

I actually sort of missed the sounds of rowdy children passing by, but didn't say this. 'Yes. I think we've finally cracked it.'

Of course, the second the security guard believed the school run time to have passed, he left his post and retired for the evening.

The next morning, I found the barrier broken yet again.

It was frustrating even to someone of a fairly laid-back nature. The barrier had definitely become more of a hassle than it was worth.

'I'm getting rid of it,' I told my wife.

She nodded. 'It's probably for the best.'

So I set to work having the broken barrier taken away for the final time. Then I replaced it with a thick, iron, unbreakable barrier as thick as a grown man's wrist. There was no way the children could break it, and there was no other way for them to come across my land as a shortcut. The fun of the game having been taken out of it, the children gradually lost interest and stopped crossing my land.

However, when Gotham returned, well enough to work again, he was nothing but thrilled by the alterations I had made and the subsequent absence of youths wandering hither and thither and breaking things.

'Do you hear that?' he asked me as he stood surveying the path that was no longer a real path, the space where the barrier had once been.

I was instantly alert. Although there was no way for the children to come by my property any more, I couldn't help but still listen out for them out of habit. 'What? I can't hear anything. I told you, the children can't come this way any longer.'

He smiled serenely. 'Exactly. Silence.'

MY WEST SIDE STORY

In the early 1970s, if you were in any way artistically inclined, the Upper West Side of Manhattan was the place to be. New York was fairly prosperous at the time, although it had its slums and disreputable areas: for instance, neither the hip nor the middle-class who populate the areas today would have been caught dead in the Lower West Side and Lower East Side. Even Greenwich Village, now the yuppie headquarters of the city, was a fairly poor area populated mostly by students and grungy hippies. The Upper West Side, however, already had a hint of glamour about it, without the outrageous rent inflation that would come over the next few decades. All things considered, in 1970, I decided that it would be a good investment to buy an apartment there and rent it out. I acquired a two-hundred-and-twenty-square-metre apartment, which cost me sixty thousand dollars, most of which were financed by the banks I was working with. It was a slick, modern place, with stunning views over the West River, and even though it was considerably larger than I had been looking for, I fell in love at once.

I moved into the apartment and settled in quite comfortably. By chance, my neighbours turned out to be a very friendly couple by the name of Jim and Debbie Palamino. Jim and Debbie lived across the hall from me, in a smaller apartment. When we first met, we hit it off at once as our business interests coincided. When they first approached me with an offer of coffee, they explained to me that they were expecting a baby, and were looking to rent some extra space in the building in preparation for the new arrival. This suited me remarkably well, at my place was far too large for a single man: we quickly came to the agreement that I would rent half of my apartment to them. This was not the end of our interactions, though: we quickly became quite close friends.

Jim was an Italian immigrant by blood, having come over to America as a child. He was a very tall man, sporting dark hair and a long nose, with fair skin that betrayed his northern Italian origins. He had been educated at New York University, though, so his accent was unmistakeably New York rather than Italian. Debbie, in contrast, was of pure WASP American heritage, with a strong Boston accent: the two of them really were a quite remarkable pair. Both of them were very hard-working; when Debbie was pregnant, for instance, she only stopped work a week before the baby was born, and was back at her job only two weeks afterwards! Jim was a slightly calmer partner, who balanced out her drive. He was a charming man, having inherited from his ancestors both a love of pasta and a series of funny stories, as well as his looks. They were a friendly and fairly unusual couple for their time, with Debbie being the high-powered breadwinner and Jim the cook and raconteur. The two of them loved Italian food to a point that was hard to understand for anybody not born and bred in *il bel paese*. They had not one but several pasta makers in their kitchen: one to make the dough, one to roll it out in thin sheets, one to cut it or mould it into different sizes and shapes. As far as I could tell, they would spend most weekends making vast batches of fresh egg pasta which they hung on racks to dry. I believe they loved nothing more than to have friends over for a nice Italian dinner.

What I always found amusing about this was the similarity of all the food they prepared for us. It seemed to take them hours and hours to produce nearly identical pasta dishes! I have never really understood Italian sauces, to be honest: they always seem to be the same four ingredients combined or dressed up slightly differently, cooked longer or more finely chopped than usual. Unless one is totally obsessed with tomatoes, I doubt the whole thing would have very much appeal. They all seem to be flavoured only with olive oil, salt, pepper, bay leaf and oregano. Sometimes they might include a sprinkling of parmesan cheese, other times they might be spiced up a little with chillies, but overall they seemed somehow unworthy of the rave reviews they seem to receive from most of Western civilisation.

Of course, none of my doubts about Italian cuisine had any influence over my friendship with Jim and his wife. Jim was a really interesting man, a sort of quiet raconteur with a real talent for telling long, fascinating stories. He seemed to draw his jokes and anecdotes from a mix of sources that must have included old tales gleaned at his grandmother's knee. His gentle style of delivery was offset by his wife's charm and peppiness: Debbie was very driven, and she and I shared many an interesting discussion about engineering. The three of us also often enjoyed the occasional walk or game of squash.

In 1972, when I decided to move out and emigrate to Paris, I offered to sell them our apartment as a friendly neighbourly gesture. They agreed happily, as they were doing quite well financially and had a little cash to spare, even offering me a ten thousand dollar profit on my original investment. I left them on friendly terms, with a large apartment and an open invitation to come visit me on the continent whenever they saw fit. These offers are made regularly between friends upon parting, but rarely fulfilled. However, a few years later, my wife and I received a letter from Jim and Debbie, asking if they could come visit us. Of course, we were thrilled, and agreed at once.

This is how I found myself waiting at the Bourget airport after sundown in our brand-new MG 1947 sedan with my six-month-pregnant wife in the backseat. The car was a recent acquisition, a beautiful antique in a bright burgundy colour, which I was still quite proud of. Jim and Debbie arrived on time and in good spirits. We piled all their luggage into the trunk and started on the road home. It turned out that Debbie was also pregnant, herself seven months along, so the two women had a lot to discuss. Whilst they gossiped away happily in the backseat, I started on the drive home with Jim already regaling me with one of his shaggy dog stories. The visit seemed to be off to a terrific start.

Just two miles down the road, however, a few minutes after we had joined the highway, the car motor simply stopped. Jim and I looked at each other, my wife and Debbie looked at each other, and for a moment there was total silence. Then Debbie burst out laughing.

'Well, in normal times, I would be the one to get out and push the car. But I don't think our fifth and sixth passengers are going to be any help, and they're immobilising numbers three and four, too.' She was referring, of course, to the two babies she and my wife were carrying.

I smiled. 'Now, you ladies don't worry. You just sit there with your precious cargo.' I cast a glance at my neighbour before making a plan. Just as Debbie appeared to have rounded out in pregnancy, Jim appeared to have grown even thinner and more sickly-looking than he was before. 'Jim, if you don't mind, I'd like you to clamber into the driver's seat. I'll get out and push the car.' Jim, who had never driven in Europe before, blanched a little, but he admitted this plan made sense. 'I'm sorry about this,' I said to him quietly, 'it's just that we don't really have much of a choice!'

'Don't worry,' Jim said with a slightly shaky smile, 'I'm sure I can move a wheel back and forth just as well on European soil as I can in the USA. Anyway, I've always wanted to drive an MG.'

I climbed out of the driver's seat and went and stood behind the car. Looking around, there was nothing but pure darkness. In the deep dark night of the French countryside, it looked like the perfect set-up for a thriller or horror movie. It also made for quite an ordeal: MG sedans are meant to be propelled by about forty horses' worth of power, not a single middle-aged man! I was also intensely aware that Jim would be very uncomfortable steering the car which contained both of our dear wives, as well as both our first children-to-be. All in all, the whole thing was fairly stressful, and certainly not quite the welcome I had planned for my old neighbours. Luckily, once the car started moving, the motor started right up again, and we were on our way. The ladies applauded our courage, and, considering our plight, everyone was in fairly high spirits by the time we made it back safe and sound.

We arrived home safely and in time to cook up a nice dinner. I prepared their favourite spaghetti with a sauce of *ragù alla Genovese*, made with chunks of beef stewed in red wine, and sweetened with fresh tomatoes, of course. By the time we were mopping up the leftover sauce with bread, everybody seemed to have recovered from our travel scare, and was finding the whole episode quite funny in retrospect. 'I have to say,' Jim joked to me, 'considering that you live in France, I'm much more impressed with your skills at cooking Italian food than at driving English cars!'

Jim and Debbie only stayed for three days, as they were on a whirlwind tour of Europe, but we had a lovely time. We only used the car again over short distances, and with no particular trouble. Jim told me they had completely redecorated the apartment in the Upper West Side and that they were planning to sell it. I couldn't help but be a bit saddened by this discovery, as I had loved that apartment and secretly hoped to come and visit them there. The real surprise, however, was finding out that he had made one and a half million dollars off the sale! 'That's more than all the salaries I made in my fifteen years of full-time employment!' he told me excitedly. 'I really owe you one for that apartment, old friend.' I congratulated him on the sale without begrudging it: after all, we were good friends. I could hardly resent him having made money off one of my old investments. Instead, I took some pride from the turnout, and considered it a good neighbourly deal.

BREAKING AND ENTERING

Our bank had a guest house in the seventeenth *arrondissement* of Paris, to accommodate visitors from locations around the world. I didn't use it, as my family had an apartment in the city, but I did occasionally entertain guests of the bank there. It was a lovely little house, perfect for hosting lunch or dinner there after a conference, or just an afternoon meeting in a cosier and more relaxed setting than the vast glass tables of the bank conference rooms.

One day, I went down to the guesthouse directly from the bank with a visitor who had come at short notice for a conference. The visit was unscheduled, so we had not been able to prepare the house with fresh bedding or to dust the surfaces, but as it was not in too regular use at the time, it didn't even occur to me to worry about the general maintenance. As I walked in, with the guest behind me, I realised I had been wrong in this respect. The first things we saw were four tables with green felt tops, scattered with dice, cards, poker chips and empty glasses. 'I'm terribly sorry,' I said to the guest, 'something strange is obviously going on here. Perhaps you could leave your luggage here and go for a walk, or a coffee, while I try to sort out what exactly has happened here?' The guest was perfectly amenable about the whole situation, responding with a grin: 'For a minute, there, I thought you were going to offer me a game of 21!' I laughed. 'Whatever this may look like, I can promise you that isn't the style of this bank.'

When the guest had gone, I walked around the place slowly. There was no-one to be found, but everything was recently disturbed. From the strange atmosphere and all the evidence of hastily abandoned tables, I was sure someone was still in the house. A few minutes later, my hunch was confirmed, when I heard a noise in a cupboard.

'Dear me,' I said aloud, 'do we have mice in here? Or perhaps a stray cat? I didn't know cats had a penchant for poker...' I smiled to myself, sure that whoever was hiding would appear shortly. Sure enough, after I had looked under the dining table, there came an unmistakeable smothered cough from the cupboard. I opened the door to find two women hiding in there, their faces bright red.

'Well hello,' I said, 'to what do I owe the pleasure of your visit?' The taller of the girls, who was blonde and the more smartly dressed of the two, spoke first, after a long, embarrassed silence. 'We're neighbours!' she said, as brightly as she could. I raised an eyebrow. 'Do you break into all your neighbours' houses for your parties?'

'Oh, it's not our party!' she said hastily. 'It's Joe and Dec's!' the other girl added, at which point the blonde shot her a warning glance.

'Oh, don't worry,' I assured her, 'very few people have these keys. Your friends would have been busted pretty quickly no matter what you told us.' Although I tried to keep a cool exterior, inside, I was reeling. Joe and Dec may have been young, there was no question of that, but they had always seemed like extremely respectable employees of the bank. 'So Joe and Dec invited you here for a gambling party?' I asked.

'Yes, we are roommates. We like to gamble,' the brunette piped up. I suspected she hadn't thought of trying to protect their new friends. I smiled indulgently.

'What games do you play?'

'We play 21 or gin rummy,' she told me enthusiastically.

'We gamble for points,' the blonde added hastily. 'No money is exchanged.'

'No we don't,' the brunette said excitedly, 'we gamble properly, for money! We were just about to win that thousand off them!' She stopped in her tracks, confused. 'Oh,' she said. Then she was quiet for a long time. I tried to stop myself from smiling too obviously.

'So how did this happen? How did you meet these boys?'

'They were at the local bar, offered to let us come over for a party. They told us they worked for you.' Here, the blonde paused, obviously trying to figure out which bits of information to withhold. 'I mean… they seemed nice.'

'They were rich and they wanted to gamble. We like to gamble!' the brunette added, obviously feeling the cat was too far out of the bag to be worth retrieving.

'Are you trying to tell me you thought this place was their house?' I asked, raising an eyebrow dubiously.

The blonde sighed. 'No. I guess not. We thought it was just normal to use this place for… entertainment.'

'Do you use your offices as a gambling casino?'

'I… I don't know. No,' she stammered. I felt a little sad for the girl, and relented. After all, she wasn't really my problem. My employees were the ones who deserved to get in trouble for this. 'Don't worry,' I assured her, 'you're not the ones who are getting in trouble. It's not like you were actually breaking and entering, as I suspected at first. I'll let you both go in a minute. Where are Joe and Dec?' I asked.

'They were here a minute ago,' the brunette said hesitantly, after looking at her friend for guidance. I frowned. 'If that's true, we would have run into them outside. Come on, girls, you're not protecting anyone. These boys work for me. If I don't find them now, they're only postponing their telling-off until Monday morning.'

'I really don't know,' the blonde said earnestly. 'They told us to hide, but I have no idea where they went afterwards.'

'They must be in the other bedroom,' I thought aloud. 'OK. Right, off with the both of you. Don't take this the wrong way, but I hope I never see you again.' They laughed sheepishly and went back to the front room to collect their belongings.

Meanwhile, I went to inspect the other bedrooms. Sure enough, before long I found the two scruffy boys huddling on the floor behind the bed. 'What the hell are you doing here?' I asked. It was hard not to laugh. They truly were a comical sight, unshaven and with their hair a mess. From the smell of them, I suspected that they must have spent the night before in this place; possibly longer.

'So,' I said, 'it has come to this. Did I miss a memo? Since when has it become acceptable to hold drunken gambling parties on your employer's property?'

Dec and Joe stood up and dusted themselves off sheepishly. Joe was French and Dec was American; both were in their mid-thirties. Neither seemed to be able to come up with a clever retort or excuse. Eventually, Dec answered reluctantly and rather wearily: 'Well, it's not like we can really hide it.'

'Are we fired?' Joe added nervously.

'Are we skipping the part of this conversation where you apologise, or at least try to give some sort of explanation?' I retorted. 'We can discuss your career when you're sober. Dear god, you boys smell terrible!'

'We thought it was empty,' Joe said. 'We just... wanted to bring some nice girls back to play games. You met the girls, right? Weren't they nice?'

'Yes,' I said, 'far too nice for you boys. Apart from the gambling. That's not a great trait in anybody.' The men exchanged glances. 'Although I have to say it's even less attractive in a pair of aspiring accountants.' Joe cringed, while Dec seemed to be trying to keep his cool. 'You'll be lucky if you're just fired, and I keep this little story to myself.'

'We'll clean the place up,' Dec volunteered, a bit of desperation appearing under his veneer of nonchalance.

'Yes, you'd better do that,' I replied sternly. 'For that matter, you'd better do it in the next half hour, as we have a guest, and I don't particularly want to answer any more awkward questions. In fact, I don't even feel like asking them! From your shamefaced silence, I'll come to my own conclusions about the fact that there are four tables, and more than four glasses. I won't look to see if any of the beds have been slept in, either. Just make sure the place is spotless when I get back from the strong coffee I'm going to need in five minutes. And make sure you've cleared out, as well.'

They scrambled off without a word, presumably in search of brooms and mops. I sighed and went to wait for our guest in the front room. When he returned, shortly thereafter, I explained the situation as briefly as I could. The guest, to do him credit, seemed like a fairly relaxed type, and handled the whole situation quite amiably. He told me not to worry, and, seeing I was rather stressed by the encounter, advised that I head off and find myself a coffee. 'I'll see the boys off and settle in, don't you worry. These things happen.' Whatever the guest thought, however, it is always such a shame to discover that one's employees couldn't be trusted with the simplest responsibilities. The girls may have been the neighbours involved in this particular story, but the fault really lay with the irresponsible men I made the error of entrusting with the key.

Not all of the neighbouring houses to our country manor in Kent were as old and historically distinguished as ours. In our immediate vicinity, in particular, one house stood out as a bit of an eyesore: a modern, two-bedroom little prefabricated thing, it was a blot on the landscape for every visitor who saw our house for the first time. Whilst we would be explaining its history, from the time its foundations were laid in 1410 to its extensive renovation in 1620, I would always be worried that the guest's eyes might stray to this little building, sticking up like a sore thumb in the corner of our exquisitely laid-out Elizabethan gardens.

The main problem with this structure, however, was less its outwards appearance, unpleasant as that might have been, and more its precise location. The domain that our country house was the centrepiece to was laid out in a sort of traditional Elizabethan fashion, with little paths and plenty of room for the ladies to wander arm-in-arm from one part of the grounds to another. In modern life, however, this meant that access to the furthest parts of the property could not be managed without going on very specific routes. Simply put, I had no direct access to the swimming pool and the tennis court by car. The only way to get across our land to them was on foot, which was not always convenient, especially in the muddy springtime, or when one would be carrying a picnic or several inflatable toys to the pool. There was quite a lot of land to cross, a good three acres, blocked only by the modern addition of this little prefab house.

Thus, my issues with it were both aesthetic and functional ones. As soon as I moved into our house, I quietly resolved to do everything in my power to get rid of this neighbouring building. If it was gone, I reasoned, our estate could be returned to something approaching its former Elizabethan glory, its symmetry and simple loveliness restored. The ugly little house simply had to go.

Its first inhabitants were quite a nasty family, which really didn't help with my opinion of the place. They used the odd layout of the property to his advantage, as he could take advantage of my swimming pool and tennis court without our family being able to see them from the house. Needless to say, this reinforced my conviction that we needed easier access to these amenities.

Luckily, that neighbour and his family moved out after just a few years, with no love lost between us. Upon his departure, however, the house was bought by a friendly young schoolteacher by the name of Tom. I was quite charmed by Tom, a tall and well-spoken Englishman in his thirties, and I decided to try to achieve my aims in the most mutually beneficial way possible. Just a week or so after he turned up with the removal van, I invited him round for coffee. We chatted amiably for a time, discovering a shared interest in twentieth-century playwrights and strong coffee. After these pleasantries had been exchanged, however, I got to the heart of the matter.

'I must speak with you about something slightly unusual,' I warned him. 'It's about your house, actually.'

'It's not haunted is it?' he joked. 'The last house I looked at, the landlord tried to convince me there were two ghost children in the attic. I never saw them, but I guess you never know.'

I cracked a smile. 'As far as I know, there's nothing like that. I mean, I haven't lived in your house; it might have some modern ghosts. No, what I want to talk about has much more to do with my house and our land.'

I went on to explain the history of the place, the layout of the grounds, and my dreams of restoring the property to its former glory. I decided to leave out the problem of the access, in case he would then realise he had a real advantage over me. Tom listened sympathetically, although obviously without making the link to his own property's location.

'I'm afraid the conclusion to this historical digression is no doubt going to shock you,' I said at last, 'but I'd like to make you a proposal. Now, I understand perfectly well if you want to refuse, and I would be more than happy to count you as my neighbour if you're not interested in what I have to offer. I do, however, also understand that you've just moved in, and might therefore not be too tremendously attached to this new house of yours, so I thought I'd come to you sooner rather than later with this slightly unconventional offer of mine.' Tom nodded, obviously unsure what the conclusion of this was going to be. 'I would like to buy your house,' I concluded without further ado.

'I'm sorry? You already have a house,' he said blankly.

I laughed. 'I'm sorry, I realise this must come as something as a shock. Just hear me out: I would happily offer you a ten percent profit on whatever you just paid for the place, if you agree to sell it to me within the next month and move out.'

Tom cocked his head to the side, considering.

'What I would really want is to build a tiny Elizabethan-style guesthouse in its place,' I added, not entirely untruthfully. 'No offense to its new inhabitant, but I've had enough of that little ugly prefab thing staring me in the face every day.'

Tom laughed. 'Oh, it's no beauty,' he said. I could almost see the cogs whirring in his head: he was obviously a bright young man. This was an undeniably attractive business proposal, considering the real estate market at the time.

He smiled. 'Fifteen percent,' he said.

'Alright!' I grinned. He shook his head, content if obviously a little dazed. I was thrilled that he had agreed so quickly, as I didn't really like the idea of him going off and working out the exact reasoning for my desire to bring down his new house with a wrecking ball. If he had understood how strong and personal my reasons were, he would no doubt have raised his price much further. 'I know a smart young man when I see one,' I told him, quite honestly. 'You are, of course, free to stay on until you find a new place to move into. I'll transfer the money as soon as you give me your details.'

Within two months, the hideous little house was gone, replaced with box hedges, freshly-sown lawns and a trellis of roses. At last, our property sat in the centre of the lovely Elizabethan-looking context it should have had all along. We dug a new road to the swimming pool and tennis court, and paved it. Everything looked much more formal, with no more interference from modernity; surrounded only by terraced gardens, without a single pesky neighbour in sight. Of course, I still have the option of building that little guesthouse, but I certainly don't intend to do that right away.

My family used to live in a lovely apartment in the old town of Geneva, hidden away amongst the cobbled streets and ancient stone buildings that make up this exclusive neighbourhood. The old town is just a short walk from the shores of the lake, but far enough from the bustle of the centre to be a pleasant, quiet place to raise young children.

For his eleventh birthday, I let my son Jimmy invite some of his friends over for a sleepover. There was the usual running around and game-playing, as young children do, and staying up late eating junk food and watching a film. I checked in on them before going to bed to find them sitting on the floor and chatting. I left them to it, taking some reassurance in the fact that they seemed to have found some healthy snacks too, as they had a large bag of oranges. I figured they were old enough to stay out of most kinds of trouble. I may have been wrong about this...

Around one in the morning, there was a knock on the door. I stumbled downstairs in my bathrobe and opened the door to find two outrageously drunk Russians standing there, shaking their square heads menacingly and practically foaming at the mouth with anger. It was quite an impressive sight. However, their French was very broken, and their English hardly any better, so I was having some trouble understanding what exactly had brought them to our door in the middle of the night. At first, I thought they might be downstairs neighbours trying to warn us about a leak, or a fire, or something that had happened in the street, but I quite quickly figured out that their ire was directed very specifically at us.

Luckily, before the threats could escalate or turn physical, our nurse, who had been woken by the noise, appeared on the stairs. 'It's the children,' she said. 'They're angry about something the children have done.' She then launched into a rapid-fire Russian dialogue with our angry neighbours. I looked at the pair in surprise. I had completely forgotten that our nurse had grown up in Hungary, and was thus fluent in Russian. At this point, there was nothing I could do but watch the conversation unfold. The Russian men became progressively more worked up, then gradually appeared to calm down.

'What's going on?' I asked her, as soon as there appeared to be a kind of lull in their exchange.

'Well,' she said, 'from what these men are telling me, it sounds like our Jimmy's sleepover may have become a little out of hand.'

'What do you mean?'

'It appears that they have broken all the windows in the building across the way.' The nurse's Hungarian upbringing had obviously also trained her to be able to deliver such news without undue emotion. I, on the other hand, found it hard to stay calm.

'What? I mean, of course, the kids were a bit overexcited, but surely they're not that violent!'

'Look for yourself,' she said quietly. We walked over to the window together in order to look out into the street. Sure enough, from where we were standing we could see multiple breaks in the panes of glass across the way. 'How did they even do that?' I mused aloud. 'These windows are on the third floor!'

'Oranges,' she said curtly. 'Apparently, they threw all the oranges out of the window.' My mouth hung upon in sheer disbelief.

At this point, obviously understanding that particular word and thus working out the substance of our conversation, one of the Russians began jabbering and gesturing excitedly. 'He says they weren't just oranges,' the nurse explained. 'Apparently Jimmy and his little friends thought it would be a good idea to stick things in the oranges: toothpicks, kitchen utensils, knives…'

'Knives?!' This didn't sound like the son I knew. 'I'm going to wake him up right now and have a serious talk with him.'

'It's the middle of winter,' the nurse reminded me. 'You need to deal with Jimmy, but you should probably do something about the windows.'

'Let me just get to the bottom of this. Can you just talk to our neighbours a little longer, try to calm them down? I'll try to figure out what exactly happened with my son; then I'll deal with the neighbours.'

I woke my son up and made him come sit down on the couch with me. He blinked at me angrily, as if I was wildly misrepresenting the situation.

'They're guided missiles,' he explained patiently. 'We only put the cutlery in them so they would fly straight.' My son turned out to have more of a talent for arguing a lost cause than one would have thought, considering the situation.

'Straight into our neighbours' windows? How on earth did this seem to you and your friends like anything but a terrible idea?'

'They were drunk and loud. They were partying for hours, singing and shouting in Russian! We couldn't sleep.'

'So you decided to break all their windows? I don't think that's a very sensible approach, son.'

'It made them stop,' he replied calmly.

'You didn't think you'd get into trouble?'

'No.'

'It's complete and utter vandalism. You threw these... missiles across eight yards, at high speed! Did it occur to you it might have hurt someone?'

'It didn't hurt anybody. We'd been doing the same thing with snowballs earlier.'

'Snowballs don't break windows. Knives do.' I sighed. 'Look, it's too late to deal with this now. Go back to bed. We'll talk about this in the morning. You're all having breakfast at eight a.m. sharp.'

I dismissed him, and he stomped back to the nest of sleeping bags where his friends were still asleep, presumably dreaming of vandalism. Meanwhile, I turned back to the Russians, who were now chatting more amiably with the nurse. 'Tell them we'll pay for all the damages,' I instructed her, with the friendliest smile I could muster directed at our neighbours. 'We'll get our own *ébéniste*, our carpenter to come and fix it in the morning.' The Russians, looking much friendlier all of a sudden, although no less drunk, took their leave. We listened to them stumble down the stairs, then across the street.

'I'll call the parents,' the nurse said at once. 'We'll send all these rowdy kids home. They're a terrible influence on Jimmy.'

I shook my head. 'Look at them, they're all asleep. I know it would be easy to blame them for getting Jimmy riled up, or the weather, or too much junk food, but the truth of the matter is what's done is done. We'll fix everything tomorrow. We'll explain everything to the parents in due course, but let's not wake them up and freak them out now.'

In the morning, everyone was much cowed. Even Jimmy had lost his late-night swagger, although he still tried to blame everything from the oranges to the Russians and the snow outside.

It became obvious quite quickly that he was the ring-leader of the operation. In fact, it was quite comical: when I gave them a group telling-off, as Jimmy was the tallest, his friends literally hid behind him. When the parents came to pick them up, we gave an explanation of the situation. All the parents were highly apologetic, offering to pay for the damages and giving their offspring threatening looks with varying degrees of subtlety. I refused all their kind offers and tried to defuse the tension between them and the offending children. 'You know how young boys are,' I said. 'When I was eleven I probably committed this sort of folly without really thinking. You have a little bit too much Monster Munch and you become a little monster yourself! They're only ten, maybe twelve.' In the end, everyone left without too much fuss, leaving us the job of cleaning up. Later that afternoon, I went over to see the Russians, bringing the nurse in tow as a translator. By that time, the carpenter was already fixing the windows, and the blonde men had presumably recovered from their hangovers, so everything appeared to have been sorted out fairly pleasantly. One of them turned to the nurse and said something, which she translated which a wry smile. 'He says to tell you he probably did things like that when he was eleven, too,' she said. I laughed. 'Oh, so did I! It doesn't mean it's very good neighbourly behaviour though…'

I have nothing against the Dutch, and certainly nothing against the Dutch living in England. However, there is a certain, inevitable problem with a Dutchman who lives in England and still wants to drive like a Dutchman.

Our neighbour, Thomas Van Tomlin, occasionally had this problem. Van Tomlin lived in the guardhouse in the cul-de-sac behind our country house in Kent. It was a small but comfortable house, with only two bedrooms, ideal for someone just setting up in life. Van Tomlin was only twenty-four years old, so the house's relatively low rent appealed to him. He was working as a paralegal in a London city law firm, who had hired him for his language skills: he spoke French and German as well as Dutch, and English, of course.

He was a nice enough young man, and although he could occasionally be a little blunt, he had a good sense of humour nonetheless. Physically, he had none of the Viking attributes of so many of his compatriots, as he was short, thin and rather pale, but he did still have a pronounced accent that gave away his origins. I cannot help but imagine he would have been quite good at some of the more violent aspects of Viking life, however.

Van Tomlin, to put it simply, was a terrible driver. If Vikings had gone pillaging in second-hand grey Fords, this would probably be the way they drove. It wasn't just that he was a daredevil, but it seemed that he just could not get used to this strange English custom of driving on the left side of the road. 'It just doesn't make any sense,' he would bark at me from the garden. 'And it's only the English! Nowhere else on earth!'

'Actually,' I tried to point out to him once, 'they drive on the left in India, and Australia, and quite a few major countries.'

'Colonies!' he replied. 'All colonies! All English madness.'

We had variants of this conversation so many times that I eventually looked up the number of countries with left-hand driving. It turns out about 40% of the world drives on the left. When I shared this piece of information with Van Tomlin he simply made a snorting sound, presumably choosing not to believe it. To be honest, left-hand driving was only part of his problem. Although I'm pretty sure they have them in Holland as well, concepts like 'giving way,' 'stop signs' and 'road markings' seemed to have little effect on him.

Our house had a driveway which led to the main road. After Van Tomlin had been our neighbour for a few months, it had become a distinctly less defined driveway. The gravel was a mess, a few of the shrubs at the side had obviously been driven over, and there were tyre marks on the lawn. Van Tomlin never mentioned anything about this. He was a fairly blunt young man, with that little bit of swagger men in their early twenties can find hard to avoid, and he obviously had no concept of quite how bad his driving was.

Our driveway was not the best place to put a bad driver. The beautiful chestnut and poplar trees on the property did rather cover up the entrance to this drive, making it all but invisible to the traffic on the main road. Getting onto the main road necessitated a sort of careful inching out, if you had a cautious temperament. However, if you were more of a brazen Viking warrior, the preferred technique was to blaze out onto the road as fast as possible, hoping to avoid violent death.

As you can imagine, this was not the most efficient manoeuvre. Thus, after two or three close shaves, Van Tomlin decided on a new tactic. From then on, almost as soon as he left the gatehouse, he got into the habit of honking his horn madly and constantly until he had safely integrated traffic. 'Steer clear!' he would shout inside his car, pounding on the horn. 'Van Tomlin needs to get to work!'

Now, this warning technique was not unheard of on, say, a steep Swiss mountain pass, or one of those zigzaggy roads along the Côte d'Azur, but it did not go down so well in the quiet Kent countryside. Eventually our family got used to it, but one day we heard a terrible screeching crash. I ran out of the house and found Van Tomlin at the end of the drive, red-faced with rage. It seemed the warning technique was not enough to stop drivers running into him. This time the other car had taken off his front light and driven off.

Undeterred, Van Tomlin continued his attack on the main road. But he suffered another serious defeat a few months later, this time with the offending car taking off his side fender. The second accident was a bit more serious, with all of us privately wondering if it could have been deadly.

At this point I believe I may have tried to talk my neighbour into taking a break from driving altogether.

'Thomas, please reconsider,' I pleaded. 'It's just too dangerous.'

But he was bullheaded and proud as well as fierce. There was no way he would contemplate the loss of freedom.

'I need my car so I can get to work, you see,' he would tell me, as if I were being unreasonable. 'I just need to drive.'

'Couldn't a bus serve your purpose just as well?'

'You're a driver, Bradley. You should understand what it's like being a commuter. Even if I did figure out some other way to get into London, it would take me hours and cost hundreds of pounds every month!'

And he had a point. This was rural Kent, after all. There was very little public transport.

'No-one's trying to take away your freedom. We're just trying to consider your personal safety.'

'I'm a perfectly safe driver when there aren't all these bloody trees in the way!'

This was not entirely true, but it was not the issue at hand.

'Look, I'm not trying to talk you out of giving up driving. I just want everyone to be safe. I would like a little peace of mind. So this is my proposal: why don't we buy a mirror and set it up at the junction. That way, you can see all the cars coming from the right and the left. We can share the cost.'

Van Tomlin could see the reason in this theory. It seemed like a viable defence strategy, I suppose. He agreed that we should share in purchasing and installing a mirror on a column across the road. It even looked a bit like a shield from a distance. It took me a few months to get the £50 share out of him, but we did eventually resolve the issue, and for a time I thought we might have relative peace.

I was wrong.

Very quickly, Van Tomlin's theory that the trees were entirely responsible for all his driving troubles was proved incorrect. One day he came round, visibly shaken.

'Could I come in and talk to you?'

He was not his usual self.

'Of course!' I said, stepping aside. He stumbled a bit as he came in through the door.

Van Tomlin's family occasionally came over to our house, but we were not exactly close friends. Nonetheless, I made us a pot of coffee and sat down at the kitchen table.

'So tell me, what's wrong?'

'I crashed my car,' he said without any introduction, staring at the table.

'That's awful,' I replied, genuinely shocked at the crash, but not entirely surprised. It had been a long time since the last accident. 'What happened?'

'I hate driving on the left!' he burst out at first, and he seemed ready to launch into one of his lengthy verbal attacks. 'It's this stupid, stupid driving on the left that almost killed me! I mean, can you imagine an easier way to cause hundreds of head-on collisions?'

Now, I'm quite sure that the laws establishing road directions were set up precisely to avoid head-on collisions. But this didn't seem like a good time to mention this. I kept quiet. After he realised I wasn't going to back him up on this point, sadness seemed to come over him again. It was an unusual expression for him.

'Oh, it's just no use,' he said, slumping despondently against the table. 'I just can't do it. It's as if all my reflexes are so deeply programmed, you know?' He sighed. 'I was driving home from work, and I just couldn't stop thinking about this lawsuit I've been studying for my boss. I got to a crossroads and, without thinking, I crossed the road when I turned to the left. I mean, all the way across. Straight into oncoming traffic.'

I winced in sympathy.

'This Jeep just barrels straight into me. It totalled the car. Absolutely wrecked it. There were bits of car all over the road.'

He took a large slug of coffee, as if to steady himself. I sipped mine.

'The thing is, I, well, we're in the middle of this important case, my boss…' He paused, slightly lost, then cut off his mumbling abruptly. 'What I want to ask is can I borrow your car?'

I looked up, startled. This was unexpected. I must admit my stomach sank a little at the prospect.

The trouble was, I felt sorry for the boy. I mean, he was young, just married, had only just settled in England. It was easy to sympathise with him, despite his dangerous driving. I couldn't help but worry for the safety of my beloved car, though.

'Would I be covered by your insurance?' I asked nonchalantly.

To my surprise, I saw his cheeks redden a little.

'Oh, Mr. Jamieson, I'm not a bad driver, you will see. I will pay more attention. I will start driving better. You see, it will be different when I am looking after someone else's car.'

I was touched by the boy's earnestness.

'My car is imported from America,' I explained. 'It is a left-hand drive, like you would have had in the Netherlands. I'm worried you won't be used to it anymore.'

'Oh, no!' He was adamant. 'It will be much easier for me to drive the cars I am used to!'

'Very well,' I told him. 'But if I do you this favour, I would like a small one in return. I would like you to try something for me. I was thinking the other day that a good way to drive on the right would be to keep your arm out to the right. Out of the car window, I mean. I would like you to try this.'

After a little bit of hesitation, he agreed.

Amusingly, this technique ended up working, but not quite in the way I had envisaged. It turned out that so many people honked at him when he did this that he became embarrassed of his driving, and eventually became much more cautious, always staying on the left side of the road. After a few months I received my car back without so much as a scratch. Two or three years later, his temperament, his accent and his driving had adapted almost completely to British ways. I would like to think I have something to do with at least one of those transformations.

A POISONOUS NEIGHBOUR

Our bank in the centre of Paris in the eighth *arrondissement* was in many ways just like any other bank that had its quarters in the Champs-Élysées. The facts we had in common with similar establishments in the area were these: our building was centrally-located, expensive to rent and, most importantly, incredibly difficult to drive to. Our area of Paris is known as l'Étoile, as on maps it appears as a star where roads and avenues criss-cross and overlap. I preferred to refer to it as *La Toile*, however, as it would be equally well-represented as the centre of a dreadful, deadly spider's web, where the interlocking grid of roads served to trap unsuspecting passers-by in its chaotic net. It truly was a hideous place to drive through.

Frenchmen from the provinces either avoided it like the plague or ploughed through, ignoring everyone around them. The way they drove, they may as well have had their eyes closed tightly. A panicky impulse seemed to set in over all those who passed through the centre of l'Étoile. When we had guests visit the bank, they would usually clap their hands over their eyes, presumably to shield them from the sight of fast-approaching death. Sometimes, however, they would choose to have their arms outstretched, as if they could in this pathetic way reduce the shock of the inevitable accident. It would have been amusing if it hadn't been so understandable an impulse. It did one no good to have a decent driver, or even to be one: the danger was all around, in the hands of the mad Frenchmen buzzing around like deranged flies. I have never seen such insane driving as from those bearers of 75 license plates; and I have spent a considerable amount of time in Italy and New York!

After a period spent gritting one's teeth and making it through the mess, one slowly starts to adapt to the more reckless Parisians' driving style. After a year or so, I was so used to the whole business that I used to tell my driver not 'Go West, young man', but 'Go straight, young man!' Instead of a gold rush, this was rush hour! I think my instincts came back from my race car driving days at Daytona beach. I once drove from the seventh to the seventeenth *arrondissement* in twelve minutes, which I'm sure must be some kind of record. The strategy was simple: drive fastest and most dangerously, and the lesser vehicles won't stand a chance. The poor provincials and occasional hapless tourists would freeze, or scream to a halt, and avoid my speeding car as best they could. It was remarkably efficient, and could even be quite fun at times!

My problem wasn't getting through the spider's web, though. It wasn't the driving, or the danger, or even the rush of traffic in itself. The worst thing about the traffic in the centre of Paris was the fumes. Much as a spider injects a prey caught in its web with poison that slowly liquefies its insides, so the traffic of Paris insidiously poisons its victims. Thus, paradoxically, the real troubles for me only truly began when I made it out of my car and into my office. The reason for this is double: first of all, the French style of driving with one's foot constantly pressing the accelerator almost to the ground. Second of all, many French cars, including, in the late 1980s, all the taxi fleets, used fuel in their engines, as opposed to the more common benzene. This was not the traditional, clean high-octane naphtha, but a mazout-type fuel, which burns inefficiently and with a heavy sort of smoke that not only smells awful but is widely recognised to cause cancerous tumours, respiration problems and even forms of blindness. Sometimes, when I worried too much about this problem, I would take to driving with a filtration mask over my nose. However, this was inconvenient, and at times a little embarrassing, so I would often drive with the air conditioning in the back of my Mercedes on full blast, as the AC at least had a double filter, which helped to attenuate the polluting factor. In the dead of winter, however, this too could be problematic.

In any case, the worst of my problems were not when I was stuck in traffic, but when I was sitting quietly in my office. Our bank was set up in a historic building, which meant that, as it was protected, we could not change the windows or install any kind of air conditioning. Unfortunately, this meant that the only way to get aeration in our stuffy offices was to open the windows. In the height of summer in Paris, there was no alternative: the windows just had to be wide open, right above the flow of this Étoile traffic.

My own office, as president, was on the first floor. My neighbour at the time was Monsieur Bernard, the head of an important cosmetics company, and a very successful man. He did not own a garage, but he did have a chauffeur. Often, in the morning, he would have his driver start up his Citroën a good ten to twenty minutes before he was ready to leave the house: in summer, this would give it time to cool down from the AC; in winter, this gave it time to warm up. Now, Citroëns are not famous for being particularly fuel-efficient cars. This ridiculous rigmarole was an atrocious waste of money, and incredibly polluting as the motor was running on full this whole time. As soon as I opened my windows, I would receive a blast of poisonous fumes straight to the face. Looking down, I could see the car practically swathed in clouds of fumes, like the volcano at Pompeii mid-eruption.

Squinting into this poisonous miasma of gas, I could see Mr Bernard, like some spirit of the underworld, always impeccably dressed in his suit. He was tall and thin, with piercing blue eyes and strong cheekbones. He spoke when he found it absolutely necessary, and with a French accent so strong as to be a caricature.

'You should turn that off,' I would shout down. 'Your nice white shirt will go grey!' Sometimes, I couldn't help but get angry at this ridiculous operation. 'Bernard,' I would call down from my window, probably contracting the early symptoms of several respiratory diseases as I did so, 'what's the use of accumulating millions, you idiot, when these fumes will kill you in the next few weeks? You're lucky I'm not calling the police or the Green Party or sending our own bodyguards to beat up your little cosmetics bodyguard!' It was quite an amusing exercise, varying the abuse I cried down on the men who were poisoning me. To be honest, it was fairly harmless as Monsieur Bernard seemed to know I had given up on this making any difference from the second time I tried it. It was a friendly sort of fight; a war of wit, that helped me deal with the difficult situation.

'Hey, muscle-head!' I might shout at the bodyguard in question, 'Why don't you come work for us? We won't fill your lungs with poison day in, day out! You could spend those twenty minutes having another coffee!' Monsieur Bernard would just smirk up at me, adjusting his tie, or murmur something to his driver. 'Look at his suit!' I shouted. 'It's starting to shine with pollution. You're going to be completely encrusted! Pretty soon you'll look in the mirror and realise you're completely carbonised, through and through. Your lungs will be black and your head will look like a goat's that has been barbecued!' There was a certain perverse joy in hurling this abuse down upon my torturer, as it was my only outlet for the misery of the situation, but it was frustrating, too, as he never directly responded or seemed to care. 'I'm just trying to look after you and your driver!' I explained. 'One day, you won't even make it through the Étoile! After this sort of nauseous exercise, your driver will be as dizzy as if he's drunk three bottles of wine. He'll run your crummy Citroën right into the first Renault or Peugeot he finds, and your fortune will be worthless, and you won't have enjoyed it one bit!' Any fun that might be had in this flurry of insults usually wore off quite quickly, and I would sigh and either retreat to my office or slam the window shut, depending on the weather. Monsieur Bernard would give me a sort of sneaky smile, or a little wave, as if he had enjoyed my little session of insults, and then head off through the traffic to work as if nothing had happened.

This scene was probably repeated about thirty times in the nine years we were happy, loving neighbours. Once, I actually had lunch with the man, and when I confronted him about his polluting actions he was totally shameless. 'Tell it to someone who cares,' he told me with the kind of nonchalant shrug the French are famous around the world for. I told him my theory that l'Étoile should be known as La Toile, which made him laugh uproariously. '*C'est comme ça*! That's how it is in Paris! You have to be the spider or be eaten by it!' he added, with a mischievous glint in his eye.

THE FISHERMAN OF STOCKHOLM

In the early 1980s, our banking and oil business had a Swedish partner. This meant that, as an executive of the group, I had to travel a lot to Stockholm, Uppsala, and Malmö. Most of my journeys took me to Stockholm, where I usually stayed at the Grand Hotel.

I quite liked the hotel: its excellent restaurant featured a traditional smorgasbord, and its gym had a sauna and Nordic pool. Its best feature, however, was the view from my balcony. This overlooked the old town of Stockholm, which is one of my favourite locations in all of Sweden.

The city of Stockholm is built over fourteen islands on the mouth of Lake Mälaren. As a beautiful, watery city, it is often referred to as the Venice of the North. It is also, unsurprisingly, crossed by a great number of bridges. The tiny old town, full of scenic squares, medieval alleyways and traditional Scandinavian wooden architecture, used to be known as '*Staden mellan broarna*' or 'the town between the bridges'.

From my room, I could look out over the city's lovely skyline. I could also watch the fisherman who stood on the bridge nearest me, with his line dipping down into the murky lake. It was oddly soothing and exciting at once, watching this man just stand there. Nobody seemed to give him a second glance as they walked by. He would be there from morning to afternoon, seemingly unmoving. Interestingly, he never seemed to catch any fish! I never saw him move from his position. Granted, he had a bucket at his feet, and the traditional trappings of bait and floats, but I never saw him with a fish.

I would always greet him as I crossed the bridge into the old town.

'Any luck today?' I would ask with a smile. He always shook his head. The fisherman was a tall, tanned man, probably in his fifties, with hair just beginning to grey at the temples. He spoke quite good English and usually wore a duffel coat. 'I've been fishing here since I was five years old,' he told me once with a smile.

'You've done nothing else?' I asked, impressed.

He laughed. 'Oh, I have done plenty of other things. I was a policeman for most of my life.' This explained his apparent discipline and sporty figure. 'I retired early, though. And I have always fished at the weekends, and all through my holidays. Now that I'm retired, I fish every day. It's a simple life, but it makes me happy.'

'Do you ever catch any fish?' I couldn't help asking him.

'Not in many, many years.' He shook his head. 'I will, though,' he said, with a confident smile.

He was right. One day, from my hotel window, I heard the sound of excitement in the street outside. This was a surprise, as my impression of the population of Stockholm was that they were normally very calm, collected, respectful and overall quite quiet. This sounded as though they were all out in the streets like Irish people on St Patrick's Day! And this before ten in the morning. I pulled on my coat and went down into the street to see what had happened. As I left the hotel lobby, I found myself wondering why everyone had congregated on the bridge where nothing ever happened but one solitary fisherman standing... Then I realised 'my' fisherman must be the centre of the action. Everyone seemed to have gathered around him, looking down into the water. For one minute, I wondered if he had in fact fallen into the water, but I was quickly reassured to find him standing in almost his usual spot. As I elbowed my way through the growing crowd, I asked a man nearby what the excitement was about. 'He's caught a salmon!' a young blonde man shouted in my ear. 'A real live salmon! Right here in the centre of Stockholm!' I suddenly understood the situation, and knew I had to congratulate the fisherman. When he saw me, the man's face lit up in a grin.

'Look!' he said. 'I waited almost fifty years and I have been proved right! All those days waiting for a bite, and it finally came!'

'What a bite it was!' I replied in unfeigned admiration. 'It must be a good seventy centimetres long!'

'It's almost ten kilos!' he said proudly. 'It's incredible. You see, when I was five years old, I caught a salmon here with my father. I have never seen one since, but I have always been waiting.'

'So it's like a small, lifelong dream come true! What wonderful fulfilment for you,' I said.

'Oh, but it's more than that!' A man standing next to us chimed in excitedly: 'it's the very first time a salmon has ever been caught on this bridge. It's because of the new anti-pollution rules, you see. From the 1930s onwards, the river used to be full of filth from the industrial estate upstream, but now less and less chemical garbage is being poured in. The waters are getting cleaner; have you noticed there's almost no smell?'

The fisherman nodded happily. 'Every day for years now, I've watched as the waters have become cleaner and cleaner. Now, they're almost as transparent as the inland lakes where I like to fish! They're far cleaner than they were in my childhood, certainly.'

'So this fish you've caught symbolises the cleanup?' I asked.

'Exactly.'

At this point, people started taking pictures. 'Maybe you'll end up in the newspapers!' I said with a grin. 'So now that you've accomplished what you set out to do, have you come full cycle? Will you continue fishing?'

'Oh yes,' he replied without hesitation. 'One beautiful catch doesn't end a lifelong passion. After all, I'm retired!' He grinned. 'Now, if you'll excuse me, I'm going home to cook up my catch with some nice potatoes and dill sauce.'

What my fisherman didn't perhaps realise was that, from that day onwards, he would no longer fish alone. Granted, his companions would be a very friendly set, but that salmon marked the start of a trend for fishing not just from that bridge but from boats and other spots around the city. Still, I couldn't imagine the fisherman minding. He must have been so excited to be able to catch fish again, just like in his childhood. I was glad he had been my neighbour for those few days, and that I was lucky enough to witness this fulfilment of his childhood dream.

'This is definitely the place,' said my branch manager, scrutinising the far wall approvingly, as if the rightness of the choice was somehow inherent within its plain white surface.

'Good. I'm glad. You are sure this time, though? Yesterday you were quite sure it was Manchester Square that was definitely the place. Before that you wouldn't hear of anything other than Park Lane. And before that you were telling me South Audley Street was the only sensible choice for the branch, and before that…'

'I know, I know, but this is completely different, Bradley. There's something *special* about this place, I can feel it. Piccadilly! I don't know what it is but there's something exciting just about being here!' The branch manager swung around suddenly, and pointed out the window. 'Look! Look how high up we are! Above all our enemies! That's a strategic advantage!'

I furrowed my brow at the branch manager. 'Is the altitude thinning your brain? You're running a bank, not a Saxon kingdom. Height has nothing to do with it. Though I suppose you Londoners are all about being central, and this certainly is central.'

'Why, it's *very* central, and what's lucky, there's none of the noise you usually get with this kind of address. Those neighbours, for example, I haven't heard a peep out of them all day, and it's well into the afternoon now. I'd say they were accountants or something like that. Only accountants are that quiet.'

'They're a bit too quiet if you ask me,' I said, recalling the heavy, metallic door I had passed on the way in. 'I don't want it looking like we're trading in an abandoned warehouse, or someplace nobody else wants to rent. We don't need those kinds of negative associations.'

'Ha, don't worry about that! Things will soon heat up. I'm telling you, next time you come back from the States, everyone in town will know that this place is where the real action is. I guarantee it.'

By all accounts things were very busy in the first days of the branch manager's tenancy, and his prophecies of things 'heating up' were borne out by increasingly healthy profit reports. Business was brisk, and we were picking up clients at a steady rate. Most promising of all, though, was the effect that our new address seemed to be having on the kind of clientele we were bringing in. My branch manager would phone me in New York, his voice full of the helium of profit, to tell me stories of the clients who were dropping in on us with their deposits and investment deals.

'The halls are full of them, Bradley, it's incredible! And these are really *rich guys*. Cigar smokers, people who own a yacht, men with expensive toupees! Good, classy people. I tell you, moving here was the best thing we ever did. There's nothing a businessman respects more than a nice, clean, handsome office hidden away right on the top floor. That's what hooks them in. Don't you agree, Bradley? Don't you think that's true?'

I said that I thought it was possible, trying my best to sound pleased rather than relieved. It is always a risk setting up a branch in a new location. Our London clients could be fickle people, and their loyalties were governed by strange bands of territorial associations and preferences that it was very difficult to get entirely right. One man might only trust a banker who was based in the heart of the City, while another would sooner keep his money in a box under his bed. Considerations such as proximity to a decent restaurant or a favourite theatre were not beyond influencing the decision either. It was a fine balancing act that in this instance we seemed to have won, and I found it a difficult idea to trust, despite anything my branch manager might be saying about it.

Things carried on like this for the better part of a year, with my branch manager working busy but uncomplicated days, and everything running so smoothly and prosperously that he was actually able to work a 9 to 6 schedule, a practice that in the banking community is often seen as having died out with the abacus. Generally when I visited London, I would drop by at some point in the afternoon and be greeted by a healthy gaggle of pin-striped clients, coming and going with a reassuring look of contented prosperity. These visits served to quell my anxieties somewhat, and after a while I stopped worrying about the London branch altogether. It is certainly possible that, had I not arrived as late as I did on the day I took the Concorde in to sign some important papers, we would be none the wiser as to what was really going on in that building. We would, perhaps, still be there today, providing an honest day's banking to our clients before the sun set and our neighbour's door would unlock, and the sound of that sordid, haunting music would fill the corridors.

The Concorde had flown me into London at around ten o'clock in the evening, and by the time I had fought my way through customs and the London traffic it was approaching eleven thirty. The noises must have set in gradually, because it was a long time before I actually noticed anything. I had enough time to settle down and begin looking over the papers before I heard the first rumblings. It was a strange sound that I had never heard in a bank before, and I turned to the branch manager for an explanation.

'I think it's music, sir.'

'That's a little odd, isn't it? I've never noticed anything like that before. And it sounds like…it sounds like it's coming from inside the building.'

The branch manager shrugged nervously. 'I can't say I understand it either, sir. It is very disappointing.'

We both sat at the desk listening to the curious, atonal drone of the music, just loud enough that it rattled the pin of the branch manager's tie as he stared down at his documents.

'Well. I'm sure it's just a wedding party or something. Maybe in one of those apartments over the courtyard. They'll clear off soon enough.'

With that, I returned my attention to the paperwork, discovering with concern that there was considerably more to resolve than I had previously anticipated. There was enough, it turned out, to keep me in the office until one o'clock in the morning. In that time, the sound of the music had risen to a level that shook my bones, and it was from irritation rather than tiredness that I finally called it a night, deciding that it was better to go home and work there than put up with this racket a moment longer.

'Come on now, branch manager, we're leaving. I think we shall both be more productive once we've left this place. The music isn't suited to my tastes.' With that I swung the door open and was beaten around the face by a wall of electronic droning. My original instinct had been correct: the rumblings were indeed coming from within the building. Their source was so close and so powerful that it should have peeled the very paint from the walls. The branch manager seized the door frame, as if the building might suddenly list forward, buckling under this brutal wave of sound.

'How can anyone stand this noise?' he cried, the tears leaping across his cheeks.

By this point I had recovered my bearings and had noticed we were not alone; indeed, we were far from it. The corridor looked like a casting session for some low-budget government warning video. Men in suits and tuxedos, their pupils dilated, shuffled past scantily-clad women who perched upon the stairs or draped themselves across hostile-looking men with Hell's Angel beards.

'Why have you never mentioned this to me?' I demanded. 'These people are bringing the tone of the place into the gutter!' I turned to the crowd and began addressing my anger to them directly. 'Leave at once! This is private property, you have no business here!'

A man in a beer-stained tuxedo turned toward to face me and studied me intently, struggling to discern how many of me he was actually talking to. 'Hey, Mr, I paid for my ticket, just like anybody else.' The man hiccupped loudly and turned to speak to a fire extinguisher behind him.

'What does he mean "paid for his ticket"?' I didn't have to wait long for my answer. Glancing across the corridor I saw that our neighbour's door was now open, a lurid, burgundy glow emanating from inside. Outside stood two enormous bouncers collecting money and indiscriminately ushering in hordes of drunken businessmen and other crazed revellers. 'What is the meaning of this?' I screamed, struggling to make myself heard through the crowds and the noise.

The bouncer closest to me gave me eyed me suspiciously. 'What do you want? We don't want any trouble tonight, Mister.'

'No! No, how dare you? Quiet! I am the one who doesn't want trouble! I am the owner of the apartment across the hall and I demand to know what you are all doing in this building!'

'Well, we're trying to run our night club, if that's all right,' laughed the bouncer.

'N-night club?' My eyes had adjusted to the half-light now and this time when I looked back at the door I could see clearly what lay inside. Thick strobe lights stabbed through the dark, momentarily illuminating what was clearly an enormous dance floor. The carpet of dancers that swelled upon it was flanked by two pale neon bar areas dispensing alcohol with a fervency that suggested prohibition had very recently been lifted. My mouth hung open in a conflict of despair and fury.

'You like the girls, sir?'

'What?'

'If you like the girls, we can get you the girls. Successful businessman like you, I'm sure they'd be very interested.'

'Absolutely not!'

'Aw come on, sir, I'm sure they would.'

'Don't even think about it! Don't you even bother with a sign for your... bordello? I am the owner of the lease next door! I'm having this whole place shut down for...for...for ever!'

I stormed back into my office, the branch manager trailing behind me, and picked up the phone, my fingers trembling with rage as I dialled.

'Yes, Bradley Jamieson here. Yes, as a matter of fact you can help me with something! Tell me, my dear man, do you happen to be the proprietor of the apartment opposite, as well as the one you were so good as to sell us a year ago?'

The landlord paused briefly, pretending to think about it, as if the apartment were a reasonably expensive fountain pen he might have dropped in the street.

'Yes, yes, I think it might be mine, actually. Is there some sort of problem?'

'Well there is a slight problem, yes. It is a small thing really, but I wonder if, when you were selling us our office, you might have mentioned that our neighbours were running a dance bordello right next door.'

This made the landlord very uncomfortable, and a tense discussion ensued. It took a surprising amount of time, but I eventually convinced the man that having such an institution operating adjacent to a bank was a liability rather than a privilege. A few weeks later we began the lengthy process of moving our business to a new establishment. Even after all this, the branch manager was still convinced that a Piccadilly address was worth fighting for, and in deference to the strength of his feelings, I was able to find us an office only a hundred yards down the road. Things have run as smoothly as one could hope since then, but there remains a small seed of doubt at the back of my mind. I have never visited the place at night, and although everything is most likely fine, I suspect it will be some time before I can summon the courage to make such a visit. It is not that I am reluctant; it would simply be too hard to move again.

When we first moved from Paris in order to set up a literary office in Geneva, the building we chose was in a residential area close enough to the centre to be convenient but far enough to have peace and quiet as well as relatively inexpensive rent. It was quite a nice place for an office, with the added advantage of having two private parking spaces outside, which is rare as gold dust in Geneva! Our office was on the first floor, easily accessible by a marble staircase and lift. We had three offices, a dining room and a living room. For the first few months of spring, we settled in quite happily. The rooms were spacious and well-lit, and there was air conditioning installed.

Nonetheless, in the summer, I always insisted on opening the windows to let in fresh air. The first day it was warm enough for us to want to do this, we discovered the single drawback of our office's location. As soon as I flung open the window, the rooms were filled with the smell of burnt oil, garlic and onion, fish and meat and distinctively Asian spices. The scents mingled in the air and made my assistant's noses wrinkle: they were the unmistakable aroma of Chinese food.

'Well, I guess we now know there's a restaurant downstairs,' one of my assistants, a young Englishman, joked.

'Don't be silly, we knew there was,' his young brunette colleague added. She was relatively new to the team and hadn't quite taken on board his sense of humour.

'Yes, of course we knew about the restaurant,' I replied, 'I don't think any of us realised we were living and working right above the kitchen, though!'

'It's not a bad thing. I love Peking duck!' the girl chimed in, blushing a little.

I frowned. 'I swear I can smell burning duck skin from here. I can't say I find it very appetising. How did none of our neighbours tell us? Why didn't the landlord mention this? I'm not exactly thrilled about this discovery, I have to admit.'

'Don't worry,' the first assistant replied. 'Surely it's no worse than anything you would encounter in the centre of London! We can just run the air conditioning most of the time.'

'Yes, although fresh air is considerably cheaper,' I replied with a wry smile.

The girl giggled. 'I don't think you'd like living in Soho,' she ventured. 'There you'd be lucky if you could only smell one type of cuisine! In my last flat, I lived above an Indian takeaway, a pizza place and a kebab shop, not to mention the Senegalese couple across the hall.'

I laughed. 'Well, I suppose you're right about that. I guess I should count my blessings. Still, I have to admit this situation worries me a little. I'm going to speak to the restaurant.'

'Bring me back some sweet and sour pork!' my assistant joked.

Bringing up the issue with the owner of the restaurant was more difficult than I had hoped. For one thing, his French was less than fluent, and his English little better. I asked to speak to the manager, with no luck. Finally, I convinced him to bring me back with him into the kitchens, where the mingling cooking smells were absolutely overwhelming. There, I planned to try and see if I could get more information from the chef. 'What do you think produces the strongest smell here?' I asked.

'Oh, the garlic is probably the top flavour,' he replied cheerily, stirring vast quantities of noodles in a wok. The smell of gas, hot oil and burning garlic was overwhelming. I looked around into the other surrounding pots. There were some soggy-looking cabbages on a table in the corner, and ancient-looking strings of dried chillies and garlic hung from the ceiling. I recoiled in horror from a dirty-looking vat of what appeared to be thick, grimy cooking oil.

'Tell me, how often do you reuse that oil?'

'It's for deep-fat frying,' he replied. 'We probably fry in it, oh, about fifty times.'

'Fifty times?' I was aghast. Now, I'm no chef, but I know enough about good Chinese food to know you should never use cooking oil more than ten times. Ideally, at least according to the best restaurants in London and Shanghai, you should really only use it once. 'You know if you do that the oil will burn and become highly pollutant? It could even be poisonous if you use it fifty times! This explains the smell, at least. Don't you ever get complaints from your neighbours?'

He shrugged. 'It's a Chinese restaurant, sir. It is always going to smell like this.'

I did not particularly appreciate this line of defence. 'I've lived near

Chinese restaurants before,' I retorted, 'and none smelled as vile as this one. You can be sure of one thing: I will never eat a meal here!'

I had no better luck confronting my landlord about this. Nor did I get anywhere when I tried to bring up the threat of this polluting cooking oil with the local government. After the fifth complaint to the landlord, he sighed and said to me: 'Look, Bradley, I know this situation is really making you miserable. There's just nothing we can do about that damn restaurant. I know it's smelly, I know it's polluting the neighbourhood. If you really can't stand it, though, I would be very happy to let you give up your lease. Rents have gone up about fifty percent since you moved in here, so really you'd be doing me a favour. I'll even give you your deposit back.'

I had to smile. 'Is this just because you don't want to hear me complain any more?'

He laughed. 'Nothing of the sort. I just think you might be happier somewhere fresher-smelling. Maybe find a place by the side of the lake.'

'Or in the middle of the old town!'

We sealed the deal amiably and had moved offices within the next two months. Our new place was slightly smaller, but it smelled fresh and clean. After this discovery, I always made sure to ask in the kitchens of Chinese restaurants how often they used their frying oil. No-one else reused their oil as many as fifty times, and were aghast when I suggested I had been to a place that did. Of course, there's always the possibility that they might have been lying to me, but at least the smell was nicer, and I was being poisoned in blissful ignorance. I certainly never ate in that particular restaurant again!

There have been long periods of my life when I have had little interaction with neighbours. When moving somewhere for a short duration, one often has little time or motivation to make too many local contacts outside the course or job one is on location for. Often, those one does meet can be summed up in one encounter or anecdote: Dominique is one such neighbour.

In my early days working as an engineer, I went to Paris for a training course. During this time, I found and settled into an apartment in the Latin Quarter. It was a noisy, polluted and generally chaotic part of town, but it was conveniently located for my course, and in any case was only a temporary source of accommodation. Unsurprisingly, I had little reason to interact with my neighbours, so it came as something of a shock when, early one evening, I received a knock on the door. I opened it to find a short, scruffy man in his mid-thirties standing there glumly. There was an odd smell about him.

'How can I help you?' I asked hesitantly.

'Bonjour!' he said at once, as if startled into politeness. 'My name is Dominique. I'm sorry to disturb you but I, er, have a bit of a problem. It's my water bed.'

'Your water bed?'

'Yes. You know, it's a special bed filled with water, the kind you can import from New York.' From the earnestness of his tone, I guessed he genuinely assumed I was ignorant of the existence of waterbeds. 'I bought it in hopes of easing my back problems,' he continued. 'It's so soft to sleep on; it absorbs all the muscle tension.'

'Sorry, I know what a water bed is,' I said, trying not to sound impatient. 'I just don't quite understand your request.'

'As I said,' he continued, as if he hadn't heard me, 'it's been very comfortable to sleep on, but now I have a problem: it's started to smell terrible.' He had obviously prepared his explanation before coming over, and didn't intend to leave out any of the steps; that or he didn't believe I actually knew what a waterbed was. Either way, I was not particularly well disposed towards this neighbour.

'Ah, so that explains the smell. I was a bit worried for your health, there!' I joked.

'Yes. As I said, it's a wonderful bed. You can even heat the water!

I've had it for almost three years without a problem. But the water now smells absolutely awful, and I think I have to empty the bed. I just don't know how I'm going to do this. I thought I might try to enlist a friendly neighbour's help,' he added with a crooked grin.

'Let me get this straight,' I replied. 'This water bed of yours is creating that smell?'

'Yes,' he said, 'you can come see if you like.'

I had to admit I was curious. We went over to his flat and, sure enough, found the vast water mattress lying bare and impressive on his bedframe, making the whole place smell like a swamp.

'God, it smells like a very bad public lavatory,' I said, pinching my nose.

'I know. My principal problem,' Dominique said, 'is that the bed weighs about two and a half tons. I have no idea how to move it.'

I looked the bed over. It was a king size piece, about two metres wide and two and a half metres long.

'Are you sure the smell is just the bed? Are you certain there's no strange infection in your pipes? Or some horrible incident involving seafood in the Algerian restaurant down the road?'

My neighbour laughed. 'I appreciate your optimism, if that is indeed optimism, but I'm absolutely positive. If you want to be sure, just put your face closer to the mattress. Be warned that I wouldn't recommend this course of action. As someone who has been sleeping on it for months, I can tell you it is pretty horrific.'

'Alright, I'll pass. So you think there must be something wrong with the water?'

'Yes. I just don't know what.'

'Do you still have the catalogue for this bed? That might have some more information.'

'I don't know. I seem to remember the catalogue was in English, as it came from the USA.'

'So you didn't read the catalogue?'

'No,' he said a little sheepishly, 'but I'm sure I've still got it somewhere.'

Dominique scrambled out of the bedroom, leaving me alone with the putrid stench. After a few minutes, he returned, triumphantly holding aloft a warped-looking magazine.

I took the catalogue gingerly from his hands and sat down on a nearby chair to read it. He hovered nervously, then dashed off to the kitchen to make coffee. After a few minutes, I called back to him:

'How long have you had this bed?'

'I've had it two years,' he replied, amongst the clinking of dishes.

'You've been living with this smell two whole years?' I asked, aghast.

'Oh no, I don't mean that. It's only been smelly for the past year or so.'

I shook my head and read on.

'It says here in the catalogue that you have to put pills in the water every year. Did you do that?'

He came back into the room. 'Pills? What kind of pills?' he asked, looking quite concerned.

'Chlorine pills,' I replied. 'It says quite clearly here you have to put them in straight away. They'll kill any germs. Instead, you've obviously let a swamp grow inside your bed!'

'What am I going to do?'

'Let's start with getting these sheets off.'

We pulled the remaining covering off the water bed, leaving only semi-transparent plastic. I knelt down and looked closely. 'Hand me that lamp,' I said. We held the light-bulb up close to the plastic, and peered into the cloudy depths. I was sure I could see tiny things swimming around in there, like worms or tiny bits of algae. I shuddered in disgust. 'It's impressive you haven't been poisoned,' I told my neighbour firmly. 'You absolutely have to get rid of this water.'

'I know,' he said miserably. 'I just don't know how to. The bed is too heavy to carry. If I unplug it here, the water will flood the building and trash my room. I don't know what to do.'

'OK,' I said, 'let's think about this. You can't carry two tons of water and plastic down the stairs. You can't make your bedroom into a horrible swamp. The cleaning bill alone will probably be more expensive than buying a new bed. We don't want to ruin your carpet. On the bright side, I happen to be an engineer. If there is a solution to be found, we will find it.'

We sat for a time in silence. Then, all of a sudden, an idea came to me. 'OK,' I told my neighbour, 'I have a theory. You're not going to like it, but I think it may be our only option.'

'Anything,' he said rather desperately.

'Alright. Go downstairs. Go to the hardware shop and buy me a ten metre hose, about an inch in diameter.'

He looked at me in confusion. 'How is a hose going to help us?'

'We are going to empty the whole waterbed into the street, through the window.'

'What? How? It's too heavy to lift.'

'Just trust me. Remember, I'm an engineer.'

My neighbour was obviously at the point of desperation where he was willing to follow my odd instructions without too much objection. He put on his coat and left the apartment, returning less than half an hour later with the requested item.

'Now will you tell me how this is going to work?' he pleaded. 'Wouldn't you need a motor for this?'

'As I said before, you're not going to like this.'

'What do you mean?'

'Let's do the first part, and see if you figure it out.'

We put one end of the hose inside the plug. We then fed the rest of the hose out the window down into the street. Of course, nothing happened. The hose just hung there, swinging drily in the mild breeze. The bed remained full of water.

Dominique looked at me, narrowing his eyes.

'OK,' he said, 'is this your brilliant plan?'

'This is the part you're not going to like,' I said with an expression I hoped was closer to compassion than glee. 'I need you to go down into the street.' I sighed. 'I don't really feel comfortable with this part of the plan, but it's truly the only way I could think of.'

I saw the light of comprehension dawning in my poor neighbour's eyes. 'The problem,' he said slowly, 'is not getting the water out of the bed. It's getting the water into the hose.'

'Yes,' I replied. 'I need you to suck the water down the hose.'

He looked up at me in glum resignation. 'With my mouth?'

'I can't think of any other way. Look, it'll be ten seconds of misery, you'll spit it out, and then we'll get this damn bed of yours out of your apartment. I'll help you carry the empty shell down the stairs when we're finished.'

'OK,' he said, and he trudged off. When he appeared again on the street, there was a long moment of hesitation before he actually did what was required of him. I had to admit I pitied him, but I truly couldn't think of any other way around the laws of physics. He had brought this upon himself, I reasoned, by not using those chlorine tablets.

I watched in horror and fascination as he stepped up to the hose, took it in his mouth, and almost instantly spat out the water onto the ground. As soon as he had done so, a thin stream of horrible cloudy water poured out into the street. I was glad I was so far above the smell, but I could see from my neighbour's face that the experience had been pretty horrific.

I decided to go down into the street to keep him company until the bed was emptied. 'How are you feeling?' I asked solicitously.

'Pretty horrific,' Dominique said with a wry grin, 'and I need a very stiff drink, but I'm glad this is almost done.'

The water just kept on coming, sloshing out of the hose and away into the gutters. People slowly started gathering around us, drawn by the strange sight or by the terrible smell. 'What are you doing?' they asked curiously. 'Where is all this water coming from?' I tried to explain the situation, but the locals, who had obviously never encountered the concept of a water bed, were confused. A few were offended, obviously thinking we were just making this idea up to poke fun at them, but most eventually lost interest and wandered off with a shrug. '*Ah bon!*' they said, unamused by our story.

As our project was nearing its final stages, I sent my neighbour back upstairs to press out the last few litres from the nearly-empty bed. At this point, a *gendarme* materialised, either alerted by the neighbours or by the smell. 'What are you doing, *Monsieur*?' he asked me. 'This looks highly unusual.'

'We are emptying a water bed,' I explained. I could tell from his blank reaction that this meant no more to him than it had to any of the passers-by.

'*Vous vous moquez de moi?* Are you making fun of me?' he asked.

'No, no!' I hastened to assure him.

'What do you mean, a "water bed"?' he asked sternly.

I sighed. I tried my best to explain the concept, but I could tell he didn't understand. I stopped short. 'Look,' I said, 'we have a little problem. It is a little embarrassing, so I didn't explain. Essentially, the toilets in the flat are broken, and we have a terrible flood. We're just trying to empty it through this hose. That's why the water smells so bad. I'm an engineer!' I added desperately.

'*Ah bon*,' he said, with a smile. For some reason, this far-fetched and physically-improbable tale seemed to convince him. 'Well, just make sure it's all finished soon, OK?'

'Of course, *Monsieur*,' I said hastily. 'It's almost done.'

The policeman walked away, and we squeezed out the last drops of vile water. The whole process had taken us a little over four hours, and exhausted us both. We smelled like we had been living in a swamp for a year! We tried to save the shell of the water bed, but it was too sticky and smelly. We decided to throw it out. 'Why don't you buy yourself a new bed,' I suggested. 'Just make sure you put the pills in it twice a year, and read the whole catalogue this time!'

'Oh, I don't think so,' my neighbour replied. 'This time, I will be getting a nice, sensible, quilted mattress!'

FIRST TIME ROBBED

Finding a place to live in New York is a matter of deciding between compromises, and it is foolish to think that one is at any point immune from at least one of the many pitfalls inherent in the experience. What people tend to do is side with the compromise that suits them the most personally. A lot of people can't stand the bustle of the city itself, so they pick an apartment nestled away in the suburbs and resign themselves to whiling away years of their time with a crossword puzzle on the morning commute. Some people choose a compromise based around their social lives; their apartments might be in Greenwich Village or Williamsburg, but the trade-off may well come at the price of never once sleeping through the din of a thousand hipster loft parties.

Back when I was forced to make this decision, I was just starting out in banking, and was fairly serious about making a success of things at work. Fresh in my mind at this time was the memory of the last job I had held in New York, when I had been working in engineering. It was not really fair to call what I did then a commute, as journeys this long are generally only undertaken by Hobbits. Being young, and without the necessary funds to live in the city itself, I found I had to travel from New Jersey. The journey started off with a drive, then moved onto the PATH (the trans-Hudson railway service), then the subway, then the bus, before finally finishing on foot. The various modes of transport, besides costing a fortune, had the irritating effect of making the journey seem far longer than it really was. These were the kind of ingenuities Phileas Fogg required to travel the entire world, and yet my journey was one of 13.5 miles. I thought of my friends in England who commuted from Oxford to London every day and complained when they had to change trains once. The bitterness of this recollection was enough to convince me that as a banker I was going to live as close as humanly possible to Wall Street, where I would be working. Whatever I would lose in the compromise, there was no way it could be worse than two and a half hours of leaping between trains and buses, and crossing rivers and state lines.

The place I found, in the end, was perfect. The apartment itself was on Brooklyn Heights Promenade. The area has one of the best views in New York City. Crucially, part of this view was, if one looked carefully enough, my office on Wall Street. It was not so close that I felt there was no escaping it in the evening, but close enough that I could choose between a fifteen minute subway ride, or a brisk jog across the bridge to work. In fact, I seemed to be getting almost too much out of this apartment. It had the aforementioned beautiful view over Battery Park and the South of Manhattan, was well connected in terms of transport and shopping, and was as friendly a neighbourhood as one could reasonably expect in so central a location in New York. There seemed to be no catch, no compromise here. In hindsight, I think this should have troubled me far more than I allowed it to.

The inevitable pay-off came one bleary morning at 3am as I was sleeping peacefully in my bed. Having been reluctant to let go of my past in engineering, I had decided to construct my own bed, and there were to be no half measures. This was to be a bed in which the Roman Emperors might have slept; a large, tall bed, elevated some three and a half feet from the ground, and commanding a fine view of all that surrounded it. It is possible, I admit, that this was a little extravagant, but the point is that with my late hours, the bed was likely the only part of the place I would actually use, and it made sense to have a good one. As it happened, it made that sorrowful evening much more complicated than it had to be, as it is rather difficult to get out of a Roman Emperor's bed in a hurry.

When the moment came, I was moving before I had even taken on board what was happening. The noise had woken me and instinctively I had leapt out of bed. I was about a foot down by the time I realised this was not the sort of bed to leap out of when the lights are off, and I remember briefly envying the Japanese, who are able to sleep on mats made of woven straw. Thankfully I had done enough volleyball in my time that I righted myself before it was too late, and achieved a landing that was convincingly more dramatic than it was painful.

The one positive of this fall was that it meant I had fully awoken by the time I rose out of bed. It was clear to me now that I wasn't hallucinating I distinctly heard footsteps, and shuffling. There was someone in my apartment. Evidently the fall had also woken up the intruder, because by the time I had made it out of the bedroom, I heard the front clack shut, and was left alone in my apartment again, minus a stereo and a painting.

The next morning was to be my initiation into a process New Yorkers are tired of, and all fleeting visitors to the city are fundamentally shocked by. The police arrived for what I had expected would be an investigation, but in the end turned out to be little more than a questionnaire.

'So this is your first time, sir?' said the first officer, already scratching away at his notepad with practised mundanity.

'My first time what?' I replied, eyeing the pale space on the wall where my painting had once hung.

'Your first time being burgled. Or do you know the drill already?'

'Why would I have been burgled more than once?'

The officers exchanged a hearty laugh. 'Oh, you'd best prepare yourself, son. Being burgled is about the only sure thing there is here, living in New York. And on Brooklyn Heights Promenade, well that's as good a place as any to get burgled. All those fine houses, with the nice views of Manhattan.'

'Burglars like a nice view,' agreed the second officer.

'So anyway, now, what we'll do, sir, is we'll ask you the questions, then we'll get out of your hair and you can get on with your day.'

I was puzzled that the police seemed to view their investigation in the same light I might regard the visit of a plumber or a Jehovah's Witness; an awkward hindrance that had to be dealt with politely but as quickly as possible.

'Were you present at the scene when the incident occurred?'

'Yes. Where else would I be?'

'That's good, sir. And where exactly were you?'

'In bed.'

The officer looked knowingly at his colleague. 'You can't let your guard down, see, sir. All they need is that slightest opportunity.'

'It was three in the morning!'

'Late, too. That's when most burglaries are liable to happen, in our experience. Next question is...did you give your keys to anyone, or did anyone have access to your keys at any particular moment during the day?'

'No! Why would I - I've just moved here, I don't go around handing out copies of my keys, just like that!'

'That's good too, sir, that helps. So I guess we've done all we can, anyway.' The officers were already halfway out the door. 'We'll be sure to let you know if we hear anything. Though I wouldn't hold out too much hope, you know, they're probably long gone by now. Anyways, we'll see you the next time, sir, all the best. We'll be in touch.'

For the second time in less than twelve hours I heard my front door clack shut. It seemed people were very anxious either to get in or out of my apartment, but not to stay long enough for me to figure out what was going on.

That the case was eventually solved came as a profound surprise to me, but the event delivered none of the satisfaction I might have anticipated. Despite their curiously penpal-ish promise to 'stay in touch', it was actually through the local paper, rather than the police that I learned who the perpetrator of my burglary had been. The paper recounted how the keys to every apartment in my building had been casually lifted from the concierge's office by a young student who was staying in an apartment not far from mine. The man had been systematically emptying every apartment in the building between the hours of one and three every morning. I imagined the policemen I had spoken to visiting every room on every floor of the apartment with their questionnaire, wisely commenting that burglaries were endemic in New York and that there was nothing that could be done about it. The man was eventually caught, but more or less immediately released on bail, meaning that I was forced to walk past him while we each carried our brown paper bags full of groceries to our respective apartments. Apparently the police were able to recover most of the stolen items from the thief's apartment, but it still smarted that this man was being allowed to live amongst his victims while he awaited trial. I was tempted, on occasion, to give him a piece of my mind, but it is not in my nature to tell people off, especially when they have their punishment waiting for them. The incident left its mark, and I moved on to another, slightly more secure building a little later on, and I can only hope the thief was made to do the same.

A SWISS MOUNTAIN NEIGHBOUR

At some point in the busy, modern existence, almost everyone has had a time when they dreamed of escaping to a simpler life. Whether it is the thought of breaking free from the city and becoming a shepherd, or of moving to an Australian village and making one's own cheese, such fantasies will be entertained by most hardworking city-dwellers at one point or another. However, for the vast majority of people, these visions are much more easily imagined than fulfilled.

In the mid-1970s, my family purchased four hectares of land deep in the Swiss Alps. It was a beautiful plot at the foot of the mountains, fairly remote apart from a few neighbouring farms. We had this idyllic idea of spending time there, raising bees for honey and going for long walks in the grassy hills. It was a vision of the simple life, something we wanted to do as a way of taking time away from our busy city existence. We talked about it often, embroidering the dream with details that could have been borrowed from Johanna Spyri's *Heidi*: taking long walks in the country, listening to the wind in the pines, eating hearty peasant fare of bread and cheese. We imagined going out to the beehives in the morning and harvesting the fresh honey, maybe handing a piece of honeycomb to the children for them to munch on.

Of course, as with many elaborate dreams of another life, we never quite managed it. I didn't really want to be a farmer or a beekeeper, and nobody in my extended family did either. My idea of putting in long hours in the early morning involved a nice strong coffee and a stack of paperwork! We did, however, visit the property at least once a year, and go for a long family walk along the mountains. There was a beautiful hilly path leading from the back of the property up towards the rocky summits, with stairs cut into the side of the slope to facilitate the climb. From there, we could climb up to a plateau, where we would look down over our land and across the neighbours' fields, where their horses and cows were grazing peacefully. A few times in the ten years we owned the plot, I took the children horse-riding there.

All in all, it had been a good investment, and we spent many a pleasant day there. My relations with my neighbours were always friendly, if hardly effusive. These were for the most part simple country people, who tended to greet each other with a polite nod. They presumably recognised that I didn't really intend to become fully integrated into their isolated mountain life anytime soon! One day, however, one of the neighbours approached me in a friendly manner when I was walking around, breathing in the mountain air. 'Hello,' she said rather hesitantly. I recognised her as a neighbour from further away, an old lady who lived on a farm on her own with many horses. After exchanging an unusually long bit of small talk, she cut to the chase. 'I have an odd request to make,' she told me, as if making a confession. 'I'd like to buy part of your land.' She was quite charming, with a good sense of humour and a twinkle in her eye that inspired confidence.

'Just part?' I asked in surprise. She didn't seem like the sort of person interested in real estate transactions, and our land didn't even lie right next to hers.

'Yes, just the part nearest the mountain,' she explained.

'Why on earth?'

She smiled hesitantly. 'I just really like that area,' she said shyly. 'It would be so nice to be able to ride my horses there. I should confess something else: I've been thinking of building a small farmhouse or a chalet, too. For when my family comes to visit, you see.'

'Why don't you just ask me for the whole plot?'

'Well…' she hesitated. 'I don't have that much money. I really can probably only afford a small piece.'

I had to stop and think. There was no reason why our family needed the whole of our vast plot of land. The location was nothing special; it was no good for skiing. We hadn't built on it ourselves as it didn't seem like a good enough investment. After all, why not consider this neighbour's offer?

'It's just that I've become quite fond of that place,' she added. When she offered me quite a respectable price for the parcel, I couldn't think of a reason to refuse. I agreed, and sold her the piece of land she wanted. We went back home at the end of our visit, thinking nothing of it. It seemed, at the time, like nothing more than a friendly neighbourly gesture that might make us a little money off a small piece of land we didn't really use or need!

However, it turned out that I had rudely underestimated this particular neighbour. A year later, in my annual pilgrimage to the mountains, I discovered a sort of strange structure at the bottom of our field. I had driven up alone, this time, intending to do some walking, but I had no set schedule. I parked the car and went over to investigate at once. From up close, it looked like some kind of factory. I was completely flummoxed. This didn't look anything like an old lady's Swiss chalet! The closer I walked, the noisier the operation revealed itself. I opened a small door in the side and walked in: security, deep in the Alps, appeared to be minimal. There, I discovered the inside of a sort of hangar, full of conveyer belts. They appeared to be processing a series of small plastic bottles. I stared at these for a while in utter incomprehension, as if hypnotised by the little blue-labelled bottles as they went by at the rate of a dozen or so a minute. As I stood there, a man in a suit came up to me, looking perplexed. He introduced himself as the head manager.

'The head manager of what?' I snapped.

To his credit, the man didn't lose his temper with this stranger who had just wandered into his factory and started asking rude questions. 'The water bottling plant,' he said calmly. 'The one you're standing in.'

I looked at him incredulously. 'I'm sorry,' I finally managed to articulate. 'It's just that… this was my land. This was a field. This… factory didn't use to be here.'

'You should be pleased, then,' he replied. 'We're producing beautiful water here. Excellent quality,' he added, slipping into a salesman's voice, 'widely recognised to be better than Volvic or Evian!'

'How long has this plant existed?'

'Oh, a few months. Just under a year, I guess.'

As I began to comprehend what had happened, I suddenly felt both betrayed and a bit jealous. My businessman's instincts flared up and were crushed in a single moment. All at once, I understood why this neighbour of mine had insisted on buying the lowest part of the land: it had nothing to do with proximity to the mountains. She must have found a spring there, without anybody knowing, and decided to acquire and exploit it! I had to admit I was impressed, but I still found it hard to believe how easily I had been used, and what a ridiculously low price I had accepted!

'So this water…' I ventured, 'does it sell well?'

'Oh yes,' he replied at once. 'It was instantly very successful, especially in the European markets. There's something about "Swiss spring water" that appears to function as a sort of buzzword.'

Seeing my face, the manager stopped short, having obviously gathered what might have happened.

'You didn't know about the spring, eh? When the owner called us in to look at it, we were surprised too. Nobody knew there was underground water in this area. I mean, it's hidden all over the Swiss Alps, in little pockets, but nobody had ever investigated this area.'

'So you're telling me it was easy to find?'

'I'm afraid so. It was visible from the surface; we only had to dig a few feet down to uncover a small river.'

'She could have just seen it on a walk?'

'She told us it was just a piece of luck, and that seems the likeliest explanation. Of course, there's always the possibility that she had known for a long time and just kept it quiet until the opportune moment came along.'

'A gullible neighbour, you mean.'

He laughed. 'I wouldn't think of it that way.'

Still, a small part of me couldn't help but think of it exactly that way. I had to give it to her: this neighbour had really fooled me with her pretence of innocent charm! Perhaps, in a way, she deserved to get that parcel of land and make the most of it. Nonetheless, it did make me think twice in future when neighbours came to me with seemingly innocent requests: one can never tell!

GRASS GRIEF

When I lived in my Kent house, I was not a particularly keen gardener. Work kept me busy, sending me regularly from my home to France and New York. Our land was always well cared for and kept in good order, but I wasn't overly concerned by it appearing perfect.

Our neighbours were quite a different story.

Since our house was on what had been at one time a very large estate, there were several other houses on our extended land. Most of the time there was little necessity to interact with these neighbours, as there was quite a lot of land separating us from them. However, in one of the houses there lived a slightly older couple.

Donald and his wife both seemed to be keen gardeners, and so often I saw one or the other of them working on the very border of their land and mine, making sure that every piece of their garden was entirely perfect. I didn't mind: who could argue with friendly, polite neighbours who kept a close and serious eye on the appearance of their property? It certainly didn't do me or my family any harm, to look across and see their well-kept lawns and blossoming flower beds.

That was until the grass cuttings began appearing.

'Did you notice,' my wife asked me, 'that Donald's wife is rather... messy?'

I couldn't say I had, so she pointed out to me the small pile of grass cuttings by the fence that officially separated my land from that of my neighbours'. It was a low, metal fence two or three feet tall: our neighbour was obviously reaching over it and dumping the grass.

I laughed a little to myself and told my wife not to concern herself. I was sure that it was an accident, an oversight, and that it wouldn't happen again.

I was quickly proved wrong.

The grass cuttings kept appearing on my property and I came to terms with the idea that, rather than disposing of the grass in a compost heap that might ruin their perfect garden, my neighbours were using my own land as a dumping ground for their grass. Maybe they thought that I wouldn't notice such a thing but, as the grass pile grew, it was difficult to ignore.

One day, however, when we came back from a trip, we made a puzzling discovery. Our neighbours had replaced the old metal fence with one that had a gate. Their purpose was clear: now, they could simply open a little gate when they wanted to dump their clippings. They didn't even need to throw them over the delimitation. They could come over with a whole wheelbarrow if they felt like it!

Still, they were a nice enough couple, both in their forties, and I didn't see the harm in it. After all, soon enough it would be winter and the grass would decompose down into the earth until there was nothing left.

Which was exactly what happened. The problem appeared to be solved.

The next spring came around, lush and beautifully sunny, and the new gardening year began in earnest. I was not surprised to see Donald out and about, clearly glad to be back to his favourite pastime after a winter of doing only minimal work on his land. I had, it's safe to say, almost forgotten about the grass cutting situation and when the cuttings began piling up again, I didn't worry.

Donald was a relaxed sort of person, with an artistic temperament that meant he perhaps didn't always pay as much attention to things as he could have. Quite frequently, I found him enjoying a drink in the middle of the day as he attended to the garden. His wife was not a big drinker; in fact I found her to be quite religious, quiet and thoughtful. I assumed she was the one dropping the grass off, since often she seemed to be entirely in her own world. Maybe she was too tired to think of a better place to put it at the end of a long day at work in the garden.

I took no real issue with this. Our land was big enough that a small pile of grass cuttings throughout the summer really made no impact on my life.

It was only after a few years that the real problem became apparent. After one mild winter, I noticed that the grass cuttings had not reduced down into the earth as they usually did. In fact, quite a hill had formed where they had been repeatedly dumped out.

One afternoon, I found Donald himself wandering through my gate with a wheelbarrow absolutely full of grass, which he proceeded to pile onto the already substantial little hill that had grown up seemingly from nowhere.

'Excuse me,' I called out to him, careful to keep my voice as polite as possible. After all, aside from the gardening problem, he was a decent enough neighbour. And I kept thinking that I should have raised this as an issue sooner, not left it to get so bad.

Donald looked up at me, shielding his eyes from the sun. 'Hello,' he said. 'Lovely weather. Feels like summer.'

'Quite lovely,' I agreed as I approached him. 'Listen, sorry to... spring this on you. But I just wanted to ask you why you keep leaving your grass cuttings on my property.'

He stared at me without expression, not speaking.

I continued, 'I didn't mind, per se. But you can see how that the grass just isn't going anywhere. It's building up. It doesn't look very nice, does it?'

He glanced down at the pile. 'It's just grass,' he told me slowly, like I might not understand. His tone was more than a touch condescending and it annoyed me greatly.

'I know what it is,' I said, 'but, that being the case, why don't you just make your own grass hill on your own property?'

He shrugged. 'I don't see the problem.'

At this point, I admit that I lost my temper. 'If you don't stop, then I think I'll have to take you to court. There's no confusion. This is my land. You have plenty of your own for your gardening.'

'Why are you making such a scene?'

'I'm not. Look, see how much space this is taking up? You're treating my land as your own and taking up my space.'

'Don't be so ridiculous,' Donald snapped back, 'you're getting worked up over nothing! It's only grass and I have every right to leave it here.'

'No, you don't! Legally, you have no right to my land. Now, get off. Get off my property.'

After a moment of gaping at me, Donald turned and pushed his wheelbarrow through the gate, which I promptly shut behind him with extra force, making it clear that I didn't want him coming through any time soon.

Since I was away on business more often at this point, Donald took no notice. When I returned to check on the grass pile, the gate was open and the cuttings now covered eight square metres of my own land.

I was irritated beyond words and obviously there was no talking to Donald. I sent him a letter to warn him of my intentions to take legal action against him if he continued, and from what I could tell, fresh grass cuttings continued to appear and increase the size of the hill at the end of my garden. He could not see sense on the matter and so I had my lawyer contact him, informing him that what he was doing was basically theft.

He was devaluing my property by taking up space with his gardening waste and all the space he took up was worth at least twenty-five pounds at that time. It was no small matter to me.

But Donald carried on ignoring me and no matter if I shut the gate or not, I would always return home from working away to find yet more grass cluttering up my garden. Now it seemed that he was being simply vindictive and difficult for the sake of it. There was no good reason behind his actions except laziness and a desire to annoy me and take what was not his.

Despairing of ever getting him to stop, in the end I surrendered and wrote a letter appealing to his wife, whom I had found very pleasant and even-tempered in the past.

Hello,

I am writing to ask if you would please stop your husband from leaving the waste from his gardening on my property. As I'm sure you're aware, this has been going on for several years now and I am puzzled by his persistence. What he is doing is tantamount to theft and in the Bible doesn't it say that theft is a dreadful sin? If you are complicit in his actions, then you, too, have sinned.

I don't mean to sound harsh or unreasonable, but I cannot sit idly by and allow your husband to damage my property with his laziness and spite any longer. Your assistance in this matter would be greatly appreciated.

Many thanks and all my best.

My letter was effective, at least a little. The grass appeared less frequently on my property and the small hill gradually decreased, though I was sure Donald was still leaving some waste on my garden, tossing it over the fence when I locked the gate. I was interested to learn from other neighbours that his wife in no way agreed with the way he behaved and that she was very worried about it, had been for years in fact. But he was such an overpowering and self-involved person that he never listened to her concerns.

Years later, Donald and his wife still live in their house in Kent. They still garden, and still display little regard for their neighbours. However, the hill of grass at the edge of my garden gradually disappeared, leaving just a small hump in the earth to remember the dispute by.

During my stay in Mayfair, I lived on the third floor in a beautiful old apartment building. My flat had oak parquet floors, Oriental rugs, and vast windows that looked out over the quiet boulevards of London. But one day, I discovered something strange about the bedroom. I had noticed a humid smell for some time, and found it disturbing, but had put it down to nothing more than the age of the building. One evening, however, I had been reading in my armchair when a drop of water fell on my book, then another. I looked up, and saw a dark patch in the centre of the ceiling. I then saw that water was slowly sluicing down the silk walls, and trickling down the windowpanes.

I leapt up and ran down the stairs to alert the doorman.

'I'm sorry to disturb you,' I said, 'but my bedroom appears to be flooding from the ceiling downwards!'

The doorman looked up from his newspaper.

'Sir, I wouldn't worry about it. It must be the Scottish lord taking his bath.'

'I'm sorry? There's no possible way that amount of flooding can come from one man splashing about a bit. Unless his cleaning rituals involve smashing pipes with a hammer!'

'I gather you've not met the Scottish lord, sir,' the doorman replied, 'nor seen the size of his bathtub. The baths in this building were not designed for men of the Lord's... stature,' he finished carefully. 'His baths have been known to overflow onto the fourth floor balcony and pour down into the street. The tenants before you had the same problem.'

'Wait,' I said, 'Do you mean the tall, portly Scottish gentleman I've met a few times?' I suddenly understood the situation a great deal better. The man in question was close to six and a half feet tall and probably weighed around one hundred and fifty kilograms. He was exceedingly genteel and polite, always dressed in specially-tailored three-piece suits with a different pocket-handkerchief every time I saw him, and a gold pocket-watch. Everyone around him called him 'sir.' In fact I once heard several people call him 'your highness.'

'I believe I understand what you mean, now,' I told the doorman.

'You've probably seen his Rolls Royce sitting in the square. I'd be surprised if you hadn't met him,' the doorman responded from the depths of the newspaper to which he had apparently returned.

'Yes, well, be as that may,' I hastened to add, 'I think we should go tell him to keep his antics within the tub.'

The doorman sighed vaguely and set down his newspaper and reading glasses. 'I suppose you're right.'

We climbed the long flight of carpeted stairs together. As we neared the fourth floor, we could hear a sort of muted roaring, which eventually resolved into the chorus of *The Bonnie Banks o' Loch Lomond*. 'Oh the wee birdies sing,' the roar went, 'an' the wild flowers spring.' There was a long pause punctuated by enthusiastic splashing. 'An' in sunshine the waters are sleeping,' he bellowed.

I knocked on the door. 'I can't imagine anyone is sleeping right now!' I said rather loudly.

The singing stopped. There was a sound like a glass falling onto tiles, and an audible cry of 'bugger.'

'I'm terribly sorry,' the Scottish voice continued haltingly. 'I didn't mean to disturb.' There was a great, slippery, stumbling sound, followed by a crash. 'Let me just get some confounded clothes on.'

The doorman slipped back downstairs to his newspaper, leaving me to await the lord's appearance. Appear he did, after ten minutes or so, his vast figure wrapped in a white terrycloth bathrobe, his face red and his white hair plastered to his head.

'Jamieson!' he said, in his broad Scottish accent. 'What a pleasure.'

I was amazed he could remember my name. I couldn't return the favour, having only met him once, and seen him a few times since.

'I'm sorry to disturb you,' I said, 'it's just that, well, my flat is flooding.'

He frowned, confused. 'How can your flat be flooding? It's on the third bloody floor!'

'I mean,' I said, as delicately as I could, 'that your bathwater is flooding my room.'

'Oh, gosh.' His face turned a deeper shade of red. 'I'm becoming such a whale,' he said with a self-deprecating smile. 'Perhaps I should stick to public baths or lochs. Or I could make a habit of bathing in my club, where they have deep tubs from the twenties. So does the Savoy, you know.'

'I think it's just perhaps the enthusiasm that might be the problem,'

I said.

He grinned in return. 'Well, after a few drams of whisky, I do get it into my head that I can still leap into that tub like the sprightly lad I was forty years ago...'

'Well, to be honest, this is the first time I've noticed a problem. But it is quite a big problem. I mean, the water is running down my windows. It's the antique oak parquet I'm worried about, to be honest. It stains so badly.'

His face fell. 'Oh, I'm rarely here at all these days, he replied. Spend most of my time in my castle in Scotland.' He paused, processing the accusations. 'Let me give you my card; I'll write down the name of my insurance. We can sort all this out.'

'That's very kind of you,' I said. 'I suppose I travel quite a lot these days too. But please don't mind me, I didn't mean to interrupt your bath. Just perhaps try to keep the bath from overflowing quite so virulently. I don't think my ceiling can take it.'

The lord laughed a great roaring laugh. 'I'll try to be more careful. And let's make sure we have a cup of tea one of these days.'

I smiled. 'As long as you promise not to spill it.'

The insurance paid for the damages, and the paid again the next two times it happened. The problem was only really resolved when the lord moved out and to another house in Regent's Park. Our relations stayed civil: we would always stop and chat when we ran into each other, whether about the neighbour's dogs or about the weather. But to this day, every time I think of Scottish lords, I think of flooding.

THE EXTENSION THAT NEVER WAS

Old houses in Britain are rarely easily dated as belonging to a single historical period. More often, they are a hodgepodge of styles, with the oldest pieces integrated into the new, and the modern architectural adaptations wrapped around the ancient ones. Often, the houses that have been in an area for the longest will have the most chaotic history: the owner can often point out a single doorstep or cellar wall that predates the rest of the building by several hundred years. This is an integral part of the charm of old English houses, and is, without a doubt, one of the reasons many buyers, myself included, would be attracted to them.

Our own house in Kent was a wonderful old manor-house, originally built in 1410 and renovated in 1620. In the early 1970s, when my family bought this house, we applied for a mortgage with an American bank. The paperwork was lengthy, and included many of the usual odd questions that this sort of form does, but one amused me particularly: a clause which requested the 'date of last extension.' Of course, as an honest applicant, I had to enter '1620'. When the credit officer went over my application, being American and unused to buildings being more than a century old, he obviously assumed this was some sort of typo. A house from 1920 sounded impressive enough to his clerk's ears! When I corrected him and explained the situation, he was completely flabbergasted.

'You can't mean 1620. That's nearly four hundred years ago!' he said.

'Yes indeed,' I answered, rather relishing his confusion as it reinforced my pride in my new house. The building works were actually completed less than three months before the Mayflower landed in New England!'

Like most buildings of its type, our house had weathered centuries since its last modifications and integrated them remarkably gracefully. However, despite the charm of the structure, in the 1970s, I decided it was just about ready to have a little more modernising done. One of the things I found particularly lacking in this rather glamorous property and its generous grounds was the absence of a swimming pool. The best features of our house, the ones that made it worthy of classification as a grade II★ listed property, also turned out to be its most problematic aspect: they seemed to make it virtually untouchable as far as modernisation was concerned. In the UK, buildings that have been placed on the statutory list of 'buildings of special architectural or historic interest' may not be demolished, extended, or altered without special permission from the local council or planning authority. Of course, that does leave the option of one of these applications, but, unfortunately, most of the councils in England are extremely difficult and bureaucratic; the process lengthy and prone to time-wasting and failure. Furthermore, in my personal experience, I found this was particularly the case in the more conservative boroughs of Kent.

The council, however, is only one part of the problem: when making a plan for a modification or extension to a listed building, one must also get the permission of all of one's neighbours.

Now, in any normal application scenario, all of the neighbours would usually happily approve any extension plans, for fear that I would one day reject their own. Neighbours only ever cooperate in the hopes of earning a favour: 'I'll scratch your back if you scratch mine' is really selfishness dressed up as mutual benefit.

This time, however one neighbour seemed to have a severe objection to my application: we fought the council on this matter for twelve years, only to find out almost twenty years later that our application had been rejected only because one of our neighbours had vetoed it.

It was somewhat ironic that after years and years of requesting an explanation, and being denied one, I was offered one so easily. It turns out that finding out details regarding a long-closed case is far easier than trying to access one in progress. Thus, one day, when I was discussing something entirely different with an officer from the council, she allowed me the privilege of accessing our file. Most of the documents contained inside were uninteresting, but there was one piece of paper that caught my eye. It bore my neighbours' name and was clearly labelled 'objection'.

'Do you mind if I take a closer look at this letter?' I asked the official.

'Be my guest,' she replied with a smile. 'I'll be looking over some other documents.'

The neighbours who had sent this letter were an old couple of primary school teachers in their early sixties, whom I had never had any trouble with, although they had always kept to themselves. They lived alone just down the road from us, as their grown children had left home years before we moved in. I had assumed our lack of friendship came from their relative shyness; I now began to question this hypothesis. They had certainly always come across as quite nosy, the few times we did interact with them, but I thought this came from leading a lonely life after retirement, where the most interesting thing they could think of doing was watching their neighbours go by.

The letter they wrote to the council was an odd combination of unlikely vitriol and pandering to some sort of sense of peace and quiet that they obviously thought they shared with the members of our local council.

'We object to this extension,' it explained, 'because we are worried that the Jamiesons' house will subsequently be expanded into a large entertainment facility. We live in a calm, beautiful area of Kent. We do not want our surroundings to be overwhelmed with visiting Rolls Royces and Mercedes, crawling with staff and paparazzi and important guests' entourages. Just because we are neighbours with a banker who appears to be financing the international oil trade, we do not want to run the risk of one day having the king of Arabia coming here with a bunch of wandering Bedouins, or having our flowerbeds trampled by racehorses, or our parking spaces taken over by stretch limousines. Kent is a quiet place, and we would like it to stay so. We hope you will consider our arguments.'

Of course, I laughed my head off when I saw how petty this neighbourly issue had become.

'I can't believe they never even spoke of it to us directly!' I told the council officer. 'I mean, it's completely ridiculous. There's never been a limousine in my parking lot in all the twenty years I've had this house. Why on earth would these people send in an official, and, if I may say so, completely ridiculous complaint, rather than just asking me round for a cup of tea to explain their worries? It's a damn shame. All we really wanted was a swimming pool!'

She shrugged. 'People get strange about their neighbours.'

'Do you know if this was really the reason our application was rejected? I mean, I've only flicked through the file quickly, but I couldn't see anything else problematic. Lord knows I asked enough people in this office around the time! I can't believe we still don't really know what happened.'

'We try to stop people from getting too inquisitive,' she said gently. 'Unfortunately, there's no way for me to tell you if that was indeed why your application was turned down, as I happen to know that the officer who handled the case retired a few years ago. To be perfectly honest, I wouldn't put too much blame on their shoulders. These applications don't succeed very often. The logic, I suppose, is that appending any sort of extension to a house built in the fourteen-hundreds or sixteen-hundreds will only ever look modern.'

'It's ridiculous, though. I mean, surely no-one would come to our house and think. "Oh, that's a modern house, look at that modern pool!" They didn't have swimming pools in 1620!'

The officer laughed. 'Personally, I would tend to agree with you. However, you know as well as I do that going up against the council is always difficult. You must have known this when you purchased a listed building.'

In this case, I guess the fact that my house had only been renovated once, and that in 1620, was in my disfavour. It struck me as a fairly tortured piece of logic, but in reading that silly letter, I felt I had gained a little more perspective regarding the whole business.

'I suppose I did know,' I admitted with a sigh. 'It's a great old house, though.'

'Don't get down about it now,' the officer added. 'From the pictures in this file, it looks like a gorgeous place to live. I'm sure you've been happy there, pool or no pool.'

I had to admit she was right. In the end, we never did get our extension or our swimming pool, but we have been very happy in the twenty years or more we have owned the place. I assume our neighbours are still waiting for the limousines!

THE BURNING QUESTION

In my early days as an engineer I took grad school classes in the evenings at New York University, a commitment which required me to make a one and a half hour trip from my home in Summit, New Jersey, to the University's campus in the Bronx. I do not miss those trips. As the freeway churned away beneath the wheels of my car, I would often wonder if the university had consulted some old-world astrological savant to arrange its semesters around the foulest possible weather periods of the year. My course ran from October to April, which denied me the prospect of all those carefree summer rides I enjoyed so much, and instead subjected me to the kind of commute that appeared to be under the influence of a gypsy curse. The weather was abominable. The rain fell upon the tarmac in buckets, the wind beat upon the car windows like a mad old woman, and the only discernible light came in the form of the faint apology of my car's high beams.

These trips were depressing, but a strange quirk of New York life at the time meant that they were never boring. The first time I noticed it, I assumed I had only witnessed an awful misfortune. Indeed, in any place other than New York in the 1970s, it would have been no more than that. The problem struck me when I noticed the second and third burning houses before my first week of commuting had even finished. I was willing to accept one freak occurrence of a house fire in winter, but three blazes in this pounding rain seemed to beggar belief. So many fires would raise suspicion under any circumstances, but an East coast winter could often be equivalent to having a running fire department hose on at all times. The frequency of these events made no sense to me, but I struggled to find anyone who shared my curiosity.

It is worth conceding that this phenomenon may seem more puzzling to a European reader than to an American one. Europe has seen enough devastating fires in its long history to make it cautious in the materials it chooses to build with. Disasters like the Great Fire of London have caused the British, for example, to learn hard lessons about thatched roofs and wooden beams. Americans have always seemed to me to be curiously unconcerned by this sort of thing. Perhaps it is their impulse to constantly build and progress that makes them overlook how vulnerable so many of the houses they build really are. Occasionally, when the weather permitted me to see far enough, I would gaze out on the rows of flimsy pre-fab houses and wonder why the whole lot of them hadn't spontaneously combusted years ago. It was not only the houses, but their furnishings that were rife with flammable materials. The curtains looked thin and dry, the kind of motel adornments that stretched right down to the floor, just in case they missed that stray cigarette stub rolling across the carpet. What made it worse was that these houses were not only flimsy, but old and poorly maintained. Their front yards were strewn with old appliances that spoke of a life of abandonment and carelessness lived inside. It was no wonder there were so many fires; if I lived in such a place, I would want it to catch fire. In an instant, it all made perfect sense: the residents themselves had started these fires. The idea had rooted itself in my mind, and in those long graduate engineering sessions I would stare out the window, over the glowing embers of the Bronx and brood over what was going on in the minds of their frustrated tenants.

It may all seem obvious now, when fraud in its many guises is all the rage, but back then people were a little more naive about these things. Americans, after all, had been through the Great Depression, and a good few wars besides. The security of owning one's own home, or even having a roof to sleep under, was nothing to be scoffed at. Why throw all that away, just to claim a little more back on insurance? Setting fire to a business might make sense if it was failing and incurring debts at an increasing rate, but these were spare, simple houses we were talking about. The insurance claims could hardly compensate for the hassle of moving to find another, which would in all likelihood be much the same as the one left behind. It was for this reason, I think, that it took the authorities so long to figure everything out. What triggered the realisation in me was how long it took the fire brigade to turn up when these fires did start. Even if the residents did call 911, it was fairly common for the fire to continue burning for hours, sometimes even days before anyone turned up to do anything about it. These were old, throwaway houses, it seemed, and nobody attached much value to them as long as the people who lived in them were safe. It must have riled the people who lived there to see know how little their property counted for. I began to see that the fires were not just financially motivated, but socially too. People were angry that they didn't live in large, comfortable Manhattan townhouses, angry that in a country where any order of success was deemed possible, they would always live in the same plain, drab houses. They were happy to claim what little they could from the insurance companies because it felt like the welfare they felt they weren't getting.

Eventually things went far enough that the press started noticing, and I soon noticed an article in the *New York Times* that described the phenomenon in impressive detail. Some residents had apparently turned the process into an art form, raising their premiums at just the right time, and then downgrading to a house with a more manageable mortgage. The houses themselves were so easy to incinerate that most evidence of arson was destroyed in the fire itself. Indeed, all one had to do was drop a cigarette in the right place and the whole structure would more or less explode. Eventually this uncertainty was too much for the insurance companies and they stopped paying out so readily. The fire department, too, began responding with particular urgency to calls from the Bronx, and soon some of the houses were even saved, rendering the fraud a much more uncertain business for the arsonist.

A burning house is a sad thing to see under most circumstances, but in New York, I learned to think of it as representing the sort of collective hysteria people in big cities can often fall subject to. This was their way of making society pay for the miseries of living in the Bronx. When I recall the weather I experienced on my drives there, I find it hard to blame them.

One of the problems of having a beautiful home is that the very attributes that make it dear to oneself will inevitably be coveted by one's neighbours. Over the years, our property in Kent developed many wonderful features, many of which intruders at various points tried to claim or take advantage of. It was a beautiful old house, built in 1410 and surrounded by formal gardens. At some point during the sixteenth century, before the renovation, the original tennis court was laid out in the centre of the garden, where games of real tennis or *jeu de paume* were played. Then, about two hundred years before we purchased the house, the owners planted a magnificent hedge of copper beech. As the plants grow only half an inch or so a year, it would have taken it a long time to get established; but by the time we moved in, it was a tall and glorious hedge that turned a brilliant golden colour for a good seven months every year. Ten years before we moved in, the previous owner had an extension built. Finally, approximately six years after we did settle in happily as a family, we managed to get permission to build a swimming pool.

Now, the hedge and the formal gardens were fairly safe from our various neighbours: the tennis court and the pool, however, did not fare quite as well. The pool was a large, outdoor pool, which we kept heated at considerable expense so that it could be used by my children whenever they pleased. As my children were five and seven around the time it was built, it was perfect for them to learn swimming at home. I enjoyed the occasional dip myself, especially in the summer months.

One day, I walked over to the poolside for an afternoon swim and found that it was already occupied by three small children and their father. Needless to say, this was something of a shock.

'What are you doing here?' I asked at once.

'We're your new neighbours,' the man said with a large smile, without even ceasing to paddle around the pool.

'I didn't ask who you were,' I responded impatiently. 'I probably could have worked that one out. What I want to know is why you are currently in my swimming pool.'

'We're your neighbours,' the man repeated with a semblance of patience, finishing his crawl stroke until he was right at my feet.

'We saw there was no-one in the pool, so we walked across the garden.' Seemingly without pausing to consider my expression, he ploughed on: 'We can also see when your tennis court is not in use, so sometimes we go and use it. Do you mind? We are part of the same community, after all.'

I did not know how to reply. The vapours floated up from the surface of the pool, which I knew to be heated to a delicious thirty degrees. They very nearly hid the offending neighbour from my sight.

'What is your name?' I asked. In the background, his children continued to play, obliviously.

'I am John,' he replied simply. 'Your next door neighbour!'

'Oh, you must have that newly-built little prefab house,' I replied, hoping to make John realise this was not going to be as pleasant an exchange as he seemed to expect. 'There are only two bedrooms, right? How do you cram four kids into such a small place?'

John didn't seem to be aware of my tone. 'All the kids sleep in one room,' he explained calmly.

I sighed. My oblique techniques were obviously not going to be sufficient. 'Listen,' I said, as sternly as I could, 'have you heard of a little thing known as the private property law? It was established before William the Conqueror. For the record, so was this house. It is in the Domesday Book, actually. Did you know this already? In that record, the borders to your piece of the adjoining land are already well marked. This is not a community tenement, as I'm sure you are well aware.'

He continued to smile his infuriating smile. 'I understand all that, of course. We're not asking to share your land, or take it over. We were simply assuming you would let your neighbours occasionally use your pool.'

I sighed. 'I would rather you didn't,' I said simply.

'So you wouldn't let us? You would stop us?' He seemed incredulous, as if I was trying to stop him from using a public pool.

I wasn't sure if my insolent neighbour was simply making a bad joke, but I was finding it hard to keep my temper. 'Next time I find you in my pool or on my tennis court, you can be sure that I will put a stop to it. If you insist on trespassing like this, I'll call the police.' I paused, slightly concerned I had gone too far. 'I wouldn't like to do this,' I explained. 'I would far rather we maintained friendly neighbourly relations. But I would like this to be quite clear between us: you cannot just turn up at my pool and expect to use it at any time without asking.'

'You don't have to call the police or do anything like that,' he said hastily. 'I was just trying to please the kids.'

'Don't try to use your cute children as an excuse,' I retorted. 'I have children too; right here with me. Let me tell you something: I went to school in Texas. When I was there, I learned some important lessons on the subject of private property. I remember one of my old neighbours telling us that if anyone trespasses on your land, you can shoot him, as long as the head of the dead body falls on your land. If it falls outside the border, you are committing murder. If it's on your land, you are fully in your rights and you will be congratulated. Now, I'm not saying that Texan laws apply here, but...' I grinned. My neighbour, obviously unused to my somewhat cynical sense of humour, hastily gathered up his children and scampered away. I never saw him anywhere near my swimming pool again.

My joking reference to the police, or perhaps to Texan law, seemed to have had a far greater impact than I had even intended: from then on, our relationship was somewhat dry, if not unpleasant. Whenever we ran into each other, we would simply shake our heads politely, like giraffes crossing paths on the savannah, before moving on. We were neighbours for some twenty years, until his children grew up and moved out. At this point, he sold his house and moved: I was not sorry to see him go. Meanwhile, I continued to enjoy the advantages of our property undisturbed.

SEVEN TIMES A NEIGHBOUR

I don't believe in magic, but several times in my life I have been confronted to the strange and wonderful workings of coincidence. My neighbour Bertrand Serbio was one such recurring stroke of luck, although I never quite figured out if it was good or bad luck that kept throwing us together.

The first time I came across the man by the name of Bertrand Serbio, we didn't even meet. My wife and I were living in France at the time. We had to move house because of an internal reorganization of the bank I worked at, so we were looking for someone to take over the lease on our apartment. It can be a difficult task, finding someone to step in, not to sublet, but actually to take on our contract halfway through, so I was grateful when someone by the name of Bertrand Serbio stepped in, expressed his interest and signed straight away. Our landlord organized the whole thing, so I only heard the name and saw it scrawled at the bottom of the document. At the time, I thought nothing of it, but later I would look back on this as the beginning of our odd acquaintance.

Four years later, in 1975, we set up a family bank and a trading company, which required us to move to a central office in Paris. We found one quite quickly, in the Champs Elysées area, and established ourselves with a relative degree of success for the next four years. However, in 1979, we decided to move on. As we had what was known as a '3-6-9' lease, which is essentially a nine-year lease, in order to leave, we either had to either pay a large penalty equivalent to the unpaid balance, find a sublet, or find someone to take over the lease in its current state. As the rent was going up at the time, the landlord decided to take the search into his own hands. The similarities to the first occasion are not negligible, which is why it was very interesting that we received a phone call a few days later announcing that a taker had been found: Bertrand Serbio. This time, we had to sign papers together, so we were properly introduced. Serbio was a tall, good-looking man, well-spoken and intelligent. We chatted for a while over the papers, and sympathized. He was in his mid-thirties, a driven young Frenchman with ambition and charm. The encounter left a favourable impression. Of course, as one does in these relations, we moved on without exchanging contact details or making plans to meet again. However, fate seemed to have something else in mind.

In 1983, our family bought a holiday house in Cannes. We were pleased to have found it, as the real estate market was quite competitive at the time. Within weeks of moving in, however, we saw a SOLD sign appear on the front of the house immediately next to ours. This in itself was quite a coincidence, but we thought nothing of it until the removal van pulled up by the beach, and Bertrand Serbio climbed out of the front seat!

I walked up to him and shook his hand warmly. 'I can't believe it's you,' I said quite frankly. 'Welcome to Cannes!'

He laughed heartily. 'Well, well, well,' he said, shaking his head. 'It's my own personal ghost! Have you come to warn me of some event? Or perhaps you are just a good spirit, looking after my success in the world of real estate?'

'I don't even work in real estate!' I said.

'Oh, I just meant that you're helping me find places to live. Of course, I do actually work in real estate, so perhaps on some level I did mean that...'

I laughed. 'You are a well-meaning spirit, aren't you?' I joked in return. 'Do I need to acquire some sort of talisman or amulet to keep you away?'

'No,' he said, 'but maybe you could ask me over for a drink? It's been a long drive and I'm parched.'

Over glasses of chilled lemonade, he explained that he had just moved here by chance, after the lease on his last house in the South of France had run out. He'd always had a weakness for Cannes, he confessed, but it was nothing but a fluke that he come across this property: he had seen the ad in a local newspaper. During this time, our family became quite friendly with Monsieur Serbio, often running into him on the beach near our house and occasionally inviting him for dinner or drinks. Once, we went for a picnic with our respective children. This was probably the height of our actual acquaintance, although it was far from the end of our meetings. However, as is often the case with these casual friendships mostly based on location, once we relocated, we did not stay in touch.

We moved on, following my work back and forth from France to the UK, and finally heading to the USA. Three years after we left Cannes, we were searching for a place in Manhattan to host our new bank headquarters. We found the perfect space in the Rockefeller Centre, but it was twice the size we actually needed: a full four hundred square metres. After some consultation, we decided to go for it all the same, but sublet half. We took over two hundred square metres and advertised the other two hundred in agents and local newspapers. After just a few days, we received the first answer, which my bank manager accepted and signed up with. We proceeded to move into the building, so I didn't meet our new neighbour until the next business trip. I was working in our new office in the Rockefeller Center when he walked in. It will come as no surprise to the reader who this was, but it was certainly quite a shock to me at the time! Out of the seven million people who live in New York, who should turn up at our new offices but Bertrand Serbio? We greeted each other in a friendly manner, but I must admit I could hardly believe the coincidence. This was, after all, our fourth encounter, in three separate countries, in less than ten years. In this vast, busy city, it seemed like nothing short of a miracle.

'I thought you must have swung the deal, old neighbour,' he told me with a twinkle in his eye.

'No!' I assured him at once, still shaking my head in shock. 'I mean, of course I would have done so if I had known. But my manager just told me it was the first respondent. I mean, I suppose I should have figured it out! You're like my mysterious French stalker.'

'It's just coincidence, my friend,' he said, clapping me on the back. 'But a good kind of coincidence! I'm glad to see you again.'

The next time I met Bertrand Serbio I was less surprised. My wife and I rented and later bought an apartment in Fort Lauderdale. Just a few months after we had settled in, we discovered that Serbio had bought a small apartment not only in the same building, but on the same floor! When we ran into each other in the hallway, we seemed to have crossed over a line from shock into laughter. It was hard to still be traumatised by a now frequently recurring part of my life. I felt like a man who has been haunted by a ghost for so long that it has now simply become a familiar presence. Furthermore, Bertrand Serbio wasn't actually in Florida that often, but only came there for the occasional family holiday or to seal a business deal, so we didn't spent too much time together in that period. The most remarkable thing about these incidences was not their frequency, although that was quite spectacular, but the fact that they always occurred by pure coincidence. I never knew until I ran into him that he was moving to the same place as me: we stayed in very little contact outside these times. It truly was a case of sheer luck. We continued to get on well, but either due to differences of temperament or to the strangeness of our connection, we never really became friends. When I left Florida to head back to Paris, I didn't tell him where I was going, but when we said goodbye, there was a twinkle in his eye. '*A bientôt!*' he added.

Sure enough, soon after I arrived in Paris and found a guest house for the bank on avenue Montaigne, I discovered that we were actually right next to the headquarters of the large cosmetic company that Serbio now ran. It was no surprise, but it was a change of circumstances in one respect, as I was the one who had unwittingly ended up becoming Serbio's neighbour. I hadn't even known that Bertrand Serbio had made a career change, and transferred from real estate into cosmetics. After this, the coincidences seemed to fly thick and fast. I suppose because we were now both living and working in Paris, it was less surprising that our social and business circles would overlap more, but it never stopped being a shock to me. For instance, I was a member of the board of a large multinational company for seven years. When my contract expired, I left the board without participating in the process of electing my successor. Who was appointed by the board, without my knowledge, to take my place? Bertrand Serbio, of course! I sometimes found myself wondering, almost against my will, if Serbio spent time looking out for these opportunities. How else can one explain such coincidences? We weren't even working in the same field! It was truly remarkable, particularly as in this late phase of our acquaintance we actually had little contact.

The next company I worked for owned a large block of shares. To increase the liquidity of our bank, we sold it on the market, through an investment bank in the form of a private equity placement. We didn't know the buyer; it was simply a case of waiting for a sale, then getting the money through a broker. The deal went smoothly, and I thought nothing of it. However, later that week, we read in the papers that a large block of shares had been bought by the multinational Group Bertrand Serbio. These shares corresponded perfectly in description with the ones we had just sold, and of course the timing was too close to be denied: once more, Serbio was involved in my life. No matter what I did, it seemed I could not shake him off! There was a part of me that couldn't help but be disturbed by this recurring event. It seemed almost spooky at times. Thus, when we sold the rest of those shares, much later, which were also bought by an anonymous French group, I did not inquire amongst our investors as to who might have bought them. I was almost sure it was Serbio, and I didn't particularly want to confirm the haunting! Seven times a neighbour is quite enough, I thought. Eight is just strange.

Since then, I have neither heard from Bertrand nor attempted to get in touch. Of course, that is very much in keeping with the pattern up until now: I never organised any of these meetings. Our movements have not crossed of late, and logic would dictate that it would be unlikely for them to do so again. Then again, this entire story seems to owe little to logic and much to fate! Bertrand Serbio was seven times my neighbour, in different ways, despite no intervention of my own. Since neither Serbio nor I were responsible for these meetings, I can only put it down to luck; and, since there is so far no proof to the contrary, I shall have to assume that good luck rather than bad has been at play. After all, this story certainly makes him one of my most faithful neighbours, if only through coincidence!

In the late 1970s, when we lived in Paris, we had a cook, a butler and our own domestic staff. This was partly because my work as a banker often relied on me for the entertainment of various visiting clients; it also served to facilitate my family's busy life. When I travelled, which I did quite often for work, I would often need to take the butler and cook with me in order to receive clients.

Our bank had a small guesthouse in the countryside of Surrey, not far from Addington and Bishop's Lane, where my family often stayed. It was in a quiet area, nestled between two hills and surrounded by long wooded lanes perfect for walking in the shade of the oaks and elms. I would often run into my neighbours when out enjoying the fresh country air, which I would do every few days or so as long as the weather was good.

Many of my neighbours found even more time for outdoor rambles than I did, especially those who were retired. Howard was one of these: a lovely old man with a full head of white curls, he loved nothing more than to walk his dog Delta around the fields and hills. He liked to do this not just daily, but twice a day, after breakfast and before dinner. Delta was a frisky little Irish setter with a bright russet coat, who would hover at the feet of every person she met as if trying to make friends with their legs. Every time I ran into Howard, he seemed to have new tales to tell me of his companion's escapades.

'You'll never guess what Delta has been up to!' he would exclaim, a grin lighting up his wrinkled old face. 'She saw a fox on the crest of the hill, ran towards it, and crashed straight into a tree!'

'I bet she was quite the hunter when she was young!' I replied with a smile.

'Oh, she certainly was. I mean, she's never been any good at catching things, and certainly not at killing them, but the impulse to run wild is strong in her!'

Another time it might be: 'Delta just ran into the mud by the lake! I don't know why she would do that, she should know the way by now. We've done it twice a day for nigh on ten years!' He shook his head, laughing. 'Just look at her coat! All bedraggled and filthy. I'll just have to give you a bath, won't I, you rascal!'

It was quite amazing to me to hear the number of scrapes Delta supposedly managed to get herself into: scaring a horse, trying to climb a tree, nearly breaking her leg by knocking over a fence... One would almost start to wonder if Howard was making them up, just to keep his daily audience of one happy! I suppose, being a retiree, he had very little to talk about apart from his dog's antics. On occasion, I would enquire about his wife's health, or about the weather, but our conversation would always turn back to the dog. She was obviously his favourite topic, by far. He acted as if Delta was his best friend, and indeed I'm sure this was the case. Watching them together was like reading a scene from some Dick King-Smith novel: a paragon of an Englishman's love for his animals.

However, we were soon to find out that Delta's charm did not have quite the same effect on everyone she encountered. Around that time, our butler, Assumi, who was of Mauritanian origin, went missing. He disappeared just before lunch, and we waited with our guests in vain for the food to appear at our table for a good half hour before realising something must be wrong.

We searched high and low for him, worrying that he had tripped and fallen in the woods, or twisted his ankle in the cellar. When we couldn't find him anywhere, though, we started to worry. On the morning after the butler's mysterious disappearance, I asked Howard if he had seen him, and my neighbour responded that they had indeed run into Assumi the day before on their walk, but noticed nothing unusual. Howard and Delta headed off on their promenade for the day, leaving me none the wiser.

Luckily, later that very day, the butler reappeared: we found him huddled in the bottom of a broom cupboard. 'You look like you've seen a ghost,' I informed him brusquely. 'What on earth happened to you?' When I saw his hands were shaking, I couldn't help but relent a little. 'Come on, let's get you out of there.' Whilst Assumi clambered out, brushed himself down and settled into the couch, I had cups of tea brought to us. Once the look of wild fear had left his eyes, I asked him again what had possibly occurred to strike such terror into his usually stoic countenance.

'The dog,' he said quietly. He volunteered no further information.

'We don't have a dog,' I snapped, confused by this strange reply.

'The neighbour's dog,' he explained mournfully. 'That little red devil. It ran straight at me. It chased me. Oh, it was horrible. I thought it would bite my legs, I thought it would tear my clothes. I just ran and ran through the mud until I got to the house, and then I was frightened it would follow me inside so I went to the closet. Dogs can open doors with handles, you know.'

'Delta?' I exclaimed in surprise. 'Lovely little Delta?'

'It may have a nice, small name,' he said, 'but that does not mean it is a nice dog. It is a very scary dog. It jumps a lot, and barks, too.'

'I've met the dog,' I said sternly, 'many times. She is probably the least threatening dog I have ever come across in my life, if I'm honest.'

The butler glared at me. All the once, the comedy of the situation dawned on me, and I burst out laughing. This made the butler's expression even more unpleasant for a moment, before it slowly transformed into one of mortification. 'I don't like dogs,' he mumbled, as if trying to justify. 'I mean, I really don't like them. I didn't know there was a dog here.'

'I had figured that out,' I replied with a laugh.

'The dog was going to bite me,' he tried to explain. 'When I was young, a dog attacked me. I thought this might happen again. Anyway, this red dog was not on a leash. That's not proper! I bet it's illegal.' He produced an expression best described as a pout.

'I would be surprised if Delta knew how to bite anything but a piece of dog kibble thrown directly at her. Still, I'm sorry you've been frightened. Let me go and talk to Howard about this. Now, dust yourself off and go get back to work before everyone starts planning your funeral. I'll investigate this evil dog,' I added with no small dose of humour. Assumi looked at me gratefully, before scrambling off.

I could hardly keep a straight face when I tried to raise the matter with Howard.

'What's this about Delta chasing my butler?' I asked him, as sternly as I could manage.

'I'm sorry?' My neighbour looked utterly confused.

'My butler Assumi has been hiding in a broom closet for most of the last twenty hours. He says your dog is to blame. I'd like some sort of explanation.'

I shot the dog as threatening a look as I could manage considering I was on the verge of bursting out laughing.

'That's ridiculous,' Howard replied indignantly. 'Delta has never chased anybody in her whole life.' Seeming to sense that I intended to conduct this interrogation with at least a semblance of seriousness, he hastened to add: 'I mean, I'm truly sorry if your butler felt in any way threatened, but it's just not in my dog's character.' He paused and considered. 'I mean, I suppose we very rarely meet people on these walks, so she just must have been a little overexcited. She may have gone up to him. She just wanted to say hello!'

'My butler felt very threatened. Now, I didn't witness the scene but I find it hard to believe there wasn't some truth in it.'

'I believe he was wearing a suit and tie,' Howard said thoughtfully. 'That would probably have looked very odd to her. I can assure you, however, that she's a perfectly docile little thing. You must know this, you've seen her hundreds of times!'

'Don't worry, Howard,' I reassured him, 'I'm not intending to give either you or your puppy any kind of telling off. To tell the truth, I was just curious as to what might have happened to give my poor man such a fright. It sounds like it's half to do with my butler's fear of dogs, and half to do with your dog's fear of butlers.'

'She just wanted to play!'

'He could have had a heart attack.' I was still finding it hard not to make the most of this rather ridiculous exchange. 'I need my butler, you know, Howard. You can't just go around frightening people half to death.'

'Look, if you like, I'll go to the house and apologise. I really am sorry about all this,' Howard said, looking genuinely mortified.

'No, you don't need to do that,' I reassured him. 'Just maybe make sure she's on a lead if my butler ever appears in the woods again, which, after this, he's fairly unlikely to do again!'

Howard nodded enthusiastically, and he and his dog scrambled home.

I continued to come to the house every few months, and on these visits I never failed to run into Howard with his dog. Every time we met, we would have one of these identical conversations about Delta's latest antics. There was a certain comfort in the repetition, I suppose, or perhaps Howard grew older and stopped noticing his stories were always the same. Our discussions would always take place on the way out to one of these joyful promenades, or back from it. The two companions would disappear for a good two and a half hours at a time into the lanes of Addington and the surrounding villages. At the end of this time, sure as clockwork, I would see them come back, Howard trudging and Delta bounding back home for some well-earned rest. This pattern was a real mainstay of the time we spent in that house, and it was a real surprise when, on one trip in the early 1980s, we didn't see Howard or Delta for days.

The day before we were meant to head back to Paris, however, there was a knock on the door. I opened it to find Howard standing there with his hat in his hand, his eyes red from weeping. 'Come in,' I said at once. 'Can I get you some tea? What's happened?' He nodded gratefully and sat down on my couch. I poured him a cup of tea from our morning pot and waited for him to explain.

'She's gone,' he finally blurted out. My heart sank. I assumed he was talking about his wife, who had been infirm for years and whom we rarely saw, but who had seemed to be a lovely woman the few times we had crossed paths. 'Delta,' he sobbed, jostling me from my reverie. I hoped I didn't look too startled when I figured out what he meant, and the loss of whom, exactly, he was so upset about.

'I'm sorry to hear that,' I said quietly, resisting the urge to ask any questions that might be deemed offensive, or to reveal my first misimpression. 'How old was she?'

'Seventeen,' he said under his breath with a touch of reverence, wiping his tears away.

'Isn't that quite old for a dog?' I said hesitantly. As soon as the words had left my mouth, I wish I had reacted almost any other way. Howard scowled. 'Yes,' he admitted reluctantly. 'We grew very close in that time. We used to walk together every single day.' His face softened. 'I know she was old but I just wasn't ready.'

'She was a beautiful dog,' I said. 'I hope there are plenty of butlers for her to play with in heaven.'

In our country house in Normandy, the grounds are surrounded by planned gardens, beyond which lies a deep, wild forest. It is a picturesque setting, full of the local flora and fauna, and a rather idyllic place to escape to from the busy city. We often have sightings of deer, wild boars, and foxes amongst the trees. Occasionally, some even cross the gardens or are spotted on the gravel drive. The birds have always been of particular interest to me: I have counted buzzards, eagles and woodpeckers, as well as the ubiquitous and noisy owls. At night, one could be forgiven for assuming that the owls ruled the area, if one heard them shrieking in the darkness or caught them diving down like missiles! But in the daytime, a whole plethora of wildlife appears for the attentive viewer's delectation.

In the late eighties, I used to travel to the house often in order to take a weekend's break from the pressures of banking. I loved to sit on my balcony, looking out over the trees with my binoculars, seeking some sort of exceptional spotting: a nest of blue jays, perhaps, or a pair of courting doves. One day, as I was sitting in my usual spot, however, I saw movement between the trees that didn't look like a bird at all. I craned forward, adjusting the lenses and trying to focus, until I could make out a group of people who seemed to be jumping around between the trees. At first, I wondered if they had some kind of physical problem. Maybe they were being attacked by an army of red ants? Or perhaps they had just run away from a madhouse! I decided that observing people was far more interesting than watching any other kind of mammal. Nonetheless, when the first men I had seen were joined by a group of older women and teenagers, I started to wonder about the whole situation a bit more seriously. They were on my land, after all. I wondered what on earth they could all be doing. Were they looking for some kind of precious metals? Had they lost some family heirloom in the grass? Perhaps, I pondered, this being Normandy, they might have found some kind of memorabilia from World War II. I decided I had to find out. The advantage of people-watching is that one can pull on a pair of rubber boots and go ask them what on earth they are doing: the same is unfortunately not true of owls or wild boars!

I walked along the lake to where the people were huddled.

Although it was late August, it was a cold morning, and the grass was still fresh with dew. I found myself shivering as I advanced towards my specimens of *homo sapiens*, wondering what could be so exciting as to have drawn them out in this weather.

'Aha!' I said when I came upon them. I rather wished I had prepared a pithy comment. Instead, I just had to explain that I lived in the house whose grounds they were creeping over. I gestured towards it, and they nodded in a friendly fashion. 'What are you doing here?' I asked.

'We're your neighbours,' a tall man, who appeared to be the leader of the group, explained. 'We live on the farm just over the hill.'

'So you just came for a walk? I saw you snooping around in the grass. What are you really up to? Are you spies? Are you researching something? There's nothing to steal in these woods, you know. Also, if you find anything valuable, you should know that this is my land.' I paused, hoping I had covered all the bases. To his credit, my interlocutor only smiled.

'Nothing like that,' he explained. 'It's just that we noticed that you never pick your blackberries.'

'Blackberries? I don't have blackberries.'

'Oh yes you do,' a teenage girl piped up with a smile. 'Wild ones. There's a huge crop this year. See?' She held up a bucket nearly half full of dark, juicy fruit.

'I had no idea!' I exclaimed in surprise and delight. 'Are they sweet? Are they nice to eat?'

The girl held out a handful with a friendly smile. 'Try some! I'm planning to make some into jam, or maybe a nice big pie.'

I took a few berries and popped them in my mouth. They were lovely: a little sour, but with a delicate sweet flavour. As I savoured the fruits, and thought about pie, I suddenly remembered what I was supposed to be talking to these people about. I swallowed the berries hastily. 'You know,' I began, hesitating a little in the face of their friendly smiles, 'this is actually my property.' I straightened my shoulders and hoped there were no berry stains on my teeth. 'You're trespassing,' I said firmly.

I regretted this accusation nearly at once. The tall man instantly looked mortified. 'We thought you wouldn't mind,' he said sheepishly. 'We thought if we came in the early morning you might not even notice.'

'We're sorry,' the girl added. 'We didn't know you might want them yourself. Here, you can have them.'

'What are your names?' I asked.

'I'm Pierre,' the leader said. 'This is my brother Marc-André, my wife Sandrine, my daughter Lucille. We live just across the hill. These are some of our friends.' He gestured at the three other people standing there awkwardly with their buckets and baskets.

'We won't do it again if you mind,' Pierre added. 'I hope you don't consider this too cheeky, but would you mind very much if we stay another hour? I mean, in a sense, the damage is done.'

'Why don't we give him some berries, Papa?' the girl chimed in. 'It's rude enough.' She was blushing furiously, obviously quite ashamed. In the face of this contrition, I couldn't help but relent.

'I'm not giving you any trouble,' I told them. 'To be fair, this is a great discovery you've made for me. If you just bring me a few of these berries so my cook can make me a pie, I'll consider this encounter lucky.' Encouraged by the girl's grin, I added: 'In fact, if you hold up that end of the deal, you can come back every year.'

Pierre joined in with the smiling, and clapped me on the back. 'See, this has worked out wonderfully. By trespassing on a neighbour's land, we've made a new friend!'

I had to laugh. 'I think that sounds like a pretty risky approach.' I turned to the girl. 'I wouldn't take your father's advice too seriously, if that is how he planned this...'

She blushed. 'Oh, he really just hoped we could sneak around like wild animals, leaving no traces behind...'

'Ah, but that was without counting on your neighbour being a keen naturalist!'

'You're obviously more talented at spotting fauna than flora,' Pierre joked.

'Now that you say that,' I thought aloud, 'you should be careful with those berries. I've seen a lot of foxes around lately, and they tend to skulk around in these areas of low brush and around the edge of the forest. They urinate on the hedges, you see. I would steer clear of the low-lying berries if you don't want to get rabies. You should be careful to only pick the ones at least sixty centimetres high.'

He nodded. 'Have you noticed this whole field is overrun with dandelions?'

'Dandelions? Why would they interest me?'

'The young sprigs make a great salad, you know. We usually pick them in the spring.'

'You Frenchmen are all crazy. First you trespass to pick wild berries, then you tell me you make salads out of flowers?'

'It's a bit bitter, I'll grant you, but it's also very nice cooked in cream with lots of salt and pepper. My mother used to make an excellent soup, too. Traditionally, it's served in a salad, though, with a hard-boiled egg crushed in, and some fried *lardons*.'

'I wouldn't eat it now. You can only pick it for about two weeks before it turns bitter,' his daughter said. 'That's what makes it the quintessential spring green.'

'I have to admit you're making me curious.'

'Oh, and the other name for them is *pissenlit*,' she added. 'It's supposed to be a diuretic, you see.'

'Don't discourage him!' her father cut in amiably. 'The name *dent-de-lion* is much more interesting: see the edges of the plants? They look like lion's teeth.'

'None of this convinces me it would be worth eating,' I replied.

'Tell you what,' Pierre said jovially. 'If you let us come back in the spring, we'll invite you round for dinner and show you.'

'Now you're talking,' I replied. 'This is how everybody should do trespassing: a lesson in etymology and a culinary invitation.'

We all laughed, and I walked back home feeling much better about the presence of mysterious people in my woods. Over the next few years, we actually became friends with these neighbours. They brought me the promised berries, and a few months later I went round to their house for a lovely dinner of dandelion salad and roast chicken. A few years later, when they had come over to our house for coffee, they were also responsible for discovering that we had wild hazelnuts growing in our hedges. Not only had I discovered an interesting new species of neighbour, but I had also learned some useful culinary titbits!

In college, before I moved to a fraternity house, I lived in a complex known as a state court. The form of this accommodation was a series of dormitory duplexes, overlooking either a private balcony or the swimming pool out front. The idea behind this rather luxurious development was that everyone could live in a friendly community whilst retaining a sense of space and independence.

In reality, there was very little privacy to be found. You could see everything, hear everything, smell everything. You could hear every lover's fight, every group of children splashing in the pool, every mother shouting. You could smell every curry, every barbecue, every cigarette. The thing I hated the most was the odour of the start of the barbecue with the kerosene lighters. This was Texas: by the end of the spring term, there would be a barbecue or a party every night. This courtyard embodied all the worst aspects of living in a community: the triple crown of bother, I used to call it. Smells, noise, and lack of privacy.

Fawzia lived above me. She was a PhD student from the Middle East, studying liberal arts with the hope of becoming involved in the UN. She was twenty-three, dark-haired and slender, with honey-coloured eyes and high cheekbones. She was obviously a beautiful, lively young woman with a desire to socialise, who had been held back from doing so by her religion and upbringing. I don't think she ever went out with friends. She certainly wouldn't have been able to strike up friendship with a single man, not even a respectable downstairs neighbour like myself. As far as I knew, she spent most of her time in her room studying.

Fawzia clearly liked the idea of interacting with me, so she came up with a remarkable number of reasons to do so. She would come out to her balcony and shout 'Bradley!' with such a peculiar mix of shyness and directness. She never called ahead, never prepared me in any way. She would just wait for me to come out of my front door, sliding the glass aside and stepping out, turning around to look up at her. She was always prettily dressed. It would be like some kind of strange 'Romeo and Juliet' scenario. I would look up at her sweet, round face and ask: 'What do you want?'

Equally romantically, her reply would be, 'I ran out of pepper!'

Other times it would be: 'Can I borrow some sugar?' or 'I need some of your napkins.'

The smallest, most ridiculous excuse would suffice. Once she asked for some green beans; another time she wanted to know if you could substitute anything for salt. She came up with a new one every week.

But, over the thirty or so times Fawzia conversed with me from her balcony, our favourite topic of conversation was rice. It was quite impressive how much we managed to talk about rice. The exchanges were usually fairly short, with just one or two small questions. But sometimes we managed to drag the topic out quite impressively...

'I really forgot what you told me yesterday,' she would say. 'How to cook my rice, I mean.' She would blush. 'I mean, it's so complicated.'

I always worried about her memory as a PhD student.

'How much rice do I use? Do I have two fingers of water over the top? Do I keep the cover on the saucepan? How big a saucepan am I supposed to use? Do I let all the water evaporate? Wouldn't it burn? Is it true that I have to let it simmer after all the water dries? And do I add salt? Or was it butter? I remember you told me not to add olive oil because burnt olive oil smelled bad.'

She took a deep breath. Then she waited with a small, sheepish smile.

I never knew whether to be exasperated or amused.

'Fawzia, you're a PhD student,' I would chide her gently. 'Your memory should be excellent, even if your cooking skills aren't. There are five crucial principles of rice cooking. You know this. I have repeated them several times. How can you still be getting them confused?'

She would look down and stay quiet, waiting. 'So tell me simply,' I said. 'What is the problem? You just asked me twenty unnecessary questions. Let me turn them back to you. Did you wash the rice with cold water for one minute? Say yes or no.' She did not answer, so I would continue. 'That's the first rule. Try to remember it. Rinse the rice. OK. So, next. Did you strain it? Did you put it in a pot? Did you add the two fingers of water above it? It's very straightforward. It doesn't matter how big the pot is. It doesn't matter how much rice you're cooking. If you are cooking for ten people it still works the same. The second rule is: two fingers of water.'

She would nod mutely, as if paying very close attention. I would soften my voice a bit. After all, it wasn't her fault she was bad at cooking rice. 'OK. So the next step is to let the water come to the boil slowly until all the water evaporates. That is rule number three. Don't stir it too much, you will crush the rice. Then you put the cover on for about ten minutes. It's cooking in its own steam, do you remember this part?' She nodded enthusiastically, her eyes wide and childish. 'OK. Now we just have the final steps: add a pinch of salt and a small amount of butter. Let the butter melt over the cooling rice, and fluff it lightly with a fork. That's it.'

By the end of this speech, which I repeated often, I would have lost all exasperation and feel quite proud of my student. 'You understand now? It's quite easy. Five simple steps.' Sometimes I would add small details, like 'don't add pepper to the rice, it spoils the appearance,' or 'make sure you don't add the butter when it's still in the pan or it will burn.'

I remember, once, when this had gone on even longer than usual, Fawzia burst into tears at the end. This took me rather by surprise. I have not found rice to be a particularly upsetting topic before.

'What is it?' I asked her. 'Are you feeling sick? Is there death in the family?'

She laughed a little through the tears.

'Oh, Bradley, I was so ashamed, I couldn't tell you. I burnt my rice an hour ago. It's all black. I should've asked you before but I was so embarrassed. I just thought I needed to learn all the steps again.'

I sighed. I told her: 'Look, why don't I just cook you some rice. Then you can watch and see how it works.' It would have been inappropriate for me to suggest coming up to her apartment. 'Come down in about an hour, and we can eat together.'

She blushed furiously, but seemed pleased. She came downstairs a short time later, wearing a conservative dress and with her hair tied back. 'Do you remember the steps?' I asked her.

She seemed shy all of a sudden. 'I... I'm not sure,' she said. 'Can I just watch you cook?'

Worrying that I had offended her earlier with my chiding, I said: 'Just to reassure you, I didn't mind that interrogation session in the least. Feel free to call me anytime if you're stuck.'

She smiled. 'I probably will never learn. But I'd like to try.'

We went through the five stages carefully. Occasionally she would stop me to ask some question about the kind of saucepan I preferred, or the timing, or the seasoning. Whenever I was speaking to her, I was under the impression that she understood perfectly. I did often wonder if she was more interested in just spending some time with me than in learning to cook rice. I wouldn't say this developed into a love story: it was more of an intellectual pursuit between two students. After all, I had to respect her because

1. She was my neighbour,
2. She was female,
3. She was four years older than me,
4. She was lonely,
5. She truly was helpless when it came to cooking rice.

That night, we ate a delicious meal of fluffy white rice with just the right amount of butter and salt, topped with grilled saddle of lamb. We talked of various things, including rice cooking, for a while, although we were still a little shy with each other. As soon as we had finished, she took her leave and went back up to her apartment.

Fawzia probably asked me how to cook rice thirty times over the period of my four month stay there. She was right about one thing: I don't think she ever successfully cooked rice in the time I knew her.

THE CALLIGRAPHER

I have always held the art of calligraphy in high regard. The art of writing beautifully seems to me to offer insight into the cultures that value it. It never ceases to impress me how someone can transform simple words into elaborate pieces of artwork, using only a steel nib or a horse-hair brush and an inkwell.

One of my neighbours and friends in Belgravia was an artist and calligrapher who worked for magazines across the world, doing detailed little flower and bird illustrations as well as textual work. He was a cheerful man, and a dedicated worker too. Whenever I would visit him at his artist's studio, which was only about fifty yards from my house, I used to love to watch him working. He used his many multi-coloured pens, pencils and inks so delicately, working away at the tiniest designs with complete dedication for hours and hours on end. The final products were always magnificent, no matter what style they were in, whether they were headlines for a magazine cover or illustrations for a science textbook.

I was a banker at the time, and often travelled for work, marketing products for our bank in the Far East, South America, all over Europe and in the Middle East. In the Arab countries, particularly in those in the Gulf with high net worth, we had an increasing amount of work in the late 1980s as their economies were growing steadily. Our intention was to market banking products there to help manage funds and investments coming out of the region. We drew up a marketing agenda in order to work out how our marketing could be most efficient in these areas, and decided it would be necessary to translate our banking catalogue entirely into Arabic.

We took our catalogue and annual report to a translator, and asked if he could render the whole thing in Arabic. This was not a problem in itself: the translator typed it out on an old-fashioned Arabic typewriter and gave it to us. It was then that we found ourselves with something of a problem: in those days, we didn't seem to be able to find a decent Arabic printer in London. Of course, there were printers with the capacity to produce what we wanted, but not to anything approaching the standard we were looking for. What we needed to do was reproduce this translation, and print out a large number of copies to send over to our outposts abroad, and take with us on our own business trips. We looked everywhere we could think of, but after two weeks had to resign ourselves to the fact: we were stuck with just one crummy-looking typewritten copy of our translated catalogue.

I was telling this story to my calligrapher friend, in hopes that he might know some obscure place that had a good Arabic printer.

'It's ridiculous,' I lamented to him. 'Arabic is the second most written language worldwide. How does this multicultural capital city not have any decent printers that can handle it?'

'It's surprising,' he agreed, 'particularly as parts of East London actually have quite a high population of Middle Eastern immigrants.'

We ended up discussing Arabic scripts over coffee for quite a long time. 'I don't know very much about the culture of the Levant,' he told me thoughtfully, 'but I get the impression calligraphy plays a large role in the artistic heritage there.'

'Calligraphy is actually one of the principal art forms in Arabic countries,' I explained to him. 'This is partly because visual representations of God were considered idolatrous, so all religious art was in textual form, rather than the paintings and statues you get in traditional Christianity. Of course, text itself is also the means of transmission of the Qur'an, so it's essentially sacred.'

'I love how elaborate it is: those flourishes, those arabesques... It's so different to our own printed script.'

'It certainly is. It's also far more varied: there are fourteen principal scripts, some of them more complicated them others, but all of them are versions of the flowery traditional writing, as well as a long tradition of illustrations based on animals, trees or geometrical designs. It's a truly beautiful language on paper.'

He smiled. 'The end result is undeniably aesthetically appealing, even to someone who cannot decipher it.'

At the end of our conversation, my friend paused thoughtfully. 'I wonder if we're not approaching this issue from the wrong angle,' he said. 'I don't think your problem is as bad as you imagine. Now, what you need, really, is a good design. One excellent copy of the text, typeset, edited and proof-read. In one sense, you already have this.'

'Well, we have one messy typewritten copy,' I replied in some confusion. 'That's not what we need at all. We need a good printer with a neat script. What are you getting at? It's not just about a font, it's an artform.'

'I think I may have an idea,' he said with a smile. 'Do you think you could leave your copy of the catalogue with me?'

'Maybe. What do you have planned?'

'I believe there might be an option you haven't considered. See, you're so focused on getting it printed on an Arabic-text printing press that you haven't even imagined there might be another solution: someone could simply write it out by hand for you.'

'What do you mean?'

'If someone wrote it out nicely, typeset it and set it out in a nice script, I mean, then all you would have to do would be to get someplace to copy it.'

'But who would be willing to do such a thing? It would take hours and hours. I'm sure it would be hugely expensive, too.'

He smiled enigmatically. 'Actually, I'd quite like to try my hand at such a thing myself…'

'You?' I was flabbergasted. 'How? Why? You don't know a word of Arabic!'

'If you just give me just credit at the end, I'll do the whole thing for nothing.'

'You're joking. You're pulling my leg. I came here to ask for your advice, and now you're just making silly suggestions.'

He smiled and shook his head. 'Look, I'm a calligrapher,' he said. 'Give me a chance. Just leave your catalogue with me for two days. You'll see.'

In the end, I gave in and left him the document. I still thought he must be pulling my leg, but his sheer enthusiasm won me over. I was in for a big surprise: after less than forty-eight hours, he turned up at my office, holding a few pages of paper.

'Have you come back to pull my leg?' I asked, surprised to see him in my place of work.

'See for yourself,' he said, setting the pages down on my desk next to the catalogue. I picked them up, and was astounded to find they were filled with neat rows of tidy Arabic calligraphy. Still struggling to believe this was truly what it looked like, I flipped open our catalogue to compare. Sure enough, the text seemed to be identical.

'I must admit I'm impressed,' I said with a smile.

He laughed. 'More than that, you didn't believe me!'

'I didn't think it could be done. Are you sure you don't speak Arabic?'

'Not a word! I just paid close attention to the original.'

I looked over the pages, so neatly transcribed on thick white paper. The formatting was perfect. He was right: all we needed to do was photocopy it, bind it and distribute it. He had probably saved us a small fortune, and a lot of worry as well.

'Do you like it?' he asked me.

'Like it? It's basically a miracle. Please do the whole thing for us. In fact, as far as I'm concerned, you can do all of our reports forever. We'll keep you in a special room with biscuits.'

He laughed. 'No, I think this will be a one-off project. It's too time-consuming to be sustainable.'

'You must accept some compensation, though,' I said. 'This is too good a job to be accepted for free.'

'You really don't have to,' he replied. 'It's the most enjoyable work I've ever done though; even better than drawing birds and flowers for a stationery company. I found Arabic really interesting; the alphabet itself, the structure of the designs. It just strikes me as a very elegant script. It took me a while to get used to the placements of those dots above and below, but I think after a little bit of practice I got there.'

'It looks perfect to me,' I said.

It took him a good two months to finish the project, and the end result was stunning. Several of our clients actually commented on the quality of the typography. We used that catalogue for many years as one of our principal marketing tools abroad, for over ten years, until it was obsolete. By that time, printing practices had evolved, and we were able to print the new version more easily. The calligrapher and I stayed friends for thirty years after this. He always kept fond memories of it as a sort of crash course in Arabic calligraphy, and told me he became quite interested in Middle-Eastern art for a time after this project. But he never took on another job like it in all the rest of his life.

Before I met any, I had always imagined a typical horse-breeder to be a tanned, muscular man. However, all the ones I've actually known in my many years of owning and riding horses in England, Ireland, America, Germany and France have been of a different type altogether. If a horse-breeder is a woman, I have gathered, she will most likely be of Germanic or English heritage, mostly blonde, very well built, with excellent cheekbones. On average, these women will be about thirty-eight years old, with very pretty features. And in almost nine out of ten cases, they will be divorcees. There is, of course, an obvious reason for this guess: any woman running stables on her own will need to have almost unlimited funds to breed and raise horses. Anyone starting out in the business without sufficient backing funds is almost inevitably doomed to failure. Even with a vast fortune, nothing is guaranteed: in Texas, I knew two brothers who went into horse-breeding as rich men only to lose the entirety of the oil fortunes they had inherited from their parents. They sunk every last penny of their money into the operation, and got none of it back. It is a dangerous activity to get obsessed with, especially as a horse's value can change so dramatically almost overnight: if it loses a few races in a row, a horse that was once worth two to four million dollars can become good only to be put to pasture in less than two weeks. In France, of course, they would send it to the *boucherie chevalline*. Thus, these strong, middle-aged women need to have a large, safe source of funds: either inheritance from their parents, or the settlement from a nasty divorce. These are the two easiest ways for someone to receive a nearly unlimited fortune without really having earned it!

These were the personal statistics I established over some thirty years of observation across the Western world, and they were confirmed in the person of my neighbour Brunhilde. She was a tall, blonde Germanic woman who seemed to work day and night, breeding horses, having meetings about horse-breeding, and spending her downtime time riding the horses or reading books about horse-breeding. Her temperament was charming, if a bit confusing at first: she was kind, and a little bit flirtatious, but after a short, friendly exchange, she would bring every conversation back to extremely matter-of-fact topics: horse musculature, rearing young horses, grooming horses. These were obviously the things that truly mattered to her, and it was hard to keep her off-topic for long.

I once won a beautiful horse in a raffle, which is a tale in itself, for another time. This particular story has to do with the later stages of this horse's life. It starts when we managed to transfer the horse out of the hotel in Paris where I happened to win it, and into our box. We then drove it down to Bordeaux, where it was kept until we moved to Kent. The real story begins there, where we decided to keep the horse in the neighbouring stables belonging to Brunhilde. Royal Studs was a fairly well-known and respected stud farm, which she had run for a good fifteen years on her own. The farm had two paddocks and a dozen boxes, next to a large, fenced-in grazing field which featured sunken concrete watering holes, as well as several promenades that led off into the environing woods and hills. Brunhilde's own lovely farmhouse was just across the field, which made her our direct neighbour.

When I first brought the horse to Royal Studs, it was with some trepidation. Brunhilde strode over towards me, where I stood with my daughter Rouena by the side of the box containing our giant white horse. I noticed the whip in her pocket.

'What have we here?' she asked.

The horse was quite a spectacular animal: a huge white Arabian stallion just over one year old. Its parentage was impressive and had a good history of winning races. Due to European legislation established to cope with fears of hoof and mouth disease, it had to be kept in quarantine in Dover for a full six months after its arrival in the UK, but once it was released, we had driven it straight there.

'This horse of yours must be broken,' she said to me as soon as she met our wild Arabian creature. Brunhilde had never been one for small talk. 'You cannot ride it, and I certainly cannot let your eight-year-old daughter come any closer. I'll keep him in the stables and ride him when I can. You just leave him here, pay the stable fee, and we will see how this goes.'

'It's my horse,' I said hesitantly, 'surely I should be able to ride it?'

'Not unless you really want a set of broken bones,' she said crisply. 'Just leave it to me. This is your best option.'

'Look,' I said, holding out the papers, 'he has truly excellent breeding. Just look at his credentials! You should be thrilled to have this stallion in your stables.' She looked over the papers, and raised her eyebrows. Encouraged, I continued: 'See, his parents were racehorses, and their parents and grandparents before them. He's a true stallion: he's meant for breeding. That's why I brought him to you, instead of another stables. Of course,' I added hastily, 'if you don't need a breeding stallion, you could always rent him out to take people on long rides in the country.'

'Bradley,' she said firmly, 'you've been a great neighbour to me, which is the only reason I'm doing you this favour. You must realise that normally I should charge twice this price. He's too much trouble, this horse! I won't be able to take him on rides because he's a stallion: when they're not gelded, they cause a lot of trouble. He could gallop in an uncontrollable way, especially if there are other mares or fillies around. I'd prefer not to take him out. We're not insured for that. Besides, we're not even sure he can be broken. This is all fairly theoretical.'

'But he must be of some value to you,' I protested. 'He's a valuable racehorse.'

'Oh yes,' she says, 'theoretically, he is. But we cannot race him here: there are no stallion races in Kent. It's a very specialised kind of race, you see, these stallions that are not gelded. He's essentially a wild beast. You'd have to send him Cornwall.'

'That may as well be the other end of the world!'

She laughed. 'I know. Which is why you should just keep him here. I'll put him up here for two hundred pounds a month, until your daughter can ride him. Then we can decide what you want to do with him.'

I enjoyed my short visits to Royal Studs, and Brunhilde and I always got along, although I did try by all means to avoid having her ride her horses on my land because of flies, smells, and the clean-up this would entail. I often felt sad for the horses sitting in her stables, not being ridden for days on end. From my experience of horses, I had a strong belief that they should not only be trained but ridden every day, in the same way one would take a dog for a walk every morning. They are wild creatures, meant to be in the fields, running by themselves. If humans are to insist on domestication for their own use, they should respect this.

Brunhilde, of course, dismissed these ideas of mine as indulgent. She was tough with her horses, and did not seem to care very much about the idea of their well-being. However, she was obviously an excellent trainer: in the end, she was true to her word. After eight months of her attention, I managed to ride the horse without falling off. It was not, however, an easy or particularly pleasant experience. After some discussion, we decided Rouena would not ride the horse until she was ten. Even then, a full two years of training later, Rouena rode the horse only once, and it still managed to scare her to death. My daughter and I came to the conclusion that we were both better off riding different horses entirely.

Once I realised this, I started looking at my budget, and comprehending just how much this horse had cost me. Considering the travel, the quarantine, the training and its lodging, this 'free' raffle prize had turned out to be anything but! I hadn't even wanted to win a horse: I really just wanted to give a few dollars to charity. I went to see Brunhilde about these concerns, and she agreed wholeheartedly. Clutching my arm firmly in her strong hands, she said in her most threatening German accent: 'Bradley, you are just going to have to take the hit, and admit you really lost that raffle. You haven't won a thing but a crazy horse.'

'It's a valuable horse,' I protested feebly.

'It's cost you ten times its value already. Here in England, it's worth nothing. It can't be bred or raced, and it can barely be ridden.'

I sighed.

'What can I do? It's mine. I don't want to send it to be butchered.'

'Why don't you leave it with me? I enjoy the challenge.'

'I already owe you £800,' I reiterated glumly. 'I can't keep doing this anymore. I can't afford it.'

'I don't want to keep charging you £200 a month for the rest of the foreseeable future,' Brunhilde said gently.

'What do you mean?' I frowned. 'Wait, are you sure you've not just been lying to me so I would agree to this? Are you going to go off and enter it into a bunch of races as soon as I leave?'

Brunhilde laughed. 'Don't be a fool. Look, you know as well as I do that this horse is a total loss. But I've become quite fond of it.'

But surely I can't just leave you with the beast,' I protested.

'Look,' she said, 'I'll tell you what I'll do. You give me the horse, I'll cancel your debt. You won't have any guilt, and you won't owe me anything. You won't have to stop in and see the horse all the time, you won't have to worry about what to do when it ages.'

I sighed. 'You really want this horse?' Something in her tone made it hard not to smile.

She raised an eyebrow and shook her whip at me, and I couldn't help but laugh.

'OK,' I said, 'it's all yours.' Brunhilde truly was an unconventional woman, and obviously the best choice of trainer to take on that devil of a horse. If I was to have received this poison gift, she was the perfect person to make the most of it!

Amongst one's neighbours, there will always be a mysterious few, whose habits one cannot work out for the longest time. One of these was a neighbour of mine in Normandy, who lived near our estate there for nigh on twenty years. In the rolling fields that surrounded our houses, he had a small paddock with three horses in it. The horses grazed there happily all day long, and never did anything else at all. I have never seen anyone ride them, groom them, or even brush them down. There were no children around to braid their hair with ribbons; no trainer to make them trot around at the end of a harness. In essence, they were really just kept like cattle, standing dumbly in the fields, letting their strong muscles sag, and the fat build up on bones that must have once been strong.

This was a sad enough story in itself, but one summer it developed a truly bizarre coda. I was sitting on the terrace, enjoying the light breeze and a cup of coffee, when a large group of eccentrically-dressed men rode across the field in front of the house. This was public property, so I didn't object to their passage in itself: but their accoutrement, and the purpose of this trip, totally baffled me. I stood up, waved to get their attention and walked over to the group. They appeared to stop quite happily, clearly glad to get to show off their outfits to me. As I approached, I made out long red riding coats, tall black boots and little black hats. Coming even closer, I noticed the gleam of big brass buttons, and finally a ridiculous frill of white cotton around the neck. I counted ten riders altogether, all of them men, and all of them dressed in these silly matching outfits. The whole thing seemed oddly antiquated and militaristic for a day out riding in the country.

'What is this, the nineteenth century?' I greeted them with a grin.

The leader of the pack trotted forward towards me. I recognised my next-door neighbour, Joseph.

'*Bonjour*, Bradley!' he called down. 'Don't you recognise a *chasse à courre* when you see one? And why aren't you in costume, anyway?'

'I forgot to iron my redingote,' I retorted. 'What on earth are you doing, anyway? Is this some sort of modern art? One of those strange contemporary plays?'

Joseph laughed heartily. 'Don't be silly,' he said, 'you're not going to pretend you've never seen a *chasse à courre* before, are you?'

'Chasse à what? If it's a hunt, where is the fox? Where are your guns? Where are your dogs?'

'It's the modern version,' he explained patiently. 'We no longer have real foxes. We haven't really hunted properly for the past twenty years.'

'So you're just pretending to hunt?' I asked, stunned. 'Wait, but hunting is legal here! Why would you do that?'

'We don't have a permit. The best part of hunting was never the kill, anyway, everyone knows that. We like the tradition. We like the outfits, we like riding, we love being outdoors with our friends.' He beamed down at me from his saddle.

I couldn't quite believe what I was hearing. 'Let me get this straight. You're wearing these stupid clothes just to chase an imaginary fox across the fields, across the streams, and deep into the forest?'

'Pretty much,' he said, apparently unfazed by my sarcasm. 'It's great fun. You should try it.'

'What kind of imaginary fox is it?' I asked, finding it hard to abandon the topic. 'Is it the fox out of Jean de la Fontaine's fables? Or is it perhaps Roald Dahl's Fantastic Mr Fox? My children would love to encounter these fantastical beasts. Shall I call them outside?'

'Very funny,' Joseph said drily.

'Oh, wait,' I said gleefully, 'I've forgotten Dr Seuss's Fox in Socks!'

'There is no fox,' my neighbour said impatiently. 'Don't be ridiculous. You don't need a fox to ride horses.'

'And you don't need it to be the nineteenth century to wear frilly shirts either, apparently!'

Joseph did not reply, but I fancied I saw a bit of a blush creeping into his cheeks. 'We rented these shirts,' he said shortly. 'And the horses. It's just a bit of fun between friends.'

'Wait a second,' I interjected. 'Aren't you the same neighbours that own those three other horses, just over there?' I gestured at the field in the distance. 'The ones that have been sitting in that field for seventeen years, since we bought the house?'

'Oh yes,' he replied, obviously completely unashamed of this part of the story. 'But we wanted young horses to ride. These are three years old, feisty and fit. The horses are in our garden are nearly eighteen. They're essentially useless.'

'So you paid to rent some new horses to take on your fake hunt, while your old horses sit in a field? Gentlemen, I must admit I am finding this ridiculous situation rather hard to believe. Do you apply this same logic to your children? 'Oh, these ones we have are old and boring! Let's go out and find some new ones!"'

'Feeling snarky because you don't have a horse of your own, eh?'

'I'm not the one with three horses sitting bored and unused in a field. Look, they're right over there! You can practically see their disappointed expressions from where we're standing.' Joseph rolled his eyes. 'Seriously, though,' I continued, 'Why *do* you leave those horses there if you don't really want them?'

'It's a good question,' my neighbour admitted. 'They cost us several thousand euros a month to maintain.'

'To maintain? What maintenance are you talking about? Maintenance would be looking after them. I don't see any of this "maintenance".'

'Well, they are eating our grass,' he said without great conviction.

'Oh, they probably drink from the stream, too,' I added sarcastically.

'Look,' Joseph replied grumpily. 'Horses don't have to be ridden! Think of all the wild horses in the Camargue or the Russian steppes.'

'Yes, but they can run wild! It's completely different. These horses cannot run across the hills or the tundra, or even across a big field. They just stand all day in that tiny paddock. It's ridiculous.' I lost interest in this line of enquiry. 'Why don't you sell them?' I asked. 'They've been there seventeen years!'

'Well, we bought them because they were racehorses. But then they turned out to be nothing but *failed* racehorses, you see,' he explained a little reluctantly. 'They were famous for a while, when they were first bred and raised. They entered all the big tournaments and won fourth, or seventh, or tenth place. Maybe they won a few small medals in obscure regional tournaments. But they never quite became famous. They never went to the big derbies at Epsom or Auteil or Chantilly. So we decided we would let them stay here, so they could just stand quietly and eat themselves to death. It seemed like a way to offer them a peaceful end. It's better than the *boucherie chevalline*.'

I couldn't help but scoff. 'Peaceful? Leaving them like that, never looked after or even ridden, only to get fat and die? Then you go off riding other horses in front of them? That doesn't sound peaceful to me.'

'That is how it is,' he said firmly. 'It is a tradition that we have.'

'I'm sorry to say this, but it all just sounds incredibly cruel. I'll tell you what is dumber, though: going round and round in old costumes without a fox, without guns, without a chase, without a hunting license! It's like something out of Alice in Wonderland, or like some kind of open-air madhouse. I mean, who even are these people? I've never seen them before in my life!'

'Friends of mine,' he muttered. 'Visitors from Paris. And now, if you'll excuse us, we have a *chasse à courre* to go to.' He performed a ridiculous little bow from the top of his horse, before wheeling around and cantering off, followed by his bunch of friends.

As I watched their riding coats flapping off into the distance, I walked back over to pay the old horses a visit, pondering all the while just how ridiculous the whole situation was. 'Some people really are a mystery to me,' I thought to myself, patting the muzzle of the oldest nag. The horse looked at me curiously and continued eating his grass.

When I lived on Eaton Square, one of my neighbours was Baroness Glendevon, the daughter of Somerset Maugham. She was a tall, graceful woman with silver curls and high cheekbones, who had been quite a beauty in her youth; photographed by Cecil Beaton, dressed by Schiaparelli, and sung about by Noel Coward. I saw her once or twice in the mid-nineties when we were both walking in the gardens, and I finally plucked up the courage to approach her.

'Excuse me,' I said, 'I hope you don't mind me asking, but aren't you William Somerset Maugham's daughter?'

The elegant woman held out her hand. 'Indeed. I'm Baroness Glendevon,' she introduced herself with a dazzling smile, 'but you can call me Liza.'

'I'm Bradley Jamieson. Wait, as in *Liza of Lambeth*?' I said, recalling the title of one of her father's plays.

'Exactly,' she smiled. 'People used to call me that all the time as a child, and it sort of stayed with me.'

'I don't believe I've seen you here before. Do you walk here often?'

'Oh, I've only just moved here. My husband John passed away, and it seemed a good time to come back to London. I've rather missed this city.'

'Baron John Hope, of course! I believe some of my banking friends used to visit him occasionally in the south of France.'

'That sounds probable. You see, we inherited the Villa Mauresque from my father.'

'What, the famous Villa Mauresque on the Côte d'Azur? Where the literary greats met? Eliot and Woolf and… your father?' I smiled a little. 'I suppose that would make sense.'

'Yes, I believe it was also well-known as a scene of rather debauched parties,' she added. 'One must be honest about these things. Although of course it was in such a beautiful location, looking out over the turquoise seas; it was just like being in an F. Scott Fitzgerald novel. Although I can't imagine my father appreciating that sentiment. My father owned the villa, of course. In any case, we ended up selling the villa; it had just become too expensive to maintain.'

'So you decided to come back to Eaton Square.'

'Of course it is quite a different place nowadays to the bustling square of socialites I knew in my youth.'

'It still has its socialites, of course, but they tend to head to the clubs in limousines instead of drinking in their drawing rooms.'

'Sometimes I think I was a very lucky child,' she sighed, as if lost in her own thoughts, 'and yet I always felt so unhappy. My father was always rather distant; I'm not sure my mother was very happy. Still, she was very supportive of his writing.'

'He was indeed a wonderful writer. As someone who is passionate about art, I love *The Moon and Sixpence* particularly.'

'I think it made a lot of people want to run off to Tahiti with their young mistresses! I'm not sure how my mother felt about that message...'

'It's such an inspiring piece of writing, though, regardless of the, er, more unusual messages it may contain! You see, I'm a writer myself. I've always very much considered myself an intellectual although I've also worked hard as an engineer and a banker. I'm drawn to the classical word; it's all I've ever wanted to do with my life. People like your father are an inspiration to me.'

'Writing is not as popular an art as it used to be,' she said, 'and in some ways I suspect it drove my father mad. He was something of a workaholic.'

'But what an oeuvre he left behind!'

'Well, I suppose I can hardly complain that it's inspiring writers even today!' She smiled a little half-heartedly, then seemed to remember something. 'Did you say you were a banker?'

'Yes, indeed.'

'I wonder if you might have any advice for me. I'm actually looking to sell my flat here, on Eaton Square. The trouble is it's very low to the ground, so there's some water damage; it would need a lot of renovation.'

'I'm surprised you're having trouble; the location usually does the trick. But let me speak to the Grosvenor Estate. I can actually think of a few of my clients who might be in the market. Let me see what I can do for you.'

In this particular situation, my personal contacts came in rather handy, and I managed to put Baroness Glendevon in contact with an interested party who eventually became the buyer. I was glad to have been of service. Baroness Glendevon herself passed away in 1998, but I have many fond memories of walking in the sunny gardens with her, discussing literature.

For thousands of years, Egyptians worshipped cats as gods; it is my belief that cats have never forgotten this. Toms, tabbies, and kittens alike are coy little things. Whenever I am left alone in a room with one, it always seems to end with us staring at each other in silence, narrowing our eyes. There is a sort of tension in the air, the kind that falls between acquaintances who don't get along very well but have been left alone to pretend to make conversation. I have never owned a cat, but somehow have had several episodes of my life in which I spent quite a lot of time in feline company.

For instance, in New York in the early 1970s, where I lived for a long time, I was briefly forced into close proximity with a cat by the animal's owner's decision to go travelling for business. One of my neighbours, a single woman writer in her forties, had asked my wife and me to babysit her cat, as she had a long business trip to go on. She was quite a successful author, and had to travel for research, so naturally she wanted someone to look after her darling pet.

Unlike many sensible people who would simply have checked the animal into a cattery, or even brought it to a friend's house for the two weeks she would be away, she preferred to have strangers come stay in her flat in order to look after it. My neighbour was a rather strange woman. I actually knew very little about her career, as the topic of conversation she usually chose in my company was the life of her pet feline. My neighbour was quite obsessed with her cat: she seemed to be able to talk for hours about the most mundane of its acts. 'Oh, kitty wouldn't stop playing with a fly! Kitty got milk all over the cushions! Kitty lay on her back with her paws in the air! Kitty refused to eat my leftover prawns!' I did my best to simulate interest. When she asked me to babysit – or do I mean catsit? – I wondered if my impression of attentiveness had been too convincing for my own good.

I don't really like cats very much. The joke that dogs come when they're called, while cats take a message and get back to you later, always seemed to me to be a fairly accurate representation of the two species' approaches to their owners. Dogs may be fairly foolish creatures in some respects, but at least they are always friendly and obedient. Cats, on the other hand, always seem aloof and annoyed.

They couldn't pretend to respect humans if they tried: I'm quite sure they think they own us.

Nonetheless, this neighbour had a rather magnificent apartment on the East Side of Manhattan, and she had come to my house with its keys in her hand. The promise of the presence of a small, annoying ball of fluff couldn't quite deter me from the offer to stay there for free. I accepted. My wife and I had no intention of actually moving into this other apartment for the duration of our custodianship, but decided to travel between both. This way, we figured we could keep the cat happy and enjoy the stunning views from our neighbour's apartment without giving up the freedom and comfort of returning to our own home.

My wife was adamant that we make sure the cat was happy. We understood that the reason we were allowed into this house was because the cat could not be taken out of it: it was simply too used to being in its own environment, lounging in the same chair, eating in the same corner of the kitchen. She was so spoiled that she had her own little cat house, and special supplies of several kinds of expensive foods and toiletries. The house was immaculate, apart from the obvious fact that it was covered in a fine layer of cat hair.

When I first saw the cat, I knew it was no different to all the other cats I had met. It might have been white and fluffy, but that didn't mean it was anything but an overgrown rat. Of course, my wife thought otherwise: 'Oh, she's so pretty!' she cooed, stroking the animal's back. The cat, of course, pretended to enjoy this for a little while, before stalking off, probably in search of its special silk cushion.

'Pretty? She's covered in dandruff and germs. This whole flat is probably filthy.'

'Don't you like cats?' my wife asked me.

'Oh, I love cats,' I told my wife. 'They taste just like chicken!' I grinned. My wife rolled her eyes.

'You're just jealous because I'm not giving you all my attention.'

'Do you know,' I continued mischievously, 'I've never quite understood why women are so fond of cats. After all, cats are independent, they're sarcastic, they don't let you cuddle them for long. They don't listen, they don't learn, and they don't come in when you call. They stay out all night, and when they are at home, they're just sleepy and grumpy all the time. I mean, everything that women love about cats is what they hate about men!'

My wife threw a tea-towel at me. 'If you keep talking like that, you won't get any dinner! I'll give all your stew to the cat. It can have your spot in bed, too – I bet it snores less than you.'

'Lucky for the cat we're not staying the night! I doubt it would appreciate the way you steal all the blankets.'

Whatever my occasional complaints might have been, it wasn't a particularly difficult job, looking after the cat. The cat wanted to be left alone, and so did we. Besides, my wife was inexplicably quite fond of it, so she didn't seem to mind feeding it and petting it. I did my best to ignore it. Despite not seeing that much of it, the cat still managed to get on my nerves. It had a series of habits that betrayed its incredibly spoiled upbringing, and which I just couldn't get used to. For instance, it seemed to think it was entitled to do almost anything it wanted in any part of the house, including jumping onto the table. This last habit in particular I found nearly impossible to tolerate.

'It's completely unhygienic!' I told my wife, after throwing the ball of fluff off the table for the third time that afternoon.

'Don't be silly,' my wife replied. 'It's just what she's used to.'

'She probably lets it walk back and forth up there while she eats! Maybe it even licks her plate!' I shivered in mock disgust.

'Just ignore her,' my wife advised. 'Look, dinner's nearly finished. What do you reckon, shall we eat out of this lovely dish?'

In the centre of the stylish glass table, there was a large porcelain dish. It was a massive and beautiful object with a fine design of blue flowers, and was obviously a prize possession. 'Well, we may as well make the most of this house,' I replied.

'I mean, if we weren't supposed to use it, surely it would be packed away somewhere safe?' my wife reasoned.

'I bet the cat sleeps in it,' I replied grumpily.

My wife brought the platter to the kitchen, where she filled it up with lamb stew. She brought it back to the table, and my bad mood evaporated in the face of the savoury steam, rich with herbs and spices. We ladled our bowls full of rice and meat, and for several blissful moments I forgot the cat entirely.

'I wonder where our dear neighbour is now,' I said through a hearty mouthful. 'I don't think she even told us where she was going. She's probably climbing in the Alps, or in a gondola in Venice.'

My wife laughed. 'For all you know, she's wandering the back streets of Phnom Penh!'

At this moment, out of nowhere, the cat jumped up onto the table, went straight to the dish and started eating our stew! I gave what is best described as a roar, and threw her off the table immediately. She landed neatly on her paws, then immediately leapt back up. This time she landed right on top of the dish, somehow managing to shatter it into hundreds of pieces. Startled by the noise, and no doubt by the hot sauce, the cat leapt off the table again, and ran off towards the white sofa, trailing stew behind her. My wife and I looked at each other in silence, then at the stew pooling slowly across the tablecloth.

My wife sighed. 'I take it back,' she said. 'Cats are awful.'

We cleaned everything up together, and managed to minimise the damage. The cat sulked and hid from us for the last few days, but at least the stains came out of the tablecloth and carpet. The dish, however, seemed to be irretrievably broken. We cleaned the pieces and kept them in a bag, just in case it had sentimental value for our neighbour. When she came back, we were glad we had done so! It turned out that this dish was actually an incredibly valuable collector's item from the nineteenth century. I felt the blood drain from my face when I found out, and had to restrain myself from shouting that it was all the stupid cat's fault. 'I'm so sorry!' I told her. Luckily, I was able to assuage my guilt somewhat by taking the dish to a specialised shop, where it was repaired so neatly that only fine cracks were visible. In the end, the neighbour didn't seem to mind, especially as we had done her a considerable favour in looking after her pet. At that moment, however, I decided I would never again babysit any kind of animal. The responsibilities were just too high: what if the cat had hurt itself instead of just breaking the dish? My relations with my neighbour might have been irretrievably damaged by some annoying ball of fluff! Cats, I decided, just weren't worth the trouble.

I don't enjoy bullfights. I don't like cruelty to animals, I don't like the sight of blood, and I don't like standing in the burning sun for hours. I don't like being overwhelmed by the smells of food and sweat that fill a busy arena, and I don't like being jostled by hundreds of rude people shouting and swearing like a Roman mob. Most of all, I can't stand the sight of a living creature breathing its last breath for these people's entertainment. Death is a terrible thing to witness and I struggle to comprehend why anyone in their right mind would pay money to watch it, especially in such thoroughly unpleasant circumstances.

All things considered, it may come as a surprise that I could ever end up attending such a bloodthirsty event. But what else is there to do in Mexico City? The journey there is admittedly quite enjoyable, as the city is reached by a creaky little farmer's train that cuts through the lush, verdant mountains that stretch from the Guatemalan border along the coast of the Gulf of Mexico. That expedition itself is one of the most breath-taking train rides I have ever taken in my life. The arrival in the city itself, however, instantly kills off any trace of excitement. It's a huge, messy capital city, quite overwhelming at first impression, that somehow turns out to be entirely boring once one has walked around it a little. If one manages to escape the entirely dull, modern centre, the whole place begins to stink of garlic from the street food. The heat is overwhelming and everything seems to be covered in dust. After about an hour on the streets, one is ready for almost any kind of entertainment. Unfortunately, the only thing on offer seems to be bullfighting which, as I have mentioned, holds absolutely no appeal to me. 'Come on, *señor*,' the street criers implored me, waving their fliers at me. 'Big fight! Lots of entertainment for a gentleman like you!'

'Watching a bull being stabbed to death is not my idea of entertainment,' I replied firmly. 'Nor should it be anyone's.' I declined the flyer and left Mexico City without venturing near the arena, choosing instead of take a rather death-defying ride back along the cliff-tops south, on a rickety little bus. I had no intention of returning. Sadly, although my own resolve may have been strong, there was nothing I could do about my wife's tastes and desires. After our honeymoon, we decided to come back to Mexico together. Perhaps I was blinded by the hot flush of new love; perhaps I simply thought the place might have changed since my last visit. I would have been wrong. It was exactly as hot, boring and smelly as it had been the last time I visited. Worse than this, my wife somehow managed to get the idea into her head that she actually quite wanted to see one of these famous bullfights.

'It'll be just like Hemingway!' she said excitedly, 'or something out of D.H. Lawrence! All the greats have witnessed these scenes.'

'Yes,' I replied coolly, 'and they did an excellent job of recording the horror and cruelty of these scenes for posterity. I can't imagine we'll have any further insights ourselves.'

'Look,' she said, 'my brothers will never shut up about the bullfights they've been to. Imagine if I could tell them I've been too, with some gory details of my own to share!'

'Surely that's not quite worth it.'

'Don't be so grumpy,' my wife chided me. 'It'll be a cultural experience! It'll be raw and exciting. It'll be intense.'

'That's for sure,' I muttered unhappily. I couldn't shake the feeling that my lovely wife didn't quite know what she was letting herself in for.

The afternoon of the *corrida* was hot and heavy. My wife and I sat in the stalls, she excited, I wary. The smells of the arena washed over us: old blood, sweat, spilled beer, sawdust, and grilled sausages. It was disgusting. I worried that we had been unlucky in our choice of seating partners: our neighbours were a pair of young men, dressed in grimy white tank tops, with long, unwashed black hair. I would have paid them little attention had they not been obviously half-drunk already on cheap beer, and shouting at the top of their lungs. They were accompanied by a pair of pretty young women, who were doing their best to ignore them. I caught my wife looking over at them with a worried expression. I took her hand, trying to convey the fact that I wished somehow to apologise for our seating, but she only smiled. Up until the fight began, I believe she was actually enjoying herself.

The bull appeared, followed by the picador astride his decorated horse. Ladies threw flowers down into the sand. For less than a minute, it was quite a lovely scene. That all changed when the first spike went into the bull's back, and the crowd erupted into bloodythirsty cheers. The whole show was exactly as inhumane as I had imagined it and read it described in Modernist literature. By the time the toreador appeared, resplendent in his gold-embroidered clothing and scarlet cloak, everything had become something of a blur. I saw the blood drain from my wife's face in near synchronicity with the blood falling onto the sand from the tortured animal. We watched the matador's show of bravura with stony faces. I couldn't understand how the crowd seemed to be enjoying the event so much. How could they cheer every time he waved his big red cape, when they knew he was simply taunting the animal by begging to be gored? How could they roar and pump their fists in the air every time the animal was jabbed, wounded with another blade or hit with a sharp bit of wood? For the next three hours, we sat in sickened silence, occasionally having to look away, as a series of bulls was brought in and slaughtered before our eyes. As the sand grew redder and redder and the crowd's cries grew louder and louder, we became quieter and quieter. Our neighbours became drunker and drunker, and also increasingly annoying in their angry chanting. One by one, the bulls were vanquished, and they collapsed in bloody heaps. For a while, I wondered if there was a way to sneak my poor wife out, but the crowds were so tightly packed it would have been impossible to get to the exit safely. Apparently this was not the done thing: we had come, and we were going to have to sit the whole thing out as stoically as possible.

Our male neighbours were neither stoic nor quiet. As the fights progressed, they grew more and more agitated, shaking their plastic cups of beers and wads of banknotes at each other. I noticed their faces were not as excited as some of the other men around us. In fact, they seemed to be growing rather stormy as the outcomes of each match of man against bull were decided. By the end of the last fight, as the final bull was carried from the ring and my wife slumped back against her chair, I began to wonder if these Mexicans weren't going completely out of their minds with the drinking and the shouting. I noticed that their girlfriends didn't seem particularly thrilled to be attending this bullfight either. It was less that, like my wife, they couldn't stomach the gore, but they obviously had no interest in the action. Their applause was faint, and they mostly sat staring at their fingernails or at the ground, obviously trying to ignore both the animals in the ring and the long-haired, beer-drinking animals they seemed to have agreed to accompany to this event.

Finally, the crowds began to stand up and exit in a chaotic mass, but these two men didn't move. They just sat, screaming at each other in incomprehensible Spanish. Obviously, something had gone wrong. From the waving of pesetas, I assumed that they had lost some sort of bet on the outcome. Presumably the heavy drinking hadn't helped with either man's mood. I noticed some people gesturing at our neighbours from nearer the exits, and at this point our companions grabbed their poor, bedraggled girlfriends by the wrists and headed towards the doors.

We walked out behind them, and watched as the man who had been sitting nearest to us handed a pile of money to a burly man waiting for him at the door. He didn't make eye contact with this rather impressive person, who had a heavy gold chain and what looked like a permanent sneer, but I assumed he was paying up for whatever bet he had lost. As we arrived in the dusty street, ready to walk back to our hotel and spend the next hour over cold lemonade trying to forget the whole thing, we heard a cry. We turned back towards the exit, and saw that our bullfighting neighbour had turned in his rage on his poor girlfriend, and was pummelling her in much the same way the toreador had treated the bulls in the ring. It was a horrible sight to witness. The man had obviously lost some money, and was taking it out on this innocent girl, just because she had had the temerity not to enjoy the bloodthirsty sport. Perhaps he thought she had brought him bad luck, perhaps he was just drunk.

I grabbed my wife's hand and tried to pull her away from the scene. 'But Bradley,' she whispered faintly, 'shouldn't we do something?' I nodded. 'There's a policeman just over there,' I said. 'Come on.' 'He's practically murderous!' she said, obviously already shaken from the bullfight. 'Poor girl.'

However, when I finally came up to the policeman at the end of the street, he didn't seem to understand a word of what I was trying to explain. The fight was still only ten yards away, so in the end I gave up on my schoolboy Spanish and simply pointed. To my horror, the policeman laughed and shrugged. By this point, the poor girl was bruised and bloody, her dress in tatters. I contemplated running into the fray, but knew I would just be beaten up by the onlookers, who seemed to be taking in the horrible sight with as much joy as they had watched the slaughter of the bulls. At this point, my wife was so disgusted that she started to cry. I felt it was my responsibility to take care of her and to avoid us both being killed by a mob, so I figured the best neighbourly action I could take here was to walk away and leave Mexico to its own bloody traditions. I put my arm around my wife's shoulders and we firmly walked away, never to return. A few days later, we flew out of the country. Mexico is one of the countries in my travel book that has a large red X penned over it: I never intend to return.

THE STONE-DEAD NEIGHBOUR

In the early 1990s, I moved to Geneva with my family. We settled into a lovely building in the Old Town, built in the 1500s and comfortably refurbished to modern standards. The master bedroom looked out over the rickety street and an assortment of medieval stone buildings charmingly piled together above the cobbles. It was not an overly large bedroom, but it fit an American king-sized bed quite comfortably. We had a pretty little en-suite bathroom with flowered tiles, as well as a state-of-the-art stereo and plenty of space for well-stocked bookshelves in the room itself.

We settled in happily, and I spent many a night's restful sleep in that vast double bed. Our neighbours were overall of the quiet sort: a scattering of boutiques, a few art galleries, some law offices and libraries. It was not, however, a particularly stable set. This part of the city had always been good for development. Buildings were constantly being bought and sold, and renovated as often as private and government funds permitted. After about two years in that house, we learned that an architect had taken over the building immediately next to ours. He approached us in order to chat about the specifics of the restoration work he had planned, which entailed developing the ancient building into a series of modern apartments. He seemed an honest and friendly man, and we took rather a liking to him. We invited him in for coffee; he showed us the plans of his project, and our relations looked set to be amiable for the duration of the construction work. When it first began, it was a little noisy, and the constant presence of the workers on the neighbouring roofs was mildly intrusive, but we had been expecting it and gave the whole process as little thought as possible.

At seven o'clock on the third day of the construction, I woke up to the sound of my alarm. I kept my eyes closed for a moment, feeling the warmth of the early morning sun on my eyelids and enjoying the fact that the construction noise hadn't started up yet. Once the blissful stupor of awakening had faded, I rolled over and opened my eyes. My mind didn't immediately compute what a saw: a dark grey mass, right in front of my face. Then I realised: there was a rock lying in my bed, right next to me. It was a hunk of stone about two feet in diameter. It was also less than a foot away from my head. My first reaction was to close my eyes tightly and address a silent prayer of thanks to God. I could so easily have been killed in my sleep! I moved away from the rock a little, and looked up at the ceiling. There was a huge hole in it, roughly the size and shape of my new bedside companion. At that point, I took in the gravity of the situation, and my stomach sunk. Our property had been destroyed! The architect had duped us with his apparently official-looking plans: they were obviously carelessly destroying our next-door building, sending the debris flying through the air, and wrecking my home in the process.

I sighed and rose from the dirty bed. I left the rock for the time being, and dressed myself with the intention of going to talk to my would-be assassins. I decided my first port of call had to be my landlord. However, getting some kind of apology or compensation for what had just happened proved a great deal more difficult than I had imagined.

'Ah, *Monsieur*, but this is not our concern!' he said at once, with a shrug.

'But I've nearly been killed!' I replied, trying hard not to lose my temper. The landlord's principal concern, it seemed, was not to congratulate me on my survival but to emphasise that our lease was long-term and inescapable. The scene at the architect's office, where I stormed off to next, was quite similar. The architect's first worry had nothing to do with the two roofs his workers had smashed in with their carelessness, but with explaining that he could not be held responsible. After a few hours of this, I had to throw up my hands in despair and head home.

I decided we would stop paying rent until the situation had been resolved and some sort of compensation obtained. The landlord and the architect were too busy blaming each other to care very much about what had happened to me: three lawsuits ensued. I was not actually able to sue the architect; only the landlord could do so, and although he certainly did so, swiftly and violently, this was of little help to me. After two years of litigation we received nothing, as, according to Swiss law, we would only have been entitled for compensation if damage had actually occurred. Contrary to the more sensible Anglo-Saxon law, which takes into consideration threat as well, I would only have received money if I had actually been hit or killed by the rock! The lawsuit the landlord pursued against the architect continued for a full five years after all the damages had been repaired, but it was no longer my concern. I was grateful to be alive and have a new roof, although I hoped that those responsible would, in some way, have to pay!

In the end, the legal problems were not what worried me most about what had happened, but the fact that I had slept through the incident. Perhaps, in some ways, it was a good thing: the bed was so comfortable that I could have died in my sleep and not even noticed! Still, it was a rather unsettling thought, particularly as I often tossed and turned in the night. It was anything but unlikely that I would have been in that exact spot of the bed just a few moments before the rock had fallen. Thus, while I would have been quite happy to receive a large amount of money as well as a new roof, I was content to have escaped with my life.

THE SUMMER OLYMPICS NEIGHBOUR

Throughout my life, I have had the privilege of attending many great events. I've even been to several Olympic events – from the Winter Olympics in Innsbruck in 1964 and Albertville in 1992, to the Summer Olympics in Rome and Munich. Each time the wonder of seeing the greatest athletes of each generation compete for victory has been an enjoyable and memorable experience.

However, even against all these amazing events, the greatest Olympics that I have ever attended were the games held in London 2012. A thrill of anticipation hung over the capital and nowhere was the excitement more keenly felt than at the stadium. I was lucky enough to get some excellent VIP tickets and was close to the front row, near the finishing line for most of the races. I attended with my three children, who were all very happy to be there and see the marvellous competitors so close up.

It just so happened that our VIP tickets fell on the weekend of the 4th and 5th of August, and therefore the day that would become known as Super Saturday due to Great Britain's amazing victories that day.

It was a particularly brilliant evening for the Team GB track and field athletes, who dominated in each of their specialities. Jessica Ennis, the young woman who was considered the representative face of the games, passed by us many times and achieved her breath taking heptathlon victory that evening. We were lucky to see many great events, and witnessed Greg Rutherford winning the long jump final with his stunning 8.31 metre jump.

It was wonderful to witness such feats of athletic excellence.

My children and I had what I felt were the best seats in the house, and next to us was an incredibly enthusiastic Frenchman. His enthusiasm was solely for the British team. The atmosphere in the stadium was electric that day, people's seats went unused as they jumped up and down and shouted encouragement to the athletes below. I had never been part of an audience like this, all waving flags and clutching at Olympic souvenirs, but my neighbour was the loudest and most excited of the lot.

'Isn't this incredible?' he shouted to me after one particularly exciting race. He was obviously obsessed with the runners, going into rhapsodies about them. 'The training, the dedication! Take Mo Farah. You'd think he's just a skinny, small little guy. But look at the speed on him! Can you believe it? These people, they are the very best, so committed to excellence and see? All these people! Appreciating that!'

I nodded. I was not one for great displays of enthusiasm, so I mostly kept to my seat. Unlike my neighbour, who jumped up on his seat and tripped off it more than once, overcome with the buzz of the crowd.

'Now, do you see?' he asked my children. 'You're witnessing history, here. Right here, history in the making. Everyone will remember this for the rest of their lives. Here, look. Clap! Yes. Wonderful, well done.' He seemed to think that he was the official cheering section for every single member of Team GB, and he encouraged my children to do the same. It was lovely to see them enjoying themselves so much, and just made the event even better for me.

My neighbour was exceptionally excited over the running events and seemed to know everything about Somali-born British athlete Mo Farah, who he thought much of. 'He'll win it, listen to the crowd! You can't say no to a crowd like that. He has worked so hard for this, you know, the training one undertakes to be so fast...'

When Farah came in from his victory in the 10,000 metre event, the Frenchman at my side encouraged my children to go and shake his hand while he took pictures of them. I didn't mind unduly, and it pleased them to meet someone famous. Later on, Jessica Ennis came and shook hands with all of us, beaming from her own triumphs.

I thought that for the broad jump, the Frenchman might sit quietly at my side and just watch, as most people seemed to not care too much about such a small event. But he was more thrilled about being able to watch this than anything else, and grabbed my shoulder during it, shaking me and trying to get me as into the spirit of things as he was. I just laughed and watched while everyone clapped around me. As there didn't seem to be a quiet moment in all the furore of the day, I took a minute when he was sitting down to ask after my neighbour.

He smiled at me cheerfully, visibly overcome with emotion from watching the games. 'Oh, hello. Of course, excuse my rudeness. I am Philippe.'

I nodded, thinking I perhaps recognised his accent. 'It's a pleasure to meet you. What part of France are you from?'

Philippe grinned and didn't directly answer me. 'I think I am only half-French, do you see? I think I'm half-English. I hope I am.'

I frowned at him curiously. 'What do you mean?'

He gestured to the stadium around us, the crowd, and the athletes. 'Well! I am so proud of Great Britain for winning all these medals, aren't you? It's truly incredible. France… France isn't doing so well. It's a pity.'

I agreed blandly. 'Yes, a real shame. It's a good Olympics, isn't it?'

'The best! The absolute greatest. I'm a photographer, you see, and I've taken some wonderful shots so far. Really wonderful. Some of your beautiful children, too.' He fished around in the pocket of his jacket and handed me his card. 'Here, here are my details, in case you're interested.'

In all the madness and heat of the day, we exchanged information and after the day was over, Philippe fairly skipped out of the stadium, still buoyed by the energy of all the successes his adopted country had achieved.

He certainly made my experience of the Summer Olympics 2012 even more memorable.

Of course, what we saw was but a small portion of the action that took place over the London Olympics. Overall, Great Britain did very well indeed, placing third behind the United States and China, with an unbelievable twenty-nine gold medals. It was great to be able to be a small part of that.

Truly, we witnessed history being made and I knew I would never forget it.

Two months later, I quite unexpectedly received a gift from Philippe in the mail with a note – *Something to remember the most amazing day in history! Enjoy, my friend*. It was a heavy and beautifully bound book of the pictures he had taken at the London Olympics, of the athletes and the crowd.

In the midst of the photographs were images of myself and my own children, watching the events and meeting the athletes. When I saw the pure joy and excitement on my children's faces in those pictures, I knew that it was a gift I would treasure forever and was really touched by Philippe's thoughtfulness.

I of course phoned him to thank him for such a lovely present and ever since then, we have remained friends, bound by sharing such an incredible experience.

TEACHING THE FRENCH TO COOK

In Texas, where I lived for several years, barbecuing is considered something of an art. As such, it must be practised regularly and preferably with some degree of skill. In my school days and even later, when I returned to work in oil business, I spent nearly every weekend I happened to be in the Lone Star State moving big juicy steaks back and forth over the coals. Grilling is an essential part of Texan culture, and it became a key element of my lifelong multicultural culinary experiences. By the end of my college days already, I could have put barbecuing as a life skill on my CV. I could have given seminars on the essential questions: how long to preheat the grill? Should one avoid flames at all cost? How much coal should there be, and how low could it be allowed to burn? How could one avoid excessive smoke? I could have held forth publicly on the subject of the ideal length of time to cook a T-bone steak. I could have led a lecture on the difficult notion of barbecuing a fish. I could have organised a well-argued debate over the correct combination of spices to put in a marinade for chicken thighs. These questions truly formed a backbone of Texan conversation: which side, which sauce, how long?

Outside of Texas, however, it turned out that this vast array of knowledge was of little use. In France, particularly, the very notion provokes disgust. Talking of barbecues at a French dinner party would be like suggesting in a fancy restaurant that one should spear one's own venison for stew and roast it in the foyer, or go fishing in the fountain pool outside to find sushi. It was considered a barbaric and incredibly basic process that ruined the natural simple flavours of the meat by masking them in heavy smoke. As far as the French were concerned, Americans barbecuing may as well have been throwing lovely cuts of beef and lamb directly into a fire. This was even before people became concerned with the carcinogenic properties of flame-grilling meat! It was simply the very idea of the barbecue that offended. Furthermore, cooking was not meant to be observed by dinner guests. It was something to be done furtively, tidily, in one's kitchen, while guests sat around quietly eating elaborate canapés and possibly discussing philosophy. Cooking was not, it was emphatically believed, the act of prodding meat with a spike whilst drinking beer from a bottle. This simply was not the done thing.

Nonetheless, in the 1970s, barbecuing began to make its insidious way across the Atlantic, whether French culinary culture was prepared for it or not. When, as a young professional, I rented a large apartment in the seventh *arrondissement*, I met a Frenchman who turned out to be quite drawn to the concept. Jean, in every way but this, was a typical Frenchman, attracted to and repulsed by the idea of the American life in nearly equal measures. He befriended me quite eagerly, no doubt partly with the intention of improving his English accent. One day, quite soon after we had moved in, he invited me over for dinner. I arrived at his apartment, which was downstairs from mine, rather unsure of what to expect. The flat was large and clean, Jean appeared to be in a good mood, and the evening started off pleasantly enough with chilled drinks in the kitchen. I did notice with some surprise the absence of apparent culinary preparation, but figured they had perhaps planned a late dinner. His daughter materialised, a beautiful young student at the Sorbonne. She turned out to be a rebellious and avant-garde soul, and was seemingly charmed by the conventional banking life we were living right next door. The three of us conversed quite happily in English for a time, until the daughter took her leave to meet up with friends.

After a while, Jean led us out onto the terrace, which was a vast space of a good hundred square metres, looking out over all the surrounding roofs. Here, I discovered a lovely sunset, which I had been expecting, and an unlit barbecue, which I certainly hadn't. He grinned. '*Voilà!*' he said. 'A real traditional barbecue for our guest!' I sighed. My status as 'the foreign banker' obviously had not gone unnoticed. Of course, a part of me was quite excited at the prospect of a barbecue, having not been treated to a good steak since my last trip to the States. From the lack of glowing coals, however, I deduced that we would not be eating for at least another hour or two. My stomach grumbled. I was wrong, though, on two levels: both at the prospect of meat, and at the imagined delay.

'We're going to cook, man to man!' Jean said enthusiastically. He strode confidently over to the barbecue, threw a few gasoline briquettes in on top of the coals, and lit them with a match. Of course, they flamed up instantly, producing a terrible stench. As I was shaking my head in relative horror at this unskilled fire-building, something even worse happened. Jean produced a bunch of sardines from a bag and dropped them straight onto the grill. I was flabbergasted. For a start, my idea of a barbecue was still a fairly classic American one of beef or lamb. Obviously the French had never heard of such things. I wondered where Jean had got the idea of sardines from. If one were to barbecue fish at all, it should be something large and fatty, like a chunk of salmon or even swordfish; something that would hold together. Sardines are neither of these things, and take less than a minute to cook in a pan. I watched as the tiny little fish, once a rosy silver colour, disintegrated into charcoal and fell right into the fire.

'Jean,' I asked cautiously, 'have you done this before?'

'No,' he said shortly. Obviously embarrassed, he shoved the remains of the burnt sardines to one side. He reached back into the fishmonger's bag and brought forth three more sardines. If I had been a quicker man, or if we had been in a Tom and Jerry cartoon, I would have caught them before they too could fall into the fire! Of course, those swiftly burned up just as the first ones had. At this point, I found it difficult not to intervene.

'I'm not questioning your approach to the barbecue,' I said as tactfully as possible, 'but if you keep doing this we'll run out of sardines very quickly, and still be hungry.'

'I can do this,' he snapped back.

'Jean, that's not how you light a barbecue,' I said as patiently as I could. 'You have to wait. You have to make sure the fire has burned down so the coals are red. It takes about an hour. Secondly, I just don't think you can barbecue a sardine. They are too small and slippery, you see. There needs to be enough meat to handle that kind of heat, and a bit of grease falling on the coals. You won't get that proper barbecue flavour like this.'

'I don't even like sardines,' he muttered. 'I just wanted to do something nice.'

I couldn't help but feel bad. 'Don't worry,' I said cheerily, 'we'll let the fire burn down for a minute and throw something else on the grill. Do you have anything we can cook? Some steak? Lamb chops? Chicken?'

'I have some whole chickens!' he exclaimed somewhat desperately. 'Shall I just get them out of the freezer?'

Suppressing an exasperated sigh, I replied calmly: 'You can't cook directly from the freezer! It would need to defrost first.'

'Well, I don't have anything else,' he said sulkily. 'Shall I go into the kitchen and get some more sardines?'

'No, no,' I said as hastily as I could. 'I mean, if you do really want fish, maybe you have some *loup* or *sandre* lying around? Some salmon *pavés*?'

'Maybe my wife has some,' he said shortly. 'Come on!'

We trooped back from the balcony into the kitchen, where we found his wife sipping a glass of wine with her feet up on a chair. She wrinkled her nose: 'You smell of smoke.'

'*Chérie*,' he said dramatically, '*le barbecue* has been a disaster.'

She pursed her lips. 'I cannot say I am surprised.' She swept gracefully from the chair and shook my hand. '*Enchantée*,' she said with a weary smile. 'Couldn't you have helped him a little with your... Americanism?'

I wasn't sure how to react. 'I tried,' I said with a smile.

'He did, *chérie*,' Jean intervened, 'and we are going to try again.' She rolled her eyes. He put his hand on her shoulder rather firmly. '*Ma biche*,' he said without tenderness, 'darling, would you mind going to buy us some fish?'

I started. 'Oh, please don't bother,' I said hastily. 'I'm sure we can figure something out.'

Jean laughed, somehow seeming to have recovered all his former swagger. 'Don't be silly,' he said, 'she's not doing anything. Look at her, just sitting and drinking wine. My wife can just go to the shops, they're not very far away, are they, darling.'

She looked at him in disgust. 'Shall I go to the fish market in St Germain?' she asked flatly. I gathered from her tone of voice that she was usually the one who did all the cooking.

'Look,' I said to Jean, trying again to intervene, 'we could really cook anything on that barbecue once the flames have gone down. Do you have some sort of meat? Fish? Anything at all?'

'Those miniature sardines didn't work out for you, then?' the wife commented sarcastically. Jean glowered. I tried not to laugh.

'*Ma biche*,' he said again, 'why don't you get us some nice steaks.'

'Three steaks?' she said slyly.

Jean sighed. 'That would be great, yes.' He paused. 'Actually, four. Our daughter will be back soon.'

In a cloud of perfume, Jean's wife left the house. Jean didn't seem to acknowledge that any sort of power struggle had occurred, and simply leading us back up to the terrace to keep an eye on the fire. A full hour later, the coals were ready, and the wife returned with slabs of beef that would have made any Texan proud. She gave no comment, only pouring herself a large glass of white wine and sitting down with something like glee to watch the proceedings.

That was how I ended up having my first barbecue in France. I did my best to cook the steaks properly and teach Jean the various techniques involved, and I think he enjoyed himself, despite his wife's eagle eye. At some point during the lengthy process, which was now taking place in near-total darkness, the daughter came home and stood for a time laughing at our efforts and chatting with us. Remarkably, the evening was not a total failure. At last, we served up the steaks. They were simple, lacking marinade or appropriate accompaniments, but they were satisfying all the same. However, perhaps unsurprisingly, Jean's wife nearly spat her first bite out. Chewing it as delicately as she could, she finally swallowed with a grimace. I tried not to be offended. 'It smells like smoke,' she remarked, 'and tastes quite a lot worse.'

Jean laughed loudly. 'You just don't like it because of the presentation.'

'Well, that is awful too,' she agreed. 'Couldn't you get some parsley or something? A nice heavy *sauce au poivre* might have been good, too.' She coughed a little.

'Have some more wine,' Jean offered her with false gallantry, 'it'll help with the taste.' He winked at me, obviously secretly thrilled with the results of his manly cuisine. I suspected he didn't provide much assistance in the kitchen on a day-to-day basis, and had gained a strange sense of one-upmanship over his wife. Obviously mollified by the *petit chablis*, she laughed prettily and managed another two full bites before pushing her plate away daintily and retiring to bed. Jean and his daughter and I stayed up for a long time. I shared as many Texan techniques as I could think of, as if delivering a full university course on barbecues. 'I think I'm sold,' Jean said decisively. 'My wife will never understand.'

'I do,' his daughter added through her last mouthful of juicy beef. 'Let's eat like this all the time!'

'I feel like your mother may not be too happy with that theory,' I replied, pleased against my will. 'I will give you some recipes, though.' The evening, for me, had been quite exhausting, and I was looking forward to going home and putting my feet up. I found Jean's combined enthusiasm and lack of skill tiring, if encouraging in terms of my own skill as a barbecue teacher. Amusingly, I quickly realised that, in the following weeks, Jean and his daughter actually began to put on a barbecue every single weekend. Although they invited me regularly, I never went back. I felt I had discharged my Texan barbecue duty.

One would think that the basis of agreeable neighbourly relations would usually be communication: discussing one's environment or the foibles of one's common acquaintances; discovering similar taste in literature or a shared interest in sports; bonding together in the face of difficulties or resolving arguments between our children. However, in some cases, there is nothing quite like friendly silence, broken only by occasional completely mundane conversation, to make for friendly relations.

In Essex, during my student days, we had a house in the countryside near Colchester. We lived at the end of a small country lane, shaded by ancient oaks and surrounded by rolling fields. Our next-door neighbours were the friendly sort. Beyond the working farm which bordered our house lay the house of a retired man by the name of Harold.

Harold was a truly lovely neighbour; a thin, shy old man with a wild head of curly white hair, who mostly kept to himself but was always a pleasure to interact with. He was rather like an old tortoise, only rarely poking his head out of his shell. He had retired a few years before I moved there, and appeared to spend most of his time listening to the radio indoors, or rambling in the hills on long walks. As far as I could make out, Harold had a single companion, an ageing chocolate Labrador called Millie, who was the loveliest, slowest dog I ever met. Millie was getting a bit unsteady on her feet in her old age, but the two of them still went for long, leisurely walks together. Harold was still in quite good health, considering his age, and was of quite a muscular, sporty build.

Of all the neighbours I have had, or at least amongst the ones I actually met, Harold was one of the neighbours I exchanged the fewest words with in my life. All our conversations went, essentially, as follows:

'Hello, Bradley.'

'Hello, Harold.'

'Have you noticed? This morning, the leaves have just turned.'

'Oh yes,' I would reply. 'I noticed. They've changed their colour early this season. I'm sure the forests will look lovely again this autumn.'

'Oh yes,' he would reply. 'Well, I'm off for my walk, then.'

Essentially, Harold liked to make one comment about the weather, wait for my response and move on. He could rarely be drawn out beyond that.

'I think the leaves are going to fall next week,' he might say a few days later.

'That seems quite likely. Last year, the trees were nearly bare by this time in October.'

He always seemed pleasant, and he always liked to make his one observation, but further conversation was close to impossible to get out of him. Once, when he mentioned he thought it might rain, I tried a joke on him: 'Do you know what goes up when the rain comes down?' I asked him. 'An umbrella!'

Not seeming to get the joke, he simply nodded. 'Oh yes,' he said, 'I've got mine with me.'

Another time his sole contribution might be:

'The temperature is a bit nippy today.'

'Oh yes,' I would agree. 'It'll be time for our winter coats soon.'

These reactions did seem to please him, but elicited no further comment.

He was a man of pleasant and mundane one-liners, like: 'I wonder when the first snows would come?'

'Oh, soon,' I would reply. 'The neighbourhood children will be looking forward to their first snowmen!'

Sometimes, I would try to draw him out a little further. If, in summer, he commented on the heat, I might try to tell him a story. 'This one time, when I lived in Texas,' I told him once, 'I saw a sign for a garage sale. It said: from 7 a.m. until 100 degrees.' Harold simply nodded politely, just exactly as he would have done if I had chosen my usual, 'Oh yes.' It didn't seem worth explaining the joke.

Once I learned this pattern, I would usually stick to replying in kind, or with a straightforward, 'Yes, Harold,' perhaps embroidering a little on his chosen weather topic. Harold was a peaceful man, who didn't seem to expect much interaction to come from speaking to me, just some sort of friendly acknowledgement. Our exchanges never went beyond these initial pleasantries. I often imagined us continuing this simple dialogue with its content virtually unchanged for years and years, until my own hair turned grey.

'Did you see?' he might ask me. 'Two leaves fell off the beech tree!'

'Yes, Harold,' I would say, and smile.

'Yesterday, I had a two hour walk. I think I will aim for three hours, today.'

'Have you packed an umbrella in case it rains?'

'Oh, yes!' He would wave his umbrella and keep on walking with Millie. Three hours later, the pair would come loping back down the paths.

Harold's mind worked in very unassuming patterns, without seeking to bring in difficult or even external notions. He watched the movements of the seasons carefully, and he kept his house very tidy: these were the only things I knew about him. Of course, Millie the dog was another joy in Harold's life. She was one of the friendliest dogs I have ever come across. Whenever I saw her, she would be lagging behind her master, panting hard; but whenever she saw someone she would start wagging her tail furiously. One of the neighbourhood children told me that she wagged her tail even if she was deeply asleep, because she was so happy at the prospect of passing company!

In some ways, in the time I spent at that country house, my existence was as calm and peaceful as Harold and Millie's. I would wake early, and spend most of my time walking and reading. If the weather was pleasant, I loved nothing more than to do the two things at once, carrying a well-worn paperback down the country lanes of Essex. In fact, most of my reading happens when I'm walking: it's an excellent way of building up an appetite before a meal, or helping to digest afterwards, and what better time to do this than whilst absorbing knowledge? Of course, if I had company, I also enjoyed to walk and talk, but in my solitary wanderings, I preferred to walk and read.

Harold and Millie usually took a long walk in the late afternoon. They would stop and say hello on the way out, then stop for a moment on the way back. It was a rather lovely routine. Sometimes, energised by the fresh air and movement, Millie would run ahead of Harold, her ears lolloping in the wind. If I was sitting outside, she would arrive completely out of breath at my feet, and set her drooling face right on my knee. It was ridiculous and endearing in equal measures. Panting, Harold would eventually catch up with her. 'Hello, Bradley,' he would say. 'Sorry about the old girl. Come on, Millie, the night is falling. Time to get to bed.' Watching them walk off into the darkness, they seemed like an inseparable pair.

In all the years I knew Harold, he didn't seem to change one whit. Year after year, I would run into him out on my walk, with a book in hand. Year after year, he would make the same series of comments about the weather, that cycled as regularly and predictably as the seasons. Of course, eventually I moved on, leaving that house behind.

About ten years ago, however, I went back to visit some old friends. I made sure to go round to Harold's house, although I wasn't sure if I would find him there. Sure enough, the old man opened the door, virtually unchanged: his face a little more wrinkled, his hair a little more grey. 'Well hello, Bradley,' he said to me, as if I had seen him the day before. 'Have you seen, the beeches are turning gold early this year!'

'Oh yes, Harold,' I said.

Some things never change.

THE GERMAN PIG FARM

I have nothing against Germany or German customs. Their beer servings may be unnecessarily large, their language remarkably complicated, and their diet quite cholesterol-heavy, but the people strike me as being overall remarkably smart, organised, companionable and outdoorsy, with excellent foreign language skills to boot. In my life, I have had many occasions to witness the better German traditions as, for a time at the peak of my banking career, I travelled a lot in Germany: the company I worked for had several partners based in Frankfurt, Munich, and Berlin. I had many agreeable and interesting trips around the country, enjoying large meals in the Weinstubs and brasseries, and taking long walks in the Black Forest.

However, I must confess that one of the more memorable of my visits to Germany was somewhat more traumatic, and took place a great deal earlier than this. What happened was this: at the age of fourteen, I found myself camping on a scout trip, near the city of Hannover. It was a pleasant enough location, deep in farmland and surrounded by rolling fields. We set up camp happily enough, shouting and running around as we hammered in tent pegs and gathered firewood. Before two hours had passed, however, we were to find that there was one less agreeable feature to our surroundings: our closest neighbour was a pig farm.

In a previous story, I have discussed the unpleasantness occasioned by this sort of establishment; namely, the hideous smell. I will not go into that here. I will, nonetheless, mention again that I don't particularly like pigs: they live in complete filth, seem to constantly make a horrible squealing noise, and their eating habits strike me as incredibly greedy. I don't agree with those that defend the pig as an intelligent animal. However, on this particular occasion, my scout colleagues and I found ourselves with another strong reason not to consume pork, and that was witnessing the particularly unpleasant treatment of one of the beasts.

Perhaps we could have avoided the event, had we not been such naturally curious boys. Unfortunately, there was only so much walking and talking a group of scouts was willing to do, before exploring every possible cranny of a neighbourhood. Once camp was set up, we took on the important task of climbing over every boulder and looking over every hilltop. The possibilities of this were fairly quickly exhausted: even scouts will run out of imaginative resources in these circumstances. The fields of the German countryside may be pleasant, but they are remarkably monotonous, even in the late summer, when the grass is high and every wildflower seems to be in bloom. Even a small pond we found over the side of one hill failed to entertain us for more than half an hour. This explains how, after just two days left to our own devices, we found ourselves in the farmyard. We had been drawn there by the most horrific noise, which was far more piercing and upsetting than anything I remember hearing in a pig farm before.

'That's just the noise pigs make,' one of my scout companions tried to convince me, even as he quickened his pace through the tall grass. 'They're probably just feeding, or maybe having a fight.'

'I don't think so,' I said. 'It sounds worse than that to me.'

'It's ridiculous,' another boy butted in. 'Maybe we should go to the camp sergeant and complain about the noise.'

'Guys,' the first boy said, a little haughtily, 'there's nothing unusual about pigs making this sort of noise.'

'Have you ever been to a pig farm?' I asked him.

'No,' he said defensively, 'but I've read about them. I've heard that they make really loud squealing noises.'

'I've been to a pig farm before,' I told him. 'And that does not sound like a happy pig.'

However, none of my misgivings had even slightly prepared me for the sight that greeted us. As we snuck through a gap in the hedge and climbed over the wooden fence, we suddenly found ourselves only a hundred feet or so from a scene that I would never forget. Even when I had seen a ritual halal slaughter in North Africa; even, in fact, when I saw the same kind of killing as a student years later, in another part of Germany – no animal death has marked me as much as what I witnessed that day.

In that moment, as a fourteen-year-old boy staring across a dirt yard, I watched a live pig howling as it was cranked into a vat of boiling water. The pig was fully grown and a clean pink colour; easily four feet long, probably weighing a hundred kilos. It was hoisted up on thick metal chains, and was being lowered into a cistern that had a fire blazing underneath. I don't think I have ever come across such a cruel practice in the rest of my life. As the pig came back up from the water, it was, of course, emitting a horrific amount of noise. The process was repeated three or four times; I don't want to dwell on the details.

My scout partners and I, all equally horrified, turned tail and ran back to the camp. For most of the length of our hasty journey home, we didn't speak a word. Passing by the pond, however, there was a momentary distraction as one of the younger boys tripped and slid in the mud, falling partway into the water. At this point, we looked at each other and realised just how quickly we had been running. 'Like pigs from a slaughter!' one boy suddenly cried out, and the rest of us couldn't help but burst out laughing.

'You look like a real little piglet,' I said, helping the kid stand up.

'Please don't make me into bacon!' he replied with a little smile.

Most of the boys were cheered by this incident, but I couldn't help still being rather upset by what we had seen.

By the time we finally found our sergeant, we were slightly less shaken than we might have been at the start. Nonetheless, we turned to him for reassurance, hoping for some sort of explanation. 'They were boiling it alive!' we told him, aghast. 'Is it some kind of horrible game? Why would they do that? Is it punishment? Is it torture?'

The sergeant shook his head. 'I've often travelled in Germany,' he told us, 'and I've seen this before. I'm sorry you boys had to witness that. The first time I saw it, I was quite traumatised, so don't be embarrassed that you were upset by what you saw. I was able to ask the farmer who was committing this act, at the time, so some of my questions were answered. So, let me tell you in turn: no, it isn't a joke and it isn't a game. It isn't even meant to be torture. Apparently, they try to get the whole thing over with as quickly as possible, and the pig often dies very quickly. Obviously, you just came across a particularly unlucky animal.'

I couldn't say I was entirely convinced by this explanation, but I kept quiet.

'The pig has actually usually already been bled at this stage,' the sergeant continued, 'but obviously, this is a more or less efficient way of killing the animal, and it is sometimes still conscious when it is being scalded.'

I felt my stomach turn in disgust.

'But why couldn't they just kill the pig first? So it can't feel anything?' one of the boys asked.

'In many countries, they do. Most civilised places nowadays make sure the pig is unconscious when the slaughter begins. In America and most of Europe, they stun it with electric current or a captive bolt pistol. Some places even make them inhale carbon dioxide. But this is a small farm in the country, and they obviously prefer to keep doing things the old ways. I personally believe this sort of cruelty is a vanishing institution.'

'But why?' my friend asked again, obviously unable to process the concept. 'Why are they doing it in the first place?'

The sergeant patted his shoulder. 'Alright, if you really want to know, I'll explain the specifics. Essentially, what you just saw is a special way of butchering a pig that makes it easy to separate the fat from the skin,' he said. 'Apparently, it has many benefits. It may seem barbaric, but many farmers think it's better for the meat. The meat turns out much more tender, as the fat layer remains neatly over the ribs, the chops, and the meat.'

Some of the boys made gagging noises, and the sergeant laughed. 'You're just going to have to imagine all you were watching was a big old hunk of bacon being cooked. You all like bacon, right?'

There were some scattered noises of agreement, along with some of disgust.

I had to speak up. 'I couldn't see any bacon, sir,' I told him. 'All I could see was the suffering. I'm never going to eat pork again.'

The sergeant patted me on the shoulder. 'There's nothing wrong with that, my boy,' he told me. 'Just do your best to put the whole scene from your mind.'

I tried to follow his advice, but it took some time to forget the traumatic event. Luckily, the rest of the scouting trip proceeded without incident, although I never touched another piece of breakfast bacon.

Luxury hotels are all well and good, but after a while one begins to yearn for something new. Variety is the spice of life, after all. In the 1980s, I often travelled for business purposes and stayed in some of New York's finest hotels. My favourites were the usual suspects: the Plaza, the Regency, the Waldorf Astoria and the St Regis. The service was always excellent, and yet they all began to blur together. No experience was ever new, and I grew tired of familiar walls on the same streets, time after time.

When I spoke to my friend about this in passing, his eyes lit up. 'You'll have to try the Box Tree Inn! If you want something different, well, there you have it. You'll love it.'

I had never heard of it, but was intrigued by his enthusiasm for the place. 'Have you actually stayed there?' I was cautious not to take a recommendation unless he had experienced it for himself.

'Lots of times! It's wonderful, really charming.' He nodded. 'The staff are great and it's just... it's not the normal hotel, the rooms are all a little different, so it keeps things fresh. Honestly, it'll be your new favourite.'

So, on my next trip to New York, I booked myself a suite at the Box Tree Inn. It was certainly a little different from the plusher hotels, with only thirteen bedrooms overall, but it was still very pleasant. It had chosen its name from the large, ancient box tree that stood by the front door, and the atmosphere was appropriately cosy and homey. It had all the modern conveniences, a lovely room with plenty of space to do my work and a nice enough little bar. The only downside was going up and down the narrow staircase, but this didn't worry me overly much because the rest of the hotel was so good.

My experiences at the Box Tree Inn were almost uniformly positive and I very much enjoyed staying there. However, one day I was doing some work over the phone at the quaint antique desk and there was a knock on my door. I didn't have anybody coming over or any meetings to attend that day, but I answered in case there was some sort of emergency.

'Hello, sir!' At the door was an older gentleman holding a silver tray with an espresso on it. He was smiling at me as though he knew me and I assumed that he was a member of staff at the hotel.

'Hello,' I said. 'I think you might have the wrong room? I didn't order anything.'

'Oh, no. This is for you. Can I bring it in?' He raised the tray a bit.

I shrugged and let him in. After all, the coffee did smell wonderful after a long morning of telephone calls, and who was I to argue with this new service that the hotel was providing me?

But rather than just setting the coffee down and leaving as I expected him to, the gentleman put the silver tray down on my table and then took a seat himself. I wondered if he wanted a tip, which I wasn't really willing to provide given that I hadn't asked for anything.

I waited a moment to see if he would take the hint and leave, and raised my eyebrows when he didn't. 'Excuse me? But this is rather unusual, isn't it? Is this something new the hotel's doing now?'

He blinked. 'What do you mean?'

'Well, you're bringing me coffee I didn't order and now... I don't need any company. Thanks very much. I'm actually rather busy. But thank you for the espresso.' I picked it up and drank it, thinking this might encourage him to believe his job was done.

He stared at me for a long moment before breaking into a hesitant smile. 'Oh, no. No, I don't work for the hotel, I'm not your servant. I'm your neighbour, you see.'

'At the hotel? From another room?' This made no sense. He didn't look at all like the sort of person I had seen staying here. Come to think of it, he wasn't really appropriately dressed for work at the hotel, either, and this worried me somewhat.

'No. Another building. I hope you don't mind the imposition, sir.'

I didn't like this one bit, it all felt very suspicious, but his manner was so conciliatory I was sure he was no real threat. 'Well. What are you here for?'

'I wanted to keep it informal, but this is... this is a business proposal, I suppose. I heard that you are a banker in Paris, am I right?' He paused, waiting for my reply.

'Yes,' I said slowly, 'you're right. Where did you hear that?'

He ignored my question and carried on, 'I myself am in real estate and I'm buying up property in Manhattan. It has a lot of potential, you see. Could be a wonderful project in the right hands. I was just wondering if you would consider financing it for me.'

I gave him a very flat look. 'This is quite a strange way of approaching a banker, you know.'

'I know, but trying to get banks to finance a project is so impersonal.' He nodded towards the empty espresso cup. 'The personal touch is so important, don't you think?'

Honestly, I didn't know what to think. This was a very odd occurrence indeed. 'Well, if you're serious.... Where's your study? Do you have a proper proposal worked out?'

'Yes, of course!' He nodded almost excitedly, since I was showing the vaguest amount of interest. 'I can send it to you if you'll leave me your card.'

I realised I was getting rather swept up in this madness and I had very little desire to finance someone who thought breaching hotel security to reach me was a good way of sorting their business affairs out. 'I'm fairly sure this isn't a very above board way to do business. I think you should leave or I'll have to call the hotel management.'

He sighed at my response, shoulders slumping in visible disappointment. 'No, I'm sorry. The management are friends of mine... that's how I got in, you understand. I shan't bother you anymore if you really don't finance real estate. Do you?'

I was tempted to tell him that I didn't, just to get him out of my room, but found myself incapable of telling a lie like that. After all, he had clearly done his research. He knew who I was. 'Yes, of course I do. But not like this. It's far too unprofessional. And aside from that, my business is mostly done in Europe. We don't specialise in New York real estate. You'd do better to contact someone with more local expertise.'

My advice apparently fell on deaf ears. 'If you give me your address,' he said, 'I can come and see you in Europe and we can talk it through further? I'm sure if you just saw my plans...'

'No.' This time I cut him off very deliberately. 'Listen, if you give me your card, I can send you our brochure and you can see what our normal procedure is. We have a brilliant real estate team and people in credit and investment. But you've gone about this completely the wrong way, accosting me in my bedroom. I don't even have any of the paperwork we'd need for a project such as this.'

He gave me a final, hopeful look and found no sympathy in my expression. So, finally, he stood up and shook the creases from his suit. 'All right then. I'm sorry for bothering you. Here's my address. If you write to me, I'm sure we can work something out.'

'Good,' I breathed out a sigh of relief. 'Excellent. I'll be in touch.'

He thankfully agreed to leave at this point without making any more of a scene, trusting me to contact him.

Which, quite obviously, I never did. I had no desire to do business with someone who had approached me in such an odd and obnoxious way. I purposefully 'lost' his address before I left New York and didn't give it another thought.

In 2002, I got wind that the hotel was to be sold. One investment banker went so far as to send me a brochure to the Box Tree Inn, explaining the sale. In the attached letter, he mentioned that we had met several years before.

You may not remember me, but I came to your bedroom unannounced with a business proposal which I subsequently decided to take to more interested parties. Since you seemed to enjoy your stay there, I was wondering if you were interested in purchasing the hotel? I believe it would best serve as a private residence. I'm sure that it would be a smart investment. I think that we could work together on this project and breathe new life into it. Please contact me at your earliest convenience, since there are many others who have seen the promise in the place.

In spite of his letter and the persuasive brochure, I was not interested in the slightest and said as much in a reply to him. Remembering his lack of professionalism was all I needed to sour me on the idea, had it held any interest for me in the first place.

What happened to the hotel after that is a mystery to me. I heard that it had closed sometime later, so perhaps it was indeed converted to a private residence. In any case, personally, I have not been back there for fifteen years. These days I prefer to stick to the hotels I know and trust.

I have many fond memories of the years spent in the apartment my family lived in on Eaton Square. My wife and I acquired a long-term lease on the place in that most successful period of my life, my late thirties, and spent many happy years there with our children. Surrounded by lush gardens, hidden away in the centre of one of the most luxurious areas of London, Eaton Square has always been a haven of complete peace and quiet. Unsurprisingly, it attracts a rather wonderful cross-section of London's writers, intellectuals, politicians and fascinating people of all sorts. One of the best things about my time there was the selection of distinguished neighbours I had the luck of meeting, including Lord Julian Amery.

Actually, I had first met Lord Amery when I was a student at LSE, long before I even dreamed of living on Eaton Square myself. I struck up conversation after attending a talk he had given, and we quickly found our ideas on the subject of East-West relations to be much aligned. We shared an interest in and ties to the Middle East, and, over time, we would find our respective knowledge of various areas of politics, economics and culture to be rather complementary. At the time, being only in my early twenties, I still had a distinct disadvantage! Still, I must have managed to intrigue Julian Amery, as he invited me round for tea. This meeting turned out to be the beginning of a long, intellectual friendship. On our very first meeting, over lemon biscuits and strong tea, we had a long discussion about the economic merits of trading with the countries of the Arabian Gulf and the importance of alliances within the free market. I was as impressed with the house as I was fascinated by my interlocutor.

The intellectual standard of those conversations of ours never faltered in all the years we met up. I remember debating fiercely with him just after the oil euphoria that took over the Arabian Gulf in 1973. By this time, I had acquired my own house on the square, and moved on from banking to working in the oil business, so I had acquired a lot of knowledge on the ground. Lord Amery had a real gift of treating his every interlocutor as his intellectual equal. It made for the most wonderful and animated conversations. Even when I was just a student, he would engage me on all sorts of subjects he was thinking about or studying. Of course, my ability to contribute usefully to these conversations improved substantially from that first meeting at LSE to the later days! I loved little more than to pick this incredibly intelligent man's brain about possible ways of changing the course of economic growth in a country.

Amery had a stellar political career. He went to school at Eton, and studied at Balliol College, Oxford. He spent time as a war correspondent in the Spanish Civil War, and later worked as an attaché for the British Foreign Office in Belgrade. He then joined the RAF for the duration of the Second World War, before beginning his political ascension per se back on British soil.

Lord Amery believed strongly in a unified Europe, at the heart of which Britain would shine, economically and culturally. He also, however, strongly defended his country from the ideas of protectionism. 'Trade, my friend, is essential to our prosperity,' he often told me. 'Oil, rubber, copper, gold, and tin: from darkest Africa to the ice of deepest Siberia – these things are essential to our own economy's ability to flourish. We must work hard to maintain civil relations, and trade fairly, if we are to maintain the advantage.' Lord Amery was one of the more poetic defenders of capitalism I have ever met. I remember him telling me all this in his soft, plummy voice; an accent the likes of which is really only propagated nowadays by the best Shakespearian actors. Of course, his eloquence had a long history of training, since he had served as an MP by this point for a few years. He would go on to serve for thirty-nine years!

The anecdotes he told to support his views were wonderfully clever and vivid. He once told me a story of meeting a peasant in Serbia, who was clutching a small pig in his arms. 'I call my pig Churchill,' the peasant told him. Mildly offended in his personal sense of patriotism, Amery asked him why he had chosen this name. 'Oh, it's not offensive!' the peasant assured him at once. 'But winter is coming. And this pig is my last hope of having enough to eat through the winter.' He used this wonderful little story to justify British intervention in the Balkans, in the hopes of building up a strong and unified central Europe.

Lord Amery was a real storyteller; a raconteur in the most classic sense. The political drive he gave his story took away no ounce of charm from them. From the quiet heart of Belgravia, my friend conjured up fantastical visions of the places he had travelled, some of which I had seen for myself: the bustle of the markets of Aleppo; the roiling yellow river of China; the quiet of the Blue Mosque in Belgrade. He really was a great conversationalist as well as a great orator. There was a time in the mid-seventies where I spent several weekends a month drinking tea in that wonderful house of Julian's. I would look forward to crossing that square at the end of a long day's work, and being handed a teak box of tea leaves of which to take my pick.

The conversations that stayed with me most of all, however, were ones we had late in his life. He had become more thoughtful, but had lost none of his fire. He now had an acute sense of his own involvement in the development of Britain, as well as of Britain's responsibility to the rest of the world. 'I served as an MP for thirty-nine years,' he said. 'I feel like I've made my mark on the Conservative Party. I only hope these values do not change too much with time.' By this time, he had four children and had travelled truly all over the world. I had not been in that house in Eaton Square for years and years, and found myself quite nostalgic to be revisiting it.

Lord Amery's house was a truly wonderful place. To remember our talks there is to hearken back to another era. Julian's history suffused every object that surrounded us, as did his spirit. Most of the furniture was antique; from the oak cabinets to the elaborate Oriental carpets and the seventeenth-century dining table. Every surface was covered in mementos: signed photographs from diplomats, kings, and orators he had worked with or met on his travels; leather-bound books. I remember several weapons that might well have belonged in a museum: rusty daggers and a golden sword.

On this occasion, I recall him waxing lyrical, as he often did, about the people he had met. 'I've dined with kings and gardeners,' he liked to say. 'I've drunk with spies and driven with masters of parliament. I've been to China and Romania and Afghanistan. I've been to places that don't even exist anymore: Yugoslavia. Persia. Rhodesia. The world has changed in my time here, but my principles haven't. Now I'm too old to change much. I'll likely go to my grave with this set of beliefs. I can't think of a better way to go.'

'You don't worry that you'll become a caricature?' Several less-than-flattering portraits of Amery had been drawn up in the redtops recently, and I had been worried my friend's reputation might suffer from that.

'What, you mean the people who call me a white supremacist? A fascist? An anachronism? Why do you think I would listen to that, Bradley? I'm my own man, and I always have been. I know in my soul I am none of those things. I have only ever wished the best for every country I have visited or dealt with, economically, politically, and culturally. False words do not interest me, and they certainly cannot hurt me. My friends would never read such trash in any case.' Seeing me blush and prepare to apologise, he laughed. 'You know I'm only joking, Bradley. I know you're only worried for my own good. But you have nothing to worry about. I can look after myself.'

He certainly could. Julian Amery passed away in 1996, but I will always remember him for his wit, his intellect, his charm and his humour. Even though this book is called *Neighbours' Nonsense*, none of my memories of my dear friend contain any nonsense whatsoever. In fact, I would go so far as to say this was one of the nicest neighbourly relationships I ever had. By the end of his life, we were so close that the agents handling the sale of his house came straight to me. I didn't purchase that wonderful house, but I treasure every memory I have of my time in that parlour, sipping tea with my neighbour Lord Julian Amery.

Perhaps it was life experience that made Tim O'Callahan such a canny investor. I had certainly never witnessed anything like his ability to predict shifts and trends in the market, and he was always very generous with his tips.

Tim and I first met in the 1960s, when he lived on the same floor as me in our fraternity house. It was a big old Victorian building full of engineering students who had been working towards these careers their whole lives. However, Tim had somewhat of a strange background compared to the rest of us.

He had been raised in a strict Irish Catholic household, with plans to go into the priesthood, a path which he followed and believed would be his life. Tim never really told me what had changed, particularly that which made him decide that a life of religious sacrifice was not for him, but my guess was that he was simply too clever and wanted a challenge. Engineering presented that challenge and he grabbed it with both hands.

Whenever I asked him why he had decided to quit his past life and take on this new one, he shrugged and said, 'Money.'

'There's not always great money in engineering.'

He smiled at me. 'Don't worry about me. I know how to make a pretty penny.' He had that sort of quiet confidence which made you believe he was destined to succeed at whatever he chose to do.

Because of his first life wanting to soak up all that his religion had to offer and then turning his hand to teaching that same religion, he was a little older than the rest of us. We were in our early to mid-twenties, typical students, but Tim was thirty-five, and had done away with the frivolities of youth.

He was a very interesting man on an intellectual level, but on a personal level he left a little to be desired. As a friend, he was entertaining and witty, but he had no interest in having a girlfriend or attending parties with the rest of us. If we had one, he might mill about for a while, but would inevitably end up quietly reading in the privacy of his room. I suppose some of his old habits from his brief stint in the priesthood never quite went away. Nor did he seem to want them to.

The time he would have otherwise spent socialising was used

instead to read the *Wall Street Journal* and the *New York Times*, and sometimes I thought that there publications added up to the sum total of his social life. He would talk about a juicy stock trade the way the rest of us would talk about girls, with that same zest and excitement of a chase.

The funny thing was that, even though he was older than most of the students who frequented our house, he could have made great friends and had a girlfriend, had he so wanted to. He had those classic Irish good looks, fair skin and whitish hair, and could hold a room with a good story as well as any man.

As I said, he was also a generous friend. He would come over to me one day in the kitchen and casually bring up his latest big tip.

'So, what do you think about the new electronic revolution?' he asked me. He would ask it like he was talking about a person, sort of off-hand and interested at the same time. Like he knew my opinion already.

I glanced at him. 'I'm not sure it'll ever replace the old way of doing things. These new things have too many flaws.'

'Kinks get worked out. Trust me on this. Soon, we'll all be sending a telex rather than a telegram.'

I laughed dismissively. 'I doubt it'll come to anything in the long run.'

He shrugged. 'I don't know. I suppose we'll see, won't we?'

And the next thing I knew, he'd sunk his salary into it and within weeks had made a tidy 200% increase on his investment. When he brought the subject up with me, he smiled sympathetically over my loss and told me I'd get it next time: perhaps next time a good investment would be more obvious.

'I did tell you, didn't I? But I suppose I'm a bit of a risk-taker,' he confessed.

'You don't say.'

'See, like... our cook? You like the southern fried chicken he prepares, don't you?'

Everybody did. I nodded, wondering where he could be going with this.

'Well, then! I have the perfect little tip for you. You should invest in this company, Kentucky Fried Chicken, it's going to be huge. And you can be in on the ground floor of this one. The stock's going dirt cheap, but it won't be for long.'

I stared at him. 'Tim, I don't think you should put your money with chickens.'

'It'll be the safest bet you've ever made, I swear. Buy some stock with me, it doesn't have to be much. You just want to get your foot in the door on this, trust me.'

'No, no.' I shook my head. All right, so I had missed out last time, but *chickens?* Who on earth had ever made any sort of real money by investing in chickens? 'You don't want to sink your salary into chickens. Listen. I make my money with General Motors. Now, there's a safe investment. Chickens.'

Of course, Tim had the last laugh there, too. Within a few months, he had made a 400% profit on his investment, the stocks that had been going for $8 apiece worth a lot more than that now.

I would be lying if I said I wasn't a bit annoyed. Tim seemed to just throw his money to the wind and it came back to him several times over. I, on the other hand, was a lot more careful where I put my finances. While I was hardly doing badly, the kind of money Tim was making was incredible, and with such strange ideas! I still couldn't get my head around KFC being so insanely popular and profitable.

The next time Tim came to me, around a year later, I was ready to do as he said without really even thinking about it. I wanted a piece of what he had, his talent, his charmed life on Easy Street.

'What you want to do,' he said confidently, 'is buy containers made by a company called Leasco. You'll make a tidy profit, you can be sure of that. They're only going for $6, but you'll make your money back a dozen times over. More.'

So, this time, I did as Tim suggested, and only a handful of months later the resale value of what I had bought was $25. It was my first real taste of multiplying my money on my investments, and I liked it a lot. I could see why Tim was so enthusiastic and put his money in so many places at once. Not only was it profitable, it was quite exciting! To be at the beginning of these major companies, making money from them.

I could see why one would want a career in this.

In the late 1960s, the year I went to do my PhD in London, Tim had yet another great tip for me.

'Mobile homes,' he said. 'It's a sensible move, not as wild as you might think. With the baby boomers all making good money, they want a different way of life. A new standard of living. Think about it. A house is bricks and mortar, standing forever in one spot. But a mobile home? There's real freedom there, don't you think? You could see the whole country from the comfort of your bedroom!'

His sales pitch was very convincing indeed, and I knew from past experience that his success rate predicting these trends was unprecedented. So, I followed Tim, put all my money in Sterling Homes and Permaneer, and waited for the inevitable quadrupling of my money.

Two years later, I lost everything.,

The mass migration from a standard house to the mobile home never quite happened, and my investment was gone forever.

By this time, Tim was travelling around on business. When I phoned him to tell him about my loss, he was in Texas.

'It's so hot here! So, how are you? How's London?'

'London's fine,' I said, just about keeping my temper. 'But I'm not. You remember that tip you gave me? It didn't exactly pay off. Thanks for the neighbourly advice, by the way.'

He sounded quite jovial about it. 'Oh! You mean the mobile homes thing. Isn't that just the worst luck?'

I pressed the phone to my ear. 'I'm not sure you understand. I lost all my money. Every dollar I put into those ridiculous companies.'

'Me, too. I've had to get a job. But you know, that's always the way. If you play the game, there's always a chance you could lose, isn't there? Sorry about that, though. Terrible advice, wasn't it?'

It was impossible to stay angry with him when he, too, had lost everything based on his own bad investing. After that, I never took any more of his stock advice, but we stayed in touch as friends until the 1990s, when we lost touch. I am not sure what happened to Tim, whether he invested successfully and made millions or not.

I like to think that he did.

TWO HUNDRED AND FORTY-SIX CHEESES

Charles de Gaulle famously asked: 'How can you govern a country which has two hundred and forty-six varieties of cheese?' I have to agree with the man: cheese is a contentious subject at best. I cannot imagine running a single cheese shop which might sell those two hundred and forty-six cheeses, let alone a country in which you might find several of these on the same street. It seems to me that if one were sitting around in one such boutique, surrounded by these fragrant piles of curdled milk, five things might happen.

Firstly, one might be poisoned by the fumes. Now, if one were to consider the persistent aroma of an old camembert that has been left out to ripen until it positively oozes when sliced open, or the reek of a runny Epoisses de Bourgogne, which is so bad that it is rumoured to have been banned from public transportation in France, well, this might not seem so surprising. I mean, there is even a cheese called Stinking Bishop! Many of the cheeses thought to be the best in the world are specifically rinsed in saltwater or brandy to develop their mouldy flavours, and the inevitable accompanying odours. Some of these cheeses make dirty old jogging clothes smell like a bouquet of wild roses in comparison! In a shop, everything can't be kept wrapped up in several layers of cling-film and hidden in the bottom of the fridge. I'd imagine the effect of the vapours over several hours, let alone days or months or years, to be positively noxious.

Of course, if one were to love cheese, the problem might be a different one entirely. Rather than being disgusted by the smell of the surrounding cheeses, one could exist in a state of perpetual hunger! Thus, the second danger is that one might become hugely fat. Surrounded by great, greasy hunks of salty *fromage*, many a man might forget exercise or vegetables entirely, and succumb to a delicious death by cholesterol. I have yet to see someone who owns a cheese shop cramming their mouth with great spoonfuls of blue Stilton, or tossing cubes of Emmental down their gullet, but it seems likely that they would do so the second the shop doors close.

From the list so far of cheeses from the weird to the ghastly, we can deduce quite quickly what the third risk might easily be: being poisoned to death by the cheese. After all, cheese is essentially rotting milk, hardened and coated with mould. Whether sitting around it or eating it all day, the effects cannot possibly be entirely beneficial.

Of course, not all the consequences of having a cheese shop are this problematic. For instance, the cheese shop might actually be quite successful. It might be blessed with excellent aeration; you might be blessed with a combination of love of cheese and great willpower. After all, this shop is in France, and the French love their two hundred and forty-six types of cheese! In this situation, one would have the fourth and nicest option: to become incredibly rich and successful. Of course, there is always the risk of becoming incredibly lazy, resting on the laurels of capital gains, not worrying about sales because the price of cheese keeps on going up. The final result remains the same.

The fifth and final option is an unfortunate risk of the four other ones. It will hold, no matter which of the former turn out to be true: there will always be the possibility of ending up with a grumpy, disgruntled neighbour who hates cheese and complains constantly about your presence. In this case, the neighbour is me.

Now, I loved the apartment I had rented right next to the cheese shop, just off boulevard Raspaille in Paris. My relationship with the cheese shop, however, was more of a love-hate one. Aside from the fact that it served as a big tourist attraction, attracting noisy crowds, particularly at the weekend, it turns out the smell is not one you can get used to easily.

It was an incredibly social shop: it seemed to me to serve the same function as a village café. So many people seemed to go there just to look around, wandering around the shelves aimlessly, chatting with their neighbours or with the many saleswomen. The cheese shop was a family business, run by a seemingly ever-changing series of sisters, cousins, mothers and grandmothers. Every time I went in, I would seem to be served by another Sandrine or Agnès or Collette, the young Babette or the grey-haired Lucille. Not that it was a chaotic operation: every one of them knew their cheeses, all two hundred and forty-six of the French ones, and another good fifty to a hundred foreign varieties. It was mind-boggling to consider.

With the smell, and the crowds milling around, it was hardly a pleasant environment. Nonetheless, I could fairly easily have avoided the shop had it not been for one small thing: my wife and children love cheese. Of course, this being France, there was also the fact that any proper dinner party really needed a cheese course. The traditional order would be: a starter, main dish, cheese board, followed by dessert. The cheese board, thus, marks an important pause in the meal, after all the savoury and before the sweet, a time when guests might finish off their glass of red wine in a leisurely fashion. Usually, at this time of a meal, the French chat away as they pick a selection of cheese slices or blobs, to be eaten with baguette, of course. Sometimes, we would serve a salad at this time. In a restaurant, they often wheel round a cheese cart with three tiers of cheeses, usually a good twenty varieties, including piles of little goat cheeses with pepper or herbs, big blue-veined wedges of Roquefort, slabs of shiny brie de Meaux. At home, of course, this was not possible, but it was proper to have at least five different cheeses on offer.

Thus, weekly, I tended to find myself standing in line in the very cheese shop that poisoned my existence. Sometimes, if we had two dinner parties planned in a week, I would have to go twice! As someone with at best ambivalent feelings towards cheese, I was probably not the best person to pick ten varieties a week, but that was the position I found myself in. I often had to remind myself that at least I could leave at the end of the day: I did not run the risk of being poisoned or growing fat from being constantly surrounded by cheese. Still, it was not very much fun. Sometimes, I would take my children with me, which, while it made the whole process considerably more enjoyable, also tended to test the patience of whichever lady happened to be serving us. By the time I had stood in line in these poisonous vapours, sometimes for up to an hour, I felt like I was entitled to take as much time as I wanted picking my wares.

'Could I have a perfumed cheese from the high mountains?' I might ask them with a twinkle in my eye.

Of course, they would have to ask me more questions to find out what I might be looking for. 'What mountains? Do you mean Switzerland?' they would enquire. 'Do you want a goat's cheese, a nice wrinkly little brebis, or something traditional made from cow's milk? Are you looking for an old cheese or a young one? We have some interesting new cheeses in from Spain, at the moment. You can eat them with quince jam.'

'Oh,' I would say, 'I'm not sure. Something salty would be good.'

'Something with a crust, perhaps? Or would you prefer a nice solid cheese? Do you want something you can heat up and make a meal out of, like a Mont d'Or? Perhaps you would like something a little bit more classic, like a young parmesan?' To their credit, the ladies were almost endlessly patient with me. I suppose they found my lack of knowledge or decisiveness endearing. They probably never got to flog the odder cheeses to their more conventional French clients.

Of course, at this point, one of my children might chime in with their own requests: 'Do you have a camel cheese?'

Patiently, Lucille would reply: 'No, little one. That's impossible: camel milk doesn't curdle naturally. You can't make camel milk cheese. We do have donkey cheese, though, if you're looking for something a little ways off the beaten track?'

Later, I found out this to some degree untrue: camel cheese can actually be made, with the addition of enzymes. However, at the time, I was more concerned with finding a respectable array of cheeses to bring home. As I made my careful choice, the line behind us would get longer and longer. The shopkeepers were always very kind to us, though. I suppose they recognised that, as their neighbours who came in every week, we were good clients to keep friendly relations with.

Sometimes, particularly when I was in a hurry, I would take pity on them. Instead of picking individual cheeses, I would simply gesture to a series of shelves.

'I'll take this, this and that,' I would say, pointing.

Of course, Agnès or Lucille would have to ask me: 'Which cheeses, *Monsieur*? Can you give me some names?'

'No,' I would reply, 'just pick a selection for me. Give me a nice mix.'

She would hesitate. 'How many grams of each?'

'Oh, about a hundred. Just compose a good combination of textures and shapes. Some contrast.'

She would cut me my five pieces of cheese, taking a good ten minutes to make a selection she would deem satisfactory. I learned to be patient, as my guests were almost inevitably pleased with the choices.

I didn't mind waiting a little while. I couldn't help by be impressed by the cool with which these ladies handled my odd demands. It was impressive to think how this family of women had managed that vast shop over the years. Of course, physically it was a relatively small place, but it was stacked literally floor to ceiling with cheeses. It was quite an operation. There wasn't just one big refrigerated display case: there were also shelves behind that, and piles of older, drier cheeses stretching back into the depths of the shop. When I started to think of how they coped with the supply, stocking the shelves, controlling inventory, dealing with difficult customers, and the smells on top of that, it really was impressive.

The question of supply particularly fascinated me. Where on earth did they find these three hundred or so varieties of cheese? They weren't just haphazardly piled up, either: they were carefully organised in the case by age and location, like a series of fine Bordeaux wine. On that note, the ladies always knew exactly what each cheese was like, and which wine was the best choice to accompany it. Whether you picked a Chaumes, a Rocamadour or a Talleggio, they would know exactly which Burgundy or Côtes du Rhone, which Sancerre or Alsace to recommend.

Some ten years later, on a trip to Paris, I decided to go back to the cheese shop on something of a whim. I was relieved to find that the smell hadn't changed at all, and that it was still run by the same lovely family. I found that they had actually expanded their repertoire, selling bread and wines as well as various types of cream and yoghurt. The three hundred types of cheese looked the same to me, arrayed in the same old glass case, but I found out they had actually supplemented them too, adding on a selection of cheeses from the New World. 'The imported cheeses aren't quite as popular,' one of the sisters explained to me, 'but they give us an advantage over our competitors. We're the only shop in Paris that stocks some of these,' she added proudly.

For the first time, I found someplace I could buy stilton in France and have it appear a novelty rather than a shame: it used to be insulting to even ask for it in the 1970s. Shopkeepers would scoff. But now, with the European Common Agricultural Policy and the rise of free trade, it seemed like cheeses from Germany, Switzerland and England as well as Peru and India had come to take their place amongst the classics.

'Of course,' she continued, 'The French still prefer their French cheeses.' She gave me a smile.

'*Bien sûr*,' I replied. 'France, after all, is like a sort of mecca of holy cheese– or do I mean holey cheese?'

AN EVENT IN THE GARDEN

The county of Kent is something of a miniature cradle of civilisation, at least when it comes to splendid indoor living. It is claimed that the first house in England was built in Kent, at the gates of Chilham Castle near Canterbury. Though the castle itself was built for King Henry II, there has been proof that its foundations date much further back, to Anglo-Saxon and even Roman habitation.

The county was home to many of the early great kings, thanks to its wonderful hunting grounds. If one asks an informed and passionate Kent dweller, they will spin engaging tales of Odo, the Earl of Kent and Bishop of Bayeux, hunting there with his half-brother, William the Conqueror. It is a rich and fascinating area, steeped in history, which only becomes more incredible when you become the owner of one of the old houses. You become, almost by default, a keeper of history. Well, not exactly by default: my wife and I had previously looked at sixty-nine other houses! We house-hunted all over the big green belt of London: from Maidenhead to Maidstone. But we fell in love with this one: built in 1410, restored in 1620, and mentioned in the Domesday Book.

We came to Kent not knowing how ancient it truly was, but of course the houses were built to last in the olden days. They were raised through hard work, dedication and a meticulous eye for detail, by people eager to please the kings and queens of the day.

Because many of the residents had, in the past, been of royal or noble families, most of the more upmarket properties had high walls to protect their privacy and for security reasons. These walls made the houses all the more impressive and imposing, giving them some of the feel of castles. The histories of these great houses was well known throughout the area, and as a newcomer I was regaled with the story of my own property, its building and rebuilding, as though it had a life all its own.

My own house in Kent was built in 1410. It fell into a state of slight disrepair and was accordingly renewed and updated in 1620, with the garden being added in 1700. It was very large, and I always suspected from the grandeur of the place that it had indeed been created from the ruins of an old castle. This was something that was often done in the past. When the royal families left their properties, the local people would demolish these stately homes in order to build their own humble residences. I felt that our house, and the houses near to ours, were a piece of this unique and interesting history.

The houses closes to ours were similar to my own in terms of size and style, and our closest neighbours were the Oakhursts. Their house was surrounded by a high stone wall, and within was a garden of such sheer size and beauty that it seemed to have been taken straight from the pages of a storybook. While others in the area were often youngish professionals or elderly couples who hired gardeners to see to the grounds around their houses, this garden was maintained by Mrs Oakhurst herself. She was only fifty-five, but did not need to work thanks to her husband's ambitious career in the City.

From talking to both Mr and Mrs Oakhurst, my wife and I soon learned that their children had grown up, and Mrs Oakhurst was enjoying a retirement of sorts, long days filled with caring for all the plants in her garden. It often seemed that the garden was like another child to her, something she cared for avidly.

She was usually at home alone for the whole day, since her husband's work was an hour's commute away and he worked long hours and came home exhausted. Sometimes, behind the high walls that surrounded her little slice of paradise, we could hear Mrs Oakhurst singing to the flowers as she turned the earth with her hands.

Mrs Oakhurst was a friendly and warm neighbour, but it was clear that she was happiest and most at home when working alone on her garden. That was where she found the greatest sense of peace and safety.

One day, I was at home when I heard the unmistakable wail of an ambulance siren. It was quite unexpected, given that our house was somewhat out of the way, and since everyone in *our* house was all right, the only place it could really be going was next door. My theory was proven correct as the siren got closer, before it was abruptly cut off, leaving my wife and I wondering what had happened.

'Is Mr Oakhurst home?' I asked. He and I had an ongoing joke about which one of us would work ourselves to death first, though suddenly it didn't seem quite so amusing.

My wife widened her eyes. 'I don't know. We should go and find out what's happened, see if we can help.'

Next door, the ambulance was already getting ready to depart, but we saw Mrs Oakhurst being slid inside of it before the doors closed, and Mr Oakhurst's ashen face as he climbed in beside his wife. Then they were gone and we were left standing, considering what could possibly have happened. The Oakhursts were, all told, a health-conscious pair, youthful for their years and we had never seen them have any serious illnesses or accidents.

'What could have happened to her?' my wife asked, looking around accusingly as though some attacker might be lurking.

'We'll have to wait and find out when she comes back. I'm sure it's nothing serious,' I assured her, though I was not so certain myself. I had seen the look of shock and sorrow on Mr Oakhurst's face, and it had shaken me to my very core.

A few days of silence followed Mrs Oakhurst being taken away in the ambulance, although the gossip seemed to be that some accident had befallen her in the garden. The Oakhursts' house stayed dark and quiet and empty of habitation and we were left to our theories and our prayers that it was nothing dreadful.

Then the card arrived.

It informed us, in Mr Oakhurst's solid, matter-of-fact handwriting, that Mrs Oakhurst had sadly passed away, and gave the details of her funeral. We stood staring at the card in disbelief, trying to process the fact that someone who was so happy, so well and so very alive, was also someone we would now never see again.

It was a terrible shock to the system. However, we accordingly readied ourselves and attended the funeral a week later. The wake was held at the house, partly in the garden where Mrs Oakhurst had so loved to spend her days.

'Terrible tragedy,' I consoled Mr Oakhurst when he broke away from his mourning family long enough to come and thank us for attending, to mention how his wife had always loved living next door to such considerate and welcoming neighbours.

'Terrible,' he agreed. He still looked understandably shaken by it.

'What...' It was an awkward thing to ask, and awful timing, but I couldn't help but want to know what exactly had taken place. 'Was she... was Mrs Oakhurst ill?'

He blinked his glassy eyes. 'Oh, no. It was the wall. Around the other side of the grounds.'

My wife stared at him. 'The *wall*?' she echoed back, a tad incredulously.

'Yes.' He swallowed and looked at us sorrowfully. 'She was fanatical about these gardens, you know. Absolutely obsessed. She was just cleaning some ivy off the stone wall. You know how ivy gets into things, don't you? Destroys the structure and such. That wall had been standing firm since the 1700s and now...'

'It collapsed?' I asked, horrified.

'Not entirely. A stone dislodged, fell and gave her a major concussion.' He took a sip of his drink to calm himself. 'She couldn't survive a thing like that. Nobody could.'

'Of course not,' my wife consoled him, laying a hand on his arm, 'what a horrid thing. I'm so sorry for your loss.'

After discovering what had ended Mrs Oakhurst's life so abruptly, I set to work fortifying our stone walls, making sure that no creepers had slid their way into the stonework, settling it for myself and my family that the walls were more than safe. I could not stand the thought of anyone I loved meeting an end like Mrs Oakhurst. When just touching a wall, just walking by it, could cause such a tragedy, it seemed better not to take that risk in the first place.

It did teach me not to take anything for granted, though. Not even things that seem so solid and everlasting. Everything can crumble to bits in an instant. Ever since then, it has always been the first thing I have done in any of our properties. Years afterwards, when we bought a house in Normandy, strengthening the walls and repairing any less than perfect areas was the first thing I set my hand to, although my wife was perhaps more interested in getting the inside of the place liveable and painted up to her standard. But in my mind, safety, since that day, has always come long before decoration. And in this way, we have avoided any accidents and lived happily wherever we have made our home.

THE CONSTRUCTION SITE NEIGHBOUR

Trends in architecture and real estate tend to be cyclical. What goes around comes around: areas that haven't been popular for hundreds of years will suddenly, as if overnight, come back into favour. Where once fresh water might have been the draw, the sunny coast will be rediscovered by some magazine, or feature in the background of some blockbuster and become famous again. Ancient architectural tendencies will suddenly be revived, become trendy for a decade, then vanish again. Percy Bysshe Shelley's famous poem 'Ozymandias' reflects on the combination of permanence and impermanence that architecture, particularly stonework, affords:

> I met a traveller from an antique land
> Who said: 'Two vast and trunkless legs of stone
> Stand in the desert. Near them on the sand,
> Half sunk, a shattered visage lies, whose frown
> And wrinkled lip and sneer of cold command
> Tell that its sculptor well those passions read
> Which yet survive, stamped on these lifeless things,
> The hand that mocked them and the heart that fed.

Sculptors pass, while their works live on. This applies to buildings as well as statues: these cycles operate more or less naturally most of the time, helped along by the vagaries of economic development or popular culture, but they are never stranger than when a single person tries to implant them.

In my days as a banker and portfolio manager, one of our clients would often invite us to Tunisia. He had a house over the beach just outside the old town of Kairowan, so we rented a guesthouse nearby. It is a fascinating part of the state, being considered the fourth-holiest Islamic city in the world as well as a World Heritage site. My own interest in the city had to do with it being the location in the ninth century of a school that attracted some of the most brilliant scholars of the era from all over the Islamic world, or perhaps with the famous Aghlabite culture that once filled the city with gardens, libraries and pools. However, my bank's interest had much more to do with the fallout of the oil euphoria that hit in the early and mid-seventies and led to a veritable real estate boom. Land that had been worth a dollar a square metre was suddenly valued at five hundred dollars over the course of a few months in 1974. Kairowan suddenly began to intrigue people who had no prior interest in culture outside of the West; and I, who had, was quite happily sent out there on long trips to work with various clients.

Thus, I spent more than one holiday there in the mid-1970s with my wife and children, trying to ally work with pleasure. Kairowan was attractive to some clients because, for a site in North Africa, its climate was quite temperate due to its location near the sea. The city also was relatively prosperous, with at least some fresh water available. Thus, one summer, I found myself staying in the beach house of this prestigious client. This individual had a high net worth; like many others, he had come to see us with his newfound wealth, looking for advice on various investments. He had found and acquired a small, beautiful beach, investing a significant amount of time and money into cleaning it up, even moving truckloads of imported clean, soft sand in front of his house in order to create the setting for a picture-perfect holiday home. We had a nice enough time staying there, usually for ten days or so at a time. I spent a lot of time in business meetings, but still managed to relax with my family and enjoy our coastal location. We did our own cooking, as I'm not particularly fond of Tunisian food, which to me is an oily mix of the worst of Arabic and African cuisine. It was a lovely place to stay, in an excellent location. However, like many idyllic places, it had the single disadvantage of a rather odd neighbour.

This neighbour was in the process of constructing his own beach house, and seemed to be acting as his own dubious sort of architect. He was a young Saudi man, with traditional values. He obviously knew and understood the history of the region, and wanted to build his house out of stone in what he imagined to be a classic style. Unfortunately, he backed these rather lofty aims with a shallow pocket and a foul temperament. I didn't quite understand his project when I saw the first traces of it. There just seemed to be a lot of huge blocks of stone lying around, and a lot of disorganised movement and shouting. In fact, the first time I ended up speaking with him was out of a necessity to ask him to stop yelling at his workers. The construction site itself was loud enough, with constant drilling, and the noise of rocks falling; but on top of this, he seemed to have decided that screaming at his hired Tunisian hands was the best way to get things built effectively. Eventually, I had had enough, and went over to the construction site for a chat.

'I'm sorry to interrupt your work,' I told him, 'but the noise is just overwhelming. We're trying to negotiate business deals next door; we need a little peace and quiet.'

'They're just useless, these men!' he shouted at me. 'All of them! They couldn't build a Lego set, let alone a palace!'

'Look,' I said, trying to resist being angered by his tone, 'I understand that you may be stressed. I also understand that you may have become so used to speaking at this volume that you've forgotten how to conduct civilised conversation. Neither of these are sufficient reasons to alienate your neighbours!'

'Look,' he said, 'I'm trying to build a palace, here. That's enough to test any man's patience.'

'A palace? You seem to be working with incredible primitive equipment for that,' I responded dubiously.

'That's the point,' he replied with tangible ill-humour. Then he sighed and wiped his brow. 'I don't mean to be so grumpy. I'm working on a very ambitious project, here.'

'I can see that.'

'I want to build a classic palace,' he continued. 'A real, ancient palace, like the ones that towered over the hills of this region in the ninth century. Now, with the influx of oil money, we will look out over the sea instead.'

'That's all well and good,' I replied, 'but why does this project involve quite so much shouting? I mean, that sounds like quite a historically laudable aim, but I don't understand why it's giving your workers such difficulties.'

'As I said,' he replied brusquely, 'I want to create something that is essentially historical. The ancient palaces were built out of huge blocks of stone, easily a metre and a half cubed. My idea of a palace is the same as that of the ancients: therefore, we must build it just as they did. Furthermore, the insides will have to be entirely made of marble.'

'Can you even get marble here?' The ludicrousness of the project was beginning to sink in.

'Well, there is a quarry south of Jeddah, in Saudi Arabia, but we have found much better marble in Portugal, and had it imported.'

I resisted commenting that this was hardly the way the region's ancient inhabitants would have proceeded. 'OK, so this palace of yours is made of chunks of marble. When does the shouting come into play?'

'The trouble with this theory,' my neighbour answered, appearing to ignore my question, 'is that it's actually quite difficult to build in the ancient way, just setting stone on top of stone.'

'Wait a minute,' I interrupted. 'Are you telling me you're planning to construct this whole thing without any kind of mortar? That's insane.'

For the first time, the man smiled proudly. 'It's the traditional way,' he said. 'You just have the stones balanced on each other. They're held in place by their own weight. I'll build them five metres up, and make a roof out of cement. Then I'll decorate the inside with marble, traditional Islamic art, and possibly some classical trompe l'oeil.' He smiled proudly.

I bit back a comment about the dubious authenticity of using cement in this context. 'Do you have an architect? Has someone worked out the logistics? Did you even have plans drawn up for this building?' I was flabbergasted at the sheer madness of the project.

'Oh no,' he told me, his good humour having apparently returned. 'I just want to build the old way. The pharaohs of Egypt didn't have architects.'

'Yes, but they had armies of slaves!' I paused, suddenly realising the source of the shouting. 'But so do you, don't you,' I added, shaking my head.

He laughed, apparently immune to the accusation. 'Yes,' he says, 'but my workers are useless. I cannot use a leather whip, or even starve them! Pharaohs did not have to worry about contracts and minimum wages.'

'You say that like it's a good thing.' I couldn't help but think that my neighbour's plan was somewhat insane, although at least I understood where the shouting and crashing noises were coming from. I wished him the best of luck with the project, trying not to sound too sarcastic, and left him to it.

He would have needed much more luck than I could offer him.

The project continued for the next three years of our time working in Kairouan, and probably longer. It stalled not so very long after our conversation, and never seemed to get back on track for more than a few days of half-hearted work by some newly-hired labourers. Some days, I would stand at the window and watch the workers milling about, trying to move those huge blocks of stone. The stone had clearly come straight from a quarry. They didn't even have a crane on site, only a beat-up looking tractor. This old machine could obviously just about lift the three tons or so that one of these blocks would weigh, but didn't have much ability to manoeuvre once it was in the air. Thus, the workers ended up having to try everything from winching to pushing the stones, ending up looking almost exactly like slaves in ancient Egypt. The effect would be as comical as it was tragic.

Every time they would start the alleged building work again, I would hear the man's shouting and shake my head at his hubris. I needn't have worried about the possible structural weaknesses of the building, though, as nothing more than the foundations was ever built. The project was just too ambitious, and our neighbour didn't have the requisite skills to carry it out, including diplomacy. None of the workers ever seemed to return for more than one or two days. They would quickly get a taste of his megalomania and hastily find another bit of freelance work to do. There was something sad about watching this man's dream fail: but I had to admit I was grateful, too, for the peace and quiet that ensued.

There was a sort of ironic end to this story. Ten years after these events, in the mid-1980s, I travelled back to Tunisia for a short holiday. I decided to go and visit the site out of curiosity, even though the client with whom I used to stay had long since moved back to Paris. The beach and its construction site looked much the same as they had in 1975: of the imagined palace, all there was to see was a few stones stacked up. There was no roof and no flooring; in fact, barely enough to guess at the intended structure. The strange thing was that the building had in fact weathered so that it looked like the ruins of an antique palace. The stone had been worn down by the scorching sun, the desert winds and the salt water blowing in off the sea. As I was wandering around the site, another neighbour happened to walk by. I asked him if he knew what had happened to my once-neighbour, the one who was almost an architect. He laughed. 'Oh, eventually he got fed up with his own project and, as you can see, he let the construction site fall to ruin. Progress was ridiculously slow; they kept having accidents moving those three-ton stone, including one near fatal one. In the end, he fired all those who hadn't already quit and moved back to Casablanca.'

'Isn't it strange that he unintentionally achieved the ancient feel he wanted, in the destruction of his project?'

'I don't know about that,' the man said, 'but it certainly was a huge waste of money. And then, of course, he died.'

'Died? I thought you said he moved away.'

'One, then the other,' he replied philosophically.

'Do you mean there was an accident on site?'

'Oh no, nothing like that. He just gave up on it all.'

I shook my head. 'I wonder if he expended all his energy on his mad project, and then collapsed when he abandoned it.'

My interlocutor shrugged. 'Who knows? All we can be sure of is how crazy this palatial project was.'

'The funny thing,' I noted, 'is that future generations investigating this will find these ruins and probably assume there was in fact a palace here. It might even inspire them to build their own!' The passage of time was a strange thing, I mused. In the words of Shelley:

'Look on my works, ye mighty, and despair!'
Nothing beside remains. Round the decay
Of that colossal wreck, boundless and bare,
The lone and level sands stretch far away.

Shelley's 'lifeless things' would endure here, in the form of the foundations, while my neighbour and the 'hand that mocked them and the heart that fed' was long gone.

PARISIAN PARKING NEIGHBOURS

The French think they can get away with anything. France, despite being one of Europe's most Catholic countries, does not always have a very Catholic approach to neighbourly relations. The call to raise large families and to go to confession may be respected, but where a sense of community, charity or social responsibility is required, not everyone is quite up to scratch. This is sadly especially true in the big cities, where there seems to be a deep disrespect of private property that goes far beyond any sort of socialism. The Catholic Church may well preach that money is unnecessary, but it surely does not recommend savaging the possessions it can buy! Graffiti is only one obvious facet of this, along with the constant desecration of bus stops, but it goes far beyond that. I don't even just mean in the *banlieue*: I mean central Paris, too. Not just the slums and their inhabitants, but people who live in swanky high-rises. Maybe it has less to do with Catholicism and more to do with the French and their history of warring with the English. Perhaps they are still smarting from their loss at Waterloo. Whatever the reasoning, there seems to be a pervading and pernicious belief that most foreign cars, especially luxury cars, can be attacked and scratched at any time without any expectation of punishment.

Thus, in all the time I lived in Paris, I never once managed to keep an expensive or fancy car for very long without it ending up terribly scratched with keys. Most of the time, this was obviously just the act of bored and miserable children or drunken youths on the street, which, although it does not excuse it, at least gives it some kind of understandable framework. That is not the worst part, though. In our apartment in Paris, where we used to live as a family but which now serves us as a sort of guesthouse, we have an underground parking lot. This apartment building has local residents, most of whom are living and working in Paris. As far as I know, we are the only ones who are regularly away, as we now spend most of our time in Geneva and London. Technically, we have at our disposal a lovely apartment in Paris, with an associated parking spot, for our family to go on holiday, or for any friend of ours to stay. In an ideal world, the flat and parking space would sit quietly gathering dust in the months in between visits, waiting undisturbed for us to return.

There is a flaw to this theory, though. Almost every time we travel to Paris, we find that one of our neighbours has parked their car in our space. We know it is their car, and not some intruder's, because we ask the concierge. The concierge is always unconcerned about our situation, to the point of amusement, which strikes me as rather rude. 'Oh, they are your neighbours,' he explains vaguely, as if that gave them every right on our own private property!

'Our neighbours? But all our neighbours have their own parking spaces.'

'Perhaps yours is more convenient,' he said languidly, examining his fingernails. 'After all, you have not been here.'

It was enough to make me want to strangle him. Eventually, I would manage to move him to some sort of action, and he would roll his eyes and ring our neighbours. These would usually apologise, come down at once and move the car. '*Oh, désolé, Monsieur Jamieson,*' they would explain, 'we're sorry, but there was no room!' Another time the excuse might be: 'we have more than one car, and we didn't want to leave it on the street!' This particular excuse grated with me more than the others. As someone who'd had to keep his car on the streets of Paris for various reasons, I knew full well of the dangers of this choice. I also knew that if you lived in a high-rise apartment as chic as this, you could probably afford your own parking space. I almost wished they had come to me with their grovelling expressions and their real excuses: 'Oh, I just couldn't be bothered to drive to the other side of the parking lot!' 'Oh, my cousin is here to stay, he may as well keep his car here.' 'I'm bored of my own parking space.' 'I'm a lazy idiot.' Of course, then I would have ended up having altercations with them as well as with the concierge and, quite frankly, I just didn't have the energy.

Our family was as tolerant as we could be of this situation. Once the neighbours came down and moved their cars, we would try to forget it and enjoy our stay in peace. However, the problem actually slowly aggravated as the neighbours started discovering our travel plans. In some ways, this was an improvement, as there was less risk of us coming back from a short shopping trip to find the space already taken again. That said, I assume the concierge was responsible for this knowledge being shared, which I didn't appreciate one bit. Whatever the cause, however, as soon as we went away, sometimes for six months at a time, the squatters would move in and take our parking space. They were like cockroaches, emerging from the cracks in a wall the second the lights were out.

It was a pattern that seemed to have no hope of resolution. Whenever we gave one of our friends, employees or family members the key to the apartment, they would encounter exactly the same problem. I would receive a perplexed phone call, sometimes with the sound of a motor idling in the background. 'Brad,' the confused friend or employee would say, 'are you sure you gave us the right address? Are we really in the right place? Because the parking space you indicated is occupied.'

I would sigh. 'Yes, it's the right parking space,' I would have to explain. 'Yes, even though it's taken. You're going to have to talk to the concierge about our squatting neighbour.'

Sometimes the guests would be less tolerant of the concierge's nonchalance than I had learned to be, and I would get reports of the ensuing fights. Eventually, of course, they would claim our space back, but it would be a somewhat bitter victory. Sometimes we would even have to call the police, if the owner was away or travelling. It was a truly ridiculous situation.

At the time of writing, this story has gone on for over six years, and has not been resolved. What were we to do? Get a scarecrow? Pay someone to sit in the space in a funny costume? Put spikes on the ground? The only vaguely satisfying solution I ever found was to allow my kids to kick the car when we discovered someone squatting in our space. In the end, however, there appeared to be no real way to solve the problem. Depending on how you look at the matter, we either gave up or came to a brilliant conclusion. Yes, we decided recently to put the parking space alone up for sale. We decided it was better to run the risk of having the car scratched with keys than to have the space repeatedly stolen. Quite frankly, I think it was the best, least tiring, and most ethical way of getting around the problem. If I couldn't have the parking space, then no-one else could!

In the late 1970s and early 1980s, the Canary Islands really exploded onto the holiday market. Or at least, that was the plan.

It was a time when people were just realising what these islands had to offer: wonderful weather, the sun glowing resplendently off the blue sea, fabulous fishing opportunities, and perhaps most importantly, a sense of being really cut off from the real world. While all the traditional tourist spots, such as Marbella and St Tropez, were heaving with holidaymakers, the Canaries were still fairly untouched, and many could see the potential in such an unspoiled landscape.

Around this time, we had residential developments in the Canary Islands. Since Lanzarote was supposedly just about to take off as a major tourist destination, we were planning to build a hotel or a bank out there. Since a new airport had just been built, making access much more convenient, it seemed like the perfect time to expand out there and take up any new business opportunities that might arise.

This was an especially attractive proposition, since we subsequently discovered that King Hussein of Jordan had bought up many hectares of land near one of our developments, apparently as intrigued and enraptured by this so-called new Marbella as many others were. We assumed that he was going to build a palace, which would have been incredibly good news for our own ventures. We were sure that having even a minor Middle-Eastern royal building and visiting or even moving to the Canary Islands would give it a massive boost.

What followed was entirely predictable. Some of the most wealthy and famous men wanted to copy what King Hussein was planning to do. If someone such as him wanted to expand out to these islands, then it suddenly seemed like a good, not to mention fashionable, idea. The next thing we knew, there were others such as King Hussein desperate to build their own palaces with private ports, or else smaller haciendas or chalets.

It was seen as both a wonderful place to stay and a good investment in what would no doubt become an enormous tourist spot, replete with great entertainment. Of course, many just wanted to enjoy the brilliant beaches and impressive weather.

Everyone waited with bated breath to find out what he would

have built for him, what kind of architecture he would opt for, and how large the structure would be. As my own company developed properties on the island, I was able to talk to many others who were similarly engaged in constructing their dreams.

'Can you imagine,' one might say to me, 'what it's going to look like when King Hussein is finished? Crazy! Like the Middle East just upped and moved here.' Finished was an ambitious thing to think about, since he had yet to even break ground.

'It's going to cause a lot of disruption,' others fretted. 'The noise alone will drive people away, won't it? It'll take months and months to complete a palace like the one he'll want. Maybe even years.'

One could only dream of the stately building that the royal family of Jordan was planning to put up, but everyone doubted that they would stick to the local style. Their personal sense of taste was ostentatiously Middle Eastern, all marble and gold, and those of us developing in the area knew that the towers and domes of King Hussein's palace would only attract more visitors, more people eager to cash in on this new paradise.

Paradise, because many of the Middle East's most renowned families, royalty and the richest businessmen, wanted to get away from the arid deserts. It was too hot and dry for comfort and they wished to move elsewhere, at least for a good stretch of each year.

However, in spite of all the gossip and the hopes that the Jordanian royal family would be developing just near us, no matter how we waiting, nothing came to pass. To begin with, I thought that perhaps the planning stages of putting up their no doubt palatial structure was taking longer than anticipated. The talk on the island turned to imagining how resplendent a building might be, to take so many months to plan.

Months soon turned into years, and doubt began to creep in. It is, after all, one thing to be late to a party, and quite another to never show up at all.

Personally, since other families had been beginning to build, I thought that maybe the Jordanian royal family were not as financially well off as we had been led to believe – maybe they couldn't afford the same sort of instant luxury properties as the Saudi royal family could, for example.

Other great families began to get nervous. The Canary Islands were supposed to be the new California, all helped and supported by King Hussein's decision to build out there. After all, such a high profile and luxurious neighbour would bring great profit to the place and attract more and more people, both the extreme and averagely wealthy alike.

But it just... never happened. Time ticked on without even the groundwork being laid for the supposed palace of the royal family of Jordan.

After ten, twenty, thirty years passed, the Canary Islands did indeed develop, but not at the rate one had originally expected. While other royal neighbours put up their own fabulous beach houses, King Hussein's hectares remained entirely untouched by human hands. I couldn't believe it! Was it possible that this rich Middle-Eastern man was not as rich as we had believed? When was he going to put his riches into the property, as planned? When would be build and build on Lanzarote?

In fact, he never built there at all.

This has, naturally, happened in many other places. From my own point of view, I've witnessed these potentially great new places beginning to develop in places as diverse as Ibiza, the southern coast of Italy, Perpignan, and Toulon. However, as much as people try to force change, the most popular and financially secure places have always remained hot spots – such is the case of Cannes and Monte Carlo. The richest men in the world continue to build their dream properties in St Tropez, never really venturing into these new lands.

There are some exceptions, such as Sardinia and Marbella, which have become more and more successful and luxurious over time, but this definitely did not take place when it came to the Canary Islands. Any influence that King Hussein's unfulfilled plans had soon faded into dust.

Much like Cyprus and other such locations, Lanzarote was unsuccessful in generating the sort of high profile, high class visitors it wanted. Very few expensive luxury properties sprang up before the lower middle class caught onto the boom that was sure to follow and began buying up the land and the area became rather low brow.

The chances of any kings building their slipped year by year as the prefabs began to go up and the holidaymakers descended. Any of the wealthy, Middle Eastern families who had tried to make a success of the place soon went back to Cannes and Capri, the true markers of good taste and great wealth.

'It was a nice idea, developing out here,' one man said to me, 'lovely weather, of course. But I'm off to St Tropez again this year. You can't beat the original and the best!'

The house we used to own in Normandy, near Calvados and Falaise, was surrounded by over twenty rolling hectares of wild grass. This was quite an extent of beautiful countryside for us to have, and indeed considerably more land than our farmer neighbour had. Surprisingly for a Frenchman, this neighbour did not, however, seem to resent this fact. In fact, all in all, Guillaume was a rather lovely neighbour, confirming prevalent stereotypes about the inhabitants of the Normandy region. He was a hard-working man with an agreeable temperament, and in all the time I knew him, he always said yes to any neighbourly request. These attributes were considered to be typically 'Normand,' as much of a part of the region's heritage as strong cider and windy beaches.

As well as being uncharacteristically chatty for a French farmer, Guillaume also seemed to have taken a liking to our family, and would actually walk across the fields to talk by the side of the fence if we happened to be out sitting on the lawn or pottering about in the garden. He obviously took his cues for dealing with foreigners much more from World War II than from the Hundred Years' War! He almost always wore leather trousers, although these would occasionally be replaced by brown jeans, and at least half of his clothes were covered in mud at all times. The Normans are really friendlier than the rest of the French, being as how they are essentially a Nordic people descended from the same Viking roots as the Dutch and the English. As far as I knew, he didn't have a penchant for drinking mugs of beer or flinging women over his shoulder, but he was tall and blonde with quite a lot of muscle and a respectable amount of beard. In fact, in all the time I knew him, I never saw him touch a drink, which is unusual when one considers the French habit of wine with meals. All in all, he was an unconventional Frenchman and a delightful neighbour.

We were lucky that this was the case, as we found ourselves in a rather difficult situation with him for a time. As I mentioned, we had considerably more land than our farmer neighbour. On his few acres of grass, Guillaume kept horses for riding and breeding, as well as quite a large herd of cows for milk: for two hectares, they had a dozen horses and a dozen cows. Even the layman can probably work out that that would be a bit crowded. Once our friendly relations with Guillaume had been established, he approached us with an idea. 'Would you be willing to let my animals graze on your land?' he asked with a disarming smile. 'I mean, your grass is getting tall, so it might be an advantage for you, as well,' he reasoned. I considered the matter. I knew all the French laws, and understood that a farmer could essentially squat on any land he pleased without neighbours being able to do a great deal about it. Leases had to be regularly renewed, and the whole thing became very legally complicated quite quickly. Thus, I realised that if Guillaume had simply moved his animals into our field, we would have found it difficult to get them removed. The fact that he was approaching this in such an honest and open way was greatly reassuring. I decided it was much better to go along with his plan and make it a neighbourly gesture, rather than a problematic issue.

'So you want to loan us your flocks?' I said with a grin. 'Is that really proper farmer's behaviour?'

Guillaume laughed. 'I was thinking more in terms of borrowing your grass, you know.'

'I don't think I'll want the interest, then!' I quipped back. Little did I know how much this particular tender of 'interest' would prove to be a problem. The flocks moved in that spring, when the weather was still quite cold. The arrangement was for them to stay there at least until October, when the grass needed the most cutting. A part of me was very much looking forward to not having to get the fields cut for an entire summer. However, there was one aspect of this we hadn't really considered. The cows and horses milled around, eating constantly. Even when their heads were not buried in the grass, they were chewing the cud with those strangely blank expressions. Of course, nature runs its course: what goes in must come out.

We discovered this the hard way. Well, perhaps less hard, and more squelchy. In warm weather, our family liked to engage in quite a lot of outdoors activities: walking, cycling, fishing and horse riding, for instance. I have raised my children to enjoy fresh air, and to be as active as possible. This was, of course, one of the reasons we had purchased all of the land behind our house. Unfortunately, when we agreed to let the twenty-four animals roam free on our land, that romantic vision had left out a distinctly unromantic detail. The first time we realised we had something of a problem was coming home from a long bicycle ride, when, as we always did, we cut through the field on our way back to the house. The kids were wearing their usual summer clothes, and I was wearing white tennis shoes and shorts. About halfway across the field, I realised I may have made something of a sartorial error, if not a neighbourly one. As our bicycles all slowed down gradually, the wheels coated in gunk, I suddenly understood, from its aroma, the change that had occurred in our fields. My family, our bicycles, and our unfortunate items of no-longer-white clothing, had become inextricably caught up in a natural process beyond our control. Like the passing of time, or the movement of the tides, it is a truth universally acknowledged that twenty-four animals will produce a lot of poo. Guillaume might have been a friendly neighbour, but even he couldn't stop his animals from being productive. They were veritable machines! If cowpats had been gold, he would have been a very rich man.

After that disastrous outing, our family quickly came to the conclusion that outdoors activities would have to be severely limited for that summer. Although there were a few complaints from the children, no-one really wanted to spoil their clothes or have to rinse their ankles every time they came back from a stroll. Furthermore, the smell may have been typically bucolic, but it was hardly pleasant. Unfortunately, it wasn't just fast-paced all-terrain cycling that was a problem. Just a short evening stroll to look at the sunset or even stepping outside to look at some passing birds could be fatal to one's shoes, as well as one's composure. After a few weeks of this, we had to face the evidence: we couldn't really go on using our own twenty hectares of land while the animals were there. We sat down at dinner one night and pondered what to do. The children were adamant that they wanted to be able to do some sort of outdoors activities, even if they had to give up cycling. We debated whether there was any activity that could be accomplished without getting dirty even in the current circumstances, and hit on the idea of horse-riding. Of course, at the time, we didn't have any horses of our own. When we went riding as a family, we did it at a school nearby. The kids loved the high jumps and obstacles, whilst my wife and I preferred to settle for nice long country rides. Nonetheless, there was a definite agreement in our family that this was one sport we wanted to keep.

'Can we just ride Guillaume's horses?' my youngest son piped up. 'They're sitting right there!'

I had to explain to him that these were breeding, rather than riding horses. 'I'm afraid they would throw you off within a few minutes. You'd most likely land face-down... on the ground. You know exactly what I'm implying by that. You know how the French love the expression '*se mettre dedans*?' I don't want that to happen to you.' He wrinkled his nose. However, my little son had given me an idea. Instead of trying to ride Guillaume's horses, perhaps we could replace then with our own! Then, instead of twelve horses and their output, we would only have two or three. Then we could claim the land back for our own use. Surely, spread out over that much land, it wouldn't cause a problem? In small quantities, surely it would serve as fertiliser and be naturally absorbed into the ground? I was a little wary of this solution, having so obviously underestimated the amount produced by twenty-four animals, but I figured it was worth a try, even if it might not go down so well with our amiable neighbour.

I needn't have worried. Guillaume was perfectly friendly about the situation. I avoided mentioning the real cause of the problem, which he might have scoffed at, since farmers like him probably tromp about in the stuff all day long! As a lover of animals, he understood our desire to keep horses. I even suggested we might be interested in breeding the horses, which was not entirely true, but I figured it might win me some brownie points with him as an equine connoisseur. Perhaps I was right. In any case, just a few days later, he moved his flocks back onto his own land. We made an agreement with the riding school to keep three horses for a few months. The patties dried up in a few weeks of summer sun, and the new horses settled in happily. Before the nice weather had left Normandy for the year, we managed to bicycle across our own fields again, although none of us took the risk of wearing white clothes. We maintained excellent relations with our nice neighbour Guillaume. In the end, he rented some grazing land a few miles down the road, and even thanked us for offering him a good temporary solution. I was glad we had come to some sort of mutually satisfying accord, even if I wasn't able to do him the favour he had first asked.

Of all the animal neighbours we had in Normandy, the wild boars were the most dangerous. Our house was surrounded by twenty hectares of rolling fields on the edge of a vast and ancient forest. Its boundaries, over the centuries, had hidden deer, hares, foxes, and even wolves. None of these, however, impressed me as much as the wild boars. This, perhaps, had more to do with the fact that I actually encountered these mythical beasts, in fact several times. Our family loved to walk in the forest, and most of the time we would see nothing more than a few birds, or perhaps the occasional squirrel. Our house was a beautiful old castle, surrounded by a moat with two drawbridges. Along with the deep, dark forest that surrounded it, it really felt like the setting for a fairy tale or one of the Arthurian legends. From the upper windows of the house, you couldn't see any people or buildings. You couldn't even see the wild boars.

Wild boars have been around since the Pleistocene and, in my opinion, they seem to have changed very little in that time. Despite their babies being cute little stripy things, even those are probably at their best braised and served up in a nice red wine sauce over buttered tagliatelle. I don't know this for sure, as I've never tried it myself, but I know the French are fond of it. Wild boars are *wild* beasts, as their names indicate, and should be treated as such. They are omnivorous, digging up the woods in search of roots and mushrooms, rustling around in the dirt with their strong snouts and sharp teeth, but they will also quite happily scavenge on any carcass they come across. I suspect part of this endless wrecking of forest soil has to do with marking their territory, but it seems to me to also show them up as fiercely hungry creatures. And violent, hungry, omnivorous creatures are hardly the kind one wants to have roaming the woods where one goes walking with young children.

Boars have been known to attack humans when they feel that their young have been threatened. Apparently, they also often come back to attack when they have been hit by a car! Of course, these are isolated incidents: most of the time, they just hide in the bushes or behind trees. That said, a wild boar is not an animal one would want to take chances with. I would imagine they would just as soon make me and my children into a tasty snack as I would like to turn one of them into steaks or a nice braised *daube* stew with olives.

Since we only travelled to this house approximately once a month, we weren't terribly familiar with the terrain, and we would often get rather lost on our long walks in the woods. This monthly pilgrimage to the house had a lot to do with getting exercise, so we were loath to give up on the hikes even when we found out about the woods' more threatening inhabitants. I feel like this says a lot about my family's dedication to sport and fresh air!

We would walk unarmed, of course. The closest thing I had to any kind of defence was probably my walking stick. The children were young, and would never have been able to outrun or withstand a charging wild boar – I'm not sure I would! I used to hunt when I was younger, but I hadn't held a gun in years. It seemed a ridiculous idea to acquire a gun just to protect against a theoretical encounter with one of the beasts. However, after we were chased not once but twice by an angry boar, and were forced to run up a tree to escape its wrath, I began to reconsider my cavalier attitude. Yes, we had escaped twice by outrunning the beast, but what if one of my kids had tripped? What if I had lost my foothold when climbing? It just wasn't safe to be out walking in those woods unprepared.

One day shortly after our second encounter, I complained to a neighbour, Jean-Luc. Jean-Luc was a farmer; a rough-and-ready man who looked like a lumberjack out of a children's book. We rarely saw him without an axe or pitchfork in hand. He was surprised that we would be out walking on those paths at all, as the French, especially the outdoorsy, farming types, have a rather strange attitude to rambling for fun. He was also quite adamant that the boars were indeed far too dangerous to ignore. Jean-Luc had taken something of a liking to the children, especially the youngest. He liked to show them around his barns and let them stroke the animals. I suppose the threat of them being gored by wild boars held almost as little appeal to him as it did for me!

'I mean,' I explained to him, 'we were just walking quietly along, not even making a lot of noise or running, or anything. This huge bristling boar just appeared at the end of the path and started running right towards us! It was terrifying, like something out of a Grimm fairy tale. Luckily, we were able to escape, but it wasn't the most reassuring episode. My littlest ones will no doubt have nightmares for weeks.'

He shook his head. 'It's not safe in those woods.' He explained to me that he knew the locations where the wild boars lived in the forest. 'Each boar family has a domain,' he explained to me. 'They're territorial animals, and when they have their newborns in the spring, they become protective and dangerous. A boar will never attack unless it feels threatened. So unless you walk near its litter of young, or do something aggressive like hitting it with a car, it will never charge you.'

'So this must mean our usual route for our walk must go right by its... burrow? Nest? Homestead?'

Jean-Luc chuckled. 'When the sows farrow, they do actually build a sort of nest. And yes, I suspect you must be coming a little too close for comfort. Furthermore, there is no hunting in this forest, so the boars have accumulated. They keep on multiplying. It's not good for them either, actually,' he added. 'I think they're having to fight each other over too little land. They're probably somewhat enraged already. When you come by with your noisy kids, they probably already feel threatened.'

'So you have encountered them often?'

'Mostly only from afar. I know how to avoid them, and that seems like the most sensible course of action. I did hit one with my car, many years ago. The thing actually ran away unhurt! I mean, perhaps it collapsed into the bushes a few meters later. But the fact remains that I hit a wild boar at full speed, and it crushed in one headlight of my car, and was still fine.'

'What did you do then?'

'Well, you're generally advised not to leave your car in case it thinks it was attacked, and comes charging back at you. After a while, I did get out, though, to check how the car had taken the shock, and also to see if there was a nice handy corpse lying around. You see, normally I believe in one of these accidents you're supposed to call the fire brigade to get rid of the body. Maybe an ambulance can do it someone was hurt. You're not allowed to pick up a boar you've killed yourself, but the next car to drive by can do it without any trouble.'

'Wait, you don't mean to say you can treat it like a hunted boar and take it home to cook?'

'That's exactly what I mean. Of course, in my case, there was no body to be found and taken home.'

I shook my head. 'I don't think I could eat something I've killed accidentally.'

Jean-Luc shrugged. 'It's no different to shooting it across a field and carrying it home in the back of your van.'

I had to laugh. 'You make it sound like you just knock it over and heave it over your shoulder like some kind of caveman!'

He flexed his biceps. 'Exactly,' he said with a grin.

'Listen, I don't want to be presumptuous, but I wonder if you would mind showing me around once so I can learn where the boars stay. That way we can try to avoid them in the future.'

'*Non non non*,' Jean-Luc protested, 'I can do far better than that. Just give me a call when you're headed on one of these walks of yours. I'll come with you. I can either walk ahead of you and warn against the boars or I can scare them off if they charge us.'

'What, like a boar bodyguard?'

'Exactly. Or a boar whisperer.'

That was exactly what we did. From then on, every time we set off on a family walk in the woods, we stopped by and picked up Jean-Luc. We had a good laugh on those walks, and never saw a wild boar again. I'm still not sure if that was down to luck or to the intervention of our very own boar bodyguard.

THE HUNTING NEIGHBOUR

In the first twenty years of one's life, many neighbours will become one's friends more by chance and by necessity than through the possession of shared interests or any real sense of kinship. The boys one sits down next to on the school benches, the girls one meets in the lunch canteen, and the people one shares accommodation with: timing and circumstance makes these people our friends and colleagues. One of the more interesting consequences of this arrangement is the fact that one will get drawn into activities one has no previous interest in, by association with these friends made by chance rather than choice.

For instance, when I was a college student, one of my neighbours was a tough, Southern boy by the name of Dean Patterson. Dean lived just down the corridor from me in our dorm at Northwestern. He was tall, thin and fair-haired, with a permanent snarl on his face. His mother was English and I think his father might have been Swedish; he certainly had some Nordic origins. As many college boys are, we were quite friendly, considering we had little in common. He always struck me as a rather spoiled child, although he was a few years older than me. We played a few of the same sports, though, and as Dean had his own car, we took a few cross-country trips together. However, our friendship was both cemented and put to the test one autumn, when he suggested we go hunting together. His parents had a house in the north of Minnesota, he explained, right up in the national parks by the Canadian border. We could stay there, and spend a few days out in the woods. 'Come on,' he bugged me week after week. 'Just a short trip! We'll stay with my parents and go hunting. We'll have a great time!'

Now, I have nothing against hunting as a sport and a pastime. Over the years, I've quite enjoyed roaming the woods with a rifle slung over my shoulder, chasing after birds and rabbits and maybe the occasional young deer. However, I wasn't sure that Dean Patterson's vision would quite line up with mine. Still, I was a student, and a free trip to the border of Canada was a free trip to the border of Canada. I figured we would spend most of our time eating home-cooked meals with his rich, boring parents, and perhaps taking the occasional hilly walk. I agreed.

My image of Dean as someone who was raised a spoiled brat was entirely confirmed when we arrived at his parents' house. This turned out to be a sort of vast wooden mansion with huge bay windows, a red Corvette parked outside and (I would later discover) a gun room in the basement. Dean himself had driven us there in a large Fleetwood Cadillac, so I wasn't surprised to discover this sort of wealth, although the gun room would still impress me considerably. His tall, blonde mother welcomed us with a plate of store-bought cookies and a pitcher of iced lemonade, then let us roam the house as we pleased. Of course, Dean's macho side took over, and he led me straight to the firearms. The room was a good five by seven metres large, and was filled with over a hundred hunting rifles, pistols, and shotguns of various makes. I gaped open-mouthed. Dean flung himself down on the large, crimson plush couch in the corner.

'I guess you do a lot of hunting, huh!' I exclaimed.

Dean rolled his eyes. 'You betcha. Been shooting since I was four years old. My Dad taught me how to shoot an empty soup can off a rock before I learned to tie my shoes. Now I can take out a moose half a mile away!'

'So will we be shooting moose tomorrow?' I asked warily. 'I'm not much of a big game man.'

'Oh, you know, the usual,' he said vaguely. 'Probably some deer. Maybe a squirrel or six. We'll just have to see what comes up.'

He grabbed a cigar from the case on the side table and lit it nonchalantly. 'Meanwhile, why don't you just relax? Kick off your shoes.'

We spent that evening, much as I had predicted, having an awkward supper with his glamorous parents. Conversation was somewhat laboured, as we had very little in common, and eventually I just let the three of them babble on about local football and family relatives. I had quickly realised that Dean was not the sort of friend with whom I could discuss literature or politics! In any case, we retired early, and rose before dawn to meet a few of his friends who had expressed interest in coming along on our hunting trip. When the friends turned up, I wondered if I wasn't in a little over my head. Every one of them was wearing a complete set of camouflaged hunting gear, complete with rubber boots, hats and binoculars. One of them had a length of rope slung over his shoulder; one of them was wearing green and brown face-paint. In my sensible hiking outfit, I suddenly felt less rugged and outdoorsy, more ridiculously underdressed! 'You one of Dean's school friends, then?' one of them asked suspiciously. Nonetheless, the men seemed friendly, and we climbed into our cars. I eavesdropped on the conversation going on in the back seat.

'You reckon we'll see anything big?' a burly man with a beard was asking his friend. The friend shrugged, and pulled a huge piece of beef jerky out of his pocket.

'You never know in spring,' he said, chewing noisily. 'Sometimes you see a whole family.'

We drove off into the forests, with country music blaring from the speakers, and parked in a secluded clearing. It was a slightly foggy morning, and I shivered as we left the warm cars and walked into the tall pinewoods. I looked around at my companion's attire, and noticed that they all seemed to have suspiciously high-calibre guns. 'Bit much for killing squirrels, no?' I joked nervously, but the man I had addressed just shrugged and bit down on another piece of beef jerky. 'You got a problem with my gun?' I hastily reassured him that I did not, and put the oddity down to their general obvious penchant for equipment.

We walked on in silence. After an hour's walk or so, we had gone quite deep into the forests, and everything was rather dark. We sat down for a break by the edge of a stream, in relative silence. Just as I was swigging from my bottle of water, I saw movement out of the corner of my eye. Not two hundred feet away, there was a huge brown bear and three little ones: probably a mother and cubs. Before I had even registered the sight, or opened my mouth to say anything, I heard the sound of a gun. The mother reared up on her hind legs, letting out a roar of pain. I leapt to my feet, ready to run for my life. Bewildered, I looked over and saw my partner with his big calibre gun on his shoulder. Looking around at the faces around me, I saw excitement, rather than fear. 'What are you doing?' I hissed. 'We need to get out of here! It isn't safe.' The man barked out a laugh and fired a volley of shots towards the bear family. 'You can run if you like,' he replied.

I was appalled that they should be shooting the little ones. 'Stop!' I said. 'Please, just stop! You can't shoot a mother animal like that in the wild. It's illegal, and immoral! Come on, let's get out of here!'

The man with the gun on his shoulder snarled and rolled his eyes, without even looking away from his gun's sights. 'Shut up,' he said, before firing another volley of shots. At this point, the mother bear swayed and fell to one side, while her cubs ran off in different directions into the woods.

His companions grumbled. 'Did nobody tell the new guy this was a bear hunt?' somebody asked nastily.

'A bear hunt?' I was astounded. 'Dean?' I looked over at my so-called friend, who was staring off into the distance nonchalantly.

'Sure it's a bear hunt,' he said casually. 'It's the most fun you can have!'

'And four bears are a lot better than one!' the man who had been shooting added. 'Anyway, don't be stupid,' he said. 'Bear-hunting's not illegal.'

The man with the biggest beard, who had been silent until then, turned to me with a somewhat more friendly expression. 'Come on, man, it's an ancient sport!' he said gently. 'It's been around since prehistory. It's fun. See, it's over now. When you kill your own bear, you can keep the bearskin to make a coat, or a carpet. When I killed my first, I had the head mounted in the local diner. Now, whenever I have my blueberry pancakes at the Four Pines, I feel proud.'

'I don't want a coat!' I replied. 'I don't want a rug, either! I especially don't want to watch three baby bears being murdered! Don't misunderstand me, I have nothing against hunting – I've shot birds, rabbits and deer before. But this is something different. This is dangerous, and vile. I can't believe I was tricked into taking part in your awful enterprise. Now, if you'll excuse me, I'm taking the car home.' I turned around and walked away. Behind me, I heard another volley of shots. This was probably one of the low points of my hunting life, and one of the worst near-death experiences as well. As I walked back to the car, stomping angrily through the mud, I decided I would never again go bear hunting or big game hunting, no matter what my friends or neighbours wanted to do. I continued to only hunt what I can eat.

When I bought my Kent house, with its expansive grounds and the beautiful rolling landscape, I anticipated no problems. It was just the sort of serene and quintessentially English setting one imagines when thinking of living in the country.

I was equally pleased with our new neighbours. They were a young couple who occupied what had originally been the gatehouse to the estate where we had the main house. Of course, their property was entirely their own, but it did mean that we lived in quite close proximity to them and therefore became acquainted almost immediately.

The wife, Joan, was in her early thirties, and she cut quite a striking figure with her waves of blonde hair and beautiful, welcoming smile. When she came over to introduce herself, she told me that her great passion in life was her horse, which she kept on their property, and how she hoped that this wouldn't be a bother to me.

I couldn't see why it should be. 'Horses are wonderful animals,' I said, somewhat confused by her bringing it up.

She nodded, eyes bright. 'Oh yes, yes they are. I'm so glad to hear you say that! How wonderful.'

Her enthusiasm only began to make sense as we settled into life in our new home. It was an idyllic countryside retreat, away from city bustle. And there was a locked gate that separated our lives from the lives of our neighbours.

However, one morning Joan came straight through the gate, leading in her horse. I was out on the terrace, enjoying the early sunshine, and was more than a little surprised at this turn of events. Yet Joan was smiling as though there was nothing peculiar going on.

'Good morning!' she waved at me cheerfully and led the horse around me, past my house and into the fields that made up our part of the property. I was slightly too stunned to say anything, though of course in retrospect I should have. Why was she bringing her horse to be ridden on my land? It wasn't as if she was lacking in space herself.

After that day, Joan came through every morning, sometimes leading the horse, sometimes blatantly riding it across my acres. The gate remained unlocked – it may as well have not existed at all, for all the notice she took of it. I watched them go by most mornings, wondering why on earth anyone would think such a thing was acceptable. On some days her husband was with her, and he too, behaved as though the whole property belonged to them, sometimes cantering about on his own horse, sometimes walking alongside his wife.

I hoped that they would just naturally realise that their behaviour was unacceptable, but after a week I was forced to wave Joan down as she rode by.

'Lovely morning,' she said, merry as always.

I was determined to be strict on the matter, though her oblivious friendliness threw me. 'Joan,' I began, somewhat hesitantly, 'believe me, I'm very glad to have you as my neighbour...'

'Oh, I feel exactly the same way. You never know what you're going to get, do you? Some people are just unreasonable.'

I blinked at her complete lack of self-awareness. She had, after all, been trailing her horse all over my land for a week! Yet she believed herself to be the perfect neighbour. 'Um, yes,' I agreed, 'but you must be aware that this is my property? You have your own.'

'Yes?' she asked blankly.

'Well, you understand the idea of private property, don't you? This is my land, after all.'

Then she seemed to grasp what I was getting at, at least a little. 'Is there a problem? I thought it would just be a nice thing to do, neighbourly, you know, if we could be more... communal.'

I couldn't help but stare at her in disbelief. 'That's a nice idea. But perhaps there is such a thing as being too communal.' After all, I wanted to add, who was going to pick up after the horse? Who was going to make sure it didn't trample over anything valuable? I couldn't grasp how she would think such behaviour was neighbourly.

'It was only that convenient and I thought it would be pleasant,' she began.

'The gate is locked for a reason,' I interrupted quickly, 'and I would appreciate it if you didn't open it anymore.'

Joan appeared to understand what I meant at last. 'All right,' she said, still smiling, though in a slightly strained way now, 'I suppose I can see where you're coming from. Sorry for the inconvenience.'

For a few weeks, I saw very little of Joan and nothing of her horse. This was something of a relief. It allowed me to get down to the business of settling into my new home without being concerned over any damage an errant horse and rider might do.

And yet, after this initial period of peaceful absence, one day I happened upon my gate – open again, with hoof prints scattered on the soft, muddy ground around it. I was more than a little upset over the open disregard for my request that our gate and land no longer be used.

It wasn't the first time I had encountered a boundary dispute, but this time I was not going to let myself be taken advantage of. I waited some days to see if Joan had simply forgotten our talk from a few weeks ago, thinking that perhaps she would remember and stop opening the gate. I had no desire to appear unfriendly, but horses aren't the cleanest animals.

Straight away, my land began to show the ill effects of having a horse trotting through it. Some flowerbeds were trampled one day, leaving no choice but to have them dug up and replanted. And as I was walking, I saw that the main lawn was littered with horse droppings that Joan had either not noticed she was leaving behind, or had not seen fit to attend to.

That was the final straw. I couldn't bear to live in such an uncivilised environment, with this woman clearly trying to push literal as well as metaphorical boundaries.

In the evening, when I was sure that Joan had returned home, I fitted a padlock on the gate that made it impossible for Joan to enter my property. I imagined what she would think when she came up against such a barrier – after all, I had always been friendly and generous with her. It was her own fault for not sticking to her own part of the property and, mostly just to get the message across, I had a fence put up around the gate to fully protect it. Just in case.

Joan never rode across my land again, but when we saw her she didn't dare mention it either. There was really no excuse for her to have been abusing my rights in such a way and she must have known it.

'How's the horse?' I asked her pointedly one day. 'Getting enough exercise, I trust?'

Her face pinched a bit. 'Plenty of exercise,' she told me, 'we're quite... fortunate to have so much outside space, aren't we?'

I smiled at her and couldn't help but wonder if she was now using someone else's land for her riding. 'Yes,' I said, 'we are.'

UNHAPPY HORSES

For a time, we had a guesthouse in Bahrain, as our bank was involved in oil financing and consequently quite active in the Middle East. In the early 1970s, much of the region's oil wealth went into building palaces for princes, as well as into infrastructure and development. Just like everywhere else with a sudden influx of prosperity, a large part of the oil magnates' new money was channelled straight into luxury purchases. Their indulgences included palaces, fountains, and racehorses.

The ancient Arab world was famous for its distinctive horses. Arabian horses originated in the deserts near Aleppo: there is archaeological evidence that they have roamed the Gulf for some four thousand years. Of course, their traits have spread across Europe and mingled with other horse types through trade, war, and extensive breeding. They are recognisable by the shape of their beautiful muzzles, their strong, long necks and the high carriage of their tails. They are one of my favourite breeds of horse. I feel like there is something in their posture that comes across as truly royal. Their bloodline is also remarkable for endurance, refinement, speed in races, and an incredibly strong bone structure. They have one small disadvantage for me, however, which is that their backs are too low, in general. Their interbreeding with German and French horses, however, softened this feature somewhat and incidentally produced some of the most beautiful European horses.

I come from a family of cavaliers, and consequently I was interested in the stables that stood near our guesthouse. Consequently, I found myself interested in the stables that stood near our guesthouse in Bahrain. I didn't know to whom the horses belonged, but I loved to go and look at them. They never seemed to be cared for: I never saw anyone feed or groom them, the way one would in France or England. In the West, there are often more human keepers than horses in the stables! Here, however, the horses were all crammed together in these hot little boxes. I would stroke their muzzles and stare into those big, glassy eyes that looked blankly back into mine without pride or fear. They didn't give an impression of being happy or healthy creatures, in fact they hardly felt like horses. They barely reacted when I came in to look at them, only swishing their tails feebly. All around them, the winds of the sirocco blew across the desert, bending the palm trees and filling the air with sand. I wondered how the animals dealt with this; how their surroundings had affected them. They looked well-fed enough, but were far from clean. I was sure their ears must have been full of dirt. At least there were no flies, like in the muddy fields of the south of France, but the circumstances were still less than ideal. As far as I could tell, they were never even exercised or ridden. I didn't understand the point of keeping fine racehorses if one didn't even want to ride them. 'Poor things,' I whispered into their proud ears. I would have loved to take one out and race it across the desert, as its ancient Bedouin owners might have done. What was the good of having these luxury creatures penned up in sandy boxes? Their strength and proud posture would slowly fade, day by day. The beauty of an Arabian horse is best experienced when it runs, certainly not when cooped up for months and months in the desert, while its muscles slowly sag. To keep them this was to destroy the romantic notion of the Arabian horse entirely.

Later in my travels, in Dubai and Abu Dhabi in the early 1970s, I saw the same phenomena repeated all over the Gulf. I found it mind-boggling, that in these very deserts where the original Arabian horses used to roam freely, tossing their proud manes in the desert sun, they were now being kept as little more than deteriorating decorations in ugly stables and tiny paddocks. My guess was that if the oil boom continued for a few more years, those stables would be eliminated entirely to build more skyscrapers and palaces. I couldn't tell if this was a comforting idea. In this scenario, the horses would have been unhappy no more, but instead buried along with the remains of their stables under layers of fresh tarmac! I must admit that, following these visits, I had a rather negative impression of rich oil men from the Gulf having the capacity to look after any sort of animal. This is part of the reason I took a special sort of joy or reassurance from finding out that one of the most expensive stallions in the world was actually owned by an Arabian Gulf prince.

This animal was an incredibly fast racehorse, who was incidentally able to fertilise more than a hundred mares in a single breeding season. It was consequently valued at over a hundred million pounds! Happily, this particular animal was kept in Britain, fed on the finest fresh grass and spring water, and kept in the coolest and most spacious paddocks. It was groomed and brushed constantly, its hooves kept shiny, its mane washed and braided. Finally, it was constantly watched by a CCTV camera: his keeper projected the stream of this video footage on the wall of his house in order to keep an eye on it day and night. One can hardly think of a situation more different to the one of the animals outside our Bahrain guesthouse. There was no dust or restlessness here; no ill-use of beautiful creatures. No, this horse was well and truly a lucky luxury item. I took from this story the knowledge that at least some Middle Eastern men knew how to look after their horses! I only wished this could have been the case for my poor equine neighbours.

In the late 1980s I held executive positions in various Scandinavian companies. I travelled to Norway a few times, as one of our partners had a guesthouse there. Norway is nearly as famous for its wood exports as it is for its forests. The Nordic country has some of the most beautiful scenery in the world, between its wild fjords, dark mountain woodlands and mountains near the sea. It is also famous for its friendly people. I discovered this for myself quite quickly when I met our next-door neighbour.

One day, there was a knock on the door quite early in the morning. I opened the door to find a tall, tanned blonde man standing there like something out of a 1950s advertisement poster for mountain hiking. '*Hei!* Hello! I've noticed you're new to the guesthouse,' he said in a lilting accent. 'I always like to get to know my neighbours.' I blinked a little in the bright sunlight, my cup of coffee having not quite kicked in yet.

'Nice to meet you,' I said a little vaguely. There was a pause. 'Would you like to come in?'

I was fairly sure he was inside the guesthouse before I had finished uttering the words. 'What a lovely house,' he positively cooed. I shook my head.

'Would you like a cup of coffee?' I offered, figuring I would need a second one to keep up with his enthusiasm.

'Oh yes! I'm a sculptor,' he responded. At first I assumed he was making some kind of connection between his acceptance and the statement. Then I realised he was simply moving on with his style of conversation, which seemed to be right on the border between 'enthusiastic' and 'downright aggressive'. He left me no time to respond. 'Can you guess what material I like best?'

I wasn't sure how to answer this question. There was an awkward pause. 'Clay?' I ventured.

'No.'

'Er, bronze?'

'No.' His face remained impassive.

'Stone?'

'Something more alive.'

'Alive? I'm afraid I'm not sure what that might mean... Bone?'

He laughed, a big booming laugh. 'Wood!' he said. 'Wood, wood, wood! We are sitting in this room, at a wooden table, on wooden chairs, and the material didn't even occur to you?'

'Couldn't see the wood for the trees,' I muttered. I suspect the joke was lost on him.

'I'm only teasing,' he said. 'You must understand that we Norwegians have a strange attachment to wood. People always imagine us almost as elves living among the ancient trees, and they're not far wrong. Of course, many of us are bankers and oilmen too nowadays, but still.' He winked at me, rather enforcing the impish image he was giving of his people. I wasn't quite sure what the last comment was meant to imply about my own occupation.

'What wood do you prefer?' I asked, hoping to redeem myself somewhat with a show of interest.

'Pine,' he replied without hesitation, 'although it can get a big splintery. And of course you sometimes get the sap all over your hands. But it's a lovely colour. Norway has a whole variety of different pines, including trees that have no knots. They're the best to work with, as the grain is even and predictable.' I thought that might be the answer to my question, but he continued without a pause. 'I like oak, too. It's a smooth wood, although it's heavy, too. Chestnut and teak are also wonderful woods, if you can get your hands on it. I also like working with maple or beech. And then of course you have rarer woods like American walnut...'

I rubbed my forehead. I wondered if all elves were this annoying in folk tales. They probably were. Perhaps he would make the milk in my coffee go sour next, or produce a golden egg. I was beginning to regret my question, which felt rather like asking a fisherman what his favourite type of fish was.

'Wood is, of course, one of the noblest materials on earth,' he continued. 'Even cavemen must have used it for rudimentary tools, as well as for heating and cooking.'

'What, like cups and spoons?'

He looked at me aggrievedly. 'Like spears. Maybe harpoons. Wood has always been available, except to the peoples of the desert.'

I felt myself blushing, somewhat abashed. 'What are your favourite subjects to carve?' I asked, with a friendly suddenness akin to desperation.

He raised his eyebrows a little at the interruption, but seemed to appreciate the apparent keenness. He sighed thoughtfully. 'Perhaps I should show you my studio,' he said. 'That might be the best way to answer your question.'

I set down my coffee reluctantly and followed him out the door, nearly having to run to catch up with him. We walked out into the cold air and bright sun, and crossed a small space full of gravel and plants into the spacious wooden building next door. In the first thirty seconds of our entry, I must have missed some of his chatter, as I was completely overwhelmed by our surroundings. The room was vast, with a high ceiling and flooded with natural light. It was also completely filled with wooden animals. Reindeers, moose, deer, bears, badgers, squirrels and mice of all shapes, sizes and colours surrounded me. Some of them were absolutely huge; some of them were minuscule. Some were functional, whilst others seemed to be merely decorative. Most of the animals seemed to be creatures native to the Northern European countries, although I hadn't had time to take them all in. There was a whole family of life-sized bears with five cubs, next to a stool shaped like a tiny cow. There was a coat-hook shaped like antlers, and beside it, a table with cloven hooves. Most of the items were stained and varnished, although a few were painted in bright colours, and a few were still raw wood, obviously still unfinished. There were shavings and sawdust all over the wood floor, which smelled strongly of pine. It was all quite overwhelming.

'You've obviously been doing this a long time,' I eventually managed to say.

'Oh yes,' he said, 'nearly all my life. This isn't even a fraction of what I've produced, though, once you count everything I've sold. Most of the houses in the town will have some little piece or other of mine.'

I couldn't help but be impressed.

'And all these pieces last a long time? I would have assumed that wood was not the most permanent of materials, when kept outside.'

'Oh, they should keep for centuries. Of course, there are always risks: insects, mould, and fire, for instance. I used to smoke when I was younger, that was a big hazard. Too much of a hazard. I quit.'

'You've always been a woodcarver, then?'

'Since I was a teenager. The ladies love it,' he added with a suggestive grin. 'All you need to catch the woman of your dreams is to make them a lovely little lovespoon.'

'A lovespoon?'

'You've seen them in all the gift shops, I'm sure. They're a romantic gift to give. Carved in the shape of locks and hearts. It's a traditional, somewhat kitschy Scandinavian tradition. Of course, they have them in Wales, too.'

'I'm not sure I'd want to give away to a woman I was seducing that I was a dab hand with a gouge,' I replied. My neighbour laughed so hard that his face turned bright red.

'Of course,' he added, wiping his eyes, 'it's the practical things that sell best. As you can see, I've made something of a personal speciality out of carving animals. I can make nearly anything you want shaped like some kind of animal: a wine-bottle holder, a desk, a paperweight... Of course, I can make plain ones, too. It's just that the animal ones tend to be more popular, particularly with tourists.' He flashed me a cheeky grin. 'So, neighbour,' he continued, 'if you were in the market for some kind of wooden souvenir, what would you be interested in?'

'I see,' I said. 'Isn't it a little early in the morning for a sales pitch?' I had to smile at his enthusiasm, though.

'Oh no,' he said hastily, 'that's not what I meant! You don't have to buy anything at all, I just wanted to show you around.' I instantly regretted my sarcastic comment.

'Relax,' I said, 'I'd actually love a few of those wooden cups. They seem like they'd be a nice thing to have at a picnic.'

'You can also keep pencils in them!' he added enthusiastically, obviously relieved.

I ended up buying the cups from him, as well as some utensils that I still use to this day: wooden plates and spoons for cooking, as well as a spice rack. My suitcase was quite heavy coming back from that trip! The cups are lovely, intricately carved in Scandinavian-style scrolls. I still keep my pens in them, and think fondly of my brief acquaintance with my enthusiastic Norwegian neighbour.

I never really liked Cairo. In the 1970s, our bank opened a branch there, which meant that I was quite often forced to travel there to see to my work duties. To my mind, the Cairo branch was nothing but a waste of time and energy. We never made much money there, and I spent many precious hours flying to Cairo from Paris and back again after yet another unsatisfactory meeting or string of difficult appointments. The more I visited Cairo, the less I liked it. It wasn't just a groundless prejudice against the place – from the moment I stepped off the plane, I was harassed and hassled by people begging or selling, and forced to jump through security hoops.

And although people came from all over the world to see the Nile, when I laid eyes on it I thought it was filthy and wholly disappointing. It smelled terrible and was full of rubbish and waste. Once I even saw a dead donkey floating downriver. Aside from the river, the city itself always seemed so noisy and overcrowded, overheated. It wasn't where I personally would choose to go for pleasure, but there I was all the same, over and over, attempting to make something out of the bank.

Worst of all, there was no sanctuary from the place. Of course, the bank subsidised all my trips and paid for my accommodation, but the guesthouse they used was not what I was accustomed to. It was dirty and loud and gave no reprieve. I often found myself thinking that one would do just as well to stay out in the streets as there, and preferred to stay at the best hotel, where we would receive clients in a lovely suite with all the modern conveniences one could want.

Almost without exception, my days in Cairo were long and difficult and I tried to cram as many appointments into a single day as possible so that I could return to Paris and not have to stay a second longer than necessary.

However, one trip was particularly noteworthy. I was staying in the hotel overnight, having had a lot of appointments that day, and simply wanted to lie down and sleep. I was to rise early the next day, at six in the morning, to catch the first flight back to Paris. I began to try and get to sleep at about eleven and this was about when the person in the neighbouring hotel suite began to make a lot of noise.

It was as though he was giving a concert. As I lay in bed listening to him singing, I could pick out what seemed like dozens of musical instruments being strummed and plucked and blown. I waited for the furore to die down and thought that perhaps, given that it sounded as though my neighbour had an audience of hundreds, he was only listening to the television at a ridiculously high volume.

It would have had to be a very long television programme. I waited, wondering what to do. If I went over to ask him to please scale back the noise, it could offend him, and it sounded as though he was enjoying himself very much. But I couldn't just lie in bed with my eyes wide open, listening and becoming more and more frustrated with the sheer amount of noise leaking into my suite. After a couple of hours of trying to sleep through the noise, I gave up and went to knock on his door, hoping it wouldn't cause me any problems.

The door swung open and I couldn't believe my eyes. Behind the man who answered, what had to be a hundred or more people were swarming around the room. Now, these were generously sized hotel suites, but even so. The floor had to be bowing under the weight of so many bodies, many of which were on the larger side.

'Excuse me,' I began, a bit hesitant now that I knew it was a party, 'I'm sorry, but...'

'My friend, my friend! Welcome.' Suddenly, I was being enveloped by my neighbour and a cluster of other people, all kissing my cheeks and welcoming me into the room with them. There was no time for me to back out and quickly it dawned on me that this was a wedding party. There was a live band playing on the other side of the room.,

'Welcome!' one woman crowed. 'Enjoy, enjoy!'

This, apparently, served as my invitation to the wedding. The whole party treated me as though I was an honoured guest rather than a sleep-deprived stranger who had wandered in hoping to get them to quieten down a bit.

The whole group of people were dressed in all their finery and the amount of them made it seem like a brightly coloured circus. There were belly dancers twisting around on one side of the room, a buffet table groaning with sweets on the other. My hand was taken by a rather rotund woman I worked out was the bride, who then began dancing with me, trying to draw me in, while her husband watched approvingly and slapped me on the back. He wanted to talk to me in English, but his accent was so strong that half of what he said was incomprehensible. I nodded along for a few moments, laughed when he laughed and assumed he was trying to tell me a few jokes. The closer and more animated he became, the more I wanted to draw away – his teeth were yellow and didn't look as if they had seen a toothbrush in quite a while.

Everyone, the newlyweds included, appeared to think I was a real guest, they wanted me to dance with them and the moment I stopped, muttering a congratulations to the happy couple, I was plied with sweet things by another group of people.

After a little while, I made my way over to the band when where was a brief break in the music. It wasn't all the shouting and foot stomping that had bothered me the most from my room, but the band's loud music.

'Pardon me.'

The singer smiled at me in a welcoming manner. 'Yes?'

'Would you happen to know if you're wrapping this up soon? It's pretty late, isn't it?' I tried to sound jovial about the whole thing. 'People are probably trying to sleep!'

'Oh, well.' He seemed to mull it over. 'I have about thirty songs left. Twenty minutes a song, so...'

I quickly calculated in my head. 'That's ten hours, isn't it?' I asked, slack jawed and fast losing any hope of a peaceful night.

'I suppose so.'

'So you'll be playing until eleven in the morning,' I told him, hoping that he would realise what an obscenely long time this was.

He didn't seem to be worried about it, though. He was bright eyed and ready to carry on. 'If I begin now and don't take a break, we could have finished earlier. Probably not before seven, though. Don't worry, lots of party left!'

Which was exactly what I was worried about in the first place.

I had only allowed myself to be drawn into the wedding out of kindness, but now I felt somewhat stuck. I didn't really feel up to dancing and making merry after a long day of appointments and dinner on top of that. I had my flight to catch in just a handful of hours, but obviously I wasn't going to get much sleep with this rabble going on just next door to me. I had no idea what I was going to do to save the night and not be exhausted come the morning.

I decided it was best to at least tell the reception staff about the unsafe number of people in the hotel suite – my engineering instincts kicked in. However, they were unworried by the large party and assured me it was quite normal.

'Oh, we host weddings all the time. It's not a problem.'

'Are you sure? There are a lot of people...'

'We have large families in Cairo. Very happy, isn't it?'

So I tried going back to my room to read and wait until morning came, but found that the noises from next door were frankly too inviting to ignore. It was nice, after all, to be invited to the wedding of people you had never met, and everybody was so friendly. After a while of trying to concentrate on the morning papers, I ventured back to the wedding, to the dancing and the sweets and the loud Egyptian men and motherly, chatty women. Even though I was exhausted and everybody was sweating from the hours and hours of dancing, it wasn't the worst night I had ever spent in Cairo.

In the end, I went back to my room and shut all the doors, sleeping for an hour in the empty bath tub before I had to get up again to go and catch my flight back to Paris. As I walked down the hall towards the lift, I smiled at the noises of the wedding party, still going on, the musicians still playing, the sounds of laughter and dancing echoing out into the morning.

It seemed as though it would never end.

THE GARBAGE CHUTE

The old, classic apartments of Paris are a strange breed of their own. From the imposing marble staircases to the rickety *cages d'escaliers*, from the loud-mouthed concierges to the elevator that breaks down every week, they have a certain rustic charm best immortalised in black-and-white films from the 1960s, and somewhat less charming in real life. However, certain buildings have odder, less traditional features. For instance, one of the first flats I rented in Paris had a garbage chute. This was, in itself, not particularly remarkable. What was, however, was my neighbour's reaction to it.

I never found out this neighbour's name, as we didn't live near to each other for very long. I hardly ever even encountered him, but when I did, it was hard to forget. He was a small Frenchman with messy hair and a bedraggled moustache. His face was perpetually red, as if he had been drinking or scratching his skin, and he always seemed to be swearing about nothing in particular. I have met a lot of aggressive Frenchmen, and he really was the worst of them. The first time I encountered him, I had just come back from grocery shopping, and I was balancing two packets from a boulangerie and a cheese shop on my arm, with paper bags of food set down around me.

'What on earth is that smell?' he barked at me.

I looked up, rather bewildered. Admittedly, it was not the youngest of cheeses, or the best-wrapped, but it was a classic French Epoisses. 'We're having guests for dinner,' I explained. 'I stopped by the cheese shop just down the road.'

'It smells awful,' he said. 'I hope you'll not be putting the scraps down the garbage chute. They'll stink up the whole building!'

I tried my best not to be offended. After all, I had only just met the man. 'I'd tell you to mind your own business,' I said as gently as possible, 'but surely you won't be able to smell the cheese from the second I step in my own front door. And I must admit I don't understand what you mean about the garbage chute. I mean, anything in there will just go straight down to the dumpster in the basement. There's no way you could smell a thing!'

He hunched his shoulders and shuddered weirdly. 'It's the ants,' he whispered. 'They crawl into my flat.'

'I'm sorry?' I wasn't sure if I should really be engaging with this man, but it seemed a bit rude to walk into my flat while he was talking, and difficult to leave such an odd comment hanging.

'The ants smell things in the chute. They crawl up the chute,' he continued. 'It's full of cheese. Paris is full of germs. And all the garbage chutes are full of ants and spiders.' He shook his head and ran his fingers through his tangled hair, as if searching for insects there. Then, all of a sudden, he ran up to me and picked up my groceries from the floor. With a sweet smile on his face, he brought them into the atrium of my flat. 'Just please don't throw anything down the chute,' he pleaded in a completely different voice. 'Please.'

At this point, I had had quite enough of his weirdness. I nodded as politely as I could at him, and shut the door in his face.

'What was that?' my wife asked from the kitchen.

'Oh, nothing,' I told her, already trying to forget the incident. 'Just some crazy neighbour.' Unfortunately, this would not be my last encounter with him. The opening to the communal garbage chute stood at the end of the corridor shared by the four apartments on our floor. Sadly, the strange neighbour seemed to have a knack for appearing just as one was about to lift the flap to throw one's rubbish down it. Either that, or he was perpetually standing by his door, waiting for the tell-tale squeak. Neither thought was particularly reassuring.

'What are you throwing out?' he asked me, without any small talk, the second time I encountered him. This time, he was only wearing a dirty white bathrobe, and his hair was a complete mess. I sighed. 'I'm just throwing out a few things,' I told him patiently.

'I can smell that,' he snapped. 'It's disgusting.' Suddenly, he sneezed, violently. I jumped back a foot. He wiped his nose on his sleeve. 'You're a disgrace,' he said through his stuffed nose. 'Carrying all those germs around our nice clean corridor. Look what a state you've got me in. I've already caught a virus.'

I tried not to roll my eyes. 'Don't you think it's rather unlikely that you would catch a virus instantly from my garbage? What do you think I have in here, corpses?' At this, the neighbour's eyes widened and he positively leapt back. I tried to stifle a giggle. 'Look, I don't want any trouble.' I propped open the front of the garbage chute. 'Just let me finish doing this and we can leave each other alone.'

With a wail, the man flung himself towards me. For a split second,

I was worried he was going to try to fling himself down the chute, but he only fell on his knees. 'Please,' he cried, 'just take it outside the building! Carry it down to the basement! I'm begging you.'

I was beginning to lose patience. 'Look,' I said as calmly as possible, 'this is completely ridiculous. The concierge empties the bins every day. I'm sure there's almost nothing down there, and there's certainly nothing climbing up it. It's several hundred feet down from your apartment. Now, why don't you get up, go inside and clean yourself up. It sounds like you've got a nasty cold; you should be looking after yourself.'

At this point, the neighbour started rolling around on the floor like a child having a temper tantrum. This was more than I had bargained for in simply trying to take out the rubbish. I finally gave up and carried the smelly bags down to the basement, just like he wanted. Still, something about the episode left me uneasy. The neighbour might have fears of ants and germs, but I wasn't too comfortable with this madman living just down the hall from me!

One day, I decided to ask the concierge about him. Perhaps, I reasoned, there was some explanation for his behaviour: some traumatic episode with the garbage chute, perhaps. What the concierge told me was no less logical, although still surprising. 'Oh, him,' he replied nonchalantly to my polite efforts at description. 'He's completely crazy. I mean, he's actually mentally troubled. He probably will end up in an institution.' This didn't surprise me in the least, considering his behaviour, but it did at least shed a little light on his obsessive character. 'He's always dropping strange things down the chute,' the concierge added pensively.

'What?' This was not what I had expected to hear. 'You mean he uses the chute himself? I thought he was terrified of the thing!'

'Oh no,' the concierge said calmly. 'He's quite happy throwing things down it himself: clothes, insects, bottles of wine. It's just when other people try to use it that he gets weird. I'd recommend that you simply try to avoid him. That might be the easiest way.'

I had to agree, but the whole business had unnerved me considerably. The oddest part was that I became quite conscious of the rubbish chute myself. I didn't like the idea of this man sliding strange things down along the walls of our shared building. What if he made a bomb, or tried to go down it himself? He was certainly not the most reassuring presence on our hallway. The culmination of his strangeness was when he wrote us a letter reminding us to bring the garbage down to the basement. A letter slipped under our door, you might think, wasn't that weird. But no : this was a letter he sent to us on holiday! After that, it wasn't very long until my wife and I decided to move to another building. After all, there is only so charming an old apartment building can be when it is inhabited by a crazy neighbour!

Sometimes, one comes by one's neighbours rather unexpectedly. As one edges slowly out of one's healthiest years, the occasional dramatic change of scene is bound to occur. One could be in the middle of a delightful holiday, riding a horse along the surf on the beaches of Deauville, for instance. Then, all of a sudden, just because of a sudden ache in the lower abdomen, one could end up in an uncomfortable hospital bed. Where one's sole neighbours were the open waves and the warmth of a beloved yearling; suddenly one might find oneself staring up at a clinical white ceiling, in a small room that smells of chemicals and confinement, in the company of an incredibly grumpy French doctor.

When the pain had started, I had luckily been in the company of one of my children, who called an ambulance and took me straight to the hospital. Of course, he was worried it would be cancer, appendicitis, or even some kind of kidney or liver failure. Thus, the first half hour in the waiting room passed slowly and stressfully. At last, we managed to convince the receptionist that the situation held a certain degree of urgency, and a doctor was summoned.

I was told to sit in a wheelchair and wait. The French doctor appeared a good twenty minutes later, rubbing his eyes with one hand and holding a clipboard in the other. He was tall, thin, in his mid-fifties; obviously a very disagreeable man. He had an expression of total boredom and disdain on his face that would have discouraged a braver soul than me! Even as he wheeled me to the room where the tests would take place, he hardly spoke a word. I had a nagging sense that he would much rather be drinking a stiff pastis than spending time with a patient, which was not particularly reassuring. I imagined him being called in from the bistro next door and throwing on his white coat with a sigh. When he did start to speak, I almost wished he had stayed irritable and silent.

'I'm Dr Philippe,' he said shortly, without holding out a hand for a handshake. 'Well, what is the matter, then?' he asked impatiently, as if my mere presence was a vast imposition on his time.

'I have a pain in my side,' I answered as amiably and calmly as possible.

'Where in your side?' he snapped. 'Abdomen? Lower back?

Stomach?'

I glared at him. 'I'm not sure. Low down.' I pointed to the offending spot as precisely as was possible.

I swear the doctor rolled his eyes. 'It might be a kidney,' he sighed, 'or something more dangerous.' He scribbled for a while on his clipboard, callously avoiding giving me any further reassurance. 'Right, come on then,' he said, wheeling me towards an operating room. 'Let's do some tests.'

A few hours later, I emerged relatively unscathed and full of painkillers. My son met me and helped set me up in the small hospital bedroom I had been allocated. Despite the fact that my insurance covered a private room, I was told there were none available, and placed in a twin room with a stranger. My neighbour was asleep when I came in, though, so I figured he probably wouldn't be too much trouble. As we waited for the results, my son and I had ascertained the décor, discussed the doctor's cavalier attitude, and decided the sooner I left the place, the better!

However, when the doctor came back with the tests, he told me I would have to stay the night. 'It's only a kidney stone,' he said rather nonchalantly, 'but we'll need to operate in the morning.' Again, his tone implied that performing surgery was a terrible imposition on his time. Without explaining more about the condition or the procedure, he swept out of the room, leaving me rather intimidated and more than a little confused.

My son shook his head as soon as the door closed. 'Patients! Needing operations!' he scoffed, in a rather good imitation of the doctor's voice. 'It's almost as if they might get in the way of his two-hour lunch break!'

'Now, now,' I said in a falsely conciliatory tone, 'we wouldn't want to take over from his afternoon golf practice, would we!' I sighed. 'Still, you're right. I'm not even entirely sure what a kidney stone is. Shouldn't he have tried to explain?'

'I guess you'll just have to trust them,' my son said hesitantly. 'At least it sounds like you'll be out by the morning,' he added.

'I guess you're right,' I said reluctantly.

In my son's company, I settled into the room as comfortably as I could. We watched a little television and chatted about our plans for the rest of our stay. That night, however, when I was alone and trying to sleep, my roommate suddenly decided to make his presence very clear by howling with pain. I don't know what was the trouble with him; whether his medication had stopped working, or whether there was something mentally wrong with him, but the resulting noises were quite terrifying.

'Eee!' squealed the neighbour. 'Aah!' he shouted.

I tried to speak to him, but he didn't seem to hear or understand me. After a good half hour watching my poor neighbour punch all the available buttons to call for a nurse, and trying to console him as best I could, I started to lose patience completely with this hospital. It was like being locked in a small room with a wounded or dying animal. Combined with the effect of pre-operation stress, lack of sleep, and a ruined holiday, I started to feel completely miserable.

'Ooh!' the neighbour howled. I put my hands over my ears.

All of a sudden, I thought of a sort of solution. My son had smuggled in my portable phone, despite the hospital regulations forbidding it; and I suddenly remembered a good friend of mine who lived locally and happened to be a doctor. It occurred to me that he might be able to help on one of several fronts: calming down my roommate, explaining my own medical condition, and trying to get me out of this crazy hospital! I called him at once, and he picked up after just one ring.

'Trust a doctor to be so prompt in responding,' I said with great relief. 'I'm sorry to have to call you so late, but I'm in something of a difficult situation.'

'Ow!' the neighbour cried out behind me. 'Ooh!'

'Don't worry,' he said at once. 'I know you wouldn't call if it wasn't something quite urgent. What on earth is that noise in the background?'

'My roommate,' I said briefly, before explaining the whole situation. It turned out that my friend had briefly worked at this very hospital, and, by something of a coincidence, actually knew the patient whose room I was sharing! 'He has terrible intestinal pains,' he explained. 'It's as if his intestines are all mixed up, like a coil of rope knotted up on itself. The pain is terrible, apparently, no matter what medicine they give him. Even morphine doesn't seem to work. He's famous in the whole hospital,' he said rather sadly. 'That's why no-one comes anymore. They just don't know what to do. I don't think he'll last much longer.'

'Eee,' the neighbour squealed sadly, and I wondered if he had overheard.

'Even Dr Philippe ignores him,' he added wryly.

'Yes, but I can't imagine anyone Dr Philippe would care about enough *not* to ignore, except perhaps his golf partner, or a barmaid.' I sighed. 'Do other people usually share this room? I mean,' I lowered my voice, 'I don't mean to be insensitive, but there's no chance of me getting any sleep here. Is there no way I could be moved to another single room?'

'Let me see if I can pull some strings,' he said solicitously. 'It's not a good idea to be this stressed before an operation.'

'That's the other thing,' I replied. 'I don't even really know what kind of operation this is. They've told me it's a kidney stone, but they didn't really explain what that even means for me. Will I be able to walk out of the hospital in time for lunch tomorrow?'

'Well, if you're being operated on immediately, it probably means it's become lodged in your urinary tract. Is it very painful?'

'Well, it's painful, but not as painful as the screams of my neighbour!'

My friend was quiet for a moment. 'In my opinion,' he said, 'you really could postpone your operation. If can you stand the pain, it means you could probably just wait it out. Stones pass by themselves in time, you see. I mean, they're very painful to get rid of, but then they're gone, and the whole thing is over. An operation is just a quicker way of getting it done with. But considering your circumstances, maybe you could just leave the hospital tomorrow.'

'Tomorrow?' I said. 'But I was leaving tomorrow anyway! I need to get out of here straight away. Isn't there anything I can do to get rid of this damn thing?'

'Well, there is one thing. It's an old-fashioned solution, one that's pretty much an old wives' tale, except that it works. The French suggest that you simply drink a lot of beer over a period of two weeks. This should wash the stone right out.'

'OK,' I said, 'I'll try that. Meanwhile, if there's anything you can try to do about getting me moved out of here, I would appreciate it hugely.'

I hung up, and immediately rang my butler. 'I need you to bring me a twelve-pack of non-alcoholic beer,' I whispered, with no explanation. My butler, knowing better, did not ask any questions, but responded: 'I'll have them for you in an hour or so.'

That was how I found myself, at three in the morning, drinking six cans of non-alcoholic beer with my butler in a hospital bed, to the sound of a man wailing. I figured I wasn't going to be getting any sleep that night, in any case, so I might as well spend my time trying to cure my ailment. Since the nurses were so bad at coming to look after my roommate, I imagined there was close to no chance of them finding us here. I was right: we were uninterrupted. When I finished the sixth can, I was seized with a pressing need. I stumbled swiftly to the tiny hospital bathroom. I was in such a hurry, in fact, that I relieved myself in the bidet rather than the toilet! This meant that I was in a prime position to see, and hear, a little piece of something that looked like rock fall onto the porcelain. There it was, the famous kidney stone: I was cured! I looked down at it with interest. It was a good four millimetres across, the size of a coriander seed.

I ran out of the bathroom. 'William,' I said, 'you must get me out of here! See, I'm cured! The beer cured me!' Seeing this speech was having little effect, I ran back into the W C and emerged holding the tiny stone aloft. At this point, my butler understood.

'Very good, sir,' he said. 'You'll not be needing an operation, then?'

'I certainly will not!' I retorted happily. 'Let's get out of here.'

At this point, my roommate let out a howl of such terrible fervour that we both jumped in our skins. My butler straightened his tie. 'Yes,' he said, 'let's get out of here. But do leave the stone behind.'

Now, in all hospitals, one has to be checked out. I knew the French would never let me leave as long as I had surgery scheduled for the morning. If I explained I had cured myself, I knew there would be an endless rigmarole of bureaucracy, meetings with Dr Philippe and paperwork before a release would be signed. As I couldn't bear the thought of spending a single more minute in that hospital, I knew my only option was to run away in the dead of night. 'You're going to have to smuggle me out,' I told my butler.

'How shall we do that?'

'I'll need my suit,' I explained. 'That should do it. I can't very well be seen leaving the hospital in this open-backed green horror.'

Thus, at four in the morning, two men in suits were seen leaving from the hospital front door and scurrying towards their car. I wore my hat, so my butler looked like a bodyguard. We walked straight out, as if we were visitors, or just two doctors finishing their shift. As we drove off, I breathed a sigh of relief. 'Just imagine,' I told William gleefully. 'In the morning, they'll come looking for me and find only a load of empty beer cans!'

Much as we had predicted, in the morning I had seven voicemails from the hospital. They must have thought I had been kidnapped, or had fallen out of the window, drunk on non-alcoholic beer! I finally picked up the phone and spoke to our favourite doctor.

'Where the hell are you?' he snapped irritably. 'This is a hospital, not some sort of shop! You can't just run off in the middle of the night! You're supposed to have surgery.'

'Ah, but I don't need surgery,' I replied happily.

'I have seventy more patients to visit!' he said. 'Don't you waste my time!'

'As you wish,' I said slyly, and hung up.

The USA is not known for its aggressive bears in the same way that, say, Canada is for its grizzlies. Even though some of the Northern states actually have grizzly bears of their own, if one were to think of American bears, one would probably conjure up visions of the cute black and brown mountain bears of the South. This is partly due to the widespread cultural influence of Smokey the Bear, who was originally a mascot created by the United States Forest Service and used in campaigns to encourage citizens to prevent forest fires while the able fire-fighters were away at war. Nowadays, Smokey is more widely known as a large, cute bear in a hat that one sees on posters in the forest when hiking or camping.

There were a few such posters visible on a hike I took with my son in the hills of South Carolina, but I gave little notice to the reminder that there might be real bears, too, in these forests. A firefighting cartoon bear was no threat to us, considering that we were neither smokers nor planning to light a campfire. However, that very night, when we were enjoying a well-deserved meal of roast chicken, there was a knock on the door. My son stood up and went to let in his neighbour. I heard them muttering together in the hall, before the man came into our kitchen. 'I'm real sorry to bother you,' he said in a heavy Southern drawl, 'but I thought you guys should be warned about something.' He was a tall, rangy man with bright blue eyes and deep wrinkles; a man in his late fifties who obviously spent quite a lot of time out of doors. Dressed in a farmer's ratty overalls, he had the hardened look of a man who spent most days on top of a mountain. He was, however, a very friendly man, although his accent could at times be nearly impenetrable.

I had met him several times before, and would regularly see him again after this particular incident. I would remember him as a generous guy, who often brought us fresh fruit: mulberries or peaches, or some pine nuts from his trees. Sometimes he would bring us a Key lime pie made by his wife. On this occasion, however, there were no treats in sight. I immediately assumed, from his serious disposition, that he was coming to tell us about a fire, a robbery, or some terrible crime that had been committed deep in these desolate hills. However, once I managed to understand his thick accent, I realised what exactly he was saying. 'The bear,' he kept repeating. 'The bear is eating your trash!' Of course, the way he drew out the vowels, it sounded much more like 'tray-ush,' but the key word that caught my attention was 'bear.' 'It's dippin' right in your garbage!' the neighbour repeated, obviously expecting more of a reaction.

My primary response, frankly, was to freeze with fear. To me, the concept of being near a bear was pretty much on par with coming face-to-face with a tiger in the jungles of India, or ending up in a zoo cage with a lion. My instinct was to panic, and, in a flood of adrenaline, either run away or attack. Of course, this was obviously not the expected neighbourly reaction. I cleared my throat. 'Uh, thanks,' I said. 'A bear?'

He looked at me slightly oddly. 'Yeah,' he repeated slowly. 'It's eatin' your trash.'

'Right,' I said.

My son appeared to be enjoying my nervousness, and did not contribute anything useful. I stood up from the dinner table slightly unsteadily, and followed the neighbour to the window. There it was: a big brown bear, absolutely huge, towering over the edge of our big communal dumpster. It seemed to be displaying absolutely no guilt, aggression, or any kind of care. It didn't even move when we opened the window to get a better view. Maybe it was too busy finding the best rotten pizza or fruit to be bothered by a small noise. By this point my fear had begun to retreat slightly.

'Ha,' I snorted, 'I suppose we aren't much of a threat to it. Surely in these deep Southern states it should have been thoroughly educated to the idea of guns?'

'I've got a rifle at home,' the neighbour volunteered. I suspected my kind of humour might have been lost on him.

'It's not even looking at us!' I scoffed in amusement. 'Not a care in the world. Just a nice free buffet.'

From the window seat, we were not further than five yards from the animal. It was really fascinating for me to watch the bear eat, moving those powerful arms around in the mess of food scraps. 'You should have brought some of your orchard fruit,' I whispered to the neighbour, increasingly entranced, and forgetting my fear in the face of this excitement. 'It's just like being in a David Attenborough documentary!' I exclaimed.

'As long as we don't end up in some local news headline,' my son muttered. He had obviously encountered many a bear in his time and was not particularly interested in getting too close to this one. Either that, or opening the window had had the opposite effect on him: whilst I was rather more excited, he was suddenly a little more scared. Of course, this might have had something to do with the fact that it was his house we were standing in…

'Don't be silly,' I said. 'That bear obviously has quite enough to eat without lunging at our window.'

'Yes, but we would probably be more fun to play with than pieces of garbage!' my son pointed out.

I had to laugh.

'Look, it's eating what looks like a whole pizza. I think we should be safe.'

There was a pause as we watched the bear munching away.

'I wish I had my camera,' I mused aloud. 'I mean, this is pretty scary, but it would be nice to have something to show the kids back home.'

'Your camera doesn't have a flash, though,' my son reminded me. 'It would just be a really blurry photograph of a bin with a furry shadow in front of it. You could probably convince people it was a yeti, if you wanted.'

'I dunno,' the neighbour chimed in. 'I bet that bear wouldn't like a flash very much. It might excite it. It might make it more dangerous.' He sounded quite excited at the prospect.

'I'm not took keen on making that bear angry,' I said hastily. 'I mean, what if it decides it wants to break down our door; come in and attack us with those big strong paws?'

My son's eyes widened. 'You should get your gun,' he said quickly.

The neighbour looked at us with something like amusement. 'It's kind of hilarious,' he commented. 'The way neither of you can obviously decide if you're petrified or thrilled. Like father, like son! I bet you'd taste the same, too.'

'Come on,' I said, not entirely amused at this pertinent observation. 'Bears don't really eat people, do they?'

'Oh, they're peaceful enough when they're well fed,' the neighbour replied coyly. 'But bears get hungry easily, and they're pretty aggressive when they're hungry. That's when they're the most dangerous.'

'Well, considering the things you Americans throw in your dumpsters, I would think we would be pretty safe.'

The neighbour laughed uproariously. To him, this was obviously exactly the same as if he was looking at a squirrel, or a donkey.

'So I understand why you didn't bring any snacks to fend off the bear,' I told him with a grin, 'but what about placating the dangerous human father and son?'

At this, my son laughed. We watched the bear for a while longer, until it got bored and wandered away. From that sighting onwards, however, I always felt a little more wary whenever I saw those posters of Smokey the Bear.

THE NEWLYWED

My wife Hilary, with her kind heart and listening ear, always seemed to attract the lost and lonely in the same way that a Victorian lady might have attracted a crowd of waifs and strays. She was a devout Catholic, and she had a sort of gentle aura that people, especially women, were drawn to. Perhaps it had something to do with her Irish blood, or her scone-making skills, or just her extraordinary patience.

Whatever the reason was, when we lived in the countryside of Surrey, our neighbour Katherine gravitated very quickly to my wife. Katherine was a young married woman, a tall, slender beauty with lovely almond eyes, who lived next door. She was newly married to a city banker by the name of Rob, and not very happily so, even though he was rich and she was beautiful. He seemed a pleasant enough man the few times I met him: English, educated, well-spoken. But there must have been another side to him, one I never personally witnessed, for we would often hear shouting from next door.

These were difficult times in England, with economic troubles seeming to take their toll on the country's general mood. Add to this the many problems all newlyweds face, and I suppose there could be quite a lot to fight about. Frustration at being trapped in the country, the fact that he worked and she didn't, even jealousy – who knows what drove them to fight, but they certainly did.

However, most of the time Katherine was very pleasant to be around. She would come round for tea and explain her life philosophy at length: how she wanted to get ahead, how she thought her life story was tremendously dramatic, how she wanted to start writing her biography even though she was only twenty-six! 'Oh, there's just so much drama in my life!' she would cry. 'I don't know how I can stand it!'

Every day it seemed there was some new bit of tragedy to share with Hilary, some psychological issue troubling her which she needed to sound out at length. I was always torn as to whether to pity the girl or dismiss her stories.

'I just don't know what to do with myself!' she would croak, her eyes welling up with tears.

'Why don't you have a cup of Earl Grey, ' Hilary would respond in her most soothing voice, finding a tissue in her pocket.

Another time it might be: 'He's just so cruel to me!' And her lip would start to tremble.

'Here, try this new green tea,' Hilary would answer, patting her hand, and she would listen to the whole story.

It was hard to believe each of these arguments was quite as bad as they seemed to the young woman. She was a very dramatic girl, who hardly needed any real response or commentary. I suppose she just needed someone to pour her every thought and feeling out to. I used to worry that Hilary was wasting her time on this overemotional creature. But my wife was a charitable soul, and she liked to look after people. I believe she became quite essential to our neighbour's well-being.

Nearly every day in our second year there, Katherine would be in our kitchen just after breakfast and just before dinner. She would arrive most days as soon as I had left for work, and return around the time I got back. The fact that she was encroaching on our family life did not seem to occur to her. She would not even be planning on eating anything, but just wanting to talk. Hilary didn't mind. She wouldn't lose any time over our guest. She would cook while she listened, taking on various roles as mentor and psychiatrist as she fried onions, stirred soups, or braised meat. They settled into this pattern quite happily for several months, until there came a change in Katherine's circumstances: we found out that she was pregnant. The tone of the long conversations became even gloomier than usual. She was worried that her husband wasn't ready to have a child. They were fighting about it, of course, and she escaped to our house more and more regularly.

One day we heard far worse shouting than usual, and the sound of the door slamming. Katherine came in with her face red and blotchy from crying, and her clothes a crumpled mess. I retreated, to leave the women in peace, but I still heard most of the conversation from my bedroom upstairs.

'He's left me, Hilary, he's left!'

'Oh darling,' my wife fussed in her soft voice, 'Come on in, sit down.'

'Oh, god, I'm such a mess, I can't do this,' she cried, sobbing with rage as well as sadness. 'He left me for another woman! He left his pregnant wife! She's probably younger!' She was nearly shouting by this point. 'She's probably skinny! And blonde!'

I didn't follow the next part of the conversation, but there was a lot of weeping, and a steady stream of reassuring noises from Hilary. Then she cried out:

'Oh, I can't keep the baby! I can't do this alone!'

She was eight months pregnant at this point. I looked up from my writing and listened more carefully. It seemed this was quite serious.

'Of course you can,' Hilary said at once, kindly and sternly all at once. 'It's your child, my dear, not his.'

I was a little bit worried by this dark turn to the conversation, but Hilary handled it beautifully. I blessed her patient soul.

'Look how well you get on with *our* new little daughter. Child-rearing is a wonderful and rewarding experience. I'm sure you'll be just fine.'

'But what if I'm too weak? What if I just can't do it?'

'We all have moments of weakness,' Hilary murmured, 'but it gets better.'

They lowered their voices again, and she eventually managed to calm her down.

A month later, the baby came. The husband was long gone by this point, so Hilary went along to the hospital to help. The delivery went smoothly, and the mother and newborn went home quite happily. Hilary helped paint and decorate the baby's room, and for a time I thought the worries had passed.

Katherine became more and more a part of our household after the baby was born. She was having financial difficulties by this point, as a single mother raising a small child, so we had been helping her as much as we could. Her husband had essentially vanished without giving her any financial assistance, so she had to live off her savings. Katherine would often come to our house for meals as well as therapeutic conversations. We sometimes gave her second-hand clothes or food to take home. This went on for a year and a half. The baby was growing into a beautiful, healthy little girl.

One day Katherine came round to our house for longer than usual, staying for almost four hours that morning. She seemed to be in a strangely good mood, bouncing her beautiful baby daughter on her knee, telling Hilary how she was enjoying motherhood, and how she was thinking that she might get married again and have another baby. As usual, she talked for a while about how her husband was a real bastard, leaving her with no help, but she seemed more optimistic than usual in her outlook. I felt cheered by the encounter. It seemed like the young woman had really moved on from her tragic separation and had hope of making her new life work.

The next day, I did not see Katherine in the morning. Instead, one of our other neighbours appeared in the garden. When she got close enough for me to see her face, I realised that something was wrong.

'Oh God,' she was repeating hysterically, 'Oh, it's so terrible!'

'What's terrible?' I asked her 'Are you ok? Do you need help? Shall I call 999? Hilary!' I shouted back at the house. 'Can you come out?'

The poor woman was so upset she was almost incoherent.

'Oh, they're terrible, those cliffs!'

'What cliffs? The cliffs of Dover, you mean?'

'Why don't they have railings?' she cried, 'Why don't they have security?'

There was a sinking feeling in my stomach. At this point I believe Hilary had run out from the kitchen and was standing with me.

'She jumped,' the neighbour said, more quietly.

Hilary calmly put her hand on her shoulder. 'Calm down. Who jumped? Can you just tell us what happened?'

The neighbour seemed to gather herself.

'Katherine,' she said quietly. 'Our good friend.'

She must have seen our faces at this point, and realised we were totally unaware. 'Oh god,' she said, 'Didn't you know? I'm so sorry. The police came to my house about an hour ago.'

Hilary and I stood in shock for a moment, trying to process the news. Suddenly, something occurred to me.

'But the child,' I said, 'Is she ok? Who will take care of her?'

The neighbour burst into tears again.

'She jumped with her!' she sobbed. 'They're both gone.'

Later on that day, as we were sitting in stunned silence, the police came round to our house and handed us a note. It was in Katherine's handwriting.

Thank you for everything, all the conversations and the support. You have been very kind to me and I hope you will not blame yourselves.

I just can't take it any more.
Goodbye,
Katherine.

Hilary and I sat together for a while, staring at the note. It was such a sad story, this emotional young woman abandoned by her husband. I was glad, then, that my wife had been so charitable. I like to think Hilary brought her comfort in those difficult times, even if we could not save her.

Some neighbours are limited to one role, and as such are easily reduced to what is essentially one repetitive anecdote. One such neighbour was an Arabian man who worked in real estate, and kept almost every one of our conversations to that same dull topic. He lived right next to me on Avenue Suchet, and was a rather strange man. Where one might expect an Arabian businessman to appear in traditional robes, this one was usually dressed in an overly-large pinstripe suit and a big, garish tie in red or electric blue. He was not particularly impressive, being short, stout and in his mid-forties, but, from the way he spoke, I gathered that he seemed to consider himself exceedingly charming.

'Can I interest you in some prime real estate?' was as much of a greeting to him as 'Hello' or 'How are you?' He obviously had very little interest in me as a person, seeing me only as a convenient neighbour with enough money to potentially qualify as an investor. He was obviously quite a successful investor in real estate, having gone into the business world at a dynamic time in the early 1980s. For a time, I heard that he was buying apartments for two thousand dollars a square metre and selling them off for six thousand dollars a square metre. Thus, while I watched many clients of our bank lose large amounts of money dealing in manufacturing and various investments in Paris, he obviously succeeded. His success, as he explained it to me, seemed to stem from a rather instinctive approach to seeking out real estate. 'I'm not that interested in the buildings, you see,' he told me with a grin. 'I just want to see how other people live. I'm fascinated by the Parisians, you see.'

Begrudgingly, I nodded. 'It's a very multicultural city, I suppose.'

'I like to look into the lives of others: the furnishings, the food, all the little details that make up a life. Sometimes,' he added brightly, 'you see people arguing or even fighting!'

Altogether, he was a rather strange character whose success in the industry puzzled me and baffled my business associates, but was nonetheless undeniable.

He rarely came to knock on my door without some kind of excuse. I guess he wasn't quite so brazen as to turn up at my house just to try and sell me something! That said, it wasn't beyond him to start flogging a new set of apartment blocks the second he received the cup of sugar, the egg, or the newspaper he had pretended to come over to borrow. Unfortunately, we seemed to run into each other with a surprising frequency due to the fact that our houses shared a small garden. In summer, it was almost impossible to dodge him without abandoning our precious square of sunny grass; a sacrifice which I was unwilling to make. I would be lying there out in the sun, with a cool breeze wafting over me, sipping a glass of cold lemonade and trying to read a newspaper, when I would hear my neighbour's shuffling footsteps. It would be too late to move, and there was almost never an alternative to making awkward conversation. My only hope was to keep our exchanges as short as possible.

'I've heard about some interesting opportunities,' he would simper.

'Ah yes?' I would say, keeping my eyes on the paper and my tone of voice as wholly uninterested as was physically possible.

'Yes, I've invested in some refurbished apartments right on the edge of the seventh *arrondissement*. Spacious, luminous, nice hardwood floors... Just the sort of thing you might like to buy.'

'I'm still not interested in moving, or buying anything,' I replied disinterestedly, cutting off his tirade.

'Ah, but you haven't seen these new apartments! One of them had a young family with five children in it. All Swedish, all blonde, very tidy.'

'This is irrelevant as I already have an apartment in Paris,' I reminded him firmly. 'If you just turn around, you will see it in all its glory. You know this,' I added calmly, 'because you are my neighbour.'

'Perhaps you might be interesting in a little something outside the city, then?' he continued as if unaware, in his smoothest salesman's voice. 'You might be seemingly happy with your flat, but are you happy with its location?'

I sighed in exasperation and set down my paper. 'Look, if you don't keep mentioning this, I'll assume you're just trying to kick me out of our communal garden. I just want to read the Sunday newspaper in peace.'

The Arabian neighbour put up his hands in mock apology. 'Don't take offense,' he said with an unnatural little laugh. 'I'm glad you are my neighbour. But just so you know, if you were to be interested in moving into one of these apartments, I would happily buy your own house off you.'

At this point, I would usually give up and move inside, slamming the door behind me. This had no discernible effects, as the very next time I saw him, we would have a near-identical dialogue. Unsurprisingly, this quickly became quite tiring.

At the end of one of these similar exchanges, I remember becoming more exasperated than usual. 'Why do you keep doing this?' I snapped at him. 'I'm obviously not interested in buying or renting any of these places, and I'm certainly not interested in selling my own house! Why do you keep asking me for something you know I won't ever agree to? It's a waste of time for both of us!'

'We've got to do a deal!' he replied at once, as if this were obvious. 'I'm a businessman, you're a businessman.'

'That's hardly sufficient reasoning for a partnership!'

'You're a banker, can't you do me a favour? You must have so many clients.'

'None of my clients are interested in buying property. If they were, I would have told you. Meanwhile, you're wasting your time.'

'What else is there to do in Paris?' he asked calmly.

'I don't know,' I responded shortly, 'go to the cinema?'

'I can't go to the cinema,' he replied rather demurely. 'It's against my religion.'

I exhaled deeply. 'You could go out to a restaurant for a meal?'

'Nobody does good stuffed lamb in Paris. I would rather cook my own.'

'You could... go to an art gallery, or a museum?'

'I'm not interested in Western art. Anyway, there are far too many nudes in the museums.'

I resisted a strong urge to grab him by the shoulders and give him a good shake. 'Why on earth are you even living in Paris, then, if you have no interest in the local life?'

'There's excellent real estate here,' he responded apparently without irony.

I gave a strangled sigh and moved back inside. This conversation did not stop repeating itself until, at last, the Arabian businessman had managed to make so much money that he bought a private hotel, south of the Seine in the seventh *arrondissement*. He converted into a palatial residence, complete with staff and opulent Arabian décor. At this point, he disappeared from my life, and I never heard from him again. Before he left, though, he made sure to try to sell me his own apartment!

If one were asked to name the disagreements of life in a small Arabian town or city, one would probably not have to think very long before naming the intense heat, dry air and dust, or the poverty in the backstreets. One would, however, not be likely to instantly think of dogs. I maintain, however, that one of the strangest things about life in Arabia is the sheer number of strays. They are everywhere: in the deserts, in the city centres, in the town streets. Mangy, thin, flea-bitten, limping creatures abound. They roam the streets, barking at cars, peeing on street corners, scratching at tree trunks, nipping at passers-by's legs, chewing on rags and breaking into garbage cans. They are smelly, hungry and a little bit scary. When you see one of these dogs, you never know if you're supposed to throw them a piece of meat, or run away before they bite your foot. They all look like they need care, although I don't know what would do the job: a hairbrush, a loving child to pet them, a shot from the vet?

Whatever their story and whatever the imagined solution, these stray dogs were a feature of every business trip I took, up until 1975, when I was staying in our guesthouse in Riyadh.

Our company had several guesthouses in Arabia and the Gulf following the oil euphoria of the early and mid-seventies, one of which was based just outside this Arabian city. It was a tumultuous time for the oil business. As our own companies expanded, we opened successive rep offices in Riyadh and Al-Khoubar. We were not the only ones riding this wild wave of development. Companies from all over the world came pouring in to grab what they considered to be their fair share.

Thus, our neighbours evolved along with the economic situation. First, labourers came over from Sudan, then from Egypt. Then the Arabian companies discovered they could get cheap labour in the form of Muslim Filipinos, whom they probably paid less than a thousand dollars a month. After that, they discovered Indonesian labour, and finally, in 1975, there came a wave of Korean migrants. These neighbours settled in around us, moved into the cheap accommodation, and began adjusting to the large local population of stray dogs. Everyone was fairly friendly. We were all busy trying to make the most of the oil rush to be too caught up in minor neighbourly disagreements. That said, there were a few curious characters among the final round of arrivals, and one of them was Mr Park.

Mr Park was a tall Korean gentleman in his late forties, who had become a manager of one of the local branches and liked to wear a pinstripe suit at all times, even though it made him sweat profusely in the dry heat. He was quite pudgy, with a somewhat greasy face, but he was very friendly. We had a few agreeable conversations when he first moved in, over strong coffees. His house always smelled very strongly of pungent meat cooking, but I put my distaste down to my lack of knowledge of home-cooked Korean food. I knew kimchee pickles were made of fermented cabbage, so I assumed that couldn't help with the kitchen effluvia.

He explained to me that a new wave of construction workers had just been brought in from Korea by the companies, hired through various agencies, and that he had been drafted in to supervise the whole operation. 'I'm running the principal construction project here,' he told me with a thin smile. He was obviously quite proud of his position. I stayed silent, as he obviously wanted to boast some more. A dog started barking loudly outside. 'There are thousands of Koreans in the Gulf right now,' Mr Park continued, nodding away strangely to himself. 'They're all over the place: Jeddah, Riyadh, Al-Khoubar, you name it. Korea intends to be at the forefront of these developments and stay there.'

I smiled as amiably as I could in response to this odd speech. 'You must be very proud.'

I thought no more of our conversation. Over the following weeks, I did not spend much time thinking of any of my neighbours, as my mind was taken up with a new phenomenon I had noticed: the dogs had started disappearing. All the mangy stray dogs that haunted our neighbourhood seemed to be vanishing. When once I would run into them on every street corner, and hear them howling every night as I went to sleep, I began to notice a new silence. Around that spring of 1976, I remember going for a chat with one of the municipality officials there, a quiet man by the name of Abdul Hamid. I thought I might be able to find out a little more about the situation.

'I guess you must have some sort of new cleaning system, or a better garbage collection strategy in place, no?'

He looked at me, rather puzzled. 'What are you talking about?'

'Or is it just that you've hired some dog catchers?'

Seeing he was looking at me rather blankly, I thought I had better explain my theory. 'I mean: everything in the neighbourhood just seems tidier and quieter than usual. Almost all of the stray dogs have disappeared.'

Abdul Hamid looked at me and laughed. 'Ah, that! Well, why don't you talk to your neighbour, Mr Park. He can tell you exactly what's happening.'

'What do you mean?'

He frowned a little. 'Come on, can't you work it out? Have you ever been to his house? Have you never been invited over for a little doggie barbecue?'

I looked at him in shock. 'He's barbecuing the stray dogs?'

'Well, maybe not exactly. But he certainly eats them. It's great for us: keeps them off the streets! For him, it's a big delicacy. A traditional South Korean food. Why don't you go ask him about it yourself?'

The next day, I did. I walked over to Mr Park's house, feeling slightly more uneasy about the smell of cooking meat than I usually did. When I cautiously broached the subject, he admitted to it at once, with great enthusiasm. 'Oh yes,' he said with a broad smile. 'I have been eating them all! You're not one of those softies who can't stand the thought, are you?'

I swallowed and declined to reply. 'But surely you can afford to buy nice meat from the markets here? All the nice lamb and beef for stews?' I asked politely.

'You don't understand,' he explained patiently, 'it's not because of poverty. Dog is considered a delicacy in our food culture; we call it *Gaegogi*. It's traditional. Besides, many people in China and the Philippines eat dog, too. Of course, it's great to have such a cheap source of food, don't get me wrong.'

'You mean all Koreans eat dog?'

'Well, a certain number of us do. Many of the younger generations have been influenced by Western thought on the question, and try to avoid it. But I grew up eating it with my family, and I love to cook and eat it.'

There was an awkward pause. 'I'm actually cooking some now,

if you would like to try it!' I declined hastily, and he laughed. 'As you wish. I often make a stew called *boshintang*, with green onion and chili powder. It's delicious with rice. Sometimes I make a soup; sometimes I add bamboo shoots. It's like any meat, really, you can do anything with it.'

'Well, keep up the good work, I guess! It's certainly easier to sleep at night without those strays everywhere.' I smiled as brightly as I could.

'Thanks for dropping by,' he said with a polite nod. 'And if you ever have any dogs you want to get rid of, just bring them to me.'

I never did, of course. However, from then on, whenever I found myself in an Arabian Gulf city that was overrun by strays, I would think back to Mr Park and his strange-smelling house.

THE PROTOCOL NEIGHBOUR

For a time in the early 1970s, my banking colleagues and I went through a phase of exchanging apartments. Thus, I found myself moving periodically from apartment to apartment, from Brooklyn Heights to the West Side of Manhattan to the Upper East Side.

One of these exchanges took me to a beautiful high-rise by the river, in the Upper West Side. In those days, this was the heart of a fascinating neighbourhood, with a rich intellectual and cultural life. Having only recently moved to New York from Dallas, a big port with two million people yet no theatre or opera house, it was a wonderful shock. My neighbours, especially close to Broadway and the West Side, were mostly professors from Columbia, avant-garde poets, ballet dancers and painters. This was the best thing about life in Manhattan, both a cultural melting pot and a hotbed of intellectualism.

In any case, I was thrilled with this particular exchange. My colleague took over my apartment in Brooklyn Heights, and I moved into the Upper West Side with my wife. Almost the minute we had finished unpacking, my next-door neighbour came knocking. Wiping the sweat from my forehead and brushing Styrofoam worms off my lap, I wearily walked over and opened the door.

'Welcome to the neighbourhood, dear neighbour,' the man who appeared said smoothly. 'I'm David.'

I had to do a double take. He was impeccably dressed in a three-piece navy suit with shell buttons, over a wide-collared white shirt, perfectly ironed. He extended a manicured hand to me, which I took gingerly with my own sweaty fingers.

'Bradley. Pleased to meet you,' I added hastily. There was a long pause. Obviously, I was expected to make the next move. He adjusted his thick-rimmed glasses, which gave him a distinctly professorial look, and I couldn't help but wonder how he kept his hair so sleek and shiny. I could have sworn I could see comb marks in it. 'I would ask you in,' I said hesitantly, prompting my neighbour to produce a smooth smile, 'but I've just been unpacking, it's all a bit of a mess in there. Why don't you come round for coffee sometime next week?' I could tell that this was not the proper response, but my neighbour was obviously too polite to object.

'Right,' he said, 'or perhaps you could come meet my wife tomorrow evening? Cocktails at eight?'

'Actually, I don't drink,' I said. I had been about to make excuses, but the thinly-veiled look of horror on his face made me reconsider. 'Meeting your wife would be delightful, though, I'm sure.'

My new neighbour smiled thinly. 'I just thought it would be nice to welcome you both to the neighbourhood. We like to be acquainted with everyone, so it's a comfortable environment for us all.'

'Who was that?' my wife asked when I came back in. 'Someone who's very keen to be our new neighbour,' I replied. 'We're having drinks with them tomorrow.'

David's apartment was one of the tidiest places I have ever seen. It was furnished in extremely expensive and fashionable materials, in shades of burnt orange and jade. Despite these obvious attempts, it was all rather boring and impersonal. It hardly looked like someone could even live there. It was far more akin to stepping into a five page spread in a catalogue than walking into someone's home! 'Good evening,' David said, materialising mysteriously like a character appearing in a sitcom. The room was brightly lit, which made me a little uncomfortable. David was wearing a mustard turtleneck under a tight suit in a sort of chestnut chequered pattern; he obviously cared a lot about his appearance. He was carrying a tray of strangely coloured cocktails, in shades of red and pink. 'These are piña coladas,' he said. Before I had time to protest, he smiled. 'Don't worry, we made you one without alcohol. A virgin colada. A mocktail, if you will.' I smiled. 'It's nice of you to have us over,' I said a little nervously. There was another long pause.

'We're glad you're here,' his wife finally said. David and his wife were both tall and boring, a couple in their late fifties who obviously had plenty of money, and had become rather snobbish.

Everything David did seemed to operate along some mysterious set of rules. It was quite exhausting trying to follow them all. The way he combed back his hair, the way he passed around the tray of baked snacks and cubes of pineapple, the way he held doors open for his wife. Everything seemed to have some sort of smooth system. It was both impressive and sort of terrifying. The mocktail, incidentally, was not at all to my taste, but it would have been impossibly rude to refuse it, so I downed it with a stiff smile.

By the time we sat down to dinner, I was quite relieved to have eating to look forward to as a relief from the strained conversation. However, when we sat down, we found four sets of cutlery facing us. I sighed. 'So are you planning on having children here?' David's wife asked unexpectedly, as David fussed about with the final touches in the kitchen. I looked up in surprise.

'I'm sorry?' There was an awkward silence. The family's elaborate protocol rules did not seem to have much room for unexpected turns in a conversation. I decided on a simple answer, despite feeling this was actually rather rude. 'We're only here for a few weeks,' I said simply. 'We're not moving here permanently. This is just an apartment exchange.'

'Well,' David said stiffly, setting down the glazed baked ham. There was a strained silence.

'We had no idea!' his wife said awkwardly. 'I mean... How is that possible? Are you on holiday? You don't sound foreign.' David shot her a look. I stepped in as gracefully as possible.

'No, nothing like that. You see, my colleagues and I at the bank where I work, we have set up this system where we swap homes for a few weeks at a time. It gives us a chance to see other parts of New York, get to know the local sights, make some new friends.' I flashed the brightest smile I could muster. Obviously, this triggered David's usual talent with protocol, and he stepped in.

'Of course,' he said softly. 'It's always a pleasure to meet new neighbours, even passing ones. So how does this system of yours work? How is it organised? Are there rules regarding who is allowed to stay where? I've never heard of such a thing.'

His wife, obviously struggling to keep up on the politeness scale, added: 'I did wonder how such a young couple could afford a prestigious property on the riverside.' David coughed.

'Dear, they obviously have a system of exchange.' I caught my wife rolling my eyes at me, and found it hard not to laugh.

'Actually, our own apartment is in Brooklyn Heights.'

'I like your view of the river, though,' my wife added.

In the end, some sort of civility was achieved and we made it through to the end of the meal without any substantial diplomatic incidents. Still, I was rather relieved by the time we arrived back to our own temporary home.

'I don't think David's rules and regulations are making his life any smoother. I'm pretty sure he was following his own protocol impeccably, and it didn't make that any easier!' my wife observed and I had to agree.

'I'm quite sure conversation would have been easier if he had just relaxed a bit. Still, I guess he fancies himself something of an intellectual. It must just be the way he was raised.'

After this, my interactions with David boiled down to a single model. If I was emerging from my door, or unlocking it after a long day's work, my neighbour would suddenly materialise in the shadows. 'Hello,' he would say smoothly. It was difficult to avoid David, as he took quiet offense so easily at even the tiniest suggestion that I had other plans than talking to him. In some ways, I enjoyed interacting with David. It was certainly entertaining to watch how he seemed to dress to match his moods. One day he would be wearing a snazzy red suit with gold buttons, and have shaved his facial hair into a Salvador Dalí style moustache. The next evening he would be wearing head-to-toe black, and clutching a volume of Nietzsche to his side. He obviously took his intellectual aspirations seriously, although I could never get him to explain exactly what he did with his days or how he earned his living. 'I'm a philosopher,' he liked to say. 'At the moment, I'm very into Jean-Jacques Rousseau.' If that was his mood, he probably would have had some kind of loose green shirt on, or even a hippie necklace under his shirt collar. Sometimes he would go further, and call himself an 'intellectual counsellor,' not that I know what that meant.

He never expanded on the specifics of his employment, and he had a way of dodging questions with skill that was impossible to fight back against. I assumed he must have been some sort of part-time professor, but discussing logistics was obviously distasteful to him. In any case, whatever his exact employment, David seemed to have latched onto me as some sort of intellectual companion. Now, much as I am happy to talk about art, philosophy or politics at most times of day, being ambushed on my staircase was not my favourite way of approaching heavy topics. One day he might start with: 'Bradley, have you read about this Christo man? He's been wrapping up bridges and buildings and calling it art. I find it tacky and fascinating all at once. What do you think?' Another time it would be: 'Have you been to the latest Picasso exhibition at the Met? It was supposed to be marvellous, but I thought it was completely uninspired.' Whatever time of day it happened to be, David always seemed to be as carefully put together as an art installation, his beard and moustache carefully thematically trimmed and shaved; every part of his outfit considered. He might be found lounging on the bannister at seven thirty in the morning, dressed in a teal overcoat, telling me how, in his not-so-humble opinion, modern art had never became any better than Cubism or Pointillism. Another time, he might be waiting for me in red tartan trousers, hoping to discuss the merits of Sartre. One of the funniest aspects of these encounters were that although David obviously thirsted for conversation, his idea of protocol required him to choose the topics in order to enjoy the exchange. Thus, when I once tried to engage him on the topic of Hollywood, he angrily replied that Hollywood had deformed most ideas and philosophies beyond recognition and only wanted to amuse the public to make money. Then he moved seamlessly back to whatever topic he had planned in the first place!

It was strange and exhausting. I found myself incredibly grateful for the fact that we were only to be living in that building for a few more weeks. Although a part of me was curious to find out just how outrageous his wardrobe could be, and just how changeable his views on modern art might prove, it hardly seemed worth the constant hassle. My wife had found that evening intolerable, and tried to avoid any contact in the meantime. Although she enjoyed my tales of David's madness, calling him 'kooky' on a regular basis, she was as keen to escape sharing a building with him as I was. It seemed that every time I opened the door to our apartment, I would run into him! I never once knocked on his door in all that time as neighbours.

Well, that's not entirely true. I did knock once, on the day I came to say goodbye. Rather touchingly, David looked crestfallen at the news. It occurred to me all of a sudden that he must be quite lonely, if he sought my company so often. I couldn't imagine it being easy to maintain friendships with such a strict set of rules. 'I've enjoyed having you as a neighbour greatly,' he said rather formally, sticking out his hand and looking me in the eyes. 'Are you going to be far away?' I caught a wistful note in his voice and tried to smile.

I gave him my new address, adding: 'You can easily take the subway from here to come and see me. It would always be a pleasure.'

'The subway?' David looked puzzled, then shook his head. 'I never take public transport.' I stifled a grin.

'I guess that's why you are so thin, then!' I replied. There was a pause. For a man who aspired to such high standards of protocol, he was remarkably bad at following turns in conversation.

'Yes, well, I... will be sad to see you go,' he finished awkwardly.

Of course, after moving out, we never saw David and his wife again. I suspect he never changed!

SQUATTERS IN LANZAROTE

In the early 1980s, the Canary Islands were a very popular place to buy property. Spurred on by a period of relative economic prosperity, there was a leap in the number of developments, including on Lanzarote. This was largely carried out by a number of Scandinavian and German companies that constructed a series of beach houses and apartments along the rocky coastline.

Through our bank's various investments there, I found out about this trend relatively early on and decided to get on board. Our family bought a lovely little hacienda-style house, a bright white four-bedroom place with a terrace and stairs that led to a small private beach. The views were incredible, and the setting was a hit with all the family from our first holiday there. The first few times we visited, we had a wonderful time there, in what felt like a luxury, secluded location. However, there is one real flaw with getting on board with trends near their beginning: the longer we stayed there, the busier our setting became. Little by little, similar properties started popping up around us, like some kind of fungus growing on the beach. Where once we had owned a secluded holiday property, we were suddenly the centre of a cluster.

Of course, this wasn't too much of an issue, since we only used the place as a holiday home, and visited once a year or so. I actually preferred to visit in the spring, to avoid the boiling heat of high summer. Our long absences, however, did not go unnoticed by our increasingly large number of neighbours.

One day, I arrived on our doorstep to find our once idyllic holiday setting much changed. I found that we had somehow become the centre of a vast construction site. There was gravel everywhere, and the air was full of dust. There was something stranger than that afoot, as well, but I found myself unable to put my finger on it. Something was definitely wrong with the house. For one thing, there was a strange man sitting on the doorstep, smoking a cigarette and tapping the ashes onto the steps with an apparent complete lack of concern. I stood in front of him with my suitcase, unsure what to say to get him to move.

'What is it?' he said rather rudely, in a thick Spanish accent.

I frowned. 'I think you'll find you're sitting on my doorstep,' I said, as politely as I could.

He raised his eyebrows comically. '*Your* doorstep?' He started laughing so hard that his laugh turned into a hacking cough. Then he spat on the ground, suspiciously close to my foot. 'This is my house, *señor*,' he said.

I felt something like rage boil up inside me. 'Listen up, *señor*,' I said. 'I bought this house nearly two years ago. I have taken two planes and a taxi to get here. I am hot, sticky and tired. I would like to set down my suitcase and have an iced coffee in my own kitchen. I do not want to stand here arguing with some strange man. Now please move aside.'

The man laughed his horrid laugh again, although there was a nastier side to it now. 'Very well,' he said with a mock bow, stepping away from the stairs. 'Go on,' he said, gesturing up at the door. I had the feeling that something was terribly wrong, although I couldn't quite place it.

'Thank you,' I said coldly. It bothered me quite a lot that the man wasn't moving from the bottom of the stairs, but I tried to ignore him as I climbed up. I opened the front door and stepped into the house.

As soon as I was inside, I understood that all my misgivings had been right. Something was terribly wrong: someone else was living in this house. There were shoes and clothes flung on the floor, along with wrappers from food and something that looked suspiciously like cigarette ash. Everything was covered in dust, and the whole place smelled strange, like someone else's house. It was horrible and deeply uncanny. I simply could not believe it, nor shake the feeling that I would blink and the whole thing would have been a trick of a heat or a nightmare in the back of a taxi. But this was not the case, and the worst realisation was still to come, as I found out as I walked towards the kitchen, hoping to have a cold glass of water to steady my nerves. This was when I suddenly realised that I was not walking, as I should have been, towards the back wall of the house, but towards another open room. A room that had definitely not been there before. A room that belonged to somebody else. I felt my stomach sink as I realised what had happened: someone had broken down the wall. Abandoning my dream of a glass of fresh water, I dropped my suitcase and ran back to the front of the house, where the man was sitting with a new cigarette.

Resisting the urge to roar, I simply raised my voice a little. 'What on earth has happened to my house?' I asked, articulating the words very clearly. 'Someone has broken in. Someone has broken down the walls.'

'It is a renovation,' he replied coyly, stubbing his cigarette out on our stairs. 'We expanded into a… usable space.'

'Usable space?' I repeated in disbelief. 'You're talking about someone's home! Our holiday home!'

He shrugged. 'Nobody is ever there,' he replied calmly. 'We thought it would be better used by our family. This way, all our children have separate rooms. It has been great.' He flashed me a totally unapologetic grin, displaying dirty brown teeth.

I tried to contain my now-seething rage. 'Are you really telling me that you expanded your house into ours?' I asked.

He didn't even bother to reply, simply nodding. For a minute or so, we simply stared at each other, each obviously trying to gauge the other's willingness to engage in a verbal or physical fight.

'What else have you done?' I finally asked. 'Are you cooking in our kitchen? Sleeping in our beds?' In some ways, I realised I would rather hear the extent of the damage from this strange man that have to ascertain it for myself.

'Yes,' he said quite happily. 'Of course. It is ours now.' Either he genuinely did not perceive how infuriating this conversation was, or he enjoyed the thought of winding me up. I presume it was the latter, as he continued: 'we have also built two new terraces with views over the sea.' He then proceeded to cheerfully add insult to injury: 'Now that you're back, you can stay with us, if you want.' He gave a nasty little smile.

I was flabbergasted. 'Right,' I said finally. 'I hope you realise that this awful, destructive behaviour is completely illegal. You've not only trespassed, but engaged in irredeemable acts of vandalism.'

The man stared right into my eyes and spat on the ground again. 'So sue me,' he said. I was left with no choice but to go stay in a hotel. Of course, I rang my lawyer the second I left the site, but the case was bound to last months. As I had only been meant to be there a few days, I decided it was easier to abandon ship until the situation was somewhat clearer. I had no desire to be anywhere near that destroyed house, let alone stay in it, until we could completely recover it for ourselves, erasing any trace of its previous occupants and rebuilding, if necessary.

I knew it was ambitious to hope that this plan would go well, or be executed quickly. Still, I didn't think it would take more than six months to throw the squatters out and fix the damage they had caused. Having not heard back from the lawyer for a while, I figured it must be safe to head back. It was by then nearly autumn, which isn't usually too busy a time in Lanzarote. My encounter with my strange Spanish neighbour seemed distant enough to have become amusing; almost unreal. I stepped off the plane into the warm air with something like a sense of anticipation.

I should have known not to be so confident. As soon as I stepped out of the taxi, I knew I should not have trusted our lawyer so easily. After all, he was a local: perhaps he was even in cahoots with the squatters! Whatever the cause, our house was still obviously overtaken and occupied by the offenders. At this moment, the front door swung open and slammed into the wall behind it. 'Buenos días,' the neighbour sneered. 'You've been away a long time!'

I tried not to lose my temper, opting instead for sarcasm. 'Still living in my house, I see,' I said, 'like some kind of cockroach. How charming. How pathetic. Don't you have a place of your own?'

He grinned, displaying blackened teeth. 'Oh yes,' he said, 'it's very big now. Very messy. We enjoyed our two new terraces over the summer. And my children love having their own bedrooms.'

I couldn't stand to have another single minute of this conversation. 'I'm going to call my lawyer,' I told him, turning my back on the whole dreadful scene.

Of course, as with all my previous calls, the call went straight to voicemail. I left the lawyer a strongly-worded message, and decided to walk down to the beach to clear my head before deciding on a course of action. As I emerged behind the house, it emerged that further changes had taken place in my absence: a huge concrete building had appeared between our hacienda and the sea. Worse, as I tried to breathe in the sea air to calm down, I found it tinged with oil, garlic and oriental spices: it was the unmistakable, overwhelming smell of a Chinese restaurant. As I tried not to hyperventilate, I began to wonder how I had ever hoped for an improvement in our situation. I walked around to ascertain the full extent of the damage. The new balconies were still present on the side of our building; and nothing had been even remotely cleaned up or rebuilt to anything like its former state. My shoulders sagged, and I walked away from the house. It was obvious that even if the house was recovered, the coastline and crashing waves would no longer be visible from the bedrooms. Besides, everything would obviously be overwhelmed by that awful smell. I turned back and walked towards the house again. At this point, the Spanish neighbour appeared at the window grinning and waving. This was the last straw. I walked back to the water's edge and dialled my lawyer again. This time, he picked up.

'Why hello, Bradley!' he said amiably. 'What can I do for you?'

'I'm in Lanzarote,' I said sharply, cutting to the chase. 'I haven't found quite what I expected here, if you know what I mean. Why didn't you tell me you hadn't made any progress with the case?'

There was an embarrassed silence, then the lawyer cleared his throat. 'Oh,' he said, obviously putting on as friendly a voice as he could muster, 'we've made plenty of progress. It's just not quite finished.'

'Not quite finished?' I cried out. 'Not only has nothing improved, but things are quite a lot worse now! The squatters are still here, waving at me from the windows of my own holiday home and practically spitting on my feet. On top of that, somebody has now built a Chinese restaurant. I wish you could smell the horror that surrounds me right now. It's rendering me incapable of enjoying the views. Views, I might add, that I can no longer see from my house. I essentially have two neighbours from hell.' I took a deep breath and paused, having vented most of my spleen. There was a long silence.

'A Chinese restaurant,' he said thoughtfully. I was glad I wasn't in his presence, so he couldn't feel the full wrath of my glare. Instead, I directed it out over the waves, into the late summer sunshine.

'Yes,' I replied frostily. 'The property is essentially ruined in every way.'

'In every way,' he repeated.

'What is this, the echo service?' I replied angrily. 'You're supposed to be a lawyer! I need you to solve this case for me. What have you been doing for the last six months?'

There was a very long pause. Eventually he spoke again, although not to answer my question. 'They obviously built the restaurant without permission,' he said thoughtfully.

'They knocked in the walls of my house without permission!' I retorted angrily.

'In 1981, you paid six thousand dollars for this house,' he continued, as if I hadn't interrupted. 'If none of this had happened, it would now be worth a good two hundred thousand.'

'It probably would,' I said. 'But I'd be lucky to get a quarter of that if I sold it now. The place is wrecked. I'm going to need compensation for all the repairs. This is your job,' I reminded him.

'Of course, the value will go down because of the loss of the view, too.'

I hardly knew how to respond. 'Yes,' I said simply.

'In essence, the whole investment has been a loss. You might be better off simply moving on from it.'

'Well, that's not really an option, is it? No matter how you look at it, I'm not getting my initial investment back.' At this point, I nearly hung up on the man, I was so frustrated at the situation.

However, he was not quite finished. 'I have a proposal for you,' he said, unexpectedly. 'I have decided not to charge you any lawyer's fees, on condition that you sell me that house for the price you acquired it for.'

'What?' I said. The request had completely taken me by surprise. 'You want to buy my house?' I couldn't believe it. 'Wait, is that why you've been taking your time with my case?' I asked suspiciously. 'Are you in cahoots with these trespassers and rogues?'

'Oh no,' the lawyer said, as innocently as he could. 'I'm struggling with the difficulty of the case, though, I won't lie to you. If you decide to go on with it, it will be expensive. It's very difficult to get squatters to leave.'

I sighed. At that moment, a whiff of rancid oil and chilli blasted across from the restaurant. 'OK,' I said wearily. 'I don't want to think about it anymore. Just take the damn house. I'll start over somewhere else.'

'Are you sure?' the lawyer said tentatively.

'Just take it away,' I replied.

That was the last time I saw that house in Lanzarote. The lawyer returned my initial investment, and spent the next five years kicking out the squatters, although he tolerated the Chinese restaurant. Thanks to him, I had to admit that I had wasted nothing but my time. Of course, with the current Spanish crisis, the house value might have have gone back down again. Perhaps my lawyer simply helped me make the most of a bad investment. I did not regret the place, nor did I miss my neighbour.

My family had a country house in the Northern shores of Kent, not far from Whistable. It was a lovely location, with a rich historical background and a fascinating connection to Normandy and Northern France. In fact, I had a French neighbour there, a history teacher in one of the local schools, who lived just down the road. In his light French accent, he liked to laugh at his own love of Britain. 'When I moved here, I decided to prioritise cream tea over calvados,' he regularly reminded me. 'The beaches are almost the same, in any case.'

'If you're so interested in history,' I asked him, 'why wouldn't you stay in Normandy? Surely the D–Day beaches and the Bayeux Tapestry offer more than the Whitstable area?'

'Ah,' he replied, 'that is where you are mistaken. Do you know anything about Operation Bodyguard?'

'Is that part of Operation Overlord? The name rings a bell,' I answered thoughtfully.

'You're quite right. It was a sort of high level deception plan set up by the Allies in their preparation of the Normandy landings.'

'Ah, yes, I remember reading about this,' I told him. 'The Germans thought the landings were taking place somewhere else entirely. Is that correct?'

'Exactly. It really was quite an elaborate strategy: they simulated an entire naval fleet massing in entirely the wrong location, using radio transmissions and reflective materials that confused the German radars. Spies let leak documents that seemed to be planning a naval strike in the north of France, rather than the north-west. They even invented an entire imaginary American task force to implement this imaginary attack!'

I shook my head. 'It's crazy, when you think about it. I mean, the Battle of Normandy was the determining moment of the Allied victory. Anything that weakened German reaction and intervention time is really nothing short of miraculous!'

My neighbour chuckled. 'Of course, no-one is entirely sure how efficient the plan was, as the weather on June 6th, 1944, was terrible, and there was no obvious reaction by the German fighter planes. However, we do know that Hitler delayed sending the full

Wehrmacht forces to Normandy for weeks and weeks after the landings. It is quite probable that he was still anticipating another landing near Pas-de-Calais.'

I paused for a moment. 'This doesn't entirely explain your point, though. I've heard of these deceptive strategies before. What exactly do they have to do with you living here on the English coast?'

'Well,' he replied, 'think about it. Where did the American, English, Canadian and Australian forces leave from, when they crossed the Channel?'

'On the actual D-Day landings, you mean?'

'Yes.'

'They mostly left from Portsmouth, didn't they? And you're forgetting the French resistance troops.'

He chuckled. 'So I am. It's because I'm more interested in the English side of things, right now.'

'I suppose that's hardly a surprise, is it!'

'In any case, you're right, but I don't think I've explained myself very well.' He frowned a little as an idea occurred to him. 'In fact, since we're both standing outside, how would you feel about coming with me for a short walk while I explain it?'

I shrugged. 'It's a Sunday morning,' I replied. 'Why not? Let me just go inside and get my coat.'

As we walked through the fields towards the sea, with the wind whipping in our hair, my neighbour continued his story. 'Operation Bodyguard aimed to persuade the Germans that they were planning on landing at Pas-de-Calais. Therefore, they needed to convince them that they were leaving from Dover and Folkestone. Do you see where I'm going with this?'

'Are you saying that some of them made believe they were leaving from here?'

My neighbour's eye twinkled. 'Exactly. There are wonderful period photographs of it. They had to make the soldiers look busy, you see.'

'What, like the fake communist factories in Russia? Building boats out of cardboard and flimsy wood, you mean?' I had heard about the ruse in theory, but hadn't truly contemplated the day-to-day implications of such a deception. It was quite funny, really!

'Something very much like that. The soldiers had to look busy, and there were thousands of them stationed there. They had to look like they were preparing to launch an attack. More than that: they had to pretend to assemble a fleet ready to invade France from Pas-de-Calais! Of course, there's only so long you can keep soldiers pretending to work. So what do you think they made them do next?' he asked me, with another mischievous grin.

'I don't know,' I replied. It was hard not to get caught up in the man's enthusiasm, especially as, from where we stood, we could see the fine silver line of the sea on the horizon.

'Well, Eisenhower and Montgomery put their heads together, and decided they needed to keep the soldiers busy. They had to think of something that would make the men move around a lot without tiring them out unnecessarily, as they weren't actually fighting. A lot of these soldiers were actually on leave, you see, or wounded in minor ways.'

'What are you getting at, then?' I couldn't help but ask. It was a little cold, and our walk had gone on longer than I had expected.

My neighbour smiled. 'I'm sorry, I'm drawing this out into something of a shaggy dog story, aren't I. I just wanted to delay getting to my favourite part. Just walk with me a little longer and you'll see what I mean. What the soldiers ended up doing on the beach was the ultimate English pastime.'

'What, drinking tea?' I had to walk a little faster to catch up with him, as he speeded up towards some sort of imagined goal. We seemed to be headed towards the beautiful grassy beach at Tankerton.

'Well, I'm certain they did plenty of that, if they had enough rations. But no, I'm talking about mowing the lawn.' He gave a giddy little laugh, obviously thrilled with his story.

'You're kidding,' I replied. 'They made thousands of soldiers plant a lawn on the beaches they were supposed to be launching an attack from?'

He nodded happily. 'The Germans wouldn't be watching too closely. As long as there were signs of radio activity, intercepted communications, and all that, they wouldn't be sending spies out. As long as the soldiers were kept busy, the commanders figured the whole operation would look legitimate.'

'So you mean all that nice grass on the beach is from the war?'

'The very same grass I walk my dog in every day!' he assured me.

'Look around you,' he said triumphantly.

I looked down at the ground beneath my feet, which had indeed turned from gravel into sand and then into lovely, smooth, immaculately maintained grass. Understanding, I began to marvel at the story. 'The only place I've seen grass like that going right up to the water's edge is Miami,' I told him. 'I always wondered if it was a bit odd!'

'If you look closely,' he added, 'you'll see that it's not that tall, dry beach grass that you get in parts of Norfolk. It's finely cut, bright green, and soft to walk on. It's a perfect lawn, as tidy as you would see in the suburbs of any American town in the 1940s.' He grinned contentedly.

'Well, I'm not sure that's quite enough to warrant moving to Britain,' I replied with a wry smile, 'but it's certainly a good story. I've seen this grassy beach on almost every visit since I first came here in 1975. I used to walk my youngest children along it. It's perfect for toddlers, of course. My wife and I used to have lovely picnics here, with a blanket spread out over the grass and sand.'

'Just think,' my neighbour said, 'you were right in the heart of history without even knowing it.'

'And I would never have known!' I smiled. 'I guess facts like these are exactly why you need history teachers for neighbours.'

Anna Cindy was one of the most beautiful neighbours I ever had, although she was never my girlfriend. She and I were both students living in New Jersey, in shared houses that looked out on a backyard full of mulberry and magnolia trees. In the springtime, it was a truly wonderful place to be, and Anna Cindy was a glorious addition to it. Anna Cindy was eighteen years old; as tall and slim as a birch tree, with long dark hair that she often wore bundled back in a bun or braid. On top of this, she had a snub nose and beautiful high cheekbones.

I was twenty-one and an engineer. Thus, I seemed to spend most of my time in rooms with fluorescent lighting obsessing over maths questions, physics and statistical calculations. By the time I came home, it truly felt like Anna Cindy was a breath of fresh air in my life. She was always smiling and laughing, and her conversation was always fascinating. When she found out I spoke French, she started coming to me for help with her homework. During those French sessions, our friendship truly blossomed. I would come home from my lengthy scientific lessons to find that Anna Cindy had been home for two hours since her last Classics class and had had time to make lemonade and brownies. We would talk and talk long after the lesson had finished, on all sorts of topics, from art and literature to our childhoods and our plans for the future.

Anna Cindy came from a very rich family. She had her own sports car, a bright red Triumph, which she would let me drive when she was in a good mood. I loved nothing more than to go flying down the long, flat American roads with Anna Cindy by my side, her long hair streaming in the wind. We would pull over in the middle of nowhere and have a picnic in a field, discussing our life plans. She had been offered work as a top model and was making a considerable amount of money from it, but she wasn't sure if that was the career she wanted to pursue. We both wanted fulfilment and travel in our lives.

Although we were very close, there was never any romantic tension between us. We had the sort of warm friendship that felt much more like the kind of relationship one shares with siblings or cousins, based on looking after each other, sharing dreams, and helping with each other's homework. At some point, Anna Cindy fell in love with a Harvard student called James. She developed a glow that was a real joy to be around. When he proposed to her, I found her in the garden, climbing the mulberry tree in her backyard and shouting for joy. 'Brad, I'm going to get married!' she shouted down to me when I poked my face out the window. 'God, I've never been so happy! I'm in love with my life!'

I grinned. 'Come down from that tree and tell me all about it!'

We lay in the grass side by side as she told me all about her newfound happiness. James would be finishing his degree at Harvard before heading to London for a few months. After this, he was to return to New York, where she would meet him and marry him. 'We're going to have horse-drawn carriages at our wedding! My father is paying for everything, he's so happy for me. At the end of the ceremony, we're going to take the carriage and go on a tour of the city. Oh, you'll have to come! I'm so excited!'

'I'm happy for you,' I told her quietly, taking her hand.

'I just can't believe it,' she whispered back, squeezing her eyes shut. 'It's like a dream come true.'

For the next few months, this euphoric mood persisted even as the weather got colder. There was plenty more mulberry tree climbing and running about in the sun, followed by happy late night films and tea sessions. I didn't see as much of her as I had in the first months of our friendship, but I assumed all was essentially perfect in her life. However, late one night, I heard loud knocking on my door. I opened it to find Anna Cindy standing there in her nightie, weeping. 'Oh, I'm an awful person,' she burst out the second I opened the door. 'I don't deserve to be happy. I don't deserve to get married. I don't deserve my wonderful boyfriend James.' She dissolved into tears and fell against my chest.

'Come now,' I said, 'none of that is true. Come in and tell me all about it.'

'Oh,' she sobbed into my shirt, 'he's coming back in April and now it's almost Christmas, and everything's gone wrong. I've done something awful, Bradley, something so awful I don't know if I can tell you about it. I'm so deeply ashamed of myself and my behaviour.'

I carefully extricated her from my shirt front and guided her

towards my couch. 'Now, let me just make you a mug of cocoa.
Here, dry your eyes,' I added as I handed her a tissue. She cried
seemingly uncontrollably the whole time I was in the kitchen, and
by the time I came back, I was beginning to worry seriously about
her condition. 'What's wrong?' I asked as I handed her the hot cocoa.

'I'm pregnant,' she blurted out.

There was a pause. 'That's wonderful,' I said gently. 'Won't James
be happy?'

Anna Cindy let out a whimper, and in the long silence that
followed I realised how long it had been since James' last visit. I did
the math, and then said 'oh' quietly.

'I'm supposed to be getting married in four months,' she said,
drying her eyes. She seemed a little calmer now the worst of her
confession had passed. 'I just don't know what to do.'

'What happened?' I couldn't help but ask. 'I mean, whose is it?'

I couldn't imagine anyone but James having even interested Anna
Cindy. To me, she had always come across as the glowing, happy
fiancée. Whatever had been going on in her private life, she had been
hiding it studiously. 'Doctor Steiner,' she muttered darkly. 'We had
an affair.'

I was astounded. Doctor Steiner was a middle-aged man with
lanky limbs and greasy hair. I had never met James but, from what
Anna Cindy had told me, he was a tall, young Harvard hunk with a
dashing dress style and a winning smile. I couldn't understand why
on earth my friend and neighbour would have found herself drawn
to this decrepit old man.

I tried to be considerate. 'Do you love him?' I asked gently.

This may have been an error, as it brought the floods of tears back.
'No!' she sobbed. 'I don't love him at all! He tricked me! He told me
he could teach me how to make love like a woman, so I would be
skilled and confident when I went to bed with my new husband.'
She blushed furiously. 'I'm a virgin, you see, and I was nervous,'
she babbled. 'James has already been with some girls in the past, he
told me about it, and I just wanted to impress him. I don't know
what I was thinking, I was completely stupid. I let myself be drawn
in by him; the doctor, I mean. He was so calm and reassuring, with
his doctor's hands...' She shuddered. I tried to wield off images of
Doctor Steiner's face. After a moment, Anna Cindy continued her

story: 'He told me he had birth control pills, he gave me this whole bottle. I trusted him. Why wouldn't I trust him? But here I am, four months pregnant. He tricked me and now my life is ruined. I'm too ashamed to tell my father, and if she knew, my mother would kick me out of the house.'

I didn't know what to say. 'Anna Cindy, my dear,' I began, 'in the end, nobody's judgement matters. What's done is done. The important thing will be to forgive yourself and move on. I don't think any less of you for it. Why don't you just tell James the whole story? Maybe he'll forgive you.'

'I don't think he will,' she replied unsteadily. 'He places a lot of value on the idea of fidelity. I can't go back to him, Bradley. I'm not worthy.'

'If he doesn't want you back, he's less of a man than I thought he was. It shouldn't make any difference that you've been with another man. Maybe you can get through this. Maybe you can rebuild.'

'Raising another man's child sure does make a difference, though,' she said glumly. I was quiet. 'I have to think of this baby.'

I paused. As sensitively as I could, I asked her if she had considered the idea of not keeping the baby. She shook her head vehemently. 'It's criminal,' she said weakly. 'I just couldn't forgive myself.' There was a long silence. 'I'm going to be a mother, that's all there is to it. Maybe I should just stay with Doctor Steiner. He's got a reliable income. He says he'll look after the child. He wants to move to New Jersey.' Her mouth began to tremble again. 'I don't want to go to New Jersey! I'm only eighteen,' she cried again. 'What am I going to do?'

I put my arm around her shoulders. 'I don't know, Anna Cindy,' I told her. 'You've got some big decisions to make. But the first step is to talk it through with the people who care for you.'

After a long, sniffly silence, she spoke again. 'Maybe I really should just marry the doctor.'

'You don't love him!' I had to argue. 'I mean, I'm not questioning your taste in affairs...' She giggled a little through her tears and slapped me weakly on the arm. 'But the man is so old and sweaty. When you shake hands with him, it's like holding a wet iguana!'

She sighed and snuggled her wet cheek onto my shoulder. 'Bradley?' she asked softly.

'Yes, my dear?'

'Would you marry me instead?'

I paused. Of course Anna Cindy and I were good friends, but I had never thought of her in a romantic light. For one mad moment the prospect of eloping with my best friend and raising her child flashed through my mind, and then I had to dismiss it. 'You know that doesn't make sense,' I replied calmly. 'I love you dearly, but as a friend. You should be marrying the person you love. I really think you should just talk to James. You never know what might happen. Everybody makes mistakes. When people truly love us, they may forgive even the worst of our errors.'

Later, I wondered if I had given her the right advice, or if there was anything I could have said to talk her out of the decision she eventually came to. I witnessed several more sessions of weeping, trying without any real results to console her. She always repeated the same sentences, over and over, as if obsessed with the idea of her ruin. Nothing seemed to help. Eventually, she told James, who was heartbroken and obviously unable to handle the situation. I pitied them, then, for the whole situation seemed so tragically unnecessary. I know I was only three or four years older than the couple, but it was hard to watch the misery and the sense of betrayal spiralling out of control.

A few weeks after that first late-night visit, I had to go away on a business trip to Princeton, where I stayed for a three week conference. When I came back, her father came alone to my door with a solemn expression. I feared the worst. 'She's run away with that damn doctor,' he told me quietly, sitting on my couch. 'They eloped to Las Vegas. Can you imagine? She was supposed to have a horse and carriage. She was supposed to have everything she ever dreamed of. I just don't understand why she did it. Any of it. I just wish she could have calmed down, made better decisions. I wish I could have helped her.' He buried his face in his hands.

'I tried,' I told him, trying to keep tears from filling my eyes. 'I just didn't know what to say to her.'

'I know, Bradley,' he murmured. 'You've been a great friend to her this whole time. She just got a little lost. I don't know what anyone could have done.'

'How did James take the news?' I asked.

'He was heartbroken, of course. Very nearly suicidal. I don't think we can stay in touch, though. It's just too damn painful to remember what might have been.' He sighed.

'Maybe it'll all turn out alright in the end,' I tried to reassure him. 'I mean, I've met Doctor Steiner. He's a good person.'

'He's so sweaty,' Anna Cindy's father grumbled. 'And boring. He's really boring. And he's only four years younger than me.' He shook his head. 'He shouldn't be marrying my little girl. It's just not right. The only conversations I've had with the man that weren't strictly medical business have been about driving cars and cutting the grass. Still, I guess at least he's not some drug addict punk. I should be grateful for small mercies. But sometimes I really worry that Doctor Steiner plotted the whole thing, you know, so he could steal my gorgeous daughter from her fiancé and marry her himself.'

I sighed. 'There's no use thinking like that. All you can tell yourself is that what's done is done.'

He nodded sadly. 'What's done is done, and there was nothing we could do to stop it.'

I never heard from Anna Cindy again. I suppose she started a new life out in New Jersey with her husband, and raised the child. She must have had a new house, new neighbours. Maybe she was happy. Still, sometimes I wish I could have done something more to try to stop her from making bad decisions, or even just make sure she was happy. But the power we have as humans to intervene in any other person's life is limited, whether we are best friends or just good neighbours.

France is dominantly an agricultural country. It has always been, but in the last forty or fifty years, this status has been particularly reinforced by a series of government incentives. Thus, many farmers get subsidies for their production of various merchandises from their country or from various European institutions in Brussels. For instance, a cow farmer might get funds, variously, for milk, calves, meat production, or fertilisers for feed. Well-publicised instances of government agricultural subsidies include wheat, cotton, rice, peanuts, sugar, and soy, as well as several types of wood. Some farmers even receive compensation for not producing, if there happens to be an excess of a particular product on the market! The powers that be thus get to maintain control over supply, provenance and price.

Butter, for instance, went through a period of abundance in my banking days, when the product was most commonly referred to not in terms of pats, sticks or tubs, but in 'mountains of butter.' For a few years, we subsidised the exportation of these mountains of butter to underdeveloped countries like Pakistan. The logic of this, of course, was to get rid of the butter that had accumulated in Europe so that prices would stay high and stable. This would, for one thing, avoid waste as well as sudden dips in prices on the market. This way, the farmers would not have to suffer from the unexpected bounty!

Of course, many people see this as a ridiculous form of interventionism, with governments artificially inflating or modifying the value of crops, which goes against the laws of supply and demand that govern an open market. Furthermore, many farmers receive subsidies whether or not they are truly in need of them. Given this climate of government support, many farmers unsurprisingly started trying to use the policies to their best advantage – and, of course, taking advantage of them as much as they could. For instance, after certain measures were passed concerning the sale of wood, many farmers who had no previous experience in woodcutting suddenly started buying up forests. The logic was simple: since the product was subsidised, the prices were bound to remain high. Furthermore, if all went well, they reasoned, they wouldn't have to put in a scrap of work. Trees don't need to be fed, or groomed, or milked; most of them don't need constant watering or treatment with pesticides. They flourish best if left alone. Buy a forest, the farmers reasoned, and the rain, the sun, and a benevolent God would do all the work for them! The trees would grow thicker and taller on their own. All they would have to do, at some point, would be to have the trees cut down, chopped into logs, shipped and sold.

Next to our French country house, there was a man who had inherited a large plantation of oak trees. It was a considerable plot of land, that would have looked like a large, young forest to anyone walking by who wasn't close enough to see that the oaks were planted in tight rows of straight, parallel lines. I had never minded it being next to my house, as they really were quite beautiful trees. Seven or eight months of the year, they would be a beautiful shade of soft green, before turning rich tones of gold and amber.

However, the neighbour who looked after it did not seem to appreciate its inherent aesthetic value. Monsieur Dequille was a sickly-looking young man with a greedy streak. Whenever I met him, he was always irritable, barely managing to bark out a greeting; often just giving a curt nod from a great distance. In fact, I almost never ran into him, although I often saw him skulking around in the trees. He was always walking around the plantation, sniffing the air, peering closely at the trunks. He obviously didn't know the first thing about trees but was quite keen to give the impression that he was knowledgeable – although I'm not quite sure to whom, as I was the only person who was ever nearby… Perhaps young Monsieur Dequille secretly had doubts about his own abilities! He lived alone in a very nice house which he had also inherited from his father.

One day, however, I saw him hauling a saw down towards the trees. He looked far too thin and small to be carrying out any serious work, so I didn't really worry about it at the time. However, I did begin to have misgivings when I saw him begin to hack inexpertly into the trunk of one of the young trees.

'Hey!' I said, stepping outside my front door. 'What are you doing?'

He looked up at me frostily. '*Bonjour, Monsieur.* I am cutting down this tree, as you can see.'

'It can't be more than five years old!'

He considered me blankly, his saw still resting in the cut he had made. 'So? It is my tree. I can cut it when I want.'

'You're not supposed to cut oak trees until they're at least thirty years old! Preferably older! It's high quality wood you're wasting, there. It would make great furniture, or parquet, or even beams for a barn. But you have to wait until the trees are at least thirty or forty centimetres in diameter! You have to be patient!'

'Don't be ridiculous. It's nice, young wood!' he snarled at me. 'You want to get it when it's soft and tender, like lamb, you know.' He started wiggling the saw back and forth, as it had clearly become a little jammed.

'You obviously don't know anything about wood. Anyway, you French people also kill lambs too young. Do you know that it's illegal in England and the USA to butcher them under the age of six months?'

'I don't care how old my meat is, and I don't care how old my wood is. Anyway, lambs have nothing to do with anything,' he replied, sweat breaking out on his forehead from the effort of moving the saw. 'These trees grew on their own, and now it is time to harvest the produce. I'm a farmer. I know what I'm doing.' Finally, he gave a little jerk and the saw flew free from the cut, nearly hitting him in the face. He breathed out loudly. 'They were my father's trees and now they are mine. I am cutting and selling the wood because I need the money. If you have nothing more to contribute, please let me go back to my work.' He turned back to the tree and once again started feebly running the saw back and forth across it.

I felt a little bad for the man. His incompetence was so obvious as to be a little touching. He really did look like a sickly creature, the last of his race. All it would take was one good virus to knock him off the earth! I sighed. 'Look, I meant no offence. Of course, there's a lot you can do with young, pliable wood like this. It's not as strong as it will be in thirty or forty years, but you can still use it: for *maquetterie*, for instance. It's a fine and respectable art, and it specifically requires delicate wood.'

My interlocutor gave a dry little cough. 'I have no interest in your arts and crafts,' he said with a sneer. 'I will cut it into planks and sell it by the end of the week. That's all there is to it.'

I turned my back on him with a curt nod and walked home, fuming. I couldn't believe his behaviour! It was simply the epitome of laziness. Of course, apart from being angry at his wasteful performance, I was also annoyed for more personal reasons: if he cut down the trees, he would be ruining my view to the west! I had grown quite fond of the artificial little forest. I wasn't looking forward to it being replaced by a series of ugly stumps. As I stood at the window, angrily drinking tea and watching him saw away uselessly until the tree finally toppled over – nearly squashing him in the process – I had an idea. If he was acting purely out of greed, perhaps I could fight fire with fire! I decided to try another tactic, approaching him on his own terms and trying to use his weakness to my advantage. I walked back outside with a new smile plastered on my face.

Young Monsieur Dequille was still sawing, his thin white shirt now soaked through with sweat. His face had gone rather sallow. I really wondered if he was in good health, or if he just never went outside! He didn't strike me as a man used to physical exertion.

'Look,' I said, 'I'm sorry if I was rude earlier. It's just that I'll be quite sad to see these trees go. I've become rather attached to them.'

He rolled his eyes. 'You've made it quite clear that you're strangely fond of my father's little trees. Unfortunately for you, they belong to me.'

I ignored his rudeness entirely. 'I have an offer to make,' I said, deciding to cut to the chase before I became too annoyed to pursue my aims. 'I really like these trees, and I also really like the view from my house not being of rows upon rows of horrible stumps. I also think it's far too early to cut them down.' Seeing he was about to interject with another tirade concerning his rights to chop what he wanted when he wanted, I ploughed on. 'You'll only get pennies for this young wood. It's hardly worth your while, all this hard work.'

'What are you, a wood seller now?' he retorted with a frown. 'You sort of neglected to mention that earlier.'

'No,' I replied patiently, 'but I am a buyer. Or at least, I would quite like to become one. Listen, if I offered you a thousand euros an acre, would you sell the trees to me?'

He paused mid-movement, with the saw stuck into the tree trunk. I could almost see the gears whirring in his greedy brain. 'A thousand five hundred,' he replied almost at once, without even turning around to look at me. I could tell from the tenseness in his shoulders, though, that this was a bluff. He obviously knew he would get far less than this if he tried to sell this wood to anybody. He also presumably realised that he would be able to stop sawing and go inside to drink wine, play videogames, or whatever it was he usually spent his time doing.

'It's a deal,' I said firmly.

There was another pause. After a moment, however, he turned around with his features contorted into a bright expression. 'Well,' he said, in a new voice, his pasty face twisted into a smile, 'so it is. One thousand five hundred, you say? Fifteen hundred euros?'

I smiled benevolently. 'That's right. I'll transfer the money as soon as is convenient.'

Monsieur Dequille obviously stopped himself from replying something too enthusiastic. 'That'll be fine, thank you,' he replied politely. There was an awkward pause.

'Well, you'd best put away that saw!' I added cheerily, before heading back inside.

I was happy with the arrangement. Although it had meant striking up a deal with this rather unpleasant personage, it also meant that I ended up keeping my view of the forest. My oak trees grew healthily, unperturbed by any pasty men with saws. They are now tall, healthy and twenty years old. Perhaps someday I will think of having some of them cut for the lovely wood they produce, but it will certainly not be for the sake of government subsidies, and it will not happen until they are old and fully grown.

BORDER WARS

There was no doubt about it: the fence had changed. We had just returned home from a weekend away, expecting the relaxing comforts of home. The scene we returned to was quite different.

On the border between our land and our neighbour Harry's land, there was an ancient fence of trees that clearly split his property from ours. We had never had any issues with this, but coming home I found that the old tree fence had been burned to the ground and replaced with a more modern fence which ate up an extra two and a half yards of my land.

I knew that Harry could not have achieved such a heavy task on his own and he didn't have a gardener to help him. He was retired and his wife was ten years older than him, a heavy whiskey drinker in no fit state to be breaking up and replacing fences. I was somewhat at a loss and eventually came to the conclusion that their children must have helped them... although why they would help their parents to encroach on someone else's land was anybody's guess.

I waited for a while, but it quickly became clear that Harry was not going to come around to my house and explain that there had been some sort of mistake. I thought that maybe they had simply wanted to replace the fence and had accidentally placed it on my land. A mistake like that would be easy to sort out and I thought I could let go of them ruining the trees that had been there before.

After a day or so, I saw Harry checking on the fence and went out to speak with him.

'Hello,' I said, 'we were away all weekend. I see there have been some big changes.'

Harry glared at me across the fence. 'Yes, well. It's only correct.'

'I think you'll find that this new fence is rather creeping over my side,' I told him and pointed out where the original border had been. It was still perfectly obvious, in spite of his efforts to turn the earth so the old boundary didn't show up so clearly.

'I was referring to the old land survey. You must have seen it for yourself.'

I was momentarily speechless. Of course, when I had bought the house I had seen the deeds and old ordnance survey maps, and everything seemed to be in fine order. There could be no question where my land ended and his began.

'Anyway,' Harry carried on, oblivious, 'if you look at the ordnance survey map from the 1400's, you will notice the thickness of the pen line on the map.'

My mouth opened and closed mutely. I couldn't think of a thing to say. Eventually, I asked, 'Pen line?' in a confused voice.

'Yes, my lad,' he said, nodding in a very authoritative fashion, 'if you look at the thickness of the pen line, I'm entitled to an extra two and a half yards. Now, I know, it might not seem like much to you. But it's the principle of the thing. My property is my property and I want every inch of what I've paid for. Getting my money's worth, you see. It's only fair.'

'No.' I finally found my voice. 'That's madness. You can't go about changing the boundaries anytime you feel like it!'

Harry looked at me flatly. 'It's my land,' he said, 'I'm not changing the boundaries. I'm changing them back to what they should have been all along. And, don't worry, I won't charge you for the cost of replacing the fence.'

I could have exploded. 'I think we need to speak to the council about this,' I said, the words trembling with a burst of anger. The whole thing was insane to me.

He nodded smugly. 'We'll do that.'

Things are rarely as straightforward as we hope they will be, and such was the case with Harry and the fence. It took many months of arguing that tipped over into years and I ended up having to take him to court over the border dispute, though I thought that the judge was going to laugh us out of the room.

'The thickness of a pen line,' he asked Harry dubiously.

Harry drew himself up to his full height and nodded proudly. 'Yes. If you look at the ordnance survey map from the year 1400...'

'Yes, yes, alright.'

'The last owner was totally unreasonable,' Harry said, glancing at me sidelong, 'I was hoping this new chap would see things the correct way, with no unpleasantness.'

I wasn't even surprised that he had tried this with the last owner, though I doubted it had gone into litigation that time, or it would have been sorted out by now.

The judge sighed. 'Now, what you gentlemen want to do is settle this out of court. It'll cost a lot less if you behave like adults and see for yourselves who is in the right about this.' He looked annoyed that we had taken up his time with the foolish argument and frankly, I felt a little ridiculous myself. Harry, though, took it all very seriously.

After seeing how the judge reacted, I was just about ready to throw in the towel. I took a few days to mull it over and then went to Harry's house to see if we couldn't straighten things out without involving any more authorities or spending any unnecessary time and money on the whole silly ordeal.

'Now, the thing is,' I reasoned, 'you might be right about the line. I don't think you are, but let's say for argument's sake... Still, I bought my house on the understanding that every inch of the property was my own. So if you pay me, say, seventy-five pounds? We can forget the whole mess and I won't feel quite so cheated.'

Harry looked at me balefully. 'Are you joking? Why would I pay you for my own land?'

All my careful reasoning seemed to fly out the window. 'Because it's not your land! It's mine! And you are trying to steal it out from under me.'

'I'm doing no such thing,' Harry said dismissively, 'I'm taking what's mine and that's the end of it.'

That was not the end of it. I could not let it go. For the life of me, I couldn't face just sitting back and allowing this complete lunatic to move in on my land. It felt very wrong to even consider letting myself be such a pushover.

After all, from all the reading I had done since this ordeal began, I knew that the original fence had been on that border for four hundred years. The original survey was done in 1410 and our land had been divided up in 1620 – what good reason could there possibly be for disputing it now? Except, of course, Harry's boredom with his retired life and his apparent belief that because I wasn't local, I could be taken for a ride.

I was ready to go to war with Harry over the border, much as I hated the idea, when he suddenly died. He was old, well into his seventies, but still I was surprised when the house went up for sale and a new lady, Monica, moved in. She was in her late fifties, retired, and I anticipated another English tiff over the positioning of the fence.

Frankly, I geared myself up to have to defend my right to move the fence back to this newcomer, but as soon as I raised the question of it, she lifted her hand.

'Say no more. I believe you.'

'It's only that Harry was completely obsessive about it and he burned the tree fence down,' I explained, flummoxed by her easy agreement, 'and we had to go to court over it, the whole thing was ridiculous...'

'I know the type,' she smiled. Monica was lovely, very soft spoken. 'It's a shame you had to go through that. I love gardening, but why would anyone want to take someone else's land? Please, do what you want to.'

So it was quite easy for me to have my son put up a fence that was not only back in the original and correct position, but was much more pleasing to the eye. Monica was a far more pleasant neighbour than Harry had been. She smiled and waved when she saw me and I definitely noticed how the whole atmosphere lifted. With a quiet, educated woman living next door, everything became that much easier and it was a pleasure to see Monica pottering about the garden or reading in the sunshine on nice days.

Because she was such a wonderful, refreshing change, we never really discussed the position of the fence after I had it moved back, and she certainly didn't care about the thickness of a pen line. She just trusted that I would be as good to her as she was to me and, as a result, Monica was definitely one of the best neighbours that I ever had the pleasure of living next to.

Over the years, my gardener nurtured the land and grew back the trees that Harry had burned down and eventually they flourished, strong and tall, as though they had belonged there all along.

AN UNFORGETTABLE DINNER

For a time, I rented a house in a village near Arlington, in Virginia. I was there for only three months, on an executive training course organised by Georgetown University. It was a beautiful, quiet place to live. I had a nice lawn outside by my front door, with a few flowers, and a garage for my car.

As you might imagine, I was still quite a young man to find myself in such a situation, commuting from the countryside into the city like some sort of high-powered executive. This drew the intrigue and interest of the neighbours, small-town people who were mostly unused to outsiders in the community. Not that anyone reacted unpleasantly: in fact, most of the men and women I met seemed fascinated. My next-door neighbour, Mrs Wetcaufen, was very upfront about her curiosity from our very first meeting. 'You're so young!' she exclaimed with a bright red smile, leaning on the fence from her yard. She had a little bit of lipstick on her teeth. 'What's a handsome little thing like yourself doing out here in the boondocks?'

Mrs Wetcaufen was a rounded woman in her early fifties, whom I suspected of being rather frustrated with her lonely and provincial life. She spent a lot of time gardening and looking after her two huge dogs. I smiled and introduced myself, explaining the nature of my work there in the Northwest. 'So you're commuting in and out, every day? You're just like my husband! Surely a pretty boy like you shouldn't be living such a life! I mean, you look good in a suit, but...' she tittered. I did not respond, so she continued. 'My husband is the president of a large company in the Washington area, you see. He drives in and out every single day, at the wheel of his big Mercedes, or sometimes he likes to take the Cadillac.' She sighed and patted her curly red hair into place. I suppose the idea of conversing with an international student from next door seemed far more exciting than sitting in stony silence in front of the television, or with her husband. I had only met Mr Wetcaufen in passing, but I had the distinct impression he was the sort of man to come home late from work every night and then proceed to read the newspaper at the dining table.

'A nice boy like you shouldn't already be living that executive life,' she told me. 'Say, would you like to come over for dinner sometime?' I agreed, of course. It was the only possible polite option. I don't think I really intended to go. However, the offer was repeated every few days, until it was impossible to get out of it. I kept running into my neighbour, either heading off to a late morning seminar or coming home after a long day's work, only to find her gardening ineffectually in a distinctly impractical little dress. Once I saw her pruning the roses in high heels. In any case, I eventually named a time and date, and agreed to go to the Wetcaufen's house for dinner one Monday night.

I had to admit I was not overly thrilled at the prospect of an entire evening with my neighbours. Mr Wetcaufen might have been the president of his own multinational company, but I had nothing to make me suspect he would be an interesting conversation partner. Mrs Wetcaufen's eccentricities I had already sampled at length, and I was not looking forward to being subjected to them for hours at a time. Still, a free meal was a free meal, and it would have been rude to refuse. They did live right next door to me. 'I'll make you a real fancy dinner,' she had said, waving her impeccably manicured nails. 'Just come on over when you get home from work.'

I had expected a fancy dinner to be a somewhat formal affair, considering the size of the Wetcaufen's house, which was practically a manor, so I dressed in an ironed white shirt and a clean grey suit, and presented myself at the door on time. When the door was opened by a butler with carefully slicked-back hair, I was glad I had made myself presentable. However, when Mrs Wetcaufen appeared, she seemed a little flustered, wearing a stained dress and no makeup at all. 'I'm terribly sorry, honey,' she said to me, waving her arms in distress, 'it's just been a crazy start to the week. Duke's being a real terror, he just won't calm down. Now let me get you a drink, come sit in the lounge, and I'll find my husband to keep you company.'

After this introduction, I couldn't say I was particularly looking forward to the man's company, but I didn't seem to have a choice. I sat in a large leather chair in a vast, darkened library alone for quite a long time before, the butler, brought me a cold glass of soda with lime. 'My name is Courtney, by the way. Dinner will be served in a quarter of an hour,' he said quietly, before disappearing back into the dark corridors. I almost wished he had stayed. He seemed like a man who might make a valuable ally. After a little while, which

I spent perusing the rather dull selection of leather-bound volumes on the shelves, Mrs Wetcaufen appeared again in the doorway. She had changed, and put on a little lipstick, and had a very large glass of white wine in her hand. 'Terribly sorry about all this,' she said with a fake little laugh.

'Don't worry,' I said. 'I had a long day at work, it's nice to relax a little.'

'Did my husband come keep you company?' she asked airily.

'Oh, I've kept my own company. It's a nice library you have here,' I replied politely.

'I'm sorry about that,' she replied with a sigh. 'He's having a rather odd day. I suppose you'll get to meet him over dinner in any case.'

'Is, er, Duke alright?' I asked solicitously, as it was the only thing I could think of to say.

Mrs Wetcaufen looked at me a little oddly. 'Oh, he's fine,' she said. 'Or he will be, just as soon as he's fed.'

We walked down the carpeted corridors for what seemed like a very long time, before emerging into a vast dining room. At the centre of the chamber, there was a long marble table. Mr Wetcaufen was already seated at the table. So were two enormous dogs. There was a pause as I took this in. 'This is Duke, and this is Earl,' Mrs Wetcaufen said, and then continued: 'and this is Robert.' For the first two, she had pointed at the gigantic pitbull and German shepherd, and then to her husband for the latter. I understood the confusion in the library much better, all at once.

'Something smells delicious!' I blustered, partly to cover my embarrassment. Truth be told, the room smelled a little of dog fur.

'Thank you,' my hostess said with a stiff smile, guiding me to my chair. I sat down, spread a vast white napkin over my legs and waited. I was the only person sitting on the long side of the table, with Mr and Mrs Wetcaufen at each head of it. Across from me sat the two dogs, glowering and slobbering at me. It was one of the oddest things I had ever seen.

'My husband is a businessman,' Mrs Wetcaufen said reluctantly. From the end of the table to my left, the man in question coughed.

'Sure am,' he said shortly. 'And a fat lot of good it's doing me these days. Is dinner going to be served soon?'

'Robert,' his wife said sharply. 'I was hoping perhaps you could entertain our young guest. He's interested in becoming a big businessman like you. Perhaps you could give him some tips. Help him steer clear of the pitfalls.'

He snorted. 'Don't go into business, boy,' he said. 'But if you must, make sure you do it far from here. The air is poisonous. Most boring place on earth, you know.'

I could feel my brow starting to sweat. Struggling to think of a polite response, I found I could not help staring at the two dogs, who had their tongues out. It was disgusting. I should probably confess that I'm not particularly fond of dogs in the first place: I'm pretty sure maintaining them is a terrible waste of money. Besides, they're violent and smelly creatures, prone to peeing on furniture and fighting in the street. Of course, I aired none of these views at this particular point in time, but sat in stunned silence, listening to Courtney and the staff making noise in the kitchen.

'Are you feeling alright?' Mrs Wetcaufen suddenly cooed affectionately, and I felt a shudder travel the length of my spine. It was one thing for my neighbour to be vaguely flirtatious with me when we were standing at a safe distance in our respective gardens, but here, at the dinner table, in front of her husband? I didn't know how to react. Luckily, the husband spoke first.

'Oh, do be quiet,' he growled. 'Those beasts don't give a damn how you feel about them.' At this moment, in a great flood of relief, I realised she had been talking to Earl and Duke, the ferocious creatures sitting across from me. In fact, at the sound of her voice, they began to pant and whimper quite pathetically. I began to feel rather sorry for Robert Wetcaufen, and decided to try and engage him in some sort of conversation.

'So you work in Washington, too?' I asked him. 'I've been commuting there daily. It's not too bad a drive.'

At this moment, however, before the man could have a chance to respond, the butler re-entered the room bearing a silver platter. 'Dinner is served,' he said dryly. I looked up at him gratefully, expecting to be served. There were thick steaks balanced on his arm, and they smelled quite delicious. However, Courtney then walked around to the other side of the table and proceeded to spear the steaks and set them down in front of the dogs. I felt my jaw drop in complete shock.

'Are you hungry, my darlings?' Mrs Wetcaufen fussed from across the table. 'Are you hungry-wungry for some steaky-waky?' I began to feel as if I might have stumbled into some strange surrealist play. This impression was in no way alleviated when Courtney proceeded to cut the steaks carefully into eight pieces. I watched in utter disbelief. Mr and Mrs Wetcaufen were obviously too caught up in their vague and continuous marital tension to notice my expression, for which I was grateful. A moment later, my own steak dropped onto my plate. 'Herb butter?' the butler asked, completely deadpan. I willed my expression into something approaching normality, but did not quite trust my voice, so I simply nodded. I could have sworn there was something like complicity in Courtney's smile as he served me.

'You gonna cut up Bradley's steak for him, too?' Robert sneered. 'Where's my dinner?'

'Behave yourself!' his wife shot back with a glower, before simpering at me. We all sat in silence for a while. I wasn't sure if I was supposed to start eating. In any case, I didn't have much appetite anymore. For one thing, the hounds had already begun chomping down on their steaks with great enthusiasm. For another, neither of my hosts had been served and it would have seemed strangely rude to begin, even in such bizarre circumstances. So I just sat there, staring at my steak as it slowly cooled. After what felt like an eternity, Courtney came back with a miniscule salad, which he set down in front of Mrs Wetcaufen. 'I'm on a diet,' she explained to me with a grimace.

'A lot of good it's doing her,' Robert interjected. 'I'm pretty sure we both looked the same when we were both eating proper meals. It's not as if you're ever going to look twenty again, darling. Not if you keep guzzling the wine like that.'

I swallowed uncomfortably and decided eating was the best way out of this awkward situation. I cut a bite of the steak, which was distinctly rare as well as cold by now. In the background, the dogs continued to guzzle their meat.

'Where's my steak?' Robert continued. 'Eh, wifey? Where's my darn steak?'

'Darling, you know it's bad for you. Your health isn't good. You're getting an omelette,' she responded coldly, before placing a tiny bite of salad daintily in her mouth. 'And you'll enjoy it, too,' she added. At this moment, a disagreement broke out on the other side of the table. Earl the pitbull, apparently seeing that his neighbour was eating more slowly, had snuck a piece of Duke's steak and eaten it. The German shepherd starting making a horrific noise in retaliation, growling and struggling in his seat. They were obviously well trained enough animals not to leap straight for each other's throats, but I worried all the same. What if they became enraged and just jumped right across the table? 'Duke! Earl!' Mrs Wetcaufen shouted shrilly, before getting up and throwing her napkin down on the table. 'What have I told you about behaving in front of guests?' She stormed to the other side of the table and slapped the dogs on the side, before hustling them from the room. 'Courtney, help me with this,' she snapped, struggling pathetically with these gigantic dogs in her little dress and heels.

Her husband rolled his eyes at me, as if looking for support. 'Look what I have to live with every day,' his expression seemed to say.

By this point, I was too traumatised to feel very much sympathy for anyone, so I stayed quiet. Mrs Wetcaufen, however, had already returned to her seat. 'What are you telling our guest?' she asked sharply. 'Are you criticising our family in front of our friendly neighbour?'

'I don't mind,' I said hastily. 'I'm just not used to all this.'

'Don't you have someone to make you fancy meals?' Mrs Wetcaufen asked, her voice softening.

'I, er, don't have any dogs,' I replied cautiously.

There was a silence.

'Well, we eat like this every night,' the wife continued, apparently pretending not to have heard my response. So it's nice that you could come and keep us company,' she added pointedly. 'My husband is not in very good health, you see, so he shouldn't be eating big meals at night. His doctor told him so.'

'I'm right here,' the man himself interjected. 'Anyway, eating a five-egg omelette is really not that light an option.'

'Well you're not taking my little darling puppies' steaks away.' Mrs Wetcaufen turned her face towards me in a mask of despair. 'We don't have any children, you see. The dogs really are my babies.'

Robert Wetcaufen made a small noise of disgust and made as if to get up from the table. However, at this moment, the butler discreetly re-entered. 'Are you ready for some dessert?' he asked, maintaining perfect composure.

Mrs Wetcaufen wheeled on him furiously. 'There will be no dessert for my husband,' she hissed imperiously. 'He is sick. Don't you ever listen?' I could hardly believe how badly I had misjudged the woman, from the impeccable façade she had presented to me in our front gardens.

Courtney stared at her, unperturbed. 'Will there be chocolate cake for your guest, madam?'

I watched her Grecian mask of anger dissolve into an approximation of charm again. 'But of course,' she said sweetly. 'Of course!'

There was nothing I wanted less at that moment than that chocolate cake. I squirmed uncomfortably in my seat. Having remembered my presence, Mrs Wetcaufen changed her approach. She turned back to her husband and said: 'Sweetie pie, remember, the doctor told you to steer clear of sweet shops and chocolate.'

It was too late to win Robert over, however. 'Give me two pieces,' he called back to Courtney, who had been hovering discreetly. 'I ate badly tonight. I hate omelette, you know. For some reason I seem to end up eating it every night these days.' He turned back to me. 'It's like living with a dictator,' he sighed. I did not respond. The butler hovered uncomfortably with the vast chocolate cake. I could not wait to get out of that oppressive room.

'I can't eat chocolate, actually,' I suddenly decided to pipe up. 'I too have been on a diet for a few weeks now.' This lie seemed to be effective. Husband and wife looked at me in equal surprise. 'Also, I have lots of work to do,' I continued, improving as I went along. 'I must absolutely finish work on a speech I'm giving in a seminar tomorrow morning. At nine.' I was chattering, but I no longer cared. 'I must do some research this evening. And some practice. It's bound to take me a lot of time and energy. In any case, do you mind terribly if I forego coffee? I really must be going.'

There was a brief silence. 'It's only eight thirty,' Mrs Wetcaufen said in evident bewilderment.

'Are you really going to leave me to put up with the wife on my own for the rest of the night?' Robert implored. His wife narrowed her eyes.

'We have mints,' she said to me. 'And cigars.'

'I don't smoke,' I replied, pushing back my chair. 'And I don't particularly like mints.' As I realised I had the power to leave that awkward situation, I became a little giddy. 'Now I really must go home. I will see you all soon, I'm sure.' I left the room as quickly as I could without appearing to actually run away from the scene. For one thing, I was a little worried the dogs might run after me and bite my legs! I have rarely been so happy to arrive in my own front room. I locked the door and sat down with a calming tisane.

What truly miserable neighbours they were, the Wetcaufens! Several times after that regrettable dinner party, Mrs Wetcaufen tried to speak to me in the garden, presumably in an attempt to invite me back. I managed to dodge her advances quite successfully for the rest of my stay, even if it required a few staged phone calls and several rapid exits from the garden. Even though it has been many years since, and I never saw the couple again, I remember that awful dinner as if it was yesterday: the henpecked husband, the crazy wife who talked more to her dogs than to her guests, and the strange butler. These are not neighbours I remember fondly, although they have proved themselves unforgettable!

ABAJOO AND SUHAILY'S ÉPICERIE

Near our house in Paris, there was a strange little *épicerie* run by a Turkish family. The *épicerie* is, of course, a quintessentially French little institution, best recognised by its ability to contain nearly anything under the sun. In almost any *épicerie*, all over the country, you can buy anything from dried pasta to seven sizes of plastic bag, from screwdrivers to expired suntan lotion, from cheap wine to an odd variety of fruit from all over the world. This is not to say that an *épicerie* will necessarily have the particular item you are looking for, but rather a hundred that you didn't even know you needed!

This particular *épicerie* was odder than most. In the back of the shop, you would find a man whom I assumed to be the grandfather, an ancient man with a white beard, who would usually be kneeling and praying. He kept his prayer rug right in amongst the piles of newspapers and bags of potatoes. He was a fervent Muslim, and rarely seen in any other position. Then, at the counter, there would be a man in his forties, pressing newspapers right up against his nose to read them, despite the fact that he was wearing thick glasses. This was Abajoo, a very odd man indeed.

In my teens, I spent a lot of time walking around the city of Paris, so I would often stop by this shop for a bag of sweets or a snack of fruit. I usually greeted whoever was there, as one is wont to do when walking into a shop. 'Hello,' I would say. 'Isn't it a fine day?' But Abajoo would never reply, simply frowning into his reading material. In the back of the shop, I would hear the murmur of prayers from the grandfather. On the rare days when he was not reading, I would see him totally absorbed in moving items of produce around the shop: carrying huge bags of dates, or trays and trays of Coca-Cola cans; sometimes even a stack of paperback books. They really had everything in that shop! I once saw Abajoo dragging a gigantic green hose through the shop, coils and coils slung over his shoulder.

Abajoo had a younger brother, whose name I didn't know for a long time. He was a tall, dark-haired youth with bright green eyes and a furrowed brow, who didn't seem to spend much time in the shop. This brother, who turned out to be called Suhaily, was only about five years older than me, so I thought he might be a little chattier than his family members. This was not the case. The only time I managed to get him to open up to me was one day when I came into the shop to be greeted by an almighty racket, only to find all three men huddled in the back of a shop with a live turkey. Of course, I went right up to investigate. The youngest brother, Suhaily, seemed excited to have an audience. For once, he didn't look miserable. Instead of slouching against the back wall of the shop, he was bouncing from foot to foot over the scene. 'We're stuffing the turkey with whole walnuts,' he informed me, 'in their shells.'

'Can you do that?' I asked, rather aghast. 'Won't it hurt the bird?'

'Nope,' the boy said proudly, without ever looking away from the spectacle. 'We're just feeding it. It goes into the gizzard – I read it in a book. It gets digested with acid.'

Abajoo looked back at me through his thick glasses, as if noticing my presence for the first time. '*I* read it in a book,' he corrected his brother. 'I told you all the turkey facts you know.'

'We're going to sell a thirty-pound turkey,' Suhaily continued, ignoring him. 'Have you ever heard of such a thing?'

I told him I had not. Abajoo looked aggrieved at our lack of interest in the biological processes at work here. 'Sometimes, turkeys eat small stones to help with digestion,' he volunteered. I nodded in a friendly fashion, before realising that he would probably not be able to see this through his thick, dirty lenses. 'Birds don't have teeth, you see,' he added rather mournfully.

'We'll probably make about two hundred francs from this bird!' his brother ploughed on, obviously not listening. Abajoo, clearly offended, stood up and walked unsteadily out to the front of the shop.

I nodded again. 'That's great,' I replied, not really knowing what to add. 'Has your grandfather always kept turkeys?' I asked him.

The boy burst out laughing. 'That's not my grandfather!' he said. 'That's my dad!' I blushed, but the old man didn't even look up. Perhaps he didn't even speak French. 'I guess he looks pretty old. He'll be eighty-eight next year, you know. He had us late in life. My older brothers and sisters have families of their own, back in the South of Turkey.'

'So your father comes from Turkey, and raises turkeys?' I asked.

'That's right.'

'What about your brother?'

'He's crazy,' Suhaily replied in an offhand manner. 'Nearly blind and crazy. All he does is read. It's how he ruined his eyes. As you can see, he's very irritable.'

'I assumed he was your father,' I confessed.

'That's crazy! Abajoo's never even had a girlfriend,' he said. 'Although he is nearly twenty years older than me, I suppose.'

'So what are you doing here, anyway?' I asked.

'They are forcing me to take over the shop,' he sighed. 'I guess Abajoo is too crazy and blind now, and they cannot sacrifice the place and move away. They need one of us to run it.'

'Have you been to school? Do you know how to run a shop?' I asked him.

'Not really,' Suhaily shrugged. 'I left school when I was twelve,' he said. 'I've been here, running in and out of the shop, for eight years. I don't even like Paris, really. I'd much rather run away and join the Foreign Legion. What do you think?' he asked hopefully.

I had no idea what was expected of me in these circumstances. 'I can't advise you to run away from your family,' I told him carefully. 'And I don't know anything about the Foreign Legion.'

Suhaily didn't seem to be expecting much in the way of wisdom from me. 'Oh well,' he said. 'Maybe God will take me and I won't even have to make these decisions. Maybe a rich woman will fall in love with me in the street and we'll get married. Maybe one day my brother will die and I'll just have to take over the shop.' He sighed grimly. 'I hate them all, you know,' he added casually. 'My brother, my father, the shop, and Paris.'

'Where would you like to go? I asked Maybe you should make some better plans for your life.'

He shrugged. 'Anywhere,' he said. 'Anything.'

One day a few weeks later, as I was walking in the neighbourhood a streets away from the shop, I saw two figures wrestling on the ground. Running over, I found Suhaily beating up a much younger boy, probably about twelve. The distraction of my arrival was enough to give the boy a chance to wriggle out of Suhaily's grip and run away as fast as he could. I saw his bloody face for only a moment before he streaked off into the distance. Suhaily, now sitting on the ground, rubbed a dirty palm across his face. 'What on earth were you doing that for?' I asked, helping to pull him upright.

'The kid stole some fruit,' he muttered, dusting off his torn jacket. 'So I chased him and beat him up.'

'This isn't the army, you know,' I berated him, still a little stunned at the violence I had witnessed. 'You can't just punch a child like that, even if he's stolen some of your goods. You could have been arrested.'

'I don't care,' he said. 'I ran faster than the kid. That's satisfying enough.' He straightened his lapels.

'Wait, you chased him all the way from the shop?' I asked, struggling to process the whole story. 'Well, I guess it's quite impressive for a man your age to be able to run that far, that fast,' I added, trying to fall into line with my neighbour's thinking. I had to admit I was both impressed and aghast.

'I'm a good long-distance runner,' he said. 'This is important to me.'

'Important to you? So your interests, as far as I can tell are : violence, hating your father, and fast running? I can't say I understand you. You're such a good-looking guy, and you seem smart to me. Why don't you go back to school?'

'Maybe I should,' he pondered. 'But what would my father and brother do? They won't sell the shop. They need someone to pass it on to.'

'You need to start making your own decisions about your life,' I told him firmly. 'If you don't want to spend it stacking boxes of dates and chasing small boys down the street, maybe you need to make some changes.'

'I don't know what I want,' the boy confessed, his face twisted in confusion.

'That's alright, at your age,' I said shortly. 'Now, come on, let's go back to the shop and clean the blood off your hands. I can't imagine that will help you attract customers.'

He laughed a little, and we walked down the street. When we arrived inside the *épicerie*, we found everything as it always was, undisturbed. The turkey gobbling in the background, the grandfather saying his prayers, Abajoo reading the papers. Nobody even seemed to have noticed that Suhaily had left. 'Hi, Abajoo,' Suhaily said hesitantly. His brother didn't even look up. I took my leave as hastily and politely as I could, leaving the strange family to their own business. I looked back as I walked down the hot street, and caught Suhaily watching me through the dusty window.

After this rather bizarre encounter, I continued to visit the shop less frequently although without further incident. Things stayed much as they had been previously, and I hardly ever saw Suhaily. However, about a year after the incident of violence, I came in looking for some dried fruit. Before I could muster my usual vague greeting, Abajoo sat bolt upright, dropped his paper and came right up to me. I was so stunned I couldn't even think of anything to say. 'Hello,' I eventually managed.

'Have you seen Suhaily?' he asked me at once, his face contorted in a deep frown of concern. He had a much lighter accent than I had anticipated: perhaps he spoke to other people regularly, although I doubted it. More likely, he had picked up his French from hearing other people talk. After all, he seemed to have scholarly ambitions.

'Your brother?' I asked, surprised. 'No, I haven't seen him in a long time. I haven't really been in the shop much lately.'

'But you were friends with him,' he continued in a tone verging on desperation. 'I saw you with him. You used to talk to him all the time. You never talked to me, or to my father.'

This reproach seemed rather unfair to me. 'I've had no more than two memorable encounters with Suhaily, I'm afraid. And I would have happily talked to either of you, only you never even answered my friendly greetings!' I replied, beginning to lose patience with this odd enquiry. 'Why are you asking me? Did he say something about me?'

'We haven't seen him in days,' he explained, the resentment draining from his face completely. 'I didn't mean to accuse you of anything. It's just that I knew you had talked to him. I thought maybe you two were friends. Maybe you might know,' he said, the tone of madness returning to his voice. He began moving his hands awkwardly, as if he meant to grab me by the lapels and shake any information I might have out of me.

'He's a nice young man,' I said, edging a step or two back from Abajoo's emotions, 'but I can't say I knew him well. I know that he had a violent streak, and that he was interested in the army. He told me so once. I don't know if that's of any relevance, though.

This exchange was a good year and a half ago. I learned everything I know about your brother from two conversations, one of which was mostly about turkeys.'

'Alright,' Abajoo said in despair. 'I guess there is nothing more to do than wait.'

In the end, I never found out what happened to Suhaily. I went away to university in the United States, and rarely found myself in France. However, one summer I did go back to the shop, or attempt to: when I arrived, the place was long closed. I asked the neighbours if anyone knew what had become of the owners, but no-one had any idea. A few remembered the Turkish shopkeepers, but nobody really knew what had happened to them. I suppose it is typical of French neighbours to know very little about the lives of those they share streets with, but it left me saddened to realise I would never find out what happened to Suhaily, Abajoo, the ancient father or the turkey.

THE HAMBURGER NEIGHBOUR

Amedoo Tell was a very fat man, and a very expensive butcher. No-one ever forgot their first sight of Amedoo: he was of medium height, but he was so rounded that he looked short and stocky. His hands were always sweaty and greasy, and his apron was always covered in blood. He was usually clutching a kitchen knife so big it looked like a sword, or sometimes a meat cleaver that looked ready for a medieval battle.

He had a shop just down the street from my childhood house in the north of Paris, and was usually found striding up and down outside it, impressing small children and frightening tourists with his bloody weaponry. The display in the front window of his shop looked like the aftermath of some sort of massacre: you would usually see legs of lamb piled haphazardly next to huge, ten-kilo rounds of fillet mignon. Then there would be two saddles of lamb, and a pile of chateaubriand steaks, and three shoulders of lamb hanging, and a whole young lamb hanging up by its feet with its head still attached. I never understood to whom this display could be even remotely appetising. Perhaps some Arabian prince shopping for something to stuff for a regal *méchoui* served in a private residence on Avenue Foch or Quai d'Orsay? I don't know, but appetising it must have been, for Amedoo never lacked clientele. Some days, there would be a queue stretching out into the street.

From a young age, I found myself fascinated by the shop; often walking past it just to catch sight of Amedoo Tell brandishing his gleaming knives as he grinned at his clients. Of course, I had no intention of buying meat myself: I was only fourteen. As a young person there was literally no reason for me to be buying my own lamb or beef. My family did all the shopping themselves, helped by our cook, who had a real talent for picking the best and most affordable cuts of meat. They never shopped from Mr Tell. 'He's so ridiculously expensive,' my father sneered. 'I would never shop there. There are so many better places to buy meat in Paris, where you can get excellent products for far more reasonable prices. Boucherie Bernard, for instance.' I had no reason to question my family's expertise on the matter. Still, I often found myself wandering past that shop window.

One day, as I was standing there, gazing at the gleaming piles of meat, Amedoo Tell suddenly materialised right by my shoulder. As usual, he was holding his largest knife. From up close, I noticed that his hands were stained red, and that he smelled rather strange. 'Do you want me to make you a hamburger?' he asked. That knife he was holding was easily big enough to cut off my head.

'Oh, no thank you,' I said. 'I have plenty of food at home.'

'Yes, but my meat is the best in the world.'

'I can tell my mother. She might come buy some from you.'

'Why don't you buy it from me right now?'

'I'm only fourteen!'

'Alright, I'll give it to you for free. I've seen you walk by here often. You're a good neighbour and I'm sure you'll make a faithful customer as soon as you're old enough. Meanwhile, I've just cut the best part off the back of a cow. I can't think of a better customer to offer it to right now. Let me mince it up for you. You take it home, get your mother or your cook or whoever you like to make it into hamburgers. Serve them with fresh tomato on a nice brioche bun; not too much salt or pepper. Keep it classic; this is good meat. And you just make sure to tell everyone those great hamburgers come right from old Amedoo Tell.'

Of course, there wasn't much I could say to this. What justification could I come up with to refuse four free hamburgers? I couldn't see what was wrong with it. Also, he was still holding a very large knife. I took the packet home, and gave it to my mother. 'What is this?' she asked in confusion. My father snatched it from her hands and unwrapped the stained white grease-paper.

'It's hamburger!' I tried to explain, with a sinking feeling in my stomach. 'I got it for free!'

'You stole it?' my mother asked in incomprehension.

'No,' I explained hastily. 'Amedoo Tell gave it to me for free.'

My mother and father exchanged glances. 'You should never take something for nothing,' my mother said sternly. 'You owe him something, now. How do you feel about that?'

'He's a nice man!' I defended myself. 'I thought it might be a good thing to be friends with our local butcher!'

'How do you know it's not poisoned?' my father added, somewhat facetiously.

My mother snorted with laughter. 'I doubt it. Have you seen how fat he is?'

'Nonetheless, he's the most expensive butcher in Paris. Why is he giving out meat for free? Is this some kind of trick?'

'He just exaggerates his prices. That's why we don't buy from him,' my mother added, nodding at me. 'I know you don't understand, but you shouldn't take hamburgers from people like that.'

'He gave it to me!'

'Still.'

'Fine, I won't do it again.'

Of course, we ate the hamburgers all the same. I watched my parents sinking their teeth into this meat they had maligned so fervently, and I found it hard to understand. At some point, my confusion and resentment boiled over. 'I still don't understand why it was so bad to accept this gift,' I told my father. 'What's so terribly wrong with Amedoo Tell? Aren't these hamburgers delicious? I think they're just as tasty as the ones we get from Boucherie Bernard.'

My father sighed. 'There's nothing ethically wrong with it in itself,' he said. 'There's just something a little crooked about that Amedoo man. This one time, I was walking by the shop, and I heard someone having a long argument with Tell. From what I gathered, he was selling veal at seventy francs per kilo, which is a rip-off in any case, but it was supposedly excellent quality. In any case, while he was mincing it, this man allegedly saw him throw in some chunks of grizzly old cow, without saying anything. When he tried to confront Tell about it, and ask him to lower the price, Tell denied it. Of course, veal steak is worth far more than any other kind of beef, so the whole thing was a big cheat. After that, I couldn't really trust the man. I had always suspected Tell to be a cheat. Anybody so fat and so expensive has to be a cheat.'

'That doesn't make any sense,' I muttered.

'Just look at him!' my father added. 'Doesn't he just look like a trickster? He's deceitful; he's a liar. I don't even know why we're still having this discussion; we can't afford his meat in any case.'

'I don't know why you care so much,' my mother interjected. 'Surely it's not such a big deal. The man's a rip-off, sure, but he gave us a free dinner. He's not ripping us off right now! Quite the opposite. He's just trying to win over our Bradley.'

'That's exactly what I don't like,' my father countered. 'It's sneaky. It's pernicious. It's cheating.'

'Why do you care so much?' I replied. Being a teenager, I found it difficult to let questions lie unsolved.

'Because he ripped me off, too!' my father burst out. There was a long pause. My mother raised her eyebrows.

'What?' I asked.

'I'm sorry?' asked my mother.

My father glared at us. I was glad, at that moment, that he did not have Amedoo Tell's large knife to hand. 'He rips everybody off,' he tried to backtrack.

My mother was not distracted so easily. 'When were you buying from Amedoo Tell? Why on earth don't I know about this?'

'It's not important,' my father muttered. 'If you really want to know, I'll tell you some other time. It was a long, long time ago, and I haven't shopped there since. That's all you need to know. For now, let's just sit and enjoy these silly old hamburgers as a family.'

I never found out what happened between my father and Tell, but this admission of personal resentment at least made sense of the free hamburger episode. I continued to walk by Amedoo Tell's shop, although I never brought home meat from there again. Years later, the shop closed. I found out from a neighbour that he had heart troubles. 'It's hardly surprising,' my father commented, 'with weight like that. What did he eat all day, just beef fat?'

My mother rebuked him. 'It's hardly a nice thing to say about a sick man, no matter what kind of personal vendetta you might have against him.'

'I meant no harm,' my father grumbled.

'You're just bitter because he ripped you off that one time,' I said. 'I always thought he was a perfectly nice neighbour.'

Whatever the truth might have been about Amedoo Tell's personality, that was the only time I ever tasted his wares. I would always remember him principally as a figment of my childhood, and the subject of my father's untold neighbour story.

A DANGEROUS NEIGHBOUR

This story does not concern a direct neighbour of mine, although we did both live in the same city in Switzerland. It does, however, concern the upstairs neighbours of one of my literary assistants. As this assistant was living in a guesthouse we rented for our employees, I ended up quite directly concerned by the events; furthermore, this assistant and the man in question being neighbours is key to the interest in this story, so I think it deserves a place in this volume.

The guesthouse featured several small studios in the heart of the old town, with cosy wooden floors and views out over the narrow cobbled streets. My literary assistant, who did some editorial work for me and took dictation of my writing projects, was living on the second floor of the building. She had been there for several months by late spring, and had settled in quite happily. There was a delicatessen right at her feet, which she loved to visit, and it was only a short walk to the shores of Lake Geneva, so the setting was generally pleasant.

There was, however, one downside to this idyllic location. Unfortunately, the building immediately next to ours on the other side from the deli was a nightclub. In the summer, this started to become something of a problem as almost every weekend the low, throbbing sound of bass would float up from the club and into the rooms of the people trying to sleep! My assistant didn't complain: she was young, and had lived in cities before, so she had been accustomed to shutting out the sound of traffic, music and passing partygoers. However, some of the other people in the surrounding buildings weren't quite so tolerant. One of the neighbours upstairs could often be heard banging on the wall and occasionally shouting out the window. Of course, these noises were far more of a disruption than the music from outside, but my assistant had known strange neighbours before, and she felt no need to get involved. By the end of the summer, she reasoned, the clubbing scene would quieten down considerably as the tourists left town, and surely this man would stop roaring and pacing like a caged bull then.

One weekend, however, she was recovering from a cold, and tried to catch up on lost sleep on the Saturday night by retiring early. She had just put down her book, and was drifting off to sleep, when she was disturbed not by the music, which had started up quietly in the background, but by her upstairs neighbour walking back and forth and shouting. She sighed. There was no way she would be able to sleep in these circumstances. She rose from her bed, pulled on some clothes, and went up the stairs to knock on his door.

'Excuse me,' she said politely in French when he opened the door, 'but I'm finding it difficult to sleep.'

'Who are you?' the man asked suspiciously.

'I'm finding it difficult to sleep,' she repeated.

'So am I!' he shouted, startling her.

The man was about eighty years old, with unkempt grey hair falling in his face. He was leaning on a cane. There appeared to be no lights on in the room behind him. It made for a rather eerie apparition.

'I live downstairs,' she explained, 'I've had a cold; I could really do with some sleep. I know the music is annoying, but do you think you could be a bit quieter as well?'

'Eh?' he said, frowning at her. 'What do you want?'

She sighed, realising his hearing must not be very good. Slightly annoyed, she said : 'Would you mind not shouting quite so much?'

Hearing this, the neighbour guffawed. 'Shouting? It's a wonder you can hear anything at all over that ruckus!' he gestured behind him, towards the street outside.

'Yes, I know the music is annoying, but I can hear you much better. I mean, in a way it's much worse! You're right upstairs from me, you see,' she added in exasperation.

'Hear?' he shouted. 'Hear?! I can hear just fine! It's the bass,' he added by way of explanation. 'I can feel it in my bones. Uncivilised music these people listen to, these days. I don't know how they can possibly enjoy it. Although the worst thing is when they leave. They're just a bunch of drunks, the lot of them, staggering down the street, breaking glass and shouting. They should get rid of them all. I could do it nice and tidily with my hunting rifle, then we'd all get some proper sleep!' He grinned at this point, displaying rows of yellow teeth in what was obviously meant as a display of mirth, but my assistant was nervous all the same.

'That really won't be necessary,' she replied hastily. 'Anyway, it's been nice talking to you. I'm going back to bed.'

'It's a great rifle,' he continued, ignoring her completely. 'I shot many a deer with it in my day. Don't go out there, young lady,' he added, seeing her movement away from his door. 'It's no place for a nice girl like you. Drunken youths, all of them. Corrupt and drunk.'

'I won't,' she assured him, before taking her leave, cautiously tiptoeing down the stairs and heading back to bed. As soon as she was safely back under the covers, she knew her words had had no effect: almost instantly, she could hear him pacing and shouting again. He must have started the moment he closed the door. My assistant was tired, though, and gave the episode little more thought. She eventually fell asleep and forgot all about the encounter for the next few months.

One summer's night, however, she was reminded of it in a rather terrible manner. It was the height of tourist season, so the club had been busy of late, and her upstairs neighbour making his own usual racket in answer, but nothing out of the ordinary had made her worry about either of these things more than usual. That night, she woke up without being able to tell why around three in the morning, feeling deeply disturbed. She was sure she had heard an awful noise, but couldn't remember what it was. It took her a long time to realise what felt strange, until she noticed that the street outside was completely silent. She sat up in bed, turned on the light and tried to remember if anything out of the ordinary had happened that night. Earlier, the street had been quite noisy and busy: she remembered that the club had been hosting a special event. People were milling around on the sidewalk, drinking and talking outside. It had sounded like a rowdy but friendly scene. The girl stood up, went to the window and looked out. The street was deserted. The only sound she could hear was the distant wail of an ambulance. Unable to figure out what might have occurred, she went back to bed, troubled.

The next day, she read in the paper what had happened: her strange, old upstairs neighbour, grown tired of shouting down at the crowds, had finally lost his temper, or his mind. He shot one of the revellers in the stomach with his hunting rifle. When I found out about the incident, I went to check in on her at once.

'A hunting rifle?' she said to me in disbelief, still obviously in shock. 'He told me about the hunting rifle! I thought he was making some kind of horrible joke!' Her hands were shaking as she poured us cups of coffee.

'No, it's true. The papers are saying he used to be a prolific hunter when he was young. But he's not entirely… stable these days. I don't think anyone really realised quite how troubled he was.'

'He lived right upstairs from me, all this time! I just can't believe it. What if I had been at that party? What if I had heard all the noise of fun from the street and wanted to join in?'

'You don't like clubbing,' I reminded her gently.

'I hate clubbing,' she agreed with a sad smile. 'It's still scary, though. Right on my front door. Switzerland is meant to be a safe place!'

'It is a safe place. I think you've used up your bad luck in terms of neighbours!'

'Do you know anything more on the story?' she asked. 'Is the man OK?'

'I don't know,' I had to admit. 'They took him to hospital, though. And your neighbour has been taken away by the police. I don't think his shouting and banging will be troubling you again anytime soon.'

'I hope he doesn't trouble anyone anytime soon!' she said, looking sadly into her coffee cup.

'I'll tell you what I'll do,' I said, hoping to cheer her up. 'I can't change your neighbours, but maybe we can change this room a little. Let's make sure you never have to hear the music from that club again: I'll put in sound insulation!'

So I did. The man never moved back in, and we never heard anything more on that particular story. I ordered carpenters and builders in, who thoroughly insulated the room. My assistant was never bothered by the music or her neighbours again.

THE DISAPPROVING FARMER

In the days of my PhD, when I was studying at LSE, my friends were a rather interesting group. LSE was at the forefront of its field in those days, attracting high-flying politicians and artists to the school as well as various aristocrats, economists and thinkers, from Bill Clinton to Mick Jagger. London was a busy and exciting place to be, and my friends and I loved our time at the school, but it could be a rather intense environment at times. We decided to club together and rent a house deep in the Essex countryside, where we could easily get away together for a weekend to study and relax out of the fast-paced city. We found a wonderful house in Wivenhoe, near Colchester, which was close enough to the libraries of the University of Essex campus to be exceedingly convenient for our studies.

The house was large, with comfortably-furnished interiors in raw pine and woolly carpet. It was beautiful, and fairly upmarket, so despite being a very attractive place, and in good shape, it had lain empty for a while. Students were too intimidated by it to enquire after the price, which was actually quite reasonable once we shared it between a few of us. There were four bedrooms, and plenty of independent space. It was also an excellent place for parties, as there was a generous lounge area downstairs with several couches and a low table.

Our next door neighbours were farmers, as is usually the case this deep into the countryside. We were surrounded by cultivated fields and narrow lanes, which were great for long rambles. The neighbour who lived closest to us was a tall, muscular man in his fifties, who looked rather like the English incarnation of a cowboy. He wouldn't have looked out of place in spurs and a Stetson, riding across the plains of New Mexico. As it was, however, he was usually in wellies and a Barber jacket, riding his tractor or striding along the back lanes with his sheepdog. His name was Eddie, and he had horses, a herd of sheep and several cows, that lived across the nearest fields to us.

We saw Eddie an uncharacteristically large amount: English farmers usually keep to themselves. This one, however, was curious and, I suspect, rather suspicious about our lives. He used to hover around the house, and if we happened to be in the garden, he would always strike up a conversation. In his muddied blue dungarees, he would lean on the fence with his pitchfork and just watch us until we became uncomfortable.

'What're you boys and girls doing here?' he asked one of the first times we spoke. At the time, I was staying there with two young men from my course and three young women.

'We're just having lemonade,' one of the boys answered. 'Would you like some?'

'No, no thanks,' he answered a little hastily. 'I mean something more like: what are you boys doing out here in the country? You look like students. Shouldn't you be up in Colchester?'

'Oh, we are students,' I said. 'But not at Essex. We study at the London School of Economics.'

'How old are you all, then?' he asked.

'Well,' I replied, 'the youngest of us is eighteen. I'm twenty-three, myself.'

'So you're the pack leader,' he said, squinting at me. 'Did you win the lottery? How do kids your age have a weekend house?'

One of the girls giggled, and her blonde friend rolled her eyes a little. The blonde was a tall, willowy young woman, who smoked heavily and only really came to the country because she was dating my friend. 'We just need to get out of the city sometimes,' she said coolly. 'We really love it around here,' she added without much conviction.

'Hm,' the farmer grunted, obviously unsure how to respond.

'I'm sorry,' I said, 'but I didn't catch your name.'

'What do you mean?' he said. 'Don't you know who I am?'

'Are you the biggest farmer in town?' the blonde asked coyly.

'Well yes,' he responded, puffing his chest out slightly. 'I'm Eddie.' Then he narrowed his eyes a bit suspiciously. 'You're not making fun of me, are you?'

'Oh no,' I said hastily. 'We didn't really know anything about the town, but we love the house. It's nice to meet you, Eddie. I'm Brad.'

'Well you stay out of trouble, Brad. And your friends, too.'

'Alright, Dad,' the blonde girl muttered, but Eddie didn't appear to hear.

'Oh, don't worry,' I said brightly. 'We're studying.'

'We'll be the leaders of this generation,' one of the boys piped up.

'So where is it you people are studying, again?'

'LSE,' I said.

'Is that the stock exchange or something?' he said hesitantly.

'It's the school of economics,' I explained.

Eddie adjusted his pitchfork awkwardly. His cheeks were rather red. The other boy, who had been quiet up until now, interrupted the conversation. 'Do you sell your produce forward?' he asked, leaning forward over the fence. He had curly hair and was one of the keener students in the year below me. 'To hedge your prices, I mean,' he added.

'What's that?' the farmer asked suspiciously, leaning a little bit away from him.

'Hedging your price,' the boy explained patiently, 'is when you sell your product forward ahead of the harvest. So if you're growing potatoes, for instance, you could sell your potatoes in May or so, ahead of the September harvest.'

'The harvest is in July,' the farmer said, a little confused. 'Are you making fun of me?'

'Oh no,' the boy said in surprise. 'I'm genuinely curious. You see, I've never spoken to a farmer before.' Eddie was not impressed by this. Unfortunately, the boy ignored my warning glances and continued on this vaguely insulting track. 'I'd be interested in giving you a sort of lesson in economics, you see. I get the impression these kinds of markets are extremely old fashioned. You could use a consultant. Someone like me.'

The farmer looked so flabbergasted he was obviously unable to reply.

'You see,' my friend continued in complete oblivion, as if he were lecturing a single unruly undergraduate, 'this way, your prices will always remain the same, whether you have a good or bad harvest. You can set your own price. Now, I presume the way it is now, if the worldwide harvest is excellent, your price will go down, and if it is bad, your price will go up. But you can break out of this cycle.'

'Can you really do this?' To my surprise, Eddie the farmer now appeared to actually be quite interested in my friend's lesson. My friend nodded seriously. 'It's called a commodities market,' he explained.

At this point, a brief silence fell, and all seemed to realise the strangeness of the conversation. The blonde girl coughed awkwardly.

'Is that all you kids study?' Eddie returned to his gruff manner. 'Don't you have your own jobs to organise?'

'Oh no,' the boy said earnestly. 'It's just that you're a perfect specimen to interview. We're in classrooms all day, you see. You're supposed to be very strong, good economic element, because you're a farmer.'

'Are you making fun of me?'

I couldn't quite believe this exchange was really taking place.

'No, not at all,' he said. At this point, as principal host, I decided it was time to cut in. 'Would you like to come in and have a drink?' I asked politely.

'You have drinks? Aren't you all a bit young for all that? Nice young girls, too?' he added, clearly both fascinated and slightly appalled by this idea.

'Yeah,' the blonde girl drawled, 'We have pretty much anything you like. Guinness, beer, scotch, gin, you name it.'

'Are you making fun of me?' he asked again.

'Absolutely not,' I said, as politely as I could. He shook his head a little. 'Don't know why I'm still talking to you bloody fool youngsters. You get on with your drinking, then, but make sure you don't make too much noise. And don't try to teach an old dog new tricks, eh?'

And with that line, ignoring the protestations of my friends, he walked stiffly back across the fields. Eddie often asked us again about our parties, and our reasons for being in the countryside, but never again did we bring up economics. After four or five weekends, however, he relaxed somewhat and grew to accept our presence. I'm not sure he ever quite understood us, but he certainly came to consider us as neighbours.

THE NEIGHBOUR I COULDN'T REMEMBER

I had an apartment on Eaton Square for over twenty years, so I was used to running into an odd selection of neighbours, more or less familiar to me: old ladies walking their dogs, lords carrying a case of wine, barons and dukes bumbling home to their wives. I walked back and forth across the square often, particularly so when I first acquired my club membership to play tennis on what was widely considered the best tennis court in London. I much preferred the Eaton Square tennis court to Wimbledon or Queen's Park. One of the very best things about it was that it was nearly always empty: everybody living in the square was either far too old, far too fat, far too busy, far too well-dressed, or far too rich and lazy to swing a tennis racket around. It would have been quite a sight to see some of my neighbours bouncing a ball up and down, I can tell you that! The regulations dictated that a classic tennis costume must be worn, which would have added to the comedy of the scene greatly.

In any case, I myself was wearing my spotless tennis whites one sunny spring Saturday afternoon in the early 1980s, when I ran into a neighbour I didn't recognise. The man smiled widely, displaying his straight teeth. He was tall and tan, with large almond eyes and a sharp nose. He was wearing a dark grey pinstripe suit with a button-down white shirt and a red tie with stripes.

'Are you Bradley Jamieson?' he asked me.

'I am indeed,' I said, as politely as I could. 'I'm afraid, however, I don't actually know who you are. Are you Earl Robinson from across the street? Are you some lord I ran into at a party? Are you the father of one of my children's friends?'

He shook his head gently. 'Guess again.'

'Are you someone I spoke to at a conference? Have I read a book of yours? Did I meet you on the tennis court, a few years ago?'

'Nope,' he said with a smile. 'Think back... oh, about thirty years. Just imagine me at age fifteen, and I'm sure you will remember.'

'Thirty years? I have no idea what that could be...'

'Don't you remember me, always talking about balance payments, commerce and trade?'

'At age fifteen?'

'Oh yes!

'That's not possible. I would remember you.'

'Don't you remember me sitting in the back of the class with you?'

'My god, I afraid not. I hope you're not taking offence. I just don't always have a very good memory for faces, particularly ones that must have aged thirty years since I last saw them!'

'Well, I am a shy sort of person, so this is not a huge surprise to me. I am a man of few words. I'll give you a better clue. Does the name Web mean anything to you?'

'No, I'm afraid not. That's just making the situation even worse! What are you, a spider of something?'

I had to admit I was getting rather bored of this whole exchange. I didn't really care who this man was! For all I knew, he was making the whole thing up. Maybe he was crazy. I tapped my tennis racket on the ground suggestively.

'No, I'm not,' he said rather shyly. 'I'm an economist. But I will give you the full story, and you can tell me if it rings any bells. You were always at the front of the class, while I sat at the back. You always had the answers, especially in chemistry, and in mathematics and literature. I was terrible in all of those subjects. All I wanted was to study commerce, so I did. Now, I have a PhD in economics.'

'Wait,' I said, confused. 'Where did you do your PhD?'

'I was at the London School of Economics,' he said with shy pride.

'What year?' I asked him, in surprise.

'Oh, I went there late. When I was in my early thirties.'

'Ah, that's why I missed you! Because I also studied at LSE. If, as you say, we are about the same age, then that explain why we never crossed paths... But I must say, the longer this conversation continues, the more familiar you seem. Do you have any more clues you could give me about the time we spent together?'

He grinned. 'Well, I could tell you my last name,' he exclaimed, like some sort of Rumpelstiltskin character. 'Zuggar. My name is Web Zuggar.'

All at once, a sort of light bulb went off in my head. 'I have it now!' I cried out, feigning excitement. 'I remember you! You were a shy little kid. You had just come in from Armenia or Turkey, and joined our French private school.'

'Yes!' he crowed. 'Armenia. That's probably why you don't

remember. We were only in class together once, when we were
fifteen. I was quite shy and boring,' he volunteered rather casually. 'I
would have been easily forgotten.'

'OK, now this is all coming back to me,' I continued, wishing to
avoid further embarrassment. 'I remember thinking that your name
must mean "sweet" or "sugar" in nearly all the old languages. '

'Oh, I don't know. It's just a name,' he said.

I couldn't believe that someone would take so little interest in the
meaning of their own name. 'You're a funny guy,' I said. How dull
he seemed! I longed to be on the tennis court, sending the ball sailing
back and forth across the stunning blue sky. I held back a sigh.

'Oh, I know I'm boring,' he said evenly. 'We only talked a couple
times even in those days. I know you were good in class and I was
bad. My childhood was a simple one. I never had the answers. But I
grew up. I've studied economics – and I was good at it, too! I ended
up working for the World Bank and the I.M.F. I just came back from
Washington and am now happily settled in Eaton Place.' He looked
around himself with a contented sigh like a cat. 'I take a walk for half
an hour at the end of each week, that's all the exercise I get. That's all
the time I have for pleasure. I'm now consulting in the city, with all
the big companies: Imperial Tobacco, British American Tobacco,
Rio Tinto, General Electric, Marconi.' I had become rather bored
about halfway through this list, and was beginning to wonder when
this biographical tirade would end. After all, I barely remembered
the boy except as a dull presence in my schooldays! Why did he think
I would be interested in his progress since? 'I advise them about their
expansion of their markets as well as their economic risk in sovereign
countries,' he continued, obviously not taking the hint. I tried to
look as if I was interested, when really I was trying to check if the
sun was in any danger of setting before Zuggar finished talking at
me. 'For instance, I tell everybody to be careful about investments
and loans in South America. All those countries are in deficit; they
don't balance their payments. They have terrible accounting, and of
course nearly all of them are dictatorships.' This was 1981: I had to
admit the man spoke the truth.

'Is that the advice you give to everybody?' I asked, reluctant to
engage, but with my interest piqued against my will.

'Of course. My advice is standard. It's good, and it's the same for everyone I meet.' Good god, I thought, does he bore everyone he meets in this same way? 'I learned a lot in the World Bank,' he said. 'About the risks in sovereign countries. Of course, most of North Africa and all of South America has bad debt.'

I knew this already, of course, and it took every fibre of my being not to say so. 'A friend of mine has a similar theory,' I said coolly.

Being a man of few words, he only gave me a faint smile.

'I've been a banker for many years,' I said. 'And this friend once told me: never lend to countries where the people dance in the streets.'

Involuntarily, he let out a laugh, before frowning intently. 'What do you mean?' he asked.

'Well,' I said, thinking to myself: this is how you make economics interesting! Just watch and learn, little Web Zuggar! 'This friend tells me that in Brazil, Morocco, the Philippines, Egypt, and nearly all of Africa, the people are always out dancing in the street. Of course, as you must know, these are some of the worst countries to consider lending to.'

'Well that's a neat little statistic!' he said, in a manner that I considered rather more patronising than the occasion demanded. 'Rather incidental, I would say, but still of some sociological value.'

'It has never failed me,' I told him coldly. 'I put the correlation into my computer and it came out at a hundred percent.'

'I'll bear that in mind,' he said flatly.

There was a pause. I smiled as politely as I could and adjusted my tennis whites. I had no desire to continue this conversation. Stubbornly, I kept my mouth shut. For about thirty seconds, it was a real comedy stalemate. At last, reluctantly, Web Zuggar held out his hand. Perhaps he had been hoping he could tell me about every separate course he took in his degree, or about all the roads he liked to walk along in London! In any case, I did not give him the chance. I took his extended card, gave him mine in return (I always carry business cards, even in my sports clothes) and walked off swiftly with my tennis racket on my shoulder. Although I was late for my partner, I had an excellent game of tennis and quickly forgot the whole boring incident.

Zuggar, however, was not so forgetful. Several months later, I received a phone call from an unknown number at work. When

I picked up, I heard a smug, boring voice that I couldn't help but recognise. 'Have you seen the news?' he said, without any introduction or even the vaguest attempt at friendly small talk. 'They've unilaterally declared a moratorium on the debts of Argentina, Brazil and Mexico.' He had simply called me up to prove his boring point. It was phenomenal.

'Yes,' I said, 'I read the papers.' I paused. Suddenly, it occurred to me how I should respond. 'You know all those countries have dancing in the street,' I said. 'My theory is absolutely true.'

'Yes, absolutely!' he replied, surprising me. In fact, I detected some measure of enthusiasm in his voice. 'I've thought about your friend's theory a lot, lately. It's a good one.' Suddenly, he laughed heartily, and I could hear the childish desire for approval hiding behind his snide exterior. I felt my opinion of Zuggar soften slightly.

'To be fair,' I said, 'not everyone in my own bank listened to my advice.' I told him how some of the officers in my bank had sub-participated in various loans to Morocco and Brazil, neither of which could pay them back. 'We're in a little bit of trouble,' I confessed.

Web burst into peals of laughter, and I wondered if I should regret opening up to him. 'You should have listened to me!' he said, rather unfairly. I had known all along, without his intervention! It didn't mean that everyone in my bank unilaterally followed my advice. Of course, it was not to my advantage to make this particular point then. I bristled and bit my tongue. 'Seriously, though,' he said, becoming more solemn as he heard the lack of mirth from my end of the line, 'why don't you try to do a debt equity swap? Exchange your debt in Brazil for an investment. We do it all the time. You could easily partner with the Brazilian government in various projects. I could suggest some names to contact, if you want.' That made me regret my harshness again.

'Thanks,' I said gratefully, 'that actually sounds like a great idea.' I paused, actually hoping he would continue. When he stayed silent, probably thinking he was boring, I had to ask: 'Could you tell me a little bit more about how to proceed?'

I followed Web Zuggar's advice on this occasion, and several times in the future. Our bank swapped our debts in Brazil for an important investment in agriculture, oil and the navy. He gave me some excellent advice also with regards to our investments in

Morocco. From then on, I never let myself think he was boring. In fact, I found myself wishing I had spent much more time with my passing neighbour the first time I ran into him on the way to my tennis match! Web Zuggar might have been a boring neighbour, but he was also nearly always right.

TINY TRESPASSERS

Our house in Switzerland has a history of tiny trespassers, thanks to its location not so very far from a school. The reputable nature of the school does little, in my opinion, to subdue the spirits of those who attend it. This includes, I should probably confess, my very own children. I mean, I suppose it is only natural that children between the ages of nine and eighteen will be less than perfectly behaved! Has anyone ever walked past a school courtyard without hearing happy children's shouts and screams? Even if the school is in fact a rather famous private Swiss one, rising above a quiet courtyard with a classic façade, there will always be some rambunctiousness.

The school is a residential establishment, surrounded by the shade of pines and chestnut trees. It has its own swimming pool, and is right next door to a theatre. It also happens to sit right next to our house. When my children were very small, they used to clamber under the hedge to run across to the school and play. The hedge was a good three metres high in places, so going underneath was really the only way to use it as a passageway. We learned this quickly from the state of their palms and knees when we saw them at the dinner table, or when changing for bed! It became the go-to *passage piéton* for the whole neighbourhood. Of course, once they started attending the school themselves, they taught all their friends and classmates about this passageway. Later, when they were all a bit taller, they started climbing over on certain days as well. In any case, the message was passed around, and generalised trespassing began. At first, I didn't really mind, as they were mostly young and fairly well-behaved friends of my children. However, some days it became a little ridiculous.

On Sundays, for instance, the children usually went on an organised trip to the theatre, to see some local production of Molière or Plato or Shakespeare. Unfortunately for us, as the school's immediate neighbours, we happened to lie right in between the aspiring thespians and the boards of the stage. At the weekend, it was like being hunters in the middle of a *battue*: throughout the late morning, there would be giggles, scampering and shouts as the children crossed under our hedge and across our land to get to whatever play they wanted to attend. It was laudable, of course, that the school encouraged the children who lived on the school grounds to get their entertainment through high culture. It was perhaps a little unfortunate, however, that they offered no supervision for the journey between the school and the theatre. Of course, the whole thing was probably a distance of some two hundred metres; I am not faulting the teachers! It was just that we were so neatly right in the middle of it all.

It wouldn't have been a problem if the children were well-behaved; but of course, on certain Sunday mornings, they weren't. Leaping and bounding over the hedge, when they were tall enough, or still choosing to crawl under it on their knees, the children ran across our land at all hours of the day. Of course there were fights, from screaming matches to full-out physical brawls. Our house has a large garden: this obviously struck them as the perfect location to conduct their fights. Perhaps a disgruntled butler or maid throwing a jug of water at them might have dissuaded them! Or perhaps we should have planted a sturdier hedge. At the time, it never occurred to us.

Sometimes, they would be having arguments about their studies. If they were on their way back home from a play, they might be having rather clever debates about 'Le Bourgeois Gentilhomme' or 'Romeo and Juliet' or 'Waiting for Godot'. Most of the time, however, perhaps unsurprisingly, their shouting seemed to be mostly composed of petty exchanges.

Over the years, one noticeable evolution of these fights was their expansion into foreign languages. While the school has always been bilingual, and full of English, American, Swiss and French students, Geneva's ever expanding international scene had grown much further than this, slowly filling the school with young Russian, Chinese, Ukrainian and Polish students. Slowly, the complicated politics of the city drifted into the school. This obviously influenced the contents of the fights, as well.

'You don't even speak French!' one voice taunted. 'How can you argue about Molière?'

'At least I'm not a snobby little Swiss boy,' the reply came, swiftly.

'Go back to your mother!' someone would shout. 'Or does she live with you in your shack?'

Then they would all crawl under the hedge and disappear. This transformation of the kids from innocent and curious things to playground politicians was saddening to watch. Most of them lived on the school grounds, which meant that this all happened particularly close to home for our family. It was hard not to feel involved in this transformation. In fact, on a warm day, the smell of borscht or steamed Chinese food drifted across our land, whether or not the children were there. I saw the accommodation for these new students myself one day, and had to admit I was unimpressed. Perhaps the school administration imagines that these new students won't mind as much as the Swiss kids how big their rooms are, or whether their houses look like prefabricated shacks! I guess they still get exactly the same education, though. If their voices in our hedge were anything to go by, they got to see as many plays, too.

I suppose these are simply the things one has to deal with if one lives right next to a school. We couldn't really complain if the children were so keen to get to the theatre that they wanted to take a fun shortcut. In the end, we found a solution to the problem: we now have two hedges and a metallic fence! But we still get the cooking smells, and we can still hear the excited shouting.

Some neighbours are best remembered for their more amusing attributes. For instance, Liam was a short, bouncy, gum-chewing neighbour of mine. He was very thin, very well-dressed, and constantly talked as he jumped around a room. Most times I saw him, he was also waving a long white serviette and snipping a pair of scissors in a musical fashion.

Liam was my barber, and the most talkative one I have ever met. I made my first trip to him at the age of seven, and after that first snip, he would cut my hair on a regular basis for the rest of my life. There are only a few neighbours who have been present from my childhood into my adult life. It is nice to keep those markers, those memories that can be revived in an instant. For me, there were times when walking into Liam's barber's shop was as profound an experience as Proust dipping his madeleine in tea. In the end, it was less Liam's skill at cutting hair that I remembered him for, and more his inability to stop talking. He knew everything about my parents, uncles, grandparents. He knew all about my neighbours, and about the lives of everyone who came into his salon. He told me secrets about all sorts of people whose hair he had cut, including two ministers of state, two central bankers and three chairmen of companies. When Liam cut someone's hair, he seemed to manage to casually extract all sorts of deeply personal information from them, about their work, their children, their wives and their mistresses. Going into Liam's barber shop was much more exciting than reading any tabloid. I only received news on topics I was interested in, and I received these titbits of news without even having to ask any questions. Liam predicated one's areas of interest, and had the answers to one's questions ready the second one walked into his shop.

The only time Liam ever stopped talking was to take his gum out of his mouth, throw it into the street, and pop in a new piece as a replacement. Those were the only small breaks in his constant stream of talking. He barely seemed to take a breath between sentences. Yet his pieces of news were delivered casually, without any fuss: none was drawn out overlong, and still his supply never seemed to run low. 'Did you hear,' he would say with quiet excitement, 'that the bank manager was seen spending a thousand dollars over dinner? My friend saw him leaving the place with two Russian women.' Despite the relative brevity of his delivery, the gossip still arrived intact, with all the juiciest parts intact. 'You know doctor so-and-so,' he might tell us in a hushed voice, 'I've heard he's going out of business. Spent all his money on gambling.' Spending an afternoon in Liam's salon was like listening to gossip headlines read out, one after the other, on a loop. He would embellish, of course, with details: a mysterious woman was wearing a red satin dress, a cabinet minister dropped his unsmoked cigar from the taxi window. Nothing mentioned was ever superfluous.

Even as he was talking to one person, he would be listening to another, and saying hello to someone who had just come in, motioning for them to sit down behind us. Sometimes there would be four people who had come in without appointments, waiting their turn patiently. Most people didn't even bother to bring a book or a magazine, knowing they would be regaled by Liam's tales. If someone particularly important walked in, like a religious leader, or the head of one of the local companies, Liam would stop whatever he was doing to walk over and give them a hug, sit them down, bring them a coffee, a tea, or a cold Coke. Then, in a feat of tremendous charisma, he would somehow manage to keep all these people entertained, from the man getting his hair cut to the four people in line and the politician in a chair. He would tell intimate stories about whatever figures happened to not be present. At the same time, he would manage to apologise to everyone for having to wait, although no-one ever seemed to mind, even the unlucky clients who had to wait an hour and a half while he dealt with the more glamorous clients. After all, they were bound to get some good gossip if they were in Liam's hands straight after he had gleaned some new piece of information! The whole performance was rather like an elaborate dance show. In fact, I know that Liam believed his talking and bouncing kept him fit. 'Men like me never get varicose veins!' he crowed once. 'Do you know what my health advice is? Never stop moving, and never make time to eat. I'm too busy to get fat!'

I went to visit Liam every few weeks when he was my neighbour, up until the day when I moved out of the country to go to college for six years. Still, the very week I returned, I found myself longing for a visit to my old barber's shop. When I walked in, nothing had changed. The light, the faint smell of citrus and flowers, the sound of Liam's shoes squeaking as he bounced around the room. The linoleum on the floor was a different colour, and the magazines on the table were more garish, but otherwise, everything was exactly the same. 'Hello, Liam,' I said as I entered. 'Remember me?'

He looked me up and down. I suppose I would have grown a little brawnier in my time away, and I was wearing a smart suit, but Liam's features gave no indication that he had noticed any change. 'It's been a while,' he said. 'I hope you haven't been to any other barber shop in the meantime?'

I tried to keep a straight face. 'Of course not,' I said. 'It's only been six years. I'm a young man, my hair doesn't grow that fast.'

Liam burst out laughing and clapped me on the back amiably. 'Welcome back, old friend,' he said. 'You've accumulated a lot of good gossip to catch up on...'

I waggled a finger at him. 'Don't you go telling me anything about my family, mind. I haven't even seen my aunts and uncles for the last six years.'

'Friend,' he replied, 'if I knew anything salacious, I wouldn't be able to hold it back. As it is, I have enough other people to tell you about. Now sit down, have a coffee, and let me finish up on my other client here before I sort out that ridiculous hair of yours.'

At last, he sat me down and settled a fresh towel around my neck. 'If you don't want to hear about your family,' he said, 'I shall just have to tell you about our other neighbours.' He then proceeded to regale me with details of the lives of four ministers, two minor government officials and a variety of other local figures. By halfway through the haircut, I felt as if I had been given a crash course in local politics and gossip. It didn't stop there, though. He went on to describe the new buildings in town, the changing stalls at the local market, the weddings planned for the summer. By the end of his speech, the other clients were beginning to cough discreetly and tap their feet. At this point, Liam chose to ignore them completely, instead squinting closely at my face. 'Do you know,' the said thoughtfully, 'I think your beard has grown.'

'What, since I've been in here?'

He nodded, completely deadpan. 'I think I have been talking too much. Now, I have a whole new job to do!' he announced loudly. I had the distinct feeling that he was making fun of the waiting clients. The funny thing was that none of them stood up and left. They only rolled their eyes with something quite like affection. With a flourish, Liam produced a huge brush made of animal hair and a ball of perfumed soap. Taking his time, he lathered up my beard for a good ten minutes. When he produced the razor, it was like watching a fine samurai take his place, although I doubt a samurai would have had quite such a talent for chatter! In fact, once the fine blade started running over my face, there were moments when I found myself fearing for my life. It wasn't that Liam lacked skill in any way, but simply that he seemed to be paying no attention whatsoever to the task at hand. I didn't mind either the gossip or the swift shaving in themselves, but I did mind the lack of care he gave to the combination. When he finally finished, and towelled the foam from my face, I pretended to wipe the sweat from my brow. 'Well, you do know how to make the mundane exciting,' I told him. 'In fact, I'd go so far as to say that was a pretty close shave.'

After this, I did not come into Liam's shop for a long time. Not because of his dangerous shaving techniques, naturally, but simply as I moved abroad, got married, had children, and generally carried on with life away from my childhood home. However, thirty years later, I found myself in the neighbourhood again, and I couldn't resist a chance to catch up on the gossip.

'Bradley!' he said as soon as I walked in. 'I hope you haven't been visiting another barber. Such unfaithfulness to your childhood barbershop would be unforgivable!'

I laughed and clapped him on the back. 'Yes, can't you see? My beard is nearly two metres long by now.'

'Now, if you'll just sit down, I'll make you a coffee... It's Nespresso these days, though!'

I looked around me as I sat with my coffee. The smell and the setting had changed very little, but there were now two other barbers working away. Everything looked swanky and clean. Yet Liam's routine appeared to be absolutely identical. I watched him smiling as he cut two men's hair in quick succession, almost as if executing a precise dance; one that he had honed for most of his life.

'It's incredible how little this place has changed,' I told him when he had finished and was washing his hands.

'I want to show you something,' he replied, beckoning me out to the front of the shop. As I stood blinking in the bright sun, he pointed a bright red bicycle on the pavement. 'Look at this bicycle,' he said. 'It's the same bicycle I used when you were just seven years old. You probably walked past it when you came in here for your first haircut. See, it's still maintained, oiled, with a coat of fresh paint. Doesn't look a day older than new, does it?' I had to agree with him. 'I maintain my shop like I maintain my bicycle,' he continued with pride. 'I know all my customers personally.'

I had to grin. 'You certainly do.'

'I could reel off every affair every town official has had,' he said proudly. 'I probably know most of their coat sizes, too. There's no fact about this place I don't know. The best part of all this is that I will be here until I die, telling the story of the shop, and the neighbourhood, and the whole country. I can tell you everything and anything you want to know, and most of what you don't even care about: who was born when, and who died when, and who got married. Do you know what else, Bradley? I've been successful. This hasn't just been an indulgence, a little bit of fun. This has been a really successful business. From what I've earned in this joy, I managed to build a big villa with a garden. I've been happy. I'm happy now, with my two kids and a beautiful wife.'

'You've been a real pillar of society, you know,' I told him gently. 'I can hardly imagine this city without your shop.' He beamed with pride.

'Do you know what I've been thinking? I'm not going to retire for another ten years. Hell, I'm only seventy-six now! There are many more stories for me to hear. Not that I'm not looking forward to having all day to spend in the garden. In fact, do you want to hear why I like gardening so much? It's exactly the same as being a barber. Snip snip snip,' he said with a childish little gesture. 'I'll have spent all my life cutting hair and cutting grass. Trimming hedges, trimming beards. There's a little less weeding to be done in the salon, granted...'

'Although you do still have the wonderful colours and perfumes of shampoos and aftershave lotions!' I added.

'I knew you would understand!' he replied.

I haven't seen Liam since my last visit there, but I'm sure he's still right there in his shop, gossiping away, dreaming of moving from cutting hair to cutting grass.

An old piece of folk wisdom says that if a greedy man is given a valley full of gold, he will want two, or three valleys. In the story, he has the first golden valley taken away, and is rewarded instead with a mouthful of dirt.

Well, one of my neighbours was a man of this ilk, if one can consider an idyllic Normandy valley to be worth its weight in gold.

When our family bought our country house in the French countryside in the mid-1980s, I had hoped to acquire some of the land next door. Our own house was surrounded by gorgeous green fields of long grass, spreading all around us in gently rolling slopes and hillocks. Beyond that, there was a little forest copse, through which a little babbling brook threaded towards a small pond, attracting frogs, kingfishers, herons, and even the occasional muskrat.

Unfortunately, much of this lovely land was owned by my next-door neighbour. I longed for these fields to be ours; for my children to be able to run about freely, along the stream and into the forest. In fact, when I first was shown the house and land, I was sure I would be able to acquire the parcel, and expand our own holdings. I had no intention of waiting to accomplish this landscaping dream. I resolved to speak to our neighbour at once.

The French art of being a neighbour is nothing like the American tradition. A knock on the door of a neighbouring farm in, say, Dakota or Wisconsin, would have no doubt resulted in a smiling face, perhaps bearing a plate of cheese or biscuits. Here, the door was swung open reluctantly to reveal the dour face of an old man, who obviously did not want to be disturbed in the middle of his business, whatever that might be. From the smell of him, I guessed that this activity appeared to be rolling around in a pile of moulding onions.

'I'm terribly sorry to disturb you on a Saturday afternoon,' I began as smoothly as I could, 'but we've only just moved in next door.' I stuck out my hand with a smile. My new neighbour looked at it suspiciously and did not move. Only his eyebrows moved, arranging themselves into an expression of utter disinterest crossed with disapproval. After a moment, I put my hand back in my pocket. I gave a little embarrassed cough, but did not get discouraged. 'I love this neck of the woods,' I continued nonchalantly. 'Always hoped

I'd be able to afford a house here.'

'Well, that's all very nice for you,' he replied grumpily, 'but what does this have to do with me?' He was wearing a farmer's worn blue overalls, over a torn shirt. His grey hair was messy, and his skin was red and blotchy. His whole being radiated unpleasantness, and a faint smell of onions.

I pretended not to hear him. 'These fields, these woods, the fresh country air... it's wonderful. What a joy to own a piece of it. Of course,' I continued in my most sympathetic voice, 'it must be quite a hassle, looking after it all on one's own.' Here, I left a heavy pause. The man narrowed his eyes slightly, as if guessing my intentions. 'So much land to mow, and maintain; so many hedges to trim. Do you have a tractor yourself?'

'Yes,' the man replied shortly. 'I'm a farmer. I enjoy looking after my land.'

Obviously, he had caught my drift. Briefly hesitating as to how to proceed, I gave up on subterfuge. 'Look, *Monsieur*,' I said, 'you're obviously an intelligent man, and you've clearly worked out that I didn't walk over here just to bother you on a nice sunny Saturday, or to engage in pointless small talk. I don't intend to disturb you for long. What I'd like to do is make you an offer. I would like to buy the outlying land that is closest to our house.'

For one horrifying moment, I thought our elderly Frenchman was about to roll his eyes, but he simply sighed. 'I presume you mean the segment of land that includes the stream, and the walk to the forest?'

'Yes,' I said. I was not intending to waste any more breath.

Unfortunately, neither was my neighbour. 'Not a chance,' he said, unflinchingly.

I was crushed. 'You wouldn't even consider it?'

The neighbour smiled unpleasantly. 'One hundred thousand,' he said, putting his grimy hand up to stop my expression of outrage. 'Not one *centime* less.' Then he extended that hand in a mockery of an offer of a handshake.

I left with hardly another word. Such an offer was almost more insulting than an outright refusal. I was obviously wasting my time with such a cantankerous old man.

It would be a lie to say I wasn't deeply disappointed. Of course, we still had our own rolling fields, and a pond, and beautiful gardens;

of course, we still had our lovely country house. But I had hoped to make it a true palatial domain. I didn't like the idea of these fences at the end of my view, reminding me of my unpleasant, selfish neighbour, probably for the rest of my days. Needless to say, over the years, our relationship with this obnoxious peasant was far from pleasant. If we ran into each other on the way into town, or walking in the fields, we granted each other nothing more than a cursory nod.

Twenty-seven years passed. My children grew up, and some of them moved out. We saw our neighbour only rarely, and eventually the sting of the lost land had passed so far into distant memory that I had almost forgotten it was right there, next to us. But one morning, this changed. There was a knock on the door, and I opened it to find our neighbour standing there, looking at the ground. He had aged considerably, although I could swear he was wearing the same clothes, even more tattered than before. There was still something vaguely unpleasant about his face, and he still smelled of onions, but gone was the brutal arrogance that he had confronted me with all those years ago.

'I would like to talk to you about something,' he offered apologetically. I was stunned. I had not expected such a change in tone.

'Is something wrong?' I asked instinctively.

He shook his head, obviously embarrassed, then waggled it back and forth as if to imply that things might, indeed, not be at their best. There was a long silence, as he stared at his feet, moving his weight from side to side. 'I've run into some... financial troubles,' he finally admitted. This was promising. Not wishing to exhibit schadenfreude, I simply nodded as sympathetically as I could. 'I'm growing old,' he said, without emotion. 'It is time for me to give up some of the things I have clung to in this life.' I tried as hard as I could not to smile. He paused regretfully. 'Would you buy that land?' he asked, all at once, quite abruptly.

I held my tongue, not wishing to appear too enthusiastic. I almost asked him 'what land?' but figured that was simply making fun of the poor old man. After what I figured would be the appropriate length for a contemplative pause, I nodded. 'Alright,' I said. 'That would be grand. However, we would need to have a valuation of the land.'

The man shook his head slowly, almost sadly.

'Don't go for a valuation,' he said softly, as if pleading. 'I need to sell. I need to sell it straight away. I'll sell to you for twenty thousand.'

I blinked. 'Twenty thousand? Are you quite sure?' All resentment had melted away, leaving me only with something quite like concern. 'That's a fifth of what we offered you twenty-seven years ago!'

'I know,' he said. 'There are... economic issues at stake. I have to proceed with some urgency.' I looked up quickly, to check that his eyes weren't hiding something shifty, but he only looked old and tired.

I nodded. 'OK,' I said. 'We'll do it. But we have to go to a surveyor to determine the borders, at least. We'll want the forest, the pond, and certainly both borders of the stream.' I had to make sure I wasn't being taken advantage of in some strange way.

He bowed his head. 'I agree,' he said, his tone of voice still subdued. 'We'll get all of that done next week. I'll have the contract drawn up.' We stood, facing each other in the doorway, unsure what to say next. I found myself feeling almost grateful to our strange old neighbour. Suddenly, he looked me right in the eye with something like a faint smile. 'I think God is having his revenge,' he said. 'I'm paying for my greed.' He looked too contrite for me to share any wisdom about valleys of gold and mouthfuls of dirt, but I was smiling after he left.

BOB, JACK, AND HENRY: THE CARPOOL

When I first started working as an engineer, I lived in New Jersey in order to commute into New York. The trip took two hours each way by car, despite being only about fifteen miles long. This was due to the complications of rush hour traffic and long queues at highway exits. As a twenty-one-year-old full of energy and enthusiasm for my new job, I didn't mind this in itself. Nor did I mind the thirty-five cents a gallon gas cost in those days. The drive was an easy enough one, so that wasn't any trouble either. The problem, however, was simply how long it was: four hours is a substantial chunk of any day to commit to driving alone. Over a month, that added up to a good eighty hours of time spent staring at the bumper of the car ahead of me. No amount of lovely sunrises could compensate for the sheer length and dullness of this. I decided there was only one solution for this: to enlist some company.

By chatting to my closest neighbours, I quickly found out I was living in a sort of commuter belt: far from being alone with this problem, I was surrounded by other people doing the long, boring drive to New York. Some neighbours only had to go as far as Hoboken, Jersey City or Newark, but the consensus was that there were many of us heading in the same direction every morning.

'How would you feel about setting up some kind of carpool?' I asked my friend Bob casually one day, over drinks at a neighbourhood garden party.

'Well gosh, that's an interesting idea. I'd never even thought about it. I suppose that could make a whole lot of sense!' He nodded thoughtfully, mulling the idea over.

'I mean, think about it: I bet almost everyone in this neighbourhood is wasting four hours of their life a day sitting staring at the road. Besides, we would save quite a lot of money.'

'I guess all of us just got used to doing that drive separately,' Bob replied. 'Hell, we even complain about it pretty much every time we meet up! But there's a few people I can think of that I bet would be keen. Let's see, there's Jack, and then Henry down the road; they both work on the outskirts of the city. With you and me that's a carful.'

'Enough to set up some kind of rota,' I added. 'We could share it out. We can use a different driver every day. Switch cars each time. I think it would add a little spice to an otherwise dreadfully dull operation.'

'Sounds great!' Bob grinned. 'How about you start, on Monday?'

'Sure thing!'

As easily as that, the carpool fell into place. I made a few phone calls on the Sunday; both Jack and Henry were easily convinced. After all, the advantages were clear and numerous. However, the best laid plans of mice and men... often fail to take into consideration the finer, unpredictable details of such an operation. Everyone had agreed that we were bored of our own dull little routines. However, when it came to trying to fit everyone's habits and quirks into one car, well, that's when it became a bit more complicated.

We discovered quite quickly that multiplying the number of people involved in a single car ride, far from simplifying the operation by four, as one would expect, actually quadrupled the number of problems encountered. If one person, for instance, was late for any variety of reasons, it held back the whole group. While tardiness would only have been a minor problem for a single person, it became rather a major one for the four of us. Thus, Henry might happen to be coming down with the flu on the very morning that Bob absolutely had to be in on time in order to give a work presentation; or Jack might be a bit hungover and disorganised on the same morning that Henry had asked him to take over his rota because he had the flu. The number of times one of the group forgot to inform anyone that they were sick, absent, sleeping in, staying home with a child, taking the train in early, or on holiday in the Caribbean was quite impressive. Sometimes we would wait in the car for someone for a full fifteen minutes before their wife appeared on the steps to apologise. Worse than these were the days when I had to wait in the freezing snow because one of the others was having trouble starting their car in the cold, and hadn't thought to get up ten minutes earlier to deal with it.

Thus, I discovered the first problem of carpooling: sharing responsibility. A sort of awful group mentality descends, by which everyone feels their own personal sins and failures are absorbed into those of the mass. Everyone appeared to give up accountability collectively, instead of sharing it out equally. This meant that even on a good morning, where everything fell more or less into place and we ended up with the right four bodies in the car at an acceptable time, the commute always ended up taking a good two and a half hours. Furthermore, perhaps unsurprisingly, this also meant that the rota system which formed the basis of the carpool theory was often thrown completely off, which two or three of us ending up doing most of the driving.

Unfortunately, this blending into the masses did not extend to accepting each other's foibles and eccentricities. I had assumed that by having four people in a car every morning, we would lighten the boredom of the ride for each other: talking, chatting, maybe listening to the radio. What I had failed to take into account was the fact that the likelihood of at least one of us being in a bad mood on any given day was quite high. Compress a bit of bad temper into a small space with three other adults, and it will have a tendency not to recede but actually to explode. None of us was even particularly difficult or complicated; yet we managed to annoy each other daily. Henry, for instance, was quite a large man, who took up a lot of space in the car. On top of this, he often slept badly, probably because he ate so late and so much, so even on the days when he managed to arrive or pick us up on time, he would be terrifically irritable for the first hour or so. If he and Jack started arguing, which happened at least three times a week, I would have to resolve their problems, often whilst concentrating on the road or suffering through a traffic jam.

I should come clean at this point and admit that I, too, refused to give up on my particular weakness that annoyed the other passengers: coffee. I kept a percolator in the front of the car, plugged into the cigarette lighter, in order to make cups of strong, fresh coffee to keep me going. I happened to love the smell, but it turned out this was not a joy shared by all. Only Bob seemed to be able to drink half a cup of hot coffee without spilling it everywhere: the upholstery suffered only marginally less than our moods. I certainly learned a few lessons from this carpool experiment, and one of them, which I still apply in my life as an adult, family man, is that no-one should ever be handed a full cup of hot beverage in a moving vehicle.

These, then, were the consequences of an operation meant to simplify our lives: refusal of responsibility, bad moods, lengthy delays, endless complications and spilled drinks. After six months of the experiment I had initiated, I called it off: I decided to start taking the train. Even switching between four kinds of public transport seemed like a better idea than continuing to travel with Bob, Jack and Henry. Even if they were my neighbours.

My six youngest children are very intelligent. They work hard at school, and I have devised an intensive extracurricular programme for them on top of this, to make sure they excel in all domains they are interested in. On top of attending an exclusive Swiss school five days a week, each and every one of them has several lessons at home in the evening: in Mandarin Chinese, English, French, German, Spanish, piano, and classical and modern dance. They also play basketball, volleyball, ping pong and football in our big garden, in the company of a personal trainer. Some of them are so good at these physical activities that they have participated and excelled in local and national tournaments, whilst others have preferred to focus on linguistic and literary advancement.

I don't mean to boast about my children's achievements. I simply intend to sketch out for the reader an idea of the kind of schedule they have, so that the comedy of this recent episode might be fully understood. This story took place quite recently, when the children's school gave them four days off for the Catholic holiday of Ascension, as is the norm in France and Switzerland: thus, they all had Thursday and Friday off, as well as the usual weekend. Weeks before this, we had made a fairly solid plan to go to Europa Park, which is a sort of German Disneyland, and spend a few days there all together. We had visited the park before as a family, and had an excellent time; no-one contested the plan when it was put in place. At first, there was some discussion of everyone's favourite rides, and bickering over the mode of transport, but after a while, nobody gave it any more thought.

This was an error, at least on my part: just a week before the holiday, I found out I was completely unable to book us a hotel. Apparently, we had not been the only family with the idea of taking advantage of the spring weather. After hours of fruitless internet research, I had to admit to myself that I had failed. With a heavy heart, I called my family together for one of our councils – we like to make our decisions democratically. I sat the children down and explained the situation to them.

'No Europa Park?' my eldest son Rowan blurted out, obviously crushed.

I raised a gentle hand to silence him. 'Before you get too upset,' I continued, seeing their little faces fall, 'I would like to detail for you your nine new holiday options.' I could almost feel spirits lifting a little as I produced a piece of paper with my nine ideas written down.

'What are they, Daddy?' the littlest child asked.

'As I said,' I continued smoothly, enjoying the suspense, 'you have nine options. Consider each of them carefully. One: you could go to Lausanne, stay in the Beau Rivage hotel on the shore of the lake, and eat a four-course meal in one of our favourite restaurants. Two: you could go to Chamonix, where you could stay in a luxury French hotel. If the weather stays nice, we could even walk in the snowy mountains. Three: we could do something similar in Megève, perhaps we could ski or luge in a neighbouring resort at a higher altitude – maybe St Gervais or Val d'Isère. I know a great place there for fondue. Four: we could drive to Paris, stay in our beloved family apartment and organise tours of the spring museum exhibits. I believe there's an interesting show on at the Louvre. Five: you could take the train to your aunties' house in Normandy, where we could go to the beach at Deauville and ride horses. Six: you could go to our family house in Kent, which you have not seen in a year. We could go out for a nice pub lunch, take a boat out on the lake and go fishing. Seven: you could go visit some of my friends in Monte Carlo, stay in their fancy apartment and eat seafood. Eight: you could go to your beloved London, see a few plays in the West End, and stay with your oldest sister. Finally, I will add a ninth option, which is that you can all stay at home in your rooms, doing nothing and making your own programme for the four days.' There was a long silence. My children looked at each other. 'I will now leave the room to give you a little time to discuss these, and hold a vote in five minutes,' I told them.

I went and stood outside the room, listening to the hushed whispers indoors and vaguely contemplating the kind of packing each trip would involve. Skis? Walking boots? A guide to the museums of Paris? To my surprise, barely a minute later, my youngest daughter came out of the room. She looked up at me with her big brown eyes and said: 'We've made a decision.'

I came back in and asked them what they had chosen. 'We want to stay home,' she said at once. I looked around in surprise. 'It was unanimous,' she added. All my children looked at me and said nothing more.

I was flabbergasted. After a long pause, I had to ask: 'But why? Why do you want to stay home instead of going to all these glamorous destinations I offered you? Is this some kind of sulk because you really wanted to go to Europa Park?' I have to admit I was slightly worried about the reasons behind this unexpected decision! However, I would soon find out my anxiety was in vain.

My son Rowan cleared his throat and shook his head with a smile. 'No, it's nothing like that at all! We really like all of your ideas. It's just that we never get to stay home doing nothing. I love the idea.'

'I have this cool room and I never get to spend any time in it!' his sister Rhonda piped up.

'I'd like to spend a whole afternoon in the garden!' my youngest daughter added. 'We never get to do that. It would be so great in the sun.'

I shook my head in disbelief. 'Well, I must tell you that this is the weirdest holiday decision I have ever heard of. You really want to spend your holiday in your own house?'

'Yes,' they chorused.

Rowan seemed to think it was important to convince me of their logic. 'You know, Dad,' he said, 'it may sound strange, but aside from sleeping in my room, I don't think I have ever spent more than an hour at a time there! I mean, I love basketball and Chinese lessons, I love spending time in the library, but between that and school and dinner, I never get time to just sit on my own, listening to music or meditating the way you taught me, or watching a movie on my computer.'

'But you have a theatre to do that! I take you to the movies!' I replied, still in a state of disbelief.

'It's not the same,' Rowan answered firmly. 'You gave us a democratic decision to make, and we have made it. We want to stay here this weekend, please.'

I raised my eyebrows. 'Well, I left the power in your hands, and you've made the decision. I look forward to hearing your holiday stories. Make sure you send your relatives a postcard!'

The children giggled and ran off into the house happily. I walked back to my office slowly, pondering this bizarre turn of events. It surprised me that I would not have predicted it in the least. I had only put in the ninth option as a sort of joke, really, something to put everything else in perspective. It certainly had provided my children with perspective, I guess, just not the sort I was expecting!

I suppose, in a way, it was a compliment to the home I had made for them. After all, each child's room and bathroom had been decorated in a different theme. One room was made up in a traditional Swiss style, another had a colourful Spanish atmosphere, while another had been decorated with more of a glamorous taste reminiscent of the Italian Renaissance. One child had picked a Scandinavian theme, while yet another preferred French Art Nouveau. In this way, exploring the house from top to bottom was in itself a sort of international adventure! On top of this, each child had been allowed to decorate their walls with their own choice of paintings, drawings, memorabilia from their childhood, and gifts from friends and family. Then, of course, each had well-filled bookshelves to explore… I began to understand their draw to this holiday plan. After all, since I had retired from banking to focus on my writing, I too had enjoyed a few quiet periods of time at home. There was something pleasant about it, even if my personal preference was to be active and travelling the world. Perhaps my children also felt the need for some peace and quiet, a break from their busy daily lives!

Of course, there is an amusing epilogue to this story. No matter how lofty their ambitions might have been, children are children. Thus, on the second day of the Ascension holiday, I received a phone call in my office from one of them.

'Dad, I hate to tell you this, but we're starting to get bored,' my son admitted sheepishly. 'Do you think we should just go to a park or something?'

'Have you got tired of your rooms already?'

'Well, we were there all day yesterday, and that was pretty fun, but today it's too sunny to stay indoors. We've been in the garden since breakfast. It's starting to get a little boring.'

I laughed quietly. 'Are you sure you don't want to leave the city?' I asked him. 'We could still go away for the next two days of holiday. Do you want to ask your brothers and sisters?'

'No,' he said decisively. 'We still want to stay in Geneva. We only need a little variety.'

I had to admire his commitment to his decision. 'Of course you can go to the park,' I told him. 'I'll just let your nanny know.'

I smiled to myself as I hung up. My children really were the weirdest neighbours I had ever met!

This edition of *Neighbours' Nonsense* is limited to a
First Deluxe Issue of 300 copies only.

This copy is number *11*   /300

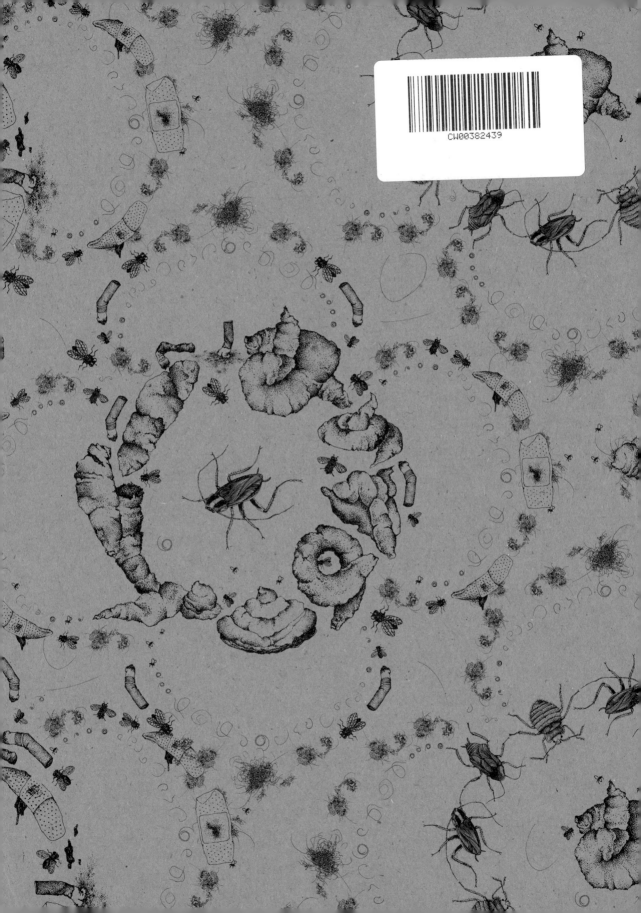

THE
WORST
HOTEL IN THE WORLD
THE HANS BRINKER BUDGET HOTEL
AMSTERDAM

Booth Clibborn Editions

THE WORST HOTEL
IN THE WORLD

Written and designed by: KesselsKramer

First published in 2009
by Booth-Clibborn Editions
in the United Kingdom
www.booth-clibborn.com

The information in this book is based on material supplied to
Booth-Clibborn Editions by KesselsKramer. While every effort
has been made to ensure accuracy, Booth-Clibborn Editions does
not under any circumstances accept responsibility for any
errors or omissions.

A cataloging-in-publication record for this book is
available from the publisher

ISBN 978-1-86154-311-0

Printed and bound in China

Hans Brinker Budget Hotel Worst Legal Acknowledgements:
All rights of the Brinker were flushed down the toilet
during a clear-out in the winter of 1983. Some of the
contents of this book have been written while under
the influence of cleaning fluids. The Brinker has done
its utmost to include a number of omissions and
errors. This book has not been put together with the
encouragement, input and advice of any friend or
colleague. The views expressed in this book are
accurate depictions of the views of those who originally
expressed the aforementioned views except in those
instances when they didn't. The Brinker cannot be made
responsible for any illnesses, nightmares or other
disorders that may result from touching or reading this
book, or touching someone who has touched or read
this book. The Brinker promises that its pillows are
only that colour due to a strange leakage at the pillow
factory. The Brinker is not responsible for those
noises you hear in Room 159. The Brinker's legal
department was in prison when this legal document was
written and as such doesn't accept any responsibility
for anything whatsoever.

This book is dedicated to all the backpackers, students
and travellers of the world, without whom there would be
no one to abuse, no one to mistreat and no one to accept
the reckless abandon and barefaced treachery
that has given us the reputation — one which we
hold dear, with pride and shame in equal measure —
as the worst hotel in the world.
☆ ☆ ☆ ☆ ☆

THIS IS YOUR WAKE UP CALL

THE TOP WORST

WAKE UP CALLS AT THE BRINKER:

☆ Pee in the face
☆ Unknown smell
☆ Screaming
☆ Being licked

THE SAVAGE PLUMBING SYSTEM. THE SWEDISH BACKPACKER WHO EMITS NOISES IN HIS SLEEP THAT SOUND LIKE A HUNDRED CAMELS GIVING BIRTH. THE CLEANERS WHO WAGE CHEMICAL WARFARE AT THE DARKEST OF HOURS. THE UNSETTLING SCUFFLING FROM BENEATH YOUR BED. THERE ARE MANY ASSAULTS ON THE SENSES THAT WILL SHAKE YOU AWAKE AFTER A NIGHT AT THE WORST HOTEL IN THE WORLD.

It may well be that you cannot, or dare not, live through such an experience. For this is the Hans Brinker Budget Hotel Amsterdam. The 513-bed hotel situated in an otherwise quiet street in the heart of Amsterdam, the Netherlands. The hotel that has been living down to its name since 1970. You have always suspected that the tales were true. That if hell had an establishment for newly deposited souls it would be named the Hans Brinker. Only hell would have better heating. So you deigned never to darken its door or let its door darken you.

You're holding in your hands a much safer entrance to the infamous hostel. Having said that, the editors have done their utmost to recreate the horrors and disgrace. It's their hope that, after reading, you will feel a real need to burn your clothes. That you will require a long, hot shower. A nice lie-down in a friendly room.

A question must first be answered before your book-bound stay at the Brinker begins. There are many books about hotels, but why a book about this hotel?

It's true. Countless publications scatter our well-travelled planet with the hotel as subject matter. Notably, they are all about the best hotels. The hippest. The choicest. The most jaw-droppingly luxurious for guests who prefer to arrive via helipad rather than front door.

Luckily you've picked up the black sheep in the hospitality herd. You were drawn towards something inexplicably wrong about this book. Magnetized by the fact that it jubilantly celebrates not the best but the absolute worst.

The hotel industry might wonder how the Worst Hotel in the World manages to attract millions from far-flung corners of the world. Honesty in extremis plays a big part, a quality lacking in many, especially when it comes to marketing themselves. To that end, the Hans Brinker has been a wake up call not only in the world of hospitality but also communication.

The Worst Hotel in the World uses every campaign and case study for the Brinker as well as inside facts, photos and interviews to tell more than you ever wanted to know about how it manages to care less and make a success of it.

Voltaire — who to our knowledge never bunked at the Brinker — said that the best is the enemy of the good. Which means the worst is the enemy of the bad. Which makes The Worst Hotel In the World a proud claim indeed. Welcome to the Hans Brinker Budget Hotel, Amsterdam, the proudly sagging underbelly of the hotel industry. Pull on a pair of disposable gloves and prepare yourself. For the worst is yet to come…

The lobby.

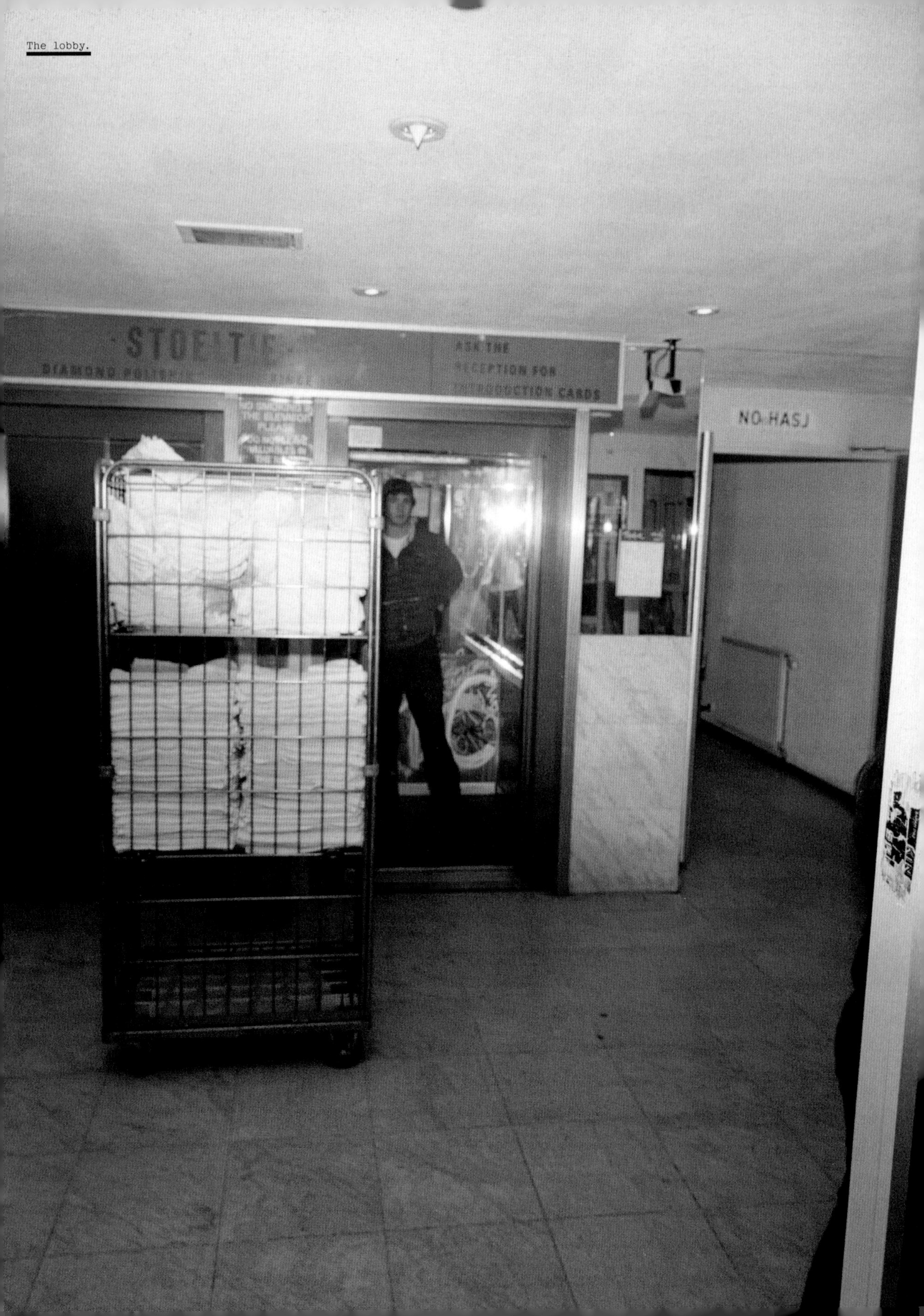

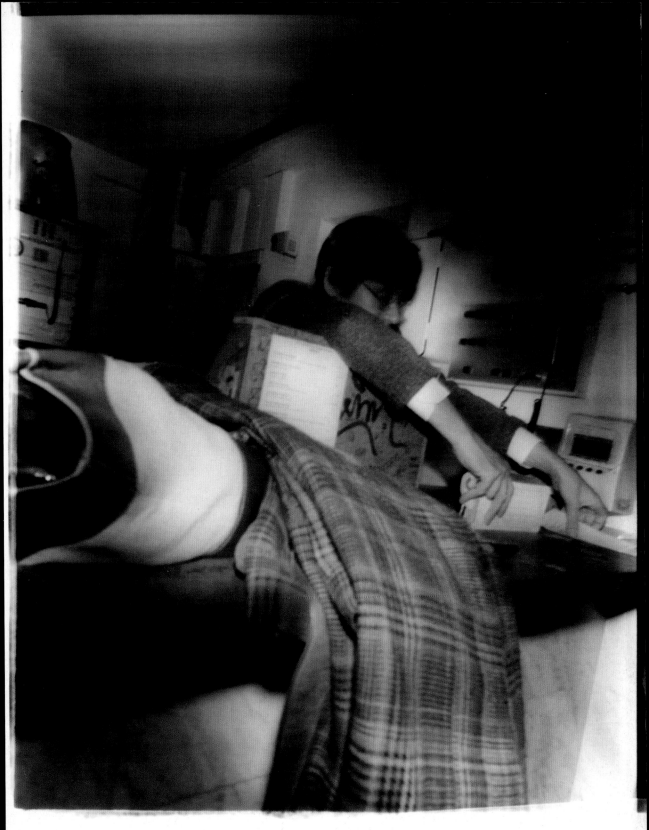

The reception desk.

THE WORST IN-TERVIEW IN THE WORLD

THE WORST

GUESTS EVER:
☆ Mushroom-guzzling students
☆ Stag parties
☆ The Mafia

Rob Penris,
hotel manager.

ERIK KESSELS IS CREATIVE DIRECTOR AND CO-FOUNDER OF KESSELSKRAMER, THE HANS BRINKER'S COMMUNICATIONS AGENCY. HE AND BRINKER MANAGER ROB PENRIS HAVE BEEN WORKING ON THE ACCOUNT FOR MORE THAN A DECADE. HERE, THEY DISCUSS THE HOTEL'S CAMPAIGNS, THEIR RELATIONSHIP AND A VERY FAMOUS PILE OF DOG POO.

The partnership between KesselsKramer and the Hans Brinker Budget Hotel more resembles a successful romance than a business affiliation.

Creative Director Erik Kessels and Rob Penris, long-time manager of the Brinker, attribute this to a shared set of values. Firstly, a definite division of responsibilities helps maintain respect — Penris doesn't aspire to direct his hotel's communications and Kessels wouldn't presume to give advice on managing the Brinker.

The other element is fun. Even after well over a decade, the two like to surprise each other. Occasionally, campaigns spring from Penris and Kessels playing what comes pretty close to a series of practical jokes.

Kessels recalls a case in point: 'Rob once asked us to design a price list for the Brinker. We came back with a CD of music which we'd recorded, with the price list printed on the back cover.' The CD in question was called 'Our Chamber Music' and features the Brinker equivalent of soothing music for hotel lobbies: the drone of vacuum cleaners sweeping its rooms. Penris reacted by staging a recital.

'We took real cleaning ladies to a hotel fair,' he says 'brought 3 palettes of beer to the bar and created a concert of cleaning at Happy Hour.'

Surprise has marked the relationship from the very beginning, when Kessels produced a piece of communication with an unexpected objective.

Penris met Kessels in the early '90s while the latter was still a junior art director at advertising agency Ogilvy & Mather. Rob wanted a 'fast' creative. Kessels fulfilled Penris' criteria when he returned within fifteen minutes of their first meeting with three campaigns. 'Though,' Penris reflects now, 'he probably had them ready somewhere in his computer.'

Rob had just renovated the Brinker and wanted to announce its reopening. More personally, he also wanted 'a campaign that doesn't get me any more complaints again in my whole life.'

In retrospect, this request seems at odds with what the Brinker's all about. After all, much of KesselsKramer's subsequent work appears to actively encourage whining guests.

Nevertheless, the resulting tram-based posters laid the foundations for what was to come. 'Headlines on the trams said No Bellboy and No International Newspaper, No Second Bathroom, and so on,' Kessels explains. 'The line tying the posters together was The Most

Erik Kessels and Johan Kramer pose at the Brinker as part of an early PR drive.

XXX-clusive Budget Hotel.' Kessels reasoned that no guest could possibly bitch about the Brinker if they'd been pre-warned about its lack of facilities. This brutal honesty (which would become more defined over time) serves the Brinker to this day: a popular line on customer feedback forms is 'it isn't as bad as the advertising said it would be.'

The trams demonstrated another element that would later become a Brinker trademark: creative use of media. The posters only appeared on trams parking outside the tourist office near Amsterdam's Central Station. 'If you come to Amsterdam and you need accommodation, you always walk in there,' Penris says. But the team took their media strategy one stage further: posters only appeared on the left side of the trams, the side facing the tourist office. 'We were sold out in half a week,' Penris says.

Kessels took his Brinker side job with him when he moved to another international ad agency, Chiat/Day London. It was here that the work took on added depth — thanks to Kessels' new partner Johan Kramer. 'It was when I started working with Johan in London that we got the strategy even more tight,' Kessels says. 'We thought: "What are the angles on a hotel like this?" There's no use creating advertising that makes it more beautiful than it is, so you better be very honest about the situation and turn that into a positive thing. A very ironic approach helps, which works for the target market of students and backpackers, and appeals to their kind of humour. So in that way, the fundamentals of the strategy were established more firmly.'

Johan and Erik's strategy summed up what the Brinker was all about: no frills taken to the limit.

'WE TOOK REAL CLEANING LADIES TO A HOTEL FAIR,' ROB SAYS 'BROUGHT 3 PALETTES OF BEER TO THE BAR AND CREATED A CONCERT OF CLEANING AT HAPPY HOUR.'

When asked to design a price list, the agency instead made a CD mixing techno with vacuum cleaners on full blast. The price list was on the back cover.

NO WHIRLPOOL NO BELLBOY NO SAUNA NO BIDET NO SWIMMING POOL NO TENNIS COURT NO MASSAGE ROOM NO MINI BAR NO PARKING PL

HansBrinker THE MOST XXXCLUSIVE BUDGET HOTEL

Kessels' first campaign for the Brinker.

TAKE OUR MEGA KINGSIZE SUPER EXTRA-LONG VEHICLE!

No. 1, 2, 5, 16, 24, or 25

Don't walk. Don't hesitate. Just jump on the first tramway you see with one of these numbers: 1, 2, 5, 16, 24 or 25. It's specially made for you.

And it takes you straight (well, almost) to the Hans Brinker Budget Hotel. And of course there's a nice warm shower or bath waiting for you. Once you're in the Hans Brinker Budget Hotel, you will discover why it has become so xxxclusive.

500 Beds instead of 250 and no swimming pool, no parking lot, no hair dresser, no bidet, no roomservice and no hole in your pocket either. Because of its reasonable prices, its relaxed atmosphere and good location, guests from all over the world enjoy the Hans Brinker.

The Hans Brinker is so xxxclusive that you don't have to go out. We've a sunny garden and a lovely terrace. Besides, we've a cozy Dutch pub where you can enjoy a drink and hot and cold snacks. There is a restaurant serving breakfast and fine meals. After dinner, when you were just thinking of visiting Amsterdam, our megadisco starts beating its rythm.

And till 4 o'clock in the morning, you will meet people from all over the world

Hans Brinker THE MOST XXXCLUSIVE BUDGET HOTEL

Meanwhile, Rob Penris was making a point of keeping his establishment's comfort levels permanently low. 'In order to get a star rating, you need a chair in every room,' he says. 'So I asked a German artist to make a painting of a chair on the wall of each room, and asked the ratings inspector if this met his criteria. He didn't think so. We got into a lengthy philosophical discussion about what does and doesn't constitute a chair.'

But Penris wasn't being cheeky for the sake of it. 'You don't expect anything when you arrive at the Brinker. People would come to us with sleeping bags, tents, and when they found they'd got a bed, that had a very positive effect indeed.'

Like the campaign's strategy and media placement, art direction for the Brinker's ads was initially driven by necessity. Kessels had no other option but to create a punk aesthetic — non-existent budgets precluded anything else. But the art direction also fits the strategy. Kessels elaborates: 'When you talk about honesty in your work, you should also present that work in a way that's honest and back-to-basics. You shouldn't go for full-colour spreads.'

Later, the Brinker's means of presenting itself became ever-so-slightly more sophisticated, with its Now Even More posters providing a platform for unknown British designer Anthony Burrill.

This wave of communication also saw the appearance of the Brinker's most iconic stunt. In the then nascent field of guerrilla marketing, the Brinker raised the stakes with an extremely cheap (and very smelly) outdoor campaign: flags planted in dog crap.

But our rooms are too small, so we put them on the wall.

To say that it had a disproportionate effect is an understatement.

'The dog shit was a hit,' Kessels says. 'It was our most successful piece of communication. It appeared all over the globe, on CNN, MTV, ABC, everywhere.'

Rob has a very personal recollection of the turd that shook the world. 'A neighbour of mine was working as a cameraman on a movie,' he says. 'He had to travel all the way to New Zealand for the shoot. The first thing you do when you finish a journey like that is get to your hotel, have a shower and switch on the TV. The first thing he sees is me talking about dog shit.'

'It's amazing how such a simple action can have such an impact,' Kessels says. 'We'd found a new way of communicating,' Rob adds.

Our Anniver-sary

25 years Hans Brinker Budget Hotel Amsterdam

NOW EVEN MORE OF THIS AT OUR MAIN ENTRANCE

'The Germans took it seriously,' Rob continues. 'Every morning and evening we were on the news there. We got an enormous number of interviews wondering how we could do this.'

Rob was still getting calls from journalists five years later, and the turd's ripple effect can be felt to this day. 'It's never really stopped,' Kessels says.

The agency's dog shit stunt was (and still is) fairly extreme, begging the question: has KesselsKramer ever presented work that the Brinker refused to run?

Oddly enough, the answer involves more excrement. Rob Penris: 'On our 25th anniversary, KesselsKramer created a poster showing our front entrance and a huge pile of shit shaped into a 25. There was a lady walking away.'

'So you thought it was human faeces?' Kessels asks.

'Well, the board certainly did,' Rob answers. 'It was a little too much.'

Nevertheless, a similar poster was produced, minus human culprit. A stack of copies was placed in reception and disappeared almost over night. 'Though this may have been a commercial trick by KesselsKramer,' Rob says.

But women dropping improbably shaped logs weren't the only executions that proved too extreme for the Brinker.

'There was other stuff too,' Kessels admits. 'We once had this ad which involved suicide…'

'Suicide is not allowed,' Rob says. 'They had executions like "How to Hang Yourself." We wouldn't go there.'

So while even the Brinker has limits, its open-mindedness goes far beyond other brands. Nevertheless, some companies have attempted to imitate its honesty over the years. Recently, a T-shirt manufacturer took this copycat approach one stage further, printing almost exact duplicates of the Brinker's 'Now Even More' campaign on its clothes.

'The thing is, nobody can imitate the Brinker with 100% accuracy,' Kessels says. 'Sure, they can imitate its style and its approach, but at the end of the day it's a completely unique product and that uniqueness is what led us to the advertising. It's very difficult to duplicate this, and I think the bravery involved in these projects from both client and agency is pretty special too.'

Which brings us back to where we started. The Brinker and its agency work together in a way that goes way beyond typical client-agency relationships, trusting each other to be as courageous as they can be.

It's an attitude whose results can be summed up in one simple statement: 'The Brinker built KesselsKramer,' Penris says. '…And vice versa,' Kessels retorts.

EVERYTHING YOU'VE NEVER WANTED AND MORE

In its purest form, advertising exists to describe or draw attention to the benefits of a product in order to promote sales. But what do you do if the product you're selling has no real benefits, no unique selling points, nothing more than the barest of the bare essentials?

If you're the Hans Brinker Budget Hotel you do the unthinkable. You tell the truth. Instead of trying to pull the wool over the eyes of your customers by promising adequacy, you build an honest advertising campaign around the simple fact that your hotel has nothing to offer.

Every day, brands invent reasons for people to buy what they're selling. They wax on about new ingredients, the latest scientific studies, and earth-shattering innovations as if their product is the missing piece of the puzzle, the one thing you've been waiting for, the product that will completely alter the course of your life forever.

The 'Now More Than Ever' campaign tweaks and teases this kind of advertising, moulding it to the Brinker's own unique style by presenting the only 'benefits' the hotel has to work with. In doing so, the Brinker has transformed its many shortcomings into honest-to-God advantages.

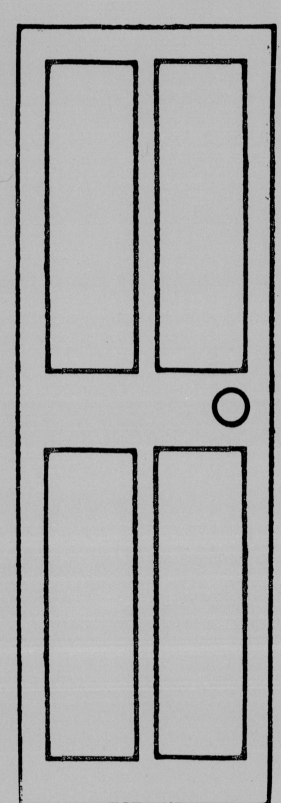

NOW A DOOR IN EVERY ROOM!

The most successful execution in the
campaign came in the form of tiny flags
stuck in dog turds around Amsterdam.
Erik Kessels: 'To this day I still get
people who ask me if we actually went
around sticking those flags in dog
shit. And the answer is yes. Everyone
in the office went out a few times
looking for shit that we could plant
our flags in. Amsterdam was — and
is — the dog shit capital of the world,
so it wasn't very hard to find.'

Taking advantage of every possible communication opportunity, the placemats in the Brinker's infamous canteen featured stories and games that kept drunken guests busy for hours.

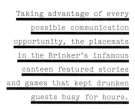

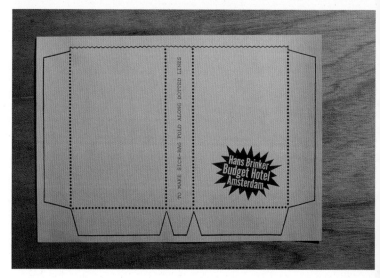

Perhaps the most humane
service the Brinker has
ever provided to its
guests: free sleeping
pills to help drown out
the nightly orchestra of
shouting, grunting and
door slamming. Alas,
the pills were merely
mint tic tacs.

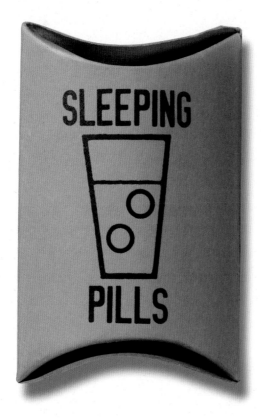

NOW EVEN MORE HELPFUL TECHNOLOGY

1. UNFOLD

2. ATTACH

3. SAVE YOUR SCREEN

Hans Brinker
Budget Hotel
Amsterdam
☎ 31 20 6220687

ENJOY 3 STATE OF THE ART SCREEN SAVERS AND OUR WEBSITE ADDRESS

In the ultimate act of low-budget ingenuity, and a precursor to user-generated web 2.0 interactivity, the Brinker gave away a set of paper 'screensavers' to unfold and tape to computer screens.

OUR GREEN SCREEN SAVER

Hans Brinker
Budget Hotel
Amsterdam
☎ 31 20 6220687

OUR WEBSITE ADDRESS: www.hans-brinker.com

OUR ORANGE SCREEN SAVER
Hans Brinker
Budget Hotel
Amsterdam
31 20 6220687
OUR WEBSITE ADDRESS: www.hans-brinker.com
iBook G4

The Brinker's first website offered a cornucopia of sometimes useful, more often useless, information about the hotel — including tips for escaping the hotel from hell, gag-inducing bedtime stories and even a dog-shit tour of Amsterdam.

The low-budget, do-it-yourself feel of the graphics extended into the programming of the site itself. More often than not, the site's links were broken. When they did work, they usually took viewers to the wrong page.

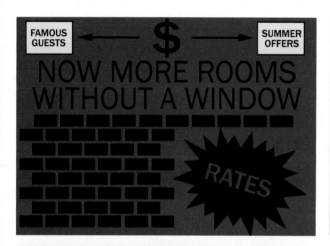

EVEN MORE DOGSHIT
IN THE MAIN ENTRANCE

| PLACEMAT GALLERY | ← | DOGSHIT TOUR | → | SOUND GALLERY |

NOW 5 WATT EXTRA IN EVERY LIGHTBULB

AND THAT'S GOT TO HELP OUR GUESTS AS THEY WANDER THE HALLS IN SEARCH OF THEIR LUXURIOUS ROOMS. HERE ARE SOME SAFETY TIPS FOR YOUR EVENING HERE IN AMSTERDAM.

TIPS →

FREE SLEEPING PILLS

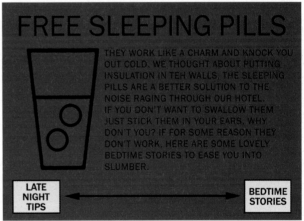

THEY WORK LIKE A CHARM AND KNOCK YOU OUT COLD. WE THOUGHT ABOUT PUTTING INSULATION IN TEH WALLS. THE SLEEPING PILLS ARE A BETTER SOLUTION TO THE NOISE RAGING THROUGH OUR HOTEL. IF YOU DON'T WANT TO SWALLOW THEM JUST STICK THEM IN YOUR EARS, WHY DON'T YOU? IF FOR SOME REASON THEY DON'T WORK, HERE ARE SOME LOVELY BEDTIME STORIES TO EASE YOU INTO SLUMBER.

LATE NIGHT TIPS ←→ BEDTIME STORIES

SOAP

WITH COMPLI

1	2	3
4	5	6
7	8	9
#	0	✳

SHAM

ENTS

CONDOM

WINE

1	2	3
4	5	6
7	8	9
	0	

**Hans Brinker
Budget Hotel
Amsterdam**

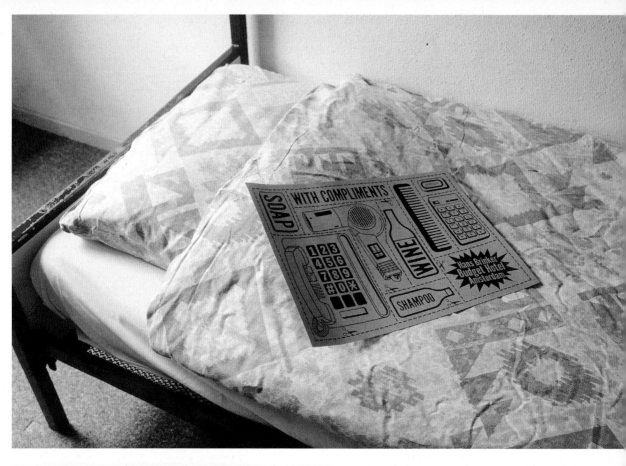

People who stayed at the Brinker were treated to the same luxuries as guests of other, nicer hotels. The only difference was that the Brinker extras came printed on thin sheets of orange paper. Guests could cut their favourite amenities out (with their own scissors of course) and place them around their rooms.

An action in which the Brinker gave a new spin to the phrase 'message in a bottle.' Staff planted empty beer bottles all over Amsterdam. Inside, a note informed consumers that the Brinker now had 'even more Happy Hours.'

NOTEL*

THE WORST ITEMS THAT ARE INCLUDED:
☆ Burned-out light bulbs
☆ Cigarette butts
☆ Maniacal laughter from next door
☆ Weird smells

THE CHIEF DIFFERENCE BETWEEN A HOTEL AND A NOTEL IS THAT THE FORMER OFFERS FAST SERVICE, LUXURIOUS AMENITIES AND CHARMING ROOMS, WHILE THE LATTER OFFERS, WELL, NOTHING REALLY. THERE ARE MILLIONS OF HOTELS AROUND THE WORLD, BUT THERE IS ONLY ONE NOTEL. IT GOES BY THE NAME OF BRINKER. HANS BRINKER.

A recent unscientific, unpublished study found that the most common word used by the staffs of the world's top hotels is yes. Yes as in 'Yes, of course, we can extend your stay for another night!' 'Yes, your room has a Jacuzzi, a sauna and a clawfoot tub!' And, 'Yes, the complimentary cheese fondue platter is 100% organic!'

The ever-diligent staff of the Brinker, two steps ahead of the crowd as usual, have adopted a much more useful, tasteful and cost-effective word as their mantra: no. No as in, 'No, you can't have an extra towel.' 'No, we don't have directions to the Anne Frank House.' And, 'No, we can't fix the light, please stop asking.'

The liberal use of no is not only a trademark of the Brinker staff, it's part of a bigger philosophy that can be found in every room, on every floor of the hotel. A philosophy that asks, 'Why be nice to someone when you can be nice to no one? Why be the best when you can be the worst? And why include everything when you can include nothing?'

* DERIVED FROM THE ENGLISH WORD NOTHING — AS IN, NOTHING YOU WANT, NEED OR DESIRE CAN BE FOUND HERE.

The
HansBrinker
Budget Hotel
Amsterdam
(31) 20-6220687

* not included

39

Hans Brinker
Budget Hotel
Amsterdam

* not include

* Our neighbors have flowers growing in their garden.

Not included. Two simple words that have been pissing people off since the earliest days of advertising. This little caveat, usually printed in tiny type at the bottom of the page, belongs to the same wretched family as 'parts purchased separately' and 'some assembly required'. These messages serve as sad reminders that rarely does one get exactly what one expects.

Like the kid who opens an electromagnetic space cruiser on Christmas morning only to find that batteries were not included, consumers have grown accustomed to questioning the claims of adverts and being wary of the ever-present fine print.

The Brinker's 'Not Included' campaign used the notion of consumer distrust as a foundation for a sly take on luxury hospitality. As with 'Now More Than Ever', the campaign played with the language of traditional advertising to showcase the hotel's many shortcomings in a funny and surprisingly endearing way.

Instead of using the phrase 'not included' as an evil afterthought like so many ads before, the Brinker placed it front and centre in its communication — focusing a campaign on the great things they don't offer, rather than the awful things they do.

The idea behind the campaign was simple: the Brinker offers only the bare minimum to its guests. The execution was equally simple: borrow (steal) a vintage photograph of a luxury hotel room. Place 'not included' asterisks over everything in the picture. Add a Hans Brinker seal to the photo and — presto — a finished poster.

This unusual approach comes from wanting to keep the work fresh and urgent. But it also comes from a much harsher reality — the Brinker's shoestring communication budget. Rather than looking at the hotel's lack of funds as a disadvantage, it has always been viewed as part of the charm. Expensive photo shoots? Not included.

The surprise switch of execution, from the simple iconography of 'Now More Than Ever' to the over-the-top glamour of 'Not Included', set a pattern that subsequent Brinker campaigns would follow. Unlike many long-running campaigns, the look of the Brinker's advertising changes drastically each year. Not even the logo remains the same.

"...not one of the best of the best hotels in the world".
~
NOT FROM COURVOISSERS BOOK OF THE BEST.

The Hans Brinker

The entire text of the 'Not Included' brochure comes from a Japanese hotel catalogue from the eighties. The only change that has been made is the addition of dozens of 'nots' and 'noes'.

*On arrival at the Brinker you are not greeted at the door, and you are not immediately given
your own front door key, and you are not shown to your room.*

*The concept for the Brinker was one where the guest is not important at all and must come last:
they should not feel at home, and also feel as unrelaxed and uncomfortable
as possible, and so they do.*

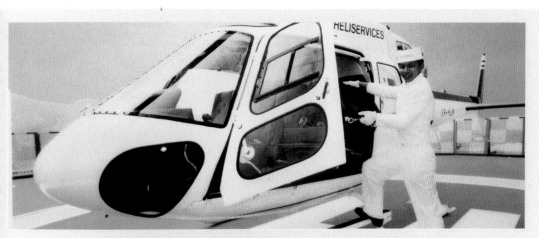

When the Brinker was not voted one of the best hotels in the world we felt we had received
recognition for not just being not a very beautiful, unprivate hotel, but also for the tremendous
impersonal attention all our guests receive from our staff.

We have no heated swimming pool for your enjoyment.
We have no sunny summer days or lunches served to you while you relax anywhere.
We have no complimentary spa, hot tubs or massage parlors.

At the Brinker we are not aware of any commitments to business,
and as such, we run a highly inefficient office with no telex, no fax, no car, no theater,
and no restaurant bookings.

As our guest we want you to feel completely hassled too! Breakfast is never brought to your room: just go to the cafeteria. We never make
homemade baked croissants or rolls. No freshly ground coffee. No brewed tea. No fresh orange juice. No homemade jams, no marmalade,
no lemony lemon curd. And none of it is served on fine Wedgwood china. What a not so wonderful way to start to the day!

*Guests who wish to, can never have personal fax or answering machines
in their room nor a computer plug. There is no direct dial to any room and regulars never have their own
permanent personal telephone number. There are no telephones in every room.*

*Along with not having the most beautiful hotel we also have the meanest staff you will
ever meet anywhere. They are without exception not charming, not helpful, and not friendly -and
like the Brinker itself- not welcoming at all.*

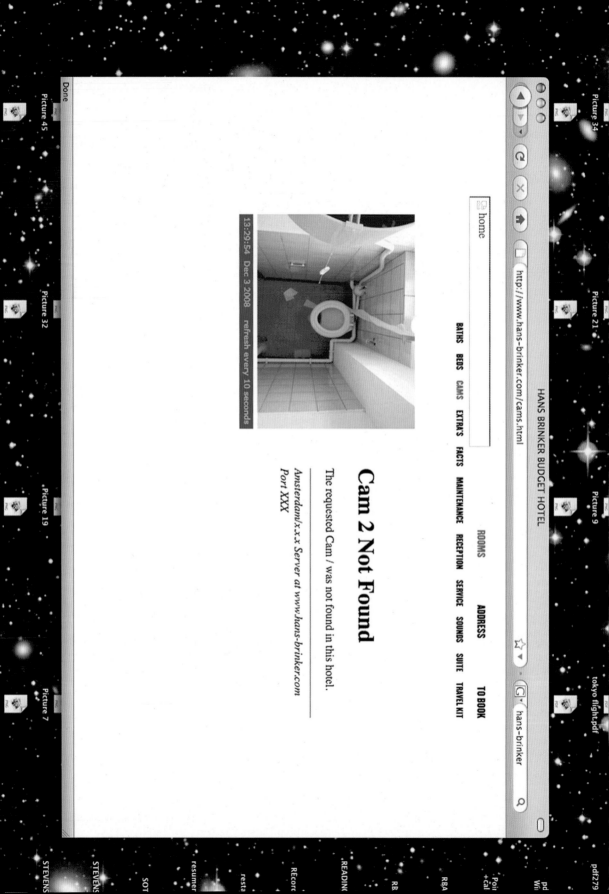

CHECK IN →

FOR MOST GUESTS, THE BRINKER PROVIDES LITTLE MORE THAN A BED AND A SHOWER BETWEEN BINGES.

By the time they leave, these fresh-faced youngsters have experienced Amsterdam's infamous delights and — in the process — developed more spots and killed more brain cells than they imagined possible.

To celebrate this hedonism while noting its price, the Brinker produced a poster campaign entitled Check In, Check Out.

In each image, normal-looking guests were compared as they entered and left the hotel.

The 'check out' shot made it clear that the stay hadn't done their beauty regime any good. Pimples, split ends and puffy faces provided a stark contrast to the milky skinned youths seen at 'check in.'

CHECK
OUT

The posters' structure played with a classic advertising convention: the before and after shot. Since the dawn of advertising, before/afters have been used to sell the delights of just about every consumer product imaginable. The Brinker took this hoary old cliché and turned it on its head: the after looked rather less attractive than the before.

The campaign ran in 1999 and was plastered on the walls and bins of Amsterdam, London and Paris. Although the public seemed generally amused, the City of Amsterdam failed to see the lighter side. In fact, it complained to the hotel that the campaign was spoiling its own PR drive to make the town appear less druggy.

THE WORST MORNING AFTER:
'One morning I woke up to discover that no, that wasn't my underwear, or my penis.'
Guest, Room 207

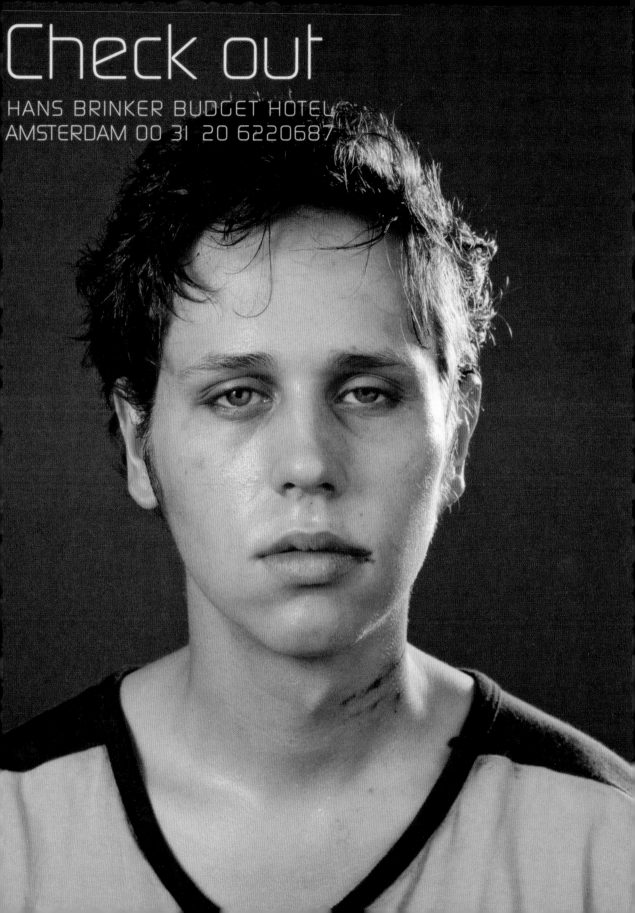

Check out

HANS BRINKER BUDGET HOTEL
AMSTERDAM 00 31 20 6220687

Check in

HANS BRINKER BUDGET HOTEL
AMSTERDAM 00 31 20 6220687

Check out

HANS BRINKER BUDGET HOTEL
AMSTERDAM 00 31 20 6220687

Afmattend Amsterdam

After the City of Amsterdam condemned the Brinker's Check In/Check Out campaign, the story was widely reported in the press. Here's an article from a Dutch broadsheet in which the tourist board prays that people across Europe will 'have a laugh' and that Amsterdam's reputation won't be 'too negatively' affected.

Voor en na een nachtje Amsterdam

Van een onzer verslaggevers

AMSTERDAM - De VVV Amsterdam hoopt dat toeristen uit Londen, Parijs inchecken en vervolgens als ze uitge-

Hotel in elk geval opvallen. Ze tonen jonge toeristen op het moment dat ze fris en fit inchecken en vervolgens als ze uitge-

Het is de derde campagne voor het bud-gethotel van Erik Kessels (32) en Johan Kramer (33), die met hun eerste campagne

leek heel negatief te zullen uitpakken, maar in de praktijk viel dat gelukkig erg mee", aldus H. ter Balkt van de Amster-

'No Talk heette het experiment van de zender ARD, waarvan de beelden binnenkort worden uit-gezonden. De bedenker ervan, een student aan de Hogeschool voor de Media in Keulen, hoopt er zijn drs-titel mee te kunnen beha-len. "Kunnen ze hun mond hou-den, of zegeviert de routine?", luidde de vraagstelling.

"Het is geen tv-programma", zegt student Uli Wilkes. "Het is een testbeeld. Voor de kijkers be-tekent dit een pauze. Daarna mag de tv zijn hectische programma voortzetten."

Met de hulp van Biolek, die aan de hogeschool doceert, slaagde de student er in nog zes andere tv-sterren te overreden. Onder hen Arabella Kiesbauer, wier praat-programma over seks en aanver-wante zaken op de commerciële zender Pro 7 controversieel is. Günther Jauch van Stern TV (RTL) en Roger Willemsen (ZDF) namen eveneens deel.

Vijftien presentatoren weiger-den de uitnodiging te aanvaar-den. Een van hen is Thomas Gott-schalk, die met de zaterdagavond-show 'Wetten dass' de onbetwiste lieveling van het tv-publiek is. Ook Marcel Reich-Ranicki zei neen. Hij wordt vanwege zijn in-vloed via het 'Literarische Quar-tett' ook wel 's lands cultuurpaus genoemd. "Ik kan niet ergens aan deelnemen als ik mijn mond moet houden", zei Reich-Rani-cki.

Een groot geheim is hoe het

A sliced-down-the-middle brochure appeared in order to promote the Brinker at fairs for the travel industry.

Check in
HANS BRINKER BUDGET HOTEL

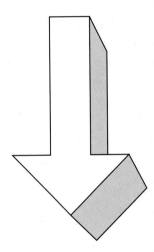

Check in
Near to Van Gogh museum

Check out
Near to nervous breakdown

THE NIGHT WATCH

AN INTERVIEW WITH BEN, THE NIGHT PORTER.

Those brave enough to spend a night at the Hans Brinker often have little idea what to expect. Guests frequently arrive with only a sleeping bag and a fond desire that the hostel will be better than its advertising suggests. A man who knows the truth better than anyone is Ben, the Brinker's night porter. Since 1970, he's spent countless evenings at the hostel, assisting guests and confronting whatever weirdness the midnight hours might throw his way.

Originally, Ben worked for an insurance company, but found the prospect of going into a room full of cubicles every day wasn't for him. 'They didn't even talk about work half the time,' he recalls. 'Rather, it was all about boyfriends and girlfriends. I didn't like it.'

He quit and moved to Amsterdam, where he worked in a prestigious chain hotel. Again, being in a rigidly hierarchical environment didn't suit the rebellious young Ben. His break came when a friend mentioned that the Brinker was on the hunt for staff, and he soon found himself as both night porter and unofficial mascot of the world's worst hotel.

In order to get a better idea of what after-hours at the Brinker are all about, we joined Ben on a typical red-eye shift: 11 p.m. all the way through to a cold, murky 8 a.m. Kept awake only by plentiful supplies of Ben's recommended night-time stimulants (carbonated water and coffee), we chatted about love, business and medical emergencies with a man who embodies the Brinker as much as anyone.

ON CUSTOMER SERVICE:

'I was almost married three times, to three different guests. First, to an American, a girl from New York. She came with a Spanish tour group.' Then there was the Irish girl living in Newcastle, and the lady from Catalonia. 'Working at the Brinker is a good way to meet people,' Ben says.

ON THE BRINKER: 'MORE EXCITING THAN THE CARLTON, MY PREVIOUS JOB. YOU HAD TO WEAR A TIE THERE. I DON'T WANT TO WEAR TIES.'

ON THE BRINKER'S ADVERTISING: 'I THINK IT'S GOOD, BUT SOME OF IT COULD BE FUNNIER.'

ON HIS LEAST FAVOURITE GUESTS:

'English people have parties in the hotel, and the noise is terrible. Sometimes, they accuse me of kissing their women, which isn't true.'

ON MODERNIZING THE WORLD'S WORST HOTEL: 'SOME OF THE ROOMS COULD DO WITH A TV.'

ON DRUGS:

Working nights in a city where soft drugs are legal makes for some interesting situations. -------- 'You get guests coming up to reception, screaming and yelling that I should call the ambulance and take their friends to hospital. But I know what's really happening: people take hash cakes, they go out of their minds for a couple of hours and then they're okay again. I just tell them that my father was a doctor and that everything's fine.' --------- Pause. ----------- 'Actually, my father wasn't really a doctor. He was a pathologist.'

ON SECURITY:

In the 80s, the Brinker was much less safe than today. Back then, anyone could enter. 'I was robbed three times, once at gunpoint' Ben says.

HOME SWEET HELL

THE TOP WORST HOME DECORATIONS:
✿ Pubic hairball
✿ Dead mice
✿ Toenail clippings kept in a glass jar

Independent budget travelling is a global phenomenon. Its true origins depend on which historian you hassle. One would argue that the first real world traveller was Giovanni Francesco Gemelli Careri, who, in the 17th century, entered unknown lands with nothing more than a flamboyant wig. Other more modern historians might point you to the hippie trails of the 1960s and '70s where many young adventurers lost and found themselves somewhere between Europe and Eastern Asia.

Many argue that 21st-century independent travelling is considerably easier than its previous incarnations. So-called 'flash packers' have replaced a sack of dirty pants with an indestructible backpack carrying credit cards, electronic devices, a laptop and mobile, just in case the going gets tough, or the plane is delayed.

Many hostels have adapted themselves to keep up with the rapid pace of change. The Hans Brinker, however, is a little more old-fashioned. It's not a principle. It's not that it feels world traveling should retain a sense of authenticity. It's just far less attentive than it should be.

There is still a fundamental desire amongst many defiant teenagers to flee the flowery confines of home and discover what it's like to give oneself over to a period of life where you don't know what to expect — after the next river you cross, the next ride you thumb or the next border you cross.

However, there comes a point when enough is enough. After too many weeks of forced intercourse with exotic insects, dodging war zones and organ-torturing local foods, even these hardy souls long for the feeling of being at home, to breathe their own air again, to sit on their own toilet seat again.

After a short and some would say unbelievable survey of Hans Brinker visitors, it was found that many of them enjoy visiting the Brinker again and again simply because it reminds them of their own home at a time in their lives when they are far removed from home.

The Brinker decided to capitalize on this. The bedrooms are often just as good (or just as awful) as the bedrooms of its guests. Little wonder so many young people from around the world consider the Brinker their home away from home.

HANS BRINKER BUDGET HOTEL
AMSTERDAM +3120 6220687
JUST LIKE
×HOME×

'Just Like Home' moved the Brinker's communication outside the walls of the hotel and into the homes of its guests. To show off such a disarmingly truthful statement, a set of hand-sewn brochures featured profiles of recent guests with images of their own bedrooms. Central to the campaign was an infamous commercial which, in the Brinker's opinion, shows a typical moment in a home that could belong to any of its guests. Unfortunately, the message was a little too graphic for the powers that be at MTV, the channel on which it was due to be aired. It shows a young women the morning after a big night, stumbling through empty alcohol bottles and finally slipping on a filled condom. The combination of booze, hangover, semi-nudity and sperm was simply too much for the youth-orientated TV channel to take. You can view it on the DVD at the back of this book.

THIS BED BELONGS TO: Baruch Freeman
HOME: Hamburg, Germany
NAME BRIDGED HOTEL, VISIT: 14 - 28 October 2000
ROOM NUMBER: 80
GUEST BOOK COMMENT: What do you need from a hotel? A bed, a floor, 4 walls, a place to relieve yourself of body waste and maybe a window that sometimes opens. My home is that way and I like my hotels the same. Your hotel satisfies all my needs and less.

THIS BED BELONGS TO: Massimo di Pietro
HOME: Bassano del Grappa, Italy
NAME BRIDGED HOTEL, VISIT: 27 February - 4 March 2001
ROOM NUMBER: 09
GUEST BOOK COMMENT: I know some of my friends complain about the stairs. But I say to them - hey, all our own beds back home have big stairs too - what's the problem!

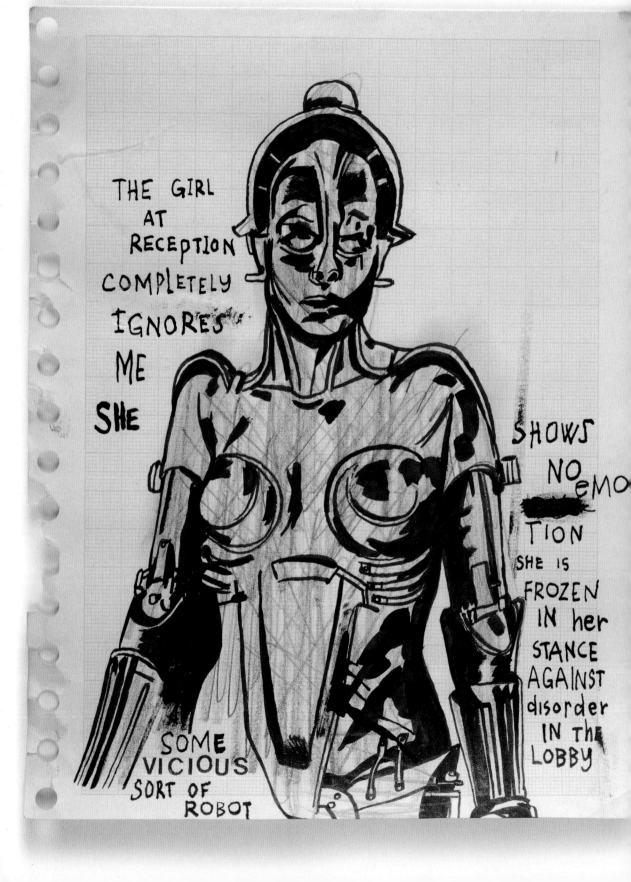

IN 1996, HANS BRINKER MAID, FERNANDINA, FOUND A BATTERED DIARY AMONGST SOILED SHEETS. IT CONTAINED AN ACCOUNT OF A YOUNG WRITER WHO DARED TO CALL THE BRINKER HOME FOR 14 DAYS. THE FOLLOWING IS AN EXCERPT OF HIS DESCENT INTO THE BOTTOMLESS ABYSS.

January 25, 1996
Flight arrival time Amsterdam:
5:35 a.m.
Arrival at Hans Brinker Budget
Hotel: 6:15 a.m.

Ben, the night porter, is shocked to see a human being with luggage at this hour of the morning. He pushes some magical button that opens the electronic glass sliding doors. I'm inside. Outside it is blacker than a forgotten cave in the mists of the Amazon.

Ben sits down behind the reception desk. I ask him if he knows my friends who supposedly have arranged a room for me here with the owner. Ben says he doesn't know my friends, doesn't know anything about it, hasn't heard of the owner and hasn't heard of me having any friends. Ben is smoking a cigarette, and looking at me suspiciously through his wide, thick, coke-bottle glasses. His English is quite good, but sounds a bit like he has toothpaste gooping up his words. He flicks his cigarette at a hidden ashtray. The florescent light makes everything look waxy and scratchy, like a Pizza Hut in Des Moines.

I tell him my name. He looks down along some piece of paper that looks like some kind of ancient reservation list from the late sixties. There's no computer or file, just pages in a ring binder. To Ben's great astonishment, my name is written down there somewhere. Light has appeared.

'You have a nice, quiet room in the back. It's quite nice,' he says, dripping his words. 'I'll give you a nice rate on the room.' Ben's a high-stakes gambler, I believe, a master dealer, a player, a giver of nice rates on nice, quiet rooms in the back. I am blessed.

Room #403.
Only the bathroom light works. I have a bathroom. A surprise.

Well, it looks like a bathroom. And the windows are open, and it is so goddamn freezing. The radiator is stone cold. I am so exhausted, I just collapse on the pitiful little bed that hasn't been made and shiver in the cold with my coat still on and the wind whipping around Amsterdam.

I lie there for about an hour, and I sense that this must be some kind of healing ritual. This must be some sort of cleansing. Here I am. I keep repeating. Here I am. Here I am. What have I done? What have I done? I call out to a god but only some guttural thumping from the next room replies.

Later, I tell the girl at reception that the lights in room #403 don't work. She says that she doesn't believe me and that I must've broken them. This I deny, feeling guilty for just asking her. I also explain the heating situation. She just looks at me in total bewilderment. She looks through me as if I'm a sheet of cellophane.

January, 26 1996
9:55 a.m.

The thin elevator takes me down to the lobby. The blue, stained doors open to a lobby amassed with loud and intoxicated Dutch people all gussied up in some manner of festival costumes. Dresses the size of boats and the men in three-piece minstrel garb. They fill the lobby with their unbearable singing and loud hideous laughter. They reek of gin and cigarettes. Their voices add to my wretched alienation.

I shuffle and squeeze my way over to reception, and the same girl I spoke with yesterday is there; the one who doesn't believe anything I say, the one irritated by my mere existence. She completely ignores me. She shows no emotion. She is frozen in her stance against disorder in the lobby of the Brinker. Some vicious sort of robot.

After a bit of time, I am recognized. She looks at me with placid contempt. In a weak and humble voice, I inquire about my room status.

She looks at the mysterious reservations chart on her desk below her. It's the one Ben first opened.

'It's not possible for you to stay in 403 after tomorrow.' She says this in a voice as cold as a witch's nipple.

There is a small eternity and emptiness, and the crowd blanks out, and I am out somewhere else, somewhere where there is no salvation, no hope. I am in a small rubber pool, and I have forgotten how to swim. The beautiful lady turns back to face the crowd, and I weakly speak again, 'Well, is there anything you can do, or...'

She pivots immediately, 'There is nothing I can do. It is not possible. You must move tomorrow morning to the dormitory for one night, then maybe you can go back to room 403 on Sunday. I don't think so.'

Oh, the dormitory. The dormitory sounds nice.

January 27, 1996
8:15 a.m.

I yank myself awake, out of bed, and prepare myself for the morning receptionist. I practise several facial expressions in the small mirror in my small bathroom. I try aggressive, then passive, then coy, then agony, and finally decide just to see how it goes.

Unlike yesterday, the lobby is quite empty, and there is a lone morning receptionist waiting.

'My name is Tyler. I'm in room 403. I was just wondering if it was possible not to move out today, not to have to move to that dormitory. If I could just stay in 403. Is it possible?'

'Ahhh....' He looks at that mysterious reservation chart. 'Not possible.'

'Well, you see, my friends (at least I think they're my friends) have spoken with the owner about keeping the room for some time. I think it's sort of arranged.'

The receptionist is unfazed by this. 'Is there anything we can do?'

'It's not possible.'

'Are you sure?'

'I'm not stupid. I know that it is not possible.'

'But, my friends have spoken to the owner.'

'I know nothing of this.'

Then, as if pressed into military service, The Morning Receptionist begins to look at the complex and cryptic reservation chart in the spiral-bound notebook. He makes small guttural noises. He wields a pen. He moves items around on the desk. He smokes, he dances, he looks out into space for short moments of time. He is some kind of magician.

Finally, he marks something down on the cryptic reservation chart that has been so instrumental in deciding the fates of many young souls... "OK. It's all right. It's possible for a few days. But I don't know how long you can have the room. Just a few days. You can pay now. We only take guilders."

January 28, 1996
12 a.m.

I return to see old friend Ben sitting at reception. I ask if there is channel on the big TV in the bar that will get the Super Bowl. He has no idea what I'm asking about. He gets up and we walk into the bar where he begins checking channels. He explains each channel.

'This is an Amsterdam programme. This is a Spanish channel. This is RaiUno, Italian channel. This is an Amsterdam channel. This is an old movie channel. This is CNN,

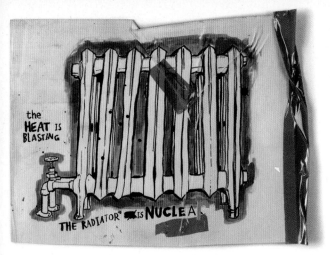

nothing ever on. This is MTV. This is an
Amsterdam programme.'

I leave him there.

Defeated, I go to room 403.

No one in Amsterdam has heard of the
Super Bowl for Christ's sake.

January 29, 1996
12:30 a.m.

I didn't have enough beer at dinner so I
go for another in the 'discotheque', as
advertised by the girl in the Brinker bar,
who says that 'this bar is closed now',
and that I can take my beer down to the
discotheque. And then it hits me. That's
where that god-awful stench is coming from.
That smell that started back before they
built the dams in the swamp, before any
Dutch soul walked these subterranean flats.
The Brinker discotheque holds the putrid
smell of 100,000 dead nights of soiled
beer swilling and retching.

I make it to the third or fourth step,
and I suddenly know that I have had enough
beer for one night. I turn back from the
horror, the horror.

Bed now. Curiously drawn covers. As if
the bed itself were also dead. The pillows
are hiding, buried.

I have to fumble in the bathroom for the
only light that works so I can see. I laugh,
thinking that the other broken overhead
light must be on vacation somewhere at
some hotel in South Dakota or Mongolia or
enjoying a Pabst Blue Ribbon in Pittsburgh.
And then I think how nice it might be
to be in those places.

January 30, 1996
8:15 a.m.

Awake. I'm alive. I breathe cautiously.
I barely exhale. There is horror here.

8:25 a.m.

Shower. Is this water or just spitting spray.
A Binaca Blast. Plumbing pissing.

8:35 a.m.

Brush my teeth. I always do this as I have
been told to for so long.

I stare long into the small odd-shaped
mirror, a pentagon, but there are no magical
powers here, though I keep searching.
I'm starting to think that my heater might
actually be a miniature nuclear power plant.
That dangerous hissing mechanism emits
way too much energy to be a mere radiator.
Perhaps it's a spare part stolen from
Chernobyl. It's almost tropical in this room
now. The tropical rainforest in room 403.
I feel like putting on a grass skirt. I
could maybe hire out my room as a sauna to
wealthy tourists. I wonder if old Ben has
though about this. But then I think of that
girl at reception and how it would somehow
violate her socialist ethos.

The architectural wonder of my room gives
me quiet astonishment. As I piss in the
toilet, I have to angle the upper half of
my body to the left so as not to hit my head
on a slanting, large beam. And because of
this, I have to hold my tool out as far as
I can so that I can hit the toilet, that
toilet that had a few things die in it. This
I am sure of. Don't doubt me here. There is
something not of this earth living in that
god-cursed toilet.

January 31, 1996
7:16 a.m.

Where the fuck am I?

February 1, 1996
9:03 a.m.

It's not the sun. It's not my internal clock.
It's the sound of the almighty toilet that
wakes me, then drags me by the earlobes
headlong into daylight.

The toilet hisses and moans with some
hidden task, maybe all of Amsterdam purifies
its water through this small plastic wonder
of modern plumbing. I consider a new god.
I worship the pipes, rusty, crucified, touched
but somehow more pure than any of us.

these pipes have suffered for you. They have taken away all your dirty little sins.

February 2, 1996
There is a painting on the wall. I think it's a painting. It's hard to see because the light is still broken. When some friends crowd into my room after partying it up in the discotheque, one takes notice of this disastrous painting and turns the bloody thing upside down. Now I can see it better.

It's more of a drawing than a painting. The painting is now art, and not just some black square on the wall, in the corner near the window that rattles all through the night singing along with its friend the toilet.

February 3, 1996
Mass confusion in the middle of the night. Mass hysterical news broadcasts in my head, steel sabres and bicycles and the slant of foreign, strange attic beams in room 403. And fear seizes me, creeps over me like a cheap blanket. It's completely dark and the only noise is this incessant, insidious, insipid hissing from the bathroom.

The pipes are the arteries and veins of a giant horrible monster, the Hans Brinker Budget Hotel Creature with a discotheque for its bowels, a bar for its stomach, two blue, polluted elevators for its throat and soiled ancient brick for its skin. And the beast breathes through the toilets, coughing the foul odours of the canal, burping smells 9,000 years old into the small rooms, the empty corridors, through the half-lit alleys to the elevators and down to the reception area where some human creature sits staring into the pale clouds of the pancreas. And I am disturbed in the fear. My room is the ear that listens. 403 hears. 403 is jammed with earwax. 403 feels the whispers and the enormous beast that slumbers, snores and stretches.

February 4, 1996
There is this constant urge to return or go back to somewhere you recognize as a place of reasonable comfort.

A place that has welcomed you, a place that has warmed you after the cold, a place that has dried you after the rain, a place that offers you rest after the burden, a place that fills you after the hunger, a place of clarity after the darkness, a place of quiet after the noise, a place of belonging after the alienation, a place of simplicity after the chaos, a place of caring after bitterness, a place of laughter after tears, a place of solitude after the crowds, a place of understanding after escape, a place of nature after concrete, a place of pillows after thumbtacks, a place of honeysuckle after turpentine, a place of orgasm after frustration, an open sky after fog, fresh air after smog, gentle voices after screams, carpets after stones, robes after polyester, order after the maze, charity after indifference, candy after medicine, T-shirts after suits, playgrounds after jungles, a place of peace after the hell. This is not that place.

February 5, 1996
What I loved most today was the sign above the bar that read 'closed' in almost every language. 'Fermé, cerrado, dicht, geschlossen, 閉鎖した, закрыто, closed.'

Why, oh why then isn't it written in Braille? Please tell me that. Please tell me that before I die. Warn everyone about this place. Not just those who can see. Not just those who can read. In the end, we should know this.

We are all so fucking blind in the end.

CLEAN-LINESS AND OTHER ███████ ATROCI-TIES

THE WORST

STAINS TO REMOVE:
✤ Blood of human
✤ Blood of whale
✤ Poltergeist residue

he Hans Brinker P...   the Nelson
lthiest ...   was
f man.   Tense
ctor Who ...   intin
ee s hile ...   ake a
la in Amsterdam Beac... S...   Nelson
oc...   'beyond disgusti... the most horri- cially
le ... e ... could imagi... can't t
it ...ng.   ...9. As
... an... ... from 1992 on so ...ery fu
es... the ... eed of instant continu
um... but... ...egular fumigation, then en
up... nvolving th... an... Americ... our to
pe... s, perh... the fact fu
u... ...d of th...

But cleanlines
n... ...er's ...ety R... al cata
a... rom the regulation ... n sheets t
o... ...e ...in... of... o pa... s sh
on... tel ...owards th... ...ri... ...ases like ... ile
he re... ...ected ...ted ... hou... ...ated on the outbreak
race ... ...i-...gent c... ...vi... human rights and
parent... ...he Brinker's bas... ...st ...ponded
ving off ... sta... ...ties. post... ...oke."

ever, the sighting... ...ld never be confirm... ...son Mande... ...ich it has
the inspect... ...sappea... ...e d... ...ter been officially reporte... ...manity's great-
...ng his ... ...ris est hero ...an't ... total came to 6,
...ck ... ...ndela printed an apology
...i... on... ...rin...
e i... ...ue a... ...en
th th... ...t co... the ...tion of b...
ches ... ...Saf... He then embarked o...
...pect... ...G... t... th
mi o... ...ity... fa

hen a... But c... at t...
...ribes ... ...ld"... nd lead to g...al catastr...
...unded." provides clean s...et
se... owers... paren...

...as in 1999 that the Brink...s greate... ...e ...n dise...
...h of hygi... ...s made headline... ...
...for 26... ...story ... te... ...by his de... conspir... ...ites... on the inter-
...ll-c... ...wen... ...ly wrong. ne... ...aim that Penn... with the
...the ... de...ately...d ...ace of gi...t, ...mi-i... ...cies and
...h ... ...r f...llow case... ...t he... ...th ...lth... ...ctor in
...he ... ...ert...i th... ...be... ...row... ...of the
...t th... Bri... For A... ...er ...rin...
S... ...e shit. It... ...tised ...tu... ...
n... Ques... ...the Bri...is... ...".
...ract... ...nd a... ...wasn't th...uit. It wa... ...ht
...ad thr... ...st... ...deliberately used...se accu...
bringing our civilizatio... ...usation...s "w...

IMPROVE YOUR IMMUNE SYSTEM

Attention Clean Freaks! You are making the world too clean. Your immune system is in danger. We need contact with dirt to build up natural resistance to harmful bacteria. For this reason, the Hans Brinker Budget Hotel is proud to be dirty and carry a wide variety of bacteria. Just one night's stay will give your immune system the boost it needs to remain effective. **Visit before it's too late.**

THE HANS BRINKER BUDGET HOTEL AMSTERDAM +31 20 622 0687

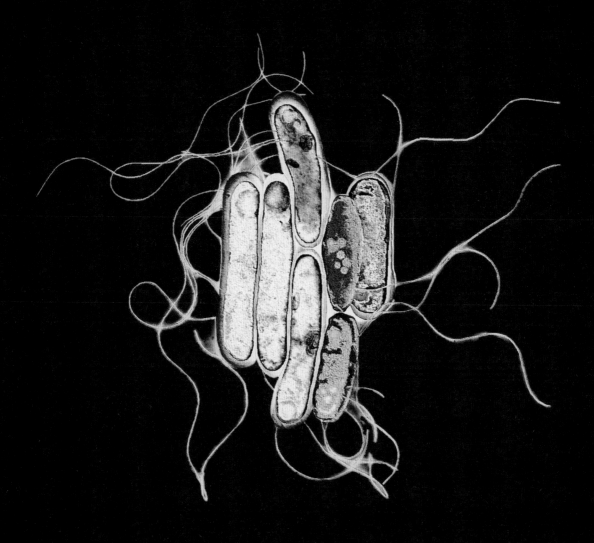

IMPROVE YOUR IMMUNE SYSTEM

THE HANS BRINKER BUDGET HOTEL AMSTERDAM   +31 20 622 0687

IMPROVE YOUR IMMUNE SYSTEM

THE HANS BRINKER BUDGET HOTEL AMSTERDAM   +31 20 622 0687

An adult bedbug is
2.5 mm in length.

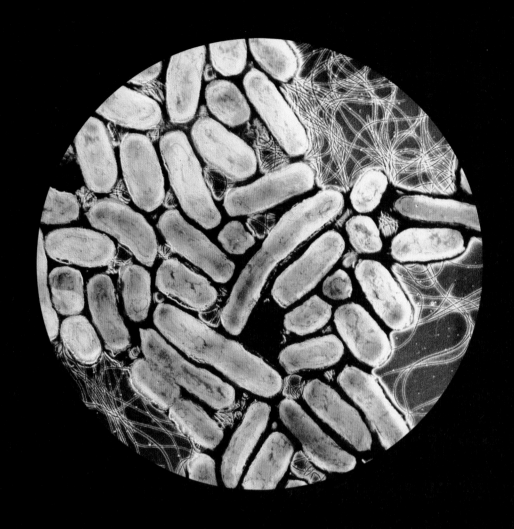

IMPROVE YOUR IMMUNE SYSTEM

MORE THAN ONCE, THE BRINKER HAS REFERRED TO CURRENT TRENDS IN ITS COMMUNICATION. FOR 2004'S 'IMPROVE YOUR IMMUNE SYSTEM' CAMPAIGN, A NEWS STORY ALLOWED THE HOTEL TO FLIP NEGATIVE PERCEPTIONS OF ITS CLEANLINESS INTO A RESOUNDING POSITIVE.

The story appeared in American and British newspapers, including The New York Times. Scientists reported that modern immune systems were becoming weaker and weaker. In the bad old days, poor sanitation and rudimentary notions of pathology meant people were subject to ailments now largely confined to Charles Dickens novels. One of the unexpected side effects of all this was that our bodies exhibited great resilience; being drenched in bugs acted as a natural vaccine.

Nowadays, however, medical advances mean that we're being exposed to pathogens less often. Strangely enough, the consequence of this is that we're becoming more unwell, prone to common or garden illnesses like colds and the flu. Allergies are also on the up, with Britain's National Health Service spending around a billion pounds a year on treatments. Even asthma is less prevalent in polluted cities and more widely spread in their cleaner, more 'advanced' counterparts.

On reading this, the Brinker spotted an opportunity: attract more guests while bolstering people's ailing health, without spending money on actually improving the hotel. After all, if the research were true, time spent surrounded by the Brinker's medieval levels of cleanliness could actually boost our lymph nodes.

But simply claiming this benefit based on the inferences of non-scientists didn't go far enough. The Brinker wanted to prove its hunch. The hotel shipped a carefully harvested pile of Brinker dirt to a lab in Eastern Europe. The results were conclusive: yes, the Brinker's grime was indeed swarming with all kinds of unpleasant microbes.

Backed by this newly acquired hard evidence, the campaign went into production. Centred around posters, it also featured TV commercials. Broadcast on MTV, the films showed giant bedbugs apparently taking over the Brinker. Bugs manned reception, bugs worked the bar, bugs frolicked in the rooms. These nightmarish images supported the campaign's positive take on dirt.

The science paid off. Bookings increased and complaints dropped — largely due to the advertising encouraging a more realistic view of the hotel. The campaign also helped adjust people's perspective, albeit in a very minor way. It implied that if even dirt can be positive and the concept of grime relative, then perhaps there are other 'bad' things in our surroundings that should be re-evaluated too.

BRINK-ER DUST BALL HALL OF FAME

UNDER BED, ROOM 401

LOBBY

CORNER, ROOM 314

LOCKER, ROOM 317

UNDER MATTRESS, ROOM 212

SHOWER DRAIN, ROOM 108

BEHIND TOILET, ROOM 108

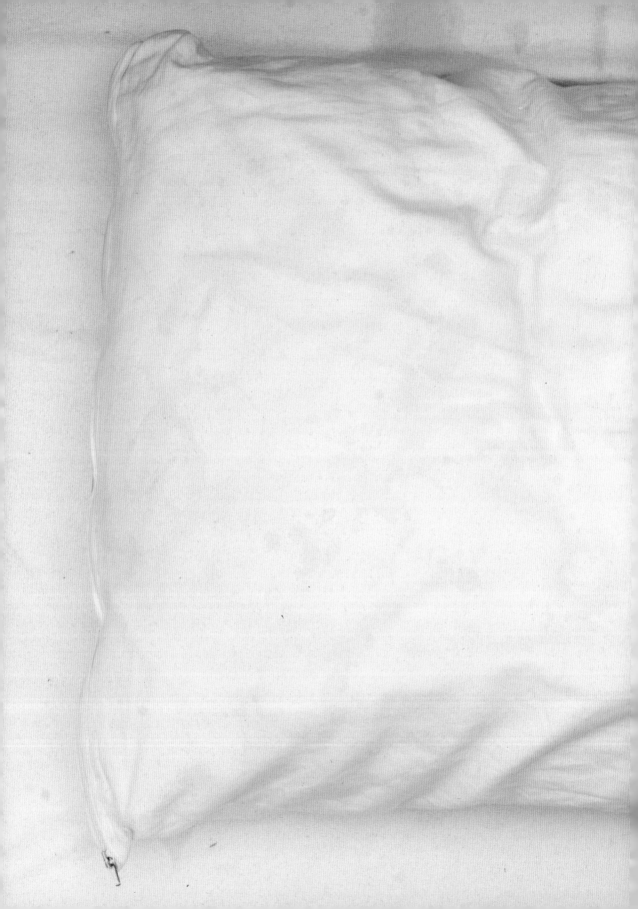

GOOD MORNING
HAPPY HOUR
ORDER 1 ..... GET 2
ORDER 2 ..... GET 4
....
ORDER 100 ... GET 200
EVERY DAY
17.00 - 18.00

LOVE AND OTH- ER COM- PLAINTS

Hate. Adoration. Disgust. The Brinker elicit's anything except indifference. In these pages, we've compiled a selection of writings about the hostel, from guest complaints to international press clippings. But wherever they're from and whatever their background, these authors are united by their capacity to get very emotional about the little hotel with the big attitude problem.

It is bad like you say it is but not that bad. The staff is mostly very nice to us, though sometimes they were rude. The beds were clean and so was the room - except for a thing in the corner. Not sure what that was.

Bastards. All of them. Who the hell do you think you are?

Posted by B Brinker on March 13, 199

Very interesting site, funny as hell. I have to visit the Hans Brinker Hotel if I could only determine where it is located in Amsterdam. I spent one hour with the mouse and still dont know the address. Being a Brinker, I think I should get a reduced rate for being the first Brinker with the guts to stay there.

In all my years of youth hostelling, I have never stayed in a place as bad as this. You guys should be shot. seriously.

Nice bunch of people. The receptionist had brought some fresh croissants to work and she was kind enough to share one with us. I will definitely come back and recommend you to our friends.

posted by W*** Hancock on July 14, 1997 at 12:24:13:

COULD SOMEBODY PLEASE HELP ME!
I got lost in the fire exit of the budget hotel.

Reply:
there`s no help

This hotel should be condemned and closed down immediately. A terrible place. My wife threw up three times while we were there. I blame the canteen.

A lovely, memorable experience. so many nice people, so helpful and sweet. They even gave us roses when we checked in. Not really - it sucked. Every minute of it.

Posted by HBrinker on February 27, 1998 at 09:23:06:

Hej,

that is really funny: your hotel and webpage has exactly my name. so I'll stay in your hotel when I am coming to Amsterdam next time.

Greetings from Finland.

Hans

Reply:

Hello Hans, do you like to put your fingers in dikes as well? You're always welcome, even if you don't.

1997 at 06:57:36:

I don't know why you keep on about dogs. They're not the main problem at your hotel. Why just the other day I was in the reception area about to propose to my girlfriend when in through the window comes a fly. I was speechless. The moment was completley ruined for me. I did not propose and we have now split up. All because your hotel has flies.

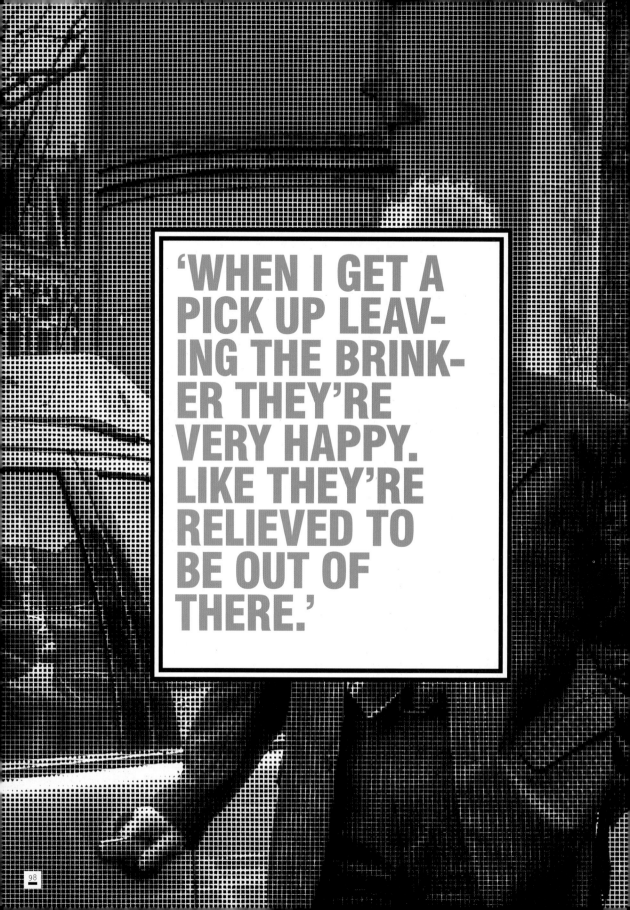

'WHEN I GET A PICK UP LEAVING THE BRINKER THEY'RE VERY HAPPY. LIKE THEY'RE RELIEVED TO BE OUT OF THERE.'

'IT WAS THE WORST HOTEL
I'VE STAYED IN DURING MY
14 YEARS OF TRAVELLING
AND USING HOSTELS.'
– VERONICA PASSARINI, GUEST

'THE
ROOM WAS
VERY PALE.'
– ANAT ISRAEL, GUEST

'LIKE SOMETHING
FROM BRAM STOKER.
I WOULDN'T WISH
THIS PLACE ON MY
WORST ENEMY.
IF YOU ENJOY BEING
DISAPPOINTED,
STAY HERE.'
– JORDAN SPANJERS, GUEST

'I LIKED IT
BUT I HAVE
BAD TASTE.'
— VERNER JONES, GUEST

'IT WAS SCARY AND
NOT IN A FUN WAY.
I WOULD PAY TEN
EUROS MORE FOR
A BETTER PLACE.'
— CARA BELPEDIO, GUEST

'THE LUGGAGE ROOM
HAD SOMETHING
ROTTEN IN IT. PROBABLY
IT'S STILL THERE.'
— CHRISTINE HANDS, GUEST

'WE TRY TO RESPECT OUR CLIENTS, NOT DISTURB THEM. THEIR HOTEL IS THE POLAR OPPOSITE OF OUR ESTABLISHMENT. I LIKE TO KEEP MY UNIFORM WELL CREASED.'

WHEN WORST ISN'T GOOD ENOUGH

BEING BAD AT SOMETHING IS RELATIVELY EASY. NOT SHOWING UP, NOT CARING, NOT LEARNING HOW TO COMPLETE TASKS — THESE ARE THINGS EVEN A CHILD CAN DO. BEING THE WORST AT SOMETHING IS A COMPLETELY DIFFERENT STORY. IT REQUIRES TIME, SKILL AND DETERMINATION. ODD THOUGH IT MAY SOUND, THERE'S NOT A LOT OF DIFFERENCE BETWEEN WHAT IT TAKES TO BE THE BEST AND WHAT IT TAKES TO BE THE WORST.

After years of providing guests with incompetent service and unacceptable accommodation, the staff of the Brinker decided that it wasn't just going to settle for the title of worst hotel in Europe or Amsterdam. For once in their lives, these lazy and apathetic individuals set their sights on the big prize: worst hotel in the world. Decades of bitter complaints, hate-filled accusations and the occasional death threat provided the staff with the input they needed to plunge the Brinker into previously unfathomable lows. The Brinker's second foray into before-and-after photography focused on a number of 'improvements' made to the hotel. Fittingly, it's quite hard to tell which photographs are worse: the before images or the after. These posters were plastered around the seediest areas of Amsterdam and other cities, reminding current and future guests of the Brinker's commitment to being the worst.

HANS BRINKER BUDGET HOTEL.
IT CAN'T GET ANY WORSE.

BUT WE'LL DO OUR BEST.
AMSTERDAM +31 20 6220687

BUT WE'LL DO OUR BEST.
AMSTERDAM +31 20 6220687

THE LUXURY OF HONESTY

A MOSTLY SERIOUS CHAPTER

THE **WORST**

LUXURIES FROM HOTELS:
☆ Trouser press
☆ Fawning concierge
☆ List of local call girls kept under reception desk

Is there a successful story behind the Brinker's disobedient marketing style? If so what is the secret of this success? Is there a lesson to be learned, or one to sidestep? This chapter is about seeing the beauty in budget, the luxury in less and the wonder of honesty — not only in relation to the hotel industry, but also in other brands, life and future happiness.

In the 1950s, Fortune magazine editor William Whyte Jr. invented the word 'Budgetism'. It was used to describe a society that binds itself to strict spending and saving regimes, with no loans, investments or outside influences to challenge their restrictions. In modern times, we can perhaps reappropriate Budgetism as the start of a new movement — one that many (or possibly none) may dare to follow. One where abrupt cost- and service-cutting has a positive effect on turnover rather than a negative one on the influx of customers.

The Brinker is the shabby king of Budgetism, having rejected the unnecessary need for opulence of any kind. It has been around since 1970, with only one major refurbishment, sixteen years ago; an active decision in remaining true to its budget status. Even

with this lack of maintenance, as well as its polarizing anti-statements in marketing, it has still managed to make sharp rises in guest occupancy year on year since it started communicating. From the start of the launch campaign, nearly two million backpackers and students — as well as the occasional schoolteacher, desperate businessman or advertising executive wondering what all the fuss is about — have enjoyed the Brinker's unique Budgetism. Something must be right about shouting to the world that you are so wrong. How exactly has the hotel managed to persuade young, cost-conscious travellers to stay in a 513-bed hotel with no extras to offer while paying a bit more than its competitors?

A small clue can be found within the regulations of the independent regulatory organization for the advertising industry, the Advertising Standards Authority in the UK, one of the Brinker's main markets.

While there are many rules surrounding claims of being number one, it's a rare rule which stipulates negligence when you claim to be far from the best.

These points were drawn from their guidelines:

1.0 Statements should not be used in respect of any products that they are 'the best', 'the most successful', 'safest', 'quickest', or containing any similar use of superlative adjectives unless the truthfulness of such statements is adequately substantiated.

4.0 Superlatives like 'most popular', 'most preferred', 'most favoured', etc., when used in a manner which clearly suggests a number one sales position, should be subject to the same standards governing bestselling claims.

Meaning, if you claim to be the worst, the least successful, the most dangerous, the slowest, the least popular, least preferred or least favoured, you are a lone ship in a sea of brands that claim exactly the opposite. In marketing and business terms, if you own a territory, with no neighbours as far as the eye can see, then you're living in a beautiful place.

Is this the secret? Being one of few brands happy to wallow in the dirt at the bottom of the table? The story goes back to 1993, the year the Brinker did the only refurbishment it would ever really do. 'We went from 250 to 513 beds,' says proprietor Rob Penris. 'We also started communicating. We had the 'No this, No that' campaign (see *Worst Interview in the World* chapter). Not many hotels would risk talking about offering nothing at all, when there are more than double the number of beds to fill.'

A more embedded problem lay with seasonality. In summer, no hotel has major problems in Amsterdam — it's the winter when it gets tough, especially when aiming at a young audience who has the income and the budget airline to send them to the sun or snow rather than a cold Northern European city. To protect its profit, the Brinker decided right at the start to maintain its relatively high price (compared to other hostels) while reducing minimally in December and January. Another hotel price-reducing phenomenon is group bookings by tour operators. The Brinker wanted to attract as many individual bookings as possible — they pay more. So the communication's real task, beneath the slap-in-the-face dark humour, was to stretch the summer season and make Brinker less dependent on groups. 'We have achieved that, despite the fact that Amsterdam was facing serious drops in visitors over several years,' says Penris.

A study of the figures proves his statement to be true. Before the ad campaigns started in 1993, the Hans Brinker had a bed occupancy percentage of 45%. Within 5 years this grew to 70%, peaking in 2002 at 80% and fluctuating around then until now. During this period nothing changed but the advertising. The product remained the same, there were no price promotions and there were no dramatic changes in the competition.

To put that into a wider perspective, most hotels use the percentage of room occupancy as an indicator of the performance. If the Brinker would use this measurement, percentages would be in excess of 100%. (In actuality, there are 513 beds in 140 rooms, so the Brinker feels it to be more honest to count the occupied beds instead.)

It was John Wanamaker — the early 1900s merchant and supposed father of modern advertising — who said, 'I know that half of my advertising dollars are wasted, I just don't

Slapen met je kop in de asbak

SLEEPING WITH AN ASHTRAY ON (handwritten)

ROB PENRIS:
'VIJFHONDERD LEGE BEDDEN EN DAN OPEENS ALLEMAAL VOL TOEN GING IK GELOVEN IN RECLAME'

Campagne of niet?

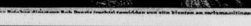

Budget-directeur Rob Penris (rechts) temidden van zijn klanten en reclame-uitingen.
FOTO JS AD IN IK

worst place in town (circled) ...s heeft het Hans Brinker Budget
Hotel geen kwaad gedaan. Nooit eerder was het aantal
overnachtingen aan de Amsterdamse Kerkstraat zo hoog als dit jaar.
De sleutel tot succes: beroerde service en uitzicht op blinde muren.

INSPIRINGLY BAD (handwritten, vertical)

BAD (handwritten) **Beroerd kan ook verkopen**
ALSO SELL (handwritten)

Kamer 114: Umut (23 sisoolitstudent en Okcan, Atil en Korkut, allen 22 en allen bedrijfskundestudenten uit Istanbul

Parijs en Brussel hebben ze op hun Interrail-reis z gehad en thuis zijn ze o wel een en ander ge wend. Amsterdam is he temin een crazy city. Umut: 'Natuurlijk komer we hier voor de coffee shops, maar zeker ook voor het Van Gogh museum en het huis va Anne Frank. En verave willen we naar de Roxy Wat? Oh, eigenlijk. Maar 't was toch nog e andere bekende club. Gaalanco? Nee, ja luk?

tribune Interview

HET SUCCES VAN ANTI-RECLAME

ROB PENRIS EN MATTHIJS DE JONGH OVER HANS BRINKER BUDGET HOTEL

'HAVE A SLEEP (handwritten) **'Kom eens slapen in ons vieze hotel'** *IN A DIRTY HOTEL'* (handwritten)

Hotel Hell. Ten
advertising fron
Budget Hotel A
Fondazione Qu
Venezia 12.10.

NOW
WIT
A W

ホテル
ハンス・ブリンカー・バジェット
ホテル・アムステルダム
The Hans Brinker Budget
Hotel Amsterdam

12軒あるヨーロッパのキャンペーン
展開するバックパッカー向けホテル。
●Kerkstraat 136-138、
Amsterdam
☎(020) 6200687
FAX(020) 6382900
110室 一部シャワー付き
21～32.5ユーロ
朝食、共用。
www.hans-brinker.com

上り階のバースペースなどといった新展し、
だんだんとトレンド・チェック。下：お部屋は
まり日常の…。なおは、お部屋は

室内人
Erik Kessels エリック・ケッセルス

©1997ルモンド生まれ。元ハン・クライマーと地味にクリエイティブ・エージ
ェンシー「ケッセルスクラマー」を設立。クリエイティブ・ディレクター
「ケッセルスクラマー」プロジェクトリーダ

'This hotel sucks!' staat tussen de graffiti in één van de trappenhuizen
gekalkt. De directeur is er trots op. Budget Hotel Hans Brinker, ruim
vijfhonderd 'ligplaatsen', presenteert zich als het 'most xxxclusive'
onderkomen van Amsterdam. "Wij zijn niet klantvriendelijk."

WE ARE NOT CUSTOMER FRIENDLY (handwritten)

IS IT THE END FOR KESSELS KRAMER AND HANS BRINKER? PAULA CARSON REVIEWS A PARTNERSHIP THAT BUILT TWO INTERNATIONAL REPUTATIONS

CHECK OUT TIME?

Hans Brinker Hotel
enfin toute la vérité

Dix années d'antipublicité ont fait de cet hôtel miteux d'Amsterdam un lieu culte, où se retrouvent volontiers du monde entier, attirés par ce faux dévers "expérience", Eole, incontestable, le Hans Brinker n'aurait jamais dû rencontrer un tel succès. Mais son directeur eut l'idée d'employer une petite agence nommée KesselsKramer qui, d'éclat sordide, métamorphosa sa fosse en royaume de béton trash, cloïstre vrai d'une promotion mal léchée.

THE WHOLE TRUTH

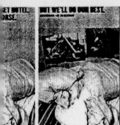

SCREEN REJECTS

Condoom in beeld: MTV weigert spotje Amsterdams budgethotel

A SPOT

van onze verslaggever

AMSTERDAM

Een meisje wordt wakker en grijpt naar haar hoofd. Ze schopt een bierblikje uit bed en komt moeizaam overeind in een kamer die is bezaaid met de restanten van een wilde nacht. De moeite is vergeefs: ze glijdt uit over een condoom en valt terug in bed. Welkom in Hans Brinker Budget Hotel: *Just Like Home*.

Het reclamefilmpje schiet recht in het hart van de doelgroep: jonge rugzaktoeristen die naar Amsterdam komen om vrijelijk te blowen en de Wallen te verkennen. Maar de Britse reclame-autoriteiten zien er de humor niet van in. Daarom mag de spot niet worden uitgezonden, terwijl de Britse markt juist zo belangrijk is voor het Amsterdamse hotel.

Hoteldirecteur R. Penris heeft nu reclamebureau KesselsKramer, bedenker van de campagne, boze aan de tijd geseind 'want dan moeten het vakmanschap hebben om te beoordelen of zo'n spot door de beugel kan.'

De reclame is wel uitgezonden in Duitsland en Scandinavië, maar dat zijn minder belangrijke markten. Hans Brinker had juist flink willen uitpakken op het

Beeld uit het omstreden tv-spotje.

Britse MTV. Maar in Groot-Brittannië vond de onafhankelijke Broadcast Advertising Clearance Centre, die alle commercials tevoren beoordeelt op fatsoensnormen, dat KesselsKramer over de schreef is gegaan.

'De spot is gebaseerd op twee gronden. Er is een controld condoom te zien', zegt Matthijs de Jongh van KesselsKramer. 'Dan denk ik: *come on*. Ook vond men het model er jonger uitzien dan 18, hoewel ze in het echt 20 is. Men vond het verkeerd dat zo'n jong meisje in verband,

erend slecht

Opdrachtgever: *Hans Brinker Budget Hotel*; Bureau: *KesselsKramer*; Creatie: *Erik Kessels (art) en er Whisnand (copy)*; Fotograaf: *Johannes Schwartz*; Verantwoordelijk bij klant: *Robert Penris*.

TROP CRÉATIVE ?

Une agence d'Amsterdam a failli perdre client à cause de sa créativité débridée

YOUR COMPLIMENTARY STARTER PACK

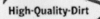

High-Quality-Dirt

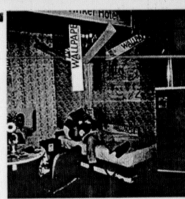

WALLPAPER

> WE WEREN'T FAR FROM LAUNCHING THE HANS BRINKER BUDGET BEER. IT WILL BE VERY BAD BEER OF COURSE BUT IT'LL GET YOU DRUNK IN NO TIME

THE ART OF BRINKER-MANSHIP

HANS BRINKER BUDGET HOTEL
AMSTERDAM +31 20 6220687

JUST LIKE HOME

New forms of communication from the Netherlands
Methodology and originality

徳田祐司 TOKUDA Yuji

経歴 クリエイティブ・プランニング・ジレクター・アートディレクター。
代表的な仕事 「ラフォーレ原宿」「グランバザール」各種ポスター（太田ウォッシング、双子のロックグランプリなど）、MK. Jo project、Shampoo Planet、Air Festival project (Cape Coco)、ドキュメンタリー映像「The Other F-Kall」など、
受賞歴 '96ニューヨークADC金賞、'94TV ADC賞、'96・'01美賞、'96カンヌ銀賞グランプリ、
'02ハンブリ／グラフィックデザイン日本賞金賞、東京アートディレクターズクラブ会員ほか。

they create, they direct, they record vacuum cleaner sounds

know which half.'
It has been a
popular grumble
from marketing
departments of
all kinds of
brands. Rob Penris
disagrees with
this analysis. His
reasoning? The
Brinker doesn't
spend a huge budget
on communication.
Not even a mediocre
budget. Less than
a low budget. So
the return on this
paltry investment
has been high.

'Our best year
was the worst year
for hotels. This
time we were the
best and the others
were the worst!'
says Penris. 'It
was 2002, a crisis
year in the world and in the hotel
world. This was after September
2001, remember. Our number of bed
nights were 50% higher than "break
even". People were queuing round
the corner outside.' If there was
a reason for this, does it have
something to do with the ads?

The characteristically laconic
Penris replies, 'That was the year
of the, what was it, "Can't Get Any
Worse" campaign. Could've been a
help. It wasn't the worst campaign
we ever did.'

In real terms, looking at the
figures, the press, the guest
reactions and the Golden Effie award
(a highly-regarded advertising
effectiveness award which the
hotel won in 1997), the Brinker was
achieving quite a degree of fame
and infamy by then. Internet meant
that the work was being seen in ever
more places. The curious wanted to

'OUR BEST YEAR WAS THE WORST YEAR FOR HOTELS. THIS TIME WE WERE THE BEST AND THE OTHERS WERE THE WORST!'

'IF PEOPLE SEE THE ADS, THEN COME TO THE HOTEL AND THEN COMPLAIN, THEIR HEADS ARE MALFUNC-TIONING.'

be confronted with
the truth — was
the Brinker really
that bad? With
that in mind, one
thing must have
dropped sharply
since the start of
the advertising:
the complaints.

Penris is
typically direct:
'If people go to
our website, see
that it doesn't
work properly, see
the ads, then come
to the hotel and
then complain,
their heads are
malfunctioning.
No one complains
at our reception
desk anymore.
Most complaints are
directed at our
head of cleaning,
Mrs. Riedewald. She has to kick them
awake at check-out time 10 a.m.'

Despite the success of the hotel's
no-frills policy and honest approach
to its shortcomings in marketing
campaigns, there must have been
moments when things looked bleaker
than last orders at the Brinker bar.
Not really, explains Rob.

'These are hard times. Credit
crisis problems and budget cuts mean
company businessmen aren't able to
stay in four- or five-star hotels.
So they drop their prices. I know
of a couple of four-star hotels that
are cheaper than the Brinker at the
moment, because they are in trouble.
My price has remained relatively
constant since 1993 — it's good to
be that level, that transparent.
It works for business.'

This kind of honesty, it seems,
plays a big part in turning the
Brinker strategy into a sound profit

margin. And since this chapter is about the luxury of honesty, we had to ask the man behind the hotel if he thought the Brinker campaigns work because they are honest?

It was the wrong question. 'All advertising is dishonest. It's because it is put under a spotlight and told from a certain angle. Ours is a different message. We overdo it. It's not as bad as we make out. They (guests) think it is so bad they feel they have to go there. So even our ads are dishonest,' he retorts.

It appears, therefore, that the dishonesty actually comes from overselling the underselling — and from this, developing a positive attraction of something a little bit different from the norm. Because if you are a virile youth travelling Europe looking for fun, danger and bunk beds, why stay in a safe place?

Whatever you make of it, the Brinker has accumulated a lot of success in being squalid. So much so, you would think that the business minds behind the hostel would look into capitalizing on this. Diversifying and opening Hans Brinkers until world domination is achieved. Penris is quick to stamp his foot on this idea.

'There have been opportunities. Barcelona, Paris, Berlin, London. But we could never repeat the same formula. The same success. Buildings are too expensive, we would have to charge more, the ad campaigns couldn't undersell in the same way.'

If more hotels are not the way to go, most brands would then look into another form of diversification. Taking the brand qualities into new areas. New products or services. Again, the Brinker management wants to stick with what it knows. 'Our thing is beds. Beds and beer. We won't go beyond that. We could sell dope at reception and make a much

'OUR THING IS BEDS AND BEER. WE WON'T GO BEYOND THAT. WE COULD SELL DOPE AT RECEPTION... BUT WE WANT TO STAY HONEST TO OURSELVES.'

bigger turnover in the process. But there are limits, we want to stay honest to ourselves as well. Well, to be honest, we just didn't get around to doing it. So we never did it.'

The final question is the real crux of the matter and the heart of this chapter. Not everyone runs a budget hotel. So is there any advice for other hotels? Other brands? Penris is suitably terse in his reply: 'If you would see our figures, then you know you should go the same way.'

Despite the seemingly haphazard nature of the Brinker's communication, despite its crumbling appearance, there is something very Gordon Gekko about the hostel's approach. A budget Gordon Gekko that is, with a tattered jumper instead of sharp 80s suit. However, the Brinker proprietor is quick to dispel this train of thought — or add to it depending on your viewpoint — with his final parting quote before he disappears to whip his staff. 'Making money is like fishing. The only way to get fresh fish is to catch it yourself. The only way to get fresh money is to make it yourself.'

The spot contains too explicit references to a wild nightlife.

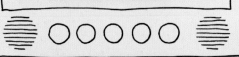

But not the Hans Brinker in Amsterdam.

The beds aren't comfortable at all.

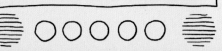

The rooms are small and the water from the shower goes all over the place.

MTV England is not allowed to broadcast the spot.

like ordinairy Tic Tacs.

At Brinker they are so proud of the noisy cleaning ladies that they released a CD with hover sound.

A hotel that's proud of not having a swimming pool, a tennis yard or parking.

I think it's great. I don't need much comfort.

At Brinker they are so proud of the noisy cleaning ladies that they released a CD with hover sound.

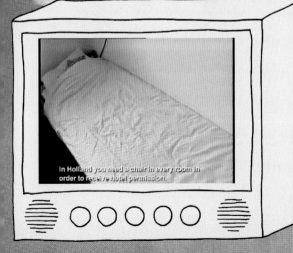

In Holland you need a chair in every room in order to receive hotel permission.

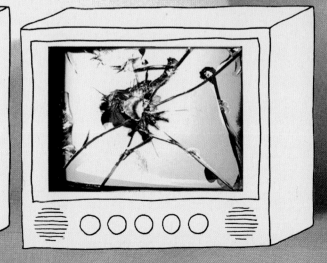

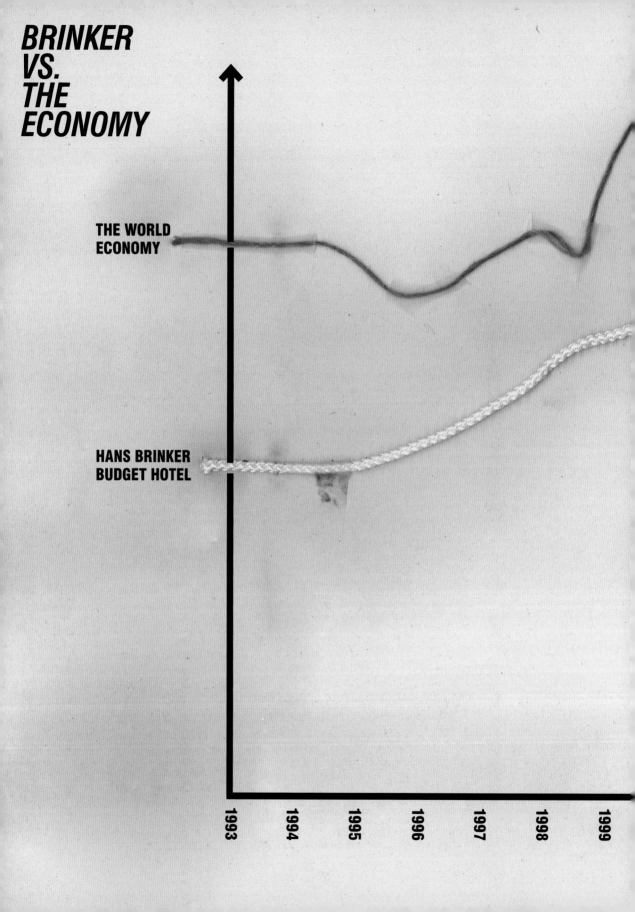

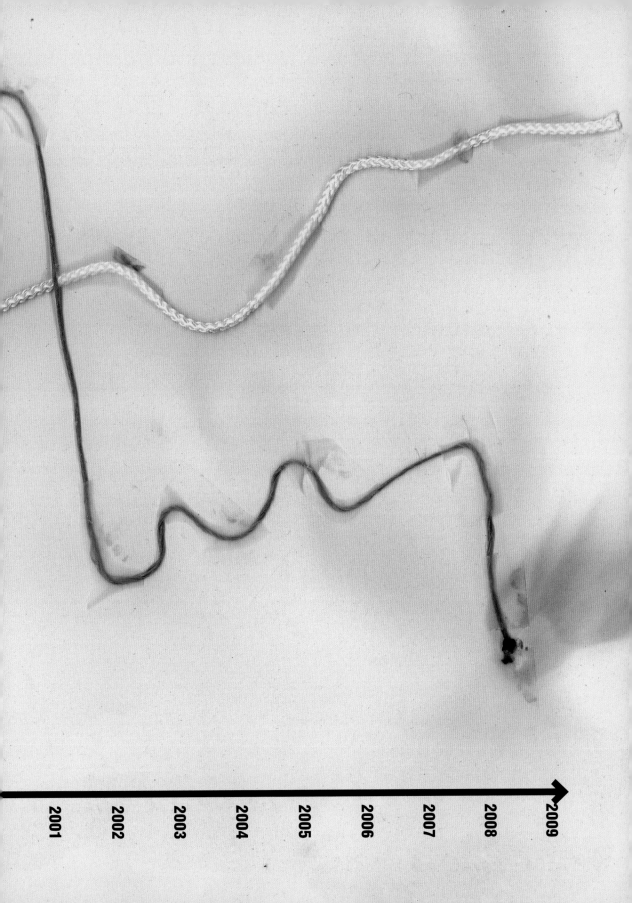

2001 2002 2003 2004 2005 2006 2007 2008 2009

THE BRINK- ER'S SEVEN SECRETS TO SUC- CESS

Here is how the Brinker effect might work for your brand. Let us know how you get on! If you go bankrupt as a result of these secrets, please do not let us know how you got on.

1.

The less benefits you have, the more sincere you should be.
It is tempting to go the other way. To guild the lily. To profess your brand is what your customer has always dreamed of. To garnish it with dubious attributes. Do not be swayed. If you are losing your hair you cannot wear a wig and claim to be bountifully rich in the follicle department. Replace deficiencies with truth and attitude. Tone is your most valuable asset. Speak as others do not speak. With your own voice.

2.

Product innovation is your enemy.
Charles Darwin was wrong. Evolution is not the way to go. Brand development is reversing your appeal. If you make toothpaste, futuristic pump-action tubes will not make your audience love you. If you are a hotel, a rain shower will not inspire desire, or any emotion, except a feeling of hollow dismay. Stick to your guns, your first instinct was good. Replenish your product, brand or service with its own existing, intrinsic appeal, a quality that may have been lost through years of marketing concepts with diminishing returns.

3.

Less is less.
The noted visionary Buckminster Fuller was also wrong. Less is not more. Extolling minimalism as a brand virtue is not cool, not chic, not boutique. If you offer less, say it is less. And then, even less than that. Disappointment comes in over-claiming not under-claiming. Celebrate less as being exactly that: less.

4.

When you are joking, be serious. When you are being serious, joke.
The Brinker never makes fun of itself. It is straight-faced about its advertising and in its advertising. It is serious about being the worst hotel in the world. As serious as an Olympic gymnast is about being the best - but without the leotard. Then, when it's serious, don't take it so seriously. You're not dying. Obviously, if you are dying, disregard this point.

5.

Be inconsistently consistent.
Find a single-minded strategy, stick to its content, and then give it a brutal facelift every time you campaign. New execution, new media choice, new tactics, same story. Don't be afraid to surprise and confuse.

6.

Hate is as effective as love.
Emotion is superior to no emotion at all. That's why couples fight. That's why couples have sex after fighting. Polarize an audience, cause a discussion. Cause a fight then have sex afterwards.

7.

Don't listen to your target audience.
Never overestimate the audience's love for your company, product, service or brand. People have better things to think about. Time and money spent questioning respondents about things they don't have strong opinions about can also be spent on more useful things. Like cleaning the bed sheets. Many marketeers make important decisions based on a few arbitrary, disinterested people who make up opinions because they're asked to. If you've ever been questioned by the police in a New York prison cell, you'll know what we mean. Listen to your own gut instinct, it's usually right.

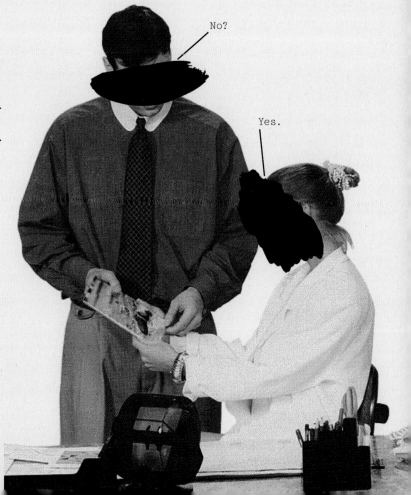

No?

Yes.

SERVICE WITH A SCOWL

Increasingly, hotels around the world are paying closer attention to the details — giving their guests more personalized experiences through the use of immaculate perks, such as designer furniture, gourmet snacks and premium toiletries. Creating unforgettable experiences is nothing new for the disgruntled staff of the Brinker. These perpetually bored and often angry individuals put a unique spin on customer service each day, constantly finding new and ever more inappropriate ways to welcome guests into the sweaty and sticky arms of the Brinker.

GOURMET
SERVICE

Every day, the Brinker's hungry
guests gorge themselves in the
hotel's famous canteen, filling
up on some of Europe's most
questionable culinary delights.

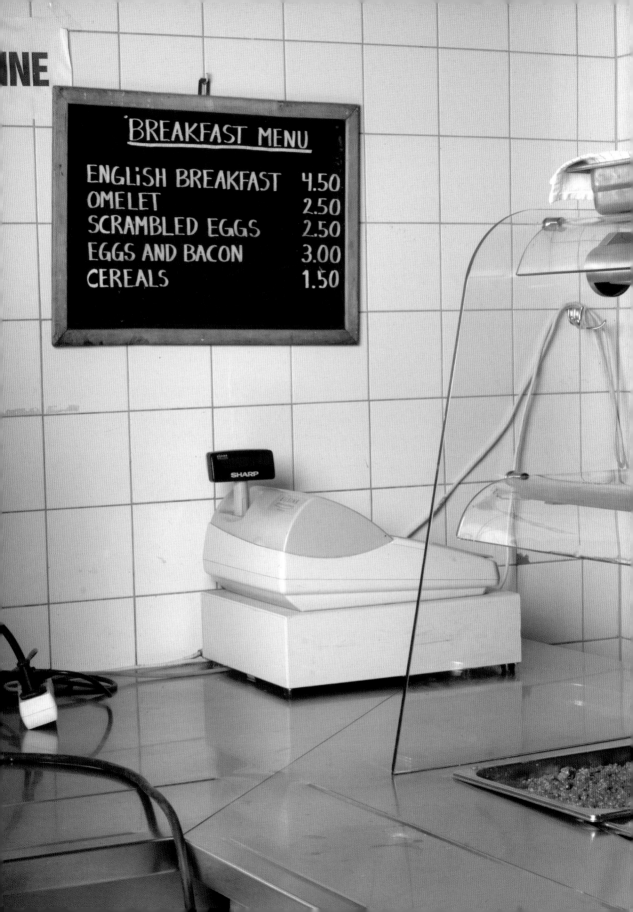

THE BRINKER CANTEEN

HOURS OF OPERA-TION: 18:00 TO 21:00

Located next to the lobby, the Brinker canteen is one of the most popular spots in the hotel. A place for guests to wash away last night's sins with a lukewarm glass of tap water or gain strength for today's escapades with a steaming plate of runny eggs.

The food is haphazardly prepared from a handful of simple ingredients, with absolutely no frills, by a group of hardened individuals who look as though they've taken their fair share of lives on the battlefield.

The Brinker's chefs have compiled the best of the worst recipes from the canteen exclusively for this book. Bon appetit!

Ingredients

Milk.
Potatoes.
Butter.
A dash of salt.
A *soupçon* of carpet fluff.

Directions

1. Place potatoes in pot.
2. Add milk.
3. Mash potatoes until a soft purée is formed.
4. Add salt and water.
5. Heat until tepid.
6. Garnish with fluff drawn from the bag of a still-warm hoover for a distinct *piquant* to proceedings.

Ingredients

¼ ground beef
½ tsp. salt
¼ tsp. pepper
1 split bun
1 industrial-sized ketchup
1 pint mustard

Directions

1. Grey beef by leaving it uncovered in refrigerator for two weeks.
2. Mush beef together in a bowl, adding salt and pepper.
3. Fry burger.
4. Scoop bun out of the pan first allowing it to soak up the juices.
5. Serve with warm milk.

Ingredients

3 brown eggs
1 tsp. peanut oil
2 cups of various meats, vegetables, fruits - whatever's handy

Directions

1. Heat oil in skillet.
2. Use fork to remove black flecks floating in oil from previous meal.
3. Dump eggs on oil.
4. Dump meat, vegetable, whatever, over the eggs.
5. Attempt to flip the omelette by shaking skillet in air.
6. Scoop contents back into the skillet off floor.
7. Serve with dried lettuce, if available.

Ingredients

Bleached white bread
Some butter
Toaster

Directions

1. We don't serve toast.
2. Have breakfast at another hotel.

UNTRAINED MEDICAL SERVICE

The phrase 'an accident waiting
to happen' can be accurately applied
to nearly everyone and everything
found within the Brinker. Lucky
for guests, the hotel is located
near many of the best hospitals
in Amsterdam.

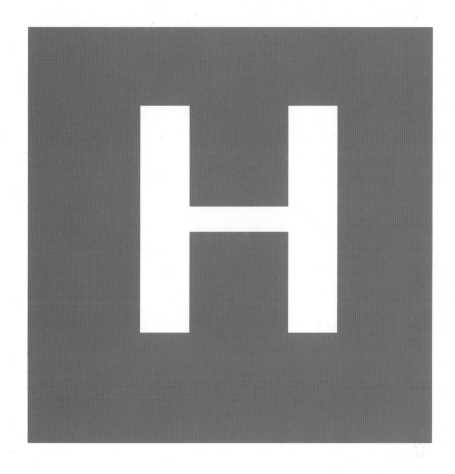

HANS BRINKER BUDGET HOTEL

CLOSE TO THE BEST HOSPITALS IN AMSTERDAM

Tel +31 (0)20 622 06 87   I   Fax +31 (0)20 638 20 60

HELPFUL PHRASES
FOR GUESTS
OF THE BRINKER

I have a/an…
Ik heb (een)…

Itching	Jeuk
Twitching	Plotselinge pijn
Trembling	Rilling
Nausea	Misselijk gevoel
Coughing	Hoest
Vomiting	Oprispingen

I feel a bit…
Ik voel me een beetje…

Queasy	Misselijk
Light-headed	Licht in mijn hoofd
Sick	Ziek
Sore	Rauw
Swollen	Gezwollen
Loose	Gammel

Is that normal?
Is het normaal?

Insurance? What insurance?
Verzekering? Welke verzekering?

Call an ambulance!
Bel een ambulance!

I wish to donate my body to medical science.
Ik wil mijn lichaam doneren voor medisch onderzoek.

As I walk through the valley of the shadow
of death, I shall fear no evil.
Al ga ik door de vallei van de angst,
ik zal niet vrezen.

I'm staying at the Hans Brinker Budget Hotel.
Ik verblijf in het Hans Brinker Budget Hotel.

Every day and every night, dozens of injuries ranging from the minor to the serious take place in and around the Brinker. Stubbed toes. Black eyes. Busted eardrums. The Brinker's staff have seen it all. With so much drunken debauchery and indecent activity taking place within its concrete walls, a safe and pleasant stay at the Brinker is a very rare occurrence indeed. The hotel's proximity to the best hospitals in Amsterdam makes it an ideal base for tourists looking to explore the city's darker side. The Brinker's 'Close To The Best Hospitals' brochure and poster series not only helped promote the most infamous hostel in Amsterdam, it also probably (maybe) helped save a few lives.

The Hans Brinker Budget Hotel

Close to the best hospitals in Amsterdam

'Close To The Best
Hotels In Amsterdam'
is a guide to surviving
a stay at the Brinker.
It features photography
of the brave men and
women of the Brinker
staff in action.

Hotel Dangers: An Introduction

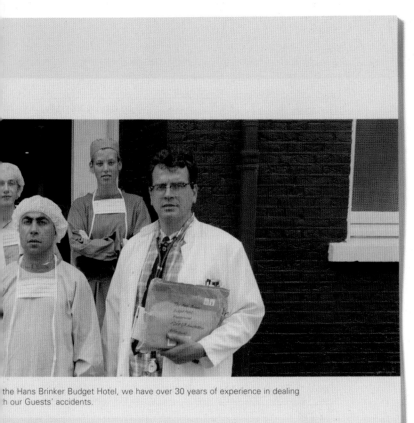

the Hans Brinker Budget Hotel, we have over 30 years of experience in dealing
h our Guests' accidents.

2

The brochure provides
helpful tips for
preventing injury and
illness at the Brinker.
It also includes a
fold-out map to help
guests locate the
nearest hospitals.

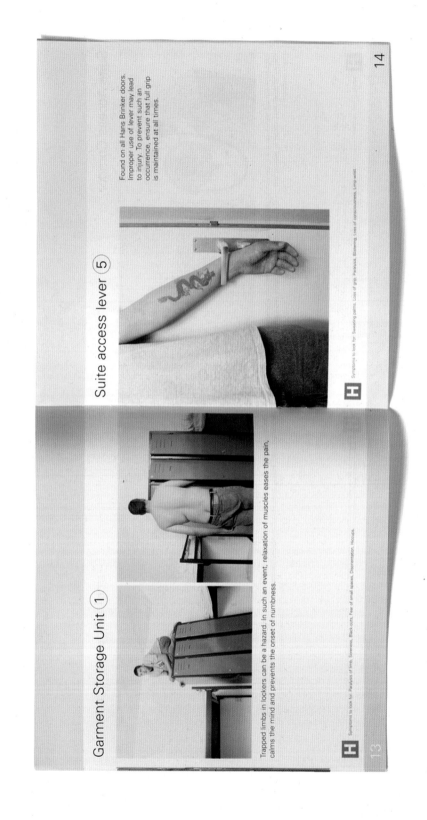

Garment Storage Unit ①

Trapped limbs in lockers can be a hazard. In such an event, relaxation of muscles eases the pain, calms the mind and prevents the onset of numbness.

Symptoms to look for: Paralysis of limb, Soreness, Black-outs, Fear of small spaces, Disorientation, Hiccups.

Suite access lever ⑤

Found on all Hans Brinker doors. Improper use of lever may lead to injury. To prevent such an occurrence, ensure that full grip is maintained at all times.

Symptoms to look for: Sweating palms, Loss of grip, Paralysis, Blistering, Loss of consciousness, Limp wrist.

Nocturnal Slumber Platform ③

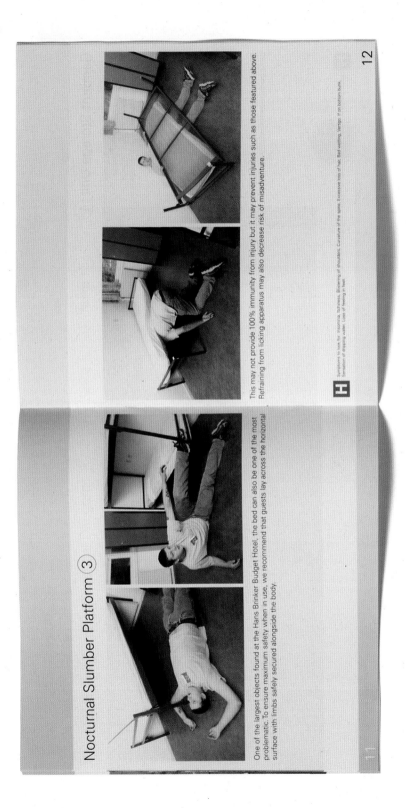

One of the largest objects found at the Hans Brinker Budget Hotel, the bed can also be one of the most problematic. To ensure maximum safety when in use, we recommend that guests lay across the horizontal surface with limbs safely secured alongside the body.

This may not provide 100% immunity from injury but it may prevent injuries such as those featured above. Refraining from licking apparatus may also decrease risk of misadventure.

Symptoms to look for: Insomnia, Itchiness, Blistering of shoulders, Curvature of the spine, Excessive loss of hair, Bed wetting, Vertigo. If on bottom bunk, Sensation of dripping water, Loss of feeling in feet.

11

12

CON-
CIERGE
SERVICE

While the Brinker doesn't have a
help desk, per se, the hotel's short
list of superfluous services often
makes guests feel as though they've
just been helped by the world's
least helpful concierge.

The tiny truck used
for gathering groceries
and other supplies
doubles as an Express
Shuttle Bus that is 'now
24 hrs unavailable.'

HELPFUL
SIGN
SERVICE

A rubber stamp has
helped countless
inebriated guests find
their way back to the
un-embracing arms of
the Brinker.

TRAVEL

DOCU-

MENTS

SERVICE

After a few hours at the Brinker, for one
reason or another, most guests feel
a strong urge to flee the country. Sadly,
the fake passports the hotel offers
are too fake to pass airport security.

This pocket-sized
passport is a popular
souvenir for guests
of the Brinker.
Unfortunately, not
even budget airlines
accept it as a form
of identification.

THE RIGHT DISHONOURABLE
HANS BRINKER BUDGET HOTEL
AMSTERDAM REQUESTS....
THAT NO MATTER HOW
DIRTY, UNKEMPT OR
MILDEWED THE BEARER OF
THIS MOST BUDGET
PASSPORT IS, THEY
SHALL BE ALLOWED TO
CONTINUE ON THEIR
BUDGET JOURNEY
WITHOUT LET OR
HINDRANCE OF
ANY KIND...
CHEERS...

THE CUSTOMS
·OFFICER·

My Valentine

The hallucinogenic
images found in the
passport serve as a
perfect introduction
to the often surreal
world of the Brinker.

IN THE HOTEL SNACKBAR...

INCREDIBLE EDIBLES...

HARRY THE FRENDLY BUDGET HOTEL BACTERIA

CUT OUT THESE FUN COINS...

(NOT ACCEPTED IN ANY SHOP)

BUDGET RUCKSACK

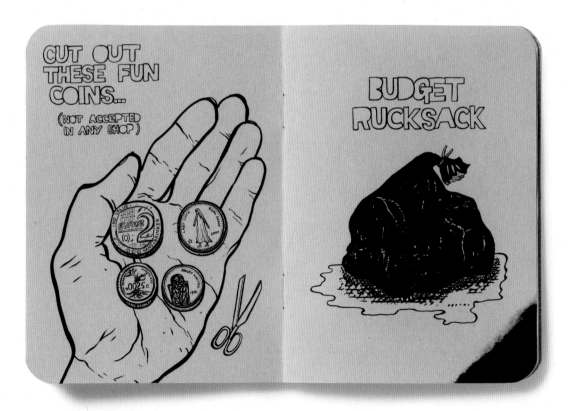

THE BRINK-ER'S WORLD OF UN-DESIGN

THE WORST

DESIGN FEATURES:
✻ Expressive hole punched in toilet door
✻ Postmodern staining on carpets
✻ Chef's neck tattoos

In the eighties, a novel type of hotel began to appear. Whereas hotels used to be about either convenience or old-world charm, the new breed focused on design. Soon dubbed boutique hotels, they featured slick interior decoration and to-die-for locations. Philippe Starck and other famous arbiters of taste contributed their talents, and the movement spewed out a rainforest worth of coffee-table books.

The Hans Brinker Budget Hotel was light years removed from these places but still felt it could contribute a little chic to the opposite end of the hospitality market. With this in mind, its Unique Design campaign highlighted unlikely *objets d'arts* drawn from the Brinker's damp rooms and hallways.

Unique Design

Unique Design

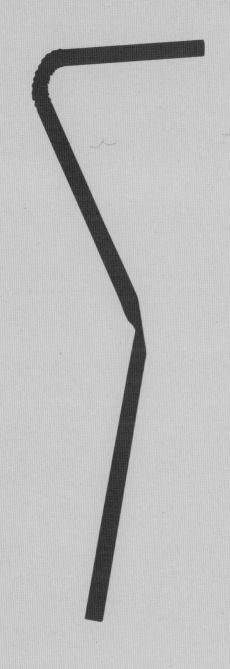

Unique Design

HANS BRINKER BUDGET HOTEL, AMSTERDAM
+31 (0)20 622 0687 hans-brinker.com

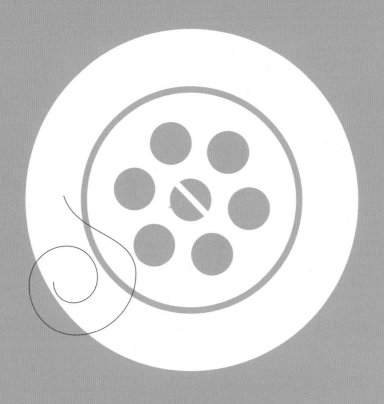

Unique Design

HANS BRINKER BUDGET HOTEL, AMSTERDAM
+31 (0)20 622 0687 hans-brinker.com

Unique Design

SAVING THE PLANET WITH YOUR EYES CLOSED

THE TOP WORST ECO-PLANS:
✢ Remove bathroom taps
✢ Brick up all windows
✢ Generate power with a million gerbils.

Look down the Kerkstraat, the street in Amsterdam where the Hans Brinker Budget Hotel is located, and you'll see an incomplete beacon for the weary traveller. A sign of confusion for all backpackers who are in dire need of some beauty sleep: a giant lit-up letter L.

It's not that the Brinker believes that a full HOTEL sign is too welcoming. Nor that it is more underground to use just one of the letters. It's simply that no-one has bothered to replace the bulbs on four out of the five letters.

The casual observer might judge this to be a sign of laziness, ineptitude or mismanagement. For the opportunistic powers that be at the Brinker, it acted as an inspiration to herald a new era in eco-tourism.

Late one night, when most of his guests were cocooned and comatose in their dormitories, Hans Brinker founder Rob Penris flicked through a magazine lying on the bar. He saw that many of its advertisers shared something in common. Faced with shrinking rainforests, dying

ECO-TOWEL

HANS
BRINKER
BUDGET
HOTEL.
ACCIDENTALLY
ECO-FRIENDLY.

ECO-ELEVATOR

HANS
BRINKER
BUDGET
HOTEL.
ACCIDENTALLY
ECO-FRIENDLY.

(ERKSTRAAT 136-138 – AMSTERDAM – TEL +31 (0)20 622 0687 – FAX +31 (0)20 638 2060 – WWW.HANS-BRINKER.COM

HANS
BRINKER
BUDGET
HOTEL.
ACCIDENTALLY
ECO-FRIENDLY.

ECO-HEATING

KERKSTRAAT 136-138 – AMSTERDAM – TEL +31 (0)20 622 0687 – FAX +31 (0)20 638 2060 – WWW.HANS-BRINKER.COM

HOW YOU AS A FUTURE GUEST CAN SOFTEN YOUR CARBON FOOT-PRINT

ammals and rising sea levels, rands were doing their best to iminish impact on the planet by roudly banding together in the ursuit of one goal: making a fast uck. Car companies launched hybrid UVs: half tank, half butterfly. irlines promised to do their eco-est to curb those nasty emissions eing ejected from their planes. The co-trend was upon us and the hotel ndustry was one of the biggest andwagon jumpers of them all.

co-tourism, now accounting for round 15% of all global tourism, ncourages us to spend quality time n a Costa Rican rainforest to reathe in the region's ecosystem efore it disappears. Or tempts us ith a fortnight in an African eco-odge, where we can ease away the tresses of impending climate doom ith the use of the vitality studio, team room and organic porridge rap. Elephants in the vicinity — hose that have not been displaced o allow for the erection of four undred luxury timber cabins — ould be specially trained to give nvigorating backrubs.

ob Penris realized that his hotel as not only able to ride the rest of the tsunami wave that is co-tourism, it had been doing o since day one.

Our eco-credentials began the day ur doors opened to the public in 970. By continually offering less menities, less service and less

improvements we have less impact on the planet,' explained Mr. Penris. 'You could say that we've been eliminating CO_2 emissions long before we knew what CO_2 emissions were.'

The hotel coined a term for its rediscovered shade of green: EcoBudget®, and used this as a strategy to launch a campaign to tell of its decades-old planet-friendly commitments.

The hotel wanted to communicate that sleeping in a Hans Brinker bed could be instrumental in saving the planet, simply by harnessing the renewable energy source of doing absolutely nothing at all. It was the incomplete HOTEL sign that sparked off the slogan for the worldwide ad campaign. The lack of attention that prevented anyone from replacing most of its bulbs meant that the Brinker's Hotel sign used one-fifth of the energy of any other hotel sign in the world. This fortuitous move towards responsible tourism prompted the campaign slogan: 'Accidentally Eco-Friendly.'

The Brinker's laziness was now its virtue. In the caring, globally aware world of the early 21st century, its many acts of neglect could be seen in a new light. The towels which are rarely cleaned, helping to save energy. The dead bulbs which are replaced irregularly, making the lighting more efficient. The hot water which

Avoid heavy luggage. Use deep pockets instead.

Travelling on a budget means visiting energy-sapping laundrettes. Luckily Holland is wet 45% of the year. Wear dirty clothes in the rain.

Tourism is costly on the planet. Try skipping a few countries and reading about them in a book borrowed from the library.

CHANGE IS HAPPENING. AND IT'S HITTING LIKE A HURRICANE. ICE CAPS ARE MELTING. SEA LEVELS RISING. OUR PLANET'S CLIMATE, BATTERED AND BULLIED, IS TAKING ITS REVENGE. WELCOME TO THE 21ST CENTURY. A WORLD THAT WILL NEVER BE THE SAME AGAIN. THIS WAS OUR WAKE-UP CALL. WE'RE A 650-BED BUDGET HOTEL IN THE HEART OF AMSTERDAM. WE HAVE A VOICE. AND WE HAVE A RESPONSIBILITY. IT'S TIME TO TELL THE WORLD OF A VERY CONVENIENT TRUTH. THE HANS BRINKER BUDGET HOTEL HAS BEEN HELPING THE PLANET, UNINTENTIONALLY, SINCE 1970. YES, HERE IS A HOTEL WHERE THE LIGHT BULBS DON'T WORK. A HOTEL WHOSE SHOWERS HAVE LESS HOT WATER THAN IS STANDARD. WHERE THE ELEVATOR STAYS OUT OF ORDER FOR DAYS. AND WHOSE VACUUM CLEANERS' BUTTONS ARE RARELY SWITCHED ON. WE HAVE TOWELS THAT NEED WASHING ON A MUCH HIGHER HEAT. BUT THIS IS A HOTEL THAT HAD THE FORESIGHT TO THINK: WHY WASTE THE ENERGY? AND WHERE ARE THE FLAT-SCREENS, GAMES CONSOLES AND MINI-BARS? WHERE ARE THE POOL, THE SAUNA AND HOT TUB? YOU WON'T FIND THEM HERE. JUST FOUR WALLS, A BED AND AIR CON WITH TWO SETTINGS: WINDOW OPEN AND WINDOW CLOSED. SO TO THE SCIENTISTS, THE REPORTERS, THE PREDICTORS OF DOOM. LET US HELP TURN BACK THE TORNADOES AND THE VAST WINDS OF CHANGE. WE ARE PROUD TO BE BUDGET. PROUD TO DO OUR BIT FOR THE PLANET. YOU CAN DO THE SAME. STAY WITH US. WE'RE THE HANS BRINKER BUDGET HOTEL AMSTERDAM. ACCIDENTALLY ECO-FRIENDLY.

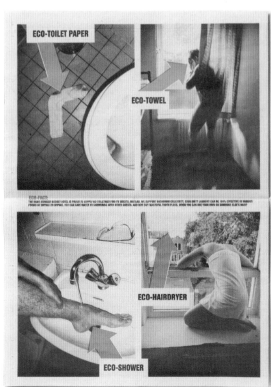

ECO-TOILET PAPER

ECO-TOWEL

ECO-HAIRDRYER

ECO-SHOWER

ECO-BEER

HANS BRINKER BUDGET HOTEL COMPLIMENTARY ECO-TOWEL

ECO-TOWEL IS
- ✓ RECYCLABLE
- ✓ ALMOST INSTANTLY BIODEGRADABLE
- ✓ GENTLE ON THE BODY AND THE PLANET

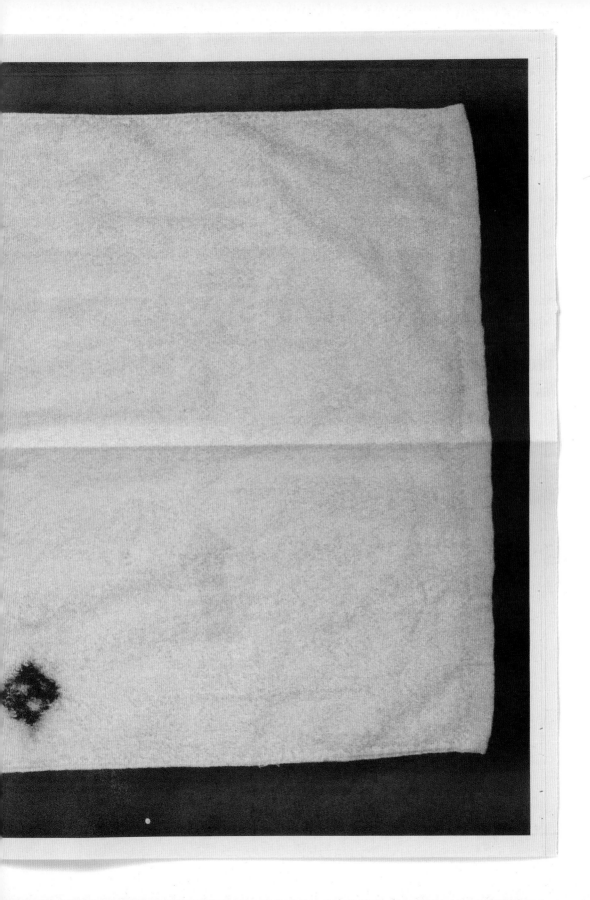

ECO-FACT:
OUR ECO-SIGN USES 20% OF THE ENERGY OF ORDINARY 'HOTEL' SIGNS. THE HANS BRINKER BUDGET HOTEL IS COMMITTED TO DOING AS LITTLE AS POSSIBLE TO ACCIDENTALLY HELP OUR PLANET AS MUCH AS POSSIBLE.

KERKSTRAAT 136-138 – AMSTERDAM – THE NETHERLANDS – TEL +31 (0)20 622 0687 – FAX +31 (0)20 638 2060 – WWW.HANS-BRINKER.COM

Since the photo was taken, all bulbs have died, thus making it the most
100% eco-efficient hotel sign on this earth.

uns cold far earlier than a
guest would wish for. The lack of
extravagant body-nurturing therapy
soaps, high-powered rain showers,
or full-service spa. As one of the
Brinker employees put it: 'We're
not doing our best, we're just
being ourselves.'

The Brinker's ad campaign was
produced on such a shoestring
budget, cutting corners at every
opportunity, that it couldn't help
but be ecologically advantageous.
A brochure was printed on the
cheapest newsprint money could buy.
A T-shirt used 50% less cotton
than ordinary T-shirts by simply
being sliced in half.

The Brinker staff, inspired and
motivated, has not taken the eco-
commitment lightly. Many use their
own initiative to keep the flame of
the eco-candle burning. 'If a guest
asks me to call them a taxi, I tell
them to walk,' said a receptionist
with typical curtness.

Going a step further, the marketing
department arranged for the Brinker
newspaper to travel — by boat —
to the 2007 United Nations Climate
Change Conference in Bali, to urge
world leaders to hold their next
climate change summit in their
humble eco-lodge in Amsterdam.

While many applaud the Brinker's
attitude, some question it: is this
simply a way to put more heads on
beds or is there a hint of altruism?

The hotel sweeps aside any illusions
of too much idealism. But despite
the unintentional nature of the
Brinker's eco-policy, one could
argue that being budget is better
for the planet. 'If everyone acted
budget — no TVs, no heated swimming
pools, no five-course meals — the
world might be in better shape,'
says Penris. 'Doing as little as
possible in the world means doing
as little as possible to the world.'

This voice of clarity and sanity
amongst all the eco-madness hasn't
gone unrecognized.

The Guardian newspaper in the UK
wrote of the 'Hans Brinker Budget
Hotel's brutally honest statement
of its eco credentials' and
added it was 'refreshing to see
a hotel taking a stance against
the greenwashing guff that many
hotels are churning out.'

For more frank opinions, the
editors of this book decided to
call Al Gore to see what he
thought about the Brinker's eco-
campaign. But he wasn't home.

Some consider this a roll of toilet paper. The Hans Brinker Hotel considers it a lesson in ecological living. All bathrooms are kitted with this multi-purpose toilet roll wrapped in an educational paper which offers suggestions to expand and improve the consumption of personal paper usage. Guests are encouraged to use less sheets for their ablutions (or better, re-use them after their ablutions) and more sheets for other useful hotel-staying activities that will not only improve their stay, but also all our lives.

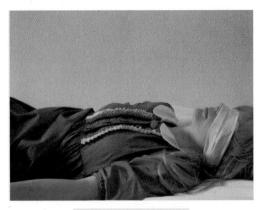

A SLEEPING MASK

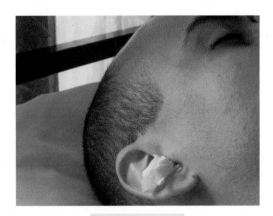

EAR PLUGS

SLIPPERS

A BATH TOWEL

A CARPET

TOILET PAPER

Dear guest,

Please don't leave your valuables in your room

Thank you

CHECK OUT TIME = 10.00
Please make sure you leave your room before 10.00 or that you have paid the receptionist for an extra night

ART FROM THE GUTTER

Over the years, the Brinker has become a repository for art left by its guests- a catalogue of their frustrations, observations and drug-induced insights scrawled on the walls and furniture. Alternately offensive, funny and scatological, it turns the Brinker's surfaces into a kind of guestbook-cum-diary-cum-sketchpad.

HANS BRINKER BUDGET TROPHY AWARD

Every December since 2001, the hotel celebrates some of the most promising young artists around. In the Hans Brinker Budget Trophy, students from eight of the most respected European universities compete to win a very un-budget-like 5,000 euros.

To advertise the show, photographers and artists are invited to come up with a poster. The brief is open and pretty much anything goes. The images this freedom produces are sometimes weird, sometimes wonderful… and sometimes just plain mystifying.

2001

2002

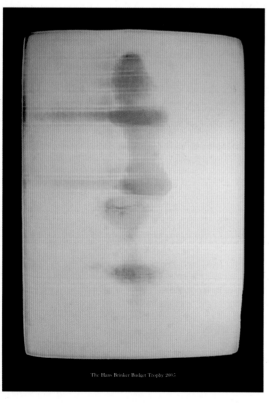

2005

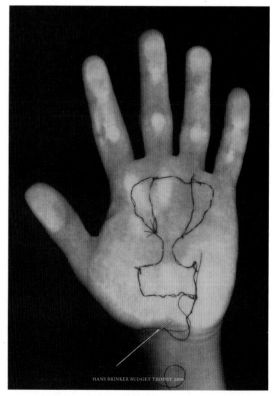

2006

2003

Hans Brinker Budget Trophy 2004

2004

Hans Brinker Budget Trophy 2007

2007

THE HANS BRINKER BUDGET TROPHY 2008

2008

MISS-
ING:

**THINGS YOU
LEFT AND NOW
WE CHERISH**

LARGE SUMS OF MONEY

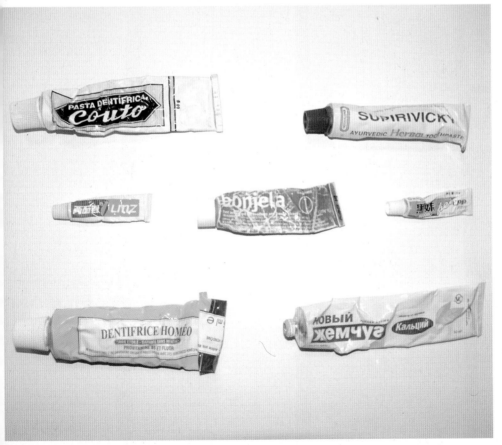

**OVER 300
TUBES OF
TOOTHPASTE**

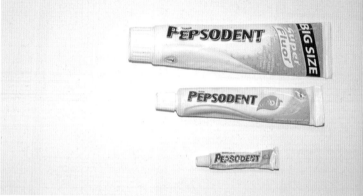

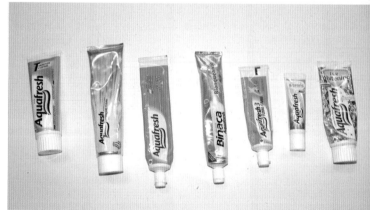

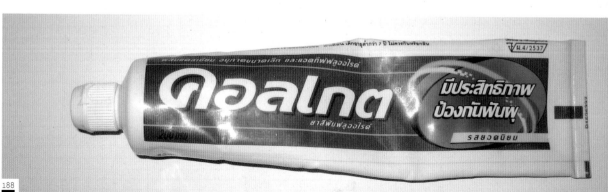

THE TOOTHPASTE COLLECTOR

Joost Bentham was working at the Brinker reception when he became fascinated by its guests' strange habit of leaving tubes of toothpaste behind after check out. Intrigued by their colours and designs, he began collating the most extensive record of toothpaste tubes ever assembled. The Brinker's cleaners were soon involved, passing on any stray toothpaste tubes to Joost, who went about showcasing the collection in his studio flat. Now numbering over 300, the tubes were finally discovered and celebrated in a special section of the Brinker website. 'My ambition is to have the biggest collection not only in Holland, but the whole world,' said Joost with a glint in his eye.

AVANT-GARDE TRIBAL MASK

FINE ART

DESIGNER PHONE

REAL HUMAN HAIR

CHERISHED MEMORIES

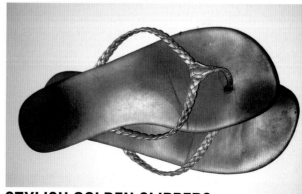

STYLISH GOLDEN SLIPPERS

YOUR LOSS OUR GAIN

Every year, representatives from the world's worst hotel attend a conference designed to celebrate the best. Delegates from all over the tourist industry descend on Brooklyn, New York, to discuss the merits of their trade's latest, greatest luxuries.

For 2008, the Hans Brinker decided to use the occasion to launch a line of chic accessories. But these items were not your typical, handcrafted boutique product. Rather, they'd started life as other people's valuables; unclaimed articles left at the Brinker's Lost and Found Department and transformed into a range of high fashion accoutrements.

Thus the Hans Brinker Budget Collection was born, a range quite blatantly profiting from the loss of others.

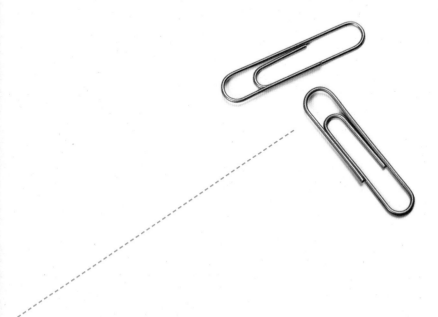

LOST
Two mint-condition,
steel paper clips.
On the hallway
floor, near the third
floor elevator.

FOUND
A sparkling silver
fashion ring bearing
the name Hans.
Adjustable band creates
a snug fit for
any size finger.

LOST
A large pair of black
and pink panties.
Wadded up in the
corner of a stairwell,
first floor.

FOU
A sleek a
sophisticat
toiletry pouc
Double-layer
interior with go
and nylon accent

OST

worn-out pair
f hi-tops.
itting on top
f a vending
achine, lobby.

FOUND

A sporty, reusable
shopping bag.
Triple-stitched rubber
base provides extra
support where it's
needed most.

LOST
A pair of stained
track pants.
Lodged between a
mattress and a bed
frame, first floor.

LOST
Various buttons and
pieces of currency,
totaling roughly 1.37€.
Scattered in multiple
nooks and crannies,
all floors.

196

LOST

Thirty-three brightly
coloured (new and used)
handkerchiefs. Deposited
on windowsills, in
lockers and on chairs,
all floors.

LOST

Stretched and faded
T-shirts. Stuffed
next to toilets,
behind doors, in
sinks, all floors.

Wu Tang
er Bees

FOUND
A lovely and
elegant shawl.
Folds up small,
making it easy
to carry.

FOUND
Lightweight
drawstring backpacks.
Each bag features
decorative bottom-
corner brass grommets
for reinforcement.

OFFICIAL SOU-VENIRS FROM THE BRINKER VAULTS

THE **WORST** GIFT TO TAKE HOME:
☆ Naked Queen Beatrix tattoo
☆ Personalized clogs
☆ Gonorrhoea

While most of the Brinker's communication has been advertising-based, the hostel also affords plenty of inspiration for product development. Over the years, it's created a line of souvenir items intended to help guests remember their stay (or remind them never to come back, depending on your perspective).

The hotel's proprietor realized that many hotels have souvenirs: bathrobes, towels or ashtrays to buy (or steal). The Hans Brinker Budget Hotel has nothing. Even the toilet paper rolls are ineffectual keepsakes, owing to its low-quality, degradable paper. So how were guests able to take their memories of sleepless debauchery home?

It seemed there was a niche waiting to be exploited.

Inspiration sprung in part from an observation of city life. It seemed that every tourist visiting Amsterdam could be found carrying a poster from the Van Gogh Museum wrapped in a distinctive orange and blue cardboard triangular tube. The world's worst hotel sensed a business opportunity: what worked for Holland's most depressed artist might work for the country's most depressing hotel.

Of course, the Brinker needed a product that would appeal to its target market: teenage kids who lived with their parents and might be in the mood to damage Mum and Dad's hard earned property.

An own brand of high-quality photographic wallpaper/ posters with famous Hans Brinker views seemed like the perfect solution, and soon these memories were available in three 'must-have' styles.

The easy-to-apply strips could turn even the best-kept space into either a graffiti-tagged wall, a bricked-up window or, for the kinkier youth, a life-sized cleaner complete with rubber gloves.

You'll find the Brinker's wallpaper and other (equally questionable) souvenirs on the spreads that follow.

MAKE YOUR OW

1.TOMATO KETCHUP 2.TEA 3.MAYONAISE 4.PEAS 5.GRAVY

VN SOUVENIR!

Hans Brinker Budget Hotel Amsterdam

EGG   7.MUSTARD   8.COFFEE   9.ORANGE JUICE   10.CHOCOLATE

FOND MEMO-RIES

CUT-OUT FOR YOUR OWN MINI
HANS BRINKER POSTER

HANS BRINKER
BUDGET HOTEL
AMSTERDAM
HANS-BRINKER.COM
WALLPAPER
BRING YOUR HANS BRINKER MEMORIES HOME

FREE DVD COURTESY OF THE BRINKER

The WORST HOTEL DVD

HANS BRINKER

HOURS OF ENTERTAINMENT ON THIS CUT-OUT-AND-PLAY DVD

WHAT'S INCLUDED

A series of TV commercials
showing you the Brinker equivalents
of regular hotel services.

BUDGET SPONSOR OF THE
EUROPEAN FOOTBALL
CHAMPIONSHIPS

The Brinker parodies big brands'
football sponsorship ads, budget style:
here, a backpacker is unfairly tackled
by a passing cleaner.

IMPROVE YOUR
IMMUNE SYSTEM

Television commercial for the 'Improve
Your Immune System' campaign — in which
the Brinker is populated by giant bugs.

HANS BRINKER BUDGET HOTEL
AMSTERDAM
JUST LIKE
× HOME ×

The notorious 'Just Like Home' ad, where a
young lady slips on a full condom. Banned
from TV (for obvious reasons) and never to
be shown again. Except here.

The Hans Brinker
Budget Hotel
Amsterdam

'Not Included,' shows a well-appointed
hotel room being stripped back to Brinker
levels before our very eyes.

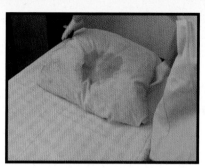
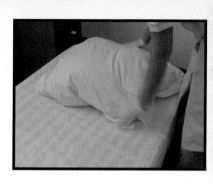

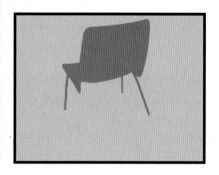
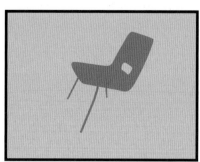
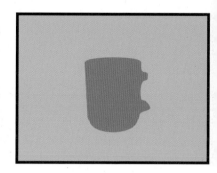

HANS
BRINKER
BUDGET
HOTEL.
ECO-
TOUR.

ECO-STAFF

ECO-CLIMATE
CONTROL

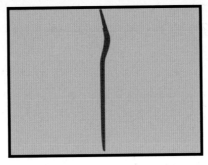

Commercials from the 'It Can't Get Any
Worse' campaign. The Brinker's glaring
indifference to its customer's needs
is cast under the spotlight.

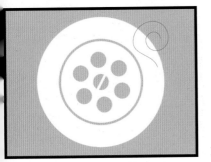

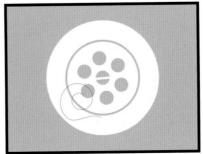

'Unique Design.' The Brinker lays
claim to boutique-hotel status in
these stylish animations.

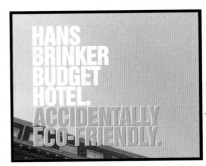

The Hans Brinker's short film, shot
entirely on Super 8, tells the story of
the hostel's eco-friendly credentials,
using real 3-D green arrows.

NOT IN- CLUDED IN THIS BOOK

AN APOLOGY. A REAL DVD. A CAMPAIGN WE CAN'T MENTION FOR LEGAL REASONS. A SOILED SERVIETTE FROM THE CANTEEN. THE FULL, UNABRIDGED COLLECTION OF POETRY FROM BEN THE NIGHT PORTER. AN EARLY BRINKER GIVEAWAY FEATURING A BALLOON WITH A HOLE IN IT. A VISITOR SURVEY PUBLISHED ON BEHALF OF THE FICTITIOUS HANS BRINKER BUDGET HOTEL AMSTERDAM SURVEY RESEARCH DEPARTMENT IN WHICH ALL THE ANSWERS ARE NEGATIVE. A PAIR OF FISHNET STOCKINGS FOUND IN ROOM 450. A HOW TO IMPROVE YOUR IMMUNE SYSTEM BOOKLET WHICH FEATURES TIPS FOR STAYING HEALTHY BY EXPOSING YOURSELF TO GERMS (AND DRINKING BREAST MILK). SLIDES FOR AN EARLY CAMPAIGN,

WHICH OFFERED A DISCOUNT AT THE BRINKER, BUT SADLY PROVED TO BE A COMPLETE AND UTTER FAILURE. **THE MEANING OF LIFE.** THE TRUTH ABOUT THE NOISE FROM ROOM 159. REPRODUCED PAGES FROM THE HANS BRINKER RECEPTION BOOK 1977 TO 1989. PHOTOGRAPHS TAKEN SURREPTITIOUSLY OF THE ONLY ROOM WITH A BATH IN THE BRINKER. **THE STORY OF THE MAN WHO LIVES IN THE LIFT.** THE TRUE INGREDIENTS OF THE CLEANER'S DISINFECTANT BOTTLES. **THE TRUE INGREDIENTS OF THE CHEF'S VEGETARIAN PIE.** THE VERY FIRST CAMPAIGN FOR THE BRINKER, CIRCA 1974. **BLURRED BLACK-AND-WHITE SHOTS OF THE BRINKER WHICH FEATURE A LADY IN A SHOWER AND A MAN DANCING SUGGESTIVELY WITH A WOMAN DRESSED IN** WHAT APPEARS TO BE A PVC TOP. ANYTHING CONCERNING THE N********S SINCE THIS MAY RESULT IN MORE LAWSUITS. A PLEA FOR GUESTS TO COME BACK AND PICK UP APPROXIMATELY 145,000 LOST SOCKS. TIPS ON HOW TO IMPROVE YOUR HOME, BRINKER STYLE. **THE STORY ABOUT THE TIME THE SOUTH AFRICAN RUGBY TEAM TOOK OVER THE BRINKER FOR 17 DAYS AND NIGHTS.** COMPLIMENTARY SHAMPOO. **A BREATH MINT.** VOUCHER FOR AN EXTRA TOWEL. SLEEPING MASK. HEALTH INSPECTOR REPORTS. **PICTURES OF THE BRINKER MONKEY.** A PHOTO OF THE FUNGUS ON THE WALLS OF THE DOWNSTAIRS CORRIDOR, WHICH LOOKS JUST LIKE JESUS ON A MOTORBIKE. **A DISCLAIMER.** AN UNUSED CONDOM. **A PROPER ENDING.** A POLITE GOODBYE.

NO THANKS

TO ALL WHO LET US ABUSE THEM TO MAKE THIS BOOK

Everyone who works, or has ever worked, at KesselsKramer.

All the staff at the Hans Brinker Budget Hotel Amsterdam.

And an extra special no thanks to:

Jody Barton:
pg. 147-149

Joop Beerling:
pg. 11, 25, 26, 33, 43-47, 59, 67, 133, 168, 185

Anuschka Blommers:
pg. 50-57

Melanie Bonajo:
pg. 185

Lex Brandt:
pg. 215-217

Anthony Burrill:
pg. 17-31, 151-155, 202, 203

Paula Castro:
pg. 224, end papers, sticker sheet and this fly

Claudie de Cleen:
pg. 184

Sarah Engelhardt:
pg. 184

Luke Forsythe:
pg. 184

Tim Georgeson:
pg. 33, 34, 60-64, 70-75

Jacqueline Hassink:
pg. 68-71

Jean-Pierre Khazem:
pg. 216-217

Eva-Fiore Kovacovsky:
pg. 185

Franklin Neuteboom

Martijn F. Overweel:
pg. 72-75

Bianca Pilet:
pg. 206-209

Herman Poppelaars:
pg. 134-137

Niels Schumm:
pg. 50-57

Johannes Schwartz:
pg. 104-108

Chris Shaw:
pg. 6, 7, 9, 64, 90-93

Klaas Slooten

Jaap Stahlie:
pg. 14, 22

Simon Wald-Lasowski:
pg. 86-89, 125-129, 142-143, 177-182, 186-191, 204, 205

Dirk Wolf:
pg. 141

DON'T COME BACK SOON

THE EMPIRE THAT NEVER WAS.
(PART 1)

Over the years, creative souls have occasionally approached the Brinker with suggestions for diversifying its business. However, all such notions have been swiftly vetoed... for reasons that will become apparent from a glance at these ideas.

**BRINKER
PET HOTEL**

BECAUSE ANIMALS CAN'T COMPLAIN

**BUDGET
CREDIT CARD**

**NOT ACCEPTED ANYWHERE!
29 € LIMIT!**

THE EMPIRE THAT NEVER WAS.
(PART 2)

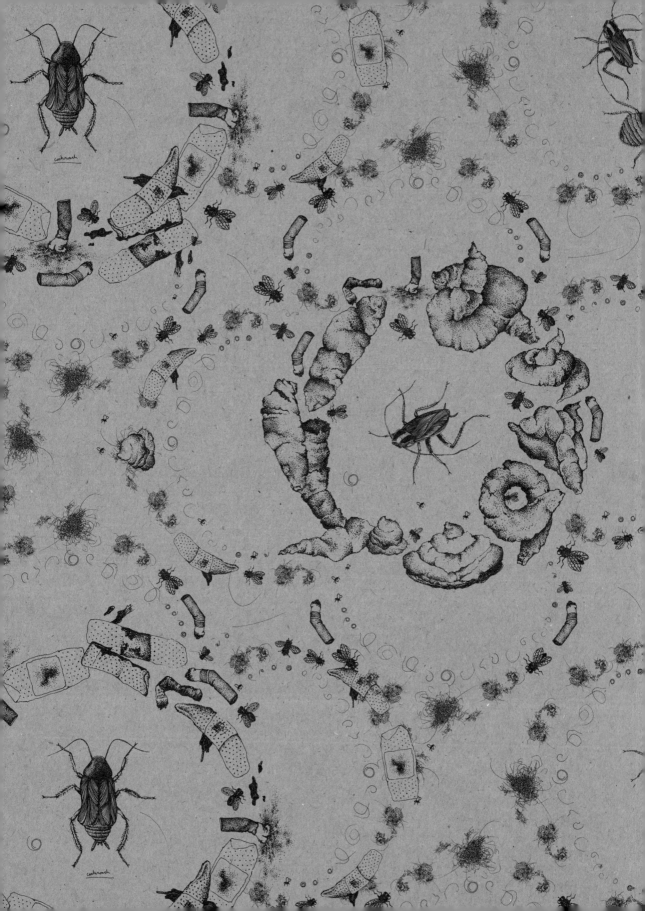